Alberto de Tornos

The Combined Spanish Method

A new practical and theoretical system of learning the Castilian language, embracing the most advantageous features of the best known methods. With a pronouncing vocabulary.

Alberto de Tornos

The Combined Spanish Method
A new practical and theoretical system of learning the Castilian language, embracing the most advantageous features of the best known methods. With a pronouncing vocabulary.

ISBN/EAN: 9783337219802

Printed in Europe, USA, Canada, Australia, Japan

Cover: Foto ©Paul-Georg Meister /pixelio.de

More available books at **www.hansebooks.com**

THE
COMBINED SPANISH METHOD.

A NEW

PRACTICAL AND THEORETICAL SYSTEM OF LEARNING

THE CASTILIAN LANGUAGE,

EMBRACING THE MOST ADVANTAGEOUS FEATURES OF THE BEST KNOWN
METHODS.

WITH A

PRONOUNCING VOCABULARY,

CONTAINING ALL THE WORDS USED IN THE COURSE OF THE WORK, AND REFERENCES
TO THE LESSONS IN WHICH EACH ONE IS EXPLAINED, THUS ENABLING
ANY ONE TO BE HIS OWN INSTRUCTOR.

BY

ALBERTO DE TORNOS, A.M.,

FORMERLY DIRECTOR OF NORMAL SCHOOLS IN SPAIN, AND NOW TEACHER OF SPANISH IN
THE NEW YORK MERCANTILE LIBRARY, NEW YORK EVENING HIGH SCHOOL, AND
THE POLYTECHNIC AND PACKER INSTITUTES, BROOKLYN.

NEW YORK:
D. APPLETON AND COMPANY,
1, 3, AND 5 BOND STREET.
1892.

NOTICE.—A Key to the Exercises of this Grammar is published in a separate volume.

PREFACE.

It is an undoubted fact that in teaching, not only languages, but any other science or art, there neither is, nor can be, any other method than that of uniting *theory* with *practice;* and the various modes of applying the one to the other, the extent of the application, and the time at which it should be commenced, have produced the great number of methods hitherto published.

This fact is now universally acknowledged, and each new author proclaims himself to be the only one who has put it into execution. The most insignificant little phrase-book does not fail to announce, in its introduction, that it combines *theory* and *practice;* and grammars containing nothing more than confused masses of rules, heaped one upon another, are entitled "*Theoretical* and *Practical.*" It is admitted on all hands that much progress has been made within the last few years in the art of teaching languages; and, in testimony of this, we have only to mention the excellent oral and practical methods of Jacotot, Manesca, Ollendorff, Boulet, Robertson, and others who have followed in their footsteps, all of which are ably treated, and have done much good in their way. But each one of the grammarians referred to, satisfied with his own invention, looked with disdain upon that of his predecessor. Hence the enmity and the almost unaccountable diversity of opinion which we observe amongst them. Had they studied each other with impartiality, and endeavored to profit by the experience and even the defects of the several systems, their labors would certainly have been attended with still more favorable results, and of course more considerable benefit would have accrued thereby to the art in general. Numberless points of excellence are to be found, scattered here and there, throughout the various ancient and modern systems, and chiefly those already alluded to; and it has been thought that, if carefully sifted out and judiciously combined, they would form a new method which would be in details essentially superior to any of the old ones.

This conviction, joined to twenty years' experience in teaching the Spanish language, sometimes through the medium of one, sometimes of another of the before-mentioned systems, has led the author to prepare and publish the COMBINED METHOD, which he now offers to those desiring to learn the noble language of Cervantes.

Whether he has successfully attained his object, the public will decide.

OBSERVATIONS

ON

SOME OF THE ADVANTAGEOUS FEATURES OF THE "DE TORNOS'S COMBINED METHOD."

1st. The advantage of presenting the verb as the first and principal part of speech, which serves as the axis upon which all the other parts revolve. These, too, have been introduced in their turn, not in grammatical order, nor by mere chance, but in the logical and natural order in which they occur in discourse, whether written or spoken.

2d. That of explaining these parts of speech in the order just mentioned, not in an isolated manner, but united to form a homogeneous whole, and in such a way that the learner will have no difficulty in finding the explanation relative to the use of each one of them respectively, as often as occasion may require.

3d. These explanations, which embrace the whole theory, and form a complete grammar of the language, are separate from and independent of the exercises; the latter being composed in strict accordance with the examples accompanying each lesson, in such a manner that those unacquainted with grammar in general, and those who have no desire to enter into the theory of the language, or, finally, those who are too young or too old to learn grammar, may acquire a thorough conversational knowledge of Spanish, by merely committing to memory the Vocabulary, studying the Compositions, and carefully writing the Exercises.

4th. From the arrangement alluded to, arises another great advantage, namely, all the elements are found in the vocabulary of each lesson, separated and detached from the examples and rules given in the explanation; thus enabling the student to see at one glance all that he has to commit to memory for each recitation.

5th. And this division of the lessons into Elements, Composition, Explanation, Version, and Exercise, enables the teacher to divide each lesson into two, three, or even four parts, according to the age and capacity of the learner.

6th. *Repetition*, and *constant repetition*, is indispensable for acquiring any language; but by repetition should not be understood the simple reiteration of single words and easy phrases; but repetition of the idioms, and of those forms of expression differing most widely from the idiomatical construction of the learner's native tongue. It is true, that though this is the proper plan for acquiring a thorough knowledge of a language, that feature might tend to make the present work appear, at first sight, more difficult than the books hitherto used; but such will not be found the case; for when there is frequent change of matter there cannot be monotony; and variety renders study at the same time easy and agreeable. This repetition, then, of useful forms of expression, and contrast of idiom, will be found in every page of our "COMBINED METHOD," in which it has been our endeavor to introduce gradually and with the necessary explanations of each, the most important idioms of the Spanish language.

7th. Although we are of opinion that to learn a language, and, above all, to learn to pronounce it, it is always preferable to have the assistance of a skilful teacher, and one who speaks his native tongue with purity and correctness; yet, as it is not always possible to procure such, we have placed at the end a Vocabulary, containing all the words used in the course of the work, and the pronunciation of each, so that nothing may be wanting to second the efforts of those who, from choice or necessity, may be their own instructors.

8th. The Vocabulary, besides giving the pronunciation and meaning of the words, indicates the lesson in which the explanation of each has been given in the Grammar. By this means the learner can with ease refer to the explanation of all those words of which it has been deemed essential to give one.

CONTENTS.

	PAGE
PREFACE,	iii, iv
A FEW REMARKS ON THE COMBINED METHOD,	v, vi
CONTENTS,	vii–xvi
PRELIMINARY LESSON ON ORTHOGRAPHY AND PRONUNCIATION,	xvii–xxiv

LESSON I.

RULE
1. Regular verbs, classified in three conjugations, ... 1
2. Roots, ... 2
3. Terminations of the three model verbs, corresponding to all the regular verbs, 2
—. Suppression of the nominative pronouns, ... 2
4. *V.* (*Usted*) requires the verb in the third person, ... 3

LESSON II.

5. *Señor, señorito, señora, señorita,* use of these words, . . . 4
6. *Don* and *Doña,* use of these words, ... 5
7. *No,* placed before the verb, ... 5

LESSON III.

8. The conjunction *y* changed into *é,* 7
9. *Qué,* interrogative pronoun, ... 7
10. *Sino.*—When *but* is to be translated by *sino,* 7
11. *Pero.*—When *but* is to be translated by *pero,* 7
12. *Español, inglés,* &c., one word may belong to different parts of speech, . 7

LESSON IV.

13. *A,* preposition *to,* used after active verbs, when the object is a person, . 10
14. *De,* used to express position or the material of which any thing is made, . 10
15. *El,* the article *the,* used to determine a noun masculine singular, . 10
—. Contraction of the article *el* and the prepositions *á* and *de* into *al, del,* . 10
16. *Un,* the indefinite pronoun used before masculine nouns, . . . 10
—. *Uno* is only used as a numeral adjective, ... 10

LESSON V.

17. *Gender,* how ascertained, ... 13
—. *Una,* used before feminine nouns, ... 13
18. *Your,* how translated, ... 13

CONTENTS.

LESSON VI.

RULE | | PAGE
19. The terminations of the persons of the present indicative; how they differ in the three conjugations, ... 16
20. *Muy*, how translated, ... 16
21. Nouns ending in *o* change that vowel into *a* for the feminine, . . 17

LESSON VII.

22. Adjectives ending in *o*, *an*, or *on* form their feminine in *a*, . . 20
—. Adjectives signifying nationality and ending in *a*, . . . 20
—. Adjectives are generally placed after their nouns, . . . 20
—. Adjectives used metaphorically are always placed before the nouns, . 20
—. Some adjectives drop their last letter or syllable, . . . 20

LESSON VIII.

23. The endings of the second and third conjugations, how they differ, . 23
24. The conjunction *ó* when changed into *ú*, ... 23
25. *Ni*, how translated, ... 23
26. The plural of nouns, ... 23
27. Adjectives agree with their nouns in gender, number, and case, . 24
28. The article agrees also, ... 24
—. Feminine nouns that take the masculine article, . . . 24
29. The neuter article *lo*, ... 24

LESSON IX.

30. *Papá*, *mamá*, *pié*, are exceptions, ... 27
31. Nouns which are not monosyllables and end in *s*, their plural, . . 28
—. Words ending in *z*, their plural, ... 28
32. Words which are compounds of two nouns, their plural, . . 28
33. The days of the week, when they take the article, . . . 28
34. *Donde, adonde, cuando*, placed before the verb, . . . 28
35. *Donde, adonde, cuando*, in interrogations require an accent, . . 28

LESSON X.

36. Irregular verbs, ... 31
—. *Tener* not included in the seven verbs, ... 31
—. Objective case of the third person *le, los, la, las, lo*, . . . 31
37. *Lo* and *le*, the difference between them, ... 32
—. *It* and *so* are translated sometimes by *lo*, ... 32
38. *Quien, cual, que, de quien*, used interrogatively do not take the article, . 32
39. When the interrogative is governed by a preposition, the same preposition must be repeated in the answer, ... 32

LESSON XI.

40. *Alguien, alguno*, the difference between them, . . . 35
—. *Any one* or *any body*, when translated by *cualquiera*, . . 35
41. *Nadie, ninguno*, their distinction, ... 35
42. *Alguno* and *ninguno*, when they lose the *o*, . . . 36
43. *Algo, alguna cosa*, used affirmatively, ... 36

CONTENTS.   ix

RULE		PAGE
44.	*Nada, ninguna cosa*, used negatively, ...	36
45.	Negatives, when placed before the verb, ...	36
—.	Two negatives render the negation more emphatic than one, . .	36
46.	*A* or *an*, when not translated, ...	36

LESSON XII.

47.	*Tener* and *haber*, their distinction, ...	39
—.	*To have* and *to be*, followed by an infinitive, how they are translated, .	39
48.	*Preterit Indefinite*, ...	40

LESSON XIII.

49.	*Mio, tuyo*, &c., change the *o* into *a* for the feminine, . . .	43
50.	Possessive pronouns agree in gender and number with the name of the thing possessed, ...	43
51.	As pronominal adjectives, *mio, tuyo, suyo* precede the noun and drop their final syllable, ...	43
52.	*Mio*, when placed after the noun, ...	44
53.	Possessives used as pronouns agree in gender and number with the nouns they represent, and take the article, ...	44
54.	When used indefinitely they take the neuter article, . . .	44
55.	When connected with the verb *to be*, the article is omitted, . .	44
56.	*Vuestro, vuestra*, when used, ...	44

LESSON XIV.

57.	Formation of compound numbers, ...	48
58.	Numbers are indeclinable, except *uno* and the compounds of *ciento*, .	48
59.	*Uno*, its agreement; when it loses the *o*, ...	48
60.	*Ciento*, its agreement; when it loses the last syllable, . . .	48

LESSON XV.

61.	*Ordinals*, their agreement and place, ...	51
—.	*Primero* and *tercero*, when they drop their final letter, . . .	52
62.	*Ordinals*, when used, ...	52
—.	N. B.—When ordinals do not require the definite article, . .	52

LESSON XVI.

63.	*Preterit Definite*, ...	56
64.	*Ante*, its meaning, ...	57
65.	*Mas* and *ménos*, how used, ...	57

LESSON XVII.

66.	*Quien*, how used, ...	61
67.	*Who*, when translated by *que*, and when by *quien*, . . .	61
68.	*Cual* and *que* relate to persons and things, ...	61
69.	*Cuyo* refers to persons and things: its agreement, . . .	61
—.	It partakes of the nature of the relatives and of the possessives, . .	61

CONTENTS.

RULE		PAGE
70.	The preposition placed before the relative,	61
71.	Relative pronouns *can never* be suppressed in Spanish,	61

LESSON XVIII.

72.	Declension of the demonstrative pronouns *este, ese, aquel*,	66
73.	*Este*, how used,	66
74.	*Este, ese*, forming one word with the adjective *otro*,	67
75.	The demonstrative pronouns used as neuter,	67
76.	*The former* and *the latter*, translated by *aquel* and *este*,	67
77.	*That of, that who*, or *that which*, translated by *el de, el que*,	67
78.	English personal pronouns rendered in Spanish by demonstrative pronouns,	67
79.	*Aquí, ahí, acá, allá*, how employed,	68

LESSON XIX.

80.	*Para* and *por*, how they differ,	72
81.	*Entre*, its meaning,	73
82.	*Hasta*, its meaning,	73

LESSON XX.

83.	*Tanto* and *cuanto*, when they lose the last syllable,	77
84.	Comparison of *equality*, how formed,	77
85.	*Cuan* may be employed,	77
86.	Comparison of *superiority*, how formed,	77
87.	Comparison of *inferiority*,	77
88.	*Mayor, menor, mejor, peor*, are already in the comparative degree,	77
89.	*Than*, translated by *de* and *que*,	78
90.	Comparison relating to *nouns, verbs*, and *adverbs*,	78

LESSON XXI.

91.	Superlatives ending in *est*, or formed by *most*, how translated,	82
92.	*Most*, or *most of*, when translated by *la mayor parte*, or by *mas*,	83
93.	*In*, preposition, when translated by *de*,	83
94.	Superlatives formed by *very, most*, etc., when formed in Spanish by *muy* and when by *ísimo*,	83
95.	Adjectives drop the last vowel on taking the termination *ísimo*,	83
96.	Other superlatives ending in *érrimo*,	83
97.	Adjectives which change their endings before the termination *ísimo*,	83
98.	Superlatives in *ísimo* irregularly formed,	84
99.	Irregular comparatives and superlatives,	84
—.	These make also a superlative in *ísimo*,	84
—.	Also with *muy*, and a comparative with *mas* or *ménos*,	84
100.	Substantives used adjectively admit the degrees of comparison,	84

LESSON XXII.

101.	*Ser* and *estar*, the distinction between them,	89
102.	" " their employment,	89

CONTENTS.

LESSON XXIII.

RULE		PAGE
103.	*Future simple,*	96
104.	The *definite article* used with numerals, indicating the hour of the day,	96
105.	*Evening* and *night,* translated by *noche,*	96
106.	The conjunction *si,* when it governs the subjunctive, and when the indicative,	96

LESSON XXIV.

107.	*Compound future,*	100
108.	*Acabar de,* its meaning,	100
—.	N. B.—How the pupil may learn a great number of words with little or no difficulty,	101
109.	Nouns ending in *tion* are the same in Spanish, changing the letter *t* into *c,*	101
110.	The days of the month are counted by the cardinal numbers, preceded by the article,	101

LESSON XXV.

111.	*Saber* and *conocer,* how they differ,	107
112.	*Aun, ya, todavía,* their different meaning and uses,	107
—.	Once, twice, &c., translated by *una vez, dos veces,* &c.,	107
—.	*Miedo, valor,* &c., take the preposition *de* after them,	107
113.	*To be afraid, to be thirsty,* &c., how translated,	107
114.	*Jamás* and *nunca,* how used,	107

LESSON XXVI.

115.	Pronoun subject, or nominative,	112
116.	Two objective cases of the personal pronouns, how used,	113
117.	The objective case, when not preceded by a preposition, is affixed to infinitives, gerunds, &c.,	113
118.	When the verb drops the final letter followed by *nos* or *os,*	113
—.	The reason of this,	113
119.	When the objective case may follow the verb,	113
120.	When the objective may be placed before the first verb, or after the second,	113
121.	Prepositions, when expressed, always govern the second objective case,	113
122.	*Mí, tí, sí,* when preceded by *con,*	114
123.	*Entre,* how used,	114
124.	The second objective case is used after comparatives,	114
125.	When the first objective case is used,	114
126.	The objective case of the third person is rendered by *le, les,* if the preposition *to* govern it in English,	114

LESSON XXVII.

127.	The third person rendered in Spanish by *se,*	119
128.	The object of the verb is to be placed last, when two *first* objective cases occur in the sentence,	119
129.	Placed first when the object of the verb is the reflective pronoun,	120
130.	Both of the objective cases belonging to the same person used together,	120
131.	The expressions *á él quiero, á ti amo,* are incorrect,	120

CONTENTS.

RULE | | PAGE
132. The pronouns *él, la, lo, los,* and *las,* how distinguished from the articles *el, la, lo, los, las,* 120
133. The adjective *mismo,* how used, ... 120

LESSON XXVIII.

134. When the *imperfect* is used, ... 125
135. When the *pluperfect* is used, ... 126
136. How the expressions *to have just* and *to be just* are translated before a past participle, ... 126

LESSON XXIX.

137. The preterit anterior, its use, ... 130
138. Derivation of adverbs of manner and quality, ... 131
139. How adverbs are formed from adjectives, ... 131
140. Adverbs terminating in *mente* admit, like adjectives, the degrees of comparison, ... 131
141. How these adverbs can be substituted, ... 131

LESSON XXX.

142. What impersonal verbs are, ... 137
143. *Amanecer* and *anocher,* used in the three persons, . . . 137
144. *Haber* and *hacer,* and other verbs used impersonally, . . 137
145. The pronoun *it,* accompanying impersonal verbs, not translated, . 138
—. Nouns taken in a definite sense require the article, . . . 138
—. Nouns used in their most general sense take the article, . . 138
146. Names of nations, countries, mountains, &c., take the article, . 138
147. Nations, countries, and provinces, when preceded by a preposition, do not take the article, ... 138
—. Names of some places that always take the article, . . . 138

LESSON XXXI.

148. *Gustar,* signifying *to give pleasure to,* how used, . . . 143
149. *Gustar,* followed by the preposition *de,* 144
150. *Gustar,* used as an active verb, ... 144
151. Verbs that require the same idiomatic construction as that of the verb *gustar,* 144
152. The verb *pesar,* when meaning *to regret,* 144

LESSON XXXII.

153. How the passive voice is formed, ... 149
154. When the passive form is used with the verb *ser* in the present and imperfect tenses of the indicative, ... 149
155. When the preposition *de* or *por* is to be used after passive verbs, . 149
156. Passive voice formed by *se,* 150
157. When the passive, formed with *se,* is to be preferred, . . 150

LESSON XXXIII.

158. *Reflective verbs,* what they are, ... 155

CONTENTS. xiii

RULE		PAGE
159.	When are the verbs made reflective?	156
160.	When a verb denotes *reciprocity*, how it is conjugated,	156

LESSON XXXIV.

161.	Which are the irregular verbs,	161
162.	Verbs which, although they undergo slight changes in their radical letters, are not to be considered as irregular,	161
163, 164.	Verbs which change *i* into *y*,	162
165.	How the irregular verbs are divided,	162
166.	What is to be observed relative to the object of the verb *pagar*,	163

LESSON XXXV.

167.	Irregularity of the verb *acostar*,	168
168.	*Imperative mood*, when used,	168
169.	The *s* of the first person plural, and the *d* of the second, suppressed before *nos* and *os*,	168
170.	The subjunctive, used when the imperative is negative in English,	168
171.	The future of the indicative, used for the imperative,	168
172.	Adjectives ending in *ous*, how rendered into Spanish,	168
173.	Nouns and adjectives ending in English in *ic* or *ical*, how rendered into Spanish,	169

LESSON XXXVI.

174.	Irregularity of the verb *mover*,	173
175.	*Se*, as the Spanish indefinite personal pronoun,	173
176.	The pronoun *se*, in its four functions,	174
177.	Nouns ending in English in *ty*, how rendered into Spanish,	174
178.	*Doler*, how used,	175

LESSON XXXVII.

179.	Irregularity of the verb *atender*,	179
180, 181, 182, 183.	*Subjunctive Mood*, when used in Spanish,	180
184.	Present tense of the subjunctive,	181
185.	Perfect tense,	181

LESSON XXXVIII.

186.	*Present Participles*,	186
187.	*Gerunds*,	186
188.	The verb *estar* used with the gerund in Spanish,	186
189.	When in English the present participle, preceded by a preposition, is used, how rendered into Spanish,	187
190.	The infinitive used as a verbal noun,	187
191.	The infinitive governed by an other verb, how rendered into English,	187

LESSON XXXIX.

192.	Irregularity of the verb *pedir*,	192
193.	The usual forms of salutations,	193

CONTENTS.

LESSON XL.

RULE		PAGE
194.	*Conducir*, its irregularity,	197
195.	*Segun* as a preposition and an adverb,	198
196.	Collective nouns,	198

LESSON XLI.

197.	Defective verbs *podrir*, *placer*, &c.,	203
198.	*Yacer*, its use,	203
199.	*Soler*, its use,	203
200.	*Desde*, its meaning and use,	203
201.	*Contra*, rendered into English by *against*,	204
202.	*Sobre*, its signification,	204
203.	*Tras*, its meaning,	204
204.	The conjunction *pues*, its use,	204

LESSON XLII.

205.	*Conjunctions*, their classification,	209
206.	What is to be observed in relation to the government of conjunctions,	210
207.	Some conjunctions that govern the subjunctive mood,	210
208.	Compound conjunctions which require the infinitive mood,	210
209.	Compound conjunctions which require the indicative,	210

LESSON XLIII.

210.	Imperfect and pluperfect of the subjunctive,	215
211.	How to render into Spanish the auxiliaries *may, might, can, could, will, would,* and *should*,	217
212.	What the imperfect subjunctive denotes,	217
213.	What the pluperfect denotes,	217

LESSON XLIV.

214.	Augmentative and diminutive nouns,	223
215.	Irregular terminations of certain diminutives,	224
216.	Diminutives may be formed from adjectives, participles, gerunds, and adverbs,	224
217.	Some of the primitive words do not admit all the diminutive terminations,	224
218.	There are derivatives which, although they appear to be augmentatives or diminutives, are not so,	225

LESSON XLV.

219.	The future simple of the subjunctive,	230
220.	How the present of the subjunctive may be substituted by the future,	230
221.	The future compound,	230
222.	The compound present of the subjunctive may be substituted by the future compound,	231
223.	What is to be observed in order not to misapply the imperfect and pluperfect,	231
224.	Government of the future simple and compound future of the subjunctive mood,	231

LESSON XLVI.

RULE		PAGE
225-226.	Interjections,	237

LESSON XLVII.

227.	Use of the article,	242
228.	The definite article used with common nouns taken in a general sense,	242
229.	The article before the names of the four parts of the globe, names of empires, kingdoms, &c.,	243
230.	Nouns of measure, weight, &c., when they require the article,	243
231.	The article repeated before every noun enumerated,	243
232.	The definite article used before nouns indicating rank, office, &c.,	243
233.	Used instead of the possessive adjective,	244
234.	Used as in English, before nouns, taken in a particular or definite sense,	244

LESSON XLVIII.

235.	Correspondence of the tenses with each other,	249
236.	When the determined verb is put in the infinitive,	250
237.	When the determining verb is *ser*, or any impersonal verb, and the governing verb has no subject,	250
238.	Put in the subjunctive when the determining verb has a nominative,	251
239.	When the governing verb is put in the present or future of the subjunctive,	251
240.	Government of the preterit indefinite, and compound future of the indicative,	251
241.	The nominative being the same for both verbs and the governing one in the indicative, in what mood the determining verb is put,	252

LESSON XLIX.

242, 243, 244, 245, 246, 247, 248, 249, 250, 251, 252.	Derivative nouns,	257

LESSON L.

253.	Compound nouns,	264

LESSON LI.

254.	The natural construction,	269
255, 256.	Figurative construction,	270
257.	Which of the two constructions is preferable,	271

LESSON LII.

258.	*Past Participles*,	276
259.	Agreement of past participles,	276
260.	When a verb has two past participles, one regular and the other irregular, how they are used,	277
261.	Irregular past participles that may be used with the verb *haber*,	277
262.	Extraordinary irregularity of the verb *morir*,	277
263.	Some past or passive participles take an active signification,	278
264.	Past participles may sometimes take the place of substantives,	278
265.	Other tenses in the infinitive mood,	278

CONTENTS.

LESSON LIII.

RULE		PAGE
266.	Idiomatic expressions, in which the English preposition differs in meaning from that which most generally constitutes its proper signification,	284

LESSON LIV.

267.	Conjunctions in English that are frequently used as substitutes for other words, how rendered into Spanish,	289
268.	Spanish conjunctions used as substitutes for other words,	289
—.	Different uses of the conjunction *si*,	289

LESSON LV.

| 269. | Some of the principal uses of the conjunction *que*, | 295 |

LESSON LVI.

| 270. | Epistolary correspondence, | 301 |

LESSON LVII.

| 271. | Observation in regard to verbs that change their meaning according to the preposition by which they are followed, | 310 |

LESSON LVIII.

272.	The verbs *to be glad* and *to be rejoiced*, how translated,	314
273.	The verbs *to be sorry* and *to grieve*, how translated,	314
274.	How the verb *caber* is used,	314

LESSON LIX.

| 275. | Idioms with the verbs *caer, dar, decir, echar*, | 320 |

LESSON LX.

| 276. | Idioms with the verbs *entrar, hacer, ir, llevar, mandar, oler á, saber á, salir, servir, tardar*, and *volver*, | 326 |

LESSONS LXI TO LXV.

On the Principal Idioms of the Spanish Language, ... 329 to 354

General observations on some grammatical and idiomatical peculiarities of the Spanish language, not hitherto treated of in the Grammar, . . . 355
Recapitulation of all the rules of the Grammar, . . . 365 to 382
Complete list of the conjugations of all the Spanish verbs, . . 383 to 438
List of all the irregular verbs, ... 439, 440
VOCABULARY, containing all the Spanish words used in the grammar, . 441 to 470

PRELIMINARY LESSON

ON

ORTHOGRAPHY AND PRONUNCIATION.

THE ALPHABET.

THE SPANISH ALPHABET contains twenty-seven letters, exclusive of *K* and *W*, which are used in foreign words only, and are pronounced as in English. The *W* appears in a very few historical names, like *Wamba*, *Witiza*. The letters are all of the feminine gender, and their names and pronunciation are as follows:

A,	a,	*ah.*	N,	n,	*aynay.*
B,	b,	*bay.*	Ñ,	ñ,	*ain-yay.*
C,	c,	*thay.*	O,	o,	*o.*
CH,	ch,	*chay.*	P,	p,	*pay.*
D,	d,	*day.*	Q,	q,	*koo.*
E,	e,	*ay.*	R,	r,	*air-ray.*
F,	f,	*ay-fay.*	S,	s,	*aysay.*
G,	g,	*hay.*	T,	t,	*tay.*
H,	h,	*at-chay.*	U,	u,	*oo.*
I,	i,	*e.*	V,	v,	*vay.*
J,	j,	*hotah.*	X,	x,	*aykiss.*
L,	l,	*a-lay.*	Y,	y,	*e-gree-ay'-gah.*
LL,	ll,	*ail-yay.*	Z,	z,	*thay-tah.*
M,	m,	*aymay.*			

All the letters are invariable in sound, except *c* and *g*, which have each two sounds, as will be seen in the proper place; and every letter is pronounced in all positions, except the *h*, which is always silent, and the *u*, which is not sounded in the syllables *gue, gui*, and *que, qui*.

So that, with a few exceptions, the Spanish language is pronounced exactly as it is written, and does not present those difficulties met with in the orthography and pronunciation of most other languages. The system of representing, in each lesson, the pronunciation of each word by an incorrect orthography only augments the doubts and labor of the learner, besides increasing unnecessarily the size of the work; one lesson of an hour's duration with a native Spanish teacher will do more toward the acquisition of a pure Castilian pronunciation, than all the works that could be written on the subject.

As the English vowels differ in sound from those of all other languages, great care ought to be taken to learn the true sound of the Spanish vowels; they are:

a, e, i, o, u.
ah, ay, e, o, oo.

Y is sometimes a vowel. (See the letter *Y*.)

A has an invariable sound, as heard in the words *art, father*; as, *arte, padre* (not varying as in the English words *fare, fat, far, fall, swallow, many, courage, mustard*).

E has the sound of *ā* in *made*; as, *hecho*.

I sounds like the first *e* in *even*; as, *inglés*. (See letter *Y*.)

O is pronounced like the English *o* in the word *ode*; as, *amo*.

U sounds as the English *u* in *bull*; as, *bula*: it is silent in the syllables *gue, gui, guerra*, except it has a diæresis marked over it, *agüero*. In the syllables *que, qui*, it is always silent.

SOUNDS OF THE CONSONANTS.

B has the same sound as in English; but in Castile and Aragon (where in other respects the Castilian language is most purely spoken and pronounced), they do not press the lips quite so close as the English do, which causes it very frequently to be confounded with the *v*, although they are distinct letters, and should be pronounced as in English.

C, when followed by *a, o, u,* or any consonant, sounds like *k*; before *e* and *i*, it sounds like *th* in *thanks*; as, *gracias, leccion, caballero.* (See letter *Z.*)

CH is not a double consonant, but a letter which, although of a double form, has by itself a particular denomination and sound; it is pronounced like *ch* in *chess*; as, *chico, chocolate.* Formerly, in words of Hebrew and Greek origin, it had the sound of *k*, when the vowel following it was marked with the circumflex accent; as, *archángel, chímica*: but this practice is obsolete, and such words are now written *arcángel, química.*

D is pronounced like the English *d*, except when found between two vowels or at the end of words, when it sounds softer than the English *d*, like *th* in the article *the*, but not like *th* lisped, as in *thin*, as Madri*d* (like *the*), not Madri*z* (like *thin*); Uste*d* (like *the*), not Uste*z* (like *thin*). This lisped pronunciation on the *d* is considered vulgar.

F is always pronounced like the English *f*, and is now used instead of *ph*; as, *Filosofía, Filadelfia,* instead of *Philosophia, Philadelphia.*

G has two distinct sounds: one, before *a, o, u,* or a consonant, is the same sound as in English *go, good*; as, *gato, gracias*: before *e* and *i* it has another strong, guttural, aspirated sound, for which the English has no equivalent, and which even a very strongly aspirated *h*, as in the words *hot, holy,* does not represent; as, *gente,* people; *gesto,* gesture; *gigante,* giant.

H is never pronounced in the Spanish language; as, *hace, higo,* pronounced as if no such *h* were there. It is, properly speaking, only a sign used to mark the etymology of words, and is now omitted in many words in which it was formerly used; as, *Cristo, Filosofía, Teatro, Pitágoras, Filadelfia.*

This letter is always written before the words that begin by *ue* and *ie*, and here it has a very soft, almost imperceptible, aspiration; as, *huevo*, egg; *hueso*, bone; *huésped*, guest; *hierro*, iron; *hielo*, ice: but great care must be taken not to pronounce it too strong, as the lower classes of certain provinces do, pronouncing *juevo*, or *guevo*; *jueso*, or *güeso*, which is considered vulgar.

J has always an aspirated guttural sound, like that which the *g* has before *e* and *i*, and is written before the vowels *a*, *o*, *u*, instead of the letter *x*, which formerly represented the same aspirated sound; as, *Alejandro*, Alexander; *Don Quijote*, Don Quixote.

L always sounds as in English.

LL is, like the *ch*, a single letter, although of double form, which therefore cannot be divided at the end of a line. It has a liquid sound, resembling that of the English *ll* in *William*, *brilliant*; as, *Guillermo*, *brillante*.

M, **N**, and **P** have the English sound.

Ñ is always pronounced like *ni* in the English word *pinion*.

Q is pronounced like the English *k* before *ue* and *ui*, in which combination alone it is now used; in all other positions it has been replaced by *c*; as, *cuando*, *cama*, *comer*, *quien*, *querer*.

R, when single, is sounded soft, as in English; as, *querido*, *oro*: and when double, or at the beginning of a word, and when it comes after *l*, *n*, or *s*, or in compound words, in which the second begins by *r*, it is pronounced with a very strong rolling sound; as, *reloj*, *malrotar*, *enriquecer*, *Israel*, *prerogativa*, *maniroto*, *cariredondo*, &c.

S is pronounced like the English *s* in *say*; as, *sabio*, wise; *solo*, alone; *señor*, sir.

T is pronounced as in English.

V has the sound of the English *v*. (See letter *B*.)

X has the sound of the *x* in the English word *tax*; as, *exámen, extrangero*. It no longer represents its former guttural sound, as has been observed. (See letter *J*.) Some replace it by the letter *s*, when it comes before a consonant, and write *estrangero* instead of *extrangero*. The grammar of the Spanish Academy does not authorize this practice.

Y is a consonant letter, but use makes it serve as a vowel when it stands alone, used as a copulative conjunction (meaning *and*); it is also used instead of the vowel *i*, in the combinations *ai, ei, ui* at the end of a word; as, *verdegay, rey, ley, convoy, muy.*

When used in its proper place, that is to say, as a consonant, it has the same sound in Spanish as in the English words *young, year.*

Z has always the sound of *th*, as heard in *thank, bath.*

SYLLABLES.

Such syllables only will be noted here as may be subject to doubt as to the pronunciation and orthography.

ca,	que,	qui,	co,	cu,
kah.	*kay.*	*kee.*	*kŏ.*	*koo.*
za,	ce,	ci,	zo,	zu,
thah.	*thay.*	*thee.*	*thŏ.*	*thoo.*
az,	ez,	iz,	oz,	uz,
ath.	*aith.*	*eeth.*	*ŏth.*	*ooth.*
ga,	gue,	gui,	go,	gu,
gah.	*gay.*	*ghee.*	*gŏ.*	*goo.*
ja,	ge,	gi,	jo,	ju,
hah.	*hay.*	*hee.*	*hŏ.*	*hoo.*
ya,	ye.	yi.	yo.	yu.

This sound cannot be properly represented in English. (See letter **Y**).

cha,	che,	chi,	cho,	chu,
tchah.	*tchay.*	*tchee.*	*tchŏ.*	*tchoo.*

lla,	lle,	lli,	llo,	llu,
lyah.	*lyay.*	*lyee.*	*lyō.*	*lyoo.*
ña,	ñe,	ñi,	ño,	ñu,
nyah.	*nyai.*	*nye.*	*nyŏ.*	*nyoo.*
cua,	cue,	cui,	cuo,	
kwah	*kway.*	*kwee.*	*kwŏ.*	
gua,	güe,	güi,	guo,	
gwah.	*gway.*	*gwee.*	*gwŏ.*	

DIPHTHONGS.

ai,	as in	dab*ai*s,	*dah'-bah-eess.*	You gave.
ay,	"	h*ay,*	*ah'-ĕ.*	There is.
au,	"	p*au*sa,	*pah'-oo-sa.*	Pause.
ei,	"	v*ei*s,	*vai'-eess.*	You see.
ey,	"	l*ey,*	*lai'-ĕ.*	Law.
ea,	"	lín*ea,*	*lĕ'-nai-a.*	Line.
eo,	"	virgín*eo,*	*veer-hĕ'-nai-o.*	Virginal.
eu,	"	d*eu*da,	*dai'-oo-da.*	Debt.
ia,	"	grac*ia,*	*grah'-thĕ-a.*	Grace.
ie,	"	c*ie*lo,	*thĕ-ai'-lo.*	Heaven.
io,	"	prec*io,*	*prai-thĕ-o.*	Price.
iu,	"	c*iu*dad,	*thĕ-oo-dath'.*	City.
oe,	"	hér*oe,*	*aï-rō-ai.*	Hero.
oi,	"	s*oi*s,	*so'-eess.*	You are.
oy,	"	v*oy,*	*vō'-e.*	I go.
ua,	"	frag*ua,*	*frah'-gwa.*	Forge.
ue,	"	dueño,	*doo-ain'-yo.*	Owner.
ui,	"	r*ui*do,	*roo-ē'-do.*	Noise.
uy,	"	m*uy,*	*moo'-ĕ.*	Very.
uo,	"	ard*uo,*	*ar'-doo-o.*	Arduous.

TRIPHTHONGS.

iai,	as in	prec*iai*s,	*prai-thĕ-ah'-eess.*
iei,	"	vac*iei*s,	*vah-thĕ-aï-eess.*
uai,	"	santig*uai*s,	*san-tē-gwah'-eess.*
uay,	"	Parag*uay,*	*pah-rah-gwah'-ĕ.*
uei,	"	averig*üei*s,	*ah-vai-rĕ-gwai'-eess.*
uey,	"	b*uey,*	*bwaï-ĕ.*

DE TORNOS'S
SPANISH GRAMMAR.

LESSON I.

REGULAR VERBS.—*First Conjugation.*

*Habl-*ar.　|　To speak.

INDICATIVE PRESENT.

Yo habl-o.	I speak.
Tú habl-as.	Thou speakest.
El or ella habl-a.	He or she speaks.
Usted (V.) habl-a.	You speak.
Nosotros, or Nosotras, } habl-amos.	We speak.
Vosotros, or Vosotras, } habl-ais.	You speak.
Ellos, or ellas, habl-an.	They speak.
Ustedes (Vds.) habl-an.	You speak.

Sí (*adverb*).	Yes.
No "	No, or not.
Señor.	Sir.

COMPOSITION.

¿ Habla V. ?	Do you speak ?
Sí, señor, yo hablo.	Yes, sir, I speak.
¿ Hablan Vds. ?	Do you speak ?

LESSON I.

No, señor, ellas hablan.	No, sir, they speak.
¿Hablais vosotras?	Do you speak?
No, señor, ellos hablan.	No, sir, they speak.
¿Habla ella?	Does she speak?
No, señor, ella no habla.	No, sir, she does not speak.
¿Hablas tú?	Dost thou speak?
No, señor, él habla.	No, sir, he speaks.
¿Habla V.?	Do you speak?
Sí, señor, hablo.	Yes, sir, I speak.
¿Hablan ellas?	Do they speak?
No, señor, no hablan.	No, sir, they do not speak.
¿Hablamos nosotros?	Do we speak?
Sí, señor, hablamos.	Yes, sir, we speak.
¿Hablais vosotras?	Do you speak?
Nosotras no hablamos.	We do not speak.

EXPLANATION.

1. REGULAR VERBS.—All the verbs of the Spanish language have their endings, in the infinitive mood, either in *ar*, *er*, or *ir*; hence their classification in three conjugations: 1st, those ending in *ar*; 2d, those ending in *er*; and 3d, in *ir*; as, *habl-ar*, *aprend-er*, *escrib-ir*.

2. ROOTS.—The letters before the terminations *ar*, *er*, *ir*, in the preceding verbs, are *habl*, *aprend*, *escrib*, and are called the roots.

3. TERMINATIONS.—All regular verbs of the *first conjugation* vary the endings in their respective tenses, so as to correspond with those of the verb *habl-ar*; all those of the *second conjugation* correspond to the terminations of *aprend-er*; and all those of the *third* correspond to *escrib-ir*.

Consequently, when the student has learned how to conjugate one of the regular verbs of each conjugation, he can conjugate all the *regular* verbs of the Spanish language (about 8,000). For this reason we recommend the scholars to devote their attention, in the *first place*, to committing to memory the different moods and tenses of these three model verbs. They will be found complete at the end of the book.

The terminations of the verbs being different for each person, as well in the plural as in the singular number, the nominative pronouns are ordinarily dispensed with, and are only used to give emphasis; except the pronoun *Usted*, which must always be expressed.—*Usted*, meaning You, is a contraction from *vuestra merced*, Your Honor; and, being a title, its omission would be considered impolite.

4. You.—In addressing an individual in Spanish, the third person is used with the pronoun *Usted*: as, *Usted habla*, you speak; the second person is employed only in speaking to relatives or intimate friends.

CONVERSATION AND VERSION.

1. ¿Hablan ellas? Sí, señor, ellas hablan.
2. ¿Hablais vosotros? No, señor; ellos hablan.
3. ¿Hablamos nosotras? No, señor; ella habla.
4. ¿Hablais vosotros? No, señor; él habla.
5. ¿Habla ella? Sí, señor, habla.
6. ¿Habla él? No, señor, no habla.
7. ¿Hablas tú? Sí, señor, yo hablo.
8. ¿Hablais vosotras? Sí, señor, nosotras hablamos.
9. ¿Hablo yo? Sí, señor, V. habla.
10. ¿Habla él? No, señor, no habla.
11. ¿No hablan ellos? Sí, señor, ellos hablan.
12. ¿Habla V.? No, señor, yo no hablo.
13. ¿No habla V.? No, señor, yo no hablo.
14. ¿No hablan ellas? Sí, señor, hablan.
15. ¿No hablais vosotras? No, señor, nosotras no hablamos.

EXCERCISE.

1. Do you speak? I speak.
2. Do they speak? Yes, sir, they speak.
3. Dost thou speak? No, sir, he speaks.
4. Do you speak? No, sir, we do not speak.
5. Dost thou speak? No, sir, I do not speak.
6. Does he not speak? Yes, sir, he speaks.
7. Do you not speak? No, sir, we do not speak.
8. Does she not speak? No, sir, she does not speak.
9. Do we not speak? Yes, sir, we speak.
10. Do they (*fem.*) not speak? No, sir, they (*fem.*) do not speak.
11. Do we (*fem.*) not speak? Yes, sir, we (*fem.*) speak.
12. Do you speak? No, sir, I do not speak; they (*fem.*) speak.

LESSON II.

MASCULINE NOUNS.		FEMININE NOUNS.	
Señor (Sr.).	Sir, Mr., or Lord.	Señora (Sra.).	Madam, or Mrs.
Caballero.	Gentleman, Sir.	" "	Lady, or My Lady.
Señorito.	Young gentleman.	Señorita (Srita).	Miss, or young lady.
Don. (Dn., or D.).	Mr., Esq.	Doña (Da.)	Mrs.

Manuel.	Emanuel.		
Español.	Spanish.		
Inglés.	English.	Luisa.	Louisa.
Frances.	French.		
Aleman.	German.		

COMPOSITION.

Señorita, ¿habla V. español?	Do you speak Spanish, Miss?
Sí, señor, hablo español.	Yes, sir, I speak Spanish.
Luisa, ¿hablas frances?	Louisa, dost thou speak French?
No, señor, no hablo frances.	No, sir, I do not speak French.
¿Hablan Vds. inglés?	Do you speak English?
Hablamos inglés.	We speak English.
¿Hablan ellos, ó ellas, frances?	Do they speak French?
Señora, ¿habla V. español?	Madam, do you speak Spanish?
Don Manuel, ¿habla V. aleman?	Mr. Emanuel, do you speak German?
Caballero, ¿habla V. español?	Sir, do you speak Spanish?
Señorita Luisa, ¿habla V. frances?	Miss Louisa, do you speak French?

EXPLANATION.

5. SEÑOR.—This word, used alone, i. e., in the vocative case, implies inferiority on the part of the speaker, and answers to the word *Lord* in English. It is used in addressing God, or the King; or by servants when speaking to their masters. With an equal, the proper term is *caballero*, gentleman; nevertheless, *Señor* may also be used among equals: in the affirmative, *Sí, señor*, or in the negative, *no, señor*, in which cases it means sir; or together with the name of the person; as, *Señor Kemp*, which means Mr. Kemp.

Señora, Señorita.—In addressing ladies, the word *Señora*, Madam, and *Señorita*, Young Lady, or Miss, may be used alone; as, *Señora*, or *Señorita*, *¿habla V. español?* Madam, or Young Lady, or Miss, do you speak Spanish?

Señorito, like *Señor*, implies inferiority on the part of the speaker, for which reason it is seldom used, except by servants.

6. Don, Mr., applies to gentlemen, and *Doña*, Mrs., to ladies. These terms are only used in conjunction with the Christian names; as, *Don Manuel, Doña Luisa*, and, still more respectfully, *Señor Don Manuel, Señora Doña Luisa*. This title, conferred, in old times, only upon members of noble families, is now used in addressing all persons, except those of very humble station, and is written in abbreviation thus, Dn., Da.

7. The negative *no*, is always placed immediately before the verb.

CONVERSATION AND VERSION.

1. ¿Habla V. español? Hablo español.
2. Luisa, ¿hablas frances? Hablo frances.
3. ¿Habla Manuel inglés? Habla inglés.
4. Caballero, ¿habla V. aleman? Sí, señor, hablo aleman.
5. ¿Hablan Vds. frances? Hablamos frances.
6. ¿Hablan ellos inglés? No, señor, no hablan inglés.
7. ¿Hablan ellas español? No, señor, no hablan español.
8. ¿Habla Luisa frances? No, señor, no habla frances; ella habla español.
9. ¿No habla Manuel aleman? No, señor, no habla aleman; él habla inglés.
10. ¿Habla V. español? No, señor, no hablo español.
11. ¿Habla Manuel español? Sí, señor, él habla español.
12. Don Manuel, ¿habla V. frances? No, señor, no hablo frances.
13. Señora Da. Luisa, ¿habla V. español? No, señor; hablo inglés.
14. Señorita Da. Luisa, ¿habla V. frances? Yo hablo frances.
15. Caballero, ¿habla V. aleman? No, señorita, hablo español.

EXERCISE.

1. Do they speak French? They speak French.
2. Do you speak English? We speak English.
3. Do they speak Spanish? No, madam, they do not speak Spanish.
4. Sir, do you speak German? Yes, madam, I speak German.
5. Does Emanuel speak French? No, sir; he speaks English.

6. Do you speak Spanish? No, sir, I do not speak Spanish.
7. Does not Louisa speak German? No, sir, she does not speak German; she speaks French.
8. Emanuel, dost thou speak English? I speak English.
9. Does Louisa speak Spanish? Yes, sir, she speaks Spanish.
10. Do you speak French? No, sir, I speak English.
11. Sir, do you speak French? No, sir.
12. Miss Louisa, do you speak Spanish? Yes, madam.
13. (Don) Emanuel, do you speak English? Yes, sir, I speak English.
14. Do we speak Spanish? We do not speak Spanish; we speak French.

LESSON III.

Estudi-ar.	To study.
Estudi-o.	I study.
Estudi-as.	Thou studiest.
Estudi-a.	He studies.
Estudi-amos.	We study.
Estudi-ais.	You study.
Estudi-an.	They study.
El (*masc. sing.*).	The.
Y or é.	And.
Qué (*interrogative pronoun*).	What or which.
Pero, sino.	But.
Bien (*adverb*).	Well.
Mal "	Badly.

ADJECTIVES.

Español.	Spaniard.
Inglés.	Englishman.
Frances.	Frenchman.
Aleman.	German.
Americano.	American.

MASCULINE NOUNS.	FEMININE NOUNS.
Alejandro. Alexander.	Margarita. Margaret.

LESSON III.

COMPOSITION.

¿ Estudia V. español?	Do you study Spanish?
No, señor, el Frances estudia español; pero yo estudio inglés.	No, sir, the Frenchman studies Spanish; but I study English.
¿ Qué estudia el Americano?	What does the American study?
Estudia español y frances.	He studies Spanish and French.
Alejandro, ¿ estudias frances y aleman?	Alexander, do you study French and German?
No, señor, estudio español é inglés.	No, sir, I study Spanish and English.
Manuel no estudia sino frances.	Emanuel studies but (only) French.
¿ Qué hablan ellos sino español?	What do they speak but Spanish?
¿ Habla bien inglés el Español?	Does the Spaniard speak English well?
No, señor, él habla el inglés mal, pero habla bien el español.	No, sir, he speaks English badly, but speaks Spanish well.

EXPLANATION.

8. Y.—The conjunction *y* is changed into *é* when the following word begins with *i* or *hi*; as, *español é inglés*, Spanish and English; *algodon é hilo*, cotton and thread.

9. QUÉ, *interrogative pronoun*, is written with an accent, to distinguish it from *que*, relative pronoun, or conjunction.

10. SINO.—When we translate *but* into Spanish, we must first ascertain its meaning; because this conjunction is used in English to express many very different things. In Spanish it is translated *sino*, when it is used in antithesis, that is, when it means *except*; and also after an interrogation, or a negation. The verb is not repeated with this conjunction; as, Él no habla *sino* inglés. He speaks but (only) English. ¿ Qué habla *sino* español? What (else) does he speak but Spanish?

11. PERO is used when it is not preceded by a negative, and the verb is repeated; as, *hablo español, pero no hablo frances*. I speak Spanish, but do not speak French.

N. B.—We will see hereafter that *but*, according to its different meanings in English, must be translated by different words in Spanish.

12. We have again introduced the words *español*, *inglés*, *frances*, and *aleman* into this lesson, because, while they were given before as substantives, they are now employed as adjectives. The pupil will observe that, in Spanish, as in English, some words are, at different times, different parts of speech; as,

LESSON III.

El Español habla *bien* frances. The Spaniard speaks French well. Here the word *Español* is used as an adjective, meaning *Spaniard*; and the word *frances* as a substantive, meaning the *French language*; *bien* is employed as an adverb, meaning *well*, and it will appear hereafter as a substantive, meaning *good*. Consequently, the learner, before translating a word, must first ascertain the part of speech to which it belongs.

CONVERSATION AND VERSION.

1. ¿Habla español Margarita? Margarita no habla español, pero habla inglés.
2. ¿Habla V. español? No, señor, hablo frances y aleman.
3. Alejandro, ¿hablas inglés? Sí, señor, hablo inglés.
4. ¿Hablan Vds. español? Hablamos español ó inglés.
5. ¿Qué hablan ellos? Hablan aleman.
6. Caballero, ¿estudia V. español? Sí, señor, estudio español ó inglés.
7. ¿Qué estudia el Aleman? Estudia español.
8. ¿Estudian Vds. español? Estudiamos frances y aleman.
9. ¿Habla bien Luisa el inglés? Habla bien español ó inglés.
10. ¿Habla bien Manuel el aleman? No, señor, habla mal el aleman, pero habla bien el frances.
11. ¿Habla bien inglés el Americano? Habla bien inglés, pero habla mal el español.
12. Señora, ¿estudia V. frances? No, señor, estudio español.
13. ¿Qué estudia Alejandro? El no estudia sino frances.
14. ¿Qué hablan ellos sino español? Ellos hablan frances.

EXERCISE.

1. Do you study German? We study French and Spanish.
2. Does Alexander speak Spanish? Alexander does not speak Spanish, but he speaks English.
3. Margaret, do you speak French? No, sir, I speak German and Spanish.
4. What do they speak? They speak Spanish and German, but do not speak French.
5. Do you speak Spanish? No, sir, I do not speak Spanish, but I speak English.
6. Does Louisa speak French well? She speaks French badly, but speaks German well.

LESSON IV.

7. What do you study? We study Spanish, and Alexander studies French.
8. What does the German study? He studies Spanish.
9. Does he study well? No, madam, he studies badly.
10. Do you speak Spanish, madam? No, sir, I do not speak Spanish, but I speak English and German.
11. Does the Frenchman speak English well? No, madam, he speaks English badly, but the Spaniard speaks English well.
12. What does the German study? He studies English, and the Englishman studies German.
13. What does Alexander study? He studies French only.
14. What do they speak but Spanish? } They speak French.
    What else do they speak but Spanish? }

LESSON IV.

Compr-ar.	To buy.
Compr-o.	I buy.
Compr-as.	Thou buyest.
Compr-a.	He buys.
Compr-amos.	We buy.
Compr-ais.	You buy.
Compr-an.	They buy.
Busc-ar.	To look for, to seek.
A.	To.
De.	Of, or from.
Al.	To the.
Del.	Of the, or from the.
Un (*masc. sing.*).	A, or an.

Libro.	Book.		
Cuaderno.	Copy-book.		
Papel.	Paper.	Madera.	Wood.
Caballo.	Horse.		
Tintero.	Inkstand.		

COMPOSITION.

¿ Qué compra V. ?	What do you buy?
Compro un libro.	I buy a book.

LESSON IV.

¿Compran Vds. papel?	Do you buy paper?
¿No, señor, no compramos papel, compramos un cuaderno.	No, sir, we do not buy paper, we buy a copy-book.
Busco al Americano.	I look for the American.
Él busca el libro.	He looks for the book.
El caballo del Frances.	The Frenchman's horse.
El tintero de madera.	The wooden inkstand.

EXPLANATION.

13. Á.—The preposition *á*, *to*. Active verbs govern their objectives with the aid of the preposition *á*, if that objective be a person; as, *Busco al Americano*, I look for the American; *Busco el papel*, I look for the paper.

14. DE.—The preposition *de*, *of*, or *from*, is used to express possession, being always placed before the possessor; as, *El caballo del Frances*: The Frenchman's horse. It is also used to denote the material of which any thing consists, or is made; as, *El tintero de madera*, The wooden inkstand.

15. EL.—The article *el*, *the*, is used to determine a noun masculine singular; as, *el libro*, the book.

N. B.—When the article *el* comes after the preposition *á* (to), or *de* (of, or from), the *e* is suppressed, and the two words compounded into one; thus, *al*, *del*, instead of *á el*, *de el*.

16. UN.—The indefinite pronoun *un* is used before masculine nouns; as, *un* inglés, an Englishman; *un* caballo, a horse.

N. B.—*Uno* is only used as a numeral adjective.

CONVERSATION AND VERSION.

1. ¿Qué compra el Francés? .Compra el caballo del Inglés.
2. ¿Qué comprais vosotras? Compramos un cuaderno.
3. ¿Qué compra V.? Compro un libro.
4. ¿Compran Vds. un cuaderno? No, señor, compramos un tintero de madera.
5. ¿Qué buscas tú? Busco un libro español.
6. ¿Qué buscais vosotros? Nosotros buscamos un tintero.
7. ¿Qué buscan ellas? Buscan el papel.
8. Alejandro, ¿buscas el papel? No, señor, busco el cuaderno.
9. ¿Estudia Margarita inglés? No, señor, estudia frances.

LESSON IV.

10. ¿Qué estudia el Americano? Estudia español.
11. ¿Estudian Vds. frances? No, señor, estudiamos inglés.
12. ¿Qué estudia ella? Estudia aleman.
13. ¿Qué compra V.? Compro el caballo del Español.
14. ¿Qué compran ellos? Compran un tintero de madera.
15. ¿Buscais vosotros al Aleman? No, señor, buscamos al Frances.
16. ¿Hablais vosotros aleman? Sí, señor, hablamos aleman.
17. ¿Hablan ellas español? No, señor, hablan frances.
18. ¿Qué estudia V.? Estudio inglés y español.
19. ¿Compra ella un libro? Sí, señor, compra un libro.
20. ¿Busca él al Frances? No, señor, busca al Aleman.
21. ¿Qué habla el Americano? Habla español.
22. Manuel ¿qué estudias tú? Estudio aleman.
23. ¿Qué compran ellos? Compran un caballo.
24. ¿Qué buscan Vds.? Buscamos el libro español.

EXERCISE.

1. What do they look for? They look for an inkstand.
2. What does she look for? She looks for a book.
3. Do you look for a copy-book? Yes, sir, we (*fem.*) look for a copy-book.
4. Do they (*fem.*) buy a wooden inkstand? Yes, sir, they buy a wooden inkstand.
5. What do you buy? We buy the Frenchman's horse.
6. Do you buy paper? No, sir, I buy a book.
7. Do you buy a copy-book? Yes, sir, I buy a copy-book.
8. What does the Frenchman study? He studies German.
9. Do you study Spanish? No, sir, I study French.
10. What does she study? She studies English.
11. What do they (*fem.*) study? They study Spanish.
12. Do you speak French? Yes, sir, I speak French.
13. Does she speak English? No, sir, she speaks German.
14. Do you speak German? No, sir, we (*fem.*) speak English.
15. Do you look for the Frenchman? Yes, sir, I look for the Frenchman.
16. Do you look for paper? No, sir, I look for a copy-book.
17. What do they look for? They look for a book.
18. Do you look for the German? Yes, sir, we (*fem.*) look for the German.
19. Do you speak French? Yes, sir, I speak French.
20. What does Margaret speak? She speaks English.

21. What do they buy? They buy a wooden inkstand.
22. What dost thou look for? I look for a horse.
23. What do you study? We (*fem.*) study Spanish.
24. What do you speak? I speak English.

LESSON V.

Necesitar.	To need, or to be in want of.
Necesit-o. *nai-thai-sē-to*	I need.
Necesit-as.	Thou needest.
Necesit-a.	He needs.
Necesit-amos.	We need.
Necesit-ais.	You need.
Necesit-an.	They need.

Mi.	My.
Su.	His, her, its, their.
Su (*n*) de V., *or* El (*n*) de V.	Your.

GENDER.

El papá.	The papa.	La mamá.	The mamma.
El abogado.	The lawyer.	La pluma.	The pen.
El comerciante.	The merchant.	La tinta.	The ink.
El lacre.	The sealing-wax.	La gramática.	The grammar.
El pollo.	The chicken.	La gallina.	The hen. *gal-y*
El algodon.	The cotton.	La seda.	The silk.
El jabon.	The soap.	La lavandera.	The washerwoman.
El pañuelo.	The handkerchief.	La camisa.	The shirt. *kah-n*
El zapatero.	The shoemaker.		*thah-pah-toŭ-ro*

COMPOSITION.

¿Necesita el abogado la pluma?	Does the lawyer want the pen?
Sí, señor, necesita la pluma y el tintero.	Yes, sir, he wants the pen and the inkstand.
¿Qué necesita comprar la lavandera?	What does the washerwoman want to buy?
Necesita comprar jabon.	She wants to buy soap.
¿Necesita el comerciante mi algodon?	Does the merchant want my cotton?

LESSON V.

Necesita comprar el algodon de V. y la seda del Frances.	He wants to buy your cotton, and the Frenchman's silk.
¿Necesita V. su pañuelo de algodon?	Do you want your cotton handkerchief?
No, señora, necesito su pañuelo de seda de V.	No, madam, I want your silk handkerchief.
¿Que necesitan Vds.?	What do you want?
Necesitamos un pollo y una gallina.	We want a chicken and a hen.

EXPLANATION.

17. GENDER.—In Spanish all nouns are either masculine or feminine; the neuter gender is only applied to those things so indefinitely used that their gender cannot be discovered.

The gender of nouns may be ascertained either by their signification or their termination.

Nouns which signify males, or which denote dignities or professions, &c., applicable to men, are masculine; and those which signify females, or professions, &c., applicable to women, are feminine, without regard to their terminations: so that, *hombre*, man; *caballero*, gentleman; *pollo*, chicken; *zapatero*, shoemaker; *abogado*, lawyer, are masculine; and *mujer*, woman; *señora*, lady; *gallina*, hen; *lavandera*, washerwoman, are feminine.

Nounds ending in *a, d,* or *ion*, are generally feminine, and those ending in other letters are masculine; as,

Papel.	Paper.	Leccion.	Lesson.
Tintero.	Inkstand.	Pluma.	Pen.
Billete.	Billet.	Ciudad.	City.

N. B.—*Una* (*indefinite article*) is used before feminine nouns.

To facilitate the pupils in the distinction of gender, the left-hand side, in the vocabulary, is reserved for masculine, the right for feminine nouns.

18. When *your* is preceded by *you*, it is sometimes translated by *Su*; otherwise, it is generally rendered by *el——de V.*, or *su——de V.*; as,

V. necesita su carta.	You need your letter.
¿Qué necesita el papá de V.?	What does your father need?
Necesita su libro de V.	He needs your book.

LESSON V.

CONVERSATION AND VERSION.

1. ¿Necesita V. mi gramática? No, señor, no necesito su gramática de V.
2. ¿Necesita ella el pañuelo de seda? Sí, señor, ella necesita el pañuelo de seda.
3. ¿Necesita V. comprar un libro? Necesito comprar un cuaderno.
4. ¿Necesitan ellas el lacre? No, señor, necesitan el pañuelo de algodon.
5. ¿Qué necesita comprar el abogado? Necesita comprar una pluma.
6. ¿Qué necesita comprar la lavandera? Necesita comprar jabon.
7. ¿Busca V. su pañuelo? Sí, señor, busco mi pañuelo.
8. ¿Busca V. el cuaderno de Manuel? No, señor, busco el cuaderno de V.
9. ¿Habla V. bien el aleman? No, señorita, hablo mal el aleman.
10. ¿Estudian Vds. frances? No, señor, estudiamos español.
11. ¿Compra V. un caballo inglés? Sí, señor, compro un caballo inglés.
12. ¿Qué compran ellos? Compran una pluma y tinta.
13. ¿Qué comprais vosotras? Nosotras compramos un pañuelo de seda.
14. ¿Qué compra la lavandera? Compra jabon.
15. ¿Busca V. á mi abogado? Sí, señor, busco al abogado de V.
16. ¿Compra la lavandera un pollo? Compra una gallina.
17. ¿Compra jabon el comerciante? No, señor, el comerciante compra algodon.
18. ¿Buscan ellas el pañuelo de V.? Buscan el pañuelo de V.
19. ¿Necesita V. hablar al abogado? Sí, señora, necesito hablar al abogado.
20. ¿Necesita V. comprar un libro? No, señor, necesito comprar una pluma y papel.
21. ¿Necesita V. estudiar inglés? Sí, señor, necesito estudiar inglés.
22. ¿Qué necesitais vosotras? Necesitamos comprar lacre.
23. ¿Necesita V. hablar al Frances? No, señor, necesito hablar al Aleman.
24. ¿Qué necesita V.? Necesito un pañuelo de algodon.

EXERCISE.

1. What do you need? I need a book and paper.
2. What does she need? She needs your handkerchief.
3. Do you need a horse? Yes, sir, I need an English horse.
4. What do you need? I need soap.

5. Does the American need the Spanish book? Yes, sir, he needs the Spanish book.

6. Do they need a lawyer? Yes, sir, they need a lawyer.

7. Do you buy a silk handkerchief? No, sir, we (*fem.*) buy a cotton handkerchief.

8. Do you look for the Frenchman's horse? No, sir, I look for the Englishman's horse.

9. Dost thou study German? No, sir, I study English.

10. What does the merchant buy? He buys cotton.

11. What does the washerwoman buy? She buys a hen and a chicken

12. Does the lawyer buy a book? No, sir, he buys paper.

13. Do they (*fem.*) speak well? No, sir, they speak badly.

14. Do you speak French, sir? No, sir, I speak English.

15. Do you study much (*mucho*)? No, sir, we study very little (*poco*).

16. Do you study fast (*aprisa*)? No, sir, I study slowly (*despacio*).

17. Do you buy cotton from the merchant? No, sir, I buy silk from your brother (*hermano*).

18. What does your papa need? He needs the lawyer's book.

19. What are they looking for? They are looking for paper.

20. Do you need a copy-book? No, sir, I need a book.

21. Do you study Spanish? Yes, madam, I study Spanish.

22. Do you need paper and pen? Yes, sir, I need paper and pen.

23. What do they need? They need a silk handkerchief.

24. What do you need? I need an English horse.

LESSON VI.

Aprend-er.	To learn.
Aprend-o.	I learn.
Aprend-es.	Thou learnest.
Aprend-e.	He learns.
Aprend-emos.	We learn.
Aprend-eis.	You learn.
Aprend-en.	They learn.
Vender.	To sell.

LESSON VI.

Muy.		Very.	
Mucho.		Much, a great deal.	
Poco.		Little.	
Aprisa.		Quickly.	
Despacio.		Slowly.	
Estudioso.		Studious.	
Holgazan.		Idle.	
Hombre.	Man.	Mujer.	Woman.
Muchacho.	Boy.	Muchacha.	Girl.
Padre.	Father.	Madre.	Mother.
Hijo.	Son.	Hija.	Daughter.
Hermano.	Brother.	Hermana.	Sister.

COMPOSITION.

¿Aprende muy aprisa el muchacho?	Does the boy learn very fast?
El muchacho estudioso aprende muy aprisa; pero el muchacho holgazan aprende muy despacio.	The studious boy learns very fast; but the idle one learns very slowly.
¿Aprenden inglés su padre y su hermano de V.?	Do your father and brother learn English?
Sí, señor, y mi madre y mi hermana aprenden frances.	Yes, sir, and my mother and sister learn French.
¿Aprende mucho la muchacha?	Does the girl learn much?
No, señor, aprende poco.	No, sir, she learns little.
¿Aprenden aprisa su hijo y su hija de V.?	Do your son and daughter learn fast?
No, señor, aprenden despacio.	No, sir, they learn slowly.

EXPLANATION.

19. THE TERMINATION of the *first person* in the present indicative is always *o* in all the verbs of the Spanish language, to whatever conjugation they may belong, except six irregular verbs, as we shall see in future; so that the only difference between the termination of the second and first conjugations is the changing the *a* into *e* in the second and third persons singular, and in all the plural.

20. MUY is generally translated by *very* or *very much*; as *muy bien*, very well; *muy bueno*, very good, &c.; but it can

LESSON VI.

never qualify a verb nor stand alone in discourse; as, Does he speak very well? Yes, very. *¿Habla él muy bien? Sí, mucho.*

21. Many masculine nouns ending in *o*, change this letter into *a* for the feminine; as,

Hermano.	Brother.	Hermana.	Sister.
Hijo.	Son.	Hija.	Daughter.
Muchacho.	Boy.	Muchacha.	Girl.

CONVERSATION AND VERSION.

1. ¿Aprende V. bien el frances? No, señor, aprendo muy mal el frances.
2. ¿Aprenden ellas aprisa? No, señor, aprenden despacio.
3. ¿Aprende mucho el muchacho holgazan? No, señor, aprende muy poco.
4. ¿Aprendeis vosotros aprisa? Sí, señor, aprisa y bien.
5. ¿Qué vende el hermano de su padre de V.? Vende algodon.
6. ¿Venden ellas papel? No, señor, venden plumas y lacre.
7. ¿Qué vende Margarita? Vende una gallina.
8. ¿Vende lacre el comerciante? No, señor, vende papel.
9. ¿Necesita V. el pañuelo de su hermana? No, señor, necesito el pañuelo de su hija de V.
10. ¿Busca su mamá de V. el pañuelo de seda? No, señor, busca el pañuelo de algodon.
11. ¿Qué necesita su hija de V.? Necesita hablar al hermano de V.
12. ¿Necesita la muchacha comprar papel? No, señora, necesita comprar un cuaderno.
13. ¿Habla V. del Frances? No, señorita, hablo del Aleman.
14. ¿Qué compra su padre de V.? Compra el caballo del hijo del abogado.
15. ¿Qué busca V.? Busco un libro y una pluma.
16. ¿Qué busca la muchacha? Busca el jabon de la hermana de V.
17. ¿Aprende mucho el muchacho estudioso? Sí, señor, aprende mucho.
18. ¿Aprende V. su leccion de frances? No, señor, aprendo mi leccion de aleman.
19. ¿Habla bien Don Manuel el español? Sí, señor, habla muy bien el español.
20. ¿Estudia V. gramática inglesa? No, señor, estudio gramática francesa.
21. ¿Compra V. un tintero y papel? No compro sino un tintero.

22. ¿Busca V. á mi padre? Sí, señorita, busco á su padre de V.

23. ¿Necesita V. comprar un tintero? No, señora, necesito hablar á mi hermana.

24. ¿Necesitamos nosotras aprender español? Sí, señor, necesitamos mucho aprender español.

EXERCISE.

1. Does your sister learn English? Yes, sir, she learns English.
2. What does your brother learn? My brother learns Spanish.
3. Do you learn quickly? No, sir, we learn very slowly.
4. Does the studious boy learn well? Yes, sir, he learns very well.
5. What does your brother sell? He sells cotton and silk.
6. Do you sell paper? No, sir, I sell sealing wax and ink.
7. Do they (*fem.*) need a French book? No, sir, they need a copy-book, a pen, and ink.
8. Do you need the English grammar? No, sir, I need the Spanish grammar.
9. Do you want to speak to my father? Yes, sir, I want to speak to your father.
10. Do you want to speak to my sister's son? No, sir, I want to speak to the Frenchman.
11. Does he want to buy a horse? Yes, sir, he wants to buy a horse.
12. Do you need my book? No, madam, I need your wooden ink-stand.
13. Do you look for the merchant? No, sir, I look for your father.
14. Do they look for papa? No, sir, they look for the lawyer.
15. Do you buy a book? No, sir, we buy a copy-book and paper.
16. Do they study English? Yes, sir, they study English.
17. Do you study German, sir? No, I study Spanish, madam.
18. Do you speak English well? No, sir, I speak English badly.
19. Does your sister speak French very well? No, sir, she speaks very little French.
20. What does your father speak? He speaks but (only) English.
21. Does he not speak German? No, sir, he does not speak German.
22. Does your daughter speak to your sister? Yes, sir, she speaks to my sister.
23. Do you learn very quickly? Yes, sir, I learn very quickly.
24. Do you sell your book? No, sir, I sell my paper.

LESSON VII.

Leer. *lai-air'*	To read.
Le-o.	I read.
Le-es.	Thou readest.
Le-e.	He reads.
Le-emos.	We read.
Le-eis.	You read.
Le-en.	They read.
Comer. *ko-mair'*	To eat, to dine.
Beber. *bai-bair'*	To drink.

MASCULINE ADJECTIVES.

Bueno.	Good. *bwai-no*
Hermoso.	Handsome.
Feo.	Ugly. *fai'o*
Pequeño.	Little or small.
Grande (*m. & f.*).	Large.
Español.	Spanish, also Spaniard.
Americano.	American.

FEMININE ADJECTIVES.

Buena.	Good.
Hermosa.	Handsome. *air-mo'-s*
Fea.	Ugly.
Pequeña.	Little or small. *Pai-kain'-yah*
Española.	Spanish. *also-pan-yole*
Americana.	American.

Pan.	Bread.	Carne.	Meat.	
Pescado.	Fish.	Leche.	Milk. *lai-chai*	
Queso.	Cheese.	Agua.	Water. *ah-gwa*	
Vino.	Wine.	Cerveza.	Beer. *thair-bai-th*	
Billete.	Billet or note.	Carta.	Letter.	

COMPOSITION.

¿Lee V. un billete? — Do you read a note?
No, señor, leo una carta. — No, sir, I read a letter.
¿Qué come el Español? — What does the Spaniard eat?
Come buen pescado, pero come mala carne. — He eats good fish, but bad meat.

¿Beben Vds. vino bueno? — Do you drink good wine?
Bebemos buen vino y buena cerveza. — We drink good wine and good beer.
¿Qué compra el Americano? — What does the American buy?
Compra un caballo pequeño. — He buys a small horse.
¿Habla V. al gran hombre? — Do you speak to the great man?
No, señor, hablo al hombre grande. — No, sir, I speak to the large man.
¿Qué vende la Francesa? — What does the French woman sell?
Vende hermosa seda. — She sells handsome silk.

LESSON VII.

EXPLANATION.

22. Adjectives terminating in *o*, *an*, or *on*, form their feminine termination in *a*. Those terminating otherwise are common to both genders; as,

El muchacho holgazan.	The idle boy.
La muchacha holgazana.	The idle girl.
El hombre comilon.	The gluttonous man.
La mujer comilona.	The gluttonous woman.
El hombre feliz.	The happy man.
La mujer feliz.	The happy woman.
La gallina buena.	The good hen.

Adjectives signifying nationality, and ending in a consonant, take an *a* to form their feminine terminations; as,

Español.	Spaniard.
Española.	Spanish.
Libro inglés.	English book.
Gramática inglésa.	English grammar.

Those ending in *o* change this letter into *a*; as,

Americano.	American.
Americana.	American.

Adjectives are generally placed after their nouns; but in poetry, or in an elevated style, and even in conversation, we place many before the noun. Reading and practice will form the ear of the scholar so as to use them properly.

Adjectives used metaphorically, or in a signification different from their proper one, are always placed before; as,

Un gran caballo.	A great horse.

Some adjectives lose their last letter, or syllable, when prefixed to the singular masculine noun; as,

Mal muchacho.	Bad boy.
Buen libro.	Good book.
Gran caballo.	Great horse, &c.

CONVERSATION AND VERSION.

1. ¿Lee V. un buen libro? Sí, señor, leo un libro bueno.
2. ¿Leemos nosotros bien el inglés? No, señor, leemos mal el inglés, pero leemos bien el español.
3. ¿Bebe V. vino? No, señor, yo bebo agua.

LESSON VII.

4. ¿Qué beben ellos? Beben cerveza.
5. ¿Comeis vosotros queso y pan? No, señor, comemos pescado.
6. ¿Qué comen los Ingleses? Los Ingleses comen buena carne.
7. ¿Qué bebe el Español? Bebe buen vino y cerveza mala.
8. ¿Qué lee la Americana? Lee un libro de mi hermana.
9. ¿Qué estudia el hijo pequeño de V.? Estudia gramática.
10. ¿Qué necesita la muchacha hermosa? Necesita un pequeño pañuelo de seda.
11. ¿Necesita V. un caballo grande? No, señor, yo no necesito un caballo grande, sino un gran caballo.
12. ¿Qué estudia la Española? Estudia inglés.
13. ¿Estudia V. la gramática francesa? No, señor, estudio la gramática inglesa.
14. ¿Come pan la Inglesa? Si, señor, come pan y carne.
15. ¿Qué beben Vds.? Bebemos leche.
16. ¿Lee V. un libro inglés? No, señor, leo un libro frances.
17. ¿Qué lee la Americana? Lee su leccion.
18. ¿Qué vende la Inglesa? Vende un pañuelo.
19. ¿Compra V. algodon al comerciante americano? Si, señor, compro algodon al comerciante americano.
20. ¿Necesita la Francesa un pañuelo grande? No, señor, necesita un pañuelo hermoso.
21. ¿Qué busca el muchacho? Busca á su hermana.
22. ¿Qué compra V.? Compro un pañuelo feo, pero bueno.
23. ¿Necesita V. seda? No, señor, necesito algodon.
24. ¿Qué lee V.? Leo el libro de mi padre.
25. ¿Que comeis vosotros? Comemos pan y pescado.
26. ¿Qué bebe el Aleman? Bebe vino y cerveza.

EXERCISE.

1. What do you read? I read a great book.
2. Do you read English well? Yes, sir, I read English very well.
3. Does the German drink wine? No, sir, he drinks beer.
4. What do they (*fem.*) drink? They drink water.
5. Do you eat meat? No, sir, I eat fish.
6. What does the Englishman eat? He eats bread and meat.
7. What does your daughter buy? She buys a silk handkerchief from the American woman.
8. Does the studious boy buy a book? Yes, sir, he buys a French grammar.
9. Does the handsome American woman buy a large book? No, sir, she buys a little book.

10. Does your mamma want a large handkerchief? No, sir, she wants a handsome handkerchief.
11. Do you need your book? No, sir, I do not need my book.
12. Do they need a Spanish grammar? Yes, sir, they need a Spanish grammar.
13. Does the woman sell bread? Yes, sir, she sells bread and fish.
14. What do you read? I read my letter.
15. What does your brother read? He reads a note.
16. Does the girl sell soap? No, sir, she sells milk.
17. Does the lazy boy learn well? No, sir, he learns badly.
18. Do you learn much? No, sir, I learn little.
19. Do you read the book? No, sir, I read the letter.
20. Do you buy cheese? Yes, sir, I buy cheese.
21. Do they buy bread? No, sir, they buy meat and beer.
22. Do you need a handkerchief? No, sir, I need soap.
23. Do you read your father's letter? No, sir, I read my brother's letter.
24. Does your father buy an English grammar? No, sir, he buys a French book.
25. Does your brother read my note? No, sir, he reads my sister's letter.

LESSON VIII.

THIRD CONJUGATION.

Escrib-ir.	To write.
Escrib-o.	I write.
Escrib-es.	Thou writest.
Escrib-e.	He writes.
Escrib-imos.	We write.
Escrib-is.	You write.
Escrib-en.	They write.
Recibir. *rai-thē-beer*	To receive.
En.	In, into, or at.
Ni.	No, neither, nor.
El (*masc. sing.*).	
La (*fem. sing.*).	
Lo (*neuter*).	The.
Los (*masc. plural*).	
Las (*fem. plural*).	

LESSON VIII.

ADJECTIVES.

Mucho.	Much.	Poco.	Little.
Muchos.	Many.	Pocos.	Few.

SUBSTANTIVES.

Periódico.	Newspaper.	Leccion.	Lesson.
Periódicos.	Newspapers.	Lecciones.	Lessons.
Ejercicio.	Exercise.	Ley.	Law.
Ejercicios.	Exercises.	Leyes.	Laws.
Zapatero.	Shoemaker.	Plata.	Silver.
Sombrerero.	Hatter.	Semana.	Week.
		Semanas.	Weeks.

COMPOSITION.

¿Escribe V. las lecciones ó los ejercicios?	Do you write the lessons or the exercises?
No escribo ni las lecciones ni los ejercicios.	I write neither the lessons nor the exercises.
¿Escriben las señoritas muchos billetes?	Do the young ladies write many notes?
Ellas escriben muchos.	They write many.
¿Recibe el comerciante plata ú oro?	Does the merchant receive silver or gold?
Él recibe oro y plata.	He receives gold and silver.
¿Escribe V. la carta en inglés?	Do you write the letter in English?
Sí, señor, escribo la carta en inglés.	Yes, sir, I write the letter in English.

EXPLANATION.

23. THE ENDINGS of the *third conjugation* and those of the second are the same, except in the first and second persons of the plural; in which the *e* of the second conjugation is changed into *i* in the third, as the learner must have observed.

24. THE CONJUNCTION *ó* is changed into *ú* when the following word begins with *ó* or *ho*; as,

Plata ú oro.	Silver or gold.

25. NI.—*Neither* and *nor* are rendered by *ni*; as,

Él no necesita ni la carne ni el pescado. | He wants neither the meat nor the fish.

26. THE PLURAL OF NOUNS is formed by adding an *s* to those terminating in a vowel not accented; as,

Ejercicio.	Exercise.	Ejercicios.	Exercises.

And adding *es*—

1st. To those ending in an accented vowel; as,

| Alelí. | Gilliflower. | Alelíes. | Gilliflowers. |

2d. To those ending in a consonant; as,

| Leccion. | Lesson. | Lecciones. | Lessons. |

3d. To those ending in *y*; as,

| Ley. | Law. | Leyes. | Laws. |

27. An ADJECTIVE *agrees* with its noun in gender, number and case, and forms the plural according to the rules laid down for nouns; as,

Buen hombre.	Good man.
Buenos hombres.	Good men.
Buena mujer.	Good woman.
Buenas mujeres.	Good women.

28. The ARTICLE *must agree also* with the noun to which it refers, in number, gender and case; as,

El libro.	The book.
Los libros.	The books.
La pluma.	The pen.
Las plumas.	The pens.
Lo bueno.	What is good.

Feminine nouns beginning with *á* accented, take the masculine article *el* in the singular number, instead of the feminine *la*, in order to avoid the disagreeable meeting of two *a*'s; as,

El alma.	The soul.
El agua.	The water.
El alba.	The dawn of day.
El hambre.	The hunger, &c.

29. The NEUTER ARTICLE *lo* has no plural number, and is placed only before adjectives used as substantives, in an absolute indeterminate case; as,

| Lo bueno. | What is good. |
| Lo malo. | What is bad. |

CONVERSATION AND VERSION.

1. ¿Escribe V. á su padre? No, señor, escribo á mi hermano.
2. ¿Qué escribo V.? Escribo una carta á la muchacha.

LESSON VIII.

3. ¿Escribe V. muchos billetes? No, señor, escribo muy pocos.
4. ¿Escriben ellos bien los ejercicios? Sí, señor, ellos escriben bien los ejercicios.
5. ¿Recibe V. libros ingleses? No, señor, recibo libros franceses.
6. ¿Qué reciben ellos? Reciben plata y oro.
7. ¿Reciben mucho oro? No, señor, reciben muy poco.
8. ¿Lee V. sus cartas ó sus billetes? No leo ni mis cartas, ni mis billetes; leo mis ejercicios.
9. ¿Necesita V. muchos pañuelos? No, señor, necesito muy pocos.
10. ¿Estudia V. muchas lecciones? No, señor, estudio pocas.
11. ¿Busca V. una pluma? No, señor, busco una gramática.
12. ¿Qué busca su hermana de V.? Busca los ejercicios en inglés.
13. ¿Estudia V. frances ó aleman? No estudio ni frances, ni aleman; estudio español.
14. ¿Necesita V. mi ejercicio? Sí, señor, necesito su ejercicio inglés.
15. ¿Escribe V. al comerciante ó al abogado? No escribo al comerciante, ni al abogado; escribo á su padre de V.
16. ¿Escriben ellas los ejercicios de inglés? No, señor, escriben los ejercicios de español.
17. ¿Recibe V. muchas cartas de su padre? No, señor, recibo muy pocas.
18. ¿Recibe el comerciante mucho algodon? Sí, señor, recibe mucho.
19. ¿Compra V. muchos pañuelos? Sí, señor, compro muchos.
20. ¿Compra su padre de V. muchos caballos? No, señor, compra pocos.
21. ¿Compra V. la gramática del muchacho? No, señor, compro el cuaderno de la muchacha.
22. ¿Habla mucho el Frances? No, señor, habla poco.
23. ¿Escribe V. bien el inglés? No, señor, escribo mal el inglés, pero escribo bien el español.

EXERCISE.

1. Does your brother write English well? Yes, sir, he writes English well.
2. Do you write to my brother? No, sir, I write to my father.
3. Do you write in English or in Spanish? I write in English.
4. Do they (*fem.*) write the lessons or the exercises? They write neither the lessons nor the exercises; they write letters.
5. Do you receive many notes? No, sir, I receive but few.
6. Do they receive gold? No, sir, they receive silver.
7. Do you receive many letters from your father? Yes, sir, I receive many.

8. Do you eat fish? No, sir, I eat bread and cheese.
9. Do the Germans drink water? No, sir, they drink beer.
10. Do you read your brother's letter? No, sir, I read my sister's letter.
11. Does the merchant sell French paper? No, sir, he sells English paper.
12. Does your brother learn German and English? No, sir, he learns neither German nor English; he learns Spanish.
13. Do you need silver or gold? I need neither gold nor silver.
14. Do you look for my father? No, madam, I look for the lawyer.
15. Do you buy a grammar from the merchant? Yes, sir, I buy a grammar from the merchant.
16. Do they study their lessons well? Yes, sir, they study their lessons well.
17. Do you speak much to your sister? Yes, madam, I speak much to my sister.
18. Do you speak Spanish or English? I speak English.
19. Do you receive French books? No, sir, I receive English books.
20. Does the merchant receive silver or gold? He receives gold and silver.
21. Do you write your exercises? No, sir, I write my letters.
22. Do you write a letter to your father? No, sir, I write to my sister.

LESSON IX.

Viv-ir.	To live.
Viv-o.	I live.
Viv-es.	Thou livest.
Viv-e.	He lives.
Viv-imos.	We live.
Viv-is.	You live.
Viv-en.	They live.
Residir.	To reside.
Mis (*plural*).	My.
Sus (*plural*).	Your.
Cuando.	When.
Donde (*without motion*). Adonde (*with motion*).	Where.

LESSON IX.

Campo, país.	Country.	Flor.	Flower.
Dia.	Day.	Flores.	Flowers.
Dias.	Days.	Casa.	House, or home.
Lápiz.	Pencil.	Nueva York.	New York.
Lápices.	Pencils.	Francia.	France.
Alelí.	Gilliflower.	España.	Spain.
Alelíes.	Gilliflowers.	Inglaterra.	England.
Cortaplumas.	Penknife.	Alemania.	Germany.
Hotel, fonda.	Hotel.	Tienda.	Store.
		Ciudad.	City.

Dias de la semana.*	Days of the week.
Lúnes.	Monday.
Mártes.	Tuesday.
Miércoles.	Wednesday.
Juéves.	Thursday.
Viérnes.	Friday.
Sábado.	Saturday.
Sábados.	Saturdays.
Domingo.	Sunday.
Domingos.	Sundays.

COMPOSITION.

¿Vive V. en el campo ó en la ciudad?	Do you live in the country or in the city?
Vivo en la ciudad.	I live in the city.
¿En dónde residen sus papás de V.?	Where do your parents reside?
Papá reside en Francia, y mamá en Nueva York.	Father resides in France, and mother in New York.
¿Cuándo come V. en casa de sus hermanos de V.?	When do you dine at your brothers'?
Los domingos, mártes y juéves como en casa de mis hermanos.	On Sundays, Tuesdays and Thursdays I dine at my brothers'.
¿Y en dónde come V. los lúnes, miércoles, viérnes y sábados?	And where do you dine on Mondays, Wednesdays, Fridays and Saturdays?
Como en casa.	I dine at home.

EXPLANATION.

30. *Papá*, papa; *mamá*, mamma; *pié*, foot; are exceptions to the general rule, and form the plural by the addition of *s*; as, *papás*, papas; *mamás*, mammas; *piés*, feet.

* All of the masculine gender.

LESSON IX.

31. *Nouns which are not monosyllables*, and end in *s*, the last syllable not being accented, do not change their termination in the plural number; as, *Lúnes*, Monday or Mondays; *Mártes*, Tuesday or Tuesdays, etc. Words ending in *z* take *es*, and change the *z* into *c* in the plural; as, *lápiz, lápices*, pencil, pencils; *juez, jueces*, judge, judges.

32. *Words which are compounds of two nouns* differ so variously that it is not possible to give rules for the formation of their plurals; but compounds of a verb and a noun in the singular number form the plural in the same manner as simple nouns; and compound words of a verb and a noun in the plural will be used the same in both numbers; as, *cortaplumas*, penknife, or penknives.

33. *The days of the week* always take the article when they are employed to mark, or express time; as,

Estudio español el lúnes y el viérnes. | I study Spanish on Monday and Friday.

34. *Donde*, where (without motion); *adonde*, where (with motion); *cuando*, when. These adverbs are placed always before the verb; as,

¿Dónde reside V.? | Where do you reside?
¿Cuándo escribe V.? | When do you write?

35. *Donde, adonde*, and *cuando*, when used interrogatively require an accent; thus, ¿*Dónde vive?* Where does he live? ¿*Cuándo lee V.?* When do you read?

CONVERSATION AND VERSION.

1. ¿En dónde vive V.? Vivo en Nueva York.
2. ¿Dónde viven sus padres de V.? Mi padre vive en la ciudad y mi madre en el campo.
3. ¿Dónde viven sus hermanos? Viven en Francia.
4. ¿Dónde come V. los sábados y los domingos? Como en el hotel de los Franceses.
5. ¿Y dónde come V. los lúnes y los mártes? Como en el hotel Americano.
6. ¿Dónde reside V.? Resido en el campo.
7. ¿Y dónde reside su mamá de V.? Reside en los Estados Unidos.
8. ¿Cuándo estudia V. sus lecciones de frances? Los miércoles y los juéves.

LESSON IX.

9. ¿Y qué estudia V. los viernes? Los viernes estudio una leccion de frances.
10. ¿Cuándo lee V. los periódicos? Yo leo los periódicos los domingos.
11. ¿Compran alelíes sus hermanas? Sí, señor, ellas compran alelíes.
12. ¿Estudia V. las leyes de Inglaterra? No, señor, estudio las de los Estados Unidos (*United States*).
13. ¿Aprende bien la muchacha el inglés? Sí, señor, aprende bien el inglés.
14. ¿Qué beben los Españoles y los Alemanes? Los Españoles beben buen vino, y los Alemanes buena cerveza.
15. ¿Dónde compra el comerciante el algodon? Compra el algodon en los Estados Unidos.
16. ¿Y dónde vende el oro y la plata? En Inglaterra.
17. ¿Cuándo necesita su hermano de V. la gramática? Mi hermano necesita su gramática el lúnes.
18. ¿En qué hotel come V.? Como en el hotel de Inglaterra.
19. ¿Qué compra el comerciante, plata ú oro? El comerciante no compra ni oro ni plata, compra seda.
20. ¿Qué estudia V.? Estudio los dias de la semana en inglés.
21. ¿Escribe V. á Francia? No, señor, escribo á Inglaterra.
22. ¿Qué escribe V.? Escribo los ejercicios de la semana en inglés.
23. ¿Dónde reside su hermana de V.? Reside en el campo.
24. ¿En qué país vive su papá? Vive en Alemania.

EXERCISE.

1. Do you live in the country? No, sir, I live in town.
2. Where does your sister live? She lives in New York.
3. Where do your parents (*padres*) live? They live in France.
4. Where does your brother reside? He resides in England.
5. Do you not reside in the United States? No, sir, in Spain.
6. In which country does your mother live? She lives in the United States.
7. Do you write to your father in Spanish or in English? I write in English.
8. Where does the merchant buy the cotton? He buys the cotton in England.
9. Which do you sell, silver or gold? I sell gold.
10. Where do you dine on Sundays and Mondays? I dine in the French hotel.
11. And where on Wednesdays, Fridays and Saturdays? In the German hotel.

12. When do they study their lesson? On (*los*) Tuesdays.
13. Does the lawyer study the laws of England? No, sir, he studies the laws of the United States.
14. Where does your mother reside? She resides in Germany.
15. When do you need your grammar? On Friday.
16. When do your sons study the French lessons? They study the French lessons on Mondays and Saturdays.
17. Where does the merchant buy the good penknives? In England.
18. What day do you (*fem.*) receive the newspapers? We receive the newspapers on Sundays.
19. Does your sister buy gilliflowers? Yes, sir, she buys gilliflowers.
20. Where do you buy your pencils? In the French store.
21. What do you study? I study the days of the week in Spanish.
22. Where do your parents reside? My mother resides in Spain, and my father in Germany.
23. Where does your sister reside? She resides in the country.
24. Do you need my books? Yes, sir, I need your books.

LESSON X.

Tener.	To have.
Tengo.	I have.
Tienes.	Thou hast.
Tiene.	He has.
Tenemos.	We have.
Teneis.	You have.
Tienen.	They have.

OBJECTIVE CASE.

Le, los (*masc. pl.*).	It, him, them.
La, las (*fem. pl.*).	It, her, them.
Lo (*neuter*).	It, (sometimes) so.

INTERROGATIVE PRONOUNS.

¿Quién, quiénes (*pl.*)?	Who?
¿Cuál, cuáles (*pl.*)?	Which one, which ones?
¿Qué?	What, or which?
De quién, de quiénes (*pl.*)?	Whose?
Con.	With.

LESSON X.

Zapato.	Shoe. *thah-prah'-to*	Botas.	Boots.
Chaleco.	Vest. *chah-lai'ko*	Casaca.	Coat.
Baston.	Cane.	Corbata.	Cravat.
Sombrero.	Hat.	Medias.	Stockings. *mai-dè-*

COMPOSITION.

¿Quién tiene mi baston?	Who has my cane?
Yo lo tengo.	I have it.
¿Qué corbata tiene V.?	Which cravat have you?
Tengo la bonita.	I have the pretty one.
¿Tienen ellos mi chaleco?	Have they my waistcoat?
No, señor, tienen la corbata de V.	No, sir, they have your cravat.
¿De quién habla V.?	Of whom do you speak?
Hablo de los Franceses.	I speak of the Frenchmen.
¿Teneis vosotros casacas?	Have you coats?
Sí, señor, las tenemos.	Yes, sir, we have (them).
¿Quién tiene sombreros?	Who has hats?
Los tiene el comerciante.	The merchant has (them).
¿Necesita V. á mi padre?	Do you need my father?
Sí, señor, le necesito.	Yes, sir, I need him.
¿Tiene V. mi casaca?	Have you my coat?
Sí, señor, la tengo.	Yes, sir, I have it.
¿Qué botas tiene V.?	Which boots have you?
¿Qué tiene V.?	What is the matter with you?

EXPLANATION.

36. IRREGULAR VERBS are those which do not retain intact the radical letters and the terminations designated for each tense and person.

The verb *tener*, to have, is the first of the irregular verbs here introduced; and, like all the auxiliary verbs, is not included in the seven groups in which the irregular Spanish verbs are classified, on account of their multifarious irregularities. The auxiliaries require, therefore, to be learned separately, or each one by itself.

A complete list of the irregular conjugations will be found at the end of the book.

When the objective case of the third person is the object of the English verb, it is translated by *le, los*, for the masculine; *la, las*, for the feminine; and *lo* for the neuter; as,

El *le* busca.	He looks for *him*.
Ella *los* compra.	She buys *them*.
Ellos *lo* necesitan.	They want *it*.

37. Lo and Le.—It must be observed, however, with regard to the objective forms *le* and *lo*, that their use is very doubtful in Spanish, since many correct writers employ the neuter *lo*, instead of the masculine *le*. Consequently, while custom or general use does not give the preference to either, the learner may use them according to his own discretion or taste, in the accusative case, masculine gender; as,

| Manuel tiene un buen libro y *lo* (le) vende. | Emanuel has a good book and sells *it*. |

Lo is sometimes employed to avoid the repetition of a whole or part of a sentence, and then it is equivalent to *so*, or *it*. Of this, however, more will be said when treating of the regimen of verbs.

38. The interrogative pronouns *quién, cuál, qué, de quién*, who, which, what, and whose, do not require the article; as,

¿ Quién habla ?	Who speaks ?
¿ Cuál tengo yo ?	Which one have I ?
¿ Qué escribe V. ?	What do you write ?
¿ De quién son los caballos ?	Whose are the horses ?

39. When, in a question, the interrogative pronoun is governed by a preposition, that preposition must also be repeated in the answer; as,

¿ *Con* quién vive V. ?	With whom do you live ?
Con mi amigo.	With my friend.
¿ *De* quién es el caballo ?	Whose is the horse ?
De mi amigo.	My friend's.

CONVERSATION AND VERSION.

1. ¿ Qué tiene V. ? Tengo un hermoso baston.
2. ¿ Tienes tú un buen sombrero ? Sí, señor, lo (le) tengo.
3. ¿ Qué pañuelo tiene ella ? Tiene el de seda.
4. ¿ Cuál tiene V. ? Tengo mi pañuelo.
5. ¿ Tenéis vosotros buenos chalecos ? Sí, señor, los tenemos.
6. ¿ De quién hablan ellos ? Hablan de las Americanas.
7. ¿ Tiene V. las corbatas ? Sí, señor, las tengo.
8. ¿ Tienen ellos los hermosos pañuelos de seda ? Sí, señor, los tienen.
9. ¿ Quién tiene las medias ? Yo las tengo.
10. ¿ Tiene V. mi chaleco ? Sí, señor, lo (le) tengo.

LESSON X.

11. ¿Quién tiene mi baston? Su hermano lo (le) tiene.
12. ¿Habla V. á su hermana? Sí, señor.
13. ¿Busca V. á su hermana? Sí, señorita, la busco.
14. ¿Estudia V. su leccion? Sí, señor, la estudio.
15. ¿Necesita V. á su papá? Sí, señor, le (lo) necesito.
16. ¿Qué sombrero tiene V.? Tengo el de V.
17. ¿Qué botas busca V.? Busco las buenas.
18. ¿Con quién aprende V. el inglés? Con un Americano.
19. ¿A quién busca V.? Busco al abogado.
20. ¿Qué compra V.? Compro lápices ingleses.
21. ¿Tiene V. una buena gramática? Sí, señor, tengo una muy buena.
22. ¿Tiene V. muchos libros? No, señor, tengo pocos.
23. ¿Tienen ellas mucha seda? No, señor, tienen muy poca.
24. ¿Dónde reside V.? Resido en el campo.
25. ¿Dónde vive su abogado de V.? Vive en la ciudad.
26. ¿Vive en Francia su hermano de V.? No, señor, vivo en España.

EXERCISE.

1. Who has the stockings? I have them.
2. What has he? He has my grammar.
3. Have they my vest? Yes, sir, they have it.
4. Which books have they (*fem.*)? They have yours.
5. Of whom do you speak? I speak of the Frenchman.
6. Who has my coat? They have it.
7. Have you my cravat? No, sir, I have it not.
8. Have we very good coats? Yes, sir, we have.
9. Who has the handsome stockings? They (*fem.*) have them.
10. Do you speak to the Frenchman? Yes, sir, I speak to the Frenchman.
11. Do you need my hat? No, sir, I have my hat.
12. Whom do you look for? I look for your father.
13. What do you buy? I buy English books.
14. Which shoes do you buy? I buy the handsome shoes.
15. Which hats have you? I have the merchant's hats.
16. With whom do you learn English? I learn with an American.
17. Have you good coats? Yes, sir, I have good coats.
18. Have they many grammars? No, sir, they have very few.
19. Where do you live? I live in the country.
20. Does your father reside in France? No, sir, he resides in England.
21. Does your mother live in Germany? No, sir, she lives in the United States.

2*

22. Do you buy many books? No, sir, I buy very few.
23. Who has my handsome boots? I have them.
24. Which hat have you? I have yours.
25. What have you? I have my stockings.
26. Of whom do you speak? I speak of your father.

LESSON XI.

Ser.	To be.
Soy.	I am.
Eres.	Thou art.
Es.	He is.
Somos.	We are.
Sois.	You are.
Son.	They are.

INDEFINITE PRONOUNS.

Alguien. *al'-găm*	Some one, somebody, anybody, any one.
Alguno. *al-goó-no*	Some, somebody, anybody.
Nadie. *nah-dĕ-ai*	No one, nobody.
Ninguno. *neen-goó-no*	None, no one, nobody.
Algo, alguna cosa. *kŏ´-sa*	Something, anything.
Nada, ninguna cosa. *rah´-da*	Nothing, not anything.
Todo.	All, everything.
Todos.	Every one, everybody.

Librero.	Bookseller.	Librería.	Bookstore.
Panadero.	Baker.	Panadería.	Bakery.
Carnicero.	Butcher.	Carnicería.	Butcher's shop.
Sastre. *sas-trai*	Tailor.	Sastrería.	Tailor's shop.

COMPOSITION.

¿Son Vds. carniceros? — Are you butchers?
No, señor, somos panaderos. — No, sir, we are bakers.
¿Es V. carnicero? — Are you a butcher?
No, señor, yo soy sastre. — No, sir, I am a tailor.
¿Tiene V. algun pan? — Have you some bread?

LESSON XI.

No, señor, no tengo ninguno.	No, sir, I have none.
¿Tienen Vds. algo?	Have you anything?
No, señor, no tenemos nada.	No, sir, we have nothing.
¿Quién tiene el sombrero?	Who has the hat?
El Americano lo tiene.	The American has it.
¿Dónde compra V. pan?	Where do you buy bread?
En la panadería.	In the bakery.
¿Dónde compra V. sus libros?	Where do you buy your books?
En la librería.	In the bookstore.
¿Eres tú muy estudioso?	Art thou very studious?
No, señor, no lo soy.	No, sir, I am not (so).
¿Tienen todos Vds. buenas gramáticas.	Have you all good grammars?
Sí, señor.	Yes, sir.
¿Quién tiene papel?	Who has paper?
Nadie lo (le) tiene.	Nobody has (it).

EXPLANATION.

40. ALGUIEN, ALGUNO.—*Alguien* refers only to persons, and always in the singular number; as,

Vivo con alguien.	I live with some one.
Escribo á alguien.	I write to somebody.

When *some one, any one* is followed by the preposition *of*, we must use *alguno* in Spanish, and not *alguien*; as, *alguno de ellos escribe en el periódico, some one* of them writes in the newspaper.

Any one, or *anybody*, not used interrogatively, is translated by *cualquiera*, as will be seen when we introduce the indefinite pronoun.

Alguien is used only in the affirmative. *Alguno* may, on the contrary, be employed either in affirmative or negative sentences; in the affirmative it always precedes the noun to which it refers, and in the negative it invariably comes after it; as,

No estudian leccion alguna.	They study no lesson (or do not study any lesson).

41. NADIE, NINGUNO.—*Ninguno* relates to persons and things, and is used in the negative in the same manner as *alguno* in the affirmative; *nadie* relates to persons only, and is used in the negative in the same way as the pronoun *álguien* in the affirmative. In a word, *nadie* and *ninguno* are merely the negative forms of *álguien* and *alguno*.

42. ALGUNO and NINGUNO lose the *o* when they come immediately before the noun.

43. ALGO, and ALGUNA COSA, are used in the affirmative; as,

Como *algo*, or *alguna cosa*.	I eat something.
¿RecibeV. *algo*, or *alguna cosa?*	Do you receive anything?

Anything, when not used interrogatively, is translated *cualquiera cosa*, as will be seen in its proper place.

44. NADA, NINGUNA COSA are used in the negative form.

45. NADA, NUNGUNO, NADIE, the adverb *no*, as well as any other words expressing negation, are placed before the verb; but when *no* precedes the verb, another negative may be placed after it, and the two negatives serve to strengthen each other, contrary to the practice of the English language; as,

No estudio *nada*.	I study nothing.
No hablo á *nadie*.	I speak to nobody, or no one.
No recibo *ninguno*	I receive none.

But in omitting the negative *no*, the words which express the negation must be placed before the verb; as,

Nada estudio.	I study nothing.
A nadie hablo.	I speak to nobody.
Ninguno recibo.	I receive none.

The two negatives are always preferable.

46. The indefinite article *a* or *an*, is not translated into Spanish when accompanied by a noun which expresses nationality, profession, &c.; as,

¿Es V. Inglés?	Are you an Englishman?
No, señor, soy Español.	No, sir, I am a Spaniard.
¿Es él sastre?	Is he a tailor?
No, señor, es zapatero.	No, sir, he is a shoemaker.

CONVERSATION AND VERSION.

1. ¿Es V. Frances? No, señor, soy Americano.
2. ¿Son Vds. Alemanes? No, señor, somos Ingleses.
3. ¿Eres tú buen muchacho? Sí señor, lo soy.
4. ¿Sois vosotros sastres? No, señor, somos panaderos.

LESSON XI.

5. ¿Es bueno el libro de su hermano de V.? Sí, señor, lo es.
6. ¿Son buenos sus zapatos de V.? No, señor, son muy malos.
7. ¿Tiene alguno mi sombrero? Sí, señor, alguien lo (le) tiene.
8. ¿Tiene alguien papel? No, señor, ninguno tiene papel.
9. ¿Tiene V. alguna cosa? No, señor, no tengo nada.
10. ¿No tiene V. cosa alguna? Sí, señor, tengo alguna cosa.
11. ¿Compran pan todos Vds.? Sí, señor, todos compramos pan.
12. ¿Dónde compran Vds. todo su pan? Lo (le) compramos en la panadería.
13. ¿Son Vds. panaderos? No, señor, nosotros somos zapateros.
14. ¿Tiene alguien mi sombrero bueno? Sí, señor, alguien le (lo) tiene.
15. ¿No compra V. algo? Sí, señor, compro alguna cosa.
16. ¿Escribe V. algo? No, señor, no escribo nada.
17. ¿Necesita V. todo el papel? Sí, señor, lo (le) necesito todo.
18. ¿Necesita V. todas las plumas? Sí, señor, las necesito todas.
19. ¿Es V. sastre? Sí, señor, yo soy sastre.
20. ¿Dónde tiene V. su sastrería? La tengo en Nueva York.
21. ¿Es su padre de V. librero? Sí, señor, lo es.
22. ¿Vende muchos libros? Sí, señor, vende muchos.
23. ¿Dónde tiene él su librería? La tiene en Francia.
24. ¿Tiene V. una panadería? No, señor, tengo una carnicería.
25. ¿Habla V. á alguien? No, señor, no hablo á nadie.

EXERCISE.

1. Are you an Englishman? No, sir, I am an American.
2. Are you good boys? Yes, sir, we are very good boys.
3. Is Louisa a good girl? Yes, sir, she is a very good girl.
4. Art thou a Frenchman? No, sir, I am a German.
5. Is yours a good book? Yes, sir, mine is a very good one.
6. Are they (*fem.*) studious? Yes, sir, they are very studious.
7. Have you anything? No, sir, I have nothing.
8. Have you nothing? Yes, sir, I have something.
9. Has anybody a good grammar? Yes, sir, the Frenchman has one.
10. Who speaks French? The American speaks French.
11. Do you write an exercise? Yes, sir, I write an exercise.
12. Where do you buy all your books? I buy them in the bookstore.
13. Are you a bookseller? No, sir, I am a baker.
14. Where have you your bakery? I have it in New York.
15. Where do you buy your coats? In the tailor's shop.
16. Have you all of your books? Yes, sir, I have all.

38　LESSON XII.

17. Do you all reside in the United States? Yes, sir, we reside in the United States.
18. Have you any bread? No, sir, I have none.
19. Do you speak to anybody? Yes, sir, I speak to the Americans.
20. Do you buy anything? No, sir, I buy nothing.
21. Are you a baker? No, sir, I am a tailor.
22. Are they French? No, sir, they are English.
23. Art thou a Spaniard? No, sir, I am an American.
24. Who is studious? Emanuel is very studious.

LESSON XII.

Haber.	To have.
He. *ui*	I have.
Has. *abs*	Thou hast.
Ha. *ah*	He has.
Hemos. *amas*	We have.
Habeis. *aba-ey*	You have.
Han. *ahu*	They have.

PAST PARTICIPLES.—*First Conjugation.*

Habl-ado.	Spoke.
Estudi-ado.	Studied.
Compr-ado.	Bought.
Busc-ado.	Looked for, sought.
Necesit-ado.	Needed.

Second and Third.

Aprend-ido.	Learned.
Vend-ido.	Sold.
Le-ido.	Read.
Beb-ido.	Drunk.
Com-ido.	Eaten, dined.
Recib-ido.	Received.
Viv-ido.	Lived.
Resid-ido.	Resided.
Escrito (*irregular in this participle only*).	Written.

LESSON XII.

Hoy.			To-day.
París.	Paris.	Habana.	Havana.
Lóndres.	London.	Viéna.	Vienna.
Madrid.	Madrid.	Filadelfia.	Philadelphia.
Paño.	Cloth.	Esquela.	Note.

COMPOSITION.

¿Cuándo ha escrito V. á su padre?	When have you written to your father?
He escrito hoy á mi padre.	I have written to my father to-day.
¿Ha recibido V. sus cartas?	Have you received your letters?
Sí, señor, las he recibido.	Yes, sir, I have received them.
¿Ha vivido V. en París?	Have you lived in Paris?
Sí, señor, he vivido una semana.	Yes, sir, I have lived a week.
¿Ha residido V. en Lóndres?	Have you resided in London?
Sí, señor, he residido algunos dias.	Yes, sir, I resided some days.
¿Han comido ellos?	Have they eaten (or dined)?
Sí, señor, han comido.	Yes, sir, they have eaten.
¿Hemos leido bien nosotros?	Have we read well?
Sí, señor, Vds. han leido muy bien.	Yes, sir, you have read very well.
¿Habeis vendido vosotros muchos pañuelos?	Have you sold many handkerchiefs?
Hemos vendido muy pocos.	We have sold very few.
¿Cuándo habeis aprendido vuestra leccion?	When have you learned your lesson?
La hemos aprendido hoy.	We have learned it to-day.
¿Habeis comprado pan?	Have you bought bread?
Sí, señor, lo hemos comprado.	Yes, sir, we have bought it.
¿Ha estudiado V. aleman?	Have you studied German?
No, señor, no lo he estudiado.	No, sir, I have not studied it.
¿Ha hablado V. con el Frances?	Have you spoken with the Frenchman?
Sí, señor, he hablado con él.	Yes, sir, I have spoken with him.

EXPLANATION.

47. TENER AND HABER. To have, used as an active verb, is translated by *tener*, as an auxiliary, by *haber*; as,

Tener caballos,	To have horses.
Tengo oro.	I have gold.
Haber hablado.	To have spoken.
Hemos hablado.	We have spoken.

When the auxiliaries *to have* and *to be*, followed by an infinitive, denote some future action, *to have* is rendered by *tener que*, and *to be* by *haber de*; as,

Tenemos que escribir.	We have to write.
Hemos de recibir dinero.	We are to receive money.

48. Preterit Indefinite.—This tense not only refers to what is past, but also conveys an allusion to the present time; as,

Alejandro ha estudiado el español.	Alexander has studied Spanish.

It must also be used when we speak indefinitely of any thing past, as happening or not happening in the day, year, or age, in which we mention it; as,

He escrito hoy muchas cartas.	I have written many letters to-day.

CONVERSATION AND VERSION.

1. ¿Ha escrito V. sus cartas? No, señor, he escrito los ejercicios de la leccion.
2. ¿Ha recibido V. su dinero? Sí, señor, lo he recibido.
3. ¿Ha escrito V. á su hermana? Sí, señor, he escrito hoy á mi hermana.
4. ¿Cuándo ha recibido V. los periódicos de Paris? Los he recibido hoy.
5. ¿Ha leido V. mi libro? Sí, señor, lo he leido.
6. ¿Han vivido Vds. en Lóndres? Sí, señor, hemos vivido una semana.
7. ¿Ha comido V.? Sí, señor, he comido.
8. ¿Ha leido V. la carta de mi hermano? Sí, señora, la he leido.
9. ¿Ha vendido V. su baston? Sí, señor, lo he vendido hoy.
10. ¿Ha necesitado V. el libro de mi hermana? No, señor, no lo he necesitado.
11. ¿Ha buscado V. bien el pañuelo? Sí, señora, lo he buscado bien.
12. ¿Ha comprado V. pan? No, señor, he comprado vino.
13. ¿Ha aprendido V. su leccion de español? La he estudiado, pero he aprendido muy poco.
14. ¿Ha hablado V. con mi padre? Sí, señor, he hablado con él.
15. ¿Ha estudiado V. el aleman? Sí, señor, lo he estudiado con un Frances.
16. ¿Ha vivido V. en la Habana? No, señor, he vivido en Filadelfia.
17. ¿Ha vendido V. muchos lápices? No, señor, he vendido muy pocos.
18. ¿Ha recibido V. sus cartas? No, señor, he recibido los periódicos del juéves.

LESSON XII.

19. ¿Ha leido V. mi esquela? No, señor, no la he leido.
20. ¿Ha buscado V. bien mi baston? Sí, señor, lo he buscado bien.
21. ¿Ha comprado V. un sombrero? Sí, señor.
22. ¿Han hablado ellos á su padre? No, señor.
23. ¿Ha aprendido V. el inglés? No, señor, lo he estudiado un poco; pero no lo he aprendido.
24. ¿Ha leido V. el periódico de hoy? Sí, señor, lo he leido.

EXERCISE.

1. Have you received your letters? Yes, sir, I have received them to-day.
2. Have you read the newspapers? Yes, sir, I have read them.
3. Have you written to my sister? No, sir, I have not written to her (*le*).
4. Have you received your letters from Vienna? I have received them.
5. Have you read the English newspapers? Yes, sir, I have (read them).
6. Have you dined with your sister? I have dined with her.
7. Have you bought your hat? I have bought it to-day.
8. Have you looked for my father in Paris? Yes, sir, I have looked for him.
9. Have you spoken with him? Yes, sir, I have spoken with him.
10. Where have you spoken with him? I have spoken with him at his house.
11. Have you studied your Spanish lesson? Yes, sir, I have studied it.
12. Have you learned it well? No, sir, I have learned it little.
13. Have the bakers sold much bread? No, sir, they have sold very little.
14. Has the tailor bought much cloth? Yes, sir, he has (bought).
15. Have they (*fem.*) dined with your sister? Yes, sir, they have dined with my sister.
16. Have they dined with your brother? Yes sir.
17. What have they eaten? They have eaten bread and meat.
18. What have they drunk? They have drunk water, wine and ale.
19. Have you spoken with the Spaniard? Yes, sir, I have spoken with him.
20. Have you spoken with him in Spanish or English? I have spoken with him in English.
21. Have you received your letters from Philadelphia? Yes, sir, I have received them.
22. Have you received them all? I have received them all.

LESSON XIII.

23. Have you lived in London? No, sir, I have lived in Vienna.
24. Have you lived with your father? No, sir, I have lived with my brother.

LESSON XIII.

Querer.	To wish, to be willing, to love.
Querido.	Wished, loved, dear.
Quiero.	I wish, or am willing.
Quieres.	Thou wishest.
Quiere.	He wishes.
Queremos.	We wish.
Quereis.	You wish.
Quieren.	They wish.
Desear.	To desire.

POSSESSIVE PRONOUNS.

Mio.	My, or mine.
Tuyo.	Thy, or thine.
Suyo.	His, hers or its.
Nuestro.	Our, or ours.
Vuestro.	Your, or yours.
Util.	Useful.
Caro.	Dear.
Barato.	Cheap.
Viejo.	Old.
Jóven.	Young.
Rico.	Rich.
Pobre.	Poor.

Amigo.	Friend.	Amiga.	Friend.
Primo.	Cousin.	Prima.	Cousin.
Dinero.	Money.	Moneda.	Coin.

COMPOSITION.

¿Quiere V. un sombrero? — Do you wish a hat?
No, señor, quiero un baston. — No, sir, I wish a cane.
¿Quiere V. mucho á su primo? — Do you love your cousin much?
Sí, señor, le quiero mucho. — Yes, sir, I love him much.

LESSON XIII.

¿Quiere V. escribir?	Do you wish to write?
No, señor, quiero leer.	No, sir, I wish to read.
¿Quiere V. hablar con mi hermana?	Do you wish to speak to my sister?
Sí, señor, quiero hablar con ella.	Yes, sir, I wish to speak to her.
¿Quiere V. comprar el caballo de nuestro amigo?	Do you wish to buy our friend's horse?
Sí, señor, quiero comprar el caballo del amigo de V.	Yes, sir, I wish to buy your friend's horse.
¿Quieres escribir á mi hermano?	Do you wish to write to my brother?
Sí, señor, quiero escribirle.	Yes, sir, I wish to write to him.
¿Tiene V. mi baston?	Have you my cane?
No, señor, tengo el mio.	No, sir, I have mine.
¿Tienen ellas nuestros libros?	Have they our books?
Sí, señor, tienen los de Vds.	Yes, sir, they have yours.
¿Es viejo su padre de V.?	Is your father old?
Sí, señor, es un poco viejo.	Yes, sir, he is rather old.
¿Es jóven su hermana de V.?	Is your sister young?
Sí, señor, es muy jóven.	Yes, sir, she is very young.
¿Es pobre el comerciante?	Is the merchant poor?
No, señor, es muy rico.	No, sir, he is very rich.
¿Ha escrito V. á su amigo?	Did you write to your friend?
Sí, señor, he escrito hoy á mi amigo.	Yes, sir, I have written to my friend to-day.
¿Ha hablado V. con su prima?	Have you spoken with your cousin?
No, señor, he hablado con mi amigo.	No, sir, I have spoken with my friend.
¿Dónde vive su primo de V.?	Where does your cousin live?
Vive en Filadelfia.	He lives in Philadelphia.

EXPLANATION.

49. Mio, tuyo, suyo, nuestro, vuestro, change the final *o* into *a*, to form the feminine termination.

50. In Spanish, the possessive pronouns always agree with the name of the thing possessed, in gender, number, and case; as,

Nuestra gramática.	Our grammar.
Nuestros libros.	Our books.

51. When used as pronominal adjectives, they precede the noun with which they agree; and it is to be observed that, in this case, *mio*, *tuyo* and *suyo* drop their final syllable; as,

Nuestros caballos.	Our horses.
Mi pluma.	My pen.
Tu papel.	Thy paper.
Su cuaderno.	His copy-book.

LESSON XIII.

Mis plumas.	My pens.
Tus papeles.	Thy papers.
Sus cuadernos.	His copy-books.

52. Mio, when used in the vocative case—that is, in addressing persons—is placed after the noun governing it; as,

Escribe, hijo mio.	Write, my son.

53. When possessives are used as pronouns, they agree in gender, number and case with the noun which they represent, and are preceded by the definite article; as,

Tu gramática y *la mia*.	Thy grammar and *mine*.
De mis muchachos y *los tuyos*.	Of my boys and *thine*.
Su hermano y *el nuestro*.	His brother and *ours*.
Sus zapatos y *los nuestros*.	His shoes and *ours*.
Tus caballos y *los suyos*.	Thy horses and *theirs*, &c.

54. Possessives are preceded by the neuter article, when they are indefinitely used; as,

Lo mio, lo tuyo, lo suyo.	What is mine, what is thine, what is his.

55. When the possessive pronoun is connected with the noun by the verb *to be*, the article is omitted; as,

Este billete es mio.	This note is mine.
Esa carta es tuya.	That letter is thine.
El caballo es suyo.	The horse is his.
Muchachos, ¿es este *nuestro* libro?	Boys, is this *your* book?
Niños, ¿es este el *vuestro*?	Children, is this *yours*?

56. Vuestro, vuestra, is chiefly used in addressing persons in very high positions; as,

Señor, *vuestra* patria lo exije.	Sir, *your* country demands it.

CONVERSATION AND VERSION.

1. ¿Quiero V. vino? No, señor, quiero agua.
2. ¿Quieren Vds. mis libros? No, señor, queremos los nuestros.
3. ¿Tienen ellos nuestros periódicos? No, señor, ellos tienen los suyos.
4. ¿Tiene V. nuestro libro? No, señor, yo tengo el mio.
5. ¿Teneis vuestros ejercicios? Sí, señor, tenemos los nuestros.
6. ¿Es vieja su amiga de V.? No, señor, es jóven.
7. ¿Es rico el comerciante? Sí, señor, es muy rico.
8. ¿Vende barato? No, señor, compra barato; pero vende caro.

LESSON XIII.

9. ¿Es útil la gramática? Sí, señor, es muy útil.
10. ¿Quiere V. mucho á su hermana? Sí, señor, la quiero mucho.
11. ¿Quiere V. beber vino? No, señor, quiero beber agua.
12. ¿Quiere V. comprar un pañuelo de algodon? No, señor, quiero comprar uno de seda.
13. ¿Quiere V. vivir en nuestra casa? No, señor, quiero vivir en la mia.
14. ¿Quiere V. estudiar español? Sí, señor, quiero estudiarlo.
15. ¿Qué quieren ellos? Quieren hablar con V.
16. ¿Quiero V. ir (*to go*) á mi casa el mártes? No, señor, quiero ir hoy.
17. ¿Necesita V. un libro? Sí, señor, necesito el mio.
18. ¿Necesita V. hablar con el abogado? No, señor, necesito hablar con el comerciante.
19. ¿Necesita su prima un lápiz? No, señor, ella no lo necesita.
20. ¿Ha querido V. mucho á su padre? Sí, señor, le he querido mucho.
21. ¿Ha necesitado V. dinero? No, señor, he necesitado amigos.
22. ¿Ha escrito V. sus cartas? Sí, señor, las he escrito.
23. ¿Ha leido V. los periódicos? Sí, señor, los he leido hoy.
24. ¿Quiero V. aprender español? Sí, señor, quiero aprenderlo.

EXERCISE.

1. Do you wish to eat anything? No, sir, I wish to drink.
2. What do you wish to drink? I wish to drink water.
3. Do you wish to speak to your brother? Yes, sir, I wish to speak to him (*le*).
4. Do you wish to learn Spanish? No, sir, I wish to learn French.
5. Do they wish to live in New York? No, sir, they wish to live in Philadelphia.
6. Have you read your note? Yes, sir, I have read it.
7. Do you want some wine? No, sir, I want some water.
8. Do they want my book? Yes, sir, they want your book.
9. Does your brother want to speak to my father? No, sir, he wants to speak to the lawyer.
10. Did you want my father's letter? No, sir, we did not want your father's letter.
11. Did you want any money? Yes, sir, I wanted some.
12. Do you wish to live in France? No, sir, I wish to live in the United States.
13. Do you wish to speak French? No, sir, I wish to speak Spanish.
14. Do they wish to buy a grammar? No, sir, they wish to buy newspapers.

46 LESSON XIV.

15. What do you wish to buy? I wish to buy a handkerchief.
16. What do you wish to read? I wish to read the English newspapers.
17. What do you wish to drink? I wish to drink some wine and water.
18. What do they want to sell? They want to sell their horses.
19. When did you receive your letters from England? We have received them to-day.
20. When did you dine with your friends? I have dined with them to-day.
21. Have you a useful book? Yes, sir, I have a Spanish grammar.
22. Does the merchant sell his hats dear? No, sir, he sells them very cheap.
23. Is your friend young? No, sir, he is old.
24. Are you rich? No, sir, I am poor.
25. Do you wish to have money? Yes, sir, I wish to have it.
26. Do your friend and cousin live in New York? No, sir, they live in Philadelphia.

LESSON XIV.

Llevar, llevado, traer.	To bring, brought, to take.
Enviar, enviado.	To send, sent.
Tomar, tomado.	To take, taken.
Pagar, pagado.	To pay, paid.

Cuanto.		How much.	
Cuantos.		How many.	
Bastante.		Enough.	
Peso.	Dollar.	Silla.	Chair.
Centavo.	Cent.	Mesa.	Table.
Café.	Coffee.	Cama.	Bed.
Chocolate.	Chocolate.		

NUMERAL ADJECTIVES—CARDINAL NUMBERS.

Uno, una.	One.
Dos.	Two.
Tres.	Three.
Cuatro.	Four.
Cinco.	Five.

LESSON XIV.

Seis.	Six.
Siete.	Seven.
Ocho.	Eight.
Nueve.	Nine.
Diez.	Ten.
Once.	Eleven.
Doce.	Twelve.
Trece.	Thirteen.
Catorce.	Fourteen.
Quince.	Fifteen.
Diez y seis.	Sixteen.
Diez y siete.	Seventeen.
Diez y ocho.	Eighteen.
Diez y nueve.	Nineteen.
Veinte.	Twenty.
Veinte y uno, etc.	Twenty-one, &c.
Treinta.	Thirty.
Cuarenta.	Forty.
Cincuenta.	Fifty.
Sesenta.	Sixty.
Setenta.	Seventy.
Ochenta.	Eighty.
Noventa.	Ninety.
Ciento.	A or one hundred.
Doscientos.	Two hundred.
Trescientos.	Three hundred.
Cuatrocientos.	Four hundred.
Quinientos.	Five hundred.
Seiscientos.	Six hundred.
Setecientos.	Seven hundred.
Ochocientos.	Eight hundred.
Novecientos.	Nine hundred.
Mil.	A or one thousand.
Dos mil.	Two thousand.
Mil ciento.	Eleven hundred.
Cien mil.	A or one hundred thousand.
Un millon.	A or one million.

COMPOSITION.

¿Han llevado mi sombrero al sombrerero?	Have they taken my hat to the hatter?
Sí, señor, lo han llevado.	Yes, sir, they have taken it.

¿ Ha enviado V. la carta á su primo ?	Have you sent the letter to your cousin ?
La he enviado.	I have sent it.
¿ Ha tomado V. café ?	Have you taken coffee ?
No, señor, he tomado chocolate.	No, sir, I have taken chocolate.
¿ Cuánto dinero tiene V. ?	How much money have you ?
Tengo bastante.	I have enough.
¿ Cuánto tiene V. ?	How much have you ?
Tengo diez pesos.	I have ten dollars.
¿ Ha comido V. con su hermano hoy ?	Have you dined with your brother to-day ?
No, señor, no he comido con él.	No, sir, I have not dined with him.
¿ Cuánto ha pagado V. al sombrerero ?	How much have you paid to the hatter ?
Ocho pesos y seis centavos.	Eight dollars and six cents.
¿ Cuántas sillas ha comprado V. ?	How many chairs have you bought ?
He comprado seis.	I have bought six.

EXPLANATION.

NUMERAL ADJECTIVES.

57. In the formation of compound numbers, the same order is observed in Spanish as in English, except as to the place of the conjunction; as,

Mil ochocientos sesenta y seis.	1866.

58. All these numbers, except *uno*, one, and the compounds of *ciento*, one hundred, are indeclinable.

59. Uno agrees in gender with the noun to which it refers, but drops the *o* when it comes immediately before a masculine noun; as,

Uno de los hombres.	One of the men.
Una mujer.	A woman.
Un hombre.	A man.
Un gran caballo.	A great horse.

60. Ciento drops the last syllable when it comes immediately before a noun. Its compounds agree in number and gender with the nouns to which they refer; as,

Cien hombres y *cien* mujeres.	One hundred men and one hundred women.
Ciento veinte y tres caballos.	One hundred and twenty-three horses.
Dos*cientos* libros.	Two hundred books.
Tres*cientas* cajas.	Three hundred boxes.

LESSON XIV.

CONVERSATION AND VERSION.

1. ¿Ha escrito V. sus cartas? Sí, señor, las he escrito.
2. ¿Las ha enviado V. al correo*? Sí, señor, las he enviado hoy.
3. ¿Ha tomado V. café ó chocolate? He tomado café.
4. ¿Tiene V. bastante dinero? Sí, señor, tengo bastante.
5. ¿Cuánto tiene V.? Tengo veinte pesos y treinta centavos.
6. ¿Cuánto ha pagado V. á su sastre? He pagado á mi sastre veinte y cinco pesos y cuarenta centavos.
7. ¿Cuándo ha comido V. con su amigo? He comido con él hoy.
8. ¿Cuántos caballos ha comprado V.? He comprado ocho.
9. ¿Ha comprado V. sillas? Sí, señor, he comprado doce.
10. ¿Tiene V. mucho dinero? Tengo cien pesos y cincuenta centavos.
11. ¿Cuánto tiene su hermano? Tiene quinientos (500) pesos.
12. ¿Dónde vive V.? Vivo en Nueva York.
13. ¿Qué número (*number*) tiene la casa de V.? Tiene el número trescientos treinta y ocho (338).
14. ¿Ha recibido V. sus periódicos de París? Sí, señor, los he recibido.
15. ¿Qué números ha recibido V.? He recibido el once, doce, trece, catorce, y diez y ocho.
16. ¿Los ha leido V.? No, señor, no los he leido.
17. ¿Cuántos años (*year*) ha vivido V. en París? He vivido cinco.
18. ¿Cuántas lecciones ha aprendido V.? He aprendido trece.
19. ¿Cuántas gramáticas tiene V.? No tengo sino una.
20. ¿Quién ha recibido hoy periódicos? Nadie los ha recibido hoy.
21. ¿Es rico el amigo de V.? Sí, señor, tiene quinientos mil (500,000) pesos.
22. ¿Ha llevado V. mis cartas al correo? No he llevado sino dos.
23. ¿Ha enviado V. mis zapatos al zapatero? Sí, señor, los he enviado hoy.
24. ¿Ha tomado V. muchas lecciones de español? He tomado doce.
25. ¿Cuánto ha pagado V. á su amigo? Tres mil ochocientos cuarenta y cuatro pesos (3,844).

EXERCISE.

1. Do you wish to send anything to your cousin? Yes, sir, I wish to send money to my cousin.
2. How much money do you wish to send? I wish to send $317.
3. Who has taken the money to the tailor? My cousin (*fem.*) has taken it.
4. Where have you sent the horses? I have sent them to Paris.
5. How many have you sent? I have sent two very good ones.

* *Correo.* post-office.

6. My son, have you taken the $31.50 to the baker? Yes, sir, I have (taken them).

7. Has your brother sent some chairs to your house? No, sir, but he has sent some to his.

8. How many has he sent? He has sent ten chairs and three tables.

9. Has the woman bought no chairs? Yes, sir, she has bought twenty-six.

10. How many letters have they written this (*esta*) week? They have written three hundred and ten letters and one thousand and one notes.

11. Which newspapers have you sent to your father? I have sent him numbers three, fifteen and eighteen.

12. Has he read them all? He has read only number fifteen.

13. Has the butcher much money? He has $1,000.

14. How much have you sent to your friend (*fem.*)? I have sent $111.17.

15. Whom do you wish to pay? I wish to pay my tailor.

16. Where does your tailor reside? He resides in Vienna.

17. When have you written to Alexander? I have written to Alexander to-day.

18. Have you received a letter from him to-day? Yes, sir, I have received six.

19. What day do you receive letters from France? I receive them on Tuesdays and Saturdays.

20. How many has your cousin written to you? None.

LESSON XV.

Pronunciar, pronunciado.	To pronounce, pronounced.
Tocar, tocado.	To touch, touched; to play, played.
Cantar, cantado.	To sing, sung.
Reinar, reinado.	To reign, reigned.
Como,	How, like, as.

ORDINAL NUMBERS.

Primero (primer *before a noun*).	First.
Segundo.	Second.
Tercero (*or* tercer *before a noun*).	Third.

LESSON XV.

Cuarto.	Fourth.
Quinto.	Fifth.
Sexto.	Sixth.
Séptimo.	Seventh.
Octavo.	Eighth.
Noveno, *or* nono.	Ninth.
Décimo.	Tenth.

Piano.	Piano.	Cancion.	Song.
Violin.	Violin.	Palabra.	Word.
Músico.	Musician.	Guitarra.	Guitar.
Pianista.	Pianist.	Historia.	History.
Cantor.	Singer.	Arpa.	Harp.
Tomo *or* volúmen.	Volume.	Obra.	Work.
Cárlos.	Charles.	Música.	Music.
Luis.	Louis.	Cantora, cantatriz.	Singer.
Enrique.	Henry.	Calle.	Street.
Rey.	King.	Avenida.	Avenue.
Trabajo.	Work, labor.		

COMPOSITION.

¿Cómo pronuncia Manuel el español?	How does Emanuel pronounce Spanish?
Lo pronuncia bien.	He pronounces it well.
¿Toca V. la guitarra?	Do you play the guitar?
No, señor, toco el violin y el piano.	No, sir, I play the violin and the piano.
¿Canta V. canciones españolas?	Do you sing Spanish songs?
No, señor, canto canciones inglesas.	No, sir, I sing English songs.
¿Quien reina en Rusia?	Who reigns in Russia?
Alejandro Segundo.	Alexander the Second.
¿En qué calle vive V.?	In which street do you live?
Vivo en la calle Once.	I live in Eleventh street.
¿Y V., dónde vive?	And where do *you* live?
Yo vivo en la calle Veinte y tres.	I live in Twenty-third street.
¿Qué toca el músico?	What does the musician play?
Toca el arpa, el violin y el piano.	He plays the harp, violin and piano.
¿Tiene V. el primer tomo de mi libro?	Have you the first volume of my book?
No, señor, tengo el segundo.	No, sir, I have the second.
¿Ha leido V. el tomo tercero?	Have you read the third volume?
No, señor, he leido el cuarto.	No, sir, I have read the fourth.
¿Cuántos años tiene V.?	How old are you?

EXPLANATION.

61. The ordinals always agree in gender and number with

the noun, expressed or understood, to which they refer, and may be placed either before or after that noun; as,

El primer tomo (or el tomo primero).	The first volume.
El primer buen libro.	The first good book.
Los primeros cuadernos.	The first copy-books.
Las primeras lecciones.	The first lessons.
El segundo tomo.	The second volume.
Las segundas intenciones.	The second intentions.

It has been seen, in the list of ordinal numbers at the opening of the present lesson, that *primero* and *tercero* lose the final letter when they immediately precede their noun, or are separated from it only by an adjective. We may observe here, that *tercero* is by some written entire; the contracted form, however, is much to be preferred; as,

El tercer tomo.	The third volume.

62. The ordinals are not so frequently used in Spanish as in English; and, except *primero*, first, their place is generally supplied by the cardinal numbers; as, for instance, in speaking of the days of the month, which are expressed by *el dos, tres, cuatro, etc.*, the second, third, fourth, &c. The following are the principal cases in which the ordinals are employed: 1st, with the names of sovereigns, popes, &c.; 2d, in the enumeration of books, chapters, lessons, &c., and a few others; but, even in these cases, after *décimo*, tenth, they are, by reason of their great length, generally replaced by the numerals; as,

Cárlos Quinto.	Charles the Fifth.
Pio Nono.	Pius the Ninth.
Capítulo décimo.	Chapter tenth.
Calle Veinte y tres.	Twenty-third street.
Luis Catorce.	Louis the Fourteenth.

N. B.—The definite article is not required in the above examples.

CONVERSATION AND VERSION.

1. ¿Pronuncia V. bien el inglés? No, señor, lo pronuncio mal.
2. ¿Es V. cantor? No, señor, pero toco.
3. ¿Qué toca V.? Toco el violin.

LESSON XV.

4. ¿Canta bien su hermana de V.? No, señor, ella canta mal; pero toca bien el piano.
5. ¿Qué leccion estudia V.? Estudio la cuarta.
6. ¿En qué calle vive su padre de V.? Vivo en la calle Catorce.
7. ¿Qué tomos ha leido V.? He leido el primero, segundo, tercero y cuarto.
8. ¿Cuántos tomos tiene la obra? Tiene seis.
9. ¿Qué libro lee V.? Leo la historia de Cárlos Quinto.
10. ¿Ha leido V. la historia de Enrique Octavo de Inglaterra? Sí, señor, la he leido.
11. ¿Qué tomo lee su hermana de V.? Leo el noveno.
12. ¿Cuánto dinero ha recibido V. hoy? He recibido cincuenta y un pesos.
13. ¿Cuántos hermanos tiene V.? Tengo cinco.
14. ¿Cuántos años tiene su hermana de V.? Tiene quince.
15. ¿Cuánto tiempo ha vivido V. en París? He vivido seis años.
16. ¿Qué número tiene su casa? El doscientos seis (206).
17. ¿Qué dia de la semana es hoy? Hoy es miércoles.
18. ¿Qué hora tiene V.? Las diez.
19. ¿Cuántos dias tiene una semana? Tiene siete.
20. Ocho y doce ¿cuántos son? Son veinte.
21. ¿Cuántos años tiene su papá de V.? Tiene sesenta.
22. ¿Cuántos dias tiene el año? Tiene trescientos sesenta y cinco (365).
23. ¿Cómo ha leido V.? He leido despacio.
24. ¿Ha llevado V. mi piano al pianista? Sí, señor, lo he llevado.
25. ¿Ha cantado V. mucho hoy? Hoy he cantado poco.
26. ¿Cuándo ha vendido V. su caballo? Lo he vendido hoy.

EXERCISE.

1. What book have you? A music-book.
2. How many volumes has it? Three.
3. Which volume have you read? The first.
4. Has your father not read the second volume? No, sir; but my cousin has read it.
5. What are you reading, miss? I am reading the History of Charles the Fifth.
6. Who has sold your sister's History of England? She has sold it.
7. Who has bought the violin? The pianist.
8. Where does he live? In Seventeenth street.
9. In what street does the butcher live? In Sixth avenue.
10. Have you bought good meat in the butcher's shop? The meat (which) I have bought is very bad.

11. What things have you sent to the tailor? I have sent stockings, vests, and pocket-handkerchiefs.

12. What day of the week is to-day? Monday.

13. Is Monday the first day of the week? No, sir, it is the second; Sunday is the first.

14. How much money does the merchant require? He requires $1,500.

15. How much money do you wish to send to your friend? I wish to send my friend $50.

16. Does he need much money? Yes, madam, he is very poor.

17. How many letters have your brothers written to Emanuel? Very few.

18. How do your sisters pronounce Spanish? They pronounce it well when they read, but not when they speak.

19. When do they write their exercises? When they have studied their lessons.

20. And you, when do you write yours? When my brothers write theirs.

21. How do the poor buy? The poor buy dear, and the rich buy cheap.

22. Has your father sold his old horse? He has sold it.

23. Have you read the History of Louis XVI.? I have read volumes first, second, and third.

LESSON XVI.

FIRST CONJUGATION—*Preterit Definite.*

Habl-é.	I spoke.
Habl-aste.	Thou spokest.
Habl-ó.	He spoke.
Habl-ámos.	We spoke.
Habl-asteis.	You spoke.
Habl-aron.	They spoke.

SECOND CONJUGATION.

Aprend-í.	I learned.
Aprend-iste.	Thou learnedst.
Aprend-ió.	He learned.
Aprend-imos.	We learned.
Aprend-isteis.	You learned.
Aprend-ieron.	They learned.

LESSON XVI.

THIRD CONJUGATION.

Escrib-í.	I wrote.
Escrib-iste.	Thou wrote.
Escrib-ió.	He wrote.
Escrib-imos.	We wrote.
Escrib-isteis.	You wrote.
Escrib-ieron.	They wrote.
Pasar.	To pass, to spend (*in relation to time*).

Ayer. Anoche.	Yesterday. Last night.
Antes de ayer, or anteayer.	The day before yesterday.
El año pasado.	Last year.
El mes pasado.	Last month.
La semana pasada.	Last week.
Ante (*prep.*).	Before, in the presence of.
Ante todas cosas.	Before all things.
Ante todo.	Above all.
Antes (*ad.*).	Before (*refers to time*).
Delante (*ad.*).	Before (*refers to place*).
Despues (*ad.*).	Afterwards, after.
Mas (*ad.*).	More.
Ménos (*ad.*).	Less, fewer.
Que (*conj.*).	That, than.

COMPOSITION.

¿Habló V. con mi padre?	Did you speak with my father?
Sí, señor, hablé con él ántes de ayer.	Yes, sir, I spoke with him the day before yesterday.
¿Han aprendido Vds. su leccion?	Have you learned your lesson?
Sí, señor, la hemos aprendido hoy.	Yes, sir, we have learned it to-day.
¿Cuándo escribió V. á su hermana?	When did you write to your sister?
Escribí la semana pasada á mi hermana.	I wrote to my sister last week.
¿Ha recibido V. sus periódicos del mes pasado?	Have you received your newspapers of last month (last month's newspapers)?
Sí, señor, los he recibido hoy.	Yes, sir, I have received them to-day.
¿Cuándo vendió V. su caballo?	When did you sell your horse?
Lo vendí el año pasado.	I sold it last year.
¿Estudia V. ántes ó despues de comer?	Do you study before or after dining (or dinner)?
Estudio ántes de comer.	I study before dining.
¿Habló V. mucho ante el juez?	Did you speak much before the judge?

No, señor, hablé muy poco.	No, sir, I spoke very little.
¿Qué libro tiene V. delante?	What book have you before you?
Tengo la gramática española.	I have the Spanish grammar.
¿Escribió V. sus cartas?	Did you write your letters?
Sí, señor, las escribí el domingo pasado.	Yes, sir, I wrote them last Sunday.
¿Come V. ménos que yo?	Do you eat less than I?
No, señor, como mas que V.	No, sir, I eat more than you.
¿Ha visto V. á su amigo?	Have you seen your friend?
Sí, señor, lo ví ayer.	Yes, sir, I saw him yesterday.
¿Dónde lo vió V.?	Where did you see him?
Lo ví delante de la iglesia.	I saw him before (in front of) the church.
¿Habló V. con él?	Did you speak with him?
Sí, señor; pero muy poco.	Yes, sir; but very little.
¿Ha comido V.?	Have you dined?
Sí, señora, he comido pan y he bebido vino.	Yes, sir, I have eaten bread and drunk wine.
¿Ha leido V. y estudiado sus ejercicios?	Have you read and studied your exercises?
Sí, señor, los he leido y estudiado.	Yes, sir, I have read and studied them.
¿Ha escrito V. á su padre?	Have you written to your father?
Sí, señor, escribí ayer.	Yes, sir, I wrote yesterday.
¿Cuándo ha recibido V. las cartas de él?	When have you received the letters from him?
Las he recibido hoy.	I have received them to-day.
¿Ha enviado V. mis cartas despues de las suyas?	Have you sent my letters after yours?
Las he enviado ántes.	I (have) sent them before.
¿Habló V. ante el rey?	Did you speak before the king?
No, señor, habló ante el juez.	No, sir, I spoke before the judge.
¿Cuánto tiempo?	How long?

EXPLANATION.

63. The Preterite Definite refers to a time past, and generally specified in the sentence, and denotes the thing or action past in such a manner that nothing remains of that time in which it was done; as,

Escribí á mi padre en el año 1864.	I wrote to my father in the year 1864.
Aprendí el frances el año pasado.	I learned French last year.

In colloquial language, the *preterite indefinite* (which has been treated of in Lesson xii.), is sometimes, though incorrectly, substituted for the *preterite definite*. The following example will show the impropriety of such a substitution:

| He escrito á mi padre ayer. | I have written to my father yesterday. |

Nothing remains of yesterday; it is time past, and has no connection with the present; and, as it has been already seen that the preterite indefinite *conveys an allusion to the present time*, the incorrectness of the foregoing example is at once apparent.

We may, however, say with propriety:

| Escribí la carta á las tres, á las cuatro, etc. | I wrote the letter at three o'clock, at four o'clock, &c. |

for the time specified is completely past.

64. ANTE.—This preposition means *before*, or *in the presence of*; as,

| Habló *ante* el juez. | He spoke before the judge. |

And it sometimes denotes priority, antecedence, &c.; as,

| *Ante* todas cosas. | Before all things. |

65. MAS, *more*; MÉNOS, *less, fewer*.—These two adverbs are used to form the comparative degree of several adjectives, which last they always precede in the sentence; as,

| El vino es *mas* caro que la cerveza. | Wine is dearer than beer. |
| Yo soy *mas* rico que V. | I am richer than you. |

When used to express some quality or circumstance respecting verbs, their usual place in the sentence is immediately after these last; as,

| Yo escribo *mas*. | I write more. |
| Tú hablas *ménos*. | Thou speakest less. |

It is needless to observe here, that *mas* and *ménos* are themselves the comparatives of *mucho* and *poco*, respectively.

CONVERSATION AND VERSION.

1. ¿Cuándo habló V. con el abogado? Hablé con él anteayer.
2. ¿Ha hablado V. con mi hermana? No, señor, hablé ayer con su amigo de V.
3. ¿Ha hablado V. con el pianista? Sí, señor, le hablé ayer.

LESSON XVI.

4. ¿Ha aprendido V. su leccion? No, señor; pero he escrito el ejercicio.

5. ¿Han aprendido ellos sus lecciones de frances? Sí, señor, han aprendido las de frances y de español.

6. ¿Cuándo aprendió su hermana á tocar el piano? Aprendió el año pasado.

7. ¿Ha leido V. la historia de los Estados Unidos? He leido el tomo primero y el segundo.

8. ¿Ha leido V. la carta de su hermana y la de su amiga? He leido la de mi hermana; pero no la de mi amiga.

9. ¿Qué ha leido V. hoy? He leido los ejercicios de la semana pasada.
10. ¿Cuándo compró V. su caballo? Lo compré el mes pasado.
11. ¿Dónde habló V. con mi padre? Delante de su casa de V.
12. ¿Leyó V. la carta de su padre ántes que la de su hermano? No, señor, la leí despues.
13. ¿Cuándo residió V. en París? Residí ántes que V.
14. ¿Cuántos años tiene su hermana? Tiene veinte.
15. ¿Cuántos pesos pagó V. el mes pasado al comerciante? Quinientos.
16. ¿Ha llevado V. mis zapatos al zapatero? Sí, señor, los llevó ayer.
17. ¿Cuándo ha recibido V. su dinero? Lo recibí anteayer.
18. ¿Ha escrito V. despues que escribió mi padre? No, señor, escribí ántes.
19. ¿Escribió V. su carta despues que recibió la de su hermano? Sí, señor, la escribí mucho despues.
20. ¿Ha hablado V. con la madre ántes que con la hija? No, señor, hablé ántes con la hija que con la madre.
21. ¿Estudió V. su leccion de ayer? No, señor, estudié la de ántes de ayer; pero no he estudiado la de ayer ni la de hoy.
22. ¿Habló V. ante el juez? Sí, señor, hablé ante el juez y ante el rey.
23. ¿Habla V. mas que yo? No, señor, hablo ménos; pero escribo mas.

EXERCISE.

1. Did you speak more yesterday than to-day? I spoke less; but I read more.

2. How many newspapers did your father read yesterday? Very few.
3. How old is your sister? She is nineteen.
4. Who took the vest to the tailor last year? The baker took it.
5. How much did the tailor pay to the baker afterwards? $59.10.
6. Did he receive the vest after or before the coat? He received it after.

7. Did your sisters sing yesterday? Yes, sir, they sang and played.
8. What did they sing? They sang Spanish songs and played on the piano.
9. Have you (*plural*) played to-day? No, madam, we have not played; but we have written our French exercises.
10. How many words have your brothers written in Spanish to-day? Fewer than last Thursday.
11. Do they speak more English than Spanish? No, madam, they speak more Spanish.
12. What have the singers received from Paris? They have received some good songs and French music.
13. Have the singers (*fem.*) enough Spanish music? Yes, sir, they have received some to-day.
14. Did they sing well last month? Not very well.
15. Who sang in your house the day before yesterday? Nobody sang.
16. How long did you reside in Vienna? Five years, six months, and thirteen days.
17. How many churches has Paris? Paris has many churches.
18. How did your cousins pronounce their Spanish yesterday? Very well.
19. Are you a musician? Yes, madam.
20. Is your sister a pianist or a singer, or does she play on the guitar? She sings and plays on the piano.
21. When did you speak before the judge? The day before yesterday and last week.
22. Do you sing much with the musicians? I sing a little; but before all things I study my Spanish lessons.

LESSON XVII.

Trabajar. trah-bah-har	To work.
Mandar?	To command, to send.
Quien, quienes,	Who.
A quien, á quienes.	Whom, to whom.
¿Qué?	What (*inter.*), who, that, or which.
Cual, cuales.	Which one, which ones.
Cuyo (*masc. sing.*), cuya (*fem. sing.*). Cuyos (*masc. plural*), cuyas (*fem. plural*).	Whose, which, or of whom.
Varios. Algunas veces.	Several. Sometimes.

LESSON XVII.

Retrato.	Portrait.	Criada.	Servant.
Pantalones.	Pantaloons.	Iglesia.	Church.
Criado.	Servant.	Calle.	Street.
Concierto.	Concert.	Plaza.	Square, market.
Teatro.	Theatre.	Compañía.	Company.
Mercado.	Market.	Juana.	Jane.
Parque.	Park.		
Juan.	John.		
Trabajador.	Workman.		
Ultimo (a).	Last.		

COMPOSITION.

¿Es viejo el caballero á quien V. habló en el concierto?	Is the gentleman to whom you spoke at the concert old?
No, señor, pero lo es la señora que ha hablado con V. en el teatro.	No, sir; but the lady who spoke to you at the theatre is (so).
¿A quién busca V.?	For whom do you look?
Busco á la señorita á quien V. busca.	I am looking for the young lady that you look for.
¿Quién es el jóven que ha hablado con V.?	Who is the young man that has spoken with you?
Es un criado del hotel.	He is a servant in the hotel.
El muchacho que lee, y al cual V. mandó trabajar, es mi hermano.	The boy that reads, and whom you commanded to work is my brother.
La gramática que él tiene, y en la cual estudia, es mia.	The grammar which he has, and in which he studies, is mine.
El caballero cuya casa V. compró es amigo mio.	The gentleman whose house you bought is my friend.
El comerciante cuyo vino V. compró, vende muy barato.	The merchant whose wine you bought sells very cheap.
El libro en que leemos.	The book in which we read (or which we read in).
La señora á quien habló es mi madre.	The lady I spoke to is my mother.
¿Manda V. sus niños al Parque Central?	Do you send your children to the Central Park?
¿A quién manda V. trabajar?	Whom do you command to work?
A mis criados.	My servants.
¡Juan!	John!
¡Señor! ¿qué manda V.?	Sir! what do you wish?
Quiero la comida.	I wish my dinner.
¿En dónde trabajan hoy los trabajadores?	Where do the workmen work to-day?
Trabajan en la calle.	They work in the street.

LESSON XVII.

EXPLANATION.

66. QUIEN.—The relative pronoun *quien* refers to persons only, and is always preceded by the preposition *á*, when governed by a verb; as,

El hombre *á quien* V. quiere.	The man whom you love.

67. WHO, coming immediately after its antecedent, is translated by *que*; when it stands alone, or is governed by a preposition, it is rendered by *quien*; as,

El muchacho *que* estudia.	The boy *who* studies.
La muchacha *con quien* hablas.	The girl with whom you speak.

68. CUAL and QUE relate to persons and things; as,

El muchacho *que* lee, y al *cual* V. mandó trabajar, es mi hermano.	The boy that reads, and whom you commanded to work, is my brother.
La gramática *que* él tiene, y en la *cual* estudia, es mia.	The grammar which he has, and in which he studies, is mine.

69. CUYO also refers to persons and things, but agrees with the word by which it is immediately followed; as,

El caballero *cuya casa* V. compró es amigo mio.	The gentleman whose house you bought is my friend.
El comerciante *cuyo* vino V. compró vende muy barato.	The merchant whose wine you bought sells very cheap.

This pronoun partakes of the nature, both of the relatives and the possessives.

70. In English the preposition does not always precede the relative pronoun; but in Spanish it is indispensable to place the preposition before the relative; as,

El libro en que leemos.	The book which we read in (or, in which we read).

71. The relative pronoun *can never* be suppressed in Spanish; so that we cannot say, as in English, the lady I spoke to, but, in full; as,

La señora *á quien* hablé, es mi madre.	The lady to whom I spoke is my mother.

CONVERSATION AND VERSION.

1. ¿A quién mandó V. ayer al mercado? Mandó á mi criado Juan.
2. ¿Cuál de sus criados trabaja mas? Juan trabaja mas que todos.
3. ¿Quién es el hombre á quién V. busca? El hombre á quien busco es trabajador.

4. ¿Quién es el caballero con quien habló V. ayer en el concierto? Es un discípulo mio.

5. ¿A quién quiere V. hablar? Quiero hablar á la señorita que toca el piano.

6. ¿Cómo pasaron Vds. el tiempo en el campo? Lo pasámos muy bien en compañía de nuestros amigos.

7. ¿Es frances el comerciante á quien compró V. el caballo? Sí, señor, es el Frances cuya casa compró V.

8. ¿Manda (envia) V. sus niños al Parque Central? Sí, señor, los mando al Parque Central.

9. ¿Con quién los envia V.? Con sus primos.

10. ¿Qué libro quiere V. leer? Quiero leer el de Manuel.

11. ¿No quiere V. leer el que yo tengo? No, señor, quiero leer el de Alejandro.

12. ¿A quién manda V. trabajar? A mis criados.

13. ¡Juan! ¡Señor! ¿Qué manda V.? Quiero la comida.

14. ¿Canta V. bien? No, señor; pero la señorita que reside en su casa de V. canta muy bien.

15. ¿Estudia V. mucho? No, señor, pero trabajo mucho.

16. ¿Ha estudiado V. hoy su leccion? No, señor, la estudié ayer; hoy he escrito los ejercicios.

17. ¿Cómo pronuncia su maestro de V. el español? Lo pronuncia bien; pero pronuncia muy mal el inglés.

18. ¿Tocó V. ayer el piano en casa de sus amigos? Sí, señor, tocámos y cantámos.

19. ¿Qué cantaron Vds.? Cantámos canciones españolas y la cancion americana llamada, "The Star Spangled Banner."

20. ¡Caballeros! ¿Quieren Vds. tomar chocolate ó café? Queremos beber vino.

21. ¿Cuántos dias pasó V. en el campo? Pasé toda una semana.

22. ¿Porqué no pasa V. un mes en el campo con nosotros? Porque necesito residir en la ciudad.

23. ¿Cuál de sus amigos habla bien español? El que estudia mucho habla bien.

24. ¿Cuál de sus hermanos estudia mas? El mas pequeño.

25. ¿De quién recibe V. cartas? De mi padre y mis hermanos.

26. ¿Es de V. el libro en el cual estudia su hermano? No, señor, es suyo.

27. ¿Trabajó V. mucho ayer? No, señor; pero he trabajado mucho hoy.

28. ¿Cuándo estudia V. sus lecciones? Las estudio los miércoles y los sábados.

LESSON XVII.

EXERCISE.

1. Whose is the portrait (which) you sent me yesterday? It is the portrait of my brother who lives in Germany.

2. Which portrait have you sent to Charles? I have sent no portrait to Charles; but I have sent mine to the musician.

3. With whom did you spend last week? I spent last week with my cousin John.

4. In which city of France does the pianist's brother live? He lives in the city in which your sister Jane resides.

5. To whom did you send the first volume of your work? I sent it to Louis.

6. Whom do you order to work? My servant John.

7. Who is the lady you are looking for? She is the mother of the singer (*fem.*) whose piano Charles bought last year.

8. With whom did you send your children to the concert last night? I sent them with a servant.

9. With which servant did you send them? With one of mine (my own).

10. In which church does Miss Garcia sing? She sings in Twenty-eighth street church.

11. How did you (*plural*) pass the time in Philadelphia? Very well.

12. Did you study many lessons? We studied very little, and neither read nor wrote our exercises.

13. How much did you write the day before yesterday? I studied a good deal, but wrote little.

14. Which volumes of Robertson's History has your son? He has received the first, second, third and fourth.

15. Did you buy any books at the bookstore in Walker street? Yes, madam, I bought the History of Charles V. and some music books.

16. Whom have you paid with the money I sent you? I have paid the man who worked in my house yesterday.

17. Does your servant work much? No, sir; but she reads a great deal.

18. From whom do you receive letters every day? I receive letters from Henry on Mondays, Wednesdays and Fridays, and from my father on Tuesdays.

19. Who has the boots that I bought in Fourth avenue? John has taken them to his cousin who lives in Philadelphia.

20. Has your servant bought any good meat in the market? He has not bought any to-day.

21. How many songs have you received from Spain? I have received several from Spain and two from England.

22. Have you sung any of them? None; but my sister sang one or two last night at the concert.

23. Are they very good? One of them is very good, and my cousin (*fem.*) sings it very well.

24. How many pencils does the hatter wish? He wants twelve pencils and three penknives.

25. Does Louisa play much on the piano? No, sir, she is very lazy, and will neither play nor study.

26. The tailor has a handsome vest, very cheap; will you buy it? I do not wish to buy a vest; but I want pantaloons.

27. Has he any pantaloons? He has none, he sold them all last week.

LESSON XVIII.

Ir. | To go.

PRESENT.

Voy.	I go (or, am going).
Vas.	Thou goest.
Va.	He, or she, goes.
Vamos.	We go.
Vais.	You go.
Van.	They go.

PRETERIT DEFINITE.

Fuí.	I went.
Fuiste.	Thou wentest.
Fué.	He, or she, went.
Fuimos.	We went.
Fuisteis.	You went.
Fueron.	They went.

PRESENT.

Venir.	To come.
Vengo.	I come (or, am coming).
Vienes.	Thou comest.
Viene.	He, or she, comes.
Venimos.	We come.
Venis.	You come.
Vienen.	They come.

LESSON XVIII.

PRETERIT DEFINITE.

Vine.	I came.
Viniste.	Thou camest.
Vino.	He, or she, came.
Vinimos.	We came.
Vinisteis.	You came.
Vinieron.	They came.

DEMONSTRATIVE PRONOUNS.
Singular.

Masculine.	Feminine.	Neuter.	English
Este.	Esta.	Esto.	This.
Ese.	Esa.	Eso.	That.
Aquel.	Aquella.	Aquello.	That (yonder).

Plural.

Masculine	Feminine	Neuter	English
Estos.	Estas.	No neuter.	These.
Esos.	Esas.	"	Those.
Aquellos.	Aquellas.	"	Those (yonder).
Ello.			It.

Aquí, acá.	Here.
Ahí.	
Allí, allá, acullá. }	There.
Porqué.	Why.
Porque.	Because.
Léjos.	Far.
Cerca.	Near.
Otro. Ambos.	Another. Both.
Ni uno ni otro (*ind. pro.*).	Neither.

Profesor.	Professor.	Juana.	Jane.
Discípulo.	Pupil.	Discípula.	Pupil.
Lado.	Side.	Zapatería.	Shoemaker's shop.
Jardin.	Garden.	Manteca.	Butter.

COMPOSITION.

¿De quién es *este* libro que tengo *aquí?* | Whose book is this which I have here?
Ese que tiene V. ahí, y *este* que yo tengo *aquí*, son del profesor. | That one which you have there, and this one which I have here, are the professor's.

¿Quién es *aquel* caballero que reside *allí* del otro lado de la calle? | Who is that gentleman who resides there on the other side of the street?
Aquel caballero es mi discípulo. | That gentleman is my pupil.

¿Adónde va V.?	Where do you go?
Voy allá, al otro lado del parque.	I go there to the other side of the park.
¿No quiere V. venir acá de este lado?	Will you not come here to this side?
No, señor, voy allá del otro lado.	No, sir, I go there to the other side.
¿Quiere V. comprar aquel libro?	Do you wish to buy that book?
No, señor, quiero comprar ese otro.	No, sir, I wish to buy that other one.
¿Quiere V. venir al teatro con nosotros?	Will you come to the theatre with us?
Eso quiero.	That (is what) I wish.
¿Llevó V. *aquello* á la sastrería?	Did you take that (thing) to the tailor's?
Lo llevó.	I did (or I took it).
¿Manda V. algo mas?	Do you command anything more (or have you any more commands)?
No, *eso* es todo.	No, that is all.
¿Envió V. el chaleco á la sastrería, y las botas á la zapatería?	Did you send the vest to the tailor's, and the boots to the shoemaker's?
Envió lo uno y lo otro (*or* ámbos).	I sent both.
¿Fueron á su casa de V. el médico frances y el profesor aleman?	Did the French physician and the German professor go to your house?
Vino *aquel*, pero no vino *este*.	The former came, but the latter did not come.
¿Habló V. de *aquello* á mi madre?	Did you speak of that to my mother?
No, señor, pero hablé de *ello* á su padre de V.	No, sir, but I spoke of it to your father.
En mi casa y en *la* de su hermano de V.	In my house and in your brother's.
El jardin de esta casa y el de la que V. compró.	The garden of this house and that of the one you bought.
Este caballo y *el* de mi amigo.	This horse and my friend's (that of my friend).

EXPLANATION.

72. The demonstrative pronouns *este*, this, *ese*, *aquel*, that, are thus declined:

Este, ese, aquel (*masc. sing.*).
Esta, esa, aquella (*fem. sing.*).
Estos, esos, aquellos (*masc. plural*).
Estas, esas, aquellas (*fem. plural*).
Esto, eso, aquello (*neuter*).

73. ESTE is used to point out what is near to us, and corresponds to the meaning of the adverb *here*; *ese* points out that which is at some distance, and corresponds to the adverb *there*; and *aquel* denotes remoteness, and corresponds to the adverb *yonder*; as,

Este libro que tengo *aquí*.	*This* book which I have *here*.
Ese que tiene V. *ahí*.	*That* one which you have *there*.
Aquel que llevó V. *allá*.	*That* one which you took *there*.

74. When the pronouns *este*, *ese* precede the adjective *otro*, another, they may sometimes be written together, so as to form but one word with it, in the following manner:

Estotro.	} This other.	Estotros.	} These others.
Estotra.		Estotras.	
Esotro.	} That other.	Esotros.	} Those others.
Esotra.		Esotras.	

These forms, however, are now rarely used.

75. The demonstrative pronouns, in their quality of adjectives, are used also *as neuter*. *Eso*, that, is the most used of the three, and almost as much as the personal pronoun *lo*, and in the same manner; as,

Eso se hará.	That will be done.
¡*Eso* es!	That is it!

76. The *former* and *the latter* is translated in Spanish by *aquel* and *este*; thus,

La aplicacion y la pereza hacen al hombre muy diferente; *aquella* le eleva y *esta* le rebaja.	Industry and slothfulness have a very different effect upon man; the former elevates him, the latter lowers him.

77. When in English the demonstrative pronoun *that* is followed by the preposition *of*, or either of the relatives *who*, *which*, expressed or understood, referring to a noun already mentioned, the definite article, in the corresponding number and gender, is employed in Spanish; as,

En mi casa y en la de su hermano de V.	In my house and in your brother's.
El jardin de esta casa y el de *la que* V. compró.	The garden of this house and that of the one (which) you bought.
Este caballo y el de mi amigo.	This horse and my friend's (*i. e.*, that of my friend).

78. English personal pronouns, followed by a relative not agreeing in case, are generally rendered in Spanish by the demonstrative; as,

Quiero comprar á *aquellos* que venden barato.	I want to buy from *them* who sell cheap.

LESSON XVIII.

79. Aquí, allí, acá, allá.—Although the adverbs *aquí,* here, *allí,* yonder, are employed as synonyms of *acá,* here, and *allá,* yonder, respectively, we must observe that *aquí* and *allí* refer to a place more circumscribed or determinate than *acá, allá*; for the same reason we can say, *mas acá, mas allá,* nearer, farther; and we cannot say, *mas aquí,* more here, *mas allí,* more there.

CONVERSATION AND VERSION.

1. ¿Viene V. del campo? No, señor, voy allá.
2. ¿De dónde viene su amigo de V.? Viene de España.
3. ¿Adónde va V. este año? Este año quiero ir á París.
4. ¿De quién es ese retrato que tiene V. ahí? Este que tengo aquí es el de mi padre, y aquel que tiene su amigo de V. allí, es de mi madre.
5. ¿Es discípulo de V. el caballero que reside en aquella hermosa casa? No, señor; pero su prima, que reside de este otro lado de la calle, es mi discípula.
6. ¿Va V. á su casa todos los dias? No, señor, voy allí los lúnes, miércoles y viérnes.
7. ¿Cuántas lecciones toma el caballero que vino ayer á su casa de V.? Toma dos á la semana.
8. ¿Quién trabaja mas, el profesor ó el discípulo? El uno y el otro trabajan mucho.
9. ¿Es este niño su hijo de V.? Sí, señor, es mi hijo Manuel.
10. ¡Manuel! ¿quieres venir aquí á mi lado? No, señor, no quiero ir.
11. ¿Porqué? Porque quiero ir con mi padre.
12. ¿Cuántos niños tiene V.? Tengo cinco, tres niñas y dos niños.
13. ¿Quiere V. venir con nosotros al Parque Central? No, señor, porque tengo que ir con mis niños al campo.
14. ¿Ha de ir V. (tiene V. que ir) hoy? Sí, señor, tengo que ir hoy.
15. ¿No quiere V. venir acá de este lado? No, señor, voy allá del otro lado.
16. ¿Llevó V. aquello á la sastrería? Sí, señor, lo llevó.
17. ¿Manda V. algo mas? No, eso es todo.
18. ¿Habló V. de aquello á mi amigo? No, señor; pero habló de ello á su hermano.
19. ¿En dónde trabajó V. ayer? Trabajó en la casa de V. y en la de su hermano.
20. ¿Trabajó V. en mi jardin ó en el de mi amigo? Trabajó en el uno y en el otro.

LESSON XVIII.

21. ¿Adónde va V. á trabajar hoy? Voy á trabajar en el jardin de esta casa y en el de la que V. compró el año pasado.
22. ¿Llevó V. mis botas á la zapatería, y compró V. el pan que necesitamos? Llevé las botas; pero no he comprado el pan.
23. ¿Qué llevas ahí, Alejandro? Llevo mis libros.
24. ¿Qué quiere tu hermano? Quiero pan y manteca.
25. ¿Pagó V. al sastre? Sí, señor, ayer pagué al sastre, y hoy he pagado al zapatero.
26. ¿De quién son esos caballos? Este es el de mi padre, y aquel es el de mi hermano.
27. ¿Cuál es el de V.? Yo no tengo ninguno.
28. ¿Quiere V. tener uno? Quiero tener muchos.
29. ¿Escribió V. la carta y la leccion? Escribí aquella, pero no he escrito esta.

EXERCISE.

1. Do you go to church every day? I only (*solo*) go on Sundays.
2. Where is your servant Jane going? She is going to the bakery to buy bread.
3. Do your music teacher (*maestro*) and your Spanish professor come to your house every day? The former comes every day, but the latter only comes on Tuesdays and Saturdays.
4. Which of the two works the more? Both have to work much.
5. Which of the two horses is the older, this one *here* or that one *there?* This one *here* is the younger.
6. Have you that letter which you received last Monday? I have not that one; but I have here the one* I received the day before yesterday.
7. Who has written these two histories, that of France and that of America? Rollin has written the former, and Robertson the latter.
8. Does the piano teacher live far from here? The piano teacher does not live far from here; but the French professor lives very far.
9. Is that all (*lo que*) your brother has studied? Yes, sir, that is all.
10. Which lesson have you studied? I have studied the one (*la que*) we read the other day.
11. Which did we read, the fifteenth or the sixteenth? We read both.
12. Which one do you wish to read first? I require to read the former.
13. Why do you require to read the former? Because I have not studied it well.
14. Which exercise have you there? I have mine and my brother's.
15. Is your brother not coming to take his lesson to-day? No, sir, he has to take his music lesson to-day.
16. John! Sir!

* La que.

17. Have you taken my coat to the tailor's? Yes, sir, I took it last night.

18. Have you paid that man? Yes, sir, I have paid him to-day.

19. How much have you paid him? I have paid him three dollars and seventy-five cents.

20. Why did you pay him three dollars and seventy-five cents? Because he worked one day in this garden, and two in that of the Twenty-third street house.

21. How many pupils have you? I have thirty: seventeen learn Spanish and the thirteen others French.

22. Do they study well? Some of them study very well; but none write their exercises well.

23. When do you sing and play on the piano? I study my lessons before singing and playing.

24. Who is that gentleman that came from Vienna last month? That gentleman is the one to whom I spoke last week at the concert.

LESSON XIX.

Hacer.	To do, or to make.
Haciendo.	Doing, making.
Hecho.	Done, made.

PRESENT.

Hago.	I do, or make.
Haces.	Thou doest, or makest.
Hace.	He does, or makes.
Hacemos.	We do, or make.
Haceis.	You do, or make.
Hacen.	They do, or make.

PRETERIT DEFINITE.

Hice.	I did, or made.
Hiciste.	Thou didst, or madest.
Hizo.	He did, or made.
Hicimos.	We did, or made.
Hicisteis.	You did, or made.
Hicieron.	They did, or made.
Partir.	To set out, to depart, to divide.
Marchar.	To go, set out, set off, to march.
Cambiar.	Change.

LESSON XIX.

PREPOSITIONS.

Para.		For, or in order to.	
Así.		So, thus.	
Por.		By, for, through.	
Entre.		Between, among.	
Hasta.		Until, even.	
Hácia.		Towards.	
Sin.	Hasta donde.	Without.	How far.

Pedro.	Peter.	Helena.	Helen.
Escritor.	Writer.	Escritora.	Writer (*female*).
Escribano.	Notary.	Tienda.	Store, shop.
Estado.	State.	Provincia.	Province.
Médico.	{ Physician.	Manera.	Manner.
	{ Doctor.	Escritura.	Writing, conveyance.
Cuarto.	Room.		
Aragon.	Aragon.	Comida.	Dinner.
Tio.	Uncle.		

COMPOSITION.

¿Qué hizo V. ayer en su cuarto?	What did you do yesterday in your room?
Estudié mi leccion.	I studied my lesson.
¿Qué ha hecho V. hoy?	What have you done to-day?
He escrito los ejercicios.	I have written my exercises.
¿Qué hace el zapatero en la zapatería?	What does the shoemaker do in the shoe-shop?
Hace zapatos y botas *para* V.	He makes shoes and boots for you.
¿Tiene V. papel *para* escribir una carta?	Have you paper to write a letter?
Sí, señora, lo tengo.	Yes, madam, I have.
¿Quiere V. escribir una carta *por* mi hermano?	Will you write a letter for my brother?
¿*Para* quién es la carta?	For whom is the letter?
Es *para* Manuel.	It is for Emanuel.
Yo parto *para* Madrid.	I set out for Madrid.
¿*Para* dónde parte V.?	For where do you set out?
Parto *para* los Estados Unidos.	I set out for the United States.
¿Habló V. á su padre *por* mi hermano?	Did you speak to your father for my brother?
Hablé *por* él á mi padre y á mi tio.	I spoke for him to my father and to my uncle.

LESSON XIX.

¿Habla V. bien el francés?	Do you speak French well?
Lo hablo muy bien, y hasta paso *por* francés.	I speak it very well, and I even pass for a Frenchman.
¿*Por* cuanto vendió V. el caballo?	For how much did you sell the horse?
Lo vendí *por* doscientos cincuenta pesos.	I sold it for two hundred and fifty dollars.
¿Necesita V. enviar *por* algo?	Do you want to send for anything?
Necesito enviar *por* el médico.	I want to send for the physician.
¿*Por* qué envia V.?	What do you send for?
Envio *por* vino.	I send for wine.
¿Vive V. *para* comer?	Do you live to eat?
No, señor, como *para* vivir.	No, sir, I eat to live.
¿Marchó ayer mucho el regimiento Séptimo.	Did the Seventh regiment march much (far) yesterday?
Marchó hasta el Parque Central.	They marched to the Central Park.

EXPLANATION.

80. Para and **Por.**—As both these prepositions very frequently answer to the English *for*, they are apt to be confounded by foreigners. Such confusion may, however, be avoided by bearing in mind the following rules:

Para expresses aim, object, destination.

Por conveys the idea of want or requirement, substitution, favor, duration of time, direction, &c. Examples:

WITH PARA.	WITH POR.
Papel *para* escribir.	Escribo *por* mi hermano.
Paper for writing.	I write for my brother.
Este libro es *para* V.	Cambió mi sombrero *por* el suyo.
This book is for you.	I changed my hat for his.
Parto *para* Nueva York.	Pasa *por* docto.
I start for New York.	He passes for a man of learning.
Comer *para* vivir.	Venderá la casa por diez mil pesos.
To eat to live.	He will sell the house for ten thousand dollars.
Trabajo *para* ganar la vida.	Trabajo *por* ganar la vida.
I work in order to earn a living.	I work to (endeavor to) earn my living.
Para el domingo.	Habló *por* tú amigo.
For Sunday.	I spoke for (in favor of) thy friend.
Este caballo es *para* su padre de V.	Envio *por* pan.
This horse is for your father.	I send for bread.
Lo haré *para* tu hermano.	Lo haré *por* tu hermano.
I shall do it for thy brother.	I will do it for thy brother (for thy brother's sake).

LESSON XIX.

81. ENTRE.—The general meaning of this preposition is *between* and *amongst*; as,

Entre los dos.	Between the two.
Entre V. y yo.	Between you and me.
Entre todos.	Amongst all.

82. HASTA signifies *till, until, even, to, as many as, as far as*; as,

Hasta el domingo.	Till (or until) Sunday.
Pasaron hasta mil.	As many as a thousand passed.
Voy hasta el Parque Central.	I go as far as the Central Park.
Estudió el español hasta que lo aprendió.	He studied Spanish till he learned it.

CONVERSATION AND VERSION.

1. ¿Escribió V. la carta para su padre, y los ejercicios de la leccion de español? Hice aquello; pero no he hecho esto.
2. ¿Tiene V. papel para escribir una carta? Sí, señor; pero tengo que escribir ántes mis ejercicios.
3. ¿Hizo el sastre mi casaca? La hizo.
4. ¿Qué ha hecho el zapatero? Ha hecho unas botas para V. y unos zapatos para Manuel.
5. ¿Para dónde parte V.? Parto para los Estados Unidos.
6. ¿Quiere V. escribir una carta por mi hermano? Sí, señor, ¿para quién es la carta? Es para *Dn. Manuel*.
7. ¿Habló V. á su padre por mi hermano? Hablé por él á mi padre y á mi amigo.
8. ¿Habla V. bien el frances? Lo hablo muy bien, y hasta paso por frances..
9. ¿Por cuánto vendió V. la casa? La vendí por ocho mil pesos.
10. ¿Por qué envia V.? Envio por mis libros.
11. ¿Vive V. para comer? No, señor, como para vivir.
12. ¿Marchó V. ayer con el regimiento Séptimo? Marché hasta el Parque Central.
13. ¿Es *Dn. Pedro* escritor? No, señor, *Dn. Pedro* es escribano.
14. ¿De qué manera hace V. eso? Lo hago así.
15. ¿Qué hizo V. ayer? Estudió la leccion de español, y hoy he escrito los ejercicios.
16. ¿Tiene V. que trabajar mas que yo? Tengo que escribir mas que V.; pero no tengo que trabajar mucho.
17. ¿Hácia donde van Vds.? Vamos hácia la iglesia.
18. ¿En dónde vive V.? Vivo en la Cuarta avenida número, trescientos treinta y ocho, entre las calles Veinte y cinco y Veinte y seis.

19. ¿Para qué quiere V. mi libro? Para leerlo.
20. ¿Quién pagó la comida? La pagámos entre todos.
21. ¿Marchan bien estos hombres? Marchan muy bien.
22. ¿Por dónde pasaron Vds. cuando fueron á la iglesia? Pasámos por la calle Veinte y tres.
23. ¿Es esa señora escritora? Sí, señor, y escribe muy bien.
24. ¿De qué país es V.? Soy de España.
25. ¿De qué provincia? De Aragon.
26. ¿Pronuncian bien el español en Aragon? Lo pronuncian muy bien.
27. ¿Hablan bien el inglés en los Estados Unidos? Lo hablan bien.
28. ¿Quiere V. venir á mi casa para comer con nosotros? No, señor, porque tengo que ir á comer á casa de mi amigo.

EXERCISE.

1. How far did the Seventh regiment march yesterday? They (it) marched to the Central Park.
2. Did your sister set out yesterday for Philadelphia? No, madam, she did not set out yesterday.
3. When does she start? She starts to-day.
4. What does your servant look for? He looks for my cousin's (*fem.*) letter.
5. What do you do to learn Spanish? I study the lessons of my Spanish grammar and read good writers.
6. To whom did you speak last night at the concert? I spoke to the physician for Peter.
7. Who is that man who came to your house last night? He is my brother's servant.
8. Do you speak Spanish well? No, sir; but I speak Italian very well, and I even pass for an Italian (*italiano*).
9. How did your uncle spend the day yesterday? Studying his lessons and writing to Madrid.
10. Will your uncle write a letter for (in favor of) Charles? He will write it.
11. Do the young ladies want to send for anything? They want to send for the physician.
12. For what do they send for the physician? To speak for their servant (*fem.*).
13. Where does he live? In Fifth avenue, between Twenty-fourth and Twenty-fifth streets.
14. Where do you send? I send to the shoemaker's.
15. What do you send there for? For some boots and shoes for Emanuel.

16. How do you write your exercises without ink? I write them with a pencil.

17. How did Louis write his exercise the other day? He and his sister wrote it between them. *El y su hermana escribi[...]*

18. Have you sold your old hat? I changed it for Peter's new one.

19. Will you pass me that paper to write a letter for my brother? This paper is not for letters.

20. What is it for? It is for my exercises.

21. Whose letter is that? This letter is for your mother.

22. Where did the singer go last year? He went to Aragon, a province in Spain.

23. What have you sent for? I have sent for nothing.

24. Will you go for wine? I do not want wine, but bread and meat.

25. Do you live to eat? No, sir, I eat to live.

26. Have you read the newspapers to-day? No, sir; but I have marched with my regiment.

27. Has the tailor made my vest? Yes, sir, he made it last week.

28. Will you go to the pianist's for my piano? No; I have to study my lessons.

29. Do you write before studying? No; I study first and write afterwards.

LESSON XX.

Salir.	To go out, to leave.
Saliendo.	Going out.
Salido.	Gone out.

PRESENT.

Salgo.	I go out.
Sales.	Thou goest out.
Sale.	He goes out.
Salimos.	We go out.
Salis.	You go out.
Salen.	They go out.

PERTERIT DEFINITE.

Salí.	I went out.
Saliste.	Thou wentest out.
Salió.	He went out.

LESSON XX.

Salimos.	We went out.
Salisteis.	You went out.
Salieron.	They went out.

Tanto.	So, so much, as much.
Cuanto.	How much.
Como.	As, how.
Presto.	Soon, speedily.
Pronto.	Promptly, quickly.
Temprano.	Early.
Tarde.	Late.
Mejor.	Better.
Peor.	Worse.

Mayor.	Greater, larger, older.
Menor.	Smaller, younger.
Mejor.	Better.
Peor.	Worse.
Prudente.	Prudent.
Imprudente.	Imprudent.
Pronto.	Prompt, quick, ready.
Presto.	Ready, prepared.
Callado.	Silent, taciturn.
Hablador.	Talkative.
Limpio.	Cleanly, clean.
Vivo.	Lively, alive.
Situado.	Situated.
Cansado.	Tiresome, tired.

| Méjico. | Mexico. | Fecha. | Date. |

COMPOSITION.

¿Es Alejandro tan prudente *como* su hermano?	Is Alexander as prudent as his brother?
No, señor, Alejandro es muy imprudente. Es *tan* imprudente *como* hablador.	No, sir, Alexander is very imprudent. He is as imprudent as talkative.
¿Son los comerciantes mas ricos que los médicos?	Are merchants richer than physicians?
Algunos son *mas* ricos; pero otros lo son *ménos* que los médicos.	Some are richer; but others are less rich than physicians.
¿Es Nueva York *mayor* que Madrid?	Is New York larger than Madrid?
Madrid es *menor* que Nueva York.	Madrid is smaller than New York.

LESSON XX.

¿Qué caballo es *mejor*, el de V. ó el mio?	Which horse is the better, yours or mine?
El de V. es mayor; pero es *peor* que el mio.	Yours is larger; but it is worse than mine.
¿Tiene V. mas *de* cincuenta pesos?	Have you more than fifty dollars?
No tengo mas *que* veinte y tres.	I have not more than twenty-three.
El tiene *tanto* dinero *como* V.	He has as much money as you.
Yo estudio *tanto como* V.; pero no aprendo tanto.	I study as much as you; but I do not learn so much.
Él habla español *tan* bien *como* V.; pero no lo escribe *tan* bien.	He speaks Spanish as well as you; but he does not write it as well.
Él tiene *tanto cuanto* quiere.	He has as much as he wishes.
Tengo *tantos* libros y *tanto* papel como él.	I have as many books and as much paper as he.
Yo escribo *mas que* V.; pero V. lee *mas que* yo.	I write more than you; but you read more than I.
Él habla ménos que V.	He speaks less than you.

EXPLANATION.
DEGREES OF COMPARISON.

83. The adverbs *tanto* and *cuanto* lose the last syllable, *to*, before an adjective or another adverb.

84. The comparative of *equality* is formed by placing the adverb *tan*, so or as, before, and *como*, as, after the adjective; as,

Alejandro es *tan* prudente *como* su hermana.	Alexander is *as* prudent *as* his sister.

85. CUAN may be employed, if the comparative is followed by an *adjective* instead of a noun; as,

Es *tan* hablador *cuan* imprudente.	He is as talkative as imprudent.

But *como* is more frequently used.

86. The comparative of *superiority* is formed by placing the word *mas*, more, before the adjective, and *que*, than, after it; as,

Él es *mas* rico *que* V.	He is richer than you.

87. The comparative of *inferiority* is formed by placing the word *ménos*, less, before, and *que* after; as,

Él es *ménos* rico *que* V.	He is *less* rich than you.

88. MAYOR, greater or larger; MENOR, smaller; MEJOR, better, and PEOR, worse, are already in the comparative degree, and do not require *mas* or *ménos* before them; as,

Esta casa es *mayor* ó *menor* que esa.	This house is *larger* or *smaller* than that one.
Este caballo es *mejor* ó *peor* que el mio.	This horse is *better* or *worse* than mine.

89. *Than*, after comparatives coming before numeral adjectives, is also generally translated by *de* in the affirmative, and *que* in the negative; as,

Tengo mas *de* cincuenta libros.	I have more than fifty books.
No tengo mas *que* veinte pesos.	I have not more than twenty dollars.

90. Comparison may also take place with relation to *nouns*, *verbs*, and *adverbs*; but its form is so similar to that laid down for the adjectives that the learner will not require any other explanation than the examples given in the Composition.

CONVERSATION AND VERSION.

1. ¿Sale V. tanto como su hermano? No, señor, mi hermano sale mas que yo.
2. ¿Cuándo salimos nosotros? Nosotros, salimos muy pronto.
3. ¿Salió su hermano temprano de casa? No, señor, salió tarde.
4. ¿Salieron Vds. pronto del teatro? Sí, señor, salimos muy pronto.
5. ¿Sale V. presto á la calle? Sí, señor, salgo muy presto.
6. ¿Salieron Vds. temprano de la iglesia? Salimos tarde.
7. ¿Cuál de estas dos gramáticas es mejor? La que V. tiene delante es mejor que la otra.
8. ¿Es malo este caballo? Es peor que el de V.
9. ¿Es buena la pluma de su hermano de V.? Es mejor que la mia y peor que la de V.
10. ¿Cuánto dinero tiene V.? Tengo cuarenta pesos.
11. ¿Cuántos libros tiene su hermana? Tiene tantos como su prima.
12. ¿Cuánto tiempo vivió V. en París? Viví cuatro años.
13. ¿Es su hermano mayor ó menor que V.? Es mayor.
14. ¿Quién de su familia de V. habla mejor el inglés? Mi hermano menor lo habla mejor que todos.
15. ¿Dónde lo aprendió? En Lóndres.
16. ¿Cuánto tiempo vivió allá? Seis años.
17. ¿Cuándo vino de allá? Vino el año pasado.
18. ¿Cuál de Vds. dos estudia mas? Él estudia ménos que yo; pero aprendo mas.

LESSON XX.

19. ¿Cuál de sus hermanos de V. es mas prudente? El mayor es muy callado y prudente; pero el menor es vivo é imprudente.
20. ¿Salieron Vds. del concierto ántes que nosotros? No, señor, salímos despues.
21. ¿Cuándo salió su amigo de Vds. de Nueva York? Salió el mes pasado para París.
22. ¿Cuando sale V. para Filadelfia? No salgo hasta la semana que viene.
23. ¿Hácia dónde vive su amigo de V.? Vive hácia la plaza.
24. ¿Por dónde vino V. de París? Vine por Inglaterra.
25. ¿En dónde vive V.? En la Quinta avenida entre las calles Treinta y Treinta y una.
26. ¿Qué caballo es mejor, el de V. ó el mio? El de V. es mayor; pero no tan bueno como el mio.
27. ¿Tiene V. mas de cien pesos? Tengo mas de ciento.
28. ¿No tiene V. mas que tres pesos? No, señor, no tengo mas que dos.
29. ¿Habla V. español mejor que Luisa? No, señor, lo hablo peor; pero lo escribo mejor que ella.
30. ¿Salió V. ayer temprano? Salí temprano; pero hoy he salido muy tarde.

EXERCISE.

1. Have you written your letter? Yes, sir, I have written it.
2. What is the date of it (what date has it)? The first of this month.
3. Do you (*plural*) go out much? We go out this year as much as last year.
4. Which is the better grammar, mine or yours? Yours is better than mine, but not so large.
5. Which of the two goes out earlier, you or your cousin? I go out earlier than he.
6. Are merchants as rich as singers? Some singers are richer than merchants.
7. Is this horse not as lively as that one? That one is a little more lively than this one.
8. Is Mexico as large as the United States? No, miss, the latter are much larger than the former.
9. When do the musicians leave for Havana? They leave next week (the week that is coming).
10. When did you take your music lesson? I took it the day before yesterday, early.

11. Did your brothers take theirs as early as you? No, sir, they took theirs very late.

12. Which of you two speaks Italian better? He speaks it better than I; but I write it better than he.

13. Do you sing much every day? I do not sing as much as last month.

14. Does the notary write as well as the physician? The former writes better than the latter.

15. Is that man not very tiresome? He is very talkative and very tiresome.

16. Is Lewis as prudent as his uncle? He is more prudent than he; but not so taciturn.

17. Are you less tall (*alto*) than Louisa? No, she is less tall than I.

18. Is your uncle, the merchant, as rich as your father? No, sir, my father is richer than he.

19. When do your cousins leave for Paris? They leave very soon.

20. Is your servant as cleanly as ours? Ours is more cleanly than yours, but not so talkative.

21. Have you any paper for writing? I have as much paper and as much ink as I wish for.

22. Is Henry very prudent? He is as imprudent as talkative.

23. Who goes to the bakery quicker than John? Nobody goes as quick as he.

24. Have the merchants sent as much silver to France as to Spain? They have sent more to France.

25. Did the shoemaker make the shoes as quickly as the tailor made the coat? The former made the shoes quicker, because he worked more than the latter.

26. Which works the later, the tailor or the baker? The latter does not work so late as the former.

27. Are your father's books larger than ours? Yours are smaller than his.

28. Are those horses bad? They are worse than the others.

29. Will you go with your friend (*fem.*) to the concert? I will not go.

30. Why will you not go? Because it is very late, and I have to play on the piano.

31. Where did your mother learn Spanish? She learned it here.

32. And does she speak it well? She does not speak it as well as she writes it.

33. How much money have you? I have not more than seven dollars.

34. Has your friend as much as you? He has more than I; he has received more than two hundred dollars from Spain.

LESSON XXI.

Saber.	To know.
Sabiendo.	Knowing.
Sabido.	Known.
Sé.	I know.
Sabes.	Thou knowest.
Sabe.	He knows.
Sabemos.	We know.
Sabeis.	You know.
Saben.	They know.
Supe.	I knew.
Supiste.	Thou knewest.
Supo.	He knew.
Supimos.	We knew.
Supisteis.	You knew.
Supieron.	They knew.
Amar.	To love.
Viajar.	To travel.

Trinidad (*fem*).	Trinity.
Sabio, sapientísimo.	Wise, learned; very, most or extremely wise.
Hábil, habilísimo.	Clever, skilful; very clever.
Difícil, dificilísimo.	Difficult, very or most difficult.
Fácil, facilísimo.	Easy; very or most easy.
Corto, cortísimo.	Short; very or most short.
Alegre, alegrísimo.	Cheerful; very or most cheerful.
Triste, tristísimo.	Sad; very or most sad.
Feliz, felicísimo.	Happy; very or most happy.
Largo, larguísimo.	Long; very or most long.
Fuerte, fortísimo.	Strong; very or most strong.
Nuevo, novísimo.	New; very or most new.
Fiel, fidelísimo.	Faithful; very or most faithful.
Alto, altísimo.	Tall; very or most tall.

LESSON XXI.

IRREGULAR COMPARATIVES AND SUPERLATIVES.

Bueno, mejor, óptimo.	Good, better, best.
Malo, peor, pésimo.	Bad, worse, worst.
Grande, mayor, máximo.	Great, greater, greatest.
Pequeño, menor, mínimo.	Small, smaller, smallest.
Alto, superior, supremo.	High, { higher, highest. / superior, supreme. }
Bajo, inferior, ínfimo,	Low, { lower, inferior, } lowest.
Combinada.	Combined.

COMPOSITION.

Es *el mas* sabio de mis discípulos.	He is the wisest of my pupils.
Esta señorita es *la mas* amable.	This young lady is the most amiable.
La mayor parte del regimiento.	The greater part of the regiment.
La mayor parte, ó *los mas*, de los soldados.	The greater part, or the most, of the soldiers.
La mejor casa *de* la calle.	The best house in the street.
Manuel, ¿cuáles son los profesores que saben mas en tu escuela?	Emanuel, which are the professors in your school who know the most?
El profesor de aritmética sabe mucho, el de frances, sabe mas; pero el profesor de historia es el que mas sabe.	The professor of arithmetic is learned, the French professor is more learned; but the professor of history is the most learned.
¿Es bueno este caballo?	Is this horse good?
Este caballo es muy bueno; pero el de V. es mejor, y el mio es el mejor de los tres.	This horse is very good; but yours is better, and mine is the best of the three.
¿Es esta leccion *muy* fácil?	Is this lesson very easy?
Es *facilísima*.	It is most, or very easy.
¿Es su casa de V. tan alta como la mia?	Is your house as high as mine?
La mia es mas alta que la de V., y la de su hermano de V. es *la mas alta*.	Mine is higher than yours, and your brother's is the highest.
Ese Frances es *muy caballero*.	That Frenchman is very gentlemanly.
¿Es alegre ó triste su amigo de V.?	Is your friend cheerful or sad?
Es alegrísimo; pero es muy niño.	He is most cheerful; but he is very childish.
¿Es muy jóven?	Is he very young?
No, señor, es viejo.	No, sir, he is old.

EXPLANATION.

91. English superlatives ending in *est*, or formed by *most*,

LESSON XXI.

are rendered by placing the definite article before the Spanish comparative; as,

El mas sabio.	The wisest.
La mas amable.	The most amiable.

92. *Most*, or *most of*, when followed by a noun (singular), is translated by *la mayor parte*; as,

La mayor parte del regimiento.	Most of the regiment.

But if the noun is in the plural, *most* may also be translated by *mas*, with the corresponding article; as,

La mayor parte, ó *los mas*, de los soldados.	Most of the soldiers.

93. The preposition *in*, after the English superlative, is translated by *de* in Spanish; as,

La mejor casa *de* la calle.	The best house in the street.

94. Those superlatives which in English are formed with the aid of *very, most*, &c., may in Spanish be formed either with the help of *muy* before the adjective, or by adding to the latter the termination *ísimo*; as,

Muy hábil, or habil*ísimo*.	Very clever.
Muy fácil, or facil*ísimo*.	Very, or most easy.

The termination *ísimo* is, however, more expressive of the positive superlative degree than is the adverb *muy*.

95. Observe that adjectives ending in a vowel drop that vowel on taking the termination *ísimo*; as,

Corto, cort*ísimo*.	Short, very short.
Alegre, alegr*ísimo*.	Cheerful, most cheerful.
Triste, trist*ísimo*.	Sad, very sad.

96. There are other superlatives ending in *érrimo*; as,

Célebre, celeb*érrimo*.	Celebrated, most celebrated.
Salubre, salub*érrimo*.	Salubrious, very salubrious.

But these forms are not the most used.

97. Adjectives ending in the following letters change them before admitting the termination *ísimo*:

Co becomes *qu*; as, rico, riqu*ísimo*.
Go " *gu*; as, largo, largu*ísimo*.
Ble " *bil*; as, amable, ama*bilísimo*.
Z " *c*; as, feliz, felic*ísimo*.

98. Superlatives in *ísimo* irregularly formed:

Bueno, good, makes *bonísimo*, very good.
Fuerte, strong, makes *fortísimo*, very strong.
Nuevo, new, makes *novísimo*, very new.
Sabio, wise, makes *sapientísimo*, very wise.
Sacro, sacred, makes *sacratísimo*, very sacred.
Fiel, faithful, makes *fidelísimo*, very faithful.

99. Irregular comparatives and superlatives:

Bueno,	mejor,	óptimo.
Malo,	peor,	pésimo.
Grande,	mayor,	máximo.
Pequeño,	menor,	mínimo.
Alto,	superior,	supremo.
Bajo,	inferior,	ínfimo.
Mucho,	mas,	lo mas.
Poco,	ménos,	lo ménos.

All these adjectives form also a superlative in *ísimo*, according to the rules already given; as, *malísimo, poquísimo, muchísimo*.

They admit also a comparative formed with *mas* or *ménos*; and a superlative with *muy*; as,

Ménos malo.	Less bad.
Los mas grandes.	The greatest.
Muy pequeños.	Very small.

100. Substantives used adjectively admit the degrees of comparison; as,

Es mas caballero que tú.	He is more gentlemanly than thou.
Es muy hombre.	He is very much of a man, or very manly.
Este hombre es muy niño.	This man is very childish.

CONVERSATION AND VERSION.

√ 1. ¿Supo V. su leccion ántes de ayer? La supe muy bien, y la sé todos los dias.

2. ¿Ama V. á su hermano? Le amo.

3. ¿Le ama á V. su hermano? No lo sé.

4. A quién ama V.? Amo á mis papás.

5. ¿Ha viajado V. mucho? He viajado mucho en Europa; pero he viajado muy poco en América.

LESSON XXI.

6. ¿Sabe V. el español? Muy poco, señorita; pero lo aprendo.
7. Y V., señorita, ¿lo sabe V.? No, señor, no lo sé, ni lo aprendo.
8. ¿Porqué no estudia V. el español? Porque aprendo la música, y no tengo tiempo para estudiarlo.
9. ¿Es muy hábil su profesor de música de V.? Es habilísimo.
10. ¿Sabe V. cantar? No, señora, pero sé tocar un poco el piano.
11. ¿No sabe V. tocar la guitarra? No, señora, toco el violin.
12. ¿Aprende bien ese caballero el español? Estudia mucho y lo aprende muy bien.
13. ¿Quién aprende mas pronto el español, las señoras ó los caballeros? Las señoras aprenden mucho mas pronto.
14. ¿Quién es el mas sabio de sus discípulos de V.? La señorita N., es la mas sabia de todos mis discípulos.
15. ¿Cuál de estos niños es el mejor? El que ama á sus padres, y estudia mas sus lecciones, es el mejor.
16. ¿Marchó todo el regimiento 7°. por Broadway hasta el Parque Central? No, señor, pero la mayor parte de él.
17. ¿Fueron al campo los soldados? Los mas de los soldados fueron allá.
18. ¿Es esta la mejor casa de la calle? No, señor, esta casa es muy buena; pero la de Astor es mejor y la de Stewart es la mejor de la ciudad.
19. ¿Sabe V. quién pasó por aquí anoche? No, señor, pero se quién pasó por la 5ª avenida.
20. ¿Es bueno este caballo? Este caballo es muy bueno; pero el de V. es mejor, y el mio es el mejor de los tres.
21. ¿Es caballero ese Frances? Sí, señor, es muy caballero.
22. ¿Es ese hombre alegre ó triste? Es muy alegre; pero es muy niño.
23. ¿Fué V. al concierto la semana pasada? Fuí ántes de ayer.
24. ¿Quiere V. tocar el piano? Quiero, pero no sé.
25. ¿Ha venido su amigo de V.? Ha venido.
26. ¿Cuándo vino? Vino ántes de ayer.
27. ¿Cuándo sale V.? Quiero salir la semana que viene.

EXERCISE.

1. Do you know French? No, sir, but my brother knows it.
2. Is that physician clever? He is most clever.
3. Which is the most skilful physician? Ours is the most skilful in the city.
4. Is Miss Louisa very amiable? Yes, she is very amiable.

LESSON XXI.

5. Alexander, which is the most learned teacher in your school? The English teacher is learned, the teacher of arithmetic is more learned; but the Italian teacher is the most learned of all.

6. Is your school-mistress cheerful, Louisa? Yes, mamma, she is most cheerful and very happy.

7. Did you know your lessons well yesterday? Yes, I knew them very well, better than to-day's, for I have not had time to study them.

8. Does your brother know his every day? I do not know; but he works very little.

9. Is he taciturn? No, sir, he is very talkative.

10. Which is the largest church in New York? Trinity Church is the largest and the handsomest in the city.

11. Whose is that handsome house there? It is my uncle's.

12. Is it not the finest in the street? No; Mr. Emanuel's is the finest in the city.

13. Did the 12th Regiment go out to march yesterday? Not all, but the greater part went out.

14. Did not all the soldiers march through Fourteenth street last Thursday? The most of them marched through Fourteenth street, but not all.

15. Is your Spanish lesson for to-day difficult? Yes, it is the most difficult (that) I have had this month.

16. Is your French lesson very difficult, Charles? No, sir; my French lesson for to day is the easiest one in the grammar.

17. Which is the best Spanish grammar? The Combined Spanish Grammar is the best and the easiest.

18. Is not your table very low for writing? Yes, it is very low; I write better on a higher one.

19. Will you take this small pen to write your exercise? No; I do not write well with my own, which is very small, but larger than yours.

20. Have you travelled much in Europe? I have travelled very much in America, but very little in Europe.

21. Which is the longest street in New York? Broadway is the longest in the United States.

22. Do you love your parents? Yes, I love them very much.

23. Why does Margaret not love her cousin? She does not love him because he is very taciturn.

24. Which of your pupils is the wisest? Henry and Louisa are the wisest of all my pupils.

25. Who reads the most newspapers in your house? I do not know; but papa reads a great many.

26. To whom have you paid the most money to-day? I have paid most to the tailor, because he has worked most for me.

27. Does not your washerwoman work very much? Yes, she works very much, but earns (*ganar*) very little money.

28. Whose horse is the most lively, yours, Charles', or mine? Charles' is lively, mine is more lively, but yours is the liveliest of the three.

29. In what street do you live? I live in Twenty-third street.

30. Is that a fine street? Yes, it is one of the finest streets up-town of the upper part (*parte alta*) of the city.

LESSON XXII.

Estar	To be (in a certain place, state or condition).
Estoy.	I am.
Estás.	Thou art.
Está.	He is.
Estamos.	We are.
Estais.	You are.
Estan.	They are.
Prestar.	To lend.

GERUNDS.

Hablando.	Speaking.
Estudiando.	Studying.
Comprando.	Buying.
Buscando.	Looking for.
Necesitando.	Needing, wanting, requiring.
Aprendiendo.	Learning.
Vendiendo.	Selling.
Leyendo.	Reading.
Bebiendo.	Drinking.
Comiendo.	Eating, dining.
Escribiendo.	Writing.
Recibiendo.	Receiving.
Viviendo.	Living.
Residiendo.	Residing.
Teniendo.	Having, holding.
Siendo.	Being.
Queriendo.	Wishing, desiring, loving.

LESSON XXII.

Llevando.	Carrying, taking.
Enviando.	Sending.
Tomando.	Taking.
Pagando.	Paying.
Pronunciando.	Pronouncing.
Cantando.	Singing, chanting.
Tocando.	Touching, playing.
Haciendo.	Doing, making.
Pasando.	Passing.
Trabajando.	Working.
Mandando.	Sending, commanding.
Yendo.	Going,
Viniendo.	Coming.
Estando.	Being (in a certain state, &c.).
Norte, sur, este, oeste.	North, south, east, west.

COMPOSITION.

¿*Es* su casa de V. grande?	Is your house large?
Es grande; pero *está* en mal estado.	It is large; but it is in a bad state.
¿En que calle *está* la casa de su hermano de V.?	In what street is your brother's house?
Está en la Cuarta avenida.	It is in (the) Fourth Avenue.
¿*Es* Luisa bonita?	Is Louisa pretty?
Es muy bonita.	She is very pretty.
¿*Está* ella contenta?	Is she contented?
No *está* contenta, porque *está* enferma.	She is not contented, because she is sick.
¿*Es* enfermiza?	Is she sickly?
Lo *es* mucho.	She is very much so.
¿De quién *es* esta casa?	Whose house is this?
Es de mi hermano.	It is my brother's.
Está muy bien situada.	It is very well situated.
Esta carta *es* para Margarita.	This letter is for Margaret.
Nueva York *está* entre el rio del Norte y el del Este.	New York is between the North and East rivers.
El señor Walker *es* pintor.	Mr. Walker is a painter
La mesa *es* de madera.	The table is of wood.
Estuve en casa hasta que V. llegó.	I was at home until you arrived.
Mi amigo *está* para partir.	My friend is about to set out.
Estoy sin comer.	I have not dined (I am without eating).
¿Qué *está* V. haciendo?	What are you doing?
Estoy escribiendo.	I am writing.

¿De quién *es* V. amado?	By whom are you loved?
Soy amado de mis niños.	I am loved by my children.
Manuel *es* bueno.	Emanuel is good.
Manuel *está* malo.	Emanuel is ill.
¿*Está* Pedro cansado?	Is Peter tired?
Está cansado y *es* cansado.	He is tired, and he is tiresome.
¿Porqué *está* tan callado Alejandro?	Why is Alexander so silent?
Porque *es* callado.	Because he is taciturn.

EXPLANATION.

101. SER and ESTAR.—These two verbs have in English but one equivalent—TO BE; but their respective significations and uses are so materially different as to constitute one of the chief difficulties of the Spanish language. By careful observation, however, of the following simple rule, the learner will, we are assured, be enabled to overcome that difficulty, and know exactly when to use the one and when the other of these two verbs.

102. Whenever we wish to express *what* persons or things *are*, and their mode of being, in an *absolute* manner, SER is the verb to be employed; but if we desire to express the *state* or *condition* of persons or things, and the mode of that *state* or *condition* in a *relative* manner, then ESTAR must be used.

The following examples will serve to render the application of this rule more clear:

1st. Esta casa *es* grande.	This house *is* large.
2d. Esta casa *está* limpia.	This house *is* clean.
3d. Esta casa *está* en Broadway.	This house *is* in Broadway.
4th. Luisa *es* bonita.	Louisa *is* pretty.
5th. Luisa *es* feliz.	Louisa *is* happy.
6th. Luisa *está* contenta.	Louisa *is* content.
7th. Luisa *está* enferma.	Louisa *is* sick.
8th. Luisa *es* enfermiza.	Louisa *is* sickly.

In the first example we use SER to express *what kind* of a house the one referred to *is*—*i. e.* large; in the second, ESTAR, inasmuch as we desire to express *how*, or in *what state* the house *is*, *i. e.* in a *clean state;* ESTAR is also employed in the third, sixth and seventh examples, the object being to make known respectively *where* the house *is*, and in *what state* or *condition* Louisa *is* or *finds herself;* while in the fourth, fifth and eighth SER again comes into play, seeing we wish to designate Louisa's *mode of being* in an *absolute manner.*

From the above general rule may be deduced the following observations:

1st. That SER must be used whenever we wish to express possession, use, purpose or destination; to point out the nationality, profession or calling of persons; the place of production of things or the materials of which they are composed; the simple fact of existence, the occurrence of events; and, finally, as an auxiliary in forming the passive voice of verbs.

2d. That ESTAR is to be employed in speaking of situation or position, place, state or condition, in making the progressive form in *ndo* (corresponding to the English *ing*) of other verbs; and, lastly, to govern verbs in the infinitive mood with the aid of a preposition, or past participles without such aid.

N. B.—The verb ESTAR can never be used with the present participles of *ir* and *venir.*

Examples of the uses of SER and ESTAR:

SER.	ESTAR.
La casaca *es* de mi hermano.	Esta casa *está* bien situada.
The coat is my brother's.	This house is well situated.
La carta *es* para Margarita.	Nueva York *está* entre el rio del Norte y el del Este.
The letter is for Margaret.	New York is between the North and East rivers.
El señor Walker *es* pintor.	*Estuve* en casa hasta que llegó.
Mr. Walker is a painter.	I was at home until he arrived.
Este vino *es* de España.	El *está* escribiendo.
This wine is from Spain.	He is writing.
La mesa *es* de madera.	Mi amigo *está* para partir.
The table is of wood.	My friend is about to set out.
Has *sido* prudente en hacerlo así.	*Estoy* por no hacerlo.
Thou hast been prudent in so doing.	I am inclined not to do it.
Hoy *es* la celebracion.	*Estamos* sin comer.
The celebracion is to-day.	We have not dined (or eaten).
Son las diez.	Esta carta *está* fechada en Madrid.
It is ten o'clock.	This letter is dated from Madrid.
Fué el caso como yo escribí á V.	
The case was as I wrote to you.	
Soy amado.	
I am loved.	

LESSON XXII.

N. B.—As it frequently occurs that, in perfect accordance with the rules of grammar, the same sentence may be construed with either SER or ESTAR, though conveying entirely different ideas, it is essential to inquire thoroughly into the respective value of these two verbs, in order to avoid the confusion which must necessarily arise from their misapplication. The important nature of this remark may be seen from the following examples:

WITH SER.	WITH ESTAR.
Manuel *es* bueno.	Manuel *está* bueno.
Emanuel is good.	Emanuel is well.
Juan *es* malo.	Juan *está* malo.
John is bad (or wicked).	John is sick.
Pedro *es* cansado.	Pedro *está* cansado.
Peter is tiresome.	Peter is tired.
Juana *es* viva.	Juana *está* viva.
Jane is lively.	Jane is alive.
Alejandro *es* callado.	Alejandro *está* callado.
Alexander is taciturn.	Alexander is silent.
Este niño *es* limpio.	Este niño *está* limpio.
This child is cleanly.	This child is clean.
Esta naranja *es* agria.	Esta naranja *está* agria.
This is a sour orange (*i. e.* of the sour species).	This orange is sour (*i. e.* unripe).

What is said in the course of the present lesson relative to SER and ESTAR, being all that is requisite to enable the student to determine which of the two is to be used in any ordinary case, his attention shall not again be called to them until we come to treat of their idiomatic uses.

CONVERSATION AND VERSION.

1. ¿Qué está haciendo el muchacho? Está estudiando su leccion.
2. ¿Ha estudiado V. la suya? La estudié ayer.
3. ¿De quién es V. amado? Soy amado de mis niños.
4. ¿Está V. escribiendo sus ejercicios? No, señor, estoy escribiendo una carta.
5. ¿Está Margarita cansada? Margarita no está cansada; pero es cansada.
6. ¿Porqué está Pedro tan callado? Porque es callado.
7. ¿Para quién es esta carta? Es para V.

8. ¿En dónde está situada Nueva York? Está situada entre el rio del Norte y el del Este.

9. ¿Es V. Español? No, señor, soy Americano.

10. ¿Es ese caballero abogado? No, señor, es médico.

11. ¿Cómo está Alejandro? Está bueno.

12. ¿Es Alejandro buen muchacho? Es bueno.

13. ¿Estuvo V. ayer en mi casa? Estuve allí hasta que su padre de V. vino.

14. ¿De qué es este tintero? Es de madera.

15. ¿Es grande su jardin de V.? Es grandísimo; pero está en mal estado.

16. ¿En qué calle está su casa de V.? Está en la Cuarta avenida.

17. ¿Es hermosa la casa de su amigo de V.? Es hermosísima.

18. ¿Es Luisa feliz? Luisa es muy feliz; pero no está contenta, porque no vino V. á verla (*to see her*).

19. ¿Es V. enfermizo? No, señor; pero estoy enfermo.

20. ¿De quién es aquella casa tan alta? Es de un amigo mio; pero quiere venderla porque está mal situada en esta calle tan fea.

21. ¿Cuándo parte V.? No sé, quiero partir hoy, porque tengo mucho que hacer.

22. ¿Partió su amigo de V. ayer? No, señor, ha partido hoy.

23. ¿Fué V. á la iglesia el domingo pasado? Sí, señor, voy á la iglesia todos los domingos, cuando no estoy enfermo.

24. ¿Vive su amigo de V. en el campo? No, señor, reside en la ciudad.

25. ¿Qué hace en la ciudad? Trabaja de abogado.

26. ¿Qué hace V.? Yo vendo y compro: soy comerciante.

27. ¿Pasó V. por Paris, cuando fué á Madrid? Sí, señor, y por otras muchas ciudades de Francia y España.

28. ¿Viaja V. mucho? He viajado mucho; pero no viajo mas.

29. ¿Viajó V. en (Sí, señor, estuve allí el año pasado.

30. ¿Es bonito país? El país es hermosísimo.

EXCERCISE.

1. Where is your house situated? In Eleventh street.

2. Is it very large? No, sir, it is not as large as my uncle's.

3. Which of the three languages* English, French or Spanish, is the richest? The Spanish is much richer than the other two.

4. Do you speak Spanish? No, madam; but I am learning it.

5. Do you and your sister take a lesson to-day? No, our teacher is not coming (does not come) to-day, he is sick.

* Lenguas.

LESSON XXII.

6. What lesson are you at (in). We are at the twenty-second, one of the most difficult in the grammar.

7. Is Louis very taciturn? he speaks very little. No, sir, he is not taciturn; but he is silent to-day, because he is unwell.

8. Why is Henry so cheerful to-day? He is cheerful because he has received letters from his father and mother.

9. Is he a good boy? He is a very good boy; he is studying his Italian lesson.

10. How is your friend to-day? He is much better than yesterday.

11. Where is that wine from that Charles is drinking? It is from Spain.

12. Has your father been prudent in selling his horse? He has been most imprudent in selling it.

13. Whom do you love? I love my father and mother, and I am loved by them.

14. Where is that letter from? It is (*comes*) from Paris.

15. Have you (*plural*) dined to-day? No, sir, we have not dined; our servant is very ill.

16. What do you do every day to pass the time? Sometimes I sing and play on the piano, and at others I read the newspapers and go out to walk (*pasear*).

17. What does Mr. Emanuel do? He is a merchant.

18. For whom is that letter that Louisa is writing? It is for her cousin (*fem.*).

19. Is Alexander a tiresome boy? No, madam, but he went to walk very early, and he is tired.

20. Was Louis at your house yesterday? Yes, sir, he was there until my uncle came.

21. How is your uncle to-day? He is very well; he is about to set out for Paris.

22. Is Henry tired? No; but he is very tiresome.

23. Whose book is that? It is my friend's; but he wants to sell it, because it is very badly written.

24. How much does he want for it? He wants five dollars and a half.*

25. Is it in French? No, sir, it is in Spanish.

26. When do you (*plural*) leave for Europe? We leave very soon.

27. Have you a garden at your house? Yes, sir, I have a very fine garden.

28. Is it very large? It is very large.

29. What is your friend doing in Paris? He is studying law (for a lawyer).

30. And you, what do you do in Philadelphia? I work as a notary.

31. Whom is this letter from? It is from the pianist, and for you.

* Medio.

LESSON XXIII.

FUTURE SIMPLE.

First Conjugation.

Habl-aré.	I shall speak.
Habl-arás.	Thou wilt speak.
Habl-ará.	He will speak.
Habl-arémos.	We shall speak.
Habl-aréis.	You will speak.
Habl-arán.	They will speak.

Second Conjugation.

Aprend-eré.	I shall learn.
Aprend-erás.	Thou wilt learn.
Aprend-erá.	He will learn.
Aprend-erémos.	We shall learn.
Aprend-eréis.	You will learn.
Aprend-erán.	They will learn.

Third Conjugation.

Escrib-iré.	I shall write.
Escrib-irás.	Thou wilt write.
Escrib-irá.	He will write.
Escrib-irémos.	We shall write.
Escrib-iréis.	You will write.
Ecrib-irán.	They will write.

Desear.	To desire.
Practicar.	To practise.
Bailar.	To dance.
Principiar.	To commence, to begin.
Acabar.	To finish.

Medio.	Half.
Próximo.	Next.
Entónces.	Then.
Anoche.	Last night.
Antes de anoche.	The night before last.
Mañana.	To-morrow.

LESSON XXIII.

Pasado mañana.	The day after to-morrow.
La mañana.	The morning.
Si.	If.

Gusto.	Taste, pleasure.	Noche.	Night.
Deseo.	Desire, mind.	Gracias.	(to give) Thanks.
Negocios.	Business, occupation.	Familia.	Family.
		Práctica.	Practice.
Oficio.	Office.	Teoría.	Theory.
Minuto.	Minute.	Hora.	Hour.
Segundo.	Second.	Polca.	Polka.
Vals.	Waltz.	Lengua.	Tongue, language.
Idioma.	Language.		

COMPOSITION.

¿Estudiará V. mañana su leccion de español?	Will you study your Spanish lesson to-morrow?
Sí, señor, la estudiaré mañana por la mañana.	Yes, sir, I will study it to-morrow morning.
¿A qué hora principiará V.?	At what hour will you commence?
Principiaré á las tres de la mañana.	I shall commence at three o'clock in the morning.
Señorita, ¿quiére V. bailar un vals?	Will you (dance a) waltz, Miss?
Gracias, caballero, no sé bailar vals.	Thank you, sir, I do not know how to waltz.
¿Bailará V. una polca?	Will you dance a polka?
Sí, señor, con mucho gusto.	Yes, sir, with great pleasure.
Hablo mal el español, porque no lo practico.	I speak Spanish badly, because I do not practise it.
V. necesita practicar mucho para aprender una lengua.	You require to practise a great deal in order to learn a language.
Practicaré en España, porque iré allí muy pronto.	I will practise in Spain, because I shall go there very soon.
¿Qué dias toma V. sus lecciones de piano?	On what days do you take your piano lessons?
Las tomo los lúnes y los viérnes, á las once de la mañana.	I take them on Mondays and Fridays, at 11 o'clock in the morning.
¿A qué hora tomará V. las lecciones de frances.	At what hour will you take your French lessons?
Las tomaré á las diez.	I shall take them at 10 (o'clock).
¿Qué hora es?	What o'clock is it?
Es la una.	It is one (o'clock).

Son las once y cuarto.	It is a quarter-past eleven.
Son las tres ménos diez minutos.	It is ten minutes to three.
Mañana iré al campo, y pasado mañana tendré el gusto de pasar el dia con V.	I shall go to the country to-morrow; and shall have the pleasure of spending the day after to-morrow with you.
Gracias; entónces seré muy feliz.	Thank you; then I shall be very happy.
¿Bailarémos en su casa de V.?	Shall we dance at your house?
Sí, señor, bailarémos, cantarémos, tocarémos y practicarémos el español toda la noche.	Yes, sir, we shall dance, sing, play and practise Spanish all the evening (the whole night).
Muy bien, muy bien; entónces serémos mas que felices, serémos felicísimos.	Very well, very well; then we shall be more than happy; we shall be most happy.
¿En donde pasó V. ayer la noche?	Where did you spend the evening yesterday?
La pasé con mis amigos los señores Martinez y su familia.	I spent it with my friends, Mr. and Mrs. Martinez and (their) family.
¿Cuánto tiempo estuvó V. en su casa?	How long were you at their house?
Fuí á las siete de la noche y salí á los once y media.	I went at seven in the evening and left (went out) at half past eleven o'clock.

EXPLANATION.

103. FUTURE SIMPLE.—This tense affirms what is yet to be or to take place at a future time (mentioned or not); as,

Seré comerciante.	I *shall be* a merchant.
Juan *estudiará* mañana.	John will study to-morrow.

This tense is also used as imperative, as will be seen when that mood is introduced.

104. The DEFINITE ARTICLE is to be used before numerals indicating the hour of the day, and the word *o'clock* is never translated into Spanish; as,

A las tres de la tarde.	At three o'clock in (of) the afternoon.

105. NOCHE (evening or night), commences at sundown; so that evening and night both are translated into Spanish by *noche*.

106. The conjunction SI, when conditional, does not govern the subjunctive in Spanish as it does in English, unless the latter be followed by *should*, as will be seen in the proper place; in all other cases, *si* is followed by the present of the indicative; as,

Si V. *tiene* papel, ¿escribirá?	If you have paper, will you write?

LESSON XXIII.

CONVERSATION AND VERSION.

1. ¿Cuándo principiará V. á escribir sus ejercicios? Principiaré mañana.
2. ¿A qué hora acabará V.? Acabaré á las diez y media.
3. Alejandro, ¿qué quieres ser, abogado ó escritor? No seré ni abogado ni escritor, seré comerciante.
4. Señorita, ¿quiere V. bailar una polca? Gracias, caballero, no bailaré, porque estoy muy cansada.
5. ¿Bailará V. la próxima? Sí, señor, con mucho gusto.
6. ¿Practicará V. el piano hoy? No, señor, hoy no tengo tiempo; pero practicaré mañana por la mañana.
7. ¿Qué hará V. mañana? Mañana por la mañana escribiré mis ejercicios y practicaré el español con mi hermano.
8. ¿Qué dias toma V. leccion de piano? Los lúnes y viérnes.
9. ¿A qué hora tomará V. su leccion mañana? A las once y cuarto.
10. ¿Vendrá V. á mi casa en el campo? Iré pasado mañana y tendré el gusto de pasar el dia con V.
11. ¿Bailarémos en su casa de V.? Sí, señor, bailarémos, cantarémos y practicarémos el español toda la noche.
12. ¿En dónde pasará V. mañana la noche? La pasaré con mis amigos los señores Martinez y su familia.
13. ¿A qué hora irán Vds. allí? Irémos á las siete de la noche.
14. ¿Hasta qué hora estarán Vds? Hasta la una y media.
15. ¿Estará V. mañana por la mañana en su cuarto? Estaré hasta las nueve y diez minutos.
16. ¿Es triste su hermano de V.? No, señora, no es triste; pero está triste.
17. ¿Es V. feliz? Soy felicísimo; pero no estoy contento esta tarde.
18. ¿Es V. mayor que su hermano? No, señora, soy el menor de toda la familia.
19. ¿Quién es el mayor? Juan es el mayor.
20. ¿Sale V. de casa temprano? Salgo tempranísimo.
21. ¿A qué hora? Salgo á las ocho y media.
22. ¿Salió V. ayer tan temprano? No, señor, ayer salí mas tarde; pero hoy he salido temprano.
23. ¿A qué hora saldrá V. mañana? Mañana saldré á la una de la tarde.
24. ¿Para quién escribe V. una carta? Escribo al abogado, por el pobre Juan, que lo necesita para un negocio.
25. ¿Partirá V. mañana para la Habana? No, señor, no partiré hasta la semana próxima.
26. ¿Es este caballo muy fuerte? Es fortísimo; pero ese que está ahí es mas fuerte y el que está allí al otro lado es el mas fuerte.

EXERCISE.

1. When shall you commence to study music? I desire to commence next month.

2. Do you know how* to dance? I do not dance very well; but I am going to take lessons soon.

3. Do you study in the morning or in the evening? I study in the morning.

4. At what o'clock do you take your lessons? At a quarter to three in the afternoon (tarde).

5. Does your teacher come so late? Yes, he has a great many pupils this year.

6. Will you dance a waltz, Miss? Thank you, sir, I danced so much the night before last that I am tired.

7. Then it will be better to talk. I shall talk with much pleasure.

8. When shall your cousin write his exercise? He shall write it to-morrow morning.

9. At what time do you receive your newspapers? I receive them every day at eight o'clock in the morning.

10. Mr. Louis, will you come and dine at my house? I shall be very happy to go with you.

11. How did you spend the evening at your friend's? Very well; his wife (lady) is most amiable.

12. Has she not travelled in Europe? No, sir; but they spoke last night of travelling very soon.

13. Is their family large? No, they have no children.

14. Does not your friend speak Spanish very well? Yes, sir, he sometimes even passes for a Spaniard.

15. Did you practise much with him? No; his cousin speaks French very well, and so we spoke that language all the evening.

16. Where shall you spend this evening? I do not know; but the day after to-morrow we shall go to your house.

17. Thank you! then I shall be more than happy; I shall be most happy.

18. How many seconds make a minute? Sixty.

19. How many minutes make an hour? Sixty minutes.

20. And how many hours has a day? A day has twenty-four hours, a week seven days, a month four weeks, and a year twelve months.

21. Peter, what o'clock is it? It is half-past two.

22. Then I am going to take my lesson: will you come? No, thank you; I wish to read this morning's paper.

23. Until what o'clock shall you be? I shall finish at one.

* *How* is not translated when it does not refer to the manner of doing anything.

24. Peter! Sir?
25. Has the tailor finished my vest? Yes, sir, here he is with the vest and the coat.
26. When will the shoemaker make my boots? He will make them for next Tuesday.
27. Have you any business in Philadelphia? Yes, sir, I am writing the history of Louis XVI., for a gentleman of that city.
28. Mr. Henry, are you happy? Yes, sir, thank you, I am very happy; but I am not very contented this evening.
29. Why are you not contented? Because my father has not written to me this week.

LESSON XXIV.

COMPOUND FUTURE.

Habré escrito.	I shall have ⎫
Habrás escrito.	Thou wilt have ⎬ written.
Habrá escrito.	He will have ⎭
Habrémos escrito.	We shall have ⎫
Habréis escrito.	You will have ⎬ written.
Habrán escrito.	They will have ⎭

Coser.	To sew.
Lavar.	To wash.
Barrer.	To sweep.
Pasear.	To walk (take a walk).

Dedal.	Thimble.	Aguja.	Needle.
Hilo.	Thread.	Primavera.	Spring.
Verano.	Summer.	Accion.	Action.
Invierno.	Winter.	Nacion.	Nation.
Otoño.	Autumn (Fall).	Afectacion.	Affectation.
Enero.	January.	Navegacion.	Navigation.
Febrero.	February.	Agitacion.	Agitation.
Marzo.	March.	Aprobacion.	Approbation.
Abril.	April.	Aceptacion.	Acceptation.
Mayo.	May.	Atraccion.	Attraction.
Junio.	June.	Conversacion.	Conversation.
Julio.	July.	Direccion.	Direction.
Agosto.	August.	Circunspeccion.	Circumspection.

LESSON XXIV.

Setiembre.	September.	Clasificacion.	Classification.
Octubre.	October.	Coleccion.	Collection.
Noviembre.	November.	Combinacion.	Combination.
Diciembre.	December.	Comparacion.	Comparison.
		Composicion.	Composition.
		Reputacion.	Reputation.

COMPOSITION.

Habré escrito mi leccion ántes de ir á casa del profesor.	I shall have written my lesson before going to the professor's.
Habré acabado á las diez.	I shall have finished at ten o'clock.
El abogado acaba de hablar.	The lawyer has just spoken.
Yo acabo de estudiar mi leccion.	I have just studied my lesson.
La lavandera habrá acabado de lavar á las cuatro.	The washerwoman will have finished washing at four o'clock.
¿ A cuántos estamos ?	What day of the month is it ?
Estamos á seis.	It is the sixth.
¿ Qué dia del mes es hoy ?	What day of the month is to-day ?
Es el primero.	It is the first.
¿ Qué fecha tiene esa carta ?	What is the date of that letter ?
El primero de Enero de mil ochocientos sesenta y seis.	January 1st, 1866.
¿ En qué año fué V. á Méjico ?	In what year did you go to Mexico ?
Fuí en Setiembre de mil ochocientos cincuenta y dos.	I went in September, 1852.
¿ Irá V. este verano á Europa ?	Will you go to Europe this summer ?
No, señor, iré en el invierno.	No, sir, I shall go in the winter.
¿ Paseará V. mucho esta primavera ?	Will you walk much this spring ?
No, señor, trabajaré mucho.	No, sir, I shall work a great deal.

EXPLANATION.

107. The COMPOUND FUTURE affirms something future that will have taken place before or at the time of some other future action or event expressed in the sentence; and is composed of the simple future of the verb *haber*, to have, and the past participle of another verb; as,

Habré escrito mi ejercicio ántes de ir á casa del profesor.	I will have written my exercise before going to the professor's.
Habré acabado á las diez.	I will have finished at ten o'clock.

108. ACABAR DE is employed before an infinitive in the

LESSON XXIV.

sense of *to have just*, and the infinitive is translated in English as a past participle; as,

Acaba de hablar.	He *has just* spoken.
Acabo de estudiar.	I *have just* studied.

N. B.—In order to facilitate the acquisition of words, we shall give now and then a few rules, with the help of which the learner will be enabled to convert several thousand English words into Spanish. And, although we have proposed not to introduce many new words or elements at one time, these observations will enable the pupil to learn a greater number of words with little or no difficulty at all, from the striking resemblance that those words bear to the English ones.

109. The greater part of English nouns ending in *tion* are rendered into Spanish by changing the letter *t* into *c*; as, approbation, *aprobacion*. It is to be observed that the only consonants that can be doubled in Spanish are *c, n* and *r*. All nouns of the above termination are feminine.

110. The days of the month are all counted in Spanish by the cardinal numbers, preceded by the article, except the first day; and there are several forms of asking the day of the month; *e. g.*,

¿Qué dia del mes tenemos?	
¿Qué dia es hoy?	What day of the month is it?
¿A cuántos estamos del mes?	

There is no preference between these; but the answer must be made in the same form as the question; as,

¿Qué dia tenemos?	What day of the month is it?
Tenemos el seis.	It is the sixth.
¿A cuántos estamos?	What day of the month is it?
Estamos á dos.	It is the second.
¿Qué dia es hoy?	What day of the month is to-day?
Es el primero.	It is the first.

CONVERSATION AND VERSION.

1. ¿Habrá V. acabado de escribir su leccion á las diez y media? No, sé; pero la habré acabado ántes de ir á casa del profesor.
2. ¿Ha hablado aquel abogado? No, señor, acaba de hablar este.
3. ¿Ha hablado bien? Muy bien, pero con afectacion.

LESSON XXIV.

4. ¿Hará V. una buena composicion para la leccion próxima? Sí, señor, si tengo tiempo, la haré.
5. ¿Lava bien su lavandera de V.? Lava muy bien.
6. ¿A dónde envia V. sus niños? Los envio á pasear con la criada.
7. ¿A dónde? A la plaza de Madison.
8. ¿Está cerca de su casa de V.? Está muy cerca.
9. ¿Barrió el criado ayer mi cuarto? No, señor, no lo barrió ayer, pero lo ha barrido hoy.
10. ¿Lo barrerá mañana? Lo habrá barrido ántes de las nueve.
11. Muchacho, ¿está el sastre en la sastrería? No, señor, acaba de salir.
12. ¿A qué hora principiaron Vds. á bailar? Principiámos á las diez de la noche.
13. ¿Desea V. practicar el inglés? Sí, señor, si tengo tiempo principiaré pasado mañana.
14. ¿Dónde está su amigo? Está viajando por Francia.
15. ¿Ama su hermana de V. mucho á sus hijos? Sí, señor, los ama muchísimo.
16. ¿Saldrá V. muy pronto para Europa? Quiero salir mañana.
17. ¿Sabe V. bailar el vals? No, señor, pero sé bailar el rigodon y la polka.
18. ¿De dónde vienen Vds.? Venimos de Francia, y vamos para Filadelfia.
19. ¿Quiere V. salir á pasear? Muy bien, irémos al Parque Central.
20. ¿Quién lavó estos pañuelos? Estan muy mal lavados. Su lavandera de V. los lavó.
21. ¿Dónde pasó V. el verano? Lo pasé en el campo. ¿Y el invierno? En la ciudad.
22. ¿Cuáles son los meses mas alegres del año? Los de la primavera.
23. ¿Sabe V. la direccion de la casa de su hermano de V.? Sí, señor, calle Catorce, número ciento veinte y cinco.
24. ¿A qué hora comen Vds.? Comemos á las tres de la tarde.
25. ¿Qué hora tiene V.? Tengo las dos y veinte.
26. ¿A qué hora salieron sus hermanas para el parque? Salieron á las seis y media de la mañana.
27. ¿Y á qué hora volvieron? A las once ménos cuarto.
28. ¡Buenos dias!—Buenos dias.—¿Está V. bueno? Muy bueno, gracias. ¿Y su familia de V.? Muy buena, gracias.
29. ¿Baila V. la polca? No, señor, estoy principiando á aprenderla.

LESSON XXIV.

EXERCISE.

1. When shall your uncle have finished his letter? He shall have it finished at eight o'clock.
2. When shall you have your letter written? I shall have it written before going to the professor's.
3. When shall the notary make the conveyance (writing)? He has just made it.
4. Shall your servant have swept my room before the lesson hour to-morrow? Yes, sir, she shall have it swept at six o'clock.
5. What day of the month is it? It is the thirteenth.
6. Does your washerwoman come to wash in your house? She does not, but she washes very well.
7. How many lessons do those gentlemen take every month? They take four every week; that makes sixteen every month.
8. Which are the best months for walking? The three months of spring, and the three of autumn (or fall).
9. Where are you coming (do you come) from? I am coming from walking.
10. Will you give* me a needle and thread and a thimble to sew? Here is the needle; I am going to look for the thread and thimble.
11. In what year did your sister Margaret go to England? She went in June, 1865.
12. What is the date of that letter? Madrid, 7th July, 1866.
13. Shall you go to Europe this summer? No, madam, I shall not go before next spring.
14. Is December a good month for travelling? No, it is one of the worst in the year.
15. How did you (*plural*) spend the day yesterday? We walked in the Central Park.
16. Did you walk the whole day? No, we walked until twelve o'clock, and then we read and played on the piano.
17. Did you not pass the evening at Mr. Martinez's? No, we did not go out all (in all) the evening, Margaret was a little sick.
18. Do you know which are the longest months? Yes; they are January, March, May, July, August, October and December.
19. And which are the shortest? April, June, September and November.
20. But what do you do with February? February is the shortest of all; it has but twenty-eight days.
21. Shall you walk much this spring? No, miss, I shall work a great deal.

* *Dar.*

22. When shall the tailor sew my vest? He shall sew it to-morrow evening.

23. Has the lawyer not spoken? He has just spoken.

24. Until what hour did he speak? Until half-past one.

25. Did he speak in Spanish? No, he spoke in French to-day; but to-morrow he shall speak in Spanish.

26. Do you not wish to practise Italian? Yes, sir, and I shall practise the day after to-morrow, if I have time.

27. If your teacher comes to-day, will you take a lesson? I shall take it if he comes.

28. Does he pronounce well? He pronounces very well, but with some affectation.

29. How many Spanish words do you know that end in *cion*? I know very many.

30. Which are they? Conversation, approbation, agitation, complication, classification, intention, desertion, circumspection, nation, navigation, and very many others.

LESSON XXV.

| *Conocer.* | To know, to be acquainted with. |

PRESENT INDICATIVE.

Conozco.	I know.
Conoces.	Thou knowest.
Conoce.	He knows.

Conocemos.	We know.
Conoceis.	You know.
Conocen.	They know.

PRETERIT DEFINITE.

Conocí.	I knew.
Conociste.	Thou knewest.
Conoció.	He knew.

Conocimos.	We knew.
Conocisteis.	You knew.
Conocieron.	They knew.

LESSON XXV.

FUTURE SIMPLE.

Conoceré.	I shall know.
Conocerás.	Thou wilt know.
Conocerá.	He will know.
Conocerémos.	We shall know.
Conoceréis.	You will know.
Conocerán.	They will know.

PRETERIT INDEFINITE.

He conocido. | I have known.

COMPOUND FUTURE.

Habré conocido. | I shall have known.

Gozar.	To enjoy.
Prometer.	To promise.

Una vez.	Once.
Dos veces, &c.	Twice.
Alto.	High, loud.
Bajo.	Low.
Siempre.	Always.
Nunca.	Never.
Jamás.	Never.
Ya.	Already, yet (*interrogatively*)
Ya (*with a negative*).	No longer.
Aun.	Still, yet, even.
Todavía.	Still, yet, even.

A menudo.	Often.
Demasiado.	Too, too much.
Bastante.	Enough, pretty.

Frio.	Cold (the).	Vergüenza.	Shame.
Calor.	Heat.	Razon.	Reason.
Miedo.	Fear.	Sed.	Thirst.
Sueño.	Sleep.	Lástima.	Pity.
Hambre.	Hunger.	Salud.	Health.
Valor.	Courage, worth, value.	Moda.	Fashion.
Maestro.	Master, teacher.	Maestra.	Mistress (school).

COMPOSITION.

¿Conoce V. á ese hombre? | Do you know that man?
No lo conozco; pero sé quien le conoce. | I do not know him; but I know who knows him.

LESSON XXV.

¿ Porqué no aprende V. sus lecciones? — Why do you not learn your lessons?
Conozco que he hecho mal en no aprenderlas; pero prometo saberlas para mañana. — I know that I have done wrong in not learning them; but I promise to know them for to-morrow.
¿ Sabe V. francés? — Do you know French?
No, señor, pero voy á aprenderlo; ¿ conoce V. un buen maestro? — No, sir, but I am going to learn it; do you know a good teacher?
¿ Estudia V. aun (todavía) el español? — Do you still study Spanish?
Ya no lo estudio. — I study it no longer.
¿ Sabe V. hablarlo ya? — Do you know how to speak it already?
No, todavía. — Not yet.
¿ Ha principiado ya su hermano de V. sus lecciones? — Has your brother commenced his lessons yet?
Ya ha principiado; pero no las aprenderá jamás (nunca), porque no estudia bastante. — He has (already) commenced; but he will never learn them, for he does not study enough.
¿ Cuántas veces ha estado V. este mes en el teatro? — How many times have you been in the theatre this month?
He estado una vez; pero el mes pasado estuve tres veces. — I have been once; but last month I was there three times.
¿ Tiene V. miedo de su maestro? — Are you afraid of your master?
No tengo miedo de él; pero tengo vergüenza de él. — I am not afraid of him; but I am ashamed before him.
¿ De quién tiene V. lástima? — On whom do you take pity?
Tengo lástima de ese pobre hombre. — I take pity on that poor man.
¿ Tiene V. calor ó frio? — Are you warm or cold?
No tengo ni calor ni frio; tengo hambre y sed. — I am neither warm nor cold; I am hungry and thirsty.
¿ Tiene razon el abogado? — Is the lawyer right?
El abogado no tiene razon. — The lawyer is not right.
¿ Tiene él razon alguna vez? — Is he right sometimes?
Tiene razon algunas veces, pero no siempre. — He is right sometimes, but not always.
¿ Hará V. eso otra vez? — Will you do that again (another time)?
No lo haré jamás (nunca). — I will never do it.
¿ Amará V. á su amigo? — Will you love your friend?
Le amaré por siempre jamás. — I shall love him always (for ever).
¿ Ha leido V. jamás ese libro? — Have you ever read that book?
Nunca jamás lo haré. — I shall never do it.
¿ Tiene su madre de V. buena salud? — Is your mother in good health (has your mother good health)?
Sí, señor, goza de muy buena salud. — Yes, sir, she enjoys very good health.
¿ Tiene V. hambre ó sed? — Are you hungry or thirsty?
No tengo ni hambre ni sed, tengo sueño. — I am neither hungry nor thirsty, I am sleepy.

EXPLANATION.

111. SABER, to know, and CONOCER, to be acquainted with.—It must be observed, in order not to confound these two verbs, that *saber* is employed to signify the act of knowing, being informed of, having learned, or having a knowledge of something; whereas *conocer* is used to express the fact of being acquainted with, perceiving, or being able to distinguish persons or things; as,

¿ *Sabe* V. quién *conoce* á este hombre ? | Do you know who knows that man ?

112. AUN, YA, TODAVÍA.—The adverb *aun* indicates that the subject of the sentence *continues* in the same state as before; quite the reverse with the adverb *ya*, which always signifies *discontinuance* of a former state (expressed or understood); *e. g.*,

¿ Escribe V. aun ? | Do you write yet ?
No escribo ya. | I do not write any longer.

Todavía, yet, still, is synonimous with *aun*; as,

Está trabajando *todavía* (or *aun*). | He is still working.

Once, twice, &c., are rendered in Spanish by *una vez, dos veces,* &c.

Miedo, valor, vergüenza, lástima, tiempo, take the preposition *de* after them; as,

Tengo *miedo de* salir. | I am afraid to go out.
Tengo *vergüenza de* ese hombre. | I am ashamed of that man.

113. When in English the verb *to be* precedes the adjectives *hungry, thirsty, afraid, ashamed, right, wrong, warm, cold, sleepy,* it is changed into the Spanish verb *tener*, and the adjective into a corresponding substantive; as,

¿ Tiene V. miedo ? | Are you afraid ?
¿ Tiene V. sed ? | Are you thirsty ?
¿ Tiene V. calor. | Are you warm ?
¿ Tiene V. frio ? | Are you cold ?

114. JAMÁS and NUNCA may be used indiscriminately, or one for the other; as,

Jamás (or *nunca*) le he conocido. | I have never been acquainted with him.

Sometimes they are used together, to give more energy to the expression; as,

Nunca jamás lo haré. | Never, no never, shall I do so.

But *jamás* has the peculiarity of being used after the words *por siempre* and *para siempre*, for ever; where, instead of being a negative, it affirms, meaning *eternally*; as,

Le amaré *por siempre jamás*. | I will love him forever.

Sometimes it is used alone interrogatively, meaning *ever*; as,

¿Ha leido V. *jamás* ese libro? | Have you ever read that book?

CONVERSATION AND VERSION.

1. ¿Dónde conoció V. á su amigo? Le conocí en París el invierno pasado.
2. ¿Sabe V. quién conoce á ese hombre? Mi padre le conoce muy bien.
3. ¿Cuándo conoceré á su hermano de V.? En el otoño lo conocerá V.
4. ¿Ha conocido V. en Lóndres á ese caballero? Sí, señor, le conocí allí el año pasado.
5. ¿Cómo está su hijo de V.? Mal; no goza de buena salud.
6. ¿Bailó V. mucho en el baile de anoche? Sí, señor, muchísimo.
7. ¿Quién es ese caballero? Es un escritor de gran reputacion.
8. ¿Tienen mucha aceptacion sus obras? Tienen muchísima.
9. ¿Sabe V. lo que han prometido sus amigas de V.? No lo sé.—Han prometido estudiar sus lecciones.
10. ¿Vendrá V. mañana á comer con nosotros? No, señor, he prometido comer con mis amigos los Alemanes.
11. ¿Habla ya español su primo de V.? No lo habla aun, y no lo hablará jamás (nunca), porque no estudia bastante.
12. ¿Barrió V. mi cuarto? No, señor, pero prometo barrerlo mañana temprano.
13. ¿Cuántas veces prometió V. buscar mi sombrero? Jamás lo prometí.
14. ¿No desea V. ya ir á su país? Lo deseo muchísimo.
15. ¿Sale V. ya á pasear todos los dias? No salgo sino algunas veces.
16. ¿Llevó V. ya mi carta al correo? Todavía no la he llevado.
17. ¿No ha estado V. jamás en París? No, señor, jamás he estado.
18. ¿No ha leido V. jamás la historia de los Estados Unidos? Sí, la he leido una vez.
19. ¿Habla bien el abogado? Habla bien, pero muy bajo.
20. ¿Comprende V. ya el español? Si hablan alto, y despacio, sí, señor.

LESSON XXV.

21. ¿Tiene V. bastante que hacer? Tengo demasiado.
22. ¿Cuántos años tiene V.? Tengo veinte y uno.
23. ¿Cuándo vió V. por última vez á su familia? El dia seis de Setiembre del año de mil ochocientos cincuenta y cinco.
24. ¿Cuándo conoció V. al pianista? Le conocí ayer por primera vez.
25. ¿Han salido sus hermanas para el campo? Todavía no, pero saldrán muy pronto.
26. ¿Qué hace su padre de Vds.? Está gozando del buen tiempo en el campo.
27. ¿Qué tiene su niño de V.? Tiene frio y sueño.
28. ¿Tienen ellos hambre? No, señor, tienen sed.
29. ¿Tiene V. valor para hacerlo? Sí, señor, pero tengo vergüenza.
30. ¿No tiene V. lástima de esa mujer? Sí, señor, tengo lástima de ella, porque no tiene buena salud.
31. ¿Tiene sueño su madre de V.? No, señor, pero está muy cansada.

EXERCISE.

1. Do you know that man? Yes, sir, that gentleman is my uncle.
2. Are you still writing? No, I am no longer writing.
3. Has Charles come from the country yet? No, he has not come yet.
4. Have you (*plural*) ever read the History of Civilization by Guizot? No, but we shall read it next spring.
5. Are you not ashamed of not having read the History of the United States? I am not ashamed, because I am too young to read history.
6. When shall you commence to read it? I shall commence next year.
7. Very well; it is a useful study (*estudio*).
8. Does your aunt enjoy good health? Yes, sir, thank you, she enjoys very good health.
9. Are you cold, madam? No, thank you, I wish to go out a minute, because I am very warm in this room.
10. Is it ten o'clock yet? No, it is but a quarter past eight.
11. Who is that gentleman to whom your cousin spoke last night at the concert? I do not know him.
12. And that gentleman who came this morning to your house, who is he? He is a Spanish writer who enjoys a high (great) reputation.
13. Has he written many works? He has already written many books, and he is going to write a history of Spain.
14. Do you know Sir Walter Scott's works? Yes, I have read them all.
15. Are they not much esteemed in Europe (have they not much estimation)? Yes, very much.

16. When did your brother become acquainted with his (*el*) Spanish friend? Last year, in London.

17. Are you sleepy, young ladies? Yes, we are very tired, thirsty and sleepy (*tener sed y sueño*).

18. Will you take a little wine? No, thank you, we never take wine.

19. Does your mother know Emanuel's address (direction)? Yes, here it is in this letter.

20. Will you read it? With much pleasure. Emanuel Martinez, Esq. (don), 113 Broadway. A thousand thanks.

21. Did your cousin's (*fem.*) friends commence their lessons the other day? Yes, they commenced, and are much pleased (content) with them.

22. Why does the lawyer speak so low? I do not know.

23. Does he not speak as low as his brother loud? He speaks low from (by) affectation.

24. Which of your servants (*fem.*) sews the best? None of them sews.

25. How many conjugations has the Spanish language? Three regular (*regular*) conjugations, and several irregular (*irregular*) ones.

26. Have you ever been in Philadelphia? I have never been there yet; but I shall go next year.

27. Did your father write the letter for Peter yesterday? No, but he promised to write it the day after to-morrow.

28. Has your shoemaker enough to do? Yes, sir, he has too much to do.

29. Will you always love your brothers and sisters? Yes, I shall love them forever.

30. Do you not pity that man? I do pity him, for he has nothing to do.

31. Have you money enough to buy a house? Yes, sir, I have enough.

LESSON XXVI.

| *Dar.* | To give. |

PRESENT INDICATIVE.

| Doy, das, da. | I give, thou givest, he gives. |
| Damos, dais, dan. | We give, you give, they give. |

LESSON XXVI.

PRETERIT DEFINITE.

Dí, diste, dió.	I gave, thou gavest, he gave.
Dimos, disteis, dieron.	We gave, you gave, they gave.

FUTURE SIMPLE.

Daré, darás, dará.	I shall give, thou wilt give, he will give.
Darémos, daréis, darán.	We shall give, you shall give, they shall give.

PRETERIT INDEFINITE.

He dado, has dado, etc.	I have given, thou hast given, &c.

COMPOUND FUTURE.

Habré dado, etc.	I shall have given, &c.

Ganar — To gain, earn, win.

Sing. Nom.	Yo.	I.
1st *Obj.*	Me.	Me, or to me.
2d *Obj.*	A mí.	
Plur. Nom.	Nosotros.	We.
1st *Obj.*	Nos.	Us, or to us.
2d *Obj.*	A nosotros.	
Sing. Nom.	Tú.	Thou.
1st *Obj.*	Té.	Thee, or to thee.
2d *Obj.*	A tí.	
Plur. Nom.	Vosotros.	Ye, you.
1st *Obj.*	Os.	Ye, you, or to you.
2d *Obj.*	A vosotros.	
Sing. Nom.	Él.	He.
1st *Obj.*	Le.	Him, or to him.
2d *Obj.*	A él.	
Plur. Nom.	Ellos.	They.
1st *Obj.*	Los, les.	Them, to them.
2d *Obj.*	A ellos.	
Sing. Nom.	Ella.	She.
1st *Obj.*	La, le.	Her, to her
2d *Obj.*	A ella.	

Plur. Nom.	Ellas.	}	They.
1st *Obj.*	Las, les.		Them, to them.
2d *Obj.*	A ellas.		
Sing. and Plur.		{	Himself, herself, itself, themselves; or to himself, to her self, to itself, to themselves.
1st *Obj.*	Se.		
2d *Obj.*	A sí.		
Neuter Form.			
Nom.	Ello.		It.
1st *Obj.*	Lo.		It.
2d *Obj.*	A ello.		To it.

COMPOSITION.

¿Conoce V. aquellas señoras? Deseo conocerlas.	Do you know those ladies? I desire to know them.
Conociéndolas las amará V.	On knowing them you will love them.
¿Me promete V. llevarme á su casa?	Do you promise me to take me to their house?
Doy á V. mi palabra.	I will give you my word.
¿Qué le dió á V. mi primo?	What did my cousin give you?
Quiso darme unas flores; pero yo no quise recibirlas.	He wanted to give me some flowers; but I would not receive them.
¿Quieres venir conmigo al teatro?	Wilt thou come with me to the theatre?
No iré contigo, porque mi padre quiere llevarme consigo.	I will not go with thee, because my father wants to take me with him.
¿Son estas flores para tí?	Are these flowers for thee?
No son para mí; son para V.	They are not for me, they are for you.
Yo te necesito.	I want thee.
Ella nos habló en el teatro.	She spoke to us in the theatre.
Él me amará con el tiempo.	He will love me in time.
Nosotros le hablámos en el concierto.	We spoke to him at the concert.
Yo le escribí una carta.	I wrote him a letter.
Ella les dió un libro.	She gave them a book.

EXPLANATION.

115. SUBJECT OR NOMINATIVE.—To what has already been said, in Lesson X., relative to pronouns as subjects or nominative cases to verbs, we shall here simply add, that they may at all times precede their verbs, unless the latter be in the imperative mood, or be used interrogatively; examples:

Yo estudio.	I study.
Tú escribes.	Thou writest.
Vengan *ellos.*	Let them come.
¿Lee *ella?*	Does she read.

LESSON XXVI.

116. Personal Pronouns.—In Spanish there is a peculiarity to be observed amongst the personal pronouns: that is, that they have two objective cases; one of which can never be used with prepositions, and the other never without one.

117. The Objective Case, when not preceded by a preposition, is affixed to infinitives, imperatives and gerunds; as,

Amar*la*.	To love her.
Amémos*le*.	Let us love him.
Amándo*los*.	Loving them.
Habiéndo*la* amado.	Having loved her.
Cómpra*les* algo.	Buy them something.
Habiéndo*los* hallado.	Having found them.

118. In some tenses the verb drops the final letter in the first and second persons plural, when they are followed by *nos* or *os*; as,

Amámo*nos* instead of amámosnos.	We loved each other.
Ama*os* instead of amados.	Love each other.

In the first case, the reason of this is perhaps to soften the pronunciation of the first word; and in the second the *d* is dropped, in order that the imperative be not confounded with the past participle. Nevertheless, we say *idos*, go, and not *ios*; but this is the only exception to the rule.

119. The objective case may sometimes elegantly follow the verb, but rarely when the sentence does not begin by the verb; as,

Llevó*me* al teatro.	He took me to the theatre.

120. When one verb governs another in the infinitive mood, the objective case referring to the second verb may be placed either before the governing verb, or after the governed one; as,

Quiero llevar*le*, *or* *le* quiero llevar.	I wish to take him.

121. Prepositions, when expressed, always govern the second objective case; as,

Para *mí*.	For me.
Sin *tí*.	Without thee.
Hácia *ellos*.	Towards them.

LESSON XXVI.

122. Mí, tí, sí, when preceded by *con*, take *go* after them, and are joined to the preposition; as,

Con*m*igo.	With me.
Con*t*igo.	With thee.
Con*s*igo.	With him, her, them, it.

123. ENTRE is used with the nominative case of the first person singular, in this expression,

Entre tú y yo.	Between thee and me;

but in every other instance it governs the second objective case; as,

Entre sí.	Between themselves.
Entre nosotros.	Between us.

124. The second objective case is always used after comparatives; as,

Te quiero mas que á *él*.	I love thee better than him.

125. When in English the objective case of the first or second person is the object of the verb, or of the preposition *to*, expressed or understood, we use the first case; as,

Yo *te* necesito.	I want thee.
Ella *nos* habló.	She spoke to us.
El *me* amará.	He will love me.

126. In Lesson X. we explained the objective case of the third person when it is the object of the English verb; but if the third person in English be governed by the preposition *to*, expressed or understood, we render it by *le*, *les*, for both genders; as,

Nosotros *le* hablámos.	We spoke to him.
Yo *le* escribí.	I wrote to her.
Ella *les* dió.	She gave them.

CONVERSATION AND VERSION.

1. ¿Qué me dará V.? Le daré á V. las gracias.
2. ¿Qué les dió V. á sus niños? Les dí veinte centavos.
3. ¿Me darás algo por mi trabajo? Algo te daré si lo haces bien y sinó, nada.

LESSON XXVI.

4. ¿Qué os dieron en casa de tu primo? Nos dieron chocolate.
5. ¿Qué le has prometido á tu prima? Bailar hoy con ella.
6. ¿Cómo serémos mas felices? Amándonos los unos á los otros.
7. ¿Cuándo vendrá él con nosotros? Vendrá mañana temprano.
8. ¿Cuándo saldrá V. conmigo á paseo? Tendré ese gusto pasado mañana.
9. ¿Quién irá conmigo al teatro esta noche? Yo iré contigo.
10. ¿Dónde hablaste á mis amigos? Les hablé en el Parque Central.
11. ¿Les leyó V. mi carta? No, les leí la de su hermana de V.
12. ¿Me envió V. los libros? No, señor, los envié á su hermano de V.
13. ¿Cómo supo V. de sus amigos? Escribiéndoles.
14. ¿Cómo conoció V. á su amiga? Bailando con ella en casa de su hermano.
15. ¿Qué le prometió V. á su prima? Le prometí llevarla á la opera.
16. ¿Nos hablaron ellos alguna vez? Nos hablaron una ó dos veces en el paseo.
17. ¿Porqué no les habló V.? Porque no los conozco bien.
18. ¿Qué le han escrito á V. sus amigos? Que vendrán á hablarnos.
19. ¿Quieres salir conmigo á paseo? Sí, saldré contigo.
20. ¿Cuándo irémos á casa de tus amigos? Irémos hoy, porque ellos tendrán mucho gusto en conocerte.
21. ¿Quiere V. pasarme el pan? Con mucho gusto.—Gracias.
22. ¿Qué le prometiste á tu prima? Le prometí ir á su casa mañana y llevarle un pañuelo de seda.
23. ¿Cuándo le habló V.? Le hablé anoche en casa de su madre.
24. ¿Quiere V. venir á pasear? Mejor será estarnos aquí.
25. ¿A qué vienen Vds.? Venimos á hablarle á V.
26. ¿Cuándo irémos al campo con nuestros amigos? Irémos mañana.
27. ¿Cómo les ganó á Vds. la lavandera tanto dinero? Lavándonos los vestidos y trabajando mucho.
28. ¿Cuántas veces á la semana habla V. con sus amigos? Nos hablamos todos los dias.
29. ¿Vendrá hoy su primo de V. á comer con nosotras? Sí, porque quiere conocerlas á Vds.
30. ¿Le dió V. los buenos dias á su prima? Le di los buenos dias ayer en la plaza y le habló de V.
31. Le doy á V. las gracias. ¿Tiene buena salud ahora? Sí, señora, está muy buena.
32. ¿Le dió á V. los periódicos? No, señora, pero prometió mandarlos mañana.

LESSON XXVI.

EXERCISE.

1. What was* that you gave to your friend last night at the theatre? I gave him the second volume of Mr. Romanos' new work.

2. Why do you not give him the first volume? I have already given it to my cousin.

3. Did you not promise last week to give me those two volumes? Yes; and you shall have them the day after to-morrow.

4. Will you come with me to the country in the summer? I will go if you set out on the first of July.

5. Will you and your uncle come with us to walk this afternoon? This evening we have to go to the concert.

6. When will you go out with us? I do not know; but I think (that) to-morrow (*creo que mañana*).

7. Have you heard (*sabido*) from your father this week? No; but we heard from our brother John last week.

8. How often has he written to you from Boston? We have received seven or eight letters from him.

9. How much did that singer make (gain) in New York? Which one? I do not know any singers.

10. Do you not know the singer who spent last week at your uncle's in the country? Yes; but it was in Philadelphia that he sang, not in New York.

11. Are you cold? No, sir; but I am hungry and thirsty.

12. When will you take Emanuel to see your children? I shall take him to-morrow.—They will have much pleasure in making his acquaintance.

13. How many languages does that gentleman speak? He only speaks his own; but his cousin speaks five.

14. Which are they? He speaks French, German, Spanish, English, and Italian.

15. How did he learn so many languages? By studying the grammar of each one of them (*cada una de ellas*), reading the works of the best writers, and practising with the natives (*natural*).

16. Does he write all those languages as well as he speaks them? He writes them better than he speaks them.

17. Did I not see you (*plural*) speaking to the notary yesterday in the park? No, it was the day before yesterday.

18. What has he done in that affair (*negocio*) of your brother's? He has done nothing yet; and as he has to leave town (*la ciudad*) this afternoon, he will do nothing all this week.

19. Who is the young lady who danced so well last night at your house? Do you not know her? she is my cousin.

---
* See the conjugation of the verb Ser, at the end of the book.

20. When did you see our friend Mr. Perez? I saw him the other day in Twenty-sixth street, and we talked for more than two hours about (*de*) theatres and concerts.

21. I saw him the night before last; but we did not talk about theatres and concerts. In whose house did you see him? At Mr. de la Rosa's.

22. At what o'clock did you go there? I went at a quarter to eight, and left at half-past ten.

23. Did you see many Mexicans there? I only saw one: that Mexican lawyer who has just written a history of his country.

24. Does he leave soon for Europe? He wishes to set out next week.

25. Did John write to his father the day before yesterday? Yes, and he has heard (*saber*) since that he set out last week for France.

26. Has your sister read the books yet which she received from Louisa last week? Yes; and she wishes to read them again (*otra vez*).

27. I shall see her this evening; and if you wish (it) I shall take them to her (*se los*).

28. Thank you. Have you much to do now? No, I never have much to do in summer.

29. Is Peter tired? No; but he is the most tiresome boy I know.

LESSON XXVII.

| *Decir.* | To say, to tell. |

PRESENT OF INDICATIVE.

| Digo, dices, dice, decimos, decis, dicen. | I say, or tell, &c. |

PRETERIT DEFINITE.

| Dije, dijiste, dijo, dijimos, dijisteis, dijeron. | I said, or told, &c. |

FUTURE SIMPLE.

| Diré, dirás, dirá, dirémos, diréis, dirán. | I shall or will say, or tell, &c. |

PRETERIT INDEFINITE.

| He dicho, has dicho, etc. | I have said, or told, &c. |

COMPOUND FUTURE.

| Habré dicho, etc. | I shall or will have said, or told, &c. |

LESSON XXVII.

Excusar.	To excuse.
Perdonar.	To pardon.
Creer.	To believe, to think.
Ofender.	To offend.
Llamar.	To call, to knock.
Enseñar.	To teach, to show.

Ahora.	Now.
Mismo (*adverb*).	Just, very.

Mismo.	Same, self.
Necesario.	Necessary.
Preciso.	Precise, needful.
Regular.	Regular, middling.

Parte.	Despatch.	Parte.	Part.
Estudio.	Study.	Falta.	Fault, mistake.
Humor.	Humor, disposition.	Esperanza.	Hope.
Sugeto.	A person, subject, topic.	Puerta.	Door.
Asunto.	Subject, business, matter.	Noticia.	News.
Ramillete.	Bouquet.		

COMPOSITION.

Le compró un ramillete, y *se* lo mandó.	He bought her a bouquet, and sent it to her.
Les escribiré tres cartas, y *se* las mandaré.	I shall write them three letters, and send them to them.
Ella *se* lo ha prometido.	She has promised it to her.
¿Qué está V. haciendo con ese libro?	What are you doing with that book?
Estoy enseñándo*selo* á Manuel.	I am showing it to Emanuel.
¿Le leiste la carta?	Did you read the letter to him?
Ya *se la* leí.	I did. (I read it to him already.)
Ella *me lo* dijo.	She told it to me.
Yo *se lo* dí.	I gave it to him.
Mi madre *me* ama á mí.	My mother loves me.
Tu amigo *te* busca á tí.	Thy friend looks for thee.
Yo *les* dí las noticias á ellos.	I told *them* the news.
Yo *se las* daré á V.?	I will tell *them* to you.
A tí *te* amo, or te amo á tí.	I love thee.
¿Qué *le* ha dicho á V. su hermano?	What has your brother told you?
No me ha dicho nada.	He has told me nothing.
¿*Le* dije yo eso á V.?	Did I tell you that?
V. no *me lo* dijo.	You did not tell it to me.

LESSON XXVII.

¿Se lo ha dicho él á V.?	Has he told it to you?
Me lo ha dicho.	He has told it to me.
¿Quiere V. decir eso á sus amigos?	Will you tell your friends that?
Quiero decírselo á ellos.	I will tell it to them.
¿Quién llama á la puerta?	Who knocks at the door?
Soy yo mismo.	It is I (myself).
¿Tiene buen humor su amigo de V.?	Has your friend a good disposition?
Sí, señor, tiene buen humor cuando le van bien los negocios.	Yes, sir, he is good humored when business goes well with him.
¿Gana ese sugeto mucho en ese asunto?	Does that man make (or earn) much in that business?
El no gana para sí mismo; pero gana para otros.	He does not make for himself; but he makes for others.
Tengo esperanza de que me perdonará.	I have hopes he will pardon me.

EXPLANATION.

127. OBJECTIVE PRONOUNS, *continued.*—The third person being governed by *to* in English, either expressed or understood, is in Spanish rendered by *se*, if the object of the verb be a pronoun in the third person; as,

Le compró un ramillete, y *se* lo mandó.	He bought her a bouquet, and sent it to her.
Les escribiré tres cartas, y *se* las mandaré.	I shall write them three letters, and send them to them.
Mi criado *se* lo dará.	My servant will give it to him.

This is done for the sake of euphony, changing the first of the two pronouns, whatever its full form may be (*le, la* or *les*), into *se*. This rule applies to all pronouns, after as well as before the verb; as,

Ella *se lo* ha prometido (instead of *ella le lo*).	She has promised it to her.
Prometiéndosela (instead of *prometiéndolelo*).	Promising it to him.
¿Le leiste la carta?	Did you read the letter to him?
Ya *se la leí*, instead of *ya le la leí*.	I read it to him (already).

128. When two *first* objective cases occur in the sentence, one of which is the object of the verb, and the other is governed, in English, by the preposition *to*, either expressed or understood, the object of the verb is to be placed last; as,

Ella me *lo* dijo.	She told *it* to me.
Yo se *lo* di.	I gave *it* to him.

129. But if the object of the verb be the reflective pronoun, it must be placed first; as,

Luego *se* me excusó.	He excused himself immediately to me.

130. Both the objective cases belonging to the same person are sometimes used together in Spanish, in order to give more energy to the expression, and then the second must always be preceded by *á*; as,

Mi madre *me* ama *á mí.*	My mother loves me.
Tu amigo *te* busca *á tí.*	Thy friend seeks thee.
Él *se* lo dijo *á ellas.*	He told it to them.
Yo *les* dí las noticias *á ellos.*	I told them the news.
Yo *se* las daré *á Vd.*	I will tell them to you.

131. The second objective case of any of the persons should never be used in the sentence, preceded by *á,* as the object of the verb, without being accompanied by the first (except after comparatives); therefore, such expressions as these: *á él quiero, á tí amo,* are incorrect, and should be thus: *á él le quiero, á tí te amo.* The place of the second objective case in sentences of this kind is restricted to the following rules:

1st. If the first objective case precede the verb, the second may be placed either before the first, or after the verb; as,

A tí te amo, or *te* amo *á tí.*	I love thee.

2d. If the first objective case follows the verb, the second must be placed after the first; as,

Amándo*le á él.*	Loving him.

132. It may appear that the personal pronouns *él, la, lo, los* and *las* might be confounded with the articles *el, la, lo, los, las,* having the same form; but they are easily distinguished, since the articles must always be accompanied by and precede nouns; as, *el tiempo, la salud, los soldados, las obras, lo bueno*; while, on the other hand, the personal pronouns are only employed with verbs, and placed before or after them; as,

La llevaron, or llevaronla.	They carried it.
Lo buscaron, or buscaronlo.	They looked for it.

133. Whenever emphasis is required to be laid on any

LESSON XXVII.

noun or pronoun, the adjective *mismo* is used in Spanish for that purpose; as,

El no ama á nadie mas que á sí mismo.	He loves no one but himself.
Este *mismo* hombre lo hará.	This very man will do it.
Yo *mismo* lo haré.	I will do it myself.

CONVERSATION AND VERSION.

1. ¿Le dijo V. eso al inglés? Se lo dije.
2. ¿Se lo dijo V. en inglés ó en español? Se lo dije en inglés.
3. ¿Le comprendió á V.? Sí, señor, muy bien.
4. ¿Y qué le enseñó á V.? Me enseñó el retrato de su hermana.
5. ¿Lo tiene V.? No; se lo envié ya.
6. ¿Me lo enseñará V.? Se lo enseñaré á V. la semana próxima.
7. ¿Ha llamado V. á la criada? La he llamado y no ha venido.
8. ¿No le perdonará V. esa falta? No quiero perdonársela.
9. ¿A quién llama mi padre? Te llama á tí.
10. ¿Quieres enseñarme tu vestido nuevo? Te lo enseñaré con mucho gusto.
11. ¿Vendrán tus amigos á darnos los buenos dias? Creo que vendrán á dárnoslos.
12. ¿Nos han enviado los periódicos? Os los enviarán mañana.
13. ¿Cuánto le ganó V. á ese sugeto? Le ganó dos mil trescientos cincuenta y cuatro pesos.
14. ¿Qué les dieron á sus amigas de V.? Prometiéronles llevarlas á paseo; pero no les dieron nada.
15. ¿Quién dijo eso? Yo mismo lo dije.
16. ¿Para quién son estos libros? Para tí mismo.
17. ¿Han mandado mis cartas al correo? Sí, señor, yo mismo las he mandado.
18. ¿Quién me ha enviado este ramillete? Su amiga misma se lo ha enviado.
19. ¿Le leiste á tu padre las noticias de Francia? El mismo las ha leido.
20. ¿Quieres enseñarme tu reloj? Quiero enseñártelo.
21. ¿Quién llamó á la puerta? Yo mismo llamé.
22. ¿Tiene V. esperanza de ver su país? Sí, señor, tengo esperanza de verlo muy pronto.
23. ¿Cantaron bien anoche en el concierto? Cantaron bien la primera parte; pero la segunda muy mal.
24. ¿Cómo está su tio de V.? Está bueno; pero de muy mal humor.
25. ¿Es hombre de mal humor? No, señor, es hombre muy amable; pero hoy está de mal humor por asuntos de familia.

LESSON XXVII.

26. ¿Creen ellos ganar dinero á ese hombre? Creen ganárselo.
27. ¿Necesita V. enviar este periódico á su hermano? Necesito enviárselo.
28. ¿Cuándo quiere V. mandar su piano al pianista? Se lo quiero mandar ahora.
29. ¿Cuándo necesita V. hablar al abogado? Necesito hablarle ahora mismo.
30. ¿Es esta la carta que V. recibió ayer? Es la misma.
31. ¿A quién ama el Mejicano? No ama á nadie mas que á sí mismo.
32. ¿Para quién trabaja esa mujer? Trabaja para sí misma.
33. ¿Qué le ha dicho V. hoy á su padre? Lo mismo que le dije ayer.

EXERCISE.

1. Good morning, sir; how are you? Very well, thank you.
2. How is your family? Very well, thank you.
3. When did you hear from your cousin Jane? I received a letter from her yesterday. But will you excuse me an instant? some one is knocking at the door.
4. Have you sent your sister the bouquet I bought for her the other day? Not yet; but I shall send it to her to-morrow morning.
5. Will you write to her at the same time and (to) tell her what Charles said? I am going to write to her just now, and I shall tell it to her.
6. Do you think my father will pardon us? I do (I think so), because Emanuel showed me a letter he received from him, in which he says he will pardon both of us.
7. And what does Henry think of the matter? He thinks the same.
8. Have the pupils shown their new books to their teacher yet? Yes, they showed them to him yesterday.
9. Does he think they are good? He says they are very good.
10. What else (more) did he say? He said that if they study them with attention they will very soon speak Spanish.
11. Is that all* he said? That is all.
12. Who is knocking at the door? is it you, Peter? Yes, it is I.
13. Why did you not come earlier? I was (have been) reading the news from Italy.
14. What is the news (what news have we)? The papers say that the Italians have gained another victory (*victoria*).
15. What did that man promise you last night? He promised to bring me some volumes of the History of the United States.

* Lo que.

LESSON XXVII.

16. Has he brought (*traido*) them to you yet? Not yet.

17. When do you think he will bring* them? He has to come to our house this evening, and I think he will bring them with him.

18. What do you wish to see? I wish to see your new dress, if you will have the goodness (*bondad*) to show it to me.

19. Will you tell the Englishman what I have told you? I shall not tell it to the Englishman; but I shall tell it to the Frenchman this very day.

20. Will he believe it? Yes, he will (believe it); he believes everything I tell him.

21. Have they taken my letters to the post-office? I took them myself, sir.

22. Who is my father calling? He is calling you to send you to the bookstore for a book.

23. Do you know why Louis does not send us the papers any more (*ya*)? He promised to send them; but you know that no steamer (*vapor*) has arrived † this week yet.

24. When does the merchant want to see the notary? He wants to see him just now.

25. There he is talking to a gentleman; will you go and (to) tell him that my father wishes to speak to him a moment (*momento*)?

26. Good morning, sir; father wishes to tell you something; will you come now? Yes, I shall go just now.

27. How is your son, Mr. Alexander? He is much better, thank you; but he would not come out this morning, because he has to study his lesson.

28. What language is he learning? He is not learning any now; he commenced to learn Spanish in the winter.

29. What is he studying, then? He takes lessons in (of) writing, history and music.

30. What part of the grammar are you in now, Peter? I have just got to (arrived at) ‡ the twenty-seventh lesson.

31. Do you require to send this paper to your brother? I require to send it to him this very day.

* Traerá.   † Llegar.   ‡ Acabo de.

LESSON XXVIII.

IMPERFECT AND PLUPERFECT TENSES.

IMPERFECT.

First Conjugation.

Habl-aba, habl-abas, habl-aba.	I spoke, was speaking, or used to speak, &c., &c.
Habl-abamos, habl-abais, habl-aban.	We spoke, &c.

Second Conjugation.

Aprend-ia, aprend-ias, aprend-ia.	I learned, was learning, or used to learn, &c., &c.
Aprend-iamos, aprend-iais, aprend-ian.	

Third Conjugation.

Escrib-ia, escrib-ias, escrib-ia.	I wrote, was writing, or used to write, &c., &c.
Escrib-iamos, escrib-iais, escrib-ian.	

PLUPERFECT.

Habia	}	hablado.	I had	}	spoken.
Habiais		aprendido.	Thou hadst		learned.
Habia		escrito.	He had		written.
Habiamos	}	hablado.	We had	}	spoken.
Habiais		aprendido.	You had		learned.
Habian		escrito.	They had		written.

Acabar.	To finish.
Entrar.	To enter, come in, go in.
Deber.	To owe.
Deber.	Should, ought, must, to be to, to be one's duty to.
Dudar.	To doubt.
Temer.	To fear, be afraid of.
Abrir, abierto (irregular in this past participle only).	To open, opened.

Ambos.	Both.

Cuidado.	Care.	Cabeza.	Head.
Deber.	Duty.	Mano.	Hand.
Prójimo.	Neighbor.	Ropa.	Clothes.

Vecino.	Neighbor.	Ventana.	Window.
Reloj.	Clock, watch.	Visita.	Visit.
		Cuenta.	Bill, account.
Marido, esposo.	Husband.	Esposa.	Wife.

COMPOSITION.

Yo escribia cuando V. vino.	I was writing when you came.
El estudiaba sus lecciones todos los dias.	He used to study his lessons every day.
Margarita bailaba mucho cuando era jóven.	Margaret used to dance much when she was young.
Yo acababa de salir cuando V. entró.	I had just gone out when you came in.
¿Abria V. la puerta ó la ventana en el invierno?	Used you to open the door or the window in winter?
En el invierno no abria ni la una ni la otra; pero en el verano abria ámbas.	In winter I used to open neither; but in summer I used to open both.
¿Habia V. escrito los ejercicios ántes de dar su leccion?	Had you written your exercises before taking your lesson?
No los habia escrito; pero habia estudiado la leccion.	I had not written them; but I had studied my lesson.
Debe V. tener cuidado no solo de estudiar la leccion, sino de escribir los ejercicios, porque si no V. no aprenderá nada.	You must take care, not only to study your lesson, but (also) to write your exercises; for if not, you will learn nothing.
¿En dónde está su vecino de V.?	Where is your neighbor?
Acaba de entrar.	He has just come in (entered).
¿Qué hora tiene su reloj de V.?	What o'clock is it by your watch (what hour has your watch)?
Son las doce y cuarto.	It is a quarter past twelve.
¿Tenia su vecino de V. cuidado de su ropa?	Used your neighbor to take care of his clothes?
Debia hacerlo, pero no lo hacia.	He should have done so, but did not.
Debemos amar al prójimo tanto como á nosotros mismos; pero mi vecino no me ama á mí ni yo le amo á él.	We should love our neighbor as ourselves; but my neighbor does not love me, nor do I love him.
No dudo lo que V. dice.	I do not doubt what you say.

EXPLANATION.

134. THE IMPERFECT is used to express what is past, and, at the same time present, with regard to something else which is past; that is, it is a past tense which was still present at the time spoken of. It may always be employed in Spanish when in English the word *was* can be used with the present participle, or *used to* with the infinitive, or when we speak of habitual actions; as,

Yo escribia cuando V. vino.	I was writing when you came.
El estudiaba sus lecciones todos los dias.	He used to study his lessons every day.

135. The PLUPERFECT is used to express what is past, and took place before some other past action or event, expressed or understood; as,

Yo *habia leido* ya los periódicos cuando V. me los dió.	I had already read the newspapers when you gave them to me.

136. ACABAR DE.—The English expressions, *to have just*, and *to be just*, before a past participle, are translated into Spanish by *acabar de*, preceding an infinitive; as,

Acabo de entrar.	I have just come in.
El *acaba de* abrir la ventana.	He has just opened the window.

CONVERSATION AND VERSION.

1. ¿Ha hablado V. con la señorita? No, ella acababa de salir cuando yo toqué á la puerta.
2. ¿Dudaba V. entrar? Sí, porque temia ofender á V.
3. No señor; ¿qué hora es? Mi reloj tiene las once y cuarto.
4. ¿Y qué hora tiene V.? Yo tengo las once y media.
5. ¿Sabe V. qué hora es en el reloj de la iglesia? Cuando yo pasaba estaban dando las once.
6. ¿Entónces ahora deberán ser no mas que las once y veinte ó veinte y cinco minutos? Creo que serán un poco ménos.
7. ¿Ha hablado V. con mi vecino? He ido á hacerle una visita, pero habia salido.
8. ¿No habló V. con la señora? Sí, estaba en la ventana cuando yo pasé.
9. ¿Tiene una mano muy hermosa? Sí, pero los ojos son mas hermosos.
10. ¿Qué tenia en la cabeza? Dos flores.
11. ¿Quién llama á la puerta? La lavandera, que viene á buscar la ropa.
12. ¿Cuánto le debo á V.? Me debe V. veinte y cinco centavos de la ropa de la semana pasada.
13. ¿No se los ha pagado á V. mi marido? No, señora, no tenia dinero.
14. ¿Duda V. lo que le digo? No, señora, lo creo.

15. ¿Está bien lavada la ropa? Muy bien; yo misma la lavé.
16. ¿Hizo V. la visita á su vecino? Fuí á su casa; pero habia salido.
17. ¿Va V. muchas veces al teatro? Cuando vivia en París iba á menudo; pero aquí voy muy pocas veces.
18. ¿Cómo debemos amar al prójimo? Tanto como á nosotros mismos.
19. ¿Quién es el prójimo? Todos los hombres son nuestros prójimos.
20. ¿Está mala su hermana de V.? Sí, señora, y de cuidado (seriously).
21. ¿Cuántas visitas le ha hecho el médico? Muchísimas.
22. ¿Deben Vds. tener mucho cuidado de ella? Sí, señora, ya lo tenemos.
23. ¿Cuántas visitas le debo yo á V.? Con esta son tres.
24. ¿No vendrá V. á comer mañana con nosotras? Mañana iré al campo con mis vecinos.
25. ¿Habia V. recibido la carta del Frances cuando recibió la mia? La recibí despues.
26. ¿Porqué trabaja V. tanto? Porque es mi deber.
27. ¿Vendrán V. y su hermana á pasar una semana con nosotros? Sí, señora, la semana próxima vendrémos ámbos.
28. ¿Quién abrió mi ventana, Juan? Señor, yo mismo la abrí.
29. ¿Habló V. con el sastre? Fuí allá, pero habia salido.
30. ¿Cuándo vino V.? Ahora mismo acabo de entrar.
31. ¿Dónde está mi padre? Acaba de salir á la calle.
32. ¿Sabes á dónde fué? Fué á comprar ropa.
33. ¿Habrá ido á la Cuarta avenida? No, señor, creo que fué á Broadway.
34. ¿Qué hora es? El reloj de su cuarto de V. acaba de dar las doce.

EXERCISE.

1. What were you doing when Alexander went into your room? I was talking to my father.
2. I thought you were writing your exercises. No, I had written them already.
3. Does the servant take care to sweep your room every day? Yes, he knows very well it is his duty.
4. Why did you not come before? you were to come at nine o'clock. I know I have done wrong in not coming earlier; but I have been writing all the morning.
5. Does your sister Margaret dance now as much as she used? When (she was) in the city she used to dance very much, but now she has no time.
6. When you lived in the country did you open both the doors and the windows? I opened neither.

LESSON XXVIII.

7. Had you finished your work before going to the concert? I had (finished it).

8. Do you doubt what I tell you? No, sir, I never doubted anything you told me.

9. Is your neighbor afraid to open his windows in winter? He is not afraid to open them.

10. Who was it that went out last night after ten o'clock? No one went out; my brother came in at that hour.

11. Did Alexander go out when your cousin came in? He had already gone out when my cousin came in.

12. Where is he now? He has just gone out to walk.

13. Will he be very long (much time)? He will not be long; he is to take his Spanish lesson this evening.

14. Did you pay (make) a visit to my neighbor last week? I went to his house, but he was not at home.

15. When did you see the pianist? He came to see me the other day, but I had gone out.

16. Do you think we shall have studied our lessons before going to the teacher's? I think we shall.

17. What o'clock is it by (in) your watch? It is seventeen minutes past three by mine; what time have you?

18. It must be (deben ser) half-past three; has the music teacher come? Not yet.

19. Will you have the kindness to go to his house and tell him I shall not take my lesson this afternoon? With much pleasure.

20. So soon! Well, did you see the teacher? No, madam, he had just gone out.

21. How much do you owe the tailor now? I owe him very little; you know I sent him some money last month.

22. I know (it); but did he not send (pasar) in another bill on Monday? If he has sent in another I have not seen (visto) it.

23. I thought you were in the country, Mr. Emanuel? I was there last week.

24. Why did you not come yesterday? I saw you were writing and I feared to offend you.

25. But you know it was your duty to come in; you know I wanted you. Well, if you pardon me this time (vez), I shall come in again (another time).

26. How often do you go to the theatre? Not very often now; I used to go every night in the week.

27. How are we to love our neighbor? As ourselves.

28. Who is our neighbor? All mankind (men) are our neighbors.

LESSON XXIX.

29. How many visits has the physician made to your uncle? He began his visits on the 30th of December, and visited him twice a week until April 4th.

30. How many visits do I owe you for now? You owed me for twelve, but you paid me for nine, and so you only owe for three now.

31. Whose letter did you receive first, mine or Jane's? When yours came to hand (my hands), I had already received Jane's.

32. Will you take your lesson to-day? I am to go to the Central Park this afternoon with my mother, and so I shall not take my lesson until to-morrow.

LESSON XXIX.

PRETERIT ANTERIOR.

Hube	}	hablado.	I had }	spoken.
Hubiste	}	aprendido.	Thou hadst }	learned.
Hubo	}	escrito.	He had }	written.
Hubimos	}	hablado.	We had }	spoken.
Hubisteis	}	aprendido.	You had }	learned.
Hubieron	}	escrito.	They had }	written.

Ver.	To see. (*See the end of the book*)
Mirar.	To look.
Esperar.	To hope, to wait for.
Así que.	As soon as.
Apénas.	Scarcely.
No bien.	No sooner.
Tampoco (*conj.*).	Neither, not either.
Tambien (*adverb*).	Also, likewise.
Tambien (*conj.*).	As well, moreover.
Además.	Moreover, besides.
Primeramente, *or* en primer lugar.	Firstly.
Segundamente, *or* en segundo lugar.	Secondly, &c.
Frecuente.	Frequent.
Frecuentemente.	Frequently.
Cómodo.	Convenient, comfortable.
Cómodamente.	Conveniently, comfortably.

6*

Incómodo.	Inconvenient, uncomfortable.
Incómodamente.	Inconveniently, uncomfortably.
Probable.	Probable, likely.
Probablemente.	Probably, likely.
Perfecto.	Perfect.
Perfectamente.	Perfectly.
Correcto.	Correct.
Correctamente.	Correctly.

Ojo.	Eye.	Vista.	Sight, view.
Correo.	Post, post-office, courier.	Comodidad.	Convenience, comfort.
Lugar.	Place.	Milla.	Mile.

COMPOSITION.

Cuando le hube conocido le amé.	When I had known him I loved him.
Apénas hubo salido él cuando yo entré.	Scarcely had he gone out when I came in.
No bien le hube visto cuando le conocí.	No sooner had I seen him than I knew him.
Así que hube escrito la carta la llevé al correo.	As soon as I had written the letter I took it to the post-office.
Cuando le conocí le amé.	When I knew him I loved him.
¿Iba V. frecuentemente al teatro el año pasado?	Did you go often to the theatre last year?
Iba frecuentísimamente, *or* muy frecuentemente.	I went very often.
El vive en esa casa cómodamente, *or* con comodidad.	He lives comfortably, or with comfort, in that house.
El escribe correcta y perfectamente; pero V. escribe mas fácilmente.	He writes correctly and perfectly; but you write more easily.

EXPLANATION.

137. The PRETERIT ANTERIOR is used to express a past action or event that took place immediately before another action or event also past. It is never used except after some of the adverbs of time; *cuando*, when; *así que*, as soon as; *no bien*, no sooner; *apénas*, scarcely; *luego que*, immediately after; *despues que*, soon after; as,

Cuando le *hube* conocido.	When I had made his acquaintance.
Apénas *hubo* salido cuando yo vine.	Scarcely had he gone out when I came.
No bien le *hube* visto cuando lo conocí.	No sooner had I seen him than I knew him.

LESSON XXIX.

This tense is very little used, not only for the reason already mentioned, of its being preceded by an adverb of time, but also because its place may be elegantly supplied by the PRETERIT DEFINITE; as,

Cuando le *conocí*.	When I had known him.
Apénas *salió* cuando yo vine.	Scarcely had he gone out when I came.
No bien le *vi* cuando le conocí.	No sooner had I seen him than I knew him.

138. The adverbs of manner and quality, in Spanish as well as in English, are generally derived from adjectives.

139. To form an adverb from an adjective, it is sufficient to add *mente* to the adjective, if the latter has the same termination in both genders; as,

Frecuente, frecuente*mente*.
Gramatical, gramatical*mente*.

If the adjective has a different termination for each gender, then *mente* is added to the feminine; as,

Incómoda, incómoda*mente*.
Perfecta, perfecta*mente*.

When two or more of these adverbs follow each other, only the last one takes *mente*, the others taking the feminine termination *a*; as,

Ciceron habló sabi*a* y elocuente*mente*.	Cicero spoke learnedly and eloquently.

140. These adverbs terminating in *mente*, being derived from adjectives, admit like these the degrees of comparison; as,

Fácilmente.	Easily.
Mas fácilmente.	More easily.
Ménos fácilmente.	Less easily.
Tan fácilmente.	As, or so easily.
Muy fácilmente, *or* facilísimamente.	Very easily, or most easily.

141. Those adverbs may, without any change in the sense, be substituted by a substantive governed by the preposition *con*; as,

Él vive cómodamente, or con comodidad.	He lives comfortably.

LESSON XXIX.

CONVERSATION AND VERSION.

1. ¿Ve V. aquella flor tan hermosa? Miro, pero no la veo.
2. ¿Ve V. qué hora es en el reloj de la iglesia? No, pero miraré en mi reloj.
3. ¿Ha visto V. á su hermano? Sí, señor, le ví apénas hubo salido del teatro.
4. ¿Lo conoció á V. mi vecino? No bien le hube hablado, me conoció.
5. ¿Han venido mis amigos? Vinieron así que hubo V. salido.
6. ¿Le dieron á V. mis libros? Me los dieron, no bien les hube hablado de ello.
7. ¿Y se marcharon muy pronto? Se marcharon así que hubieron escrito sus cartas.
8. ¿Qué hizo V. despues? Primeramente (or primero) fuí al correo y despues al mercado.
9. ¿Qué quiere V. hacer? Primeramente escribir los ejercicios y despues estudiar la leccion.
10. ¿Porqué no lo hizo V. ántes? En primer lugar porque no tenia humor y en segundo porque apénas tuve tiempo.
11. ¿Habla V. frances frecuentemente? Sí, señor, lo hablo con frecuencia.
12. ¿Lo escribe V. correctamente? Cuando lo estudiaba lo escribia con mas correccion que ahora.
13. ¿Aprende V. inglés ó español? Aprendo ámbos.
14. ¿Y su hermano de V.? Mi hermano los aprende tambien.
15. ¿Los hablan Vds. con perfeccion? Sí, señor, el inglés lo hablamos perfectamente; pero el español ni yo, ni él tampoco.
16. ¿Ha enviado V. su carta al correo? No, señor, la enviaré mañana.
17. ¿La ha escrito V.? Tampoco la he escrito, porque quiero hacerlo con comodidad.
18. ¿Ha aprendido V. la leccion de hoy? He aprendido la de hoy y la de mañana tambien.
19. ¿Cuándo piensa V. salir para París? Probablemente saldré la semana próxima.
20. ¿No vive V. cómodamente aquí? Sí, señor, pero vivo mas cómodo en Francia.
21. ¿Vivia V. cómodamente cuando estaba en Lóndres? No, señor, vivia incómodamente porque no hablaba inglés.
22. ¿Tiene V. otro libro además de ese? Sí, señor, tengo otros dos
23. ¿Está V. malo de la vista? Sí, señor, tengo malo un ojo.

LESSON XXIX.

24. ¿Porqué no ha venido aun su primo de V.? Porque quiere venir con comodidad.
25. ¿Tiene V. buena vista? Sí, señor, pero ahora tengo los ojos malos.
26. ¿Cuándo estudia V. sus lecciones? Las estudio de dia porque el estudio de noche es malo para la vista.
27. ¿Dónde estan sus hermanos de V.? Salieron á paseo no bien hubieron escrito sus ejercicios.
28. ¿Cuándo escribieron las cartas? Así que hubieron aprendido sus lecciones.
29. ¿Llevó V. mis cartas al correo? Sí, señor, así que V. hubo salido.
30. ¿Va V. con frecuencia al correo? Sí, señor, voy frecuentemente: voy todos los dias.

EXERCISE.

1. Did you go to the lawyer's as I told you? I went as soon as you told me.
2. Was he at home? did you see him? He was not in when I went; but I waited until he came.
3. Did you show him the letter? I opened it and showed it to him; but he would* not read it.
4. What did your children do after taking their lesson? They had scarcely finished their lesson when they went to bed.
5. Did you look at the horses your brother bought on Monday. I did (look at them), and I think they are very fine.
6. Have you ever taken your family to Italy? Yes, several times; last year we travelled in Italy.
7. Did you spend some time in the principal cities? Yes; but principally in Rome (*Roma*), Florence (*Florencia*) and Milan (*Milan*).
8. Where were you on the 15th of December, 1865? On the 15th we were in Florence in the morning, and in Rome at night.
9. Did you all enjoy good health in Europe? Yes, all, except (*ménos*) Alexander, who had a sore (*malo*) eye the greater part of the time.
10. Did you go often to the theatre? We generally went every evening.
11. Had you any difficulty (*dificultad*) in understanding† the language? None; you know Emanuel speaks Italian very correctly: he had learned it before setting out for Europe.
12. Did you see many Americans when you were travelling? Very many; some of them we knew very well, and others were friends of ours.

* Quiso. † Comprender.

13. Where is the letter you were writing this morning? As soon as I had finished it John took it to the post-office.

14. Do you ever write to your uncle? Very little since we left New York; but there I used to write to him very frequently.

15. Which of you three writes French the most correctly*? I know it is not I; and as to (*en cuanto á*) Peter and Louis, I think Peter writes best, but Louis writes with more ease (more easily).

16. Do you see that beautiful flower? I am looking; but I do not see it.

17. Will you tell me what o'clock it is by the church clock? I am looking at the church; but I see no clock.

18. Have you not good sight? Yes, very good; but I have a very sore eye.

19. Did my cousins not come? They came as soon as you went out.

20. Did you show them my portrait? I did; but they scarcely had time to look at it.

21. Did they say where they were going? They said they were going to the country.

22. How long are they to be there? They did not tell me that.

23. Are they not coming for me to-morrow? Yes, sir, they are coming for you to go and pay a visit to Mrs. Peñaverde.

24. Have you ever seen a more comfortable little room than this one? Besides being comfortable it is very handsome.

25. Why do you not speak Spanish with Mr. Riberas? In the first place, because I do not speak it well enough; and in the second, because he speaks English very correctly.

26. I thought you were studying Spanish? I am studying it; but studying and speaking are two distinct (*distinto*) things.

27. Did you tell the music teacher that Louisa wishes to take lessons? Not yet; but I shall see him to-morrow and tell him so.

28. Why did you not take your lesson yesterday? I was sick.

29. Have you studied yesterday's lesson, and to-day's? I have studied both.

30. Will you come to-morrow at the same hour? Probably I shall.

* Major.

LESSON XXX.

IMPERSONAL VERBS.

Llover.	To rain.
Lloviendo.	Raining.
Llovido.	Rained.

Indicative.

Present.	Llueve.	It rains.
Imperfect.	Llovia.	It was raining.
Preterit definite.	Llovió.	It rained.
Future simple.	Lloverá.	It will rain.

Compound Tenses.

Preterit definite.	Ha llovido.	It has rained.
Pluperfect.	Habia llovido.	It had rained.
Anterior.	Hubo llovido.	It had rained.
Future compound.	Habrá llovido.	It will have rained.

Amanecer.	To grow light.
Anochecer.	To grow dark.
Diluviar.	To rain like a deluge, to rain in torrents.
Granizar.	To hail.
Helar.	To freeze.
Lloviznar.	To drizzle.
Nevar.	To snow.
Relampaguear.	To lighten.
Tronar.	To thunder.

PERSONAL VERBS USED IMPERSONALLY.

Bastar.	To be sufficient.
Haber.	(Signifying) there to be.
Hacer.	(Signifying) to be.
Ser.	To be.
Convenir.	To suit, to be proper.
Parecer.	To seem, to appear.

Brasil.	Brazil.	Habana.	Havana.
Menester.	Necessity.	Nieve.	Snow.
Hielo.	Ice.	Lluvia.	Rain.

LESSON XXX.

Helado.	Ice cream.	Tarde.	Afternoon.
Trueno.	Thunder.	La mañana.	Morning.
Medio dia.	Noon.	Media noche.	Midnight.
Viento.	Wind.	Especie.	Kind.

COMPOSITION.

¿Es necesario estudiar mucho para aprender el español? — Is it necessary to study much to learn Spanish?

Es menester estudiar mucho, pero no tanto como para aprender el inglés. — It is necessary to study a great deal, but not so much as to learn English.

En Nueva York llueve y llovizna mucho, pero no diluvia como en la Habana. — In New York it rains and drizzles a great deal, but it does not rain in torrents as in Havana.

En Madrid amanece muy temprano y anochece muy tarde en el verano. — In Madrid day breaks very early and night falls very late in summer.

En la Habana amanece y anochece siempre á la misma hora, en todos los dias del año. — In Havana day breaks and night falls at the same hours every day in the year.

En el Brasil no nieva; pero truena y relampaguea mucho siempre que llueve. — In Brazil it does not snow; but it thunders and lightens much whenever it rains.

En la Habana no hay hielo, porque no hace bastante frio para helar; y por eso lo llevan de Nueva York. — In Havana there is no ice, because it is not cold enough to freeze; and for that reason they take it from New York.

En Nueva York ha helado y nevado mucho este año; pero en el pasado nevó y heló muy poco. — In New York it has frozen and snowed much this year; but last year it snowed and froze very little.

¿Hace mucho calor en este pais? — Is it very warm in this country?

En los meses de Noviembre, Diciembre y Enero hace mucho frio; pero en Junio, Julio y Agosto hace mucho calor. — In the months of November, December and January it is very cold; but in June, July and August it is very warm.

¿Qué tiempo hace? — What kind of weather is it?

Parece que va á llover, porque hay mucho viento y hace calor. — It appears it is going to rain, because it is very windy and hot.

Cuatro años há, or hay cuatro años, que no veo á mi padre. — I have not seen my father for four years.

Pero V. tiene esperanza de verle pronto, porque llegará hoy à Nueva York en el vapor "Etna" que viene de Europa. — But you (have) hope to see him soon; for he will arrive to-day in New York by the steamer "Etna" (that is) coming from Europe.

En verano voy á pasear todos los dias al amanecer. — In summer I go to walk every morning at daybreak.

LESSON XXX.

¿Va V. á la cama temprano?	Do you go to bed early?
No, señor, tarde; á la media noche.	No, sir, late; at midnight.
¿Come V. al medio dia?	Do you dine at noon?
No, señor, como al anochecer.	No, sir, I dine at nightfall.
¿Va V. á la Habana?	Are you going to Havana?
No, señor, voy á Francia.	No, sir, I am going to France.
La Francia es mas alegre que la Inglaterra.	France is more pleasant than England.
El muchacho estudia mucho.	The boy studies much.
El estudio de la gramática es necesario.	The study of grammar is necessary.
El hombre necesita trabajar.	Man requires to work.
La conversacion es muy útil para aprender una lengua.	Conversation is very useful for learning a language.

EXPLANATION.

142. IMPERSONAL VERBS are those which are used only in the infinitive mood and in the third person singular of all the tenses, and have no definite subject; as,

Llueve.	It rains.
Tronará.	It will thunder.
Nevaba.	It was snowing.

143. The verbs *amanecer* and *anochecer* are sometimes used in the three persons, both numbers; but then they are not impersonal, but neuter; as,

Yo amanecí en Nueva York, y anochecí en Filadelfia.	I was in New York at daybreak, and in Philadelphia at nightfall.

144. HABER and HACER are often used impersonally, and are in such cases to be rendered into English by the corresponding tenses of the verb *to be*.

The verb *haber*, when conjugated impersonally, has the peculiarity of taking a *y* in the third person of the present indicative; as,

Hay mucha fruta.	There is much fruit.
Habrá muchos hombres.	There will be many men.
Hizo frio.	It was cold.
Hace muchos años.	Many years ago.

N. B.—*Há* is sometimes elegantly used for *hay;* as,

Doce años há, *or* hay doce años.	Twelve years ago;

but it is to be observed that *há* always follows the time, while *hay* precedes it.

There are many other verbs which, although not impersonal, are sometimes used as such; as,

Es muy tarde.	It is very late.
Es preciso.	It is necessary.
Es menester.	There is necessity.
Parece.	It seems, it appears.
Conviene.	It suits, it is proper.
Basta.	It is sufficient, it will do.

145. As it may have been observed, the pronoun *it*, which accompanies impersonal verbs in English, is not translated into Spanish.

Nouns taken in a definite sense require the article; as,

El muchacho estudia.	The boy studies.
El estudio de la gramática es útil.	The study of grammar is useful.

Nouns used in their most general sense are preceded by the article; as,

El hombre necesita trabajar.	Man requires to work.
La conversacion es muy útil para aprender una lengua.	Conversation is very useful for learning a language.

146. Names of nations, countries, provinces, mountains, rivers and seasons, generally take the article; as,

La España.	Spain.
La Inglaterra.	England.
El invierno.	Winter.

147. Nations, countries and provinces, when preceded by a preposition, do not take the article unless they are personified; as,

Las provincias de España.	The provinces of Spain.
El valor de la España.	The courage of Spain.

Nevertheless, the article is employed under all circumstances with the names of some places; as,

El Brasil.	Brazil.
La Habana.	Havana.
El Ferrol.	Ferrol.
La China.	China.
El Japon.	Japan.
El Perú.	Peru.

LESSON XXX.

CONVERSATION AND VERSION.

1. ¿Qué tiempo hace? Ahora hace calor; ántes hacia frio.
2. ¿Lloverá mañana? Creo que nevará.
3. ¿Llueve mucho en Nueva York? Llueve y llovizna bastante; pero raramente diluvia.
4. ¿Hace mucho frio en la Habana en el mes de Enero? Hace alguno, pero nunca nieva ni hiela.
5. ¿Relampaguea? Relampaguea y llovizna.
6. ¿Porqué escribe V. tantos ejercicios? Porque para aprender una lengua no basta hablarla, es necesario tambien saber escribirla.
7. ¿Nieva mucho en el Brasil? En el Brasil no nieva, mas que en las montañas, donde hay nieve todo el año.
8. ¿Quiere V. tomar un helado? No, señor, los helados no son buenos en este tiempo.
9. ¿Cuánto tiempo hace que no ve V. á su familia? El dos de Setiembre próximo hará once años.
10. ¿Porqué no vino V. anoche? Porque llovia y hacia mucho viento.
11. ¿Tiene V. miedo de los truenos? Cuando relampaguea mucho, sí señor.
12. ¿Porqué no fué V. anoche al concierto? Porque lloviznaba y estaba nevando.
13. ¿A qué horas come V.? Al amanecer tomo chocolate; al medio dia como, y al anochecer tomo el té.
14. ¿Se levanta V. al amanecer todos los dias? Cuando es menester, sí señor.
15. ¿A qué hora salió V. del teatro el sábado? A media noche.
16. ¿Cuándo salieron sus hermanas para el campo? Ayer al medio dia.
17. ¿Cuándo volverán? Pasado mañana por la noche.
18. ¿A qué hora amanece en el verano? En verano amanece á las cinco y anochece á las siete y media.
19. ¿Porqué se marcha V. tan pronto? Porque es menester.
20. ¿Es menester salir al amanecer? No, basta salir al medio dia.
21. ¿Hay muchos Alemanes en Nueva York? Sí, señor, hay muchísimos.
22. ¿Cuántos dias hace que no le ve V.? No hace mas que uno.
23. ¿Hay algun Frances en su casa de V.? Hay cuatro Franceses y una Francesa.
24. ¿Cuándo vinieron Vds.? Ayer al medio dia.
25. ¿Cree V. qué lloverá hoy? Parece que sí, porque hace mucho viento y mucho calor.

26. ¿Llovió mucho aquí el año pasado? Aquí llovió mucho, pero en la Habana llovió mas.

27. ¿Nieva mucho en este país? En el invierno nieva mucho.

28. ¿Se hiela el agua? Muchas veces.

29. ¿Habrá mucho hielo el año próximo? En el invierno habrá mucho hielo.

30. ¿Hace mucho frio? Sí, señor, y al amanecer llovia y granizaba.

31. ¿Porqué hace tanto frio hoy? Porque nevó ayer.

EXERCISE.

1. Is it raining? I do not know.

2. You do not know? How, are you still in bed?—Yes, and I shall be until 7 o'clock.

3. At what o'clock did you go to bed? At midnight.

4. What is it necessary to do in order to learn Spanish? It is necessary to study a good grammar, talk a great deal with Spaniards, and read the works of good authors.

5. What were you doing in the garden this morning at daybreak? I was walking.

6. Have you read the Spanish newspaper yet that I lent* you? Yes, sir, here it is. Thank you.

7. What language do they speak in Brazil? Portuguese (*portugues*).

8. Do you see that lightning†? Yes, it is lightening and thundering very much.

9. Is it proper to have the windows open when it thunders? No, it is better to have them shut (cerradas).

10. I think (it appears to me) it will soon rain. Yes, I think so too; it is already drizzling.

11. John! Sir. Is there any water in my room?—No, sir, but if you wish, I shall take some there now.

12. In what months of the year does it freeze most in New York? During (*durante*) the months of January and February.

13. I believe there is a great deal of ice used (*se usa*) in New York during the summer. A great deal, and it is very cheap.

14. It appears that there will be little ice next summer. Very little, the winter has not been cold enough to have much.

15. What watch is that you have there? It is the one I always had.

16. I thought you had given your watch to Charles, and bought your (the) neighbor's? No, Charles has a very pretty little watch.

17. What o'clock is it by your watch? It is just four o'clock (*son las cuatro en punto*).

* Prestar. † Relámpago.

LESSON XXXI.

18. Who knocked at the door just now? It was Mrs. Martinez; it is thundering, and you know she is afraid of the lightning.
19. Why did she not come in? She did not like to (would not) disturb you (*molestarla á V.*) madam.
20. Do you know whether Alexander has sent the papers to his brother yet? I think he has (*me parece que sí*).
21. Did you take him the two volumes I showed him yesterday? I took them to him this morning.
22. Was he in the house when you went? No, madam, he had just gone out.
23. Will you open that window, if you please? With pleasure.
24. And this one also? No, thank you; it is better to have that one shut.
25. What kind of weather is it to-day? Very bad; it has been raining and hailing ever since (*desde*) daybreak.
26. Madam, here are two beautiful bouquets that Mrs. Garcia has sent you from her garden. She is very kind (*buena*).
27. Who brought them? Her servant (*fem.*).
28. When did she bring them? You had no sooner gone out than she came.
29. How windy it was last night! Yes, and it rained in torrents the whole night, from nightfall until daybreak this morning.
30. What news is there from Europe? I do not know; I have not yet seen the newspapers.

LESSON XXXI.

| Gustar. | To like, to please. |

PRESENT.

(A mí) me gusta *or* gustan.	I like it or them.
(A tí) te gusta "	Thou likest it or them.
(A él) le gusta "	He likes it "
(A nosotros) nos gusta, *or* gustan.	We like it "
(A vosotros) os gusta, "	You like it "
(A ellos) les gusta. "	They like it "

IMPERFECT.

(A mí) me gustaba *or* gustaban.	I liked it or them.
(A tí) te gustaba, etc.	Thou likedst it, &c.

LESSON XXXI.

| Gustar de. | To be fond of. |

PRESENT.

Gusto de.	I am fond of.
Gustas de.	Thou art fond of.
Gusta de.	He is fond of.
Gustamos de.	We are fond of.
Gustais de.	You are fond of.
Gustan de.	They are fond of.

IMPERFECT.

| Gustaba de. | I was or used to be fond of. |
| Gustabas de, etc. | Thou wast or used to be fond of, &c. |

| Gustar. | To taste. |

Placer.	To please.
Pesar (*impersonal*).	To regret.
Pesar (*in all its persons*).	To weigh.
Faltar *or* hacer falta.	To want.
Faltar.	To fail, to be wanting or missing.
Acomodar.	To suit, to accommodate.
Convenir.	To suit, to be convenient.
Importar.	To be important.

Cerca.	Near.
Léjos.	Far.
Dentro.	Within.
Fuera.	Without.

Bello.	Beautiful, fine.
Posible.	Possible.
Imposible.	Impossible.

Poeta.	Poet.	Poesia.	Poetry, poem.
Pintor.	Painter.	Pintura.	Painting.
Escultor.	Sculptor.	Escultura.	Sculpture.
Placer.	Pleasure.	Prosa.	Prose.
Dios.	God.	Fruta.	Fruit.
Pesar.	Regret, sorrow.	Manzana.	Apple.
Melon.	Melon.	Naranja.	Orange.
Melocoton.	Peach.	Artes (*plu.*).	Arts.
Arte.	Art, skill.	Arroba.	Arroba.

LESSON XXXI.

COMPOSITION.

¿Le gusta á V. la fruta?	Do you like fruit?
Sí, señor, me gustan las naranjas y los melones.	Yes, sir, I like oranges and melons.
A mí me gustan los melocotones y las manzanas.	I like peaches and apples.
¿Cuál de las bellas artes le gusta á V. mas?	Which of the fine arts do you like best?
Me gustan todas, la música, la poesía, la pintura y la escultura.	I like them all, music, poetry, painting and sculpture.
¿Va V. á la ópera muy á menudo?	Do you go to the opera very often?
Voy dos ó tres veces por semana.	I go two or three times a week.
Me parece que lloverá pronto, y me gusta porque tengo un gran placer en ver llover.	It appears to me that it will soon rain, and I am glad of it (I like it), because I find (have a) great pleasure in seeing it rain.
¡Es posible! A mí no me gusta ver llover; pero me gusta muchísimo ver nevar.	Is it possible! I do not like to see it rain; but I like to see it snow.
¿Le acomoda á V. ese caballo?	Does that horse suit you?
No me conviene, porque es muy viejo, así que no lo compraré.	It does not suit (or answer) me, because it is very old, so that I shall not buy it.
¿Vive V. cerca ó léjos de aquí?	Do you live near here, or far away?
Vivo muy cerca.	I live very near.
¿Vive V. dentro ó fuera de la ciudad?	Do you live in or out of town?
Ahora en la ciudad; pero en el verano vivo en el campo.	In town now, but in the country in summer.
¿Qué le falta á V. para ser feliz?	What do you want (is wanting to you) to be happy?
No me falta nada, gracias á Dios.	I want nothing, thank God.
Deseo conocer al pintor cuya pintura tiene V. en su cuarto.	I desire (or wish) to know the painter whose painting you have in your room.
¿Le pesa á V. de no haber estado en el concierto?	Do you regret not having been at the concert?
Me pesa mucho de no haber estado, porque no tuve el placer de ver á su amigo de V.	I deeply (very much) regret not having been there, for I had not the pleasure of seeing your friend.
A mí me pesa de ello tambien.	I regret it too (also).

EXPLANATION.

148. GUSTAR, derived from the noun *gusto*, pleasure, and signifying literally *to give pleasure to*, is the verb by which we translate *to like*; but in passing from English to Spanish, the nominative case or subject becomes the objective, and the latter is preceded by the preposition *á*; as,

¿Le gusta á V. la poesía?	Do you like poetry?
Me gusta (*or* á mí me gusta) mucho.	I like it very much.

149. GUSTAR, followed by the preposition *de*, means *to be fond of*, and sentences in which it is used are constructed as in English; as,

Yo gusto de la música.	I am fond of music.
El gusta de la poesía.	He is fond of poetry.

150. GUSTAR, used as an active verb, means *to taste*, and governs the objective, without the aid of any preposition whatever; as,

¿Gusta V. la sopa?	Do you taste the soup?
No, señor, gusto la carne.	No, sir, I taste the meat.

151. The verbs *pesar*, to regret; *faltar*, in the sense of to want, or *hacer falta*, to have need of; *acomodar*, to suit; *convenir*, to suit; *importar*, to be important; *placer*, to please, and some others, require the same idiomatic construction of the sentence as that explained in the case of *gustar*; as,

Nos falta (*or* nos hace falta) dinero.	We want (*or* are in want of) money.
A V. le importa ese negocio.	That business is important to you.
Mucho me place.	It pleases me much.

This last verb is defective, and is very little used, except in the present and imperfect of the subjunctive mood, as will be seen in the proper place.

152. The verb *pesar*, when meaning *to regret*, generally takes the preposition *de* after it; as,

Me pesa de ello.	I am sorry for it.

CONVERSATION AND VERSION.

1. ¿Le gusta á V. la ópera? Cuando era jóven me gustaba mas que ahora.

2. ¿Vendrá V. mañana á comer con nosotros? Sí, señor, no faltaré.

3. ¿Necesita V. hoy su reloj? Hoy no me hace falta, mañana me convendrá tenerlo.

4. ¿Quiere V. saber lo que he hecho hoy? No me importa saberlo.

LESSON XXXI.

5. ¿Compra V. el caballo del inglés? No, señor, no me conviene: es muy caro.
6. Dicen que es muy bueno. No importa.
7. ¿Porqué vive V. tan léjos de la ciudad? Porque no me gustan vecinos.
8. Antes vivia V. cómodamente cerca de la poblacion. Sí; pero ahora no me gusta.
9. ¿Cuántas arrobas pesa V.? Peso ocho arrobas y cinco libras.
10. ¿Ha visto V. á su prima? No, señor, y me pesa mucho de ello.
11. ¿Cuánto pesa su niño de V.? No sé, porque no lo hemos pesado aun.
12. ¿Quiere V. ir á paseo con D. Cárlos, nuestro vecino? No quiero ir con él porque habla mucho, y no me gustan los habladores.
13. No obstante, el año pasado estaba V. en buena amistad con él. Sí; pero ahora me pesa y me pesará siempre.
14. ¿Nunca serán Vds. amigos otra vez? Jamás: es imposible.
15. ¿Porqué? No puedo decírselo á V.
16. ¿Eso no le gustará á él? Nada me importa.
17. ¿Estan Vds. comiendo pan? No, señor, estamos comiendo fruta.
18. ¿Gusta V.?* Sí, comeré una manzana.
19. ¿No le gustan á V. los melones? Sí, señor; pero me gustan mas los melocotones y las naranjas.
20. ¿Quién es aquella señorita tan bella que paseaba ayer con V. en el parque? Es una amiga mia.
21. ¿Qué son los hombres que vinieron ántes de ayer con V.? El uno es poeta, el otro pintor y escultor el otro.
22. ¿Cuál de las bellas artes le gusta á V. mas? Todas me gustan; pero la poesía mas que las otras.
23. ¿Le gusta á V. leer una bella poesía? Sí, señor, me gusta mucho.
24. ¿Hace mucho frio hoy? Fuera hace bastante; pero dentro de casa hace muy poco.
25. ¿Porqué no fué V. al baile anoche? Porque no me gustan los bailes.
26. ¿Es posible que siendo tan jóven no le gustan á V.? A mí me importa estudiar; no bailar.
27. ¿Porqué no quiere V. bailar? Porque estoy cansado..
28. ¿Qué es lo que le hace falta á V. para ser feliz? Nada me hace falta por ahora, gracias á Dios.
29. ¿Qué le falta á V.? Me falta el sombrero.
30. Aquí está. ¿Se marcha V.?—Sí, señor, si V. no manda otra cosa.

* Do you wish?

LESSON XXXI.

EXERCISE.

1. Are your brothers and sisters fond of study? They are not so fond of it as some children I have known.

2. Do they ever read poetry? Sometimes, but not very often.

3. Do you understand Spanish poetry? Not yet; but I understand prose perfectly well.

4. Do you ever eat fruit? Yes, I am very fond of apples, oranges, peaches and melons.

5. Is that gentleman a sculptor? No, madam, he is a painter, and enjoys a high reputation.

6. Do you know that it is raining? Raining! no, I did not (know it).

7. Do you think it is going to thunder? I think it is (I think so).

8. Then it is imposible to go out? By no means (*de ningun modo*); we are not afraid of lightning.

9. Does it always lighten when it rains? Not always.

10. Good morning, Mr. Retortillo, how do you do? Very well, thank you; and how are you (and you)?

11. What do you wish? I have come to see if this letter is correctly written. It is perfectly correct.

12. Who wrote that letter? A friend of mine, who writes Spanish very well.

13. Why do you not learn Spanish yourself? I have no time, and I regret it very much.

14. What profession (*profesion*) do you like best? Of all professions I like that of a physician best.

15. When did you see Miss Meléndez? I had the pleasure of seeing her the other day.

16. How do you like (*qué tal*) your new piano? Very much.

17. Who is your music teacher? I have none just now; but I used to have a German teacher.

18. How much do you weigh? I weigh a hundred and sixty-five pounds (*libras*).

19. Does Charles weigh as much as Alexander? No, sir, Alexander weighs twenty pounds more.

20. Is Mr. Martínez at home? No, sir, he is out.

21. When will he be in? I do not know; he did not say (it) when he was going out (*al salir*).

22. Does your uncle live in or out of town? In summer he lives out of town.

23. When he is in town where does he live? In Twenty-second street, near Fifth Avenue.

24. How did you spend your time when you were in the country? I walked morning and evening, and during the day I read the beautiful poems of Zorrilla and Espronceda.

25. Have you ever read any of Martínez de la Rosa's poems? Yes, but I do not like them so well as those of Meléndez.

26. Which is the greatest Spanish painter? Spain has had a great number of excellent painters, but the most celebrated of all are Murillo and Velázquez.

27. Are your cousins pleased with their new house? I believe so; but they say they liked the old one better.

28. Where did they live before taking the house in which they reside now? In Fourteenth street, near Seventh avenue.

29. Are they not comfortable in the new one? It is not for that; but they are very fond of flowers, and they have no garden now.

30. Will you come out and take a walk with me? Yes, if Emanuel comes with us; if not, I shall go and practise on the piano.

LESSON XXXII.

Poder. (*See this verb at the end of the book.*)	To be able; may, &c.
Esperar.	To expect, to wait for, to hope.
Castigar.	To punish.
Engañar.	To deceive, to cheat.
Quemar.	To burn.
Tratar.	To treat; to have intercourse with.
Tratar de.	To endeavor, to try, to treat of.
Tratar en.	To deal in.
Seguir. (*See this verb at the end of the book.*)	To follow.

ADVERBS AND ADVERBIAL PHRASES.

Casi.	Almost, nearly.
¿Cuánto tiempo?	How long?
Cuanto ántes.	As soon as possible.
De Moda.	Fashionable.
De balde. } Gratis. }	Gratis; for nothing.
De cuando en cuando.	From time to time; now and then.

De improviso.	Suddenly, unexpectedly, unawares.
De veras. / Verdaderamente.	Indeed, truly.
En lo sucesivo.	In future.
Hasta no mas.	To the utmost, to the extreme.
Poco á poco.	Little by little, by degrees, gently.
Por supuesto.	Of course.
Tal vez. / Acaso.	Perhaps.

Pícaro.	Rogue (roguish).	Coqueta.	Coquette.
Bribon.	Rascal.	Sociedad.	Society.
Ejemplo.	Example; instance.	Política.	Politics.

COMPOSITION.

Mi hermano es castigado algunas veces por no saber sus lecciones.	My brother is sometimes punished for not knowing his lessons.
Y su amigo de V. Alejandro, ¿lo es alguna vez?	And your friend Alexander, is he ever punished (ever so)?
Lo es de cuando en cuando; pero mi hermana no ha sido castigada jamás, porque sabe siempre sus lecciones.	He is, now and then; but my sister has never been punished, because she always knows her lessons.
¿Ha sido V. engañado alguna vez?	Have you ever been deceived?
Hasta no mas, porque hay muchos pícaros en la sociedad.	To the utmost, for there are a great many rogues in society.
Esta casa está bien situada.	This house is well situated.
La carta estaba mal escrita.	The letter was badly written.
Manuel es amado de (or por) Margarita.	Emanuel is loved by Margaret.
El libro ha sido escrito por un Frances.	The book was written by a Frenchman.
Se quemó (or fué quemada) la casa.	The house was burnt.
Esta casa se hizo en seis meses.	This house was built (made) in six months.
¿En cuánto tiempo se hizo la de V.?	How long was yours in building (making)?
En cosa de tres meses.	About three months.
¿Cuánto tiempo necesita V. para escribir esa carta?	How long shall you be in writing that letter?
Está casi acabada; estoy con V. en un minuto.	It is almost finished; I shall be (am) with you in a moment (minute).
Poco á poco; va V. muy aprisa.	Gently: you go very quick.
Tal vez; pero tengo prisa y quiero acabar pronto.	Perhaps so; but I am in haste, and I want to get done (finish) soon.

LESSON XXXII.

¿De veras?	Indeed?
Por supuesto: tengo que ir al correo.	Of course: I have to go to the post-office.
✓ Dios está en todas partes, lo sabe y lo puede todo, y nos perdonará si tratamos de hacer nuestro deber.	God is everywhere; He knows all things, and nothing is impossible for Him (can do all); and He will pardon us, if we endeavor to do our duty.
✓ ¿Es su reloj de V. de moda?	Is your watch fashionable?
✓ Sí, señor; pero no me gusta, porque es muy pequeño.	Yes, sir; but I do not like it, because it is too small.

EXPLANATION.

153. PASSIVE VOICE.—This voice is formed by the different tenses of the auxiliary *ser* added to the past participle of the verb, care being taken that the participle agree with the subject, in gender and number, like an adjective; as,

Soy amado.	I am loved.
Hemos sido amados.	We have been loved.
Habeis sido amadas.	You have been loved.
Serás amada.	Thou wilt be loved.

(*a*). The passive voice is, however, formed in Spanish, by *estar*, instead of *ser*, when the past participle is used adjectively, that is to say, when the state or condition of the subject is described without any reference to an action; as,

Esta casa *está* bien *situada*.	This house *is* well *located*.
La carta *estaba* mal escrita.	The letter was badly written.

154. The passive verb formed by *ser* is used in Spanish in the present and imperfect of the indicative mood, only when it is designed to express a mental act; as,

Manuel *es* amado de Margarita.	Emanuel *is* loved by Margaret.

When a mental act is not expressed, the passive verb being in the present or imperfect of the indicative mood, *estar* is the auxiliary to be used, and not *ser*; as,

El libro *ha sido* escrito por un Frances, *or* el libro *está* escrito por un Frances (instead of *es escrito*).	The book was written by a Frenchman.

155. When the action of the verb refers to the mind, the preposition *de* or *por* may be used after the passive verb, before the agent, and *por* only, when otherwise; as,

Manuel es amado *de* (or *por*) Margarita.	Emanuel is loved by Margaret.

156. The passive voice in English is very frequently turned into Spanish by putting the verb which is in the participle past in English, in the same person and number as the auxiliary *to be* in the English sentence, and placing the pronoun *se* before it.

157. The latter form is preferred when the object, or receiver, of the action is an inanimate thing, or when the subject, or agent, remains undetermined; as,

Se quemó la casa.	The house was burnt.
Esta casa *se* hizo en seis meses.	This house was built (made) in six months.

CONVERSATION AND VERSION.

1. ¿No puede V. esperar? Esperaré un poco.

2. ¿No me engañará V.? Por supuesto que no; yo no soy ningun pícaro.

3. Buenos dias. ¿De qué estan Vds. tratando?—Estabamos hablando de modas.

4. ¿Puedo V. decirme si mi sombrero es de moda? No es de la última (moda).

5. ¿Cuánto tiempo hace que pasó esta moda? Habrá ya un mes, poco mas ó ménos.

6. ¿Quiere V. quemar las cartas de esa señorita? Sí, señor, porque es una coqueta.

7. ¿De veras? Yo creia que era una señorita de mucha circunspeccion. Hace algun tiempo lo era; pero poco á poco ha ido siguiendo el ejemplo de otras.

8. ¿Tal vez el ser coqueta es de moda en la sociedad del dia? Asi lo creo.

9. V. debe excusar á las niñas; ellas son inocentes y no creen hacer mal en eso.

10. ¿Ha sido V. engañado alguna vez? Hasta no mas; porque hay muchos pícaros.

11. ¿Han sido castigados sus niños de V.? Sí, señor, han sido castigados por no saber sus lecciones.

LESSON XXXII.

12. ¿Y aquel criado tan bueno que V. tenia? Es un bribon; no lo quiero ni de balde.
13. ¿De veras? V. lo trataba muy bien. Acaso por lo mismo que yo lo trataba bien, me ha tratado él tan mal.
14. ¿Le gusta á V. la sociedad? Sí, señor, de cuando en cuando.
15. ¿Porqué no vive V., entónces, en la ciudad? Porque se me quemó la casa.
16. ¿Cuánto tiempo hace? Casi un mes.
17. Y ahora, ¿no va V. nunca allá? Voy de cuando en cuando.
18. Eso es verdaderamente un gran mal; pero en lo sucesivo tendrá V. mas cuidado.—Por supuesto que sí.
19. ¿No pudo V. saber quién le quemó la casa? No; pero creo que fué un bribon, que me queria mal.
20. ¿Quiere V. acabar ya? Sí, cuanto ántes; no puedo esperar mas.
21. ¿Qué piensa V. hacer ahora? Trato de castigar al que me quemó la casa.
22. ¿Y despues? Despues veré si puedo hacer otra.
23. ¿Y no tiene V. ahora ninguna allá? Tengo una hecha de improviso.
24. Poco á poco irá V. haciendo otra. Así lo espero.
25. ¿Por supuesto que su señora vivirá en la ciudad? Sí; pero va allá de cuando en cuando; el otro dia llegó de improviso, cuando ménos la esperaba.
26. ¿No puede V. volver mañana por aquí? Mañana tal vez no, pero pasado sí.
27. Entónces lo espero á V. sin falta. Puede V. esperarme; no faltaré.
28. ¿Irá V. hoy á la comedia ó á la ópera? Tal vez iré á la ópera, porque es mas de moda.
29. ¿Nunca va V. á la comedia? Sí; voy de cuando en cuando.
30. ¿Sabe V. que se ha quemado la Academia (*academy*) de Música? Sí; anoche lo leí en los periódicos.

EXERCISE.

1. Papa, may I go out? Yes, you may go out for half an hour.
2. How long is it since your house was burnt? Only three weeks.
3. Why does that woman punish her children so much? She always punishes them when they do wrong (*obrar mal*).
4. Does she reward (*recompensar*) them when they do right? I believe she does.
5. Why do you burn all that young lady's letters? Because she is only a coquette.

6. I think you are not right; I have known her a long time, and I believe she is very circumspect (*circumspecta*).

7. Why do your family always live in the country? Because we do not like society.

8. And is it not possible to live in town without going into society? It is impossible.

9. We always live in town, and yet (*sin embargo*) we never go into society.

10. Peter, can you write that letter for me now? I can.

11. When do you want it? As soon as possible.

12. Have you ever been deceived by that man? Yes, very often; he is a rascal.

13. How long have you known him? Not long; but each time I have had business with him, he has deceived me.

14. Indeed! What business is he in? I cannot tell you.

15. Do you often go to the theatre? Never to the theatre; I go to the opera now and then.

16. Can you tell me whether my hat is fashionable? Yes, it is in the latest fashion.

17. Is Peter's the fashion too? No, those hats went out of fashion last year.

18. Where is your old servant? He lives with us no longer.

19. Did you give Charles the fruit you were to buy for him? No, he came for it the other day, but I had not had time to buy it.

20. Why did you come so late to-day to your lesson? My exercise was very difficult, and I could not finish it in time.

21. Well, I hope you will come in time in future? Yes, in future I shall come at four o'clock precisely.

22. I hope you will not deceive me? Of course I shall not; I never deceive anybody.

23. Will that young gentleman * be at the concert with you to-morrow night? Perhaps he will come with us.

24. Does he not go every night? Indeed I do not know.

25. How long is it since you began to take lessons? About (*cerca de*) four months.

26. And do your brother and sister take their lessons at the same hour as you? No, my brother takes his at ten o'clock, and my sister at twelve.

27. Where did you become acquainted with the gentleman who danced last with your cousin (*fem.*) yesterday evening? I made his acquaintance in Madrid the year before last (hace dos años).

28. Has this young man deceived you as often as his father? He has;

* Caballerito.

you know children almost always follow the example of their parents (*padres*).

29. Do you think Charles is loved by Louisa? I think she loves him as much as it is possible to love.

30. What did you tell the tailor? I told him you wanted your coat and vest for the day after to-morrow.

LESSON XXXIII.

REFLECTIVE VERBS.

INFINITIVE MOOD.

Lavar*se*.	To wash one's self.
Haber*se* lavado.	To have washed one's self.
Haber*se* de lavar.	To have to wash one's self.

GERUND.

Lavándo*se*.	Washing one's self.
Habiéndo*se* lavado.	Having washed one's self.
Habiéndo*se* de lavar.	Having to wash one's self.

INDICATIVE PRESENT.

(Yo) me lavo.	I wash myself.
(Tú) te lavas.	Thou washest thyself.
(Él) se lava.	He washes himself.
(Nosotros) nos lavamos.	We wash ourselves.
(Vosotros) os lavais.	You wash yourselves.
(Ellos) se lavan.	They wash themselves.

(*The other simple tenses are conjugated in like manner.*)

PRETERIT INDEFINITE.

(Yo) me he lavado.	I have washed myself.
(Tú) te has lavado.	Thou hast washed thyself.
(Él) se ha lavado.	He has washed himself.
(Nosotros) nos hemos lavado.	We have washed ourselves.
(Vosotros) os habeis lavado.	You have washed yourselves.
(Ellos) se han lavado.	They have washed themselves.

(*The other compound tenses are conjugated in like manner.*)

Cortar.	To cut.
Cortar*se*.	To cut one's self; to be ashamed.
Afeitar.	To shave.

LESSON XXXIII.

Afeitarse.	To shave one's self.
Levantar.	To raise, to lift.
Levantarse.	To get up, to rise.
Cansar.	To weary, to fatigue, to tire.
Cansarse.	To tire one's self, to get tired.
Descansar.	To rest.
Contentar.	To content, to please.
Contentarse.	To content one's self.
Burlar.	To mock, to jest.
Burlarse.	To jest, to make jest of, to laugh at.
Preguntar.	To question, to ask, to enquire.
Responder.	To answer.
Engañarse.	To deceive one's self.
Temer. Reir.	To fear. To laugh.

Arriba.	Up.
Abajo.	Down.
Detrás.	Behind.
Encima.	Upon, above.
Debajo.	Under.
Luego.	Presently.
Qué tal?	How; how do you do?
Descansadamente.	Easily.
De burlas.	In jest.

Descansado.	Rested.
Contento.	Content.

Barbero.	Barber.	Pregunta.	Question, query.
Cansancio.	Weariness, fatigue.	Respuesta.	Answer.
Descanso.	Rest.	Burla.	Jest.
Contento.	Contentment.	Declinacion.	Declination.
Respondon.	Ever ready to reply.	Derivacion.	Derivation.
Cuchillo.	Knife.	Disposicion.	Disposition.
Pelo ó cabello.	Hair.	Uña.	Nail (finger).

COMPOSITION.

¿A qué hora se levantó V. ayer?	At what o'clock did you get up yesterday?
Me levantó temprano; me levanto al amanecer todos los dias.	I rose early; I rise at daybreak every morning.
¿Qué hizo V. entónces?	What did you do next (then)?
Me afeité y salí.	I shaved myself and went out.

LESSON XXXIII.

¿Se lava V. ántes de afeitarse?	Do you wash yourself before shaving (yourself)?
Me afeito ántes de lavarme.	I shave before washing myself.
¿Son fáciles de aprender las palabras declinacion, derivacion, y disposicion?	Are the words declination, derivation and disposition easy to learn?
Son facilísimas, porque casi todas las palabras que acaban en *cion* son lo mismo en inglés, cambiando la *c* en *t*.	They are very easy, because all words ending in *cion* are the same in English, changing the *c* into *t*.
Tengo un barbero que afeita muy bien, pero es carísimo; ¿qué tal afeita el de V.?	I have a barber that shaves very well, but he is exceedingly high (dear); how does your's shave?
El mio no afeita muy bien; pero es baratísimo, porque me afeito yo mismo.	Mine does not shave very well; but he is very cheap, for I shave myself.
Ahora me afeita el barbero, porque me he cortado la mano y no puedo afeitarme yo mismo.	The barber shaves me at present (now), because I (have) cut my hand, and I cannot shave myself.
¿Porqué se burla V. de su amigo?	Why do you make fun of your friend?
Me burlo de él porque se levanta muy tarde.	I make fun of him because he gets up very late.
¿Se ha cansado V. de estudiar?	Have you got tired of studying?
No, señor, porque cuando me canso de estudiar, descanso escribiendo.	No, sir; because when I get tired at study, I rest myself writing.
¿Ama V. á su hermano?	Do you love your brother?
Nos amamos el uno al otro.	We love each other.
¿Le gusta á V. mas preguntar que responder?	Do you like better to ask questions than to answer?
No, señor, yo no soy pregunton, y me gusta hacer ámbas cosas.	No, sir, I am not inquisitive; I like to do both.
Yo no trabajo mucho, lo hago descansadamente.	I do not work much; I do it at my ease.
¿Se engaña V. á sí mismo alguna vez?	Do you ever deceive yourself?
V. habla de burlas; ¿puede uno engañarse á sí mismo jamás?	You speak in jest; can one ever deceive one's self?
Por supuesto que sí.	Certainly (so).
¿Está su amigo de V. abajo ó arriba?	Is your friend up-stairs or down-stairs?
¿Está mi libro debajo ó encima de la mesa?	Is my book upon or under the table?
¿Qué tal le gusta á V. Nueva York?	How do you like New York?

EXPLANATION.

158. REFLECTIVE VERBS.—Almost all active verbs may become reflective in Spanish, and be used as pronominal. The pronoun object must be of the same person as that of the subject, and each person is conjugated with a double personal pronoun. However, the pronoun subject is almost always understood in Spanish, while in English it is expressed; as,

Infinitive. Amarse.	To love one's self.
Part. Pres. Amándose.	Loving one's self.

INDICATIVE PRESENT.

Me amo.	I love myself.
Te amas.	Thou lovest thyself.
Se ama.	He loves himself.
Nos amamos.	We love ourselves.
Os amais.	You love yourselves.
Se aman.	They love themselves.

And in the same manner in all the other tenses.

159. When an agent performs an action upon a part of himself, the verb is made reflective; and the possessive pronouns, *my*, *his*, etc., are translated into Spanish by the article *el*, *la*, *los*, *las*; as,

Me corto *el* cabello.	I cut *my* hair.
Se corta *las* uñas.	He cuts *his* nails.

160. When the verb denotes a *reciprocity* of action between two or more individuals, it is formed, in Spanish, in the same manner as the plural of *reflective* verbs; as,

Nos amamos.	We love one another.
Os engañasteis.	You deceived each other.
Se temerán.	They will fear each other.

CONVERSATION AND VERSION.

1. ¿Se ha afeitado V.? Ni me he lavado ni afeitado.
2. ¿Cuántas veces lava la criada á los niños? Los lava por la mañana, al medio dia y á la noche.
3. ¿Cuándo les corta las uñas? Se las corta los miércoles y los sábados.
4. ¿Se lavantan temprano? A las seis en verano, y á las siete en invierno.
5. ¿Porqué no se levantó V. hoy mas temprano? Porque el criado no me despertó.
6. ¿No despierta V. temprano? Cuando estoy cansado, no.
7. ¿Estaba V. muy cansado ayer? Sí, señor, el paseo me cansó mucho.

LESSON XXXIII.

8. Entónces, ¿querrá V. descansar hoy todo el dia? No, he descansado ya bastante durante la noche.
9. ¿Con cuánto dinero se contenta V.? Yo me contento con poco.
10. ¿Se contentará V. con diez pesos? Se burla V. de mí.
11. No, yo solamente pregunto.—V. me pregunta y yo respondo que no.
12. ¿Habla V. de burlas ó de veras? Hablo de veras; yo no me contento con ménos de cien pesos.
13. ¿Se burla V. de mí? No, señor, yo nunca hablo de burlas; y V. tendrá que contentarse con lo que se le ha dado ya.
14. V. es quien se engaña.—El engañado será V., yo no.
15. ¿Para qué llama V. al barbero? Para afeitarme.
16. ¿Porqué no se afeita V. mismo? Porque tengo miedo de cortarme.
17. ¿Dónde está el cuchillo? Está sobre la mesa.
18. ¿Adónde va V.? Voy á cortarme el pelo.
19. ¿Dónde vive su barbero? Vive detrás de la iglesia.
20. ¿Preguntó V. al criado por mis botas? Sí, señor, me dijo que estaban bajo de la cama.
21. ¿Sale V. ahora á paseo? No, señor, saldré despues.
22. ¿Qué tal está su amigo de V.? Ahora está mas contento.
23. ¿Qué tal es el criado que tiene V. ahora? Es muy respondon.
24. ¿Dónde está su padre de V., arriba ó abajo? Antes estaba abajo, ahora me parece que está arriba.
25. ¿Qué tal ha pasado V. la noche? Muy descansadamente; he dormido muy bien.
26. ¿Cómo estan escritos los ejercicios de su gramática de V.? Estan por preguntas y respuestas.
27. ¿Hizo V. la pregunta que le dije? Sí; pero no me dieron respuesta.
28. ¿De qué trata la leccion de hoy? De la declinacion y derivacion de los nombres, y de la disposicion de las palabras en la composicion.
29. ¿Qué está V. leyendo? Las disposiciones del rey Carlos III.
30. ¿Aprende bien el español su amigo de V.? No, señor, tiene muy poca disposicion para las lenguas.
31. ¿Qué hizo V. ayer despues que se levantó? Me lavé y me afeité.
32. ¿Se cansó V. mucho ayer? Sí, señor, me cansó mucho el paseo al parque.
33. ¿Necesita V. descanso? Descanso bastante de noche.

EXERCISE.

1. Where do you sleep? In the small room on the third floor (*piso*).
2. At what o'clock do you get up every morning? I generally rise at six o'clock.

LESSON XXXIII.

3. At what hour do your children rise in summer? They rise at daybreak.
4. At what time do they go to bed? At nightfall.
5. Where do you wash yourself? I wash myself in my own room.
6. Do you wash yourself in hot (*caliente*) or cold water? I wash myself always with cold water.
7. Why do you not wash sometimes with warm water? Because cold water is much better for the skin (*cútis*).
8. Where do you go to get shaved? I go to the barber's.
9. Where does your barber live? In Broadway, near Broome street.
10. Are you tired? No, sir, I never tire myself writing.
11. Are you speaking in earnest or in jest? In earnest; I am not in a humor to jest.
12. It seemed to me you were in a humor to jest a while ago? Not at all; on the contrary,* it was my brother that was making fun of me because I had cut my hand.
13. Well, no matter; I know you are fond of jesting and laughing at everybody. You deceive yourself, my dear sir (*señor mio*).
14. Charles, can you go to the tailor's to tell him I wish to see him? It is impossible for me to go out now, I am expecting Mr. Valero.
15. No matter, I shall send John. John cannot go either; he has to be here at the same time as I.
16. Will you go to the post-office and ask if there are any letters for me? I asked this morning when I took father's letters, and they told me there were none.
17. Did you see the newspaper I was reading when your cousin came in? There it is on the table, behind the dictionary.
18. Why did you get your hair cut (*hacerse cortar*)? Because it was too long (*largo*).
19. Indeed! I thought you liked long hair? On ladies, yes; but it is not very suitable for a man.
20. Where is Peter? I think he is up-stairs.
21. Will you do me the pleasure to call him? Certainly (*ciertamente*).
22. Was the musician contented with what you gave him? He did not appear to be contented.
23. How do you like the vest that my tailor made for you? Pretty (*bastante*) well; but I like the work of my own tailor better.
24. How is your uncle to-day? The physician came to see him this afternoon, and he said he was much better.
25. What are those gentlemen doing over there? Do you not see that they are resting?

* De ningun modo, al contrario.

26. How do you know they are tired? They have been walking all the morning.

27. Then they are very right (*hacer muy bien*) to rest. Of course; rest is sweet (*grato*) when one is tired (*se está cansado*).

LESSON XXXIV.

IRREGULAR VERBS.

Acertar.	To guess, to make out, to hit the mark.

INDICATIVE.—*Present.*

Acierto.	I guess.
Aciertas.	Thou guessest.
Acierta.	He guesses.
Acertamos.	We guess.
Acertais.	You guess.
Aciertan.	They guess.

IMPERATIVE.

Acierta tú.	Guess thou.
Acierte él.	Let him guess.
Acertemos nosotros.	Let us guess,
Acertad vosotros.	Guess.
Acierten ellos.	Let them guess.

SUBJUNCTIVE.—*Present.*

Acierte.	I may or can guess.
Aciertes.	Thou mayest or canst guess.
Acierte.	He may or can guess.
Acertemos.	We may or can guess.
Acerteis.	You may or can guess.
Acierten.	They may or can guess.

Verbs conjugated like ACERTAR.

Calentar.		To warm, to heat.
Cerrar.		To shut, to close.
Confesar.		To confess.
Despertar.		To awake, to wake.
Gobernar.	Acercar.	To govern. To approach.

Merendar.	To lunch.
Negar.	To deny.
Pensar.	To think, to intend.
Quebrar.	To break.
Sentarse.	To sit down.

Verbs that are regular, although small changes are made to preserve the pronunciation of the infinitive.

Vencer.	To vanquish, to overcome.
Resarcir.	To indemnify.
Pagar.	To pay.
Delinquir.	To commit a fault, to transgress.
Escoger.	To choose.
Poseer.	To possess.
Proveer.	To provide.
Huir.	To flee, to fly.
Argüir.	To argue.

A ver.	Let us see.
Quizá.	Perhaps.

Delincuente.	Delinquent, offender, transgressor.
Inocente.	Innocent.
Franco.	Frank, open.
Cualquiera.	Any, any one, some one, whatever, whatsoever.
Cualquiera parte.	Any place.

Fuego.	Fire.	Consecuencia.	Consequence, conclusion.
Jardinero.	Gardener.		
Motivo.	Motive.	Prudencia.	Prudence.
Sofá.	Sofa.	Verduras.	Vegetables.
		Deuda.	Debt.

COMPOSITION.

¿Le gusta á V. calentarse al fuego?	Do you like to warm yourself at the fire?
Sí, señor, me gusta calentarme al fuego en el invierno cuando hace mucho frio.	Yes, sir, I like to warm myself at the fire in winter when it is very cold.
¿Qué calienta el criado?	What is the servant warming?
Está calentando el café.	He is warming the coffee.
¿A qué hora despertó V. ayer?	At what hour did you awake yesterday.

LESSON XXXIV.

¿A ver si acierta V.?	Let us see if you *can** guess?
No sé, quizá despertó V. á las cinco.	I do not know; perhaps you awoke at five o'clock.
Despierto todas las mañanas á las cuatro y media.	I awake every morning at half-past four.
¿Cierra V. la puerta ó la abre?	Are you shutting the door or opening it?
He cerrado la puerta y abierto la ventana.	I have shut the door and opened the window.
¿Es delincuente aquel hombre?	Is that man a transgressor?
Lo creo, porque huye.	I think so, for he flees.
Niego la consecuencia; V. no arguye bien, él puede ser inocente y huir por prudencia.	I deny the conclusion; you do not argue correctly (well); he may be innocent and flee (or fly) from prudence.
¿Se proveyó V. de flores?	Did you provide yourself with flowers?
Me proveí de fruta y mi hermana de verduras.	I provided myself with fruit, and my sister with vegetables.
¿Pagó V. por ellas al jardinero?	Did you pay the gardener for them?
Yo le pagué la fruta y mi hermana le pagó las verduras.	I paid him for the fruit, and my sister paid him for the vegetables.
¿Piensa V. ir á Europa este verano?	Do you intend to go to Europe this summer?
Deseo irme á alguna parte, porque confieso que tengo mucho miedo del cólera.	I wish to go somewhere, for I confess I am very much afraid of the cholera.
Hay muchos que niegan tener miedo; pero yo tengo el valor de confesarlo francamente.	There are many who deny being afraid; but I have the courage to confess it freely.
¿A qué hora se desayuna V.?	At what hour do you breakfast?
Me desayuno á las ocho, meriendo á las dos y como á las seis.	I breakfast at eight, lunch at two, and dine at six.
¿Me promete V. venir á comer conmigo hoy?	Will you (do you) promise to come and dine with me to-day?
Entre comer ó merendar con V. escojo el merendar, porque V. come demasiado temprano.	Between lunching and dining with you, I choose lunching, for you dine too early.

* Words printed in *italics* do not require to be translated into Spanish.

EXPLANATION.

161. IRREGULAR VERBS.—All verbs that are not conjugated throughout according to the model verbs already given (*hablar, aprender, escribir*), are called *irregular*.

162. It is, however, to be observed, that although some verbs undergo slight changes in their radical letters, they are

LESSON XXXIV.

not to be considered as irregular on that account, inasmuch as those mutations take place in order to preserve throughout the whole conjugation the pronunciation of the root as sounded in the infinitive. This observation should be carefully borne in mind, so as not to take for irregular verbs those which are really not so.

Many verbs ending in *car*, *cer*, *cir*, *gar*, for instance, undergo respectively such mutations as above alluded to: those in *car* change the *c* into *qu* before *e*; as,

| Tocar. | To touch. |
| Toqué (instead of tocé). | I touched; |

in those in *cer* and *cir*, the *c* is changed into *z* before *a* and *o*; as,

Vencer.	To vanquish.
Venzo (instead of venco).	I vanquish.
Resarcir.	To indemnify.
Resarzo (instead of resarco).	I indemnify;

and lastly, those in *gar* take a *u* after the *g* and before *e*; as,

| Pagar. | To pay. |
| Pagué (instead of pagé). | I paid. |

For the same reason *delinquir* changes *qu* into *c*, before *a* and *o*; as, *delinco*, *delinca*, *delincamos*; and *escoger*, to choose, changes the *g* into *j* before *a* and *o*; as, *escojo*, *escoja*.

163. The verbs which terminate in *eer*, as *creer*, to believe; *leer*, to read; *poseer*, to possess; *proveer*, to provide, in those terminations which contain an *i*, change it into *y* whenever it is to be joined with another vowel; as, *creí*, *creyó*; *leí*, *leyeron*; *poseí*, *poseyere*; *proveí*, *proveyeremos*, &c.

164. The same change is made in the verbs ending in *uir*, when the *u* and the *i* make a part of two different syllables. Thus *huir*, to fly, makes, in the third person of the preterit definite, *huyó*; *argüir*, to argue, makes *arguyó*, &c.

165. The irregular verbs, about *five hundred and fifty* in number, may be divided into seven classes, presenting each a certain regularity in their irregularity; that is to say, whose irregularities occur in the same persons and tenses, so that when the pupil has learned seven verbs, or one of each of those

LESSON XXXIV.

groups, he will be able to conjugate almost all the Spanish irregular verbs, save a few that confine their irregularities to themselves and their compounds, and of which the majority have been already introduced in previous lessons, such as *haber*, *tener*, &c.; but the learner can find them all conjugated at the end of the book.

Acertar may serve as a model for the conjugation of the first of these seven classes of irregular verbs, just as *hablar* does for the first conjugation of the regular verbs. The irregularity of *acertar*, and of all those conjugated like it, consists in taking an *i* before the last *e* of the root, in the *first*, *second* and *third* persons singular, and the *third* person plural of the present of the indicative mood, in the present of the subjunctive, and in the imperative. (*See list of the irregular verbs at the end of the book.*) In all the other tenses and moods those verbs are regular, and the learner can easily form them according to their respective conjugations.

166. PAGAR may take for its direct object either the value paid or the thing paid for, while the person paid is the indirect object. *Por* may be used before the thing paid for; as,

Pago los caballos, *or* pago *por* los caballos.	I pay for the horses.
Pago mil pesos *por* los caballos.	I pay a thousand dollars for the horses.
Pago al comerciante mil pesos *por* los caballos.	I pay the merchant a thousand dollars for the horses.

CONVERSATION AND VERSION.

1. ¿Acertará V. la casa de su prima? Sí, señor, yo la acertaré.
2. ¿Podrá V. acertar quién estuvo aquí ayer? No acierto.
3. ¿No entiende su hermano de V. lo que le digo? Sí, señor; pero no acierta á responder.
4. ¿Se calienta V. al fuego? Sí, señor, porque hace mucho frio.
5. ¿Porqué no cierra V. entónces la puerta? Confieso que no habia pensado en ello.
6. ¿A qué hora despertó V. esta mañana? Desperté á las diez.
7. ¿El que gobierna una casa y una familia, no debe levantarse temprano? No lo niego.
8. ¿Piensa V. merendar hoy? Sí, señor, nosotros merendamos todos los dias.

LESSON XXXIV.

9. ¿Porqué no se sienta V. en aquella silla, que es mejor? Porque tengo miedo de romperla.

10. ¿Le pagó V. á su criado? Sí, señor, le pagué ayer y hoy se ha huido.

11. ¿No le perdonará V.? No, señor, porque quien delinquió una vez delinquirá dos.

12. ¿Y no se resarció de su trabajo? Sí, señor, ántes se proveyó de ropa en mi casa.

13. ¿Qué lenguas posee él? El inglés, el frances y el italiano.

14. ¿Quién posee ahora la casa de campo de V.? El americano la posee.

15. ¿Se la ha pagado á V.? No, señor, no me pagó nada.

16. ¿Compró V. flores al jardinero? Le compré verduras y mi hermana le compró flores.

17. ¿Le pagaron Vds. al jardinero por ellas? Yo le pagué las verduras y mi hermana pagó por las flores.

18. ¿A quién le gustan mas las flores, á V. ó á su hermana? Creo que á ella le gustan mas las flores; pero á mí me gusta mas la fruta.

19. ¿Qué fruta le gusta á V. mas? Me gustan las naranjas y las manzanas.

20. ¿Paga V. siempre sus deudas? Las pago cuando tengo dinero.

21. ¿Piensa V. ir al campo este verano? Deseo ir á cualquiera parte, porque confieso que tengo mucho miedo del cólera.

22. ¿No tiene V. vergüenza de confesarlo? Hay muchos que niegan tener miedo; pero yo tengo el valor de confesarlo francamente.

23. ¿A qué hora despertó V. ayer? Ayer, creo que desperté á las cinco. Despierto todos los dias á las cuatro y media.

24. ¿Y á qué hora se desayuna V.? Me desayuno á las siete, meriendo á las dos y como á las seis.

25. ¿Me promete V. venir hoy á comer conmigo? No puedo prometérselo, porque no sé si tendré tiempo.

EXCERCISE.

1. How cold it is this morning! Yes, it is very cold.

2. Will you not come and warm yourself at the fire? No, thank you; I do not like to warm myself at the fire.

3. In that case it is better to shut the doors and the windows. Perhaps *it is*.*

4. Do you intend remaining (*estarse*) here during the winter? If my uncle remains, I will too.

5. Will you not choose other rooms if you remain? Yes, I intend to do so.

---

* English words printed in *italics* do not require to be translated into Spanish.

LESSON XXXIV.

6. Good evening, Charles; will you not sit down for a few minutes? With pleasure.

7. Did you find out (make out) the musician's house yesterday? I made out the house without much difficulty, but I did not see him.

8. How was that? He must have been out, for I knocked at his door.

9. At what hour do you dine? I generally dine at six o'clock.

10. Then you lunch at noon? Yes, sir, I generally lunch about that hour.

11. Do you eat fruit every day at dinner? Not every day.

12. Did your brother pay for the fruit he bought last week? No; but he has to go out to-morrow, and perhaps he will go and pay for it.

13. Let us go and take a walk. Where do you wish to go?

14. We can go to the Central Park. Very well, let us go there; I think it is the finest promenade in the city.

15. At what time do they open the park in the morning? I believe it is open in summer at five o'clock.

16. And at what time is it shut? At eleven o'clock, I believe, or perhaps a little later.

17. In that case it will be better not to go there until to-morrow; it is now rather too late (*algo tarde*).

18. How too late? It is only half-past seven, so that we have three hours and a half for walking.

19. Where are they taking that man to? They are taking him to prison (*la cárcel*).

20. What are they taking him to prison for? He must be guilty of some misdemeanor (*delinquir*).

21. Has the servant taken the letter to the pianist yet? He took it to him yesterday afternoon.

22. Have you seen the news this morning? No; what news is there?

23. There was a great fire last night in Fourth street, and twelve houses were burned.

24. Where is Alexander? He is up stairs.

25. Have any of you seen my Spanish dictionary? Yes, I had it this morning in my room.

26. What were you doing with it? I was looking for a new word which I met *with** while reading the history you lent me.

27. How did you manage (*acertar*) to wake so early this morning? My brother awoke me singing in my room, at five o'clock.

28. At what time do you generally wake? If no one comes to interrupt (*interrumpir*) my sleep, I never wake before nine.

* English words in *italics* do not require to be translated.

29. Is it not better for the health to rise early? Certainly; but then it is necessary to go to bed early also.

30. Why do you not go to bed early? I am fond of reading and study, and so I rarely go to bed before two o'clock in the morning (*de la madrugada*).

LESSON XXXV.

IRREGULAR VERBS—*Continued.*

| Acostar. | To put in bed. |

INDICATIVE.—*Present.*

| *Acuesto, acuestas, acuesta.* | I put in bed, &c. |
| Acostamos, acostais, *acuestan.* | We put in bed, &c. |

IMPERATIVE.

| *Acuesta* tú, *acueste* él, acostemos nosotros, acostad vosotros, *acuesten* ellos. | Put in bed, &c. |

SUBJUNCTIVE.—*Present.*

| *Acueste, acuestes, acueste,* acostemos, acostcis, *acuesten.* | I may, or can, put in bed, &c. |

VERBS CONJUGATED LIKE ACOSTAR.

Acostarse.	To go to bed, to lie down.
Aprobar.	To approve.
Almorzar.	To breakfast.
Contar.	To count; to relate, or tell.
Consolar.	To console.
Encontrar.	To meet.
Mostrar.	To show.
Probar.	To prove; to try; to taste.
Recordar.	To remind; to remember.
Reprobar.	To reprove.
Rogar.	To entreat.
Soñar.	To dream.

Delicioso.	Delicious.
Espacioso.	Spacious.
Industrioso.	Industrious.
Religioso.	Religious.

LESSON XXXV.

Aristocrático.	Aristocratic.
Clásico.	Classic.
Fanático.	Fanatic.
Monárquico.	Monarchical.
Tiránico.	Tyrannical.
Trágico.	Tragic.
Poético.	Poetical.
Analítico.	Analytical.
Satírico.	Satirical.
Filosófico.	Philosophical.
Cómico.	Comic, comical.
Económico.	Economical.
Lacónico.	Laconic.
Metódico.	Methodical.
Crónico.	Chronic.

Vaso.	Tumbler, glass.	Taza.	Cup.
Sermon.	Sermon.	Moral.	Moral.
Mundo.	World.	República.	Republic.
Capítulo.	Chapter.	Independencia.	Independence.
Perro.	Dog.	Religion.	Religion.

COMPOSITION.

Manuel, acuéstate temprano y levántate temprano tambien.	Emanuel, go to bed early and rise early too.
Alejandro, cuéntame lo que te dijo Luisa.	Alexander, tell me what Louisa told thee.
Ayúdate y Dios te ayudará.	Help thyself, and God will help thee.
Ama á tú prójimo como á tí mismo.	Love thy neighbor as thyself.
Sé religioso, pero no seas fanático.	Be religious, but not a fanatic.
Sé industrioso y económico y no serás pobre.	Be industrious and economical and thou shalt not be poor.
Sentémonos, que estoy cansado.	Let us sit down, for I am tired.
Amaos como hermanos y no hableis mal uno del otro.	Love each other as brothers, and speak no evil one of another.
Entre V., Dn. Pedro, y tome V. asiento, or siéntese V.	Come in, Mr. Peter, take a seat, or be seated.
No puedo, estoy de prisa.	I cannot, I am in a hurry.
Juan, cierra la puerta, pero no cierres la ventana.	John, shut the door, but do not shut the window.
Caballeros, entren Vds., y les mostraré mis libros.	Come in, gentlemen, and I shall show you my books.
Alejandro, confiesa tu falta y te la perdonaré.	Alexander, confess your fault, and I will pardon you.

No los ofendamos.	Let us not offend them.
Amigos, cantemos y bailemos y seamos felices.	My friends, let us sing, dance and be merry.
No tomarás en vano el Nombre del Señor tu Dios.	Thou shalt not take the Name of the Lord thy God in vain.

EXPLANATION.

167. The verb *acostar* changes the radical *o* into *ue* in the same tenses and persons as those in which the verb *acertar* is irregular; *i. e.*, in the present indicative, the imperative and the present subjunctive. (*See this verb and those conjugated like it at the end of the book*).

168. THE IMPERATIVE MOOD is not used in the first person singular; nor is it used in Spanish for forbidding; that is, it is not employed in the negative form; but the persons of the present subjunctive are used when a negative command or a prohibition is expressed; as,

No lo hagas. No lo hagais.	Do not do so.

169. As has already been said, the *s* of the first person plural, and the *d* of the second, are suppressed before *nos* and *os*; as,

Amémonos.	Let us love each other.
Amaos.	Love one another.

170. When the imperative is negative in English, as the subjunctive is employed in Spanish, the objective pronouns are placed before it; as,

No lo digas.	Do not tell it.
No los ofendamos.	Let us not offend them.

171. The future of the indicative is often used for the imperative; as,

No tomarás en vano el Nombre del Señor tu Dios.	Thou shalt not take the Name of the Lord thy God in vain.

172. Many adjectives ending in *ous* are rendered into Spanish by changing this termination into *oso*; as,

Delicioso.	Delicious.
Espacioso.	Spacious, &c.

LESSON XXXV.

173. Many nouns and adjectives ending in English in *ic* or *ical* have in Spanish the termination *ico*; as,

| Fanático. | Fanatic, fanatical. |
| Poético. | Poetic, poetical. |

CONVERSATION AND VERSION.

1. Luisa, estudia bien tu leccion de español y escribe los ejercicios.
2. ¿Qué me dará V., papá, si la estudio bien y no hago faltas en los ejercicios? Te llevaré conmigo al Parque Central.
3. Papá, ¿no llevará V. á Alejandro y á Manuel con nosotros? Si son buenos muchachos y estudiosos los llevaré tambien.
4. Alejandro, ven acá y cuéntame qué hiciste ayer en el campo.—Con mucho gusto. Por la mañana me levanté temprano, me lavé y almorcé y despues me fuí á pasear. Volví muy cansado y me acosté á las nueve.
5. ¡Juan! ¿Señor? Mañana me despertarás á las cinco, me limpiarás las botas y me traerás el caballo temprano, porque quiero ir á dar un paseo y tomar un vaso de leche en el hotel del Parque Central.
6. Amigo mio, no seas fanático, pero sé religioso. No seas satírico ni hablador, pero sé prudente, económico ó industrioso y serás feliz.
7. Por Dios, Don Pedro, no hable V. mas, le prometo á V. estudiar y ser buen muchacho.
8. No seas respondon, haz tu deber, ayúdate y Dios te ayudará.
9. Don Pedro, á mi no me gustan los sermones largos, siéntese V. y hablemos de otra cosa.
10. Mire V., Dn. Juan, á aquella señorita que está en la ventana del vecino; ¿la conoce V.? Sí, señor, la conocí en Filadelfia.
11. ¿Qué tal le gusta á V.? Muchísimo; es una señorita perfecta, y habla el español tan bien como el inglés.
12. ¿Quiere V. llevarme á su casa? Tengo deseo de conocerla.—Con mucho gusto, pero ántes necesito su aprobacion.
13. ¿Le aman á V. mucho sus niños? Me aman y yo los amo; y toda la familia nos amamos los unos á los otros, así es que somos felicísimos.
14. ¿Se aman Vds. los unos á los otros tanto como se aman Vds. mismos? Creo que sí.
15. Hable V. alto y despacio si V. gusta y entónces entenderé todo lo que V. dice.—Así lo haré; pero V. no pensará en otra cosa que en lo que yo digo, porque si no, no hablaré mas.
16. ¿Le conviene á V. comprar aquella casa? No me conviene, porque es muy cara y está muy léjos de la ciudad.
17. ¿Qué le parece á V. del tiempo? Hoy es el cuatro de Julio de

1866, y por supuesto hace calor; pero hace muy buen tiempo para la celebracion de la independencia de esta gran República.

18. ¿Cuántos años hace hoy que los Estados Unidos celebran su independencia? Noventa y un años.

19. ¡Parece imposible! En ménos de cien años ha llegado esta nacion á ser una de las potencias (*powers*) mas grandes del mundo.

20. Eso debia ser así, y no dude V. que llegará un dia en que la libertad y la religion reinarán en el mundo haciendo felices á todas las naciones como á otras tantas familias que tienen un mismo padre.

EXERCISE.

1. Did you get up late to-day? No; I got up at daybreak to go and walk in the country.

2. Where did you walk? I went first to the Central Park, and then to Harlem.

3. What is the first thing we read in Telemachus? We read that Calypso could not console herself for the departure (*partida*) of Ulysses.

4. Where have you been all this time, sir? it is more than a week since you last came to see us; that is not right (*estar bien*). I confess I am rather negligent (*negligente*) sometimes.

5. You have doubtless already gone to see your old friend? Yes, and he wanted to make me spend a month with him at his country house.

6. What part of the country does he live in? On Long Island, about ten miles from the city.

7. Was he not glad to see you? We looked at each other for about ten minutes without being able to say a word; at last (*en fin*) he broke the silence (*rompió el silencio*), and said to me: "What! is it you, my dear friend? After seven years' absence (*ausencia*)! How glad I am!

8. Did he know you as soon as he saw you? Yes, and I knew him, though I met him at some distance from his father's house.

9. Doubtless he asked you about your travels (voyages)? Of course. "Where have you been?" said he. "What have you done? what have you seen? are you rich? are you happy? Tell me all you have done since you went away (*irse*); all your adventures. I wish it; I desire it; I beg of you; it will give (you will do) me the greatest pleasure."

10. All that proves his joy at seeing you. Yes, I know that; but how many questions!

11. Did he want an answer to each one of them? Of course; and I answered them as well as I could.

12. What did you tell him? I told him that after having left France,

I went to Spain, and from there into Portugal (*Portugal*), and that after a few months passed in Lisbon (*Lisboa*) I went on to Italy, where I remained four years.

13. What are the hours for breakfast and dinner amongst the Italians? The Italians, like the French, usually (generally) breakfast at eleven o'clock, and dine from five to seven in the evening.

14. And do they never eat anything before the breakfast hour? Almost everybody takes a cup of coffee or chocolate in the morning soon after rising.

15. What kind of governments are there in Europe? In Europe we find almost every form (*forma*) of government, republican and monarchical.

16. What is that book you have in your hand? An analytical treatise (*tratado*) of Spanish poetry that I was going to show to your cousin.

17. Have you seen Boileau's satirical poems? My uncle has promised to bring me that work from Paris.

18. Are you fond of reading? Yes, I take (find) great pleasure in reading books of all kinds, classical, poetical, religious, analytical, satirical, philosophical, &c.

19. Do you remember the peaches our friend sent us from the country last year? Of course I remember them, and that they were delicious.

20. Charles, go and take your breakfast; I want to take you to see the fine horse your uncle has bought for Alexander.

21. Will you not buy one for me, too, papa? If you are a good boy I probably will.

22. Do you ever dream? Very often; last night I dreamed I was travelling.

23. Indeed! Where were you going to? I do not remember now.

24. What was your father saying to Peter when I came in? He was reproving him for not having written his exercise yesterday.

25. Can you tell me what day this is? To-day is Wednesday, July 4th, of the year 1866, and the ninety-first of the Independence of the United States.

LESSON XXXVI.

Respetar.	To respect.
Parar.	To stop.
Mover.	To move.

LESSON XXXVI.

INDICATIVE—*Present.*

Muevo, mueves, mueve, movemos, moveis, *mueven.*	I move, &c.

IMPERATIVE.

Mueve tú, *mueva* él, movamos nosotros, moved vosotros, *muevan* ellos.	Move, &c.

SUBJUNCTIVE—*Present.*

Mueva, muevas, mueva, movamos, movais, *muevan.*	I may or can move, &c.

Verbs conjugated like MOVER.

Llover.	To rain.
Morder.	To bite.
Doler.	To grieve, to pain, to ache.
Volver.	To turn, to return.
Antes que.	Before.
Aunque.	Although.
Como.	Since, provided.
Para que. } A fin de. }	In order that, in order to.
Todo el mundo.	Everybody.
Principalmente.	Principally, chiefly.

Antagonista.	Antagonist.	Atrocidad.	Atrocity.
Artista.	Artist.	Capacidad.	Capacity.
Materialista.	Materialist.	Claridad.	Clearness, light.
Naturalista.	Naturalist.		
Organista.	Organist.	Crueldad.	Cruelty.
Violinista.	Violinist.	Dificultad.	Difficulty.
Purista.	Purist.	Eternidad.	Eternity.
Escritorio.	Office.	Facilidad.	Facility.
Clima.	Climate.	Noticias.	News.
Dolor.	Grief, pain, ache.	Guerra.	War.

COMPOSITION.

Se dice que Maximiliano ha partido de Méjico.	It is said that Maximilian has left Mexico.

LESSON XXXVI.

¿Se cree eso?	Do they believe that?
Aquí lo cree todo el mundo; pero en Francia no se cree.	Here everybody believes it; but in France it is not believed.
¿Cree V. que se podrá pagar pronto la deuda de los Estados Unidos?	Is it thought that the United States debt can soon be paid?
No se hará muy pronto; pero se hará.	It will not be accomplished (done) very soon; but it will be done.
Aquí se habla español.	Spanish is spoken here.
Aquí se vende buen vino.	Good wine is sold here.
Se perdona algunas veces á los delincuentes, pero no siempre.	Transgressors are pardoned sometimes, but not always.
El hombre se engaña á sí mismo.	Men deceive themselves.
¿Envió V. el violin al violinista?	Did you send the violin to the violinist?
Se le envió.	I sent it to him, or did send it to him.
¿Tocan bien el piano en España?	Do they play well on the piano in Spain?
En España se toca bien la guitarra.	They play the guitar well in Spain.
¿Se habla bien el español en la América del Sur?	Is Spanish well spoken (or, do they speak good Spanish) in South America?
Lo hablan y pronuncian bien.	They speak it and pronounce it well.
¿Le duele á V. la cabeza?	Does your head ache?
Sí, señor, mucho.	Yes, sir, very much.
¿Cómo se llama V.?	What is your name?
Me llamo Juan.	My name is John.
¿Cómo se llama eso en español?	What is that called in Spanish?
¿Cómo se dice eso en español?	How do you (or, do they) say that in Spanish?
Lo mismo que en inglés.	The same as in English.

EXPLANATION.

174. MOVER, to move, changes the radical *o* into *ue*, in the same tenses and persons as the verb *acostar*; *i. e.*, in the first, second and third persons singular, and the third plural of the present indicative, and present subjunctive, and in the imperative. (*See this verb, and those conjugated like it, at the end of the book*).

175. SE is the indefinite personal pronoun of the Spanish, referring to a personal agency in such a manner as to leave undetermined both the sex and the number of the persons represented. It corresponds, in this respect, with the English *we, they, people* or *one*; in fact, with all expressions which mention persons thus vaguely and indefinitely. It is used with the third person singular of the verb; as,

Se dice.	It is said, or they say.
Se cree.	It is believed, or they believe.
No se hará.	They (people) will not do it, or it will not be done.
Aquí se vende vino bueno.	Good wine is sold here.
Aquí se habla español.	Spanish is spoken here.

176. The pronoun *se* has now been seen used in the four functions in which it can be found; it may be well to mention them all again, in order that these different offices of the pronoun *se* may be well distinguished, and to avoid all confusion. They are the following:

1st. As an indefinite subject, as has been seen in the present lesson; as,

Se dice.	They say.

2d. To form the passive voice of verbs (see Lesson XXXII.); as,

Se perdona algunas veces á los delincuentes.	Transgressors are sometimes pardoned.

3d. As a reflective pronoun; as,

Manuel se engaña.	Emanuel deceives himself.

4th, and lastly, the objective pronoun *se*, for the sake of euphony, takes the place of the objectives *le, la, lo, les* (see Lesson XXVII.); as,

Se lo pagaré á V. mañana.	I will pay it to you to-morrow.

177. Many nouns ending in English in *ty*, are rendered in Spanish by changing these letters into *dad*; as,

Actividad.	Activity.
Capacidad.	Capacity.

N. B.—All nouns of this termination are feminine. Many nouns ending in English in *ist*, are rendered into Spanish by adding to these letters an *a*; as,

Artista.	Artist.
Organista.	Organist, &c.

LESSON XXXVI.

178. Doler.—This verb is used in the same manner as the verb *gustar*, to like (see Lesson XXXI.); as,

¿ Le duele á V. la cabeza ? | Does your head ache?

The same may be expressed in the following manner:

¿ Tiene V. dolor de cabeza ? | Have you a headache?

CONVERSATION AND VERSION.

1. ¿Se vende buen vino en Nueva York? Se vende bueno y malo; pero muy caro.
2. ¿Qué noticias hay? Se dice que la Alemania y la Italia estan en guerra.
3. ¿Se cree eso? No solamente se cree, sino que se sabe que la guerra ha principiado ya.
4. ¿Se habla español en Nueva York? En Nueva York se hablan todas las lenguas, pero principalmente el inglés, el aleman, el frances y el español.
5. ¿Se aman los Franceses y los Ingleses? Creo que no se aman como hermanos; pero se respetan.
6. ¿A quién se ama mas en este país, á los Franceses ó á los Ingleses? Es cosa que no sabré decir.
7. ¿En los Estados Unidos se respetan las iglesias de todas las religiones? Sí, señor, porque hay libertad de religion; es una cosa muy buena para el país, y yo la deseo para todas las naciones del mundo.
8. Hablemos de otra cosa, porque todos no son tan liberales como V.; y no se hará V. amigos si habla tan francamente.
9. Convengo con V. en eso, además no se debe decir todo lo que se piensa; pero para aprender una lengua se debe practicar mucho y se debe hablar de todo un poco.
10. V. tiene razon en eso, y una conversacion en que no se habla, sino de "si hace calor ó frio, si ha estado V. en el teatro, en el concierto, ó en la iglesia, y de si tiene V. el sombrero y el fusil, y el vino, y el dinero do V. ó del vecino" es muy cansada.
11. Por supuesto; pero V. debe saber que lo que se llama en inglés *small talk** es muy de moda.—Lo sé, es muy de moda, y hasta necesario algunas veces.
12. ¿Le dijo V. eso á su amigo? No se lo dije, porque mi hermana se lo habia dicho ya.
13. ¿Porqué no me lo dijo V. á mi? Porque mi hermano me ha dicho que se lo dirá á V. mañana.
14. ¿Toca Dn. Pedro bien el piano? No, señor, pero se engaña á sí mismo y cree tocarlo muy bien.

* *Charla.*

15. Véngase V. esta tarde por aquí, é irémos á dar un paseo.—Bien, si V. me espera hasta las seis, vendré, pero no ántes, porque no puedo salir del escritorio hasta esa hora.

16. ¿Qué tal tiempo ha hecho hoy en la ciudad? Hoy ha hecho buen tiempo y ayer hizo buen tiempo tambien; pero mañana hará mal tiempo.

17. ¿Cómo sabe V. que hará mal tiempo mañana? Porque en Nueva York no hace nunca buen tiempo por tres dias.

18. ¿V. cree que no hace buen tiempo mas que (sino) en la Habana? Perdone V. no me gusta el clima de la Habana ni el de Nueva York.

19. Entónces, ¿qué clima le gusta á V.? El de España, porque allí tenemos verdaderamente las cuatro estaciones.

20. ¿Qué quiere V. decir? Quiero decir que en España hace calor en verano aunque no muchísimo; en invierno hace frio, pero no nos helamos; en otoño hace un excelente tiempo de otoño, y en la primavera tenemos primavera.

21. ¿Bien, y no es lo mismo en Nueva York? Escúseme V.; en Nueva York no he conocido la primavera; hay muy pocos dias de otoño, un invierno larguísimo y un verano calurosísimo.

22. ¿Y en la Habana? En la Habana hay todo el año el verano de Nueva York.

23. ¿Yo pensaba que á V. no le gustaba hablar del tiempo? V. no me ha entendido; creo que debe hablarse de todo, pero no siempre del tiempo.

EXERCISE.

1. Why do you not come quicker when I call you? I cannot come any quicker, my head aches.

2. Where do you think Spanish is spoken best? In Madrid, and in all parts of Old and New Castile (*Castilla*).

3. And is it not well spoken in South America? There is some difference in the pronunciation; but, in general, persons of education speak correctly, whether they be † South Americans or Spaniards.

4. William, will you be good enough to take this letter to the post-office when you are going to take *your* lesson? I shall take it in the afternoon, I have not time now.

5. Are there many organists in the United States? Yes; and in New York, principally, there are a great many excellent organists and pianists.

6. Do you like that man's manner of speaking? No, I do not; he is too much *of a** purist.

7. Is your brother studying natural history? I cannot tell you

---

* English words in *italics* not to be translated into Spanish.   † Ya sean.

LESSON XXXVI.

whether (si) he is studying it or not; but I know he has just bought the complete works of Buffon.

8. Who is Buffon? A celebrated French naturalist.

9. What did that man do that was taken to prison this morning? They say he was arrested (*arrestar*) for cruelty to animals.

10. Will he be punished for it? Of course; transgressors of that kind are rarely let off unpunished (pardoned).

11. What is the matter with Alexander? A dog bit him in the hand.

12. Come here, Alexander; show me your hand. Is this the one? No, it is the other.

13. Does it pain you much? It was very sore (*pained*) when I got bitten, but now it is less painful.

14. I have always told you how necessary it is to take care with dogs. I know that; and I shall do so in future.

15. Does your new watch go well? Not very well; it stops (itself) three or four times a day.

16. Is your son getting on well in his studies? Pretty well; he has a great deal of capacity, and is fond of study.

17. Look here, Charles. What do you wish?

18. Count from one to a thousand in Spanish. Oh! I can do that with the greatest ease.

19. Well, let us see? One, two, three, four, five, six, seven, eight, nine, ten, eleven, twelve, thirteen, fourteen, fifteen, sixteen, seventeen, eighteen, nineteen, twenty, twenty-one, thirty, forty, fifty, sixty, seventy, eighty, ninety, a hundred, a hundred and one, two hundred, three hundred, four hundred, five hundred, six hundred, seven hundred, eight hundred, nine hundred, a thousand.

20. How do they write that last word in Spanish? I do not remember.

21. What is that? you do not remember! Did you not learn in the lesson on pronunciation, at the beginning of the grammar, that in Spanish every word is written just as it is pronounced? Oh, yes, now I remember.

22. Tell me, if you please, Mr. R., is French as easy to pronounce as Spanish? They say it is much more difficult, on the contrary.

23. But it is not impossible to learn French pronunciation? I did not say that; I only said that they say it is more difficult than Spanish pronunciation.

24. How do I pronounce? Very well; but, when reading or speaking, take a little more care with the *z*.

25. Please to pronounce the name of that letter again (to return to pronounce)? With the greatest pleasure; it is called z.

26. What other letter (*letra*) is pronounced like (the) *z*? *C*, when it comes (finds itself) before an *e* or an *i*.

LESSON XXXVII.

Subir.	To go, or come up, to ascend.
Atender.	To attend.

INDICATIVE—*Present.*

Atiendo, atiendes, atiende, atendemos, atendeis, *atienden.*	I attend, &c.

IMPERATIVE.

Atiende tú, *atienda* él, atendamos nosotros, atended vosotros, atiendan ellos.	Attend, &c.

SUBJUNCTIVE—*Present.*

Atienda, atiendas, atienda, atendamos, atendais, atiendan.	I may, or can, attend, &c.

Verbs conjugated like ATENDER.

Ascender.	To ascend, to mount.
Descender.	To descend.
Defender.	To defend.
Entender.	To understand.
Encender.	To light, to kindle.
Perder.	To lose.
Alegrarse.	To be glad, to rejoice.
Charlar.	To prattle, to chat.
Hallar.	To find.
Llegar.	To arrive.
Enviar.	To send.
Preparar.	To prepare.

CONJUNCTIONS.

Con tal que.	On condition that; provided (that).
Puesto que.	Since, inasmuch as; supposing that.
Dado caso que.	In case.
Hasta.	Until, till.
Aun cuando.	Even, although.
Por tanto.	Therefore.
Por cuanto.	Seeing that, for.
A ménos de. } A ménos que. }	Unless.

Támbien.		Also, too.	
Además.		Moreover, besides.	
Ya.		Whether, either.	
Tampoco.		Neither.	
Ojalá.		Would to God, God grant.	
Vapor.	Steamer.	Altura.	Height.
Globo.	Balloon.	Friolera.	Trifle.
Resfriado.	Cold.	Estada, permanencia.	Stay, permanence.

COMPOSITION.

Deseo que esté estudiando su leccion.	I wish that he may be studying his lesson.
Creo que la está estudiando.	I think he is studying it.
¿Piensa V. que tiene razon?	Do you think he is right?
No pienso que la tenga.	I do not think he is.
✓No lo creeré aunque me lo digan mil.	I will not believe it though a thousand tell it to me.
Lo creo aunque él lo niega.	I believe it, although he denies it.
Dudo que venga hoy.	I doubt whether he will come to-day.
✓Dudo que haya venido.	I doubt his having come.
Dado caso que V. no me encuentre en casa, espéreme V. hasta que venga.	In case you should not find me at home, wait for me till I come.
Así lo haré con tal que V. me prometa volver pronto.	I will do so, on condition that you promise me to come back soon (or quickly).
✓Volveré tan pronto como pueda.	I shall return as soon as I can.
Temo que no haya recibido mi carta.	I fear he has not received my letter.
¡Ojalá no la reciba! pero yo temo que la recibirá.	God grant that he may not receive it! but I fear he will (receive it).
✓A ménos que V. venga primero á verme, yo no iré á verlo á V.	Unless you come first to see me, I will not go to see you.
✓Puesto que él haya venido, ¿le hablará V.?	Supposing that he has come, will you speak to him?
Aunque haya venido no le hablaré ántes que él me hable.	Although he may have come I will not speak to him before he speaks to me.

EXPLANATION.

179. ATENDER, to attend, and all the verbs conjugated like it, take an *i* before the last *e* of the radical letters, in the same tenses and persons as the verb *acertar*, and the same tense in which *acostar* and *mover* change the *o* into *ue*; *i. e.*, in the first, second and third persons singular, and third plural of the present indicative, the present subjunctive, and the imperative. (*See, at page* 394, *this verb and those conjugated like it.*)

180. SUBJUNCTIVE MOOD.—Unlike the indicative, this mood cannot of itself express an action or mode of being in such a manner as to form complete sense; but its signification is determined by another verb, to which it is subordinate, as its name indicates,* and by which it is governed, usually with the help of a conjunction, such as *que, aunque,* or a conjunctive expression, such as *á fin de que, con tal que,* &c.

As none of the moods of the English verb correspond exactly to the Spanish subjunctive; and as the tenses of the latter are often employed to express, in the Castilian language, ideas which, in English, are conveyed by those of the indicative or the potential, and, not unfrequently, by the infinitive, learners experience much difficulty in determining when the subjunctive is to be used. Were we to give all the rules necessary for the correct application of this mood, a whole volume might be filled; we shall, however, give here those most likely to guide the student in all ordinary cases.

181. The subordinate verb is put in the subjunctive when the leading verb means *admiration, wish, will, desire, consent, prohibition, hinderance, necessity, command, doubt, regret, joy, usefulness, contentment, hope, fear, surprise, ignorance, preference, negation, permission, sorrow,* &c.

The subjunctive mood is here required because we are not positive that what we wish, command, &c., will be accomplished; but the same verb which governs the subordinate one in any of the tenses of the subjunctive, when the accomplishment of the action is doubtful, governs it in any of those of the indicative when the action is regarded as certain to take place; as,

| Déselo V. á los que hayan venido. } *Doubtful.* | Give it to those who (may) have come. |
| Déselo V. á los cuatro que *han* venido. } *Certain.* | Give it to the four who have (or are) come. |

In the first example, the verb is put in the subjunctive, be-

* *Subjunctive*, something joined, *in a subordinate manner*, to what has already been said

cause the speaker is not positive how many have come, or whether any have as yet come. In the second, the indicative is employed, because the speaker is certain of the arrival of the persons alluded to, and also of their number.

182. There are in Spanish certain conjunctions which require the subjunctive mood after them, on account of the indefinite and uncertain meaning which they commonly have. Some of them, however, it will be seen, occasionally occur with a positive signification, and may, in that case, be used with the indicative after them; as,

No lo creeré aunque me lo digan mil.	*Contingent.*	I will not believe it though a thousand tell it to me.
Lo creo aunque él me lo niega.	*Certain.*	I believe it, although he denies it (to me).

183. Finally, there are other parts of speech, and even whole phrases, which, on account of their indeterminate and doubtful, or contingent, meaning, require the subjunctive after them.

184. THE PRESENT TENSE OF THE SUBJUNCTIVE marks a contingent action as going on at the present moment, or to take place at some future time; as,

Dudo que venga.	I doubt whether he will come.

N. B.—Another use of this tense has been already noticed when treating of the imperative. (See Lesson XXXV.)

185. THE PERFECT TENSE expresses a doubtful or contingent action or event, as having been completed some time past, or that will have taken place before the completion of another future action or event; as,

Dudo que haya venido.	I doubt whether he has come.
Yo le daré su libro cuando él me haya dado el mio.	I shall give him his book when he will have given me mine.

CONVERSATION AND VERSION.

1. ¿Espera V. que llegue hoy el vapor de Europa? Creo que ha llegado esta mañana.

2. Yo dudo que haya llegado todavía. ¿Quiere V. enviar su criado á preguntar si ha llegado el vapor? Con mucho gusto, porque yo tambien deseo tener noticias de Europa.

3. ¿Cree V. que llegará un dia en que podamos ir á Europa en globos

aereostáticos? Mucho me alegraré que llegue ese dia, pero creo que no lo verémos nosotros, porque es muy difícil, y quizá imposible, el hallar la direccion de los globos.

4. ¿Suben muy alto los globos? No creo que suban á mas de dos ó tres mil piés, pero si se quiere pueden subir hasta la altura de quince ó diez y seis mil piés.

5. Dado caso que llegue hoy el vapor; ¿espera V. á su amigo? Por supuesto que sí, puesto que me escribe que llegará en este mismo vapor.

6. Ojalá llegue, pero temo mucho que haya tomado otro vapor y que no llegue hasta la semana próxima.

7. ¿Duda V. que haya estudiado su leccion? Dudo que la haya estudiado, porque es muy holgazan.

8. A ménos que V. estudie bien las lecciones y haga con mucho cuidado los ejercicios de la gramática, no aprenderá V. el español.

9. Sí, pero yo creia que se podia aprender una lengua con la práctica solamente.—Así es; pero entónces se necesita practicar todos los dias con quien la hable muy bien.

10. ¿En cuánto tiempo piensa V. que hablaré yo el español? V. lo hablará cuando sepa bien todas las lecciones de la gramática, y haya practicado y escrito los ejercicios.

11. Y despues que haya aprendido toda la gramática, practicado, y escrito los ejercicios, ¿hablaré perfectamente el español? No, señor; pero hablará V. bastante correctamente para llevar una conversacion, escribir una correspondencia, y poder hacer negocios en esta lengua.

12. Yo pensaba que el español era una lengua muy fácil.—Verdaderamente lo es para aprender lo que acabo de decirle á V.; pero para hablarlo perfectamente como V. quiere, todas las lenguas son difíciles.

13. Y si V. no lo cree, hágame el favor de decirme si habla V. su propia lengua y la escribe perfectamente.—Yo confieso que todavía tengo algo que aprender en el inglés.

14. Créame V., amigo mio, el estudio de una lengua no es una friolera. —Creo que tiene V. mucha razon; pero hay muchos que quieren aprenderlo todo y muy pocos que quieran estudiar.

15. ¿Me promete V. venir á verme cuando venga á la ciudad? Aunque venga á la ciudad no podré venir á ver á V. á ménos que acabe temprano mis negocios.

16. ¿Sabe V. hacer frases (*sentences*) en español con todos los tiempos del modo indicativo? Sí, señor, y tambien con el imperativo, el presente y el perfecto de subjuntivo.

17. Muy bien, entónces hágame V. ocho frases con los ocho tiempos de indicativo, una con el imperativo y dos con el presente y perfecto de subjuntivo de cualquiera verbo.

LESSON XXXVII.

18. ¿Está V. malo? ¿Ha estado V. hoy en el escritorio? ¿Estaba V. en su casa cuando su amigo fué á verle? ¿Habia V. estado en el teatro ántes de ir al baile? ¿Estuvo V. ayer en la ciudad? ¿Qué hizo V. así que hubo estado algun tiempo en el hotel? ¿Estará V. en casa mañana todo el dia? ¿Habrá escrito V. su ejercicio ántes de las cuatro? Estudia tus lecciones y escribe los ejercicios. No pierdas el tiempo. ¿Duda V. que yo sepa mi leccion? ¿Duda V. que yo la haya estudiado?

EXERCISE.

1. John, there is some one at the door; go and see who it is. Yes, sir.
2. Is Mr. Retortillo in? Yes, sir; who shall I say wishes to see him? Tell him that Mr. Perez wishes to speak to him a moment.
3. Mr. Perez wishes to see you a moment, sir. Let (*que*) him come up.
4. Oh! I am so glad to see you! How are you? how have you been? when did you return?—I arrived by the steamer *Napoléon III.*, on Wednesday last.
5. Did you receive all the letters I wrote you during (*durante*) my absence? I received one in March, dated from Rome.
6. How did you spend the time? did you pass through Spain, as you had intended? No; while I was still in Paris, and preparing to set out for Madrid, I learned that my brother was very ill in Florence.
7. Indeed! I am very sorry to hear that. What was the matter with him (what had he)? A heavy (strong) cold, that he had caught on his way from Turin to Florence.
8. He had not, I believe, enjoyed very good health for a long time before leaving home? No, he has always been sickly; but principally for about a year before his voyage to Europe, he had colds almost every month, and I may say that he was never without headaches, day or night.
9. Had he an Italian physician to attend him? No, Dr. Perez, his family physician, who was travelling through Italy that same winter, just arrived at Florence the same day as my brother, and, hearing of his illness, went at once (*inmediatamente*) to see him.
10. How long was he ill? Nearly three weeks.
11. How? Are you going away so soon? Sit down and let us chat for half an hour about your family. Thank you; I cannot stay any longer now, but I shall have the pleasure of seeing you again to-morrow.
12. Where are your brothers? They are gone to see the balloon that is to go up this afternoon.
13. Indeed? I thought the balloon was not to go up until Saturday. It was not to have gone up before Saturday; but, on account of the fine weather, it is to go up this afternoon.

14. Will many persons go up in it? Very few, I think; people in general do not like to go to such a height.

15. Do you understand all that is said in Spanish? I understand more and more every day; but there are still many words and constructions that I do not know.

16. How long do you think it will be before I can understand all, and speak like a native? That is a hard question to answer; provided you study with attention, read a great deal, and practice with Spaniards, you will soon understand and speak with ease; but it is difficult for a foreigner to speak any language exactly like a native.

17. But do you believe it to be impossible? No, I do not say it is impossible, but it is very difficult; and, besides, I do not think it is necessary. All that is required (wanted) is correctness, and to be able to converse with ease.

18. Has John's servant lighted the fire? Not yet; John does not wish it to be lighted until he returns.

19. Well, Charles, have you found *out** the meaning of the word you asked me for yesterday? No, sir; I have searched for it in all the dictionaries, and it is not to be found in any of them.

20. Why do you not ask your teacher? he can tell you at once. Yes, I know that very well; but I do not like to ask him so many questions: every day he comes I have a new one to ask him.

21. Do not stop at trifles of that kind; your teacher is very glad to be able to answer all questions, knowing that by that means (*medio*) you will learn better and more quickly.

22. I am very glad to see you defend him, for Alexander said he was not fond of answering questions, and did not like inquisitive persons.— Neither he does; but an inquisitive person is one thing, and a person who asks questions in order to gain knowledge is another.

LESSON XXXVIII.

Sentir. (*Look for the conjugation of this verb at p.* 395).	To feel, to be sorry for.

Verbs conjugated like SENTIR.

Arrepentirse.	To repent.
Consentir.	To consent.
Proferir.	To prefer.

* English words *italicised* not to be translated.

LESSON XXXVIII.

Asegurar.	To secure, to insure, to assure.
Animar.	To animate, to encourage, to induce.
Desanimar.	To dishearten, to discourage.
Ayudar.	To aid, to help.
Enfermar.	To fall (or get) sick, to make sick.
Exigir.	To exact, to require.
Quedar.	To remain.
Perfeccionar.	To perfect, to finish.
Usar.	To use, to wear.
Generalmente.	Generally.
De memoria.	By heart.
Ambos.	Both.
De continuo.	Continually.
Perezoso.	Lazy.

Exámen.	Examination.	Helena.	Ellen.
Oficio.	Trade, office.	Persona.	Person.
Alberto.	Albert.	Lectura.	Reading, lecture.
Norte.	North.	Profesion.	Profession.
Sur, or sud.	South.	Escuela.	School.
Este, oriente.	East.	Muerte.	Death.
Oeste, Occidente.	West.	Vida.	Life.
		Promesa.	Promise.

List of the present participles or verbal nouns and adjectives formed from the verbs already introduced.

Viviente.	Living being.	Paseante.	Walker, passer-by, promenader.
Estudiante.	Student.		
Escribiente.	A lawyer's clerk, a writer in a commercial house.	Creyente.	Believer.
		Conveniente.	Convenient, suitable.
	Resident.	Importante.	Important.
Tocante (en órden á).	Concerning.	Tratante.	Dealer.
		Cortante.	Sharp, edged.
		Gobernante.	Governing.
Reinante.	Reigning.	Contante.	Ready.
Saliente.	Salient.	Doliente.	Sad, afflicted, mournful.
Amante.	Lover.		
Practicante.	Practitioner.		
Principiante.	Beginner.		

LESSON XXXVIII.

COMPOSITION.

Tocante á lo que V. me dijo el otro dia, deseo que no se hable mas de ello.	Concerning what you told me the other day, I wish no more to be said about it.
Entraron cantando.	They came in singing.
Le encontraron leyendo.	They found him reading.
¿Qué está V. haciendo?	What are you doing?
Estoy leyendo.	I am reading.
Vengo de comer.	I am coming from dinner.
Trabaja sin descansar.	He labors without resting.
El trabajar es bueno para muchas cosas.	Work is good for many things.
El descansar despues de trabajar es necesario.	Rest after labor is necessary.
La vimos bailar.	We saw her dancing.
Emanuel es un estudiante industrioso.	Emanuel is an industrious student.
¿Es V. residente de los Estados Unidos?	Are you a resident of the United States?
Él es buen creyente.	He is a good believer.

EXPLANATION.

186. Present Participles.—Many Spanish verbs have, besides the past or passive participle, another called the present or active participle. Those formed from verbs of the first conjugation end in *ante*; as, *amante*, loving, lover; and those formed from the second and third end in *iente* or *ente*; as, *asistente*, assistant, *obediente*, obedient.

Participles of this kind cannot be formed from all verbs, and indeed those already in existence can only be regarded as mere verbal nouns or adjectives, inasmuch as, with the exception of a very limited number to be found in use, such as *tocante*, they do not follow the regimen of the verbs from which they are derived.

187. Gerunds.—Instead of the present participle, as a part of the verb, the gerund is now employed, and it corresponds, therefore, exactly to the English progressive form in *ing*; as,

Entraron cantando.	They came in singing.
Le encontraron leyendo.	They found him reading.

188. The verb *estar*, as has already been mentioned, can be used with the gerund in Spanish, as in English the verb *to be*, with the present participle; as,

| Yo *estoy leyendo*. | I am reading. |
| Ellos *estan escribiendo*. | They are writing. |

189. The INFINITIVE is used in Spanish when in English the present participle, preceded by a preposition, is used; as,

| Se fué *sin verle*. | He went away without seeing him. |
| Trabaja *sin descansar*. | He labors without resting. |

190. The INFINITIVE is also used as a verbal noun or present participle, in which case it takes the masculine definite article before it; as,

| *El trabajar* es bueno para la salud. | Work is good for the health. |
| *El descansar* despues de trabajar mucho es necesario. | Rest is necessary after much work. |

191. The INFINITIVE is often rendered in English by the present participle, when in Spanish it is governed by another verb; as,

| La *vimos bailar*. | We saw her dancing. |

CONVERSATION AND VERSION.

1. ¿Le gusta á V. mas leer que escribir? Me gustan ámbas cosas, pero creo que leyendo se aprende mas que escribiendo.

2. ¿Es estudioso ese muchacho? No, señor, pero hoy estudia mucho porque mañana tienen exámenes en su escuela.

3. ¿Piensa V. que sea conveniente ese negocio? Yo pienso que lo es, pero quizá no lo sea.

4. ¿Qué está V. haciendo? Estoy estudiando mi leccion de español.

5. ¿Sintió Helena mucho la muerte de su amiga? La sintió tanto que enfermó.

6. ¿Cómo se siente ahora? Está un poco mejor.—Me alegro que esté mejor, porque es muy buena muchacha.

7. ¿Puede V. prestarme trescientos pesos? Puedo prestárselos á V., pero no me gusta el prestar dinero (to lend).

8. ¿Cómo se aprende á hablar el español? Hablando se aprende á hablar; del mismo modo que bailando se aprende á bailar y haciendo zapatos se aprende á zapatero.

9. ¿Se arrepintió aquel hombre de su mala accion? No lo creo porque es un pícaro que vive de engañar.

10. ¿Qué profesion ú oficio tiene? No tiene ni oficio, ni profesion ninguna, es un paseante.

11. ¿De dónde viene V.? Vengo de comer.
12. ¿De dónde viene el viento? Viene del Sur, pero esta mañana venia del Este.
13. ¿Llueve en Nueva York cuando está el viento al Este? No, señor, generalmente llueve cuando el viento está al Oeste.
14. Alberto, anímate, sé estudioso y aprende de memoria la leccion para mañana. Papá, hace mucho calor y estoy cansado.
15. Bien, no te desanimes, descansa un poco y vuelve á trabajar despues.—V. quiere que yo esté trabajando continuamente.
16. No, querido, no quiero que trabajes demasiado; pero acuérdate que en este mundo no se logra nada sin trabajar.—Bien, papá, yo sé que V. tiene siempre razon, descansaré un poco ahora y despues acabaré de estudiar mi leccion.
17. ¿Se quedó mucho tiempo su amigo de V. en el concierto? Ambos nos quedamos hasta que se acabó.
18. ¿Tuvieron Vds. ayer exámenes en la escuela? Ayer tuvimos exámen de gramática, ántes de ayer de historia, hoy de español y mañana lo tendrémos de aritmética.
19. Manuel, levántate y vete á la escuela. ¿No sabes qué hora es? No, señor, yo pensaba que era temprano.
20. ¿Cómo, temprano? Ya son las siete y media y todavía tienes que lavarte y almorzar; ¡vamos, vamos, perezoso, arriba!—Alla voy papá, alla voy; y excúseme V., no sabia que era tan tarde.

EXERCISE.

1. Have you heard any more concerning the matter we were speaking of the other day? Nothing further; but I expect by to-morrow to be able to tell you something more.

2. When does your friend intend setting out* on his travel to the South? Probably by the latter end (*últimos*) of November, or beginning of December.

3. Is he to be long absent? He knows nothing as yet of how long he may be absent (*ausente*).

4. Concerning books to be read in order to perfect one's self in a language, what kind do you think the best? There is little difference between books to be used for that purpose (*propósito*).

5. Are there not some better than all the others? Not that I know of: each student will prefer those that treat of the subject he is fondest of.

6. But beginners cannot do so, for there are many books too difficult for them; is it not so? Certainly; I thought it needless to say that beginners must search for books easy to be read.

* *Emprender.*

7. It seems to me that newspaper reading is very useful; what do you think? Yes, and especially for those who take pleasure in studying the politics of the day.

8. Do you think I shall be able to understand Cervantes' great work after I have gone through (*recorrer*) the whole of the grammar? No, sir, you will not; you will have to read and study a great deal before you will be able to understand thoroughly the writings of any of the Spanish classic authors.

9. Who is that young man we met when walking, and to whom you spoke? He is a lawyer's clerk.

10. Does he make much money at that occupation? I cannot tell you; but he is undoubtedly a man of talent (*talento*).

11. Are the children gone to school yet, Louisa? All but Henry, who wishes not to go to-day, if you will consent to it.

12. I am afraid he is a very lazy boy; he is continually asking not to be sent to school.

13. How can he expect to learn if he neither goes to school nor studies at home? He wants to study at home; he says that if you consent to his staying at home, he will study anything you please.

14. Well, I shall give him something to learn by heart, and we shall see what he does.—Very well; but do not give him too much to do at the beginning, for he is easily disheartened.

15. I never require of any one more than he is able to do.—That is perfectly right.

16. Tell Charles and Albert that I want to see them, and that I have two books for them.—I need not go to tell them; here they are coming.

17. Come here, boys.—Well, papa, what do you want us for?

18. To give you these two books: one for each.—How beautiful! —Yes, that is true; but they are something more than beautiful: they are good.

19. What do they treat of? This one treats of man in life and of all living beings; and that one of man's state after death.

20. Now, I wish you to read a chapter each one in his book every day, after your lessons; and then you may go out and walk for an hour. —Thank you, sir; and we can assure you that we shall do so with the greatest pleasure.

21. Tell me, Albert, where did you buy that hat? That is one of those hats that were worn three summers ago. I know that very well, for I bought it at the time they were being worn, and I have worn it ever since.

22. This author seems to have travelled a great deal; have you read any of his travels? Yes, and I like them exceedingly (*muchisimo*).

23. I am going to read them, too, as soon as I have time. In what countries did he travel principally? He has been in nearly every country in the world, East, West, North and South.

24. What is the trade or profession of that person, just gone out? He is a physician; he has been in this city for *now* nearly five years. He is an excellent practitioner.

LESSON XXXIX.

Pedir. (*Look for the conjugation of this verb at p.* 396.) | To petition, to ask for.

Verbs conjugated like PEDIR.

Competir.	To contend, to compete.
Elejir.	To elect, to choose.
Medir.	To measure.
Reñir.	To quarrel, to scold.
Seguir.	To follow.
Rendir.	To render; to exhaust, to do out, to wear out.
Repetir.	To repeat.
Servir.	To serve.
Teñir.	To dye.
Vestir.	To dress.
Divertirse.	To amuse one's self.
Casarse.	To marry; to get (or be) married.
Besar.	To kiss.
Enamorarse.	To fall in love.
Celebrar.	To celebrate, to praise, to be glad.
Cenar.	To sup.
Presentar.	To present, to introduce one person to the acquaintance of another.
Reconocer.	To recognize, to examine closely.
Estimar.	To estimate, to value, to esteem.
Agradecer.	To thank, to be thankful, to be obliged.
En hora buena.	It is well, well and good.
Asi asi.	So so.

LESSON XXXIX.

Tal cual.	Middling, so so.
Hasta la vista.	Till I see you again.
Hasta luego.	Good-bye for a while.
Sin novedad.	Well, in a good state of health.
Medianamente.	Middling.

¡Ah! (*int.*)	Ah!
¡Oh! (*int.*)	Oh!

- Respetable.	Respectable.
Delicado.	Delicate, weak.
Infinito.	Infinite.
Junto.	Near, close to, together.
Discreto. Encantador.	Discreet. Charming.

Favor.	Favor.	Tertulia.	Party, soirée.
Beso.	Kiss.	Novedad.	Novelty.
Servidor.	Servant.	Celebracion.	Celebration.
Pié.	Foot.	Servidora.	Servant.
Honor.	Honor.	Ocasion.	Occasion.
Vestido.	Dress.	Complacencia.	Complaisance.
Esposo.	Husband.	Bondad.	Goodness, kindness.
Asiento.	Seat.		
Capítulo.	Chapter.	Esposa.	Wife.
Sobrino.	Nephew.	Orden.	Order, command.
		Memorias.	Regards.
		Enhorabuena.	Congratulation.

COMPOSITION.

¿Qué le pide á V. ese hombre?	What is that man asking for?
No me pide nada; me pregunta que hora es.	He is asking me for nothing; he is asking me what o'clock it is.
Beso á V. la mano, caballero.	(*A Spanish expression of courtesy, used at meeting or parting. No equivalent in English.*)
Beso á V. la suya.	(*Reply to the above.*)
¿Cómo está su familia de V.?	How is your family?
Todos estan bien, gracias; ¿y la de V.?	All are well, thank you; and yours?
Así así; los niños estan muy buenos, pero mi esposa no se siente bien.	So so; the children are very well, but my wife does not feel well.
A los piés de V., señora.	(*Spanish expression of courtesy, used to ladies. No English equivalent.*)
Beso á V. la mano, caballero.	(*The lady's reply to the above.*)
A la órden de V., Don Pedro.	At your service, Mr. Peter.

LESSON XXXIX.

Vaya V. con Dios, Don Juan.	God be with you, Mr. John.
Buenos dias, Doña Luisa, ¿cómo lo pasa V. hoy?	Good morning, Miss Louisa, how do you do to-day?
Bien, para servir á V.; ¿y V.?	Well, thank you; and you?
Sin novedad á la disposicion de V.	I am very well too, thank you.
Señor D. M., tengo el honor de presentarle al Sr. D. P.	Mr. M., I have the honor to introduce (or present) you to Mr. P.
Caballero, celebro la ocasion de conocer á V.	I am happy to make your acquaintance, sir.
Tenga V. la bondad de darme el cuchillo.	Have the goodness to give me the knife.
Con mucho gusto.	With much pleasure.
Mil gracias.	Thank you.
Hágame V. el favor de decirme, cómo se llama esto en español.	Be kind enough to tell me what you call this in Spanish.
Sírvase V. tomar asiento.	Please to take a seat.
Lo siento mucho, pero no puedo, tengo que marcharme.	I am very sorry, but I cannot, I must be off.
Tenga V. la complacencia de ponerme á los piés de su esposa de V.	Have the goodness to present my regards to your lady (or wife).

EXPLANATION.

192. PEDIR.—A paradigm will be found at the end of the grammar, showing the tenses and persons in which this verb and all those conjugated like it change the *e* of their root into *i*.

193. THE USUAL FORMS OF SALUTATIONS, among gentlemen in greeting each other, are the following:

Beso á V. la mano.	I kiss your hand.
Servidor de V., caballero.	Your servant, sir.
A la órden de V.	Your most obedient.
Vaya V. con Dios.	Adieu, or God be with you.
Tenga V. muy buenos dias.	Good day to you.

This last expression is used from the earliest part of the morning till two or three hours after meridian; from which time till dark is used,

Buenas tardes.	Good afternoon;

and from dark until the following morning, both on meeting and taking leave,

Buenas noches.	Good night.

All these expressions are always used in Spanish in the plural number.

LESSON XXXIX.

In saluting a lady, the first expression most frequently made use of is:

A los piés de V., señora.	Madam, at your feet.

The lady's reply is:

Beso á V. la mano, caballero.	I kiss your hand, sir.

To inquire after another's health:

Cómo lo pasa V.? *or* cómo está V.?	How do you do?

To answer:

Medianamente bien.	Middling well.
Perfectamente bien.	Perfectly well.
Para servir á V.	At your service.
Muy bien, gracias.	Very well, thank you.
Así así, *or* tal cual; y V., ¿cómo lo pasa?	So so; and how do you do?
Sin novedad,	Always well.
A la disposicion de V.	At your service.

For introducing one person to another:

Señor Don M., tengo el honor de presentarle al Señor Don P.	Mr. M., I have the honor of introducing Mr. P. to you.

And the reply is:

Caballero, celebro la ocasion de conocer á V., *or*	Sir, I am happy to make your acquaintance.
Reconózcame V. por un servidor suyo.	I am entirely at your service.

For asking or requesting:

Tenga V. la bondad de darme.	Have the goodness to give me.
Hágame V. el favor de decirme.	Do me the favor to tell me.
Sírvase V., *or* tenga V. la complacencia de.	Have the kindness to.

And for returning thanks:

Mil gracias, *or*	A thousand thanks.
Muchísimas gracias.	Many thanks.
Se lo agradezco á V. infinito.	I am very much obliged to you.

CONVERSATION AND VERSION.

1. Señor D. Juan, ¿qué le pide á V. mi muchacho? No me pide nada; me pregunta qué hora es.

2. Yo creia que le pedia á V. dinero, porque él está siempre pidiendo

centavos á todo el mundo.—Vaya! no le riña V.; á todos los niños les gusta que les den centavos.—Verdad es, pero á mí no me gusta que los mios los pidan.

8. Dígame V., D. Pedro, ¿quién es aquella señorita que está sentada en el sofá junto á su esposa de V.? Esa es una señorita muy amable, hija del Señor D. Luis Martínez, familia muy respetable á quien conocí hace muchos años.

4. ¿Quiere V. hacerme el favor de presentarme á ella? Con mucho gusto; pero le advierto que no se enamore de la Señorita Martínez, porque está para casarse.

5. Pierda V. cuidado; yo solo deseo conocerla para gozar de su discreta conversacion.—En hora buena venga V. y lo presentaré.

6. Señorita Martínez, tengo el honor de presentar á V. el Señor Don Juan McLeren.—Caballero, celebro la ocasion de conocer á V.—Señorita, reconózcame V. por su servidor.

7. ¡Ah! aquí viene Don Alberto y su esposa.—Sírvanse Vds. pasar adelante.

8. ¡Oh! Señor Don Pedro, me alegro mucho de encontrar á V. por acá. Mil gracias, señora, soy muy feliz en volver á ver á Vds.

9. A los piés de V., Señorita Martínez.—Beso á V. la mano, caballero.

10. Doña Margarita, ¿cómo está su familia de V.? Todos están bien, gracias, ¿y la de V.? Así así; los niños estan muy buenos, pero mi esposa está delicada.

11. Sírvase V. tomar asiento, D. Alberto.—Lo siento mucho, pero no puedo; he prometido á mi madre volver pronto para cenar con ella.

12. Señoras, á los piés de Vds. Beso á Vds. la mano caballeros.

13. A la órden de V., D. Pedro. Vaya V. con Dios, D. Juan.

14. Tenga V. muy buenas noches, Doña Luisa, ¿cómo lo pasa V. hoy? Bien, para servir á V., ¿y V.? Sin novedad, á la disposicion de V.

15. Buenas noches, D. Pedro; hasta mañana. Hasta mañana, póngame V. á los piés de su señora.

16. Dé V. memorias de mi parte á toda la familia.—De su parte de V. lo estimarán mucho.

17. Adios, Manuel, ¿á dónde vas tan de prisa? Voy á acompañar á mi hermana al teatro, y desde allí irémos á la tertulia del, Señor Marrací.

18. Celebraré que te diviertas mucho. Yo tambien pienso ir á la tertulia del Señor Marrací; con que, así no te digo adios, ya nos verémos.—Hasta la vista.—Hasta luego.

EXERCISE.

1. Good morning, Charles! Are you never going to get up?—Why, how late is it?

LESSON XXXIX.

2. It is near nine o'clock; but it is nothing new to see you in bed at that hour. Ah! you are always making fun of me for lying so long in the morning, and I think I rise very early.

3. Up, then, and dress yourself as quickly as possible, I want you to come and breakfast with me.

4. Indeed! What good things are you going to give me? You will have a first-rate breakfast, with excellent wine, followed by delicious chocolate.

5. Tell me, my dear *fellow*: I can never remember the name of that young lady that I met at your sister's party; what is her name? Oh, no matter; my sister has invited* her to dine this evening, and if you wait for dinner with us I will introduce you to her.

6. Papa, here is my friend Mr. N., whom I have the pleasure to present to you. I am very happy to know you, sir.

7. Be kind enough to take a seat, and excuse me an instant; I shall be back immediately. Certainly, sir.

8. How are your old friends the Retortillos? They are very well, thank you; they are to be here this evening, so you can have a chat with them.

9. Why did you not introduce me long ago to your father? I am very sorry for not having done so, and my father has often scolded me for my neglect (*negligencia*).

10. Do you expect your uncle to-day? I do not; but if he comes, well and good, we shall be glad to see him.

11. Will you be good enough to give me that newspaper that is on the chair next the window? With the greatest pleasure.

12. What news is there this morning? I see that a new president (*presidente*) has been elected in one of the provinces of South America.

13. They might have chosen another occasion for electing him, I think. Ah, of course; they are at war with Spain.

14. How much do they ask for the house that is for sale in Fifteenth street? Father was saying yesterday that they are asking a very high price.

15. What do you understand by a high price? More than the house is worth (*valer*).

16. You seem very much dissatisfied at the price; have you any intention of buying the house? Yes, unless it has already been sold.

17. What news have you from Boston? is Miss Guevara married yet? I have not heard from the family for a month; but I suppose she must be married by this time; she was to be married in July.

18. Will you come and take a walk before dinner? Ah, you must excuse me; believe me, I am worn out with fatigue.

* *Invitar.*

19. What is that you said, Emanuel? I have told you once, and I shall not repeat it.

20. Do you know that young lady who is sitting on the sofa beside your niece? Yes; I will introduce you to her, if you wish.

21. When will you introduce me? Just now, on condition that you will not fall in love with her.

22. Well, will you promise? I will; you know I am going to get married, and I only wish to enjoy her charming * conversation.

23. Miss Veleta, allow me to have the honor of introducing to you Mr. Romelio. How do you do, sir? I am very happy to know you, miss.

24. Well, John, what do you think of her? That she is charming; and I am exceedingly obliged to you for introducing me.

25. Oh, Louisa! come and look at this beautiful dress.—Oh, how beautiful! How much did it cost?—Only a trifle of $120.

26. How much did you pay for that last coat of yours, Alexander? —Only eighty dollars.—Not very much at all (*no se me hace caro*).

LESSON XL.

Conducir. (*See conjugation of this verb in at p.* 398.)	To conduct, to lead, to drive.

Verbs conjugated like CONDUCIR.

Producir.	To produce.
Traducir.	To translate.
Introducir.	To introduce.
Obrar.	To act.
Envidiar.	To envy.
Olvidar.	To forget.
Existir.	To exist.
Segun (*prep.*).	According to.
Siquiera (*conj.*).	At least, even.
Colectivo.	Collective.
Particular.	Private, particular.

COLLECTIVE NOUNS.

Ejército.	Army.	Tropa.	Troop.
Gentío.	Crowd.	Gente.	People.
Rebaño.	Flock, herd.	Multitud.	Multitude.

* *Encantadora.*

LESSON XL.

Par.	Pair, couple.	Docena.	Dozen.
Centenares.	Hundreds.	Centena.	A hundred.
Millares.	Thousands.	Mitad.	Half.
El tercio.	The third.	La tercera.	The third.
El cuarto.	The fourth.	La cuarta parte.	The fourth, &c.
El dozavo.	The twelfth.	Infinidad.	An infinity.
El doble.	The double.		
Higo.	Fig.	Conciencia.	Conscience.
Carácter.	Character.	Circunstancia.	Circumstance.
Habitante.	Inhabitant.	Uva.	Grape.
Gobierno.	Government.	Especie.	Species, kind.
Recurso.	Recourse, resources.	Naranja.	Orange.
		Castaña.	Chestnut.
Monte.	Mountain.	Nuez.	Nut.
Bosque.	Wood (forest).	Cuestion.	Question.
Rio.	River.	Produccion.	Production.
Lago.	Lake.	Libertad.	Liberty.
Nombre.	Noun, name.	Causa.	Cause.
Carnero merino.	Merino sheep.	Irlanda.	Ireland.
Rincon, esquina.	Corner.	Naturaleza.	Nature.

COMPOSITION.

Obró segun su conciencia.	He acted according to his conscience.
Habla segun las circunstancias.	He speaks according to circumstances.
Lo cuento segun me lo han contado.	I tell it as it was told to me.
Entró (or entraron) en la ciudad una tropa de soldados.	A troop of soldiers came into the city.
En el ejército de los Estados Unidos habia soldados de todas las naciones.	In the United States army there were soldiers of all nations.
El tercio (or la tercera parte) de esos hombres no saben escribir.	The third of those men do not know how to write.
El gentio era tan grande que no pudimos pasar.	The crowd was so great that we could not pass.
Un par de caballos americanos vale por dos pares de caballos méjicanos.	A pair of American horses are worth two pairs of Mexican horses.

EXPLANATION.

194. CONDUCIR, to conduct, and the verbs conjugated like it, take a *z* before the radical *c* in the terminations beginning with *o* or *a*. They also take the terminations *je, jiste, jo, jimos,* *jisteis, jeron,* &c., as may be seen in the conjugation of *conducir,* at the end of the grammar.

195. SEGUN.—We class this word among the prepositions, in conformity to the general practice among Spanish grammarians, and because it sometimes has the character of such; as,

Obró *segun* su conciencia.	He acted according to his conscience.
Habla *segun* las circunstancias.	He speaks according to circumstances.

Nevertheless, in other cases it is employed as an adverb; as,

Lo cuento *segun* me lo han contado.	I tell it as it was told to me.

196. Collective nouns, in the singular, generally agree with verbs in the singular number; but when the collective noun is taken in its most extended sense, custom allows the verb to be in the plural, for in such case the numbers concurring to form the whole, rather than the whole itself, are considered; as,

Entró (*or* entraron) en la ciudad una tropa de soldados.	A troop of soldiers came into the city.

CONVERSATION AND VERSION.

1. ¿Produce España buena fruta? España produce excelente fruta de todas especies.

2. ¿Cuál es la mejor fruta de España? No sabré decir á V., porque toda es buena y hay centenares de especies, por ejemplo: las uvas son de las mejores del mundo; los melocotones y los melones son tambien muy buenos, sin contar con las naranjas, los higos, las castañas, las nueces y otra infinidad de frutas.

3. ¿Es España un país caro ó barato? Es demasiado barato. Con un peso se puede vivir mejor en España que en Nueva York con cuatro.

4. ¿Bien, entónces porqué se vino V. á vivir en los Estados Unidos? Esa es ya otra cuestion. España no tiene que envidiar á ningun país del mundo en cuanto á su clima ni á sus producciones, ni ménos en cuanto al carácter de sus habitantes; pero bajo su gobierno no se goza de la misma libertad que se goza bajo el de la República de los Estados Unidos.

5. ¿Es esta la causa por la cuál V. se vino á residir en este país? Hay muchas otras. Por ejemplo, es verdad que en España no se conocen las hambres que hay en Irlanda, Alemania y otros países, y que, como he dicho, se vive mejor allí con un peso que aquí con cuatro; pero tambien es verdad, que en cualquiera profesion ú oficio es mas fácil ganar cuatro pesos en los Estados Unidos, que uno en España.

6. ¿Por tanto V. cree que los recursos de los Estados Unidos son

LESSON XL.

mas grandes que los de otros países? Por supuesto que sí. Aquí la nacion es grande; la libertad es grande; los montes, los rios, los lagos, los bosques son grandes; la naturaleza es grande; todo es grande; Nueva York es grande y los hombres mismos son tambien grandes; pero no mas grandes que los Españoles.

7. Hablando de esto, V. se olvida que en este ejercicio tiene V. que practicar con los nombres colectivos.—V. tiene razon, se me habian olvidado los nombres colectivos hablando de las dos naciones que mas amo en el mundo.

8. En cuanto á los nombres colectivos, su práctica es muy fácil y todo se reduce á decir: que en Nueva York hay multitud de gentes de diferentes naciones, millares de mujeres y cosas buenas y centenares de hombres y cosas malas.

9. ¿Pero y qué dice V. con respecto á los rebaños, ejércitos, etc.? Que en España hay rebaños de carneros merinos que, asi como su ejército, no tienen superiores en el mundo.

10. ¿Segun eso V. cree que todo lo mejor existe en España? Todo no, puesto que mis niños son Americanos.

11. Vamos, V. se burla.—No, señor, yo hablo de veras para practicar el español.

12. V. habla segun las circunstancias.—No, señor, yo hablo segun mi conciencia.

13. Acuérdese V. que segun V. obre con los demás así obrarán ellos con V.—Muy bien y asi como yo hable de ellos, así hablarán ellos de mí; pero yo no debo hablar de ellos mejor que de mí mismo.

14. ¿Quiere V. pagarme la mitad, el tercio ó el cuarto de lo que V. me debe? Ni lo uno ni lo otro, porque no tengo dinero ahora.

15. Deme V. á lo ménos un par de pesos.—Mañana le daré á V. una docena de pesos, pero hoy ni tan siquiera un centavo.

16. A Dios, Cárlos, me canso de charlar y me voy á acostar. Buenas noches, Luis, no olvide V. de pagar sus deudas.

EXCERCISE.

1. What is the name given to a large number of sheep together? It is called a flock.

2. What were you doing so long in the street? I went to see the reason of the great crowd at the corner of the next street.

3. Well, what was it? I could not see any thing; but it seems there was a fire in some of the streets near here.

4. You seem to be very much of a Spaniard; why did you ever come to the United States? I will not deny that I like the government; yet that is not the only reason I had for coming here.

5. Can you tell me some of the others? Undoubtedly; although living is higher here than there, business of all kinds is better, and it is easier to make money here, not only than in Spain, but than any other country in Europe.

6. I am very glad you think so; how long have you been here? It will be four years next September.

7. Will you be good enough to tell me something of your country? That will give me much pleasure.

8. You talk so much about Europe in general, and about Spain in particular, that I cannot help (*no puedo ménos de*) thinking you intend to go there. You are very right; it is very possible that my brother and I shall take a trip (*viaje*) to Spain next fall.

9. Well, in order to be able to enjoy yourselves as much as possible, it will be necessary for you to know how to speak the language perfectly before starting. That we intend to do.

10. Do you think all the soldiers in the army are Americans? No, nor even the half, and perhaps not even the third.

11. How many inhabitants are there in this city? I am not able to tell you exactly; but there cannot be much less than a million.

12. Which city in the world has the most inhabitants? London; it has about three millions of inhabitants.

13. Ah! you are jesting; or else you are an Englishman. I am not jesting, neither am I an Englishman, but a Frenchman; after London comes Paris.

14. Who is that book by? This is the celebrated Don Quixote (*Quijote*), by Cervántes.

15. In how many parts is it? Two, the first containing (*contener*) some fifty-two chapters, and the second about eighty-four.

16. What effect (*efecto*) does the reading of Don Quixote produce upon you? It makes me admire, and even leads me to envy the genius (*genio*) of its author.

17. Ah! I see; you say that to please me, because you know that I too admire the grand work of Cervantes. Pardon me, sir; I never speak according to circumstances, but always according to my conscience.

18. But, have you forgotten your promise already? What promise is that? I do not remember any.

19. No matter; I see you have completely forgotten it. I am very sorry.

20. What are the best fruits that Spain produces? Spain produces so many kinds of fruit, and so delicious, that it is almost impossible for me to tell them all: You have excellent grapes, melons, peaches, apples, oranges, and an infinity of others.

21. Have the soldiers that came into the city last night gone away yet? They marched this morning at daybreak.

22. How was our old friend Harnero when you last heard from him? He was in Boston, entirely without means, having been deceived by a bad man who took the whole of his money from him, and from whom he was unable to recover (*recobrar*) even the fourth part.

LESSON XLI.

Soler.	To be accustomed to, to do, or be, usually.
Bendecir.	To bless.
Caer.	To fall, to see (understand).
Dormir.	To sleep.
Morir.	To die.
Errar.	To err.
Jugar.	To play.
Oir.	To hear.
Oler.	To smell.
Contradecir.	To contradict.
Poner.	To put.
Podrir.	To rot.
Reir.	To laugh.
Valer.	To be worth.
Yacer.	To lie.

(*See the conjugation of these verbs at the end of the book.*)

Reposar.	To rest, to repose.
Premiar.	To reward.
Examinar.	To examine.
Desde.	Since, from.
Contra.	Against, towards.
Sobre.	Above, over, about.
Tras.	After, behind, besides.
Pues.	Well, then; therefore, &c.
Helo aquí.	Here he (or it) is.
Desde ahora.	Henceforward, from now, just now.

LESSON XLI.

Desde aquí.	From here.		
En efecto.	Indeed, in effect, in fact, really.		
Eterno.	Eternal.	Afortunado.	Fortunate.
Convicto.	Convicted.	Desgraciado.	Unfortunate.
Infortunio.	Misfortune.	Carlota.	Charlotte.
Reo.	Criminal.	Creacion.	Creation.
Grito.	Cry, scream.	Caridad.	Charity.
Coche.	Carriage.	Prenda.	Pledge, quality, accomplishment.
Vicio.	Vice.		
Fraile.	Fray, friar.	Virtud.	Virtue.
Diego.	James.	Tristeza.	Grief, sorrow.
Verbo.	Verb.	Experiencia.	Experience.
Principio.	Beginning, principle.	Página.	Page.

COMPOSITION.

¿Suele V. levantarse temprano?	Do you usually rise early?
Suelo levantarme tarde.	I usually rise late.
¿Solía V. ir á pasear á caballo el año pasado?	Used you to ride on horseback last year?
No, señor, solía pasear en coche.	No, sir, I used to ride in a carriage.
Plegue á Dios que tengamos pronto lo que deseamos.	God grant we may soon have what we desire.
Desde ahora prometo servirle á V. en lo que pueda.	From this moment I promise to serve you as far as I can.
El hombre ha obrado mal para con Dios y consigo mismo desde la creacion del mundo.	Man has acted wrong before God and to himself since the creation of the world.
Desde Nueva York á Filadelfia hay ochenta y ocho millas.	It is eighty-eight miles from New York to Philadelphia.
Yo juego contra tí.	I play against you (thee).
Esta casa está contra el Este.	This house faces the East.
La ciudad está sobre un monte.	The city is built upon a mountain (or hill).
La caridad es sobre todas las virtudes.	Charity is before all virtues.
Voy tras tí.	I go after you (thee).
Sufre la pena pues lo quieres.	Suffer the consequences (pain), since such is your (thy) will.
Tras la primavera viene el verano.	After spring comes summer.
Tras ser culpado, él es el que levanta el grito.	Notwithstanding he is guilty, it is he that raises the cry.
Leeré este libro pues V. me dice que es bueno.	I will read this book since you tell me it is good.

EXPLANATION.

197. DEFECTIVE VERBS are those which are not employed in all their tenses and persons. *Podrir*, to rot, *placer*, to please, and *yacer*, to lie, belong to this class, and are found used in the following tenses and persons:

PODRIR.

Imper.	2d person plural.	Podrid.	Rot.
Subjunc. imp.	3d person sing.	Podriria.	He would rot.
Infinit.	Present.	Podrir.	To rot.
	Particip.	Podrido.	Rotten.

PLACER.

Indicat.	Pres. 3d person sing.	Place.	It pleases.
	Imperfect.	Placia.	It did please.
	Perfect ind.	Plugo.	It pleased.
Subjunc.	Present.	Plegue.	It may please.
	Imperfect.	Pluguiera. / Pluguiese.	It might please.
	Future imp.	Pluguiere.	It may please.

These persons of the subjunctive mood in this verb are only used in the following expressions: *plegue*, or *pluguiera*, or *pluguiese á Dios*, would to God; and *si me pluguiere*, if it should please me.

198. YACER.—No part of this verb is used except the third persons of the present indicative, *yace* and *yacen*, chiefly at the beginning of epitaphs.

199. SOLER is used only in the present and imperfect of the indicative mood. This verb has the peculiarity of never being employed except as a determining verb, governing the determined verb without the aid of any preposition, and always in the present infinitive; as,

Suelo pasear temprano.	I usually go early to walk.

200. DESDE, from, points out the beginning of time or place; as,

Desde la creacion del mundo.	From the creation of the world.
Desde Nueva York á Filadelfia.	From New York to Philadelphia.

For this reason it forms a part of several adverbial expressions which signify time or place; as,

Desde ahora.	From this time.
Desde aqui.	From hence.

LESSON XLI.

201. CONTRA is used in all cases as the English *against*.

202. SOBRE, upon, above, &c., serves to denote the superiority of things with respect to others, either by their material situation or by their excellence or power; as,

La ciudad está *sobre* un monte.	The city is on a mountain.
La caridad es *sobre* todas las virtudes.	Charity is above all virtues.

It has also the signification of *además*, moreover, or *además de*, besides; as,

Sobre ser reo convicto quiere que le premien.	Besides being a convicted criminal, he wishes to be rewarded.

It also signifies time; as,

Hablar *sobre* mesa.	To talk during dinner.

Security; as,

Prestar *sobre* prendas.	To lend upon pledge.

203. TRAS, behind, after, &c., signifies the order in which some things follow others; as,

Voy *tras* tí.	I follow you.
Tras la primavera viene el verano.	After spring comes summer.

It also signifies *besides*; as,

Tras ser culpado, él es el que levanta el grito.	Besides being guilty, he remonstrates.

204. The conjunction PUES, since, is used to account for a proposition brought forward; as,

Leeré este libro *pues* V. me dice que es bueno.	I will read this book *since* you tell me it is good.

CONVERSATION AND VERSION.

1. ¿Sobre qué quiere V. que hablemos hoy? No sé; de cualquiera cosa, con tal que practiquemos con los verbos defectivos y las preposiciones *contra, desde, sobre* y *tras*.

2. Que me place; pero dígame V., ¿cree V. que tenemos mucho que practicar con el verbo *yacer?* No, señor, puesto que es un verbo que solo sirve para ponerse en los epitafios.

3. Pues si V. gusta le harémos un epitafio y pasarémos á practicar con otro verbo que no sea tan triste.—Soy de su opinion de V., porque no me gustan las cosas tristes.

LESSON XLI.

4. Helo aquí:
"Aquí yace el verbo yacer,
Otra cosa no sabiendo hacer."

5. Ese epitafio me hace recordar á mi otro, oígalo V.:
"Aquí Fray Diego reposa,
Y jamas hizo otra cosa."

6. Hombre, tenga V. caridad de mí y no me haga V. reir hablando de epitafios, que es cosa mas bien para hacer llorar que para hacer reir. ¿Suele V. tener siempre tan buen humor? No siempre; pero no se gana nada con estar triste.

7. En efecto, mas vale estar alegre que triste, pero no siempre se puede estar alegre, ¿y entónces que hace V.? Entónces mando á pasear al mal humor.

8. Eso es mas fácil de decir que de hacer; ¿quiere V. decirme como lo hace V.? Convengo con V.; pero cuando el hombre quiere verdaderamente una cosa la logra casi siempre.

9. Plegue á Dios que yo logre estar siempre contento puesto que estar contento es ser feliz. ¿Qué es lo que V. hace para estar siempre contento? Yo no le he dicho á V. que estoy siempre contento, pero procuro estarlo y así logro no estar triste.

10. ¿Cómo lo hace V.? Obro segun las circunstancias. Examino la causa de mi tristeza ó mal humor; si es mi falta me consuelo porque creo que Dios me castiga para que yo me corrija, y me haga mejor con la experiencia.

11. Bien, ¿y cuando V. es inocente y le sucede un infortunio? Entónces me consuelo tambien, porque creo que todo lo que Dios nos envia es para nuestro bien.

12. Entónces es V. filósofo. No, señor, mejor que eso; soy religioso.

13. ¿Tiene V. miedo de la muerte? No, señor, porque sé que todos hemos de morir, y que tras la muerte viene la vida eterna.

14. ¿Cuántos niños tiene V.? Cinco; dos niños y tres niñas.

15. ¿Cómo se llaman? El mayor de los niños se llama Alejandro y el menor Manuel.

16. ¿Y las niñas? Las niñas son Luisa, Carlota y Margarita.

17. ¿Cuanto tiempo hace que no ha estado V. en España? Hace veinte años que salí de España.

18. ¿Y no ha vuelto V.? No, señora, y creo que nunca volveré.

19. ¿Porqué? No porque no lo haya deseado, sino porque las circunstancias no me lo han permitido.

20. Porqué habla V. tanto de sí mismo en sus conversaciones, ¿no piensa V. que eso puede cansar á sus oyentes? Así es la verdad, señora; pero para mí es la materia de conversacion mas interesante que puedo encontrar.

LESSON XLI.

EXERCISE.

1. James, do you know where Charlotte has gone to? I saw her going out, but I do not know where she has gone.
2. Can you not help your brother in his misfortune? you know he relies (*contar*) upon your aid. I shall do all in my power to serve him; but you know that is not much.
3. Margaret, go and call Charles; tell him he has played enough, and that I want him to attend to his music lessons. Why, he has been at his lessons for the last half hour!
4. Ah! that is another thing. Where is he then? Here he is, here.
5. Well, Charles, how are you getting on with your music? Very well, papa; but I think Jane will have to help me with my Spanish exercise.
6. My dear boy, always do your own exercises, then you will be sure they are well done. Oh, yes, I know; as they say: "Help yourself and Heaven will help you."
7. How beautiful that lady is! Yes; but, my dear sir, her accomplishments are much superior to her beauty.
8. I do not doubt it at all; but how do you know that? have you known her long? Long enough to find out her good qualities, which, in my opinion, are of more value than all the beauty in the world.
9. Have you found time yet to examine the books I put on your table the other day? I have, and the examination caused (produced) me a great deal of sadness.
10. How so? From the commencement, page after page, I found that the author has not the least experience of the world; and, besides, he contradicts toward the end what he has given as a general rule at the beginning of his work.
11. I am very much grieved (sorry) that such is your opinion. So am I; but you know it is better (worth more) to tell the truth, even though it should offend the author himself.
12. Can you read that epitaph? I believe it is in English. Yes; it says: "Here lies Pedro Gutiérrez."
13. Is that all it says? No, there is a great deal more; but I cannot read it.
14. Ah, indeed! I see; you do not read English as well as you thought. I do not; and I promise you that from this moment I will study it attentively until I know it thoroughly.
15. What is that you are smelling? The book that Charles has just bought.
16. What smell has it? It smells like new paper.

17. What was that man rewarded for? For having returned (*devolver*) five hundred dollars, which he found in the park, to the person that had lost them.

18. I am very glad that he has been rewarded; but virtue is always rewarded, sooner or later (*tarde que temprano*).

LESSON XLII.

Adquirir.	To acquire.
Asir.	To seize.
Caber.	To contain, to hold.
Cocer.	To cook.
Erguir.	To erect.
Satisfacer.	To satisfy.
Traer.	To bring, to carry.

(*See conjugation of these verbs at the end of the book.*)

Conseguir.	To succeed, to get.
Callar.	To be silent, to hold one's tongue.
Reprender.	To reprehend, to chide.
Divisar.	To perceive, to descry, to espy.
Fumar.	To smoke.
Establecer.	To establish.
Saber (*imp. verb*).	(*In the signification of*) to taste, or to savor.
Sorprender.	To surprise.
Entrambos.	Both.
Solo.	Alone.
Ir á caballo.	To ride on horseback.
Ir en coche.	To ride in a carriage.
De todos modos.	At all events, by all means.
De ningun modo.	By no means, not at all.
Manos á la obra.	To work!
Por mi parte.	For my part.
Así sea.	So be it, let it be so.
¡Cáspita! (*int.*).	Wonderful! too bad!
¡Vaya! (*int.*).	Come, now! indeed! go away!

LESSON XLII.

CONJUNCTIONS.

They are classified as follows:

Copulative.

Que.	That.	Además.	Moreover.
Tambien.	Also.	Y *or* é.	And.
		Ni.	Neither, nor.

Disjunctive.

O, ú, ya.	Or, either, whether.	Por cuanto.	Whereas.
		Para que.	So that, in order that.
Sea que.	Whether.		
Tampoco.	Neither.	A fin de.	In order that.

Adversative.

Más, pero.	But.
Aun cuando.	Even.
Aunque.	Although, though.

Conditional.

Si.	If.
Sino.	But.
Con tal que.	Provided.
A ménos de. } A ménos que. }	Unless.

Causal.

Porque, que.	Because.
¿Porqué?	Why?
Pues, pues que.	Since.
Por.	For.
Por tanto.	Therefore.

Continuative.

Pues, puesto que.	Since, inasmuch as.

Comparative.

Como, así como.	As.
Así.	So.

Antes de.	Before.
Léjos de.	Far from.
En lugar de.	Instead of, in place of.
Por falta de.	For want of.
De miedo de. } Por temor de. }	For fear of.

Como quiera que.	However.
Fuera de que.	Besides.
Al instante que, *or* luego que, *or* tan pronto como.	As soon as.
De manera que.	So that.
Desde que.	Since.

Acuerdo.	Advice, or opinion.	Marca.	Brand, mark.
		Fortuna.	Fortune.

Daño.	Harm, damage.	Partida.	Party, game, departure.
Ajedrez.	Chess.		
Cigarro.	Cigar.	Opinion.	Opinion.
Cigarrillo.	Cigarette.	Pipa.	Tobacco-pipe, pipe.
Tabaco.	Tobacco.		
Jaque.	Check.	Compañia.	Company.
Caso.	Case.		

COMPOSITION.

Conjunctions governing the subjunctive.

Dado que me escriba no le responderé.	Granted that he should write me, I will not answer him.
Con tal que el trabaje.	Provided he works.
A ménos que me pague.	Unless he pays me.
Sea que se vaya ó que se quede.	Whether he sets out or remains.
Calle V. no sea que nos oiga.	Be silent lest he should hear us.

Conjunctions governing the indicative.

Al instante que recibí la carta le respondí.	As soon as I received the letter I answered him.
De suerte que (or de modo que) no pudo conseguirlo.	So that he could not bring it about.
De manera que no está nada satisfecho.	So that he is not pleased at all.
¿Qué ha hecho V. desde que le he visto á V.?	What have you been doing since I saw you?
Llegué tan pronto como pude.	I got here (or there) as soon as I could.
Miéntras que V. juega él estudia su leccion.	While you play, he studies his lesson.
Yo reprendo á V. sus faltas porque le quiero.	I reprove you for your faults because I love you.

Conjunctions governing the infinitive.

Yo trabajo á fin de ganar dinero.	I work in order to earn money.
No le visitaré ántes de conocerle.	I shall not visit him before making his acquaintance.
Léjos de amarle le aborrece.	Far from loving him, he abhors him.

EXPLANATION.

205. Conjunctions.—The learner is already acquainted with the greater part of the conjunctions; but in this lesson they are again given, so that he may see how they are classified. Besides the conjunctions introduced in this lesson, there may be formed a variety of expressions which answer the same end as conjunctions; as.

Como quiera que,	However;
Fuera de que,	Besides;

and a large number of others.

206. It would require too much space to specify all the conjunctions that govern verbs in a given mood; more is to be learned from the teacher, and by constant practice in reading and conversation, than from all the rules that could be given.

207. The subjunctive should be used after the following conjunctive expressions: *Dado que*, granted that; *con tal que*, provided that; *á ménos que*, unless; *no sea que*, lest, for fear; *ántes que, sin que, sea que*, &c.; as,

Dado que me escriba no le responderé.	Granted that he should write to me, I shall not answer him.
Con tal que él trabaje.	Provided that he works.
A ménos que me pague.	Unless he pays me.

208. Other expressions having *de*, instead of *que*, require the verb in the infinitive mood; such as, *á fin de*, in order to; *á ménos de*, unless, &c.

209. Finally, other compound conjunctions govern the indicative; as, *al instante que*, as soon as; *de manera que*, so that, &c.

CONVERSATION AND VERSION.

1. Buenos dias, Don Cárlos.—Téngalos V. muy felices, Don Enrique; al instante que lo divisó desde la ventana lo reconocí.

2. ¿Cómo está toda la familia? Todos buenos; acaban de salir.

3. ¿De manera que está V. solo? Sí, señor, en lugar de salir quise quedarme á esperar á V. pues sabia que habia V. de venir.

4. ¿Quién se lo dijo á V.? A que no acierta V.—Verdaderamente no sé quién puede habérselo dicho á V.

5. Fué Helena, su hija de V., que acaba de salir á pasear con mi esposa y Margarita, mi hija.

6. Y nosotros, ¿qué harémos? Lo que V. guste.

7. Mi opinion es que juguemos una partida de ajedrez, que fumemos un cigarro, bebamos un vaso de vino de Cariñena, y vayamos despues á sorprender á las señoras al parque. ¿Está V. de acuerdo? Perfectísimamente.

8. Pues bien, manos á la obra; ¿juega V. mucho? Medianamente; pero como no lo practico temo que me gane V.

9. ¡Qué hombre! si hace lo ménos dos años que no he jugado, fuera de que jamás he sido muy fuerte.

10. ¿Cuáles quiere V., las negras ó las blancas? Cualesquiera, de todos modos he de perder.

11. Jaque á la reina Don Enrique.—Pues creo que está perdida.—Sí, señor, no puede huir—vaya pues le doy á V. la partida, puesto que sin reina es casi imposible ganar.

12. ¿Quiere V. que en lugar de jugar mas vayamos á ver las señoras? Sí, señor, luego que bebamos del vino de Cariñena.

13. ¡Hombre, sí, lo habia olvidado! aquí está, y aquí tiene V. tambien pipas, cigarros de la Habana, cigarrillos de la marca de la Honradez y tabaco de Virginia para la pipa; ¿qué prefiere V.? Yo prefiero los cigarrillos.

14. A su salud de V., Don Cárlos.—A la de V., Don Enrique.—¡Cáspita! ¡qué bien sabe el de Cariñena!

15. ¿Le gusta á V.? ¡Qué si me gusta! desde que vivo en Nueva York no he probado vino mejor.

16. Puesto que le gusta ¿porqué no repite V.? Por temor de que me haga daño, no suelo beber mucho, y temo que me ponga un poco alegre.

17. Aquí tiene V. fuego; ¿qué tal le gustan á V. esos cigarrillos? Excelentes.

18. Señor; ¿Qué quieres Juan? Los caballos estan listos.

19. ¡Qué! ¿Vamos á caballo? Sí, señor, las señoras han ido en coche.

20. ¿Qué camino tomarémos? Irémos por la Quinta avenida, que es la calle mas hermosa de Nueva York.

21. Tenemos buen tiempo, D. Enrique.—Hermosísimo, y con esto, buena salud, amigos fieles, una larga familia y una buena fortuna, ¿qué mas podemos desear?

22. Tiene V. razon, Don Cárlos, por mi parte soy feliz y solo deseo que Dios me de una larga vida para ver á todos mis hijos bien establecidos.—Así sea, Don Enrique, lo deseo para entrámbos.

EXERCISE.

1. Does your brother never go out on horseback? Sometimes; but not very often.

2. What can be the reason of that? I thought he was very fond of horses and riding on horseback. So he is; but he does not often take exercise of that kind for fear of falling.

3. How does he go to the Central Park, in that case? Why, in a carriage of course.

4. Go away! What carriage does he go in? In his cousin's, of course, for want of one of his own.

5. Who will give me a cigarette? No one here; there is nobody here that smokes any thing but cigars or pipes.

6. Too bad! May I ask why none of you use the cigarette? Certainly; and we shall tell you with the greatest pleasure: at one time we all smoked what you call "cigarette," but what we call a "poor man's cigar," until one day Henry came (you know Henry is something of a doctor), and, with his head erect, said with a voice of thunder: "What's this? smoking cigarettes?"

7. Well! what more did he say? "Don't you know that what you are smoking there is nothing more than paper? You will all be sick!"

8. What did you do then? We were at first surprised; but very soon we promised never to smoke such a thing again, for it was good for nothing, and only tasted of paper.

9. Be that as you please; for my part I shall always prefer the cigarette to the cigar (*tabaco*). Perhaps you are right; each one has his taste, and so we shall say no more about it.

10. What news do you bring from Boston? Some good, and some bad: my cousin has been very fortunate in that affair I spoke of to you; but he met last week with an unfortunate accident.

11. Ah! how was that? He was out riding in company with some friends, and in returning home he fell off his horse.

12. I am very sorry indeed; and I hope he may soon be able to attend to his business.

13. What do you think of playing a game of chess? I am ready to play one, if you wish; but you will not find my game very good.

14. Why do you not practise more than you do? I have practised very much, with a desire to become perfect in the game, but have not been able to succeed.

LESSON XLIII.

Advertir.	To take notice, to observe, to warn.
Conjugar.	To conjugate.
Desconfiar.	To distrust, to mistrust.
Cometer.	To commit.
Distinguir.	To distinguish.

LESSON XLIII.

Formar.	To form, to shape.
Devolver.	To return, to give back.
Descuidar.	To neglect, to be at ease in one's [mind.
Pertenecer.	To belong.
Molestar.	To molest, to trouble.
Resultar.	To result, to turn out.

(*The learner ought by this time to know almost all the conjugations, both of the regular and the irregular verbs; should he at any time be at a loss for some part of a verb, he may refer to the conjugations at the end of the grammar.*)

Cada.	Every, each.
Sin duda.	Certainly, without doubt.
¡Adelante!	Go on! go ahead! come in!
En adelante.	Henceforth.
Compuesto.	Compound.
Irregular.	Irregular.
Completo.	Complete.
Varios.	Various, divers, several.
Simple.	Simple.
Seguro.	Secure, sure.
Obvio.	Obvious.
Lo demás.	The rest.

Conocimiento.	{ Bill of lading. { Knowledge.	Condicion.	Condition.
		Navidad, *or* } Natividad. }	Nativity, Christmas.
José.	Joseph.		
Artículo.	Article, section.	Relacion.	Relation.
Pronombre.	Pronoun.	Duda.	Doubt.
Participio.	Participle.	Ventaja.	Advantage.
Gerundio.	Gerund.	Frase.	Phrase.
Adverbio.	Adverb.	Prontitud.	Promptitude.
Presente.	Present.	Sentencia.	Sentence.
Imperfecto.	Imperfect.	Conjugacion.	Conjugation.
Perfecto.	Perfect.	Verdad.	Truth.
Futuro.	Future.	Imprudencia.	Imprudence.
Pluscuamperfecto.	Pluperfect.	Preposicion.	Preposition.
Infinitivo.	Infinitive.	Conjuncion.	Conjunction.
Indicativo.	Indicative.	Interjeccion.	Interjection.
Imperativo.	Imperative.	Paz.	Peace.
Subjuntivo.	Subjunctive.	Molestia.	Trouble.

LESSON XLIII.

COMPOSITION.

Descuide V.	Make yourself easy (or be at ease in your mind).
¿Cuántos tiempos tiene el modo indicativo?	How many tenses has the indicative mood?
Ocho: cuatro simples y cuatro compuestos.	Eight: four simple and four compound.
Bueno fuera (or seria) no descuidarse.	It would be well not to be off one's guard.
Conviniera (or convendria) que se hiciese la paz.	It would be well if peace were made.
Aunque dijeras (or dijeses) la verdad, no te creeria.	Though thou wert to tell the truth, he would not believe thee.
¡Ojalá cesara (or cesase) la guerra! asi seriamos mas felices.	Would to God the war would come to an end! we should then be happier.
Pensó que estudiaras.	I thought thou wouldst study.
No creí que estudiase V.	I did not think you would study (or were studying).
Juzgué que estudiaria V.	I judged you would study.
Dije que leyeras.	I said thou wert to read (or wouldst read).
Dijo que leerias.	He said thou wouldst read.
Dijimos que leyese.	We said he was to read.
Deseaba que ganaras (or ganases).	He wished thee to win.
Quiso que te casaras (or casases).	He wished thee to get married.
No sé si iria ó no.	I do not know whether he would go or not.
Si tuviera (or si tuviese) buenos libros leeria.	Had I (or if I had) good books I would read.
Seria imprudencia ir con este tiempo.	It were imprudent to go in this weather.
No quiso ir.	He would not go.
Debemos perdonar á nuestros enemigos.	We should forgive our enemies.
V puede hablar, pero yo no lo puedo.	You can speak, but I cannot.
¿Si hubiera (or hubiese) V. recibido los libros me los habria V. prestado?	Had you received (or if you had received) the books would you have lent them to me?
Si los hubiera (or hubiese) recibido se los habria prestado; pero no los he recibido aun.	If I had received them I would have lent them to you; but I have not received them yet.
En lugar de venir á verme me escribió.	Instead of coming to see me, he wrote to me.
Él no jugará por temor de perder su dinero.	He will not play, for fear of losing his money.
¡Quiera Dios que se corrija!	God grant that he may change!

LESSON XLIII. 215

¡Así sea! Lo deseo para entrámbos.	So be it! That is my desire for both.
Bebo á la salud de V., Don Enrique.	I drink to your health, Mr. Henry.
A la de V., Don Cárlos.	Your health, Mr. Charles.
Señores, manos á la obra, no sea que no podamos acabar á tiempo.	To work, gentlemen, for fear we should not be able to finish in time.
De todos modos creo que no lo conseguirémos.	At all events, I do not think we shall succeed.

EXPLANATION.

210. IMPERFECT AND PLUPERFECT OF THE SUBJUNCTIVE.— Although it has been deemed expedient, in the example of the conjugation of verbs in the subjunctive mood, to give but one English equivalent for each of the three terminations *ria, ra, se*, it is not to be inferred therefrom that they may be used indiscriminately. Indeed, the correct application of each of these terminations presents as much difficulty to the student of Spanish as does that of the English signs *might, could, should, would* to the foreigner learning English. The following rules will, however, serve as a guide in all ordinary cases, and enable the pupil to surmount not a few of the most serious obstacles to the right use of the terminations in question.

1st. When the sentence begins without a conditional conjunction, the verb may take either the first or the second termination (*ria* or *ra*); as,

Bueno se*ria* (*or* fue*ra*) no descuidarse.	It would be well not to be off one's guard.
Convend*ria* (*or* convinie*ra*) que se hiciese la paz.	It would be well if peace were made.

2d. In sentences beginning with *si, sino, aunque, bien que, dado que*, &c., or with an interjection expressive of desire, either the second or third termination may be employed (*ra* or *se*); and were it necessary to repeat the same tense in the second clause of the sentence (in order to show what would take place as the result of the condition expressed in the first clause), the first termination (*ria*) may then be used; as,

Aunque dije*ras* (*or* dije*ses*) la verdad, no te cree*ria*.	Though thou toldest (or wert to tell) the truth, he would not believe thee.

3d. When the imperfect of the subjunctive is preceded by a verb in the preterit definite of the indicative, signifying *pen sar*, to think, *decir*, to say, or such like, any of the terminations may be used; but it must be observed that the idea conveyed will be different, according to the termination employed; as,

Pensé que estudia*ra* V., *or* que estudia*ria* V.	I thought you would study.
No creí que estudia*se* V.(*or* estudia*ra*) V.	I did not think you were studying, or I did not think you would study.
Juzgué que estudia*ria* (*or* estudia*ra*) V.	I judged you would study.
Dije que ley*era* (*or* lee*ria*) V.	I said you would read.
Dijo que ley*ese* (*or* ley*era*) V.	He said you were to read.
Dijimos que ley*era* (*or* ley*ese*).	We said he was to read.

4th. But if this tense be preceded or governed by a verb in any of the past tenses of the indicative, signifying *desear*, to desire, *querer*, to wish, or by any verb of such nature, then the second termination (*ra*) or the third (*se*) must be used, and never the first (*ria*); as,

Deseaba que gana*ra* (*or* gana*se*) V.	He was desirous that you might win.
Quiso que V. se casa*ra* (*or* casa*se*).	He wished you to get married.

A glance at the foregoing rules and examples will suffice in order to observe that the first and second terminations (*ria* and *ra*) may be used one for the other, without any change in the sense of the phrase; that the second may also be used for the third (that is to say, *ra* for *se*), but that the first and third are of an entirely different meaning, and, in consequence, can never be substituted one for the other. Another peculiarity of the first (*ria*) is, that it can never be preceded by a conditional conjunction, while the second and third may.

5th. When, in translating into Spanish, *whether* is to be translated by *si*, *would* or *should* must be rendered by the termination *ria*; as,

No sé *si* i*ria*.	I do not know whether he would go.

6th. The inverted forms *had I*, *had he*, &c., meaning *if I had*, *if he had*, &c., are always to be turned into Spanish by either of the terminations *ra* or *se*, preceded by the conjunction *si*; as,

Si tuvie*ra* (*or* tuvie*se*) buenos libros, lee*ria*.	Had I (or if I had) good books, I would read.

LESSON XLIII.

7th. *Were*, used in the place of *would be*, may be translated by either *ria* or *ra*, never by *se*; as,

Seria (*or* fuera) imprudencia ir con este tiempo.	It were imprudent to go in this weather.

211. The English auxiliaries, *may, might, can, could, will, would* and *should* are sometimes to be translated into Spanish by principal verbs of the same meaning, and not merely rendered by corresponding terminations; as,

No *quiso* ir.	He would not go.
V. *puede* hablar, pero yo no lo *puedo*.	You may (or can) speak, but I cannot.

In the first example we see, that by *would not* is conveyed the idea of the want of *will* or *desire* on the part of the person alluded to, and not the idea of that person's *going* or *not going*, as dependent on a condition. Had the latter been the sense intended, we should then have rendered *would* by the termination *ria* of the verb *ir*, to go; thus,

Él no *iria*.	He would not go;

for, in that case, the object would have been simply to *predict* that he *would not go*, as dependent on some such condition as, if I did not go too, *si yo no fuese tambien*. Hence, the closest attention is required, in order to find the real meaning of the auxiliaries above mentioned, before attempting to translate them.

212. The imperfect of the subjunctive denotes a contingent action that took place some time ago, or that is taking place at the present time, or that will take place after the completion of the action expressed by the determining verb.

213. The pluperfect represents a contingent action as completed before some period of time already past, or before some other action which is now also completed, or which would be now completed had it taken place.

The closest attention to the foregoing remarks is essential, in order to avoid the improper substitution of the tenses of the indicative for those of the subjunctive, which all foreigners, and especially the English, are most liable to commit.

LESSON XLIII.

CONVERSATION AND VERSION.

1. ¿Duda V. que se haga la paz este verano? Convendria (*or* conviniera) que se hiciese la paz; pero temo que no se haga.

2. ¿Iria V. á Europa si tuviera (*or* tuviese) tiempo? No iria aunque tuviera tiempo, si no tuviese dinero.

3. ¡Ojalá! tuviera V. (*or* tuviese) mucho dinero, porque entónces me prestaria V. alguno; ¿no es así? Si tuviera mucho le prestaria á V. alguno; pero con la condicion de que me lo devolviese pronto.

4. ¿Teme V. acaso que no se lo devolviera? Todo pudiera suceder, amigo mio.

5. Si V. me hubiera (*or* hubiese) prestado algo, y yo no se lo hubiese (*or* hubiera) devuelto, V. tendria razon en desconfiar.—Todo eso está muy bien; pero si, en lugar de ser V., fuera yo el que necesitara dinero, y V. el que lo tuviera, ¿me lo prestaria? Por supuesto que sí.

6. Pues con todo eso yo no sé si V. lo haria.—¿Porqué piensa V. tan mal de mí?

7. ¿Ha olvidado V. ya que el año pasado, por Navidad, fuí á pedirle á V. cien pesos y me los negó V.? Mal pudiera yo prestárselos á V. cuando yo no los tenia; pero esté V. seguro, Don José, que yo hubiera tenido un gran placer en habérselos prestado á V. si los hubiera (*or* hubiese) tenido.

8. ¿Si V. supiera usar correctamente los tiempos y modos del verbo, sabria V. hablar español? Sí, señor, con los conocimientos que ya tengo de las demás partes de la oracion, creo que hablaria bien el español si supiera usar bien los tiempos y modos del verbo.

9. ¿Qué es lo mas importante al aprender una lengua? El conocimiento de todo lo que hace relacion al verbo.

10. ¿Porqué cree V. que el verbo es lo mas importante? Porque sin los verbos no se puede formar una sola sentencia.

11. ¿Luego, segun eso, bastará aprender la conjugacion de los verbos regulares é irregulares para hablar una lengua? No, señor, si uno sabe conjugar los verbos como regularmente se conjugan en las gramáticas; pero sí sabiéndolos conjugar como se debe.

12. ¿Pues qué, hay algun otro modo de conjugar los verbos? Los verbos deben conjugarse formando sentencias completas en todos sus modos y tiempos.

13. ¿Qué ventajas resultan de esto? Las ventajas son obvias, pues formando sentencias completas con cada tiempo y modo se aprende á distinguir estos tiempos y modos, acabando por usarlos correctamente.

14. ¿Y cree V. que hablaria bien el español si pudiese hacer sentencias en todos los tiempos y modos del verbo? Sin duda alguna, una vez que

LESSON XLIII.

V. forme estas sentencias con prontitud y sin cometer faltas, hablará V. español.

15. Pues manos á la obra, ¿quiere V. que haga algunas en el modo indicativo? No, señor, en las lecciones pasadas ha practicado V. bastante con ese modo, haga V. algunas ahora con el modo subjuntivo.

16. Presente: ¿Desea V. que yo aprenda el español? ¿Es correcta? Perfectamente; adelante.

17. Perfecto de subjuntivo: Temo que la guerra no haya acabado en Europa. ¿Está bien? Sí, señor, está muy bien; pero no necesita V. preguntarme á cada sentencia que haga, si está correcta, porque yo tendré buen cuidado de advertírselo á V. cuando no sea así.

18. Pluscuamperfecto: Si yo hubiera creido que esto le molestaba á V. no se lo habria preguntado.—Esto no me molesta de ningun modo y espero que V. no se moleste tampoco por lo que yo acabo de decir.

19. Imperfecto: ¿Seria suficiente hacer una frase en cada tiempo? Seria suficiente si cada tiempo se usase en un solo caso; pero como hay muchos y muy varios, convendria practicar en todos tanto como fuese posible.

EXERCISE.

1. Before going out, Henry, I wish to give you a *piece of* advice. Well, go on!

2. What is that advice* you have to give me? Hold your tongue, and hear what I have to tell you.

3. Did you warn your cousin not to lend his carriage to that young man who asked him for it? Yes, but he said he would do so, and that he did not distrust that young man at all.

4. Do you know how to conjugate all the verbs in the Spanish language now? I am not sure; my memory is not very good; and so I always like to look at my grammar, for fear of making (committing) mistakes.

5. Can you tell me how many conjugations of regular verbs there are in Spanish? Yes, sir, there are three.

6. When you see a new verb, how do you know to what conjugation it belongs? By the termination of the infinitive mood.

7. Can you tell me to what conjugation the verb *comprar* belongs? Certainly; it belongs to the first.

8. How do you know that? I see the characteristic termination of the first conjugation, which is *ar*.

9. And of which conjugation is *entender?* The second; its termination being *er*.

10. Very well. Now, if I say *existió*, can you tell me all about that verb? Yes, sir, it is a regular verb, third person singular, of the preterit

* *Consejo.*

definite tense of the indicative mood; it belongs to the third conjugation, its infinitive being *existir*.

11. Are there in Spanish no other conjugations than those which you have just told me? Yes, very many. Those I have mentioned (*mencionar*) already are the three regular ones.

12. What do you understand by "regular verbs"? Regular verbs are those which are conjugated in all their moods and tenses exactly like the models (*modelos*) given in different parts of the grammar.

13. And "irregular verbs," what are they? Those whose conjugation is different from the models.

14. If you could speak Spanish as well as English, do you think you would prefer it to your own language? I would like to be able to speak it as well; but there is no language in the world that I would prefer to my own.

15. If I were to lend you this phrase book would you return it to me next week? I would if you wanted it, and that I promised to return it to you at that time.

LESSON XLIV.

Aproximar.	To approach, to draw near.
Apurar.	To perplex, to press.
Aullar.	To howl.
Ladrar.	To bark.
Cuidar.	To take care of.
Dejar.	To leave, to let.
Emplear.	To employ.
Matar.	To kill.
Permitir.	To permit.
Robar.	To rob, to steal.
Imponer.	To impose.
Tantico.	Somewhat; a little.
Vaya de cuento.	To begin my story.
Como iba diciendo de mi cuento.	As I was saying (in my story).
A mi costa.	At my expense, to my cost.
Ya le veo á V. venir.	I see what you are at.
Venir á pelo.	To suit exactly, to be apropos.

LESSON XLIV.

De sopeton.	Unexpectedly.
Cuanto mas.	The more.
¡Por Dios!	For Heaven's sake!
¡He!	Ho! hoa! What?
¡Oiga!	Indeed! Just listen!
Chico.	Little, small.
Revoltoso.	Noisy.
Caliente.	Hot, warm.
Apurado.	Embarrassed.
Burlon.	Jester, scoffer.
Natural.	Natural.
Aumentativo.	Augmentative.
Diminutivo.	Diminutive.
Pícaro.	Rogue, rascal.
Satisfecho.	Satisfied, contented.

Cuento.	Tale, story.
Corro.	Group of persons.
Cojo.	Lame.
Brazo.	Arm.
Ademan.	Attitude.
Francisco, Paco (*dim.*).	Francis, Frank.
José, Pépe (*dim.*).	Joseph, Joe.
Caldo.	Broth.
Calducho.	Poor broth.
Pistoletazo.	Pistol shot.
Poetastro.	Poetaster.
Lugar.	Place.
Garrote.	Bludgeon.
Garrotazo.	Blow of a bludgeon.
Cañon.	Cannon.
Cañonazo.	Cannon-shot.
Ladron.	Thief, robber.
Anécdota.	Anecdote.
Casuca.	Miserable house.
Mosca.	Fly; tiresome person.
Necesidad.	Necessity, need.
Pierna.	Leg.
Boca.	Mouth.
María, Mariquita (*dim.*).	Mary.
Concepcion, Concha (*dim.*).	(*No English equivalent.*)
Pistola.	Pistol.
Estratagema.	Stratagem.
Josefa, Pépa (*dim.*).	Josephine.
Francisca, Paca (*dim.*).	Frances, Fanny.
Costumbre.	Custom.
Clase.	Class.

COMPOSITION.

Lo aprendí á mi costa.	I learned it to my cost.
Antes no le habia comprendido á V., ahora ya le veo venir.	I did not understand you before, but now I see what you are at.
Él me dió la noticia de sopeton.	He gave me the news unexpectedly.

LESSON XLIV.

¡Por Dios! D. Francisco, no hable V. de eso.	For Heaven's sake! Mr. Francis, do not speak of that.
¿Conoce V. á aquel hombron?	Do you know that big man?
Sí, señor, es el marido de mi vecinita Mariquita.	Yes, sir, he is the husband of my little neighbor Mary.
V. me sorprende. ¡Es posible que sea aquel hombronazo el marido de esa mujercita!	You surprise me. Is it possible that that enormous man is that little woman's husband!
¿Es ese hombre cojo?	Is that man lame?
Sí, señor; en la última guerra recibió un pistoletazo en una pierna.	Yes, sir; in the last war he received a pistol shot in one of his legs.
¿Ha matado V. alguna vez á alguno?	Did you ever kill any one?
Sí, señor, el año pasado maté de un garrotazo al perro de mi vecino, porque no me dejaba dormir, aullando todita la noche.	Yes, sir; last year I killed my neighbor's dog with a bludgeon, for he would not let me sleep, howling the whole night over.
Ese hombre es un picaronazo, que no hace sino beber y no atiende á las necesidades de su familia.	That man is a great rascal who does nothing but drink, and does not attend to the wants of his family.
Este perro es chiquito, pero yo tengo uno chiquirritito.	This dog is pretty small, but I have a very little one.
Carlotita, ve á cuidar de tu hermanita.	Charlotte, go and take care of your little sister.
Ese niño es un picarillo.	This child is a little rogue.
Esta niña es una coquetilla.	This little girl is a little coquette.
Mi pobrecico hijo está muy malo.	My poor little son is very sick.
Pépe, ¿has visto mi caballito?	Joe, have you seen my little horse?
Sí; pero yo en tu lugar, Paco, le llamaria caballejo, porque creo que no merece el nombre de caballito.	I did; but if I were you, Frank, I would call it a nag, for I think it is not worthy the name of (little) horse.
Pépe vino callandito.	Joe came in softly.
Mi amigo está apuradillo.	My friend is a little embarrassed.
Esa niña está muertecita de frio.	That little girl is almost dead with cold.
Tu casa está lejitos.	Your house is pretty far away.
Él no es poeta, sino poetastro.	He is no poet, but a poetaster.

EXPLANATION.

214. AUGMENTATIVE AND DIMINUTIVE NOUNS are those derivatives which serve to augment or diminish the signification of their primitives; not only in regard to size, but also to esteem, character, dignity, importance, &c.

They are formed by adding various terminations to the primitive nouns, dropping generally the vowel, if it end in one.

LESSON XLIV.

The terminations which are used are very numerous; but those most frequently adopted are *azo, on, ote* for the augmentive masculine, and *aza, ona, ota* for the augmentive feminine nouns. These terminations are equivalent in their meaning to the English words *big, large, stout, tall,* and such like; as,

PRIMITIVES.		DERIVATIVES.	
Hombre.	A man.	Hombr*on*, hombr*azo*, hombr*ote*.	A tall, or large, man.
Mujer.	A woman.	Mujer*ona*, mujer*aza*, mujer*ota*.	A tall, or large, woman.

But the nouns which have those terminations are not always augmentatives, since the nouns *pistoletazo,* pistol shot; *cañonazo,* cannon shot; *garrotazo,* blow of a bludgeon, do not augment the signification of their primitives, *pistola, cañon* and *garrote,* and consequently are not augmentatives.

Familiar use has introduced many other augmentative and diminutive terminations; as,

Hombron*azo*.	A very large man.
Picaron*azo*.	A very great rascal.

The terminations most used as diminutives are *in, illo, ito, ico, ete, uelo* or *ejo,* for the masculine; the feminine are formed by adding *a* to the termination *in,* and by changing the final vowel of the others into *a*.

Many of the diminutive terminations may acquire a still further diminutive signification, by adding other terminations to them; thus,

Ch*ico*.	Small.
Chiqu*ito*.	Very small.
Chiquirrit*ito*.	Very, very small.

The manner of applying these terminations, as much for their different meanings as for their various orthographical accidents, admits of so much variety that practice seems the only means of acquiring the proper use of them; as,

Mi herman*ito*.	My dear little brother.
Un hombrec*ito*.	A dear little man.
Un viejec*ito*.	A dear little old man.
Él es un picar*illo*.	He is a dear little rogue.
Carlot*ita*.	Dear little Charlotte.

Una pobre viejec*ita*.	A poor dear little old woman.
Ella es una coquet*illa*.	She is a dear little coquette.
Mi probrec*ico* hijo (*or* mi pobre hij*ito*).	My poor little son.
Un caball*ejo*.	A miserable little horse, a nag.
Un pobre*te*.	A poor useless creature.
Un ladronz*uelo*.	A petty young thief.
Un reyez*uelo*.	A petty king.

215. Besides the terminations mentioned, there are many others which may be called *irregular*, inasmuch as they can be affixed to certain nouns only, among them the most irregular are those of persons; as,

Francisco, Paco, etc.	Francis, Frank.
Concepcion, Concha, etc.	(*No equivalent in English.*)
José, Pepe, etc.	Joseph, Joe.
María, Mariquita, etc.	Mary.

216. Although the diminutives proceed in general from substantive nouns, as we see by the preceding examples, they are also formed, in familiar style, from adjectives, participles, gerunds, and even from adverbs; thus we not unfrequently say:

Revolto*sillo* es el muchacho.	The boy is rather turbulent.
Muertec*ito* de frio.	Half dead with cold.
Tod*ito* el dia.	The whole day over.
Pan calent*ito*.	Warm bread (slightly warm).
Apurad*illo* estuvo.	He was somewhat embarrassed.
Vino callandi*to*.	He came softly.
Lej*itos* está tu casa.	Your house is pretty far away.

217. Primitive words, ending of themselves in any diminutive termination (such as cep*illo*, brush; aban*ico*, fan; esp*ejo*, looking-glass, &c.), cannot take an additional termination similar to their own, without producing a disagreeable sound, which ought always to be avoided. Words ending in *ito* or *ita* are excepted.

The same termination may often serve to express *affection*, *pity*, *contempt*, &c., being in this respect like the interjections, and it is consequently very difficult to classify them. Very often their real meaning can be distinguished only by the nature of the conversation and the intonation of the voice. They are, nevertheless, not to be used too profusely, because when they come too close together they render the discourse monotonous, in consequence of the similarity existing between them.

218. There are in Spanish other derivatives, formed more or less at fancy, and which are not augmentatives or diminutives, although they may appear to be such; these might be called depreciatives (*despreciativos*), because there is always in them something of censure, maliciousness, or mockery; as,

Casa, casuca.	House, miserable-looking house.
Poeta, poetastro.	Poet, poetaster.
Caldo, calducho.	Broth, poor broth.

CONVERSATION AND VERSION.

1. ¿Tiene V. lástima de aquel pobrete? No tengo lástima de él, porque es un ladronzuelo.

2. ¿Le ha robado á V. algo? No, señor, él sabe muy bien que si se atreviese á robarme yo lo mataria de un pistoletazo.

3. Y ¿porqué no de un garrotazo, ó un cañonazo? ¿Porqué? No sé porqué, probablemente he empleado la palabra pistoletazo porque tengo una pistola y no tengo ni garrote, ni cañon.

4. No, señor, esa no es la razon; ¿quiere V. que yo se la diga? Bien, veamos.

5. V. no tiene valor para matar una mosca cuanto mas á un hombre; pero V. queria practicar con las palabras *matar* y *pistoletazo* y esta es la sola razon por la cual V. iba á cometer un homicidio.

6. Vaya, Don Francisco, V. es poeta, hombre de ingenio y de buen humor y quiere divertirse á costa mia, ¿no es verdad? Ya lo veo á V. venir, V. quiere hacerme decir que no soy poeta sino poetastro introduciendo esta palabrita mas de la leccion.

7. Solo le faltaba á V. llamarse Quevedo para serle parecido en todo, hasta en el nombre.—Mil gracias por el honor de la comparacion, pero volviendo á lo del pistoletazo.

8. ¡Por Dios! D. Francisco, no sea V. tan burlon y déjeme V. estar en paz.—Lo dejaré á V., Don Pepe, si me permite contarle un cuentecito; y para que le parezca á V. mas interesante, se lo contaré á V. introduciendo tantos aumentativos y diminutivos como me sea posible.

9. Con esa condicion le escucho á V.—Pues bien; vaya de cuento: Habia un hombrecillo en cierto lugarcillo.—Y observe V., D. Pepito, que para el cuentecito lo mismo hubiera dado que el hombre hubiera sido

hombron y el lugar lugaron.—Adelante con el cuentecillo que me va gustando un tantico. Pues es el caso que este hombron, hombrecito, hombrecillo, hombrote, hombrecico, hombrazo, hombronazo, hombracho, ó como V. quiera llamarle. . . .

10. Yo no quiero llamarle nada, V. le ha llamado ya suficiente; pero al cuento, al cuento ó se acabará el ejercicio sin que lleguemos al fin.— Pues este hombrezuelo no sabia mas que un cuentecillo; pero lo contaba á todo el mundo que encontraba.

11. Pero yo no comprendo como podia hacer que su cuento viniese á pelo y V. sabe que no se cuenta un cuento así de sopeton, como se dan los buenos dias.—Al principio, el viejoto se encontraba apuradillo para conseguirlo; pero el picaruelo inventó despues una estratagema por medio de la cual hizo que su anecdotilla viniera á pelo siempre.

12. ¡Oiga! ¿y que estratagema fué esa? Oígala V.; pero ántes debo advertir á V. que en su anécdota habia algo que hacía relacion á cañonazos y pistoletazos.

13. ¡Hó! ¡Ya vuelve V. á los pistoletazos! Pues bien, como iba diciendo de mi cuento, se aproximaba el buen viejecito callandito á cualquier corrillo que encontrase y poniéndose el dedo índice sobre la boca en ademan de imponer silencio, les preguntaba. "¿Han oido Vds. un cañonazo?" No, señor, era naturalmente la respuesta; pues bien, respondia mi hombre muy satisfecho.—Ahora que hablamos de cañonazos les contaré á Vds. una anécdota . . . . y aquí contaba su cuento.

14. Yo no veo la aplicacion de su cuento de V. todavía, Sr. D. Francisco.—¡Cómo! D. Pepe, ¿no ha oido V. un pistoletazo?

EXERCISE.

1. How did you like that story by Fernan Caballero which I lent you? Very much indeed; it gives a very good idea of the manners, customs and language of the low classes in Andalusia (*Andalucia*).

2. What did that man want? He is a poor lame man asking for a piece of bread, or a few cents to buy some.

3. He is lame, you say; how did that happen to him? He says he was at the war and received a pistol shot in the leg.

4. What does the physician give to your cousin since he has been sick? He has given him some medicine (*medicina*), and says he must take broth three times a day.

5. Do you like broth? Yes, very well; but not such poor broth as they make for my cousin.

6. How does that poor man make his living since he lost both his arms? He can do nothing in the world, and lives on what little money he gets from his brother, who is rather embarrassed himself just now.

7. Come nearer to the fire, Louisa; it is a little cold this morning. Thank you, I do not feel the cold much; but I would be obliged to you if you would call Fanny in to warm herself; she is half dead with cold.

8. Is Henry going to be employed by that merchant to whom you spoke for him some time ago? Yes, I think it is probable, and I shall be very glad, for the poor *fellow** is a little embarrassed, and has been so for a long time.

9. If I were in your place I would not allow that dog to howl so the whole night over. My father will not let me speak about it to our neighbor, who lives in that miserable old house next to ours; it is his dog, and he ought not to let it howl in such a manner.

10. Just listen to him! as if I could not go and kill it with a bludgeon.—Kill it! There would be no necessity for killing it; just give him one good blow with the bludgeon you talk of and he would let you sleep in future.

11. Have you ever read Don Quixote? No; why? If you take the trouble to read it you will find a very good anecdote of a madman (*loco*) and a dog, in the first chapter of the second part of that justly celebrated work.

12. Have you paid attention to what is said in to-day's lesson on augmentatives and diminutives? Yes, madam; and it seems to me that the proper use of them must make a language expressive and elegant in a high degree (*grado*).

13. Is *Concepcion* a very common name for ladies in Spain? There are a great many called by that name; the diminutive is *Concha*.

14. Is your mother satisfied with her new servant? Very much so.

15. Why did she let the other one go away? She was very glad to see her go away, because she used to steal everything that came to her hand.

16. Is that coffee warm? No, sir; but I could warm it in a few minutes, if you wished.

LESSON XLV.

Avisar.	To advise, to notify, to let one [know
Admirar.	To admire.
Aconsejar.	To counsel, to advise.
Apremiar.	To urge, to compel one to do any thing by order of court.

* Remember that English words *italicised* are not to be translated.

Afectar.	To feign, to affect.
Compadecer.	To pity.
Convertir.	To convert.
Desertar.	To desert.
Empeñar.	To pledge, to engage.
Explicar.	To explain.
Fusilar.	To shoot.
Guardar.	To guard, to observe, to keep.
Librar.	To free, to liberate, to deliver.
Mentir.	To lie.
Mencionar.	To mention.
Permanecer.	To remain.
Relatar.	To relate.
Santificar.	To sanctify.
Suceder.	To happen, to succeed.
Sonar.	To sound.
Volar.	To fly.

¡Ah bah!	Oh, pshaw!
¡Toma!	Indeed!

Ancho.	Wide, broad.
Falso.	False.
Calvo.	Bald.
Famoso.	Famous.
Notorio.	Notorious, well known.
Crédulo.	Credulous.
Crítico.	Critical.
Formal.	Formal, straightforward.
Supersticioso.	Superstitious.
Escéptico.	Skeptic, skeptical.

De todo corazon.	With all my heart.
En su interior.	In his mind.
Ya caigo.	I see (or understand).
Bien venido.	Welcome.
A cual mas.	Vieing with each other.
De buena fé.	In good faith.
Esto es.	That is.
Ya lo ve V.	So you see.

Sol.	Sun.	Oracion.	Prayer.
Amor.	Love.	Tierra.	Earth, land.

LESSON XLV.

Cielo.	Sky, heaven.	Calva.	Baldness, the bald part.
Reino.	Kingdom.		
Fin.	End, purpose.	Ana.	Ann.
Deudor.	Debtor.	Voluntad.	Will, choice.
General.	General.	Profecía.	Prophecy.
Cuervo.	Raven, crow.	Fisonomía.	Physiognomy, countenance.
Agüero.	Omen.		
Interior.	Interior.	Tentacion.	Temptation.
Espíritu.	Spirit.	Sinceridad.	Sincerity.
Lodo.	Mud.	Injusticia.	Injustice.
El padre nuestro.	The Lord's Prayer.	Ridiculez.	Ridicule.
Tren.	Train.	Compasion.	Compassion.
Parroquiano.	Parishioner, customer.	Materia.	Matter.
Lector.	Reader.	Fé.	Faith.
		Bolsa.	Purse.
		Excepcion.	Exception.
		Frente.	Forehead.
		Formalidad.	Formality.

COMPOSITION.

Dios te lo premie.	May God reward you for it.
Si para fines de año no hubiere pagado, le apremias (*or* apremiale, *or* le apremiarás).	If at the end of the year he has not paid you, compel him to do so.
Si viene (*or* como venga) será bien recibido.	If he comes, he shall be well received.
Quien tal diga miente.	Whoever says such a thing lies.
Si así lo haces, Dios te lo premie.	If you do so, may God reward you.
Si al salir de tu casa vieres volar cuervos, déjalos volar y mira tú donde pones los piés.	If on going out of your house you should see crows fly, let them fly, and look where you put your own feet.
Todo hombre calvo no tendrá pelo; y si tuviere alguno no será en la calva.	Every bald man will be without hair; or if he should have any, it will not be on the bald part.
Le perdonarán todo lo que hiciere.	They will forgive him every thing he may do.
Le escribiré á V. lo que me dijere.	I will write to you what he may (happen to) say to me.
Si permaneciere aquí algun tiempo se lo avisaré.	If I should (or should I) remain here any time, I will let you know.
Le escribiré á V. lo que diga.	I will write to you what he may say to me.

LESSON XLV.

Le perdonarán lo que haga.	They will forgive him every thing he may do.
Si hubiere salido cuando V. llegue.	If he should have left when you arrive.
Aunque hubiere llegado ántes que reciba la carta.	Although he may have arrived before he receives the letter.
Aunque haya llegado ántes que reciba la carta.	Although he may have arrived before he receives the letter.
El general mandó que todos los que desertaran fuesen fusilados.	The general ordered that all those who might (happen to) desert should be shot.
El general mandó que todos los que hubieran desertado fuesen fusilados.	The general ordered that all those who might have deserted should be shot.
El general ha mandado que todos los que desertaren sean fusilados.	The general has ordered that all those who may desert (*i. e.* may happen to desert) should be shot.
El general ha mandado que todos los que hubieren desertado sean fusilados.	The general has ordered that all those who may have deserted be shot.
Quien lo dijere miente.	Whoever should say so will lie.
Si viniere, será bien recibido.	If he should come, he will be well received.
Si así lo hicieres.	If you should do so.

EXPLANATION.

219. THE FUTURE SIMPLE of the subjunctive mood represents a contingent action as to take place some time hence; as,

Le escribiré á V. lo que me *dijere*.	I will write to you what he may (happen to) say to me.
Le perdonarán todo lo que *hiciere*.	They will forgive him everything he may do in future.
Si *permaneciere* aquí algun tiempo se lo avisaré.	If I should (or should I) remain here any time I shall let you know.

220. THE PRESENT of the subjunctive may be substituted for the foregoing tense, except when the verb is preceded by the conditional *si*; as, *Le escribiré á V. lo que diga*; *Le perdonarán lo que haga*.

221. THE FUTURE COMPOUND, which is not so much used as the simple, denotes a contingent action subordinate to a future event; as,

Si *hubiere salido* cuando V. llegue.	If he should have left when you arrive.

LESSON XLV.

Aunque *hubiere llegado* ántes que reciba la carta. | Although he may have arrived before he receives the letter.

222. THE COMPOUND PRESENT of the subjunctive may be substituted for the above tense, except when the verb is preceded by the conditional *si*; as, *aunque* haya llegado *ántes que reciba la carta.*

223. In order that the imperfect and pluperfect of the subjunctive, which also express a future contingent action or event, be not misapplied, as too frequently they are, and confounded with the future simple and compound future of the same mood, the following distinction must be attentively observed:

1st. That the *imperfect* and *pluperfect* may be employed when the actions or events expressed in the sentence are future only in reference to some other time expressed, or merely implied, in the sentence.

2d. That the *future simple* and *compound future* must be used when the contingent action or event implied in the sentence is future with regard to the action expressed by the determining verbs; as,

El general mandó que todos los que *desertaran* fuesen fusilados.	The general ordered that all those who should (might happen to) desert should be shot.
El general mandó que todos los que *hubieran desertado* fuesen fusilados.	The general ordered that all those who had (might have) deserted should be shot.
El general ha mandado que todos los que *desertaren* sean fusilados.	The general has ordered that all those who desert (*i. e.* may happen to desert) shall be shot.
El general ha mandado que todos los que *hubieren* desertado sean fusilados.	The general has ordered that all those who have deserted shall be shot.

224. The future simple and the compound future of the subjunctive also act as determining verbs; but they govern the subordinate verb only in the present or the future simple of the indicative, and in the imperative; as,

Quien lo *dijere, miente.* | Whoever should say so will lie.
Si *viniere será* bien recibido. | If he should come, he shall be well received.

Si así lo *hicieres*. Dios te lo premie.	If you do so, may God reward you for it.
Si para fines de año no *hubiere pagado*, le *apremias*, or *aprémiale*, or le *apremiarás*.	If at the end of the year he has not paid you, compel him to do so.

These determining sentences of the future simple of the subjunctive may be turned to the present indicative in certain cases, and to the present subjunctive in others; as,

Si *viene*, or como *venga*, será bien recibido.	If he comes, he shall be well received.
Quien tal *diga* miente.	Whoever says so lies.
Si así lo *haces*, Dios te lo premie, etc.	If you do so, may God reward you for it.

CONVERSATION AND VERSION.

1. Don José, me han dicho que es mal agüero al salir uno de su casa ver volar cuervos; ¿qué piensa V. sobre ello? Yo pienso como Don Francisco de Quevedo.

2. ¿Y qué es lo que pensaba ese famoso escritor sobre esta materia? Oiga V. lo que él decia.

3. Si al salir de tu casa vieres volar cuervos, déjalos volar, y mira tú donde pones los piés.

4. ¡Ah! ¡bah! Quevedo era un criticon que no perdonaba nada, pero allá en su interior quizá creia un poquito como todo el mundo en los agüeros; ¿no cree V. así? ¿Qué si creia? Por supuesto que sí. Vea V. aquí otro de los agüeros en que creia.

5. Si vas á comprar algo, y al ir á pagar no hallares la bolsa adonde llevabas el dinero, es agüero malísimo, y no te sucederá bien la compra.

6. ¡Toma! Esa es una verdad de Perogrullo, y ya veo que V. no cree en los agüeros pero al ménos V. creerá en las profecías; ¿no es verdad, Don José? ¡O! sí, señora, mucho, sobre todo en las de Perogrullo.

7. ¿Qué profecías son esas, que nunca las he oido? Señora no podré relatárselas á V. todas, pero le diré á V. algunas si V. lo desea.

8. Con mucho gusto, hágame V. el favor. Pues bien, oiga V.: "Si lloviere habrá lodos." "El que tuviere tendrá."

9. ¡Ah! ya caigo; es por esto que se llama cualquiera verdad que es muy notoria, verdad de Perogrullo. ¡Vamos! aquí viene Don Enrique, puede ser que él crea en algo, porque V. no cree en nada.

10. A los piés de V., Doña Anita.—Beso á V. la mano Don Enrique.

LESSON XLV.

11. A las órdenes de V., Don José.—Bien venido, Don Enrique.—Aquí tiene V. á Doña Anita empeñada en hacerme supersticioso.

12. Y V. es tambien escéptico, no cree V. en sueños, en espíritus, en fisonomías, ¿en qué cree V., Don Enrique? Yo, señorita, soy un hombre muy crédulo, creo en todo, creo hasta las mujeres.

13. Mil gracias, Don Enrique; yo creia que la sinceridad estaba siempre de parte de la mujer y no del hombre, pues son Vds. todos á cual mas falso.—Señorita, ó V. nos hace una injusticia, ó yo soy una excepcion; pero volviendo á lo de las creencias, confieso de buena fé que soy un poco supersticioso.—Me alegro mucho, de ese modo me ayudará V. á convertir á Don José que no cree en nada.

14. Perdone V., señorita, yo creo en una de las cosas que V. ha mencionado, esto es, en las fisonomías.—¡Bien, bien! explíquenos V., entónces, su significado.

15. El que tuviere la frente ancha tendrá los ojos debajo de la frente, y vivirá todos los dias de su vida.—¡Por Dios! Don José, hable V. formalmente.

16. Pues bien, con toda formalidad. Todo hombre calvo no tendrá pelo, y si tuviere alguno no será en la calva.

17. ¡Ya lo ve, V.! se burla de todo, y no cree en nada, es un escéptico completo. Defiéndase V., amigo Don José, ó quizá es verdad que no cree V. en nada. Entónces le compadezco á V. de todo corazon.

18. ¡Hombre! déjeme V. en paz, y guarde V. su compasion para todas esas pobres gentes que creen, ó afectan creer, todas esas ridiculeces; yo creo lo que veo; creo lo que siento, y creo lo que mi razon me aconseja creer; por eso creo en el sol, en el amor, en Dios.—¡Vamos! ahora va á hacernos creer que es hombre muy religioso.

19. Señor Don José, esta señorita y yo tenemos grandes deseos de aprender el Padre nuestro en español; ¿lo sabe V.? No solamente lo sé, sino que es una oracion que me gusta mucho.

20. ¿Quiere V. hacernos el favor de decírnosla? Con mucho gusto, hélo aquí.

21. "Padre nuestro, que estás en los cielos, santificado sea tu nombre, venga á nos el tu reino. Hágase tu voluntad, así en la tierra como en el cielo. El pan nuestro de cada dia dánosle hoy. Perdónanos nuestras deudas, como nosotros perdonamos á nuestros deudores. Y no nos dejes caer en tentacion. Y líbranos de mal," Amen.

22. Mil gracias, Don José; voy á aprenderlo de memoria porque me suena muy bien en español.

EXERCISE.

1. At what o'clock does the sun rise at New York in the month of September? The sun rose here this morning at twenty-seven minutes past five o'clock.

2. What did your teacher say to you to-day when your lessons were finished? Nothing to me in particular; he spoke to all of us about reading good books, as very necessary in order to acquire the love of truth and sincerity in all our actions.

3. Here are the works of Francis de Quevedo; have you ever read them? Yes, very often; and I admire very much his profound knowledge of the human heart.

4. He is also somewhat of a jester; is he not? Yes, but for a very wise end; he shows all the ridicule of the belief in auguries, omens—for instance, the flight (*vuelo*) of crows, &c.

5. What do you think of his prophecies? The only end of his prophecies seem to be to divert his readers, telling them that all bald persons will have no hair, or if they should have any, it will not be on the bald place.

6. Do you know what the general has ordered? He has given orders that all the soldiers that desert shall be shot.

7. Do you pity that poor soldier who is to be shot? I did not know there was one to be shot; what crime did he commit? He deserted.

8. What will they do to that robber if they find him? He will be shot.

9. Do you not think he deserves to be shot? There can be no doubt of it: he who kills a man must die by the hand of man.

10. Are there still superstitious people in the world? Yes, a very great many; and I must say, that, even amongst the learned, we find a great number whose education should lead* us to have a higher opinion of them.

11. Has that gentleman paid you yet the money he owed you such a long time? Not yet; indeed I begin to fear he will never pay me.

12. If he should not pay you before he leaves the country, compel him to do so. So I intend to do.

13. How long does your father intend to remain in Germany? Perhaps two or three months; but should he remain longer, he will write for me to go to him.

14. Welcome, Mr. Martinez! how long have you been in town? Only a few days; and I shall return home as soon as I hear from my brother.

15. What a fine forehead that young lady has! I have never seen such a beautiful countenance, with the exception of that of a lady whom I met in Spain a few years ago.

* Debería hacernos.

LESSON XLVI.

Adivinar.	To guess.
Acordar.	To agree, to tune.
Acordarse.	To recollect, to remember.
Colocar.	To lay, to place.
Meter.	To put, to make (noise).
Peinar.	To comb.
Picar.	To prick, to chop, to hash.
Persistir.	To persist.
Romper.	To break.
Coger.	To take, to catch.
Esconder.	To hide, to conceal.

INTERJECTIONS.

¡Ay!	Ay!	¡Zape!	Heaven preserve us!
¡Ea!	Cheer up! come, come!	¡Victoria!	Victory!
¡Eh!	Oh! ah!	¡Cómo!	How!
¡Huy!	Whew!	¡Anda!	Go! go away!
¡Ox!	Get you gone!	¡Calle!	Strange!
¡Sus!	Come! come!	¡Chito (or chiton)!	Hush!
¡Uf (or huf)!	Ugh!		
¡Hola!	Halloa!	¡Diantre!	The deuce!
¡Tate!	Take care!	¡Cuidado!	Look out! Take care! [us!
¡Ca!	Pshaw!		
¡Viva!	Hurrah!	¡Dios nos libre!	Heaven preserve
¡Dale!	Go!	¡Vamos!	Come!
¡Qué horror!	O horror!	¡Vuelta!	Turn about (or round)!

Finalmente.	Finally.
Llevar á cabo.	To accomplish.
Llevarse chasco.	To be disappointed.

Cabal.	Just, exact.
Fresco.	Cool, fresh.
Listo.	Ready, quick.
Restante.	Remaining, remainder.
Telegráfico.	Telegraphic.
Extraordinario.	Extraordinary.
Dichoso.	Happy.

LESSON XLVI.

Aire.	Air.	Camisa.	Shirt, chemise.
Cambio.	Change.	Cuenta.	Account.
Alfiler.	Pin.	Empresa.	Enterprise.
Atlántico.	Atlantic.	Cualidad.	Quality.
Éxito.	Issue.	Austria.	Austria.
Buen éxito.	Success.	Palangana.	Wash-basin, wash-bowl.
Cable.	Cable.		
Peine.	Comb.	Prusia.	Prussia.
Presidente.	President.	Procesion.	Procession.
Ruido.	Noise.	Constancia.	Constancy.
Chasco.	Disappointment.	Prueba.	Proof, trial.
Patio.	Yard, pit (theatre).	Tranquilidad.	Tranquillity.
Tratado.	Treaty, treatise.	Victoria.	Victory.
Dolor.	Pain, grief.	Gaceta.	Gazette, newspaper.
✓Asombro.	Amazement.		
Maullido.	Mewing.		
Gato.	Cat.		

COMPOSITION.

¡Ah! que desgracia!	Ah! how unfortunate!
¡Ay de mí!	Woe is me!
¡Oh! dolor!	Ah! how sad!
¡Ah! bribon!	Ha! rascal!
¡Ah! que alegría!	Ah! what joy!
¡Oh! asombro!	Oh! wonder!
¡Ay, si le cojo!	Let me get hold of him!
¡Oh! ya nos verémos!	Oh! I shall see you again!
¡Bah! no hables de esa manera!	Pshaw! don't talk that way!
¡Huy! me quemé con el cigarrillo!	Whew! I have burned myself with the cigarette!
¡Uf! que calorazo!	Oh! how warm it is!
¡Ea, á trabajar!	Come to work!
¡Tate! tate! no pase V. por ahí, que veo un hombre escondido!	Take care! don't go that way; I see a man hiding!
✓¡Zape! ese gatazo no me deja dormir con sus maullidos!	Heaven preserve us! that confounded cat will not let me sleep with its mewing!
¡Toma! toma! eso ya lo sabia yo.	That's all, eh! I knew that much myself.
¡Viva la libertad!	Hurrah for liberty!
¡Diantre de muchachos! y qué ruido meten!	Did you ever hear such children? what a noise they make!
¡Hola! D. Francisco! dichosos los ojos que lo ven á V!	Halloa! Mr. Francis! it is good for sore eyes to see you!

¿Qué me sé yo?	How can I tell?
La cuenta está cabal.	The account is exact (correct).
✓Espero no llevarme chasco, y que llevaré á cabo mi empresa.	I hope not to be disappointed, and that I shall carry out my undertaking.

EXPLANATION.

225. INTERJECTIONS are words which serve to express the different emotions and affections of the soul. There should be a separate interjection to express each passion or emotion; but this not being the case, we often use the same ones to express joy, grief, affright, astonishment, mockery, anger, &c., the signification of each interjection changing according to the voice, gesture and manner of the speaker.

The exclamations that are properly called interjections in Spanish, inasmuch as they have no other use, and because they consist of only one word, are the following: *Ah, ay, bah, ca, eh, huy, oh, ox, sus, uf, ea, hola, ojalá, tate, zape,* and a few others.

Ah, ay and *ó* are used indifferently to express pain, joy, mockery, surprise, scorn, anger, or admiration; as,

¡*Ah!* que desgracia!	Ah! what misfortune!
¡*Ay* de mí!	Woe is me!
¡*Oh!* dolor!	Ah! how sad!
¡*Ah!* bribon!	Ha! rascal!
¡*Ah!* que alegría!	Oh! what joy!
¡*Oh!* asombro!	Oh! wonder!
¡*Ah!* que necio!	Ah! what a fool!
¡*Ay* si le cojo!	Let me get hold of him!
¡*Oh!* ya nos verémos! etc., etc.	Oh! I shall see you again!

226. ¡*Bah!* expresses displeasure, and sometimes wonder and admiration. ¡*Hé!* besides being used to attract the attention, is often employed in the sense of alas! ¡*Sus!* serves only to encourage. ¡*Huy!* is an exclamation expressive of pain. ¡*Ea!* serves to encourage, and sometimes to call the attention. We use ¡*hola!* to call our inferiors, and intimate friends, and to manifest joy and surprise. ¡*Tate!* expresses surprise, and serves to warn any one of some danger. ¡*Ojalá!* serves to manifest ardent desire for something.

LESSON XLVI.

CONVERSATION AND VERSION.

1. ¡Ea! ea! muchachos, arriba! que ya es hora de levantarse.—¿Pues qué hora es, papá? Ya son las seis y quiero que os vistais, laveis y tomeis el café prontito, para ir á tomar el aire fresco de la mañana en la plaza de Madison.

2. ¡Sus! arriba! y el que se me presente primero listo irá á comprarme el *Heraldo* y tendrá el centavo del cambio.—Helena, ponme agua para lavarme.—No, Helena, no ayudes á Alejandro que ese ya puede vestirse solo, ayuda á Carlotita y á Manolito.

3. Luisa, dame mis zapatos y mis medias.—Búscalos tú mismo, yo no voy á ayudarte para que te vistas ántes que yo.

4. ¡Cuidado! ¿no veis que vais á romper esa palangana? Es este Manuel que todavía no se ha puesto mas que una media y un zapato y se quiere lavar ántes que yo, que me he puesto ya la camisa, los zapatos y el pantalon.

5. ¡Ay! ay!—¿Qué es eso, Luisa? Me he picado con el alfiler que estaba poniendo en mi vestido.

6. ¿En dónde está el jabon? Qué me sé yo.

7. ¿Carlota, me quieres dar el peine, ó te vas á estar peinando todo el dia? Déjame en paz, ahora acabo de principiar.

8. Mamá, mire V. que Alejandro no me deja ayudar á vestir á Manuel. ¿Mamá, en dónde esta mi sombrero?

9. Papá, ya estoy listo, déme V. el dinero para comprar el *Heraldo*—No, no, papá; mire V. que se ha puesto el sombrero sin peinarse.

10. ¡Cómo! eso no, Alejandro, no se sale á la calle sin peinarse.—Papá, ya estoy listo.—Y yo.—Y yo.

11. ¡Chiton! ¡Diantre de muchachos y que ruido meten! Aquí teneis diez centavos, cuatro para el *Heraldo* y de los seis restantes uno para cada uno, cuenta cabal, me traeis el *Heraldo* y despues os vais á la plaza y no volvais, á lo ménos en un par de horas.

12. Margarita, ahora que tenemos tranquilidad tráeme la pipa, ántes de ponerme á escribir, fumaré un poco y leeré las noticias en el patio al fresco.

13. Hola! grandes noticias! ¿Qué hay de nuevo? El *Great Eastern* ha llegado, y se dice que el gran cable telegráfico ha sido finalmente colocado, uniendo así la Europa y la América.

14. ¡Es posible! entónces pronto tendrémos noticias todos los dias de Europa.—Así lo espero, pero no debemos estar muy seguros de ello, porque ya te acordarás del chasco que llevámos años pasados.

15. ¡Ah! sí, ya me acuerdo; en 1858, cuando se celebró el éxito del cable telegráfico con aquella grande procesion, y se vendia por la calle la gaceta extraordinaria con el parte telegráfico de la Reina Victoria al

Presidente de los Estados Unidos.—Espero que no nos llevemos ahora el mismo chasco.

16. ¡¡La extraordinaria!! ¡¡La gaceta extraordinaria!! ¡Eh! muchacho, aquí, aquí.

17. ¿Cuánto vale? Diez centavos.

18. ¡Victoria! ¡Viva! ¡Viva! ¿Qué dice de nuevo? El cable del Atlántico ha tenido buen éxito, el primer parte recibido por él es el tratado de paz entre el Austria y la Prusia.

19. Esta es una prueba mas de lo que puede llevar á cabo el hombre, si tiene constancia y persiste en una empresa.—¿Cree V. que yo tambien tendré buen éxito en mi empresa?

20. ¿Qué empresa es esa? ¡Cómo! ¿no la adivina V.? La empresa de aprender el español.

21. ¡Ah! No dudo que V. hablará español si persiste y tiene constancia; puesto que con estas cualidades se ha logrado que hable el cable del Atlántico.

EXERCISE.

1. Can you tell me what kind of weather we will have to-morrow? Oh, what a question! Do you suppose that I can guess the weather we will have before it comes?

2. Did the pianist say he would come to tune the piano? He said he would come to-morrow, but that he could not come to-day.

3. Have you seen that the Atlantic telegraph cable is laid at last? Yes; I am glad to see that the undertaking has been so successful.

4. Do you know who sent the first dispatch by the cable? I am not sure; but I remember that the first, at the time of the former cable, in 1858, was that sent by the President of the United States to the Queen of England.

5. What was the reason of laying a second cable? Ah, come now! do you not know that the first one, having broken shortly after it had been laid, became entirely useless (*inútil*)?

6. Have you seen the news to-day by Atlantic telegraph? No; what is the news? That a treaty of peace has been signed (*celebrar*) between Prussia and Austria.

7. Charles, go and find the comb, wherever you put it when you had done with it. I have not seen it since Henry was using it; and even if I had, I would not tell you where it was.

8. Ah, you little rogue! there, you have broken the wash-basin. It is not my fault, Henry wanted it first, and I had already commenced to wash myself; but he persisted and would take it from me.*

9. O horror! *just* look at the state his hair (*pelo*) is in! Go this

---

* Persistió en quitármela.

LESSON XLVI.

instant and get the comb and comb your hair before you dare to appear before me.

10. Have you a pin to give me? Yes, here is a paper of pins; take all you want and give me back the rest.

11. Did you know your lessons well this morning? Yes, very well, and the proof is that papa allowed me to go to see the procession.

12. What did you kill that poor little fly for? Have I not told you many times that I don't wish you to catch or kill flies?

13. Is that bread fresh? Yes, sir, the baker has just brought it a few minutes ago.

14. We were to have gone to the yard to play at twelve o'clock. You may go now; but do not make much noise.

15. Where were you going when I met you? We were coming home to dine.

16. Has the shoemaker sent you his bill? Yes, but it is not correct.

17. Has not your uncle written to you since he went away? He has sent several telegraphic dispatches to my father on business; but he has not written to us once (*una sola vez*).

18. Is there not to be a new opera to-night? No; but I understand there is to be a new play (*comedia*) at the theatre.

19. That is nothing extraordinary; there are new pieces very often now.

20. If Louisa were a little taller would she not be handsomer than Jane? She would at least be quite as handsome.

21. Would you wish to have the window opened? I think it would be much cooler if it were open.

22. Would you not like me to repeat to you that story I told you the other day? If you had time I should be much obliged to you to tell it to me once more.

23. Would not quietness be much better for that gentleman than so much noise? He could not live without noise.

24. Might you not have broken your arm or your leg when you fell out of your carriage? Yes, if I had not taken care.

25. If I had wanted money when I was in the country would you not have brought me some? If I could have got (*conseguir*) it I would.

26. Would your aunt not have been disappointed if she had not been in time to take the three o'clock train? She would have been terribly disappointed, for she was going to spend the day at a friend's, about ten miles out of town.

LESSON XLVII.

Acompañar.	To accompany.
Cargar.	To load, to charge.
Curar.	To cure, to attend (as a physician).
Dañar.	To injure, to damage.
Deleitar.	To delight.
Incomodar.	To incommode.
Incomodarse.	To get out of temper.
Equivocar.	To mistake.
Evitar.	To avoid, to shun.
Instruir.	To instruct.
Ocupar.	To occupy.
Padecer.	To suffer.
Solicitar.	To solicit, to apply for, to urge.

Dímes y dirétes.	Ifs and ands.
El no sé qué.	An inexplicable something.
Dolor de cabeza.	Headache.

Masculino.	Masculine.
Amable.	Amiable.
Agradable.	Agreeable.
Extrangero.	Foreign, foreigner.
Interesante.	Interesting.
Moribundo.	Dying.
Valiente.	Valiant, arrant.
Femenino.	Feminine.

Acento.	Accent.	Alma.	Soul.
Bolsillo.	Purse.	Comedia.	Comedy.
Autor.	Author.	Vara.	Rod, yard (*measure*).
Esfuerzo.	Effort, bravery.		
Efecto.	Effect. [ness.	Libra.	Pound.
Fastidio.	Unease, uneasi-	Manteca, *or* Mantequilla.	Butter.
Ciudadano.	Citizen.		
Hospital.	Hospital.	Calidad.	Quality.
Método.	Method.	Cantidad.	Quantity.
Trabajo.	Labor, work.		
Nápoles.	Naples.		
Real.	Real.		
Sonido.	Sound.		
Chelin.	Shilling.		

11

COMPOSITION.

El porqué de todas las cosas.	The why and the wherefore of all things.
Los ayes del moribundo.	The groans of the dying.
Los dimes y dirétes.	The ifs and ands.
El cuando.	The time.
El no sé qué.	I know not what.
El tener amigos no daña.	It is hurtful to no one to have friends.
Hay hombres de un saber extraordinario.	There are men of extraordinary knowledge.
Un nada le incomoda.	A mere nothing incommodes him.
La constancia y el trabajo son necesarios al hombre en todas sus empresas.	Constancy and labor are necessary to mankind in all their enterprises (or undertakings).
La América es mayor que la Europa.	America is larger than Europe.
La Francia es una nacion muy poblada.	France is a very populous nation.
El clima de España.	The climate of Spain.
Los esfuerzos de la España.	The bravery of Spain.
Cuatro pesos la vara.	Four dollars a yard.
Dos reales la libra.	Two reals a pound.
Treinta centavos la docena.	Thirty cents a dozen.
Dos veces al dia.	Twice a day.
Cuatro pesos por vara.	Four dollars a yard.
La fé, la esperanza y la caridad.	Faith, hope and charity.
El Señor De Vargas tiene tres niños.	Mr. Vargas has three children.
La Señora Martínez es muy prudente.	Mrs. Martinez is very prudent.
Ella me dió la mano.	She shook hands with me.
Puso la mano en el bolsillo.	He put his hand in his pocket.
Muchos caballeros solicitaron mi mano.	Many gentlemen have solicited my hand.
El caballero á quien vió V. ayer en mi casa.	The gentleman whom you saw yesterday in my house.

EXPLANATION.

227. USE OF THE ARTICLE.—All or any of the parts of speech, and sometimes even whole sentences, may be used as nouns, and as such admit the article, as has just been observed in the COMPOSITION of the present lesson, in which we see examples of verbs, adverbs and interjections preceded by the article, and treated in every respect as nouns substantive.

228. THE DEFINITE ARTICLE is to be used before all common nouns, taken in a general sense and in the full extent of their signification; as,

| La constancia y *el* trabajo son necesarios al hombre en todas sus empresas. | Constancy and labor are necessary to mankind in all undertakings. |

229. The article is expressed before the names of the four parts of the globe: before the names of empires, kingdoms, provinces and countries; and before the four seasons of the year; as,

La América es mayor que *la* Europa.	America is larger than Europe.
La Francia es una nacion muy poblada.	France is a very populous nation.
El invierno en *el* Sur es mas agradable que el verano.	The winter in the South is more agreeable than the summer.

But it is omitted before the names of kingdoms, provinces, &c., when they are preceded by a preposition; unless they be personified, as has been observed in Lesson XXX.; as,

| El clima *de España*. | The climate of Spain. |
| Los esfuerzos *de la España*. | The bravery of Spain. |

Kingdoms bearing the same name as their capitals do not admit the article; as, *Nápoles*, Naples.

230. Nouns of measure, weight, &c., when preceded by the indefinite article in English, as an equivalent to *each*, require the article; as,

Cuatro pesos *la vara*.	Four dollars a yard.
Dos reales *la libra*.	Two reals a pound.
Treinta centavos *la docena*.	Thirty cents a dozen.
Dos veces *al dia*.	Twice a day.

If the preposition *por* be used, we omit the article; as, *cuatro pesos por vara*, &c.

231. The article is generally repeated before every noun enumerated, especially if they differ in gender; as,

| La fé, *la* esperanza y *la* caridad. | Faith, hope and charity. |
| Los dias y *las* noches. | The days and nights. |

232. The definite article is used before nouns indicating rank, office, profession or titles of persons, when these are spoken of, but not when spoken to; as,

El General Sheridan es valiente.	General Sheridan is brave.
El Señor De Vargas tiene tres niños.	Mr. De Vargas has three children.
La Señora Martínez, es muy prudente.	Mrs. Martinez is very prudent.

LESSON XLVII.

233. The definite article is used instead of the possessive adjective when the possessives refer to parts of our own body; as,

Me he cortado *la mano*.	I have cut my hand.
Me duele *la cabeza*.	My head aches.

This applies even to parts of the body of other persons; as,

Ella me dió *la mano*.	She gave me her hand (or shook hands with me).
Puso *la mano* en el bolsillo.	He put his hand in his pocket.

But the pronoun must be used when the personal article would occasion ambiguity; as,

Muchos caballeros solicitaron *mi* mano. | Many gentlemen solicited my hand.

234. The definite article is also employed, as in English, before nouns taken in a *particular* or *definite* sense; as,

El caballero á quien vió V. ayer en mi casa.	The gentleman whom you saw yesterday in my house.

We forbear from adding many more rules which we might give, if they were not subject to numerous exceptions, and, especially, if we were not of opinion that practice and reading will teach better than any rules when to employ and when to omit the article.

CONVERSATION AND VERSION.

1. ¿Cuál de las partes del mundo es la mayor? El Asia es la mayor.
2. ¿Es Asia nombre masculino? No, señor, es femenino.
3. Entónces, ¿porqué le pone V. el artículo masculino? Por evitar el mal sonido que resultaria de poner dos *aes* juntas.
4. ¿Luego, V. pone siempre el artículo masculino delante de todo nombre femenino que empieza por *a*? No, señor; esto solo sucede en singular, y cuando sobre dicha vocal carga el acento de la palabra.
5. ¿Ha leido V. el "Sí de las niñas" de Moratin? Sí, señor, lo leí hace muchos años; pero á mí me gusta mas la "Comedia nueva" del mismo autor.
6. ¿Qué tal le gusta á V. su nueva vecinita? Dicen que es muy bonita.—En efecto lo es; pero á mí no me gusta, porque anda siempre en dimes y diretes, y un nada la incomoda.
7. ¿Cuáles son las virtudes del alma? La fé, la esperanza y la caridad.
8. ¿Tiene V. alguna cosa interesante que decirme hoy? Muchísimas

LESSON XLVII.

interesantísimas ó importantísimas . . . . . para practicar y aprender el español.

9. ¡Uf! ya va V. á principiar con sus adverbios, preposiciones y artículos; va V. á decirme, por supuesto, que estas partes de la oracion unas veces se ponen ántes las unas que las otras, y vice versa; que las unas gobiernan á las otras y las gobernadas gobiernan á su vez á otras, que se acuerden ó no entre sí. ¿Creé V. que todo eso será interesante para mí con el fastidio que tengo, y el dolor de cabeza que padezco? ¡Calle! entónces, caballerito, V. ha equivocado la casa.

10. ¿Qué quiere V. decir con eso de equivocar la casa? Quiero decir que, en lugar de venir á la clase, debió V. ir hoy al hospital y de allí al teatro.

11. ¿Para qué? Para que le curasen en una parte de sus dolores y en la otra del fastidio.

12. Sí; pero, Señor Profesor, yo siempre creia que el mejor método de enseñanza es aquel que "instruye deleitando." V. tiene mil razones, pero ha olvidado una pequeña circunstancia que requiere su método.

13. ¿Y cual es esa circunstancia? Que no puede aplicarse sino con aquellos discípulos que se deleitan aprendiendo.

14. Y ahora volviendo al artículo.—Señor Profesor, V. me escusará, pero no volvamos al artículo porque no puedo quedarme mas aquí hoy.

15. ¿Cómo es eso? el tiempo de la leccion no ha acabado todavía.—V. tiene razon; pero hoy es necesario que me vaya temprano, porque he prometido acompañar á unas señoritas á la opera.

16. ¡Oh! entónces es necesario no faltar á su palabra.—Señor Profesor, buenas noches (este buen señor me fastidia con sus explicaciones). —Diviértase V. mucho, Señor Don Pepito (este amable jóven aprenderá español, para el tiempo que yo compre una casa en la Quinta Avenida, enseñándolo).

EXERCISE.

1. If I should come for you this evening, would you come with me to see the Martinez? I would, with great pleasure, if Charlotte would accompany us.

2. How does that lady speak French? They say she speaks very correctly, though with a slightly foreign accent.

3. Might he not be cured if he called in a good physician? He is of opinion that physicians do more injury than good to mankind.

4. Do you know any thing of the author of that play? Yes, I have read (or heard) all his plays; they are very interesting, and delighted me exceedingly.

5. What is death? The separation of soul and body.

6. Can one be a citizen of the United States without having been born (*nacer*) in the country? Yes, after having resided in the United States a certain number of years any one may become a citizen.

7. Where is that poor man going? To the hospital; he has broken his leg.

8. Pardon me, I think you are mistaken; it is rather his arm that is broken, for if his leg were broken he could not walk.

9. Do you remember the name of the principal city of Naples? Yes, the name of the principal city is that of the kingdom also.

10. Did you shake hands with that young lady? Yes, as soon as she saw me she came towards me and gave me her hand.

11. Is that cloth (*paño*) sold very high? Not very; it costs only three dollars a yard.

12. How often do you take your Spanish lessons? Twice a week.

13. Would you not learn faster if you took a lesson every other day (*un dia si y otro no*)? My teacher says I would; but I have not time to take lessons so often.

14. Would you like summer to return again? No, thank you, I am glad it is past, for I assure you I have suffered enough with the heat.

15. How sad it is on the field of battle (*campo de batalla*) to hear the groans of the dying! Yes; and, notwithstanding, men will persist in killing each other for a foot* of ground (*terreno*).

16. How is butter sold a pound? Thirty cents for one kind, and forty cents a pound for the best.

17. Do you think it can injure any one to have friends? No, it can injure nobody to have friends.

18. Is not that person very amiable and agreeable? Very rarely, for a mere nothing incommodes him.

19. Are there many learned men in that country? There have been and there are at present men of extraordinary learning.

20. Which are the three principal virtues? Faith, hope and charity.

21. Is Miss Cabargas married yet? Not yet, although a large number of gentleman have solicited her hand.

22. I suppose you have all read some Spanish comedies? Several Spanish and some French comedies, by the best dramatists.

23. Which of all the French comedies that you have read do you like best? Those of Molière.

---

* *Palmo* (literally a span).

LESSON XLVIII.

Afirmar.	To affirm.
Afligir.	To afflict.
Admitir.	To admit, to accept.
Atreverse.	To dare.
Criticar.	To criticise.
Condescender.	To condescend, to consent.
Convencer.	To convince.
Declarar.	To declare.
Depender.	To depend.
Disponer.	To dispose, to arrange.
Diferenciar.	To differ.
Edificar.	To edify, to build.
Entretenerse.	To amuse.
Fabricar.	To construct, to make, to build.
Suponer.	To suppose.
Nombrar.	To name, to appoint.
Influir.	To influence, to affect.
Ocultar.	To conceal, to hide.
Observar.	To observe.
Obedecer.	To obey.
Proporcionar.	To proportion, to procure, to offer, to afford.
Pretender.	To pretend, to lay claim to, to aspire to, to sue for.
Publicar.	To publish.
Quejarse.	To complain, to moan.
Regularizar.	To regulate.
Reflexionar.	To reflect.
Ridiculizar.	To ridicule.
Reformar.	To reform.

Lo que sé decir.	What I know.
Sin que V. me lo diga.	Without you telling me.
Volver á las andadas.	To do so again, to return to (one's) old habits.
Para mi tengo.	It is my opinion.
A trueque.	On condition.
Sin embargo.	Nevertheless, notwithstanding.
Cándidamente.	Candidly.
De modo.	In such a manner, that, so that.

LESSON XLVIII.

¡Bravo!	Very good! Bravo!
Bruto.	Brutish.
Cierto.	Certain.
Aéreo.	Airy, aerial.
Angelical.	Angelical.
Ideal.	Ideal.
Interior.	Interior.
Incompleto,	Incomplete.
Imperfecto.	Imperfect.
Exterior.	Exterior.
Extraño.	Strange.
Igual.	Equal, the same.
Humano.	Humane.
Positivo.	Positive.
Real.	Real, royal.

Arquitecto.	Architect.	Carrera.	Career.
Anciano.	Old man.	Desgracia.	Misfortune.
Ciego.	Blind.	Diferencia.	Difference.
Cal y canto.	Stone.	Curiosidad.	Curiosity.
Bruto.	Brute.	Exageracion.	Exaggeration.
Idiota.	Idiot.	Franqueza.	Frankness.
Espacio.	Space.	Juventud.	Youth.
Complemento.	Complement.	Ilusion.	Illusion.
Goce.	Enjoyment.	Felicidad.	Happiness.
Mal.	Evil.	Risa.	Laugh, laughter.
Material.	Material.	Realidad.	Reality.
Objeto.	Object.	Ruindad.	Meanness.
Palacio.	Palace.	Riquezas.	Riches.
Pájaro.	Bird.		
Enfermo.	Sick.		
Prisionero.	Prisoner.		
Pensamiento.	Thought.		
Castillos en el aire.	Castles in the air.		

COMPOSITION.

Adivino el motivo por el cual nos habian adulado los mismos que despues nos critican, criticaban, criticaron, han criticado, criticarán.

Leiamos una noticia que acababa (or acaba) de publicarse.

I guess the motive for which those same persons who had flattered us before, criticise, did criticise, criticised, have criticised, will criticise us afterward.

We were reading some news just published (that had just been published, or has just been published).

LESSON XLVIII. 249

✓Contaba la desgracia que los afligió.	He was telling the misfortune that afflicted them.
No seré yo el primero que se atreva.	✓I shall not be the first to dare.
Aprended vosotros, los que os quejais, quejabais, quejasteis, habeis quejado, quejaréis.	Know, you who complain, were complaining, complained, had complained, will complain.
Él quiere jugar.	He will (is determined to) play.
Nosotros queremos estudiar.	✓We will study.
✓Él hubo de condescender.	He had to consent.
Tengo que callar.	✓I have to be silent.
Ellos deben estar muy ocupados.	They must be very busy.
Quiero (or pienso) salir.	I wish (or intend to) go out.
Afirmo (or declaro) que saldré.	I affirm (or declare) that I shall go out.
Digo que saldré.	I say that I shall go out.
✓Es útil estudiar las lenguas.	It is useful to study languages.
Conviene á los hombres instruirse.	✓It is man's interest to acquire knowledge.
El estudio de las lenguas es útil.	The study of languages is useful.
La instruccion conviene á los hombres.	Knowledge is useful to man.
Conviene que yo estudie.	It is my interest to study.
↳ Es útil que los hombres se instruyan.	It is useful to mankind to possess knowledge.
Les mandó callar. } ✓Les mandó que callasen. }	He ordered them to be silent.
Impedir que se cometan injusticias es el objeto de las leyes.	✓To prevent the commission of injustice, such is the object of laws.
Deseo que me comprendas.	✓I wish you to understand me.
No lograrás que le castiguen.	You will not succeed in having him punished.
Se le ayudará si fuere necesario.	He shall have help if it be necessary.
He sentido que no se convenza (convenciera or convenciese).	I was sorry he would not be convinced (or was not convinced.)
Habrá llamado para que le abran (abrieran or abriesen) la puerta.	He knocked, of course, in order that the door may (or might) be opened.
Creo que le convenceré fácilmente.	✓I think I shall convince him easily.
Reflexionaré lo que he de hacer.	✓I shall reflect on what I shall do.
Pensé que iba á matarla.	✓I thought he was going to kill her.
Pensé que enviara (or enviaria) la carta.	✓I thought he would send the letter.

EXPLANATION.

235. CORRESPONDENCE OF THE TENSES WITH EACH OTHER.—When one verb is connected with another by a relative, there are many combinations in which the *determining* and the *de-*

11*

termined verbs may be found; both may be in the indicative or in the subjunctive mood, or one in the indicative and the other in the subjunctive; but both cannot be in the infinitive or in the imperative; as,

Adivino el motivo por el cual nos habian adulado los mismos que nos *critican, criticaban, criticaron, han criticado, criticarán.*	I guess the motive for which those same *persons* who have flattered us *before*, criticise, did criticise, criticised, have criticised, will criticise us afterward.
Leíamos una noticia *que acababa* (or *acaba*) de publicarse.	We were reading some news that had (or has) just been published.
Contaba la desgracia *que los afligió.*	He was telling the misfortune that afflicted them.
No *seré* yo el primero *que se atreva.*	I shall not be the first to dare.
Aprended vosotros los que os *quejais, quejabais, quejasteis, habeis quejado, quejaréis.*	Learn, you who complain, were complaining, complained, had complained, will complain.

236. The determined verb is put in the infinitive whenever it has the same subject as the determining verb; as,

Él quiere *jugar.*	He wishes to play.
Nosotros queremos *estudiar.*	We wish to study.

This is the reason why the auxiliaries *haber de, tener que, deber*, always require the governed verb in the infinitive, because the subject, or nominative, is the same for both verbs; as,

Él hubo de *condescender.*	He had to consent.
Tengo que *callar.*	I have to be silent.
Ellos deben *estar* muy ocupados.	They must be very busy.

An exception to this rule occurs when the determining verb expresses a firm and decided affirmation; and so we say:

Quiero (or pienso) *salir.*	I wish (or intend) to go out.
Afirmo (declaro) que *saldré.*	I affirm (or declare) that I shall go out.

We must also except the verb *decir*, which cannot govern another verb in the infinitive, because whenever we employ it to announce our own actions it is not with the purpose of relating them, but to manifest our resolution to execute them; as,

Digo que *saldré.*	I say I shall go out.

237. When the determining verb is *ser*, or any impersenal verb, and the governed verb has no subject, the latter is placed in the infinitive; as,

Es útil *estudiar* las lenguas.	It is useful to study languages.
Conviene á los hombres *instruirse*.	It is the interest of mankind to acquire knowledge.

And such is the natural construction, because the true subject of this proposition is the very infinitive itself, which stands there as a noun, an office that cannot be performed by the other moods. The above sentences are equivalent to these:

El *estudio* de las lenguas es útil.	The study of languages is useful.
La *instruccion* conviene á los hombres.	It is the interest of mankind to acquire knowledge.

238. But if the determined verb also has a nominative, then it must be placed in the subjunctive; as,

Conviene que yo *estudie*.	It is my interest to study.
Es útil que los hombres se *instruyan*.	It is useful to mankind to possess knowledge.

Those verbs that express command, govern either of the two forms, since we say equally well:

Les mandó *callar*. Les mandó que *callasen*.	He ordered them to be silent.

239. When the determining verb is in the infinitive, in the present or future of the indicative, or in the imperative, connected with the governed verb by a conjunction, this latter verb is put in the subjunctive mood, ordinarily in the present or in the future; as,

Impedir que se *cometan* injusticias es el objeto de las leyes.	To prevent the commission of injustice, such is the object of the laws.
Deseo que me *comprendas*.	I wish you to understand me.
No *lograrás* que le *castiguen*.	You will not succeed in having him punished.
Se le *ayudará* si *fuere* necesario.	He will have help if it be necessary.

240. The preterit indefinite and compound future of the indicative govern the determined verb in the present or imperfect of the subjunctive; as,

He *sentido* que no se *convenza* (*convenciera* or *convenciese*).	I was sorry he should not be (or was not) convinced.
Habrá llamado para que le *abran* (*abrieran* or *abriesen*) la puerta.	He knocked, *of course*, in order that *the door* may (or *might*) be opened.

241. When the determining verb is in the indicative, it generally governs the determined one in the same mood, if the nominative is the same for both verbs; as,

Creo que le *convenceré* fácilmente.	I think I shall convince him easily.
Reflexionaré lo que *he* de hacer.	I shall reflect on what I have to do.

But if each verb has a different nominative, the second verb may be placed in the indicative or in the subjunctive; as,

Pensé que *iba* á matarla.	I thought he was going to kill her.
Pensé que me *enviara* (or *enviaria*) la carta.	I thought he would send me the letter.

Much more might be said upon this subject, did we not fear to exceed the limits prescribed by the nature of the present work.

CONVERSATION AND VERSION.

1. Doña Luisita, ¿Le gusta á V. formar castillos en el aire? Mucho; pero creo que formo demasiados.

2. Me alegro mucho que, como á mí, le guste á V. el mundo de las ilusiones, y tambien apruebo su franqueza de V. en confesarlo.—Y ¿porqué lo habia de ocultar? ¿Qué mal hay en eso?

3. No sé si hay mal ó no, lo que sé decir es, que todo el mundo afecta no formarlos y con cierta risita burlona pretenden ridiculizar á los que, como V. y yo, confesamos cándidamente que los hacemos.

4. ¿Y cree V., D. José, que esas gentes vivan sin ilusiones de ninguna especie? No, señorita, no lo creo. Dios ha dado á todo hombre, á diferencia del bruto, un mundo ideal interior además del mundo positivo exterior, á excepcion de los idiotas.

5. ¡Cuánto me alegro de oirlo! ¡porque yo tenia tanta vergüenza de mis pobres castillos en el aire! ¿De modo es que V. cree que yo no soy sola? De ningun modo, todo el mundo los forma, la diferencia solo existe en la manera.

6. ¡Ah! Don José, V. me va pareciendo un buen arquitecto de castillos en el aire y uno de estos dias voy á pedirle que me muestre uno de los muchos que habrá edificado.—Con mucho gusto, señorita, á trueque, sin embargo, de que V. me admita en uno de sus palacios aéreos.

7. No, eso no, jamás podria yo poner en evidencia mis castillos; pero V. dice que la diferencia solo existe en la manera de formarlos; explíqueme V. esto, quizá así lograré reformar los mios, porque he observado que son incompletos; siempre les falta algo.—Pues es extraño, señorita, por-

LESSON XLVIII.

que yo creia que solo las cosas humanas eran imperfectas y sus ilusiones de V. siendo. . . . .

8. Por supuesto, ¡angelicales! ¡Vamos! déjese V. de cumplimientos, ya sabe V. que no me gustan, y respóndame V. á mi pregunta si V. gusta, porque tengo curiosidad de saber cómo forman otros sus castillos. —Obedezco, señorita, y para principiar debo decir que yo me equivoqué cuando dije que solo se diferenciaban en la manera, porque tambien influye mucho el material.

9. ¿Cómo el material? ¡si se fabrican en el aire! ¡Espero que no los fabrique V. de cal y canto!—No, señorita, no de cal y canto; pero se fabrican; y si se fabrican, de algo se fabrican.

10. ¿Pero de qué, señor, de qué? Yo formo castillos, pero no necesito nada para hacerlos; vuelo mas que los pájaros, mando hasta en las voluntades de los otros, hago volver al tiempo en su carrera, dispongo del espacio, de la fortuna, y hago que me obedezca hasta el amor.—Eso lo creo sin que V. me lo diga, señorita.

11. ¡Dale! no vuelva V. á las andadas, y cuénteme V. qué materiales son esos de que V. me hablaba.—V. misma acaba de nombrar algunos.

12. ¿Cuáles? ¡Cómo! ¿qué mas materiales quiere V. para formar un castillo en el aire, que poder disponer, como V. dice que puede, de las voluntades de los otros, del tiempo, del espacio, la fortuna y hasta del amor?

13. ¡Toma! Pero yo no poseo ninguna de esas cosas en realidad, y sin embargo mis castillos me entretienen y divierten mucho.—Perdone V., señorita, V. las posee y con ellas forma V. ese bonito mundo interior, que le proporciona á V. los goces que no le da el exterior.

14. Y en eso tiene V. razon, que mis ilusiones, ó sea como V. las llama, mi mundo interior, me consuelan muchas veces de la ruindad del mundo exterior.—Eso sucede á todo el mundo, de ese modo, el ciego ve, el enfermo goza de salud, el prisionero de libertad, el pobre de las riquezas y el anciano de la juventud, las ilusiones hacen los males menores. En este mundo ideal es en donde los hombres son verdaderamente iguales, y para mí tengo que no es ilusorio, sino real, puesto que de él depende nuestra felicidad.

15. ¿No cree V. que hay alguna exageracion en lo que V. dice? No, señora, pero sí, creo, que debemos tener buen cuidado de regularizar nuestros pensamientos y de basar siempre nuestros castillos en el aire en la virtud y la religion.

16. ¡Bravo! bravo! muy bien, así me gustan á mí los castillos en el aire.

LESSON XLVIII.

EXERCISE.

1. Who built the house you are living in at present? An excellent architect, a friend of my father.

2. Are you certain it was an old man that was suing for her hand? I cannot affirm that it was an old man.

3. What a misfortune that he will not study! It would be a real misfortune if it were true; I think it is not true.

4. Do you ever build castles in the air? Seldom; for, in my opinion, real castles built of stone are to be preferred to the aërial ones you speak of.

5. What a pretty bird you have there! does it sing? It sings the whole day long.

6. Do you think our young friend is really as happy as he appears to be? No, there must be some exaggeration in what he says.

7. In what respect do these two authors differ from each other? Read the works of both, and you will observe for yourself.

8. Do they both write equally well? No, one of them arranges his thoughts in a very strange manner, so that it is sometimes impossible to understand his meaning,* and at all times disagreeable to read him.

9. Is Peter punished now in school as often as formerly? As often as ever; but it is useless to punish him, for though he is good for a few days, yet he always gets back to his old habits.

10. Does that man always say what he thinks? *I am sure* I cannot say; but it seems to me that there is in his manner of speaking a something I cannot explain that hides his real thoughts.

11. Is he liked in general by those who know him? On the contrary, everybody hates him and ridicules him for his meanness.

12. Have you any curiosity to see the interior of a royal palace? If the occasion offered (presented itself), I would like to see it; otherwise I am perfectly content with the interior of my own house.

13. You are wise for that; happiness is not at all times to be found in palaces. Ah! I see you are† something of a philosopher.

14. How is this, sir? your exercise is incomplete. I confess that had I wished I might have finished it; but you will find that, as far as it goes, it is not imperfect.

15. That is to say that the quality does not depend on the quantity. Precisely *so*; you may complain of my not having done the whole of the exercise, but I do not think you can criticise the part I have brought to you.

16. What size‡ is the book your friend has just published? The same size as the one he published before.

---

* *Lo que quiere decir.*   † *Tiene V.*   ‡ *Tamaño.*

LESSON XLIX.

Acudir.	To hasten (to a place), to refer.
Agregar.	To add.
Añadir.	To add.
Componer.	To compose, to mend, to fix.
Contener.	To contain.
Incluir.	To include.
Facilitar.	To facilitate.
Ofrecer.	To offer.

Por instruido que sea.	However learned he may be.

Anteriormente.	Formerly, previously.
Comparativamente.	Comparatively.
Corrientemente.	Currently, fluently.
Flúidamente.	Fluently.
Suficiente.	Sufficient.
En general.	In general.
Generalmente.	Generally.
Considerablemente.	Considerably.
Particularmente.	Particularly, privately.

En cuanto á.	As to, as for.

Artificial.	Artificial.
Anterior.	Anterior, previous.
Aborrecible.	Hateful.
Celeste, azul celeste.	Celestial, sky-blue.
Celestial.	Celestial, heavenly.
Célico.	Celestial, heavenly.
Chinesco.	Chinese.
Creible.	Credible.
Despreciable.	Despicable.
Familiar.	Familiar.
Gigantesco.	Gigantic.
Terrestre.	Terrestrial, earthly.
Territorial.	Territorial.
Terroso.	Terreous, earthy.
Terrado, terrero.	Terrace.
Terrenal.	Terrestrial, earthly.
Terron.	Lump (or clod) of earth.

LESSON XLIX.

Ricacho.	Very rich.
Picaresco.	Roguish.
Patronímico.	Patronymic.
Propio.	Proper, own.
Mudable.	Changeable.
Verbal.	Verbal.

Arenal.	Sandy (ground).	Arboleda.	Grove.
Ascenso.	Promotion.	Ascension.	Ascension.
Alvarez.	Alvarez.	Carnuza.	Bad meat.
Calvinista.	Calvinist.	Creencia.	Belief, credence.
Catolicismo.	Catholicism.	Ciencia.	Science.
Diccionario.	Dictionary.	Gentualla.	Rabble.
Escobajo.	A bad broom.	Madrastra.	Step-mother.
Boticario.	Druggist, apothecary.	Terminacion.	Termination.
		Dicha.	Happiness.
Domínguez.	Dominguez.	Isla.	Island.
Fernández.	Fernandez.	Educacion.	Education.
Idiotismo.	Idiom.	Escoba.	Broom.
Filosofastro.	Philosophaster.	Excusa.	Excuse.
Hijastro.	Step-son.	Explicacion.	Explanation.
Hermanastro.	Step-brother.	Espada.	Sword.
Hombracho.	Corpulent.	Exclamacion.	Exclamation.
Libraco.	A contemptible book.	Firma.	Signature.
		Gota.	Drop.
Pajarraco.	An ugly bird.	Figura.	Figure, appearance.
Latinajo.	Dog Latin.		
Manzanar.	Apple orchard.	Faccion.	Feature.
Pinar.	Pine grove.	Factura.	Invoice.
Protestante.	Protestant.	Facultad.	Faculty, power.
Padrastro.	Step-father.	Adquisicion.	Acquirement.
Significado.	Signification, meaning.	Astronomía.	Astronomy.
		Afluencia, fluidez.	Fluency.
Vinacho.	Bad wine.		
Protestantismo.	Protestantism.		
Habanero.	Havanese.		
Madrileño.	Madrilenian.		
Rodríguez.	Rodriguez.		
Sánchez.	Sanchez.		
Amante.	Lover, sweet-[heart.		
Arbol.	Tree.		
Amador.	Lover.		

LESSON XLIX.

COMPOSITION.

¿Porqué lee V. ese libraco?	Why do you read that contemptible old book?
Porque no tengo otro; pero V. se equivoca, es un libro clásico excelente.	Because I have no other; but you are mistaken, it is an excellent classic (book).
¿Conoce V. á aquel ricacho?	Do you know that rich man?
Le conozco; pero no le trato, porque es un hombracho que solo le gusta tratarse con gentualla.	I know him; but I have no intercourse with him, because he is a low man, whose taste is to associate only with the rabble.
Juan, no barras con ese escobajo, que ensucia mas que limpia.	John, do not sweep with that old stump of a broom; it dirties more than it cleans.
La carne buena se vende á treinta centavos la libra; la carnuza á veinte.	Good meat sells at thirty cents a pound, poor (bad) meat at twenty.
Ese estudiante suele decir latinajos, pero no sabe Latin.	That student is in the habit of reciting dog Latin, but he does not know Latin.
En la América del Norte hay mas protestantes que católicos.	There are more Protestants than Catholics in North America.
Los boticarios en los Estados Unidos no solo venden medicinas, sino perfumeria, cigarros y otras muchas cosas.	In the United States the druggists sell not only medicines, but perfumery, cigars, and many other things.
¿Vive el Señor Fernandez con su padre?	Does Mr. Fernandez live with his father?
No, señor, porque no quiere vivir con su madrastra y hermanastros.	No, sir; because he does not wish to live with his step-mother and step-brothers.
¿Es V. madrileño?	Are you a Madrilenian?
No, señor, soy Habanero.	No, sir, I am a Havanese.
Aquel filosofastro es despreciable.	That philosophaster is a despicable (man).
Esa señorita es muy amable; pero muy mudable.	That young lady is very amiable, but very changeable.

EXPLANATION.

242. DERIVATIVE NOUNS.—These nouns constitute one of the chief sources of the richness of the Spanish language; we have already introduced some of them in previous lessons, when treating of augmentative and diminutive terminations.

These terminations are very numerous, both for the substantives and adjectives, and each one of them determines the general signification of the derivative noun. As it would be impossible to give in this place a complete list of all these terminations, we shall endeavor to lay before the student such of them as are to be found in most common use.

243. The terminations *aco, acho, alla* and *uza*, denote inferiority; as

Libr*aco*.	A contemptible old book.
Pajarr*aco*.	An ugly bird.
Vin*acho*.	Bad wine.
Gentu*alla*.	Rabble.
Carn*uza*.	Bad meat.

The termination *acho* is sometimes augmentative; as,

Ric*acho*.	Very rich.
Hombr*acho*.	A big (or corpulent) man.

244. *Ajo* implies meanness, and the consequent contempt inspired by it; as,

Escob*ajo*.	An old stump of a broom.
Latin*ajo*.	Dog Latin.

245. The terminations *al, ar, ego, ico, il, isco*, in adjectives, commonly denote the quality of the thing; as,

Artifici*al*.	Artificial.
Famili*ar*.	Familiar.
Gigant*esco*.	Gigantic.
Picar*esco*.	Roguish.
Clás*ico*.	Classic.
Chin*esco*.	Chinese.

246. In substantives the same terminations, *al, ar*, and also *eda* and *edo*, serve to form collective nouns; as,

Arbol*eda*.	Grove.
Aren*al*.	Sandy ground.
Manzan*ar*.	Apple orchard.
Pin*ar*.	Pine grove.

247. The terminations *ante, ario, ente, ero, ista* and *or* are for the most part expressive of use, sect, profession, trade, or occupation; as,

Estudi*ante*.	Student.
Botic*ario*.	Druggist.
Zapat*ero*.	Shoemaker.
Organ*ista*.	Organist.
Protest*ante*.	Protestant.
Calvin*ista*.	Calvinist.
Pint*or*.	Painter.

248. The termination *astro* signifies inferiority in a superlative degree; as, *filosofastro*, a despicable philosopher; *poetastro*, poetaster; and it is curious to observe that it also serves to express the degrees of relationship existing between those persons who more generally hate than love each other; as,

Herman*astro*.	Step-brother.
Hij*astro*.	Step-son.
Padr*astro*.	Step-father.
Madr*astra*.	Step-mother.

249. *Ble* corresponds to the same termination in English; as,

Aborreci*ble*.	Hateful.
Crei*ble*.	Credible.
Muda*ble*.	Changeable.
Ama*ble*.	Amiable.

250. *Ismo* corresponds to the English termination *ism*; as,

Catolic*ismo*.	Catholicism.
Protestant*ismo*.	Protestantism.

251. The names of nationalities are also derivatives, and have their terminations in *ero*, *es*, *eño*; as,

Haban*ero*.	Havanese.
Franc*es*.	French, Frenchman.
Madril*eño*.	Madrilenian.

252. Many patronymic, or family, names are also derivatives; for instance, *Alvarez, Domínguez, Fernández, Rodríguez, Sánchez*, &c., were the names that were given to the sons of the Alvaros, Domingos, Fernandos, Rodrigos, Sanchos, &c., changing the final *o* into *ez*.

LESSON XLIX.

CONVERSATION AND VERSION.

1. ¿Es necesario para hablar una lengua aprender todas las palabras que contiene dicha lengua? De ningun modo, además, yo no creo que exista un hombre, por instruido que sea, que las sepa todas.

2. ¿Cuántas palabras piensa V. que sean suficientes para poder hablar el español corrientemente? De tres á cuatro mil palabras primitivas con sus derivados es todo lo que se requiere, para hablar una lengua flúidamente.

3. Sí, pero probablemente los derivados serán en tanto ó mayor número que los primitivos.—Así es, pero una vez que se conocen las terminaciones, es muy fácil el formarlos, aunque nunca se hayan visto anteriormente.

4. ¡Es posible! entónces esto debe facilitar mucho el estudio de la lengua.—Muchísimo, porque, como ya hemos dicho, sabiendo los primitivos no tiene mas que añadírseles las terminaciones, segun el significado que quiera dárseles.

5. ¿Quiere V. hacerme el favor de formar algunos derivados? Sí, señor, con mucho gusto; déme V. los primitivos.

6. ¿Cuáles son los derivados de cielo? Celeste y celestial.

7. ¿De tierra? Terrestre, terrenal, y otros.

8. ¿Porqué no me los da V. todos? Porque me parece mejor que aprenda V. primeramente los de mas uso, pues sobre haber muchos, los hay de poco uso comparativamente.

9. Cuáles otros se pudieran formar de cielo y tierra? Célico; terroso, terron, y otros muchos.

10. ¿Se pueden formar derivados de los verbos? Sí, señor, y á estos se les da el nombre de verbales.

11. ¿Cuáles se derivan del verbo amar? Amador, amante, amado, amable.

12. ¿De ascender? Ascenso, ascension.

13. ¿De creer? Creyente, creencia, creible, crédulo, crédito.

14. ¿De estudiar? Estudiante, estudio; pudiendo agregar además los aumentativos y diminutivos que tambien son derivados, como estudiantillo, estudianton, etc.

15. ¿De qué se derivan los nombres de familia González, Domínguez, etc.? Se derivan de los nombres propios Gonzalo, Domingo, etc.

16. ¿Cuántas palabras cree V. que contendrá esta gramática? Mas de tres mil palabras primitivas y un gran número de derivadas.

17. ¿En acabando la gramática podré traducir y hablar sobre cualquiera materia que se ofrezca? Podrá V. hablar de todo y seguir una conversacion en general como V. ve que ya lo hacemos; pero para tra-

LESSON XLIX.

ducir y hablar de cualquiera ciencia, arte ú oficio en particular, tendrá V. que acudir al diccionario, porque es imposible introducir en una gramática todas las palabras necesarias para poder hacer esto.

18. Y en cuanto á los idiotismos de la lengua, ¿se hallarán todos en esta gramática? Tampoco, puesto que se podrian componer tres ó cuatro volúmenes como este y quizá no incluirian todos los de la lengua.

19. ¿Cómo los aprenderé entónces? En la conversacion de personas instruidas y en la lectura de buenos libros.

EXERCISE.

1. Did Charles go to another regiment at the time of his promotion? Yes, he left the 71st and went to the 7th.

2. What do you know about the names Sánchez, Domínguez, and all those ending in *ez*? That they mean son of Sancho, son of Domingo, and are formed from those names by adding the termination you have just mentioned.

3. To whom does that magnificent pine grove belong? To the stepson of the gentleman who owns that pretty little house you see over there in the distance (*á lo léjos*).

4. What contemptible old book is that you are reading so attentively? It is no contemptible old book at all (*ninguno*), it is the dictionary; I always go to the dictionary for a word of which I do not know the meaning.

5. Do you know the names of all the heavenly bodies? No, nor you either; the science of astronomy is still imperfect, and there are besides many of the heavenly bodies hidden from human sight.

6. Is not that young gentleman a great lover of the sciences? Yes, but most particularly of the exact sciences.

7. Why do you sweep with that old stump of a broom? It is the best I have.

8. Did you say he was a philosopher? No, on the contrary, I said he was but a miserable philosophaster.

9. How does that rich fellow amuse himself? Reading history in general, and that of his own country in particular.

10. I observe that you speak German very fluently now; have you changed your book? No, I have still the same one, but I myself study more than I did formerly.

11. Do you know whether your cousin speaks as fluently as your sister? Mrs. Alvarez says that in familiar conversation they speak equally fluently.

12. Do you do any compositions? Yes, our father requires us to do two compositions a week on the idioms of the language.

13. Is it not a despicable habit to offer to do things we never intend to perform (*llevar á cabo*)? I should say it is more than despicable, it is even hateful.

14. Does not the study of grammar considerably facilitate the acquisition of a language? Yes, but that alone is not sufficient: something more is required.

15. Have you much fruit at your house in the country? We have a very fine orchard of apples.

16. What language was that your young friend spoke in a moment ago? What he takes for Latin; but what is not in reality any thing but dog Latin.

17. Would not that letter have been better if you had not added that last word? It appeared to me to be necessary to add that to what I had already said, so that the meaning might be more easily understood.

LESSON L.

Amenazar.	To threaten, to menace.
Apoyar.	To lean upon, to support.
Disgustar.	To displease, to disgust, to grieve.
Recurrir.	To recur, to have recourse.
Sacar.	To take out.
A pesar de.	In spite of.
Y diciendo y haciendo.	And suiting the action to the word.
¡Todo sea por Dios!	I hope all will be for the best!
Tomar las de villadiego.	To take to one's heels, to make off.
Sobre todo.	Above all.
Desproporcionadísimamente.	Without any proportion.
Adverbial.	Adverbial.
Antisocial.	Antisocial.
Antepenúltima.	Antepenultimate.
Inútil.	Useless.
Componente.	Component.
Izquierdo.	Left.
Derecho.	Right.
Penúltima.	Penultimate.
Superlativo.	Superlative.

LESSON L.

Anteojos.	Spectacles.	Equivocacion.	Mistake.
Aguardiente.	Brandy.	Ganapierde.	A game in checkers.
Barbilampiño.	Beardless.		
Correveidile.	Tell-tale.	Barbería.	Barber-shop.
Bienhechor.	Benefactor.	La derecha.	The right hand.
Director.	Director.	La izquierda.	The left hand.
Dolor de muelas.	Toothache.	Sinrazon.	Injustice.
Dentista.	Dentist.	Partícula.	Particle.
Disgusto.	Disgust, grief.	Quijada.	Jaw.
Hazmereir.	Laughing-stock.	Las damas.	Draughts, checkers.
Condiscípulo.	Schoolmate.		
Pisaverde.	Fop, coxcomb.		
Pormenor.	Detail.		
Puntapié.	Kick.		
Parasol.	Parasol.		
Paraguas.	Umbrella.		
Quitasol.	Parasol.		
Socialismo.	Socialism.		
Sacamuelas.	Tooth-drawer.		
Pueblo.	People, town.		
Vicerector.	Vice-rector.		

COMPOSITION.

No le está bien á un anciano el ser pisaverde, eso es propio de barbilampiños.
It is not becoming to an old man to be a fop; that belongs to beardless boys.

¿Quién ha dado un puntapié á aquel muchacho?
Who gave that boy a kick?

Yo se lo he dado, porque es un correveidile.
I did, for he is a tell-tale.

Este hombre juega muy bien á las damas, sobre todo á la ganapierde.
This man plays very well at draughts, and especially at *ganapierde* (give away).

¿Tiene V. un quitasol ó un paraguas?
Have you a parasol or an umbrella?

Tengo ámbos.
I have both.

Ese jóven bebe mucho aguardiente y no hace caso de los consejos de su bienhechor.
That young man drinks a great deal of brandy, and pays no heed to the advice of his benefactor.

Esa es la razon porque es el hazmereir de todo el mundo.
That is the reason why he is the laughing-stock of every one.

¿Tiene V. buena vista?
Have you good sight?

No, señor, y esta es la razon porque uso anteojos.
No, sir, and that is the reason why I use spectacles.

Mi condiscípulo Manuel me ha ayudado á hacer la composicion.
My school-fellow Emanuel has helped me to do my composition.

Es inútil que me cuente V. los pormenores.	It is useless for you to tell me the details.
El director y el vicerector de la escuela son hombres excelentes.	The director and sub-director of the school are excellent men.
Me disgustan las sinrazones.	Unreasonableness disgusts me.
El socialismo, á pesar de la opinion de los que lo apoyan, es antisocial ó imposible.	Socialism, in spite of the opinion of those who support it, is antisocial and impossible.

EXPLANATION.

253. COMPOUND NOUNS.—These are very numerous in the Spanish language; some are formed of two nouns, as *barbilampiño*, beardless; *puntapié*, a kick; *aguardiente*, brandy; others are formed of a noun and a verb, as *quitasol*, parasol; *sacamuelas*, tooth-drawer; others of an adjective and a verb, as *pisaverde*, coxcomb; others of a noun and an adverb, as *bienhechor*, benefactor; others of a noun and a preposition, as *anteojos*, spectacles; others of two verbs, as *ganapierde*, a mode of playing draughts; others of two verbs and a pronoun, as *hazmereir*, laughing-stock; three verbs, a pronoun and a conjunction enter into the formation of *correveidile*, tale-bearer; and, finally, others are composed of a noun and some one of the following component particles: *a, ab, abs, ad, ante, anti, circum* or *circun, cis, citra, co, com, con, contra, de, des, di, dis, e, em, en, entre, equi, es* or *ex, extra, im, in, infra, inter, intro, o, ob, per, por, pos, pre, préter, pro, re, retro, sa* or *za, se, semi, sesqui, sin, so, sobre, son, sos, su, sub, súper, sus, tra, trans* or *tras, ultra,* and *vice* or *vi*; as,

*Anti*social.	Antisocial.
*Com*posicion.	Composition.
*Con*discipulo.	School-fellow.
*Di*rector.	Director.
*Dis*gusto.	Displeasure.
*Im*posible.	Impossible.
*In*útil.	Useless.
*Por*menor.	Detail.
*Pos*puesto.	Post-fixed.
*Sin*razon.	Unreasonableness.
*Vi*cerector.	Sub-director.

LESSON L.

We call them *component particles*, because the majority of them—although they are true Latin and Greek prepositions—have no signification in Spanish, except as prefixes, in which case they serve to augment, diminish, or modify the signification of the simple word in proportion to the strength or value they have in the languages from which we have taken them.

CONVERSATION AND VERSION.

1. Don José, ¿sabe V. el significado de las palabras penúltima y antepenúltima? Sí, señor, porque corresponden á las palabras inglesas *penultimate* y *antepenultimate*.
2. Pues bien, ahora, que hablamos de "cañonazos," quiero decir, ahora que hablamos de estas palabras, le contaré á V. un cuentecito.—Muy bien, á mí me gustan mucho los cuentos, sobre todo cuando no son largos y vienen á pelo.
3. Pues este viene á pelo y no es largo.—Entónces cuentémelo V., Don Pedro, escucho con la mayor atencion.
4. Pues vaya de cuento: Un caballero tenia un fuerte dolor de muelas, y fué á un *sacamuelas* para que le sacase una.
5. ¡Hombre! ¿y porque no fué á casa de un dentista? Porque en aquel pueblecito no habia dentistas y tuvo que ir á una barbería, cuyo barbero unia á su oficio el de sacamuelas.
6. ¡Pobre hombre! adelante.—Este barbero, ó sea sacamuelas, pero que de ningun modo era dentista, le preguntó:
7. "¿Qué muela le duele á V.?" "La *penúltima* del lado izquierdo de la quijada inferior."
8. "Muy bien," y diciendo y haciendo le sacó, no la penúltima, sino la última.
9. "¡Huy! ¿qué ha hecho V., hombre? yo le dije á V. que me sacase la penúltima, y V. me ha sacado la última."—"¡Calle! pues yo creia que penúltima y última era todo una misma cosa."
10. "No, hombre, no; la penúltima es la que está ántes de la última."
—"¡Diantre! Mil perdones, y siéntese V. que esta vez no me equivocaré."
11. "¡Vamos, y todo sea por Dios!" "¡Ay! ay! hombre dado á Barrabas!"
12. "¡Toma! ¿y ahora porqué se queja? ¿no vengo de sacarle la que estaba ántes de la última?" "Sí; pero V. olvidó contar la que me sacó anteriormente, de modo que ahora me ha sacado la *antepenúltima*."—La ante . . . . ¿qué? Pero no importa, dejemos estos malditos nombres, que han sido causa de mi equivocacion, y siéntese V. que yo le aseguro á V. que." . . . .

12

13. Pero el parroquiano, dándolo á todos los diablos, tomó las de villadiego, y se cree que nunca mas recurrió á un sacamuelas para que le sacase la penúltima muela.

14. ¿Cuál es la palabra compuesta mas larga en español? *Desproporcionadisimamente.*

15. ¿De qué palabras se compone? De la partícula componente *des*, el nombre *proporcion*, la terminacion superlativa *sima* y la termininacion adverbial *mente.*

EXERCISE.

1. Do you use spectacles because it is fashionable with some people to wear (*gastar*) them, or because you cannot see without them? Because I cannot see without them.

2. My toothache is not any better yet. Then you had better go to the dentist's and get him to extract (*sacar*) the tooth.

3. Do you often see the beardless youth who came to walk with us without being asked * last evening? Not often, nor do I care to see him very often, he is too much of a fop for my taste.

4. Which way do I turn here to go to the new hotel? Turn to the right; it is not more than two streets to the hotel.

5. What did he do when you said that? He took to his heels, and I have neither heard of nor seen him since.

6. What were your two school-fellows doing at the door a few minutes ago? One of them had told the director of a mistake in the other's exercise, and this one threatened to punish him for his trouble (*molestia*); so, suiting the action to the word, he gave him a kick, and called him a despicable tell-tale.

7. Has your brother bought the house yet that he intended to buy? No; when he came to examine the details he found the price of the house entirely out of proportion to the value.

8. Do you always take an umbrella when it rains? I seldom use an umbrella; when it rains I never go out, if I can avoid it.

9. What a strange man that is! Yes, he is the laughing-stock of every one who knows him.

10. What kind of wine do they give you in your hotel? They give us very poor wine, and so I drink very little of it; I prefer water.

11. Do you often play at draughts (or checkers)? Very often; but I prefer the losing game.

12. What is that man's business? He keeps a barber's shop in Sixth or Seventh Avenue.

13. I want you to be good enough to translate this letter for me. Oh!

* Invitasen.

it is useless to talk to me of translating any thing just now (*por ahora*), for I have a headache.

14. Where is that family living now? In a small town in the western part of the State.

LESSON LI.

Atravesar.	To traverse, to cross.
Atropellar.	To run over, to hurry one's self too much.
Causar.	To cause.
Correr.	To run.
Calcular.	To calculate.
Dividir.	To divide.
Exponer.	To expose.
Extrañar.	To wonder at.
Hospedar.	To lodge and entertain.
Incendiar.	To set fire to.
Llorar.	To cry, to weep.
Manifestar.	To manifest, to show, to inform.
Ordenar.	To order, to arrange.
Oponer.	To oppose.
Proponer.	To propose.
Parar.	To stop.
Procurar.	To procure, to try.
Resistir.	To resist.
Rivalizar.	To rival.
Simpatizar.	To sympathize.
Ni con mucho.	Far from, far from it.
A decir verdad.	To say the truth.
En lo que respecta.	With respect to.
En marcha.	Let us go, let us start.
A lo largo.	Lengthwise.
A esta parte.	Within the last.
A pié.	On foot.
En frente.	In front, opposite.
Continuamente.	Continually.
Perpendicularmente.	Perpendicularly.
Alrededor.	Around.

LESSON LI.

Admirable.	Admirable.
Apto.	Apt.
Curioso.	Curious.
Desocupado.	Disengaged, unoccupied.
Directo.	Direct.
Indirecto.	Indirect.
Figurado.	Figurative.
Inepto.	Unsuitable.
Gramatical.	Gramatical.
Complemento.	Complement.
Cosmopolita.	Cosmopolite.
Carruaje.	Carriage.
Delito.	Crime.
Dibujo.	Drawing.
Individuo.	Individual, member.
Literato.	Man of letters.
Gozo.	Enjoyment.
Museo.	Museum.
Paseo.	Promenade.
Punto.	Point, place.
Edificio.	Edifice.
Peligro.	Danger.
Omnibus.	Omnibus.
Soltero.	Bachelor.
Público.	Public.
Trascurso.	Course (of time).
Rincon.	Corner.
Tablero de damas.	Checker-board.
Academia.	Academy.
Admiracion.	Admiration, wonder.
Arquitectura.	Architecture.
Construccion.	Construction.
Belleza.	Beauty.
Frase.	Phrase.
Distancia.	Distance.
Esquina.	Corner.
Lágrima.	Tear.
Laboriosidad.	Industry.
Marcha.	March.
Metrópoli.	Metropolis.
Madurez.	Ripeness, maturity, prudence.
Permanencia.	Permanence, stay.
Sorpresa.	Surprise.
Vista.	Sight, view.
Orilla.	Bank, border.
Batalla.	Battle.
Remuneracion.	Remuneration.

COMPOSITION.

Oriente y Occidente. — East and West.

Cielo y tierra. — Heaven and earth.

El hombre discreto ordena siempre las cosas con madurez. — The sensible man always arranges his affairs with prudence.

La casa de Juan se ha incendiado. — They have set fire to John's house.

Un individuo inepto para escribir puede ser apto para otras cosas. — An individual that is unsuited for writing may be apt at other things.

El reo, á quien se castiga, ha cometido grandes delitos. — The culprit that is being punished has committed great crimes.

LESSON LI.

Un hombre pobre es muy diferente de un pobre hombre.	A poor man (a man in poverty) is very different from a poor fellow.
Hemos dado un gran paseo.	We have had an excellent walk.
Hemos dado un paseo grande.	We have taken a long walk.
Lo que V. dice es una cosa cierta.	What you say is certain.
Yo he observado cierta cosa.	I have observed a certain thing.
Madrid, á 23 de Agosto de 1866 (or Madrid, Agosto 23 de 1866, or Madrid y Agosto 23 de 1866).	Madrid, August 23d, 1866.
Yo soy quien probaré que tú te equivocas.	It is I who shall prove that you are mistaken. ✓
✓ Dios es admirable en todas sus obras, pues todas ellas manifiestan su poder y su bondad (or admirable se muestra Dios en todas sus obras; su poder y su bondad manifiestan todas ellas).	God is wonderful in all His works, for they all set forth his power and His goodness.
Solo Dios es grande, hermanos mios.	God only is great, my brethren.
Adios, Juan; ¿qué tal?	Good morning, John; how do you do?
Hasta mañana. Buenos dias.	I shall see you to-morrow.
Nueva York, ciudad de los Estados Unidos.	New York, a city of the United States.
Yo mismo le ví llorar lágrimas de gozo.	I myself saw him shed tears of joy.
✓ Pronto se calmarán las borrascas que agitan la nave del Estado.	The tempests by which the ship of State is tossed shall soon be calmed.
¿Ha estado V. alguna vez en el Museo de Nueva York?	Have you ever been in the New York Museum?

EXPLANATION.

Notwithstanding we have already made some general observations relative to the place each part of speech occupies in sentences, we deem it expedient to add here a few rules which the learner will find of considerable utility in composition.

254. THE NATURAL CONSTRUCTION demands that the substantive be placed before the adjective, because the thing is before its quality; that the governing word precede the one governed, for it is natural that the former should present itself to the mind before the latter; that the subject precede the verb; that the verb precede the adverb by which it is modified; that the complement come after the verb and the adverb, if there be one; and that when two or more things are to be expressed, of which one, from its nature, comes before the other, this order be preserved; as,

Oriente y Occidente.	East and West.
Cielo y tierra.	Heaven and earth.
Norte y Sur.	North and South.
Este y Oeste.	East and West.

255. FIGURATIVE CONSTRUCTION.—The genius of the Spanish language, and, above all, use, allow us to depart in some cases from the above rules; thus avoiding the monotonous uniformity which would otherwise take place, and leaving the writer more latitude for the construction and arrangement of his periods. So long as sense and perspicuity do not suffer, there is ordinarily no fixed position for any of the parts of speech. Therefore:

1st. Personal pronouns subjects of verbs may, with a few exceptions, be expressed or suppressed at will.

2d. When the pronoun subject is expressed, it may be placed either before or after the verb.

3d. The same liberty exists with respect to the verb, adverb and complement.

4th. Nevertheless, for the sake of clearness in our sentences, it is essential that certain words which together form a whole (such as adjectives with the substantives they qualify, or parts of sentences, acting the part of subject or complement) should be arranged in the same order as that in which the ideas they express are naturally presented to the mind.

5th. There are also certain words which, when placed before certain others, have a signification very different from that which they have when placed after them.

Of all the modern languages the Spanish is certainly the most flexible; indeed, in no other can the same idea be expressed with the same words in so endless a variety of constructions.

Let the following sentence serve as a proof of the truth of this assertion:

Esta señorita era hija de Don Manuel Sánchez.	This young lady was the daughter of Mr. Emanuel Sanchez.

LESSON LI.

256. Words which, from their nature, cannot be separated: *Esta señorita. De Don Manuel Sánchez.*

Natural Construction.		Esta señorita era hija de Don Manuel Sánchez.
1st *inversion.*		Era esta señorita hija de Don Manuel Sánchez.
2d	"	Era hija esta señorita de Don Manuel Sánchez.
3d	"	Era de Don Manuel Sánchez hija esta señorita.
4th	"	De Don Manuel Sánchez era hija esta señorita.
5th	"	Hija era esta señorita de Don Manuel Sánchez.
6th	"	Hija de Don Manuel Sánchez era esta señorita.
7th	"	Hija de Don Manuel Sánchez esta señorita era.
8th	"	De Don Manuel Sánchez hija era esta señorita.

257. The natural construction is, of course, the most grammatical, but the best writers generally give preference to the figurative, as being more easy and elegant, and as giving at the same time more freedom to imagination and genius, and finally, as being better suited to express the grand emotions of the soul.

CONVERSATION AND VERSION.

1. ¡Oh! amigo mio, V. por Nueva York! ¡Cuánto lo celebro! Sí, señor, aquí me tiene V., Don Fernando, no he podido resistir la tentacion de venir á ver la América.

2. ¡Me alegro infinito! ¿Pero porqué no se vino V. á hospedar á mi casa? En primer lugar, porque llegué anoche muy tarde; y en segundo, porque á los solteros nos gusta la libertad y la vida del hotel.

3. Bien, no me opongo, á condicion de que vendrá V. á pasar con nosotros algunos dias.—Lo haré así con mucho gusto, además, Don Fernando, que, como no sé hablar inglés y esta ciudad es tan grande, tengo miedo de perderme si salgo solo, y quisiera que, durante mi permanencia en ella, tuviese V. la bondad de ser mi *cicerone*, de modo es que me propongo, pasar la mayor parte del tiempo en su compañía.

4. En eso me hara V. mucho placer, además de que yo gozaré tanto como V. con la sorpresa y admiracion que le causarán á V. las vistas de esta metrópoli. ¿Ha estado V. jamás en Lóndres ó en Paris? No, señor, jamás he salido de España hasta ahora.

5. ¿Cuándo quiere V. que principiemos nuestros paseos? Cuando V. guste; ahora mismo si está V. desocupado, porqué, á decir verdad, tengo una gran curiosidad.

6. ¿Quiere V. que vayamos á pié ó en coche? A pié, si V. gusta; me parece que podrémos ver mas cómodamente; pero tomarémos un coche cuando haya que salir de la ciudad.

7. Pues en marcha, venga el brazo.—Yo temo que voy á molestar á V., Don Fernando, porque soy muy curioso, como dicen los franceses, soy un *flâneur*, y me llaman la atencion hasta las cosas mas pequeñas.

8. Entónces simpatizarémos, porque á mí me gusta observarlo y criticarlo todo.—¿ Qué calle es esta en que estamos ahora ? Esta es la Cuarta Avenida, y esa que la atraviesa es la calle Veinte y tres.

9. ¿ Cómo es eso ? Las calles en Nueva York estan divididas en avenidas, que son las que atraviesan la ciudad á lo largo, y en calles, que la atraviesan de occidente á oriente, cortando las avenidas en ángulos rectos y formando toda la ciudad como un tablero de damas, de modo que sabiendo el número de la calle ó avenida y el de la casa á donde se va, puede calcularse fácilmente la distancia.

10. Y este edificio de arquitectura tan curiosa de la esquina, ¿ qué es ? Esta es la nueva academia de dibujo, donde se exponen al público muy buenas pinturas.

11. ¿ Hay aquí tan buenas pinturas como en el musèo de Madrid ? No, ni con mucho; este país es aun nuevo, y aunque puedan hacerlo en otras cosas, todavía no pueden rivalizar en lo que respecta á las bellas artes con Europa.

12. ¡ Hombre, qué hermosa plaza ! Esta es la plaza de Madison y todos estos bellos edificios que V. ve á su alrededor, y la plaza misma, han sido hechos de veinte años á esta parte.

13. ¿ Qué edificio es aquel de enfrente que es tan grande como un palacio ? Ese es el hotel de la Quinta Avenida, y en efecto V. tiene razon en compararlo á un palacio, porque los hoteles son en realidad los palacios de los Estados Unidos, y se dice que son los mejores del mundo.

14. ¡ Cuidado ! hombre, por poco se deja V. atropellar por el ómnibus. —¡ Cáspita ! ¡ qué mujer tan hermosa !

15. Sí ; pero no debe V. pararse á admirar las bellezas, en medio de Broadway en su punto de reunion con la Quinta Avenida, porque corre V. peligro de ser atropellado por los carruajes de todas especies que continuamente lo atraviesan.

16. Don Fernando, ¿ son todas las señoras en Nueva York tan hermosas como esa que acaba de pasar ? No sé, porque yo solo miré dónde ponia los piés, procurando escapar al mismo tiempo de los carruajes; pero sí podré decirle á V. que mujeres mas hermosas que las que he visto yo en Nueva York no creo que se encuentren en ninguna parte del mundo.

17. ¡ Oiga V. ! ¿ no hablan español esos que van delante de nosotros ? Eso no debe V. extrañarlo ; esta es una ciudad cosmopolita ; en ella hay gentes de todas las naciones y V. oirá en el trascurso de poco tiempo hablar aleman, español, frances y otras muchas lenguas.

LESSON LI.

EXERCISE.

1. What do you understand by the complement of a verb? It is a phrase or a part of a phrase that serves to complete the idea expressed by the verb.

2. Can you tell me what a cosmopolitan is? A cosmopolitan is one who is not a stranger in any country, a citizen of the world.

3. Where does that gentleman live? In Fifth Avenue, on the corner of Twenty-second Street.

4. How long has your uncle been a member of the Royal Academy of Madrid? He is not a member of the Royal Academy of Madrid; but he has been a member of the Academy of Sciences for the last ten years.

5. Take that book from Charles and give it to Peter. I will give him some other book, because if I took that one from Charles he would cry.

6. Is your friend *a* married *man*? No, sir, he is a bachelor.

7. Have you ever seen Da Vinci's celebrated painting of "The Last Supper"?* No; but I have seen the engraving of that painting, made by Morghen, and it is a truth admitted by every one, that, notwithstanding the absence of coloring, that engraving is a happy expression of the original.

8. How long does it take to go from here to the Central Park? But a short time; the distance is not very great.

9. Could you run there in as short a time as one could go in a carriage? I do not doubt that I could, if I started from the same place and at the same time as the carriage.

10. How are the several States of the Union divided? Into Northern, Southern, Eastern, and Western.

11. Is that not the tallest man you have ever seen? Far from it; I have seen several much taller.

12. Have they been able to fill that office (or position) yet? I believe not; I understand that one of our friends was about to apply for it (*pretenderlo*), but his father was opposed to his doing so, and so he would not persist.

13. How far did you go before you found him? I walked about half an hour by the river side, inquiring of every one I met whether he had seen a young man on horseback; and at last an old man told me he had seen him cross the river, nearly opposite the new building they are putting up (erecting), at a short distance from the entrance to the public promenade.

14. Are there any fine public walks in the metropolis? About seven or eight beautiful ones, the most of which have been made within the last five years.

* La cena.

LESSON LII.

Aconsejar.	To counsel, to advise.
Aprovechar.	To profit, to embrace (profit by).
Consistir.	To consist.
Colorir.	To color (paintings).
Citar.	To quote, to cite.
Costar.	To cost.
Comunicar.	To communicate.
Demostrar.	To demonstrate, to point out.
Deteriorar.	To deteriorate.
Expresar.	To express.
Freir.	To fry.
Grabar.	To engrave, to fix (in the memory)
Tomarse (el trabajo).	To take the trouble.
Prender.	To take up, to arrest.
Perfeccionar.	To perfect.
Merecer.	To merit, to deserve.
Reunir.	To gather, to assemble, to reunite.
Remunerar.	To remunerate.
Visitar.	To visit, to search.
Por ejemplo.	For instance.
Que yo sepa.	For all I know.

List of the Irregular Past Participles of all the Verbs already introduced.

Abierto.	Opened.	Frito.	Fried.
Bendito.	Blessed.	Hecho.	Done.
Contradicho.	Contradicted.	Impuesto.	Imposed.
Convicto.	Convicted.	Muerto.	Died.
Compuesto.	Composed.	Manifiesto.	Manifested.
Dicho.	Said, told.	Oculto.	Hidden, concealed.
Devuelto.	Given back, returned.	Opuesto.	Opposed.
Dispuesto.	Disposed.	Preso.	Taken, arrested.
Escrito.	Written.	Puesto.	Placed, put.
Electo.	Elected.	Provisto.	Provided.
Expreso.	Expressed.	Roto.	Broken.
Expuesto.	Exposed.	Satisfecho.	Satisfied.
Visto.	Seen.	Vuelto.	Returned.

LESSON LII.

Amplio.	Ample.
Actual.	Present.
Antiguo.	Ancient, old.
Contemporáneo.	Contemporary.
Enemistado.	At variance, on bad terms.
Dramático.	Dramatic.
Moderno.	Modern.
Honroso.	Honorable.
Político.	Political.

Cocinero.	Cook.	Amenidad.	Agreeableness, amenity.
Capitan.	Captain.		
Acierto.	Success.	Biblioteca.	Library.
Colorido.	Coloring.	Cena.	Supper.
Grabado.	Engraving.	Comedia.	Comedy, play.
Fresco.	Cool, refreshing air.	Costumbre.	Custom, habit.
		Erudicion.	Erudition.
Empleo.	Employment.	Fuente.	Fountain, source.
Drama.	Drama.	Existencia.	Existence.
Estilo.	Style.	Elegancia.	Elegance.
Jóven.	Youth.	Instruccion.	Instruction, learning.
Mercader.	Dealer.		
Paisano.	Countryman.	Ignorancia.	Ignorance.
Hecho.	Action, fact.	Mencion.	Mention.
Siglo.	Century.	Literatura.	Literature.
Verso.	Verse.	Medianía.	Moderation, mediocrity.
Soldado.	Soldier.		
		Prosa.	Prose.
		Novela.	Novel.
		Política.	Politics.
		Tragedia.	Tragedy.
		Vasija.	Vase, vessel.

COMPOSITION.

Está enemistado con su primo.	He is on bad terms with his cousin.
Colocado en vasijas.	Placed in vases (or vessels).
Ha cantado una cancion española.	He has sung a Spanish song.
Los caballos que han comprado los mercaderes no son buenos.	The horses the dealers have bought are not good.
Los caballos que fueron comprados por los mercaderes son buenos.	The horses that were bought by the dealers are good.
Estan (or quedan) demostradas estas verdades.	These truths are (or remain) demonstrated.

La cocinera habia frito (or freido) el pescado.	The cook had fried the fish.
Han prendido (or preso) al culpable.	They have arrested the offender.
No sé si habrán ya proveido (or provisto) el empleo.	I do not know whether they have already provided (a person to fill) the office.
Has roto el vaso.	You have broken the glass.
¿Ha visto V. un caballo muerto?	Have you seen a dead horse?
No, pero he visto un caballo matado.	No, but I have seen a horse with a sore back.
¿Quién ha muerto á ese caballo?	Who killed that horse?
Un paisano le ha muerto.	A countryman killed it.
El capitan fué muerto por sus soldados.	The captain was killed by his soldiers.
El se ha matado.	He killed himself.
El se ha muerto.	He died.
Ese es un jóven muy leido, muy aprovechado y muy callado.	That young man is well read, makes the most of his opportunities, and talks little.
Es un hecho que la Cena de da Vinci está felizmente expresada en el grabado de Mórghen, no obstante que le falta el colorido de la pintura.	It is a fact that Da Vinci's "Last Supper" is happily expressed in Morghen's engraving, notwithstanding the latter lacks the coloring of the painting.
Aunque el fresco de la Cena, hecho por da Vinci, está mal colorido y deteriorado, ha sido grabado con acierto por Mórghen.	Although the fresco of the "Last Supper," made by Da Vinci, is badly colored, and deteriorated, it has been engraved with success by Morghen.

EXPLANATION.

258. PAST PARTICIPLES.—Some past participles retain the regimen of their verbs; as,

Enemistado con su primo.	On bad terms with his cousin.

259. The past participle must agree in gender and number with the subject or determining verb, except when that determining verb is *haber*; in which case the past participle is indeclinable, whatever be the gender and number of the subject; as,

Ha cantado una cancion.	He has sung a song.
Los caballos que han comprado los mercaderes.	The horses that the dealers have bought.

But the past participle, if it comes after the auxiliaries *ser*,

LESSON LII. 277

estar, *quedar*, or any other, except *haber*, agrees with the subject in gender and number; as,

Los caballos que fueron comprados por los mercaderes.	The horses that were bought by the dealers.
Estan (*or* quedan) demostrad*as* estas verdades.	These truths are (or remain) demonstrated.

260. Some verbs have two past participles, one regular and the other irregular. These are used very differently, since the irregular one, being a true noun, is employed in an absolute sense only, and never signifies motion, whether in the active or in the passive form. For this reason the latter may be accompanied by the verbs *ser*, *estar*, *quedar*, and others, but never by the auxiliary *haber*; inasmuch as it would be improper to say: *hubo convicto, he contracto*, instead of, *hubo convencido, he contraido*.

261. The irregular participles *frito*, fried; *preso*, taken prisoner; *provisto*, provided, and *roto*, broken, are the only ones that can be used with the verb *haber*, to form the compound tenses; as,

La cocinera habia *frito* (or *freido*) el pescado.	The cook had fried the fish.
Han *prendido* (or *preso*) al culpable.	They have taken (or arrested) the offender.
No sé si habrán ya *proveido* (or *provisto*) el empleo.	I do not know whether they have already provided (a person to fill) the office.
Has *roto* el vaso (*sounds better than* has *rompido* el vaso).	You have broken the glass.

262. The verb *matar*, in the sense of to take away life, has the extraordinary irregularity of appropriating for its past participle that of the verb *morir*; the participle *matado* being used to express wounds or sores in animals, resulting from the rubbing of the harness, or from cruel treatment; as,

Un caballo *matado*.	A horse with a sore back.
Un caballo *muerto*.	A dead horse.
Un paisano le ha *muerto*.	A countryman killed him.
El capitan fué *muerto* por sus soldados.	The captain was killed by his soldiers.

But in speaking of a person that has committed suicide, we must say:

Se ha *matado* (and not Se ha *muerto*).	He has killed himself.

263. Some past or passive participles take an active signification, but only referring to persons; as,

Un jóven *leido, aprovechado, callado*. | A well read, thrifty and silent youth.

264. Past participles may sometimes take the place of substantives, and the difference can be known only by the antecedents and subsequents, as in this sentence:

Es un *hecho* que la Cena de da Vinci está felizmente expresada en el *grabado* de Mórghen, no obstante que le falta el *colorido* de la pintura. | It is a fact, that "The Last Supper" by Da Vinci is happily expressed in the engraving of Morghen, notwithstanding the latter lacks the coloring of the painting.

Where the words *hecho, grabado* and *colorido*, are substantives. The same words appear as participles in the following phrases:

Aunque el fresco de la Cena, *hecho* por da Vinci, está mal *colorido* y deteriorado, ha sido *grabado* con acierto por Mórghen. | Although the fresco of "The Last Supper," made by Da Vinci, is badly colored and deteriorated, it has been engraved with success by Morghen.

265. Other grammarians add one more tense in the infinitive mood; as,

Haber de amar. | To have to love.
Habiendo de amar. | Having to love.

But such a classification is no longer essential, nor even correct. In early Spanish literature that form frequently occurs, performing the office now almost exclusively filled by the regular terminations of the tenses, and chiefly those of the future indicative and the imperfect of the subjunctive.

CONVERSATION AND VERSION.

1. ¿Qué le gusta á V. mas, la conversacion ó la lectura? Ambas cosas me gustan mucho.

2. ¿Qué género de lectura le gusta á V. mas? La historia, la comedia, y la novela.

3. ¿Prefiere V. la prosa al verso? No, señor, la poesía me gusta mas; pero ha de ser muy buena, porque en poesía no me gusta la medianía.

4. Que autores, en la literatura moderna, me aconseja V. que lea

para perfeccionarme en el español.—En historia y política lea V. á Lafuente, y á Miñano.

5. ¿Y para la comedia? A Moratin, Breton de los Herreros y Don Ventura De la Vega.

6. ¿No tienen Vds. otros? Sí, señor; pero yo le cito á V. solamente los mejores y solamente á los contemporáneos.

7. ¿Y poetas? Zorrilla, Espronceda, Hartzenbusch, y otros muchos.

8. ¿Tienen Vds. algun buen crítico contemporáneo por el estilo del antiguo Quevedo? Yo creo que no pueden encontrarse dos Quevedos; pero, sin embargo, tenemos críticos de costumbres muy buenos, tales como Larra (Figaro), Don Ramon de Mesonero Romanos, Pelegrin, y otros.

9. ¿Tienen Vds. buenos autores para la tragedia y el drama? Sí, señor, muy buenos, por ejemplo, Martínez de la Rosa, García Gutiérrez, Gil y Zárate, etc., etc.

10. Yo no sabia que tuviesen Vds. tantos autores buenos en la literatura actual.—Yo pudiera citarle á V. otros muchos; pero si V. reune las obras de los catorce mencionados logrará V. tener una pequeñita librería de literatura moderna, que le enseñará á V. mas español que todas las gramáticas y métodos que se han compuesto para enseñar esta lengua hasta el dia, y que le remunerarán á V. ampliamente por el trabajo que le ha costado el aprenderla, con el placer y la instruccion que le comunicarán.

11. ¡Es posible! Yo habia oido decir, y así lo habia llegado á creer yo mismo, que España no poseía nada que mereciese mencion en su literatura moderna, y á decir verdad, los únicos libros buenos que creia que Vds. poseian eran el Don Quijote de Cervántes y las obras dramáticas de Calderon de la Barca.—Así lo he oido yo decir tambien, y en verdad que es una cosa que no puedo comprender, esa general ignorancia de la existencia de una literatura española contemporánea, que ha producido mas y mejores obras que las que se han producido en algunos siglos no solamente en España sino en otras naciones.

12. ¿Se conocen en España nuestros autores ingleses contemporáneos? Se conocen mucho mas de lo que aquí son conocidos los españoles; la prueba es que la mayor parte estan traducidos al castellano, y Vds. no tienen ninguna traduccion, que yo sepa, de todos esos autores que acabo de citarle á V.

13. Probablemente consiste en que los Americanos é Ingleses no aprenden mucho el español.—Entre los Americanos debo hacer tres honrosas excepciones, que son: Washington Irving, Prestcott, y Ticknor. Estos distinguidos escritores no solo aprendieron el español, sino que viajaron en España, visitaron nuestras mejores bibliotecas y quizá adquirieron en

aquellas fuentes mucho del saber, la erudicion, el gusto y la elegancia en el decir que comunican á sus obras tanto interés y amenidad.

EXERCISE.

1. Ought we not to make the most of (profit by) every occasion that offers for acquiring knowledge? That is the only way to arrive at the possession of knowledge.

2. Tell the cook I do not wish that fish to be fried. It is too late to tell her so; she has already fried it.

3. Has that work been translated into Spanish? Not that I know; but it was translated with success into French, by M. de l'Orme, a few years ago.

4. Is not that gentleman to whom you introduced me a short time since a dramatist? He is, and his plays might serve as a model of elegance for many dramatists of higher pretensions (*pretensiones*) than he.

5. Have they found out yet who set fire to your uncle's house? Yes; and the offender has been arrested and convicted of the crime.

6. Would you be good enough to lend me that novel of which you read a chapter to me the day before yesterday? I would with great pleasure if it were mine; but it belongs to Alexander; and, as we are on bad terms at present, I should not like to ask him for any favors.

7. Would that painting be deteriorated * by being exposed to the heat of the sun (*sol*)? Certainly; and the heat of a strong fire would produce the same effect upon it.

8. Did your friend, the captain, return with his regiment from the war? No; he was killed in the first battle that took place after his arrival at the seat (*teatro*) of war.

9. I saw no mention made of his death in the newspapers. No; I believe his name did not appear in the list (*lista*) of the killed; but the sad news was communicated to his brother by an officer of the same regiment.

10. Do you like to walk in the garden in the morning before breakfast? I generally go to the garden every morning and evening to read and smoke in the cool *air*.

11. I wish you had bought that work on English literature. So do I; it would have been very useful to Louisa, who is so desirous of becoming perfect in that language.

12. Did your father think Peter merited the remuneration he received? I do not know whether he did or not; but, at all events, Peter must have merited some remuneration, or else he would have got none.

* *Deteriorar.*

13. Are you going to have your name engraved on your watch? I shall only have my initials (*inicial*) engraved on it.

14. What kind of literature does your aunt like best? Ha! you ask me more than I can tell you; I really cannot say whether she has any taste in the matter; for the fact is, never having taken her for a woman of much erudition, I have not taken the trouble to ask her.

LESSON LIII.

Agradar.	To please.
Aguantar.	To bear with, to put up with, to suffer.
Alcanzar.	To reach, to overtake, to catch.
Alimentar.	To feed.
Armar.	To arm.
Bajar.	To go (or come) down.
Corretear.	To run about.
Conceder.	To concede, to grant.
Distar.	To be distant.
Descomponer.	To decompose, to put out of order.
Determinar.	To determine, to induce.
Echar.	To throw, to put (in).
Exceder.	To exceed.
Hinchar.	To swell.
Nadar.	To swim.
Prohibir.	To prohibit.
Quitar.	To take off, to take away.
Contrario.	Contrary.
Descompuesto.	Decomposed, out of order.
Dotado.	Endowed, gifted.
Excelente.	Excellent.
Indigno.	Unworthy.
Improviso.	Improvised, unexpected.
Terrible.	Terrible.

Antojo.	Desire, longing, whim.	Alabanza.	Praise.
		Apariencia.	Appearance.
Alcance.	Reach.	Estocada.	Thrust.

Consejo.	Counsel.	Busca.	Search.
Discurso.	Speech, discourse.	Comida.	Dinner.
Gatillo.	Pincers (dentist's).	Custodia.	Keeping.
Juicio.	Judgment, trial.	Edad.	Age.
Juramento.	Oath, affidavit.	Hermosura.	Beauty.
Mar.	Sea.	Obligacion.	Duty.
Navío.	Ship.	Vela.	Sail, candle.
Piso.	Floor, story.	Travesura.	Trick, pertness.
Tiro.	Shot.	Corrida de toros.	Bull-fight.
Precepto.	Precept.	Oposicion.	Opposition.
Torero.	Bull-fighter.		
Toro.	Bull.		
Tribunal.	Tribunal, court.		

COMPOSITION.

Correr por las calles.	To run about the streets.
Habló de (or sobre) ese negocio.	He spoke about that affair.
¿Qué está V. haciendo?	What are you about?
Estaba para decírselo á V.	I was about to tell it to you.
No alcanzo á comprenderlo.	It is above my comprehension.
Hace las cosas á su antojo.	He does things after his own fancy.
Iba en busca de un amigo.	I was in search of a friend.
Me opuse á ello.	I set my face against it.
A lo largo del rio.	By the river side.
Venga V. conmigo.	Come along with me.
No sé qué determinar.	I am at a loss how to act.
De ningun modo.	Not at all.
Está comiendo.	He is at dinner.
Entró por la ventana.	He came in by the window.
Delante de mi ventana.	Before my window.
Ante el juez.	Before the judge.
Antes de ahora.	Before now.
Tales acciones son indignas de un caballero.	Such actions are beneath a gentleman.
Parecia fuera de sí.	He appeared to be beside himself.
Excede á toda alabanza.	It is beyond all praise.
Sin duda alguna.	Beyond all doubt.
De dia.	By day.
Uno á uno.	One by one.
¿Por dónde le vino á V.?	How did you come by it?
Luego.	By and by.
Por mar.	By sea.
A la mano.	At hand.

Échelo V. en tierra.	Throw it down.
En cuanto á mí.	As for me.
Dígaselo V. de mí parte.	Tell him that from me.
A consequencia de eso.	In consequence of that.
De acuerdo con.	In accordance with.
Tenía esperanza de que serviria.	I was in hopes that it would do.
Bajar al jardin.	To go down to the garden.
Todos nosotros.	All of us.
Le pido á V.	I beg of you.
¿Cuánto dista?	How far is it?
De improviso.	Off-hand.
Quítese V. el sombrero.	Take off your hat.
Se la llevó.	He carried her off.
Le dejé ir.	I let him off.
Por ese motivo.	On that account.
Adelante.	Go on.
Sobre mi palabra.	On my word.
Al contrario.	On the contrary.
No se tratan.	They are not on good terms.
Les impuso esa obligacion.	He imposed that duty upon them.
Alimentarse de esperanzas.	To live on hope.
Venga V. el doce de Mayo.	Come on the 12th of May.
Al (or del) otro lado.	Over the way, on the other side.
Se acabó.	It is all over.
Vuelva V. á leerlo.	Read it over again.
De miedo.	From fear, for fear.
Fuera de peligro.	Out of danger.
Fuera de casa.	Out of doors.
Está sin dinero.	He is out of money.
Descompuesto.	Out of order.
Perdió el juicio.	She is out of her mind.
Por curiosidad.	Out of curiosity.
Estar de mal humor.	To be in bad humor.
Pasaré á su casa de V.	I will go round to your house.
Pasámos por Francia.	We passed through France.
Le atravesó de parte á parte.	He ran him through.
Por él.	Through (*i. e.*, on account of) him.
Por medio de él.	Through (*i. e.*, by means of) him.
De dia en dia.	From day to day.
Segun las apariencias.	By all appearances.
Eso está aun por venir.	That is yet to come.
Diez contra uno.	Ten to one.
Hasta hoy.	To this day.
El navío está á la vela.	The ship is under sail.

LESSON LIII.

Es menor de edad.	He is under age.
Bajo de juramento.	Under oath.
Hácia allá.	Up that way.
¿Están levantados?	Are they up?
Al segundo piso.	Up two flights of stairs.
Que suban la comida.	Let them bring up the dinner.
Lo pusieron en custodia.	He was taken into custody.
Hincharse de soberbia.	To be puffed up with pride.
No la puedo aguantar.	I cannot put up with her.
Armese V. de paciencia.	Arm yourself with patience.
Su hermosura me sorprendió.	I was struck with her beauty.
No la conozco.	I am not acquainted with her.
Dotado de virtudes.	Endowed with virtues.
Me agradó su discurso.	I was pleased with his discourse.
A tiro de pistola.	Within pistol-shot.
A mi alcance.	With my reach.
No hay nadie en casa.	There is nobody within.
Asomado á una ventana.	At a window.

EXPLANATION.

266. IDIOMS are certain peculiar modes of expression which cannot be translated literally into another language. We have already introduced some Spanish as well as English idioms; but they are very numerous in all languages, and it would be as unnecessary to give within the compass of a grammar all those peculiar to the Spanish language, as it would be to introduce all its words. The learner will find them in the several dictionaries, and principally in the works of good writers.

However, we have introduced in the "Composition" of this lesson as many as the limits of this book would allow; giving examples of phrases in which the English preposition differs in meaning from that which most generally constitutes its proper signification, and consequently must be translated by words corresponding to those in whose place it stands; as,

No sé qué determinar.	I am at a loss how to act.
De ningun modo.	Not at all.

CONVERSATION AND VERSION.

1. ¿En dónde está Alejandro? Está corriendo por las calles.
2. ¿Porqué no me lo dijiste ántes? Estaba para decírselo á V.

LESSON LIII.

3. Yo no quiero que ande correteando calles.—Creo que iba en busca de su amigo.

4. Se lo tengo prohibido; pero el no me obedece, y hace las cosas á su antojo.—Yo me opuse á ello, y le dije qué V. quería ir á paseo con todos nosotros.

5. Don Cárlos, si V. quiere, iré á buscarlo.—De ningun modo, V. no lo encontraria; lo que temo es que haga alguna travesura que le cueste cara.

6. Yo creo que subiendo á lo largo del rio lo encontraré, porque si no me engaño le oí decir que queria ir á nadar.—No sé qué determinar, pero no, mejor será dejarlo, vámonos nosotros á paseo (or vamos).

7. Su hermano Manuel es muy diferente, excede á toda alabanza y siempre obedece los preceptos de su papá.—Sin duda alguna Manuel es un excelente muchacho.

8. ¡Hola! aquí viene Juanito. ¿Viene V. al campo con nosotros? Con mucho gusto; pero ántes tengo que pedir á V. un favor.

9. Délo V. por concedido.—¿Palabra de honor?—Sobre mi palabra. ¿Qué es?

10. Que perdone V. á Alejandro.—¡Vaya! sea así, puesto que dí mi palabra; ¿pero dónde está? Se escondió y no se atreve á presentarse de miedo, pero ahora lo veo asomado á una ventana en el segundo piso de su casa de V.

11. Yo creo que ha perdido el juicio ese muchacho; venga V. aca, señor mio, y cuéntenos qué ha hecho en todo este tiempo que ha estado fuera de casa.—Papá, perdóneme V., que no lo volveré á hacer otra vez.

12. Bien, bien, dejémoslo así por esta vez.

13. ¿Don José, como está su hermana de V.? Está mejor y esperamos que ya está fuera de peligro.

14. ¿Mató el torero al toro á la primera estocada? Sí, señor, á la primera estocada lo atravesó de parte á parte.

15. ¿No se trata V. con su vecino? No, señor, es un hombre lleno de soberbia, á quien no puedo aguantar.

16. ¿Se dió el navío á la vela para la Habana? Sí, señor, el navío está á la vela.

17. ¿Pusieron al culpable en custodia? No, señor, le dejaron bajo juramento de que se presentaria en el tribunal.

18. ¿Conoce V. á la Señorita Sánchez? Hace poco tiempo que hice su conocimiento, su hermosura me sorprendió y es una señorita dotada de grandes virtudes.

19. ¿Viajó V. el verano pasado por mar ó por tierra? Por supuesto por mar, puesto que fuí á Europa.

20. ¿Pasaron Vds. por Francia? Sí, señor, pasámos por Francia, y el doce de Mayo entrámos en Paris.

21. ¿Está V. de mal humor? Sí, señor, malísimo, porque tengo un terrible dolor de muelas.

22. Le aconsejo á V. que se arme de paciencia.—Mil gracias, por su buen consejo, pero creo que será mejor armarse de un buen gatillo.

EXERCISE.

1. How does that man spend his time? He seems to do nothing but run about the streets.

2. Is your uncle's sight not good? No, sir; and that is the reason why he wears spectacles.

3. Is that the way you spell (*escribir*) that word? Oh, no, of course not; I must take out one of the *e*'s.

4. Does your watch keep good time (*andar bien*)? Yes, when it goes, which occurs very rarely*; it gets out of order about twice a month.

5. Did you see the Spanish man-of-war (ship of war) that came into port (*puerto*) last month? Yes, I saw it the day it set sail (*darse á la vela*) to return to Spain.

6. Did you go to see a bull-fight during your stay at Madrid? I did; and although I do not like it myself, yet I could not help (*no poder ménos de*) admiring the amazing dexterity of the men (bull-fighters) who dared to expose their lives attacking the furious animal.

7. How many stories are there in the house you live in? Three; I generally sleep on the third floor.

8. Can you not induce him to stay at home? No, he wants to go; it is a whim of his, and he will not bear with any opposition.

9. Were you in court at the time of the trial? No, I could not go down town that day.

10. How far had he gone before you overtook him? I caught up with him at the corner of the street.

11. How is your cousin getting on? Pretty well; but his arm is still swollen, and to all appearance it pains him very much.

12. I wonder how he can bear up under so much suffering. He lives in the hope of getting better one day or other.

13. Did that man swear he had not been there? He made (*prestar*) affidavit that he had never set (put) his foot in the house.

14. What a beautiful young lady that is! That is true; but her learning by far exceeds her beauty.

* *Rara vez.*

LESSON LIV.

Apegarse.	To adhere to, to be attached.
Criar.	To raise (breed), to bring up.
Concebir.	To conceive.
Continuar.	To continue.
Encerrar.	To shut up.
Guardar.	To guard, to take care, to keep.
Pintar.	To paint.
Presidir.	To preside.
Ponderar.	To make much of, to praise.
Combatir,	To combat.
Reducir.	To reduce.
Rodar.	To roll.
Sacudir.	To shake, to shake off.
Tirar.	To pull, to draw, to throw, to throw out (or away).
Llenar.	To fill.
Entusiasmar.	To render enthusiastic.
Al cabo.	After all, finally, at the end.
De repente.	Suddenly, on a sudden.
No obstante.	Notwithstanding.
Si acaso.	If at all, in case.
Si bien.	Although.
Amarillo.	Yellow.
Azul.	Blue.
Anaranjado.	Orange.
Atento.	Attentive.
Confuso.	Confused.
Feroz.	Fierce.
Bondadoso.	Kind.
Favorito.	Favorite.
Griego.	Greek.
Añil.	Indigo.
Ligero.	Light, slight, speedy.
Lleno.	Full.
Montaraz.	Mountaineer, wild.
Vistoso.	Conspicuous, showy.
Colorado, rojo.	Red.

LESSON LIV.

Romano.	Roman.
Particular.	Particular, private, rare.
Picante.	Pungent.
Temerario.	Daring, rash.
Violado.	Violet (color).
Verde.	Green.
Prismático.	Prismatic.

Cabo.	End.	Algazara.	Shouts (of joy).
Circo.	Siege, circus.	Autoridad.	Authority.
Color.	Color.	Confusion.	Confusion.
Bullicio.	Rumpus, noise, bustle.	Carcajada.	Burst of laughter.
		Corrida.	Fight (bull), race.
Ceremonial.	Ceremony.	Violeta.	✓ Violet (flower).
Espectro solar.	Solar spectrum.	Diversion.	Diversion.
Goce.	✓ Delight, joy.	Clase.	Class.
Dicho.	Saying.	Infancia.	Infancy.
Desierto.	✓ Desert.	Idea.	Idea.
Interés.	Interest.	Fiesta.	Feast, festival.
Guante.	Glove.	Guiñada.	Wink.
Leon.	Lion.	Ocupacion.	Occupation.
Local.	Situation.	Corrida de toros.	Bull-fight.
Entusiasmo.	Enthusiasm.	Pelota.	Ball.
Enemigo.	Enemy.	Plaza de toros.	✓ Arena.
Lloros.	Tears, cry.	Proeza.	Prowess, exploits.
Paso.	Step, pace.	Sonrisa.	Smile.
Prisma.	Prism.	Valentía.	Bravery.
Rumor.	Rumor.	Jaula.	✓ Cage.
Sér.	Being.		
Traje.	Dress, costume.		
Recibimiento.	Reception.		
Suelo.	Ground.		
Grito.	Shout, cry.		

COMPOSITION.

✓ Los vímos cuando entrabamos.	We saw them as we were going in.
✓ Si no hubiera sido por mí, le habrian matado.	But for me, they would have killed him.
✓ Yo iria si no creyera que fuese inútil.	I would go, but that I think it useless.
Diga V. si vendrá ó no.	Say whether you will come or not.
Que venga ó que no venga.	Whether he come or not.
Dudo que lo sepa.	I doubt whether she knows it.

Por atentos y bondadosos que sean (or no obstante lo atentos que son) y por bondadosos que sean.	However attentive they are, and however kind they may be.
Es menester que se cuide V., porque si no se enfermará.	You must take care of yourself, for if you do not you will be ill.
Es menester que obedezca V. las órdenes; de lo contrario sufrirá las consecuencias.	You must obey the orders; for if you transgress them, you will suffer the consequences.
O yo tengo razon ó él la tiene.	Either I am right or he is.
Ni prometas ni obres sin pensar.	Neither promise nor act without thinking.
No lo haria si me importara la vida (i. e., aunque, or por mas que me importara la vida).	I would not do it, though my life were at stake.
Valiente si los hay.	A valiant man, if there are any in the world.
Tuvo el valor, si tal nombre merece una accion temeraria de combatir solo contra tantos enemigos.	He had the courage, if the rash action of fighting alone against so many enemies is worthy of such a name.
Quiero saber si emplea bien el tiempo.	I wish to know whether he employs his time profitably.
¿Si habrá llegado el correo?	If the mail should have arrived?
Mira si viene.	See if he is coming.
No sé si lo haga.	I do not know whether to do it or not.
Si (es que) acabo de entrar.	I have but just come in.
Si (cuando) él al cabo ha de venir.	For, after all, he must come.
Si (es que) no es eso.	But that is not it.
Si (ya) lo dije.	But I said so.
Si (porque) no hay cosa que yo haga.	For I do nothing at all.
Apénas si se oia el confuso rumor de los pasos.	The confused tramping of feet could scarcely be heard.

EXPLANATION.

267. There are several conjunctions in English that are frequently used as substitutes for other words; these conjunctions are generally rendered in Spanish by the words which they stand in the place of; as,

Los vímos *cuando* entrabamos.	We saw them as we were going in.
Diga V. *si* quiere venir ó no.	Say whether you will come or not.

268. The Spanish conjunctions are also often used as substitutes for other words of very different meanings. Let *si* and *que* serve as examples:

LESSON LIV.

Si, as an adverb, is, as we have already observed, affirmative, except when employed ironically.

Si, as a conjunction, may be employed in a variety of significations. The following are some of its principal uses:

1st. To denote the condition on which depends the accomplishment of an action; as,

Si quieres acompañarme, voy á salir.	If you will accompany me, I am going out.

2d. To express indispensable conditions; as,

Tendrás el caballo *si* lo pagas.	You will have the horse if you pay for it.

3d. In the sense of although, or even though; as,

No lo haria *si* me importara la vida (*i. e., aunque* or *por mas que,* me importara la vida).	I would not do it, even though my life were at stake.

4th. In familiar conversation this conjunction is often employed in meanings very different from those we have just explained. For instance, it is often used instead of *es que,* it is because; *cuando,* when; *porque,* because; and not unfrequently instead of *ya,* already, as we read in one of Moratin's comedies:

Si (es que) acabo de entrar.	I have but just come in.
Si (cuando) él al cabo ha de venir.	For, after all, he must come.
Si (es que) no es eso.	But that is not it.
Si (ya) lo dije.	But I said so (or did say so).
Si (porque) no hay cosa que yo haga.	For I do nothing at all.

5th. It is often used redundantly; as,

Apénas *si* se oia el confuso rumor de los pasos.	The confused tramping of feet could scarcely be heard.

CONVERSATION AND VERSION.

1. ¿Iria V. á ver á su hermano si tuviera tiempo? Yo iria si no creyera que fuese inútil.

2. Diga V. si vendrá ó no.—Amigo mio temo salir, porque hace mal tiempo, y es menester que me cuide porque si no enfermaré.

3. ¿Estuvo V. ayer á ver el recibimiento del Presidente? No, señor, mis ocupaciones no me lo permitieron.

4. ¿Cuáles son los colores en que se descompone el espectro solar? Violado, añil, azul, verde, amarillo, anaranjado y rojo.

5. ¿De qué color tiñe V. sus guantes? Los tiño de amarillo.

6. ¿Qué tal le gusta á V. este ejercicio? No me gusta de ningun modo, y si continúa tan interesante como hasta aquí, creo que me hará dormir.

7. ¿Qué costumbres le gustan á V. mas, las de España ó las de los Estados Unidos? Naturalmente, como español, me gustan mas las de España.

8. Pero ¿cuáles son las mejores? No sabré decírselo á V., cada nacion tiene las suyas y cada individuo se apega desde su infancia á las de su propio país.

9. ¿Cuál es la diversion favorita del pueblo español? Las corridas de toros; esto se entiende hablando del pueblo en general y aun de muchos caballeros de la primera clase de la sociedad; pero no de todos, porque hay muchos, principalmente, señoras, que jamás han visto una corrida de Toros.

10. Debe ser una diversion muy cruel y muy peligrosa.—No deja de ser peligrosa, pues los toros de España son mas feroces y ligeros que los de ninguna parte del mundo, criados con este objeto montaraces, de modo que cuando de improviso se encuentran en la plaza muestran una ferocidad y una valentía en nada inferior á la de un leon de los desiertos del Africa, que se encontrase de repente en estos circos llenos de séres humanos.

11. ¿Quiere V. hacerme el favor de relatarme una corrida de toros? Lo haria con mucho gusto; pero sé que no podria hacerlo como merece esta antigua diversion, en algo semejante á los circos de los Griegos y Romanos.

12. ¡Vámos! pruebe V.—Pero si es imposible, y aunque llegara á pintarle á V. el local, los vistosos trajes, tanto del pueblo como de los toreros, los curiosos ceremoniales de la fiesta, las autoridades que la presiden, las tropas que la guardan; la música, el bullicio, los dichos picantes, las sonrisas, las guiñadas, los lloros y carcajadas, todo esto no serviria de nada para hacerle á V. concebir una pequeña idea del gozo y entusiasmo que anima al pueblo español en una corrida de toros.

13. ¡Es posible! ¡Con que todo eso hay! pues yo creia que se reducia á una carnicería de vacas y caballos.—Pues si V. estuviera en Madrid le sucederia como á todos los extrangeros, que á pesar de criticarnos esta diversion, jamás pierden una corrida de toros.

14. Pero ¿en qué puede consistir ese goce que V. me pondera? ¡Goce! hombre, he visto yo tirar á la plaza el baston, el bolsillo y hasta el reloj, entusiasmado de la proeza de algun toreador. Eso era lo que yo le decia á V. que no era fácil de pintar, porque no consiste en la cosa misma por

mas interés que tenga sino en la disposicion particular y el entusiasmo de cada uno. Y si no dígame V. en el juego del fragata* americano en que no se ve otra cosa que una pelota que rueda por el suelo, ó se eleva por el aire, despedida por un garrote. . . . . ¡¡¡Qué es lo que mueve toda aquella algazara y ruido y confusion y gritos de, Hola!!! Willie!!! Charley!!! Here!!! Here!!! Run!!! James!!! Hurra!!! Hurra!!!

15. Ha, ha, ha; V. me hace reir con su corrida de toros. ¡Vaya! me alegro, algo se ha ganado, porque al principio yo creia que V. se iba á dormir.

EXERCISE.

1. Had you not better leave a line for him in case he should come? I think it would be better; notwithstanding that it seems impossible for him to get here to-night.

2. Do the boys still continue to take lessons? One of them still continues, although the least studious of the three; the other two gave up all of a sudden last month.

3. What shouts are those I hear up-stairs? Charles has some friends with him, and they are getting enthusiastic on the occasion of the President's visit to the city.

4. Do you know how to keep a secret? I want to know that before I tell you this one.—I do.—Well, so do I.

5. I suppose† they gave the General a grand reception when he returned from the war? A magnificent‡ one, fit for a king; it was Peter's uncle that presided at it.

6. Can you tell me how many prismatic colors there are, and their names? I shall try; let us see: Green, blue, violet, red, orange, yellow, indigo.

7. What is the best time for learning a language with the least trouble? During infancy; in that age the study of languages is reduced to its simplest expression.

8. What would the earth be without the light and heat which we receive from the sun? A perfect desert; man nor no living being could exist, and there would be no vegetation, for all animated nature is sustained by the vivifying (*vivificador*) effects of the sun.

9. What is the use of the prism? It possesses the power of decomposing the sunbeam (*rayo del sol*), thus enabling (*poder*) us to see separately the rays of different colors which unite to form what is called light.

10. Where are you going now? it is not yet time for the theatre. Why, it is half-past seven, and the play begins at eight precisely.

11. If my friend should have come while I was out? Oh, I imagine that if he had come he would have left some word (*dejar dicho*) for you.

* Base ball.   † *Suponer.*   ‡ *Magnífico.*

12. What is that confused tramping of feet* that I hear in the street? A crowd of people running to see a fire in the next street.

13. Do you hear how that lady praises† the courage of the man who has just got into the lion's cage (*jaula*)? I do, and I was just thinking she might find an occupation of more interest; besides, I do not see any proof of courage in such a rash action as to shut one's self up with a ferocious animal like the lion.

14. What sort of a dress did Miss H. wear at the ball? A blue silk (*seda*) dress, with violet and orange trimmings (*guarniciones*). Can you conceive of any thing more detestable?

LESSON LV.

Afianzar.	To secure, to fasten, to prop.
Conquistar.	To conquer.
Construir.	To construct, to build.
Fundar.	To found, to go upon (a principle).
Medir.	To measure.
Portarse.	To conduct one's self, to behave.
Tirar.	To throw.

Desigual.	Unequal.
Extremado.	Extreme.
Horrendo.	Horrific.
Distinto.	Distinct.
Ridículo.	Ridiculous.
Inmemorial.	Immemorial.
Recto.	Right, straight.

Auxilio.	Help.	Andalucía.	Andalusia.
Castellano.	Castilian.	Castilla.	Castile.
Arabe.	Arab.	Cataluña.	Catalonia.
Crimen.	Crime.	Corona.	Crown.
Catalan.	Catalonian.	Avila.	Avila.
Cimiento.	Foundation.	Galicia.	Galicia.
Dialecto.	Dialect.	Isabel.	Elizabeth, Isabella.
Fulano.	Such a one, so and so.	Imperfeccion.	Imperfection.
Gallego.	Galician.	Irregularidad.	Irregularity.
Modelo.	Model.	Guipúzcoa.	Guipuzcoa.

* *Rumor de pasos.* † *Aplaudir.*

LESSON LV.

Defecto.	Defect.	Igualdad.	Equality.
Mérito.	Merit.	Medida.	Measure.
Reino.	Kingdom.	Pesa.	Weight (for weighing).
Terreno.	Ground.		
Título.	Title.	Nobleza.	Nobility.
Vascuence.	Basque.	Persona.	Person.
Zutano.	Such a one.	Moneda.	Coin.
Escritorio.	Office.	Regularidad.	Regularity.
		Valencia.	Valencia.
		Vizcaya.	Biscay.
		Universidad.	University.

COMPOSITION.

Tratemos ahora de descansar que será lo mejor.	Let us try to rest now; that will be best.
Si no hay virtudes, que son el cimiento de la libertad, no se afianzará esta en los pueblos.	If there are no virtues, which are the foundation of liberty, the latter will have no firm foothold among nations.
¡Qué hermosa que estás!	How beautiful you are!
Ese sí que es un modo de portarse con honor.	That, now, is an honorable mode of acting.
Que llaman.	Some one is calling (knocking).
Que me deje en paz.	Let him let me alone.
¡Qué me matan!	Murder!
En muchas obras no se encuentra otro (or mas) mérito que el estilo.	Many works are void of all merit save the style.
Es que estoy ocupado.	Well, but I am busy.
Es que se encuentra sin ningun auxilio.	Well, but he is entirely forsaken.
Con la pérdida de su madre está todo el dia llora que llora.	She does nothing the whole day over but lament the loss of her mother.
¡Qué no lo hubiera yo sabido!	Ah! could I but have known it!
¿Qué siempre has de ser un holgazan?	Are you always to be a sluggard!
¡Qué hermoso cielo!	What a beautiful sky!
¡Qué horrenda noche!	What a horrific night!
¡Qué cielo tan hermoso!	What a beautiful sky!
A que sí.	I will bet you it is.
A que no.	I will bet you it is not.
A que lo digo.	I will bet you I can say it.
A que lo hago.	I will bet you I can do it.
¡Qué de crímenes se vieron!	How much crime there was!
¡Qué de injusticias no se cometen!	How much injustice is there not committed!
¡Qué! ¿no vienes?	What! are you not coming?

LESSON LV.

¡Fulano!—¿Qué?	Such a one! What?
Iré á paseo, que no estaré siempre metido en casa.	I shall go and take a walk, for I will not be always stuck in the house.
Qué quiera que no quiera.	Whether he will or not.
No es hijo mio, que si lo fuera	He is no son of mine, for if he were ...

EXPLANATION.

269. Que, as a conjunction, is employed in so many different ways and meanings, tending to perplex the learner, that we deem it essential to mention here some of its principal uses:

It is employed as a copulative; as,

Tratemos ahora de descansar, que será lo mejor.	Let us go to rest now; that will be best.

It sometimes serves to introduce an incidental proposition dependent on the principal one; as,

Si no hay virtudes, que son el cimiento de la libertad, no se afianzará esta en los pueblos.	If there are no virtues, which are the foundation of liberty, the latter will have no firm foothold among nations.

It is employed instead of *sino*, but after either of the adjectives *otro* or *mas*; as,

En muchas obras no se encuentra otro (or mas) mérito que el estilo.	Many works are void of all merit except the style.

It is employed instead of *pero*, but in the phrase *es que*, with which we convey the reason why something is or is not done; as,

Es que estoy ocupado.	But I am busy.
Es que se encuentra sin ningun auxilio.	But he is entirely forsaken.

The conjunction *que*, placed between two words of the same meaning, besides uniting them as a conjunction, gives more energy to the expression; as,

Con la pérdida de su madre está todo el dia llora que llora.	She is the whole day over lamenting the loss of her mother.

At other times it serves to confirm more and more the expression; as,

¡Qué hermosa que estás! (*instead of*, ¡Qué hermosa estás!)	How beautiful you are!
¡Ese sí que es un modo de portarse con honor! (*instead of* ¡Ese sí es un modo de portarse con honor!)	That, now, is an honorable mode of acting!

LESSON LV.

The conjunction *que*, at the beginning of a sentence, implies a proposition going before it; as,

Que llaman.	Some one is calling.
Que me deje en paz.	Let him let me alone.
¡ *Qué* me matan !	Murder !

In all these examples a proposition is understood before the *que*; as, *mirad*, in the first; *deseo* or *quiero*, in the second; and *reparad* or *sabed*, in the third.

When the sentence is interrogative or exclamatory, *que* denotes desire and expostulation; as,

¡ *Qué* no lo hubiera yo sabido !	Ah ! could I but have known it !
¡ *Qué* siempre has de ser un holgazan !	Are you always to be a sluggard !

In an exclamatory sentence, and when it precedes a noun adjective, it is equivalent to *cuán*; as,

¡ *Qué* hermoso cielo !	What a beautiful sky !
¡ *Qué* horrenda noche !	What an horrific night !

But if in these sentences the substantive comes first, the particle *tan* must be put between, because we cannot say: ¡ *Qué cielo hermoso!* but, ¡ *Qué cielo tan hermoso!*

In some sentences a determining verb is understood; as,

A *que* sí.	I will bet you it is.
A *que* no.	I will bet you it is not.
A *que* lo digo.	I will bet you I can say it.
A *que* lo hago.	I will bet you I can do it,

in which is understood the present indicative *apuesto*, I bet.

In other sentences it is equivalent to a collective noun or a plural adjective, and requires to be followed by the preposition *de*; as,

¡ *Qué de* crímenes se vieron !	How much crime there was !
¡ *Qué de* injusticias no se cometen !	How much injustice is there not committed !

instead of saying: ¡ *Cuántos crímenes!* ¡ *Cuántas injusticias!* or, ¡ *Qué multitud de crímenes é injusticias!*

It also denotes surprise, and is used as an interrogative, and for answering; as,

¡ *Qué!* ¿no vienes ?	What! are you not coming ?

LESSON LV.

and is equivalent to an entire proposition answering; as,

| ¡Fulano! ¿Qué? (*i.e.* ¿Qué quieres?) | Such a one! What? (*i.e.* What do you want?) |

At other times it is employed instead of the adversative *sino*, and the copulative *y*, in periods where the second member denotes opposition to what is expressed in the first; as,

| No lo conseguirá; *que* se quedará con el deseo (*instead of* sino *que* se quedará, etc.). | He will not get it, but will remain with the desire. |
| Iré á paseo, *que* no estaré siempre metido en casa (*instead of* y no estaré, etc.). | I shall go out to walk, for I will not be always stuck in the house. |

It is not unfrequently used in the place of a disjunctive conjunction; as,

| *Que* quiera *que* no quiera (*i.e.*, quiera ó no quiera). | Whether he will or not. |

It is sometimes substituted for one or other of the causals, *pues, porque, pues que*; as,

| No es hijo mio, *que* si lo fuera... (*i.e.*, porque *or* pues, si lo fuera). | He is no son of mine, for if he were... |

In this meaning it is more used in poetry than in prose; as,

" *Que* quien se opone al cielo,
Cuanto mas alto sube, viene al suelo."

CONVERSATION AND VERSION.

1. ¿Se habla el castellano en todas las provincias de España? En los tribunales, universidades, y oficinas públicas, sí señor; pero el pueblo habla diferentes dialectos.

2. ¿Qué dialectos son estos? El catalan, que se habla en Cataluña; el valenciano, en Valencia; el gallego, en Galicia; y el vascuence que se habla en las provincias vascongadas, que son Alava, Guipúzcoa y Vizcaya; se cree que este último es lengua madre y una de las mas antiguas de Europa.

3. ¿En dónde se habla el castellano? En las demás provincias, Castilla, Aragon y Andalucía.

4. ¿Porqué no se habla el español en toda España? Porque España estuvo anteriormente dividida en varios reinos; de estos algunos fueron conquistados por los Arabes, otros pertenecieron á Francia, y otros finalmente permanecieron independientes por muchos siglos, hasta que Fernan-

do ó Isabel, echando á los Arabes de España, reunieron las coronas de Aragon y Castilla.

5. ¿Son diferentes las costumbres de las provincias de España? Mucho; no solamente no se habla la misma lengua en todas, sino que hasta poco tiempo hace cada provincia tenia leyes diferentes, y aun hoy dia tienen pesas, medidas, traje y hasta caractéres muy distintos.

6. Pues eso debe ser muy incómodo; en los Estados Unidos tenemos la ventaja de hablar una misma lengua y tenemos las mismas pesas, medidas y monedas.—Verdad es, pero tambien es cierto que Vds. han hecho todo esto con la experiencia adquirida en el antiguo mundo.

7. ¿Y porqué no lo hacen Vds. así en España? Porque nosotros tenemos ya establecidas estas cosas de tiempo inmemorial, y no es fácil cambiar costumbres arraigadas por tantos siglos.

8. Cuando Vds. fundan una ciudad en este nuevo mundo, eligen el terreno necesario, tiran Vds. líneas rectas y trazan calles y plazas; para esto no siguen el modelo de una antigua ciudad de Europa, pero las antiguas ciudades de Europa con sus imperfecciones ó irregularidades les han mostrado á Vds. el modo de construir ciudades, cuyo solo defecto consiste en su extremada regularidad.

9. ¿Y no cree V. que de esta igualdad resultan grandes ventajas? Sin duda alguna, y seria de desear que en todo el mundo se hablase la misma lengua, hubiese la misma moneda, pesas y medidas, y, tanto como el clima, las costumbres y otras circunstancias lo permitiesen, las mismas leyes.

10. Tambien me han dicho que hay en España varias clases de sociedad; ¿no es así? Sí, señor; pero eso sucede en todas las naciones del mundo.

11. No en los Estados Unidos. V. vé que aquí no se dan títulos de nobleza, no hay diferencia en el traje, y decimos Mr. Johnson, hablando del presidente, and Mr. Johnson, hablando de un carnicero, y el mismo Presidente Johnson era ántes sastre, de modo que la igualdad existe en las personas como en las cosas.

12. No olvide V., sin embargo, que Dios no ha hecho dos cosas iguales en el mundo, y que los hombres son quizá mas desiguales entre sí que las mismas cosas.—Concedido, y no hay cosa que mas ridícula me parezca que las lavanderas vestidas de señoras, y los *rowdies* del Bowery afectando ser caballeros.

EXERCISE.

1. Did you meet them as you were going in, or as you were coming out? As we were going in.

2. What is the name of that province in Spain in which they speak the Catalonian language or dialect? Catalonia.

3. In which province do they speak the Basque? In the three Basque provinces.

4. And do these dialects differ very materially* from the Castilian language? Yes, very materially; in general they are more like the French than the Spanish.

5. Have you ever heard the Spanish name for the natives of Galicia? Yes, sir, for I am well acquainted with several Galicians living in New York.

6. Can you tell me the weights and measures principally used in the Peninsula (*Península*)? The principal weight, entirely different from all those of the United States, is the *arroba*.

7. How many Isabellas have there been on the throne of Spain? Two; the first was Isabella the Catholic, and the present queen is Isabella II.

8. By what event is the reign of Isabella the Catholic distinguished from all other reigns? By the discovery of America by Christopher Columbus (*Cristóbal Colon*), in the year 1492.

9. Was there not some other very important event that occurred about the same time? Ah! yes; at the commencement of that queen's reign; you mean, I suppose, the conquest of the Arabs, and union of the crown of Castile and Aragon.

10. Are railroads very common in the Peninsula? Not so common as in other European countries; but of late years the spirit of enterprise seems to be revived in Spain, and to the few which now exist we shall soon see a large number of others added.

11. Let us sit down and rest for half an hour, for I am very tired, and you must be so too.

12. How beautiful the sky looks (is) to night! That is true; but how it rained all day!

13. How long has that newspaper been published? Ten years, for it was established (founded) in 1856.

LESSON LVI.

Apreciar.	To appreciate.
Apresurar.	To haste.
Favorecer.	To favor.
Invitar.	To invite.

* *Mucho.*

LESSON LVI.

Apreciable.	Appreciable.
Corriente.	Current, fluent.
Estimado.	Esteemed.
Excelentísimo.	Very (or most) excellent.
Favorecida.	Favored.
Invariable.	Invariable.
Intimo.	Intimate.
Fino.	Fine.
Servidor.	Servant.
Mercantil.	Mercantile.

Comercio.	Commerce, trade.	Atencion.	Attention.
Corazon.	Heart.	Correspondencia.	Correspondence.
Convite.	Invitation, feast, banquet, party.	Esquela.	Note.
		Fórmula.	Form, formula.
Formulario.	List of formulas.	Expresion.	Expression.
Respeto.	Respect.	Estructura.	Structure.
Sobrescrito.	Address.	Intimidad.	Intimacy.
Corresponsal.	Correspondent.	Inicial.	Initial.
Giros.	Manner (of style).	Residencia.	Residence.

COMPOSITION.

Señor D. José Romero.	Mr. Joseph Romero.
Muy Sr. mio.	Dear Sir, My Dear Sir.
Muy Sr. nuestro.	Dear Sir.
Muy Sres. mios.	Gentlemen.
Muy Sres. nuestros.	Gentlemen.
Señora Da. Isabel Jiménez.	Mrs. Isabella Jiménez.
Muy Sra. mia.	Madam.
Muy Sra. nuestra.	Madam.
Hemos recibido su ap^{ble}, apreciable (or su est^{da}, estimada, or su favor^{da}, favorecida).	We have received your favor (or your esteemed favor).
Las de V. del 2 del corriente (or cor^{te}).	Your favors of the 2d instant.
4 del pp^{do} (próximo pasado).	4th ult.

Se repite á las órdenes de V.
    S. S. S.
      (Su seguro servidor).
    Q. S. M. B.
      (Que su mano besa).
                M. De. T.
    Q. S. P. B.
      (*To ladies*, que sus piés besa).
	Yours very truly.

LESSON LVI.

Muy Sr. mio y amigo.	My Dear Sir and Friend.
Mi querido amigo.	My Dear Friend.
Mande V. con toda franqueza á su invariable amigo y S. S.	Command with freedom your true friend and faithful servant.
El Sr. A. De L. presenta (*or* ofrece) sus respetos al Sr. D. I. De H., y le hace saber que.	Mr. A. De L. presents his compliments to Mr. I. De H., and begs to inform him that.

Sr. D. José Martínez,
    Del Comercio de Madrid.
	Mr. Joseph Martínez,
	    Merchant, Madrid.

Sres. D. Francisco Sánchez,
    Hermanos y Ca.,   Cádiz.
	Messrs. Francis Sánchez Bros. & Co.,
	    Cadiz.

Señora Da. Teodora Jiménez y Arteta,   Calle Mayor No. 10,
    Zaragoza.
	Mrs. Theodora Jiménez y Arteta,
	    10 Mayor Street,
	    Saragossa.

Al Exmo. (Excelentísimo),
    Sr. D. Juan Valero y Arteta.
B. L. M.,
    Al Sr. De V.
        S. S. S.,
           A. De T.
	To His Excellency, John Valero y Arteta.
	(Form of addressing letters, notes, &c., to persons living in the same place as the writer.)

EXPLANATION.

270. EPISTOLARY CORRESPONDENCE.—We could not, without overstepping the limits of a grammar, give here all the terms peculiar to mercantile correspondence; those desirous to become perfect in that branch may consult the several works written on the subject, among which we particularly recommend Mr. De Veitelle's "Mercantile Dictionary," published by D. Appleton & Co. We merely give here the general forms for beginning and ending letters.

In addressing persons of different classes of society, except those having titles, letters begin as follows:

Muy Señor mio.	My Dear Sir.
Muy Señor nuestro.	Sir; Dear Sir.
Muy Señores mios. Muy Señores nuestros. }	Gentlemen.

And to ladies:

Muy Señora mia.	Madam.

These expressions are most generally abbreviated thus:—
Muy Sr. mio; *Muy Sr. n^{ro}*; *Muy Sres. mios*; *Muy Sres. n^{ros}*; *Muy Sra. mia*; *Muy Sra. n^{ra}*; *Muy Sras. n^{ras}*.

LESSON LVI.

In the body of the letter, *su ap^{ble}* (su apreciable), or *su est^{da}* (su estimada), or *su favor^{da}* (su favorecida)—*carta*, letter, being understood—are equivalent to *your favor* or *your esteemed letter*.

Such expressions as these are translated thus:

Las de V. del 2 del cor^{te} (corriente); 4 del pp^{do} (próximo pasado); 8 de Mayo, etc.	Yours of the 2d inst.; 4th ult.; 8th of May, &c.

The following forms are employed at the end of letters:

Se repite á las órdenes de V., S. S. S. (Su seguro servidor). Q. S. M. B. (Que su mano besa).	I am, Dear Sir, Yours respectfully.
Manden Vms. cuanto gusten á S. S. S., Q. S. M. B.	Command at pleasure your faithful servant.

To a lady, the form is the same, only changing the letter *M.* into *P.*, thus:

S. S. S.,
   Q. S. P. B.
     (Que sus piés besa).

In a more familiar style:

Muy Sr. mio y amigo.	My Dear Sir and Friend.
Mi querido amigo.	My Dear Friend.
Mande V. con toda franqueza á su invariable amigo y S. S.	Command with freedom your true friend and faithful servant.

Esquelas, notes, are also written in Spanish, as in English, in the third person; as,

El Sr. A. De L. presenta (*or* ofrece) sus respetos al Sr. Dn. I. De H., y le hace saber que, etc.	Mr. A. De L. presents his respects to Mr. I. De H., and begs to acquaint him that, &c.

The most usual manner of addressing letters is:

    Sr. Dn. José Martínez, del Comercio de Madrid.
    Sres. Dn. Fran^{co} Sánchez, Hermanos y Ca., Cádiz.
    Sra. Dña. Teodora Jiménez y Arteta, Calle Mayor N°. 10.
    Al Exmo Sr. D. Juan Valero y Arteta, Madrid.

LESSON LVI.

In the city:

TO A GENTLEMAN.
B. L. M.,
Al Sr. D. P.,
S. S. S.,
A. T.

TO A LADY.
B. L. P.,
A la Sra. Da. F. V.,
S. S. S.,
A. T.

CONVERSATION AND VERSION.

1. ¿Le gusta á V. escribir cartas? Me gusta escribir á mis amigos íntimos; pero me gusta mas recibir cartas que escribirlas.

2. Yo no sé bien el ceremonial ó formulario de cartas, ¿quiere V. hacerme el favor de decirme cómo se principia una carta? Con mucho gusto, pregúnteme V. aquello que no sepa.

3. ¿Cómo se principia una carta dirigida á una persona cualquiera con quien no tenemos intimidad? Si es un caballero, principiamos con la fórmula de *Muy Sr. mio*, y si es una señora con la de *Muy Señora mia*.

4. ¿Y para acabar? Escribiendo á un caballero solemos decir entre otras muchas expresiones, "Queda de V.,
S. S. S.,
Q. S. M. B.,
Fulano de tal."

5. ¿Y si es una señora á quien escribimos? Lo mismo, solo cambiamos la inicial de *mano*, M., en la inicial de *piés*, P., así,
"Queda de V.,
S. S. S.,
Q. S. P. B.,
Fulano de tal."

6. ¿Y cuándo es á un íntimo amigo? Entónces es mas parecido al inglés y principiamos diciendo: "Querido amigo," y para acabar, cualquiera de las muchas expresiones que se usan, como:
"Tu amigo que te ama de corazon,
Fulano de tal."

7. ¿Cómo se escriben las esquelas de invitacion, etc., á las personas que viven en la ciudad? Se escriben, como en inglés, en la tercera persona.

8. ¿Quiere V. escribirme una esquela invitándome á comer? Sí, señor, vea V. así: "Los Sres. De V. presentan sus respetos á los Sres. De T., y les suplican que les hagan el honor de venir á comer con ellos el mártes á las cinco. Lúnes, Abril 8 de 1866."

9. Veamos si V. puede responderme en español.—Vea V., "Los Sres. De T. se apresurarán á acudir al amable convite de los Sres. De V., y les presentan sus mas finas atenciones."

10. Muy bien, muy bien, ahora solo falta poner la dirección (el sobre).—Estando las personas á quien me dirijo en la ciudad, creo que el sobrescrito debe ponerse así:

B. L. M.
Al Sr. De V.
S. S. S.,
A. De T.

11. ¿Cree V. que podré ahora traducir una carta mercantil en inglés? Sí, señor, y escribirla tambien, puesto que V. sabe ya la estructura de la lengua, además de poseer un gran número de sus giros, idiotismos y palabras mas necesarias; pero todavía tendrá V. necesidad de acudir al diccionario, porque no es posible introducir en una gramática todas las palabras y frases que requiere una correspondencia mercantil.

EXERCISE.

1. Do you ever do any of the correspondence in your office (*escritorio*)? Not often, for I do not know how to write letters in Spanish, and the greater part of our correspondence is carried on (*llevar*) in that language.

2. You ought, in that case, to make that branch the object of particular study for a time. That is what I desire to do; and I would be obliged to you to give me some instructions (*instruir*) in the forms most observed in Spanish houses.

3. I shall have much pleasure in showing you all I know myself; but as I have never been in business, there are many points of which I am ignorant (*ignorar*).

4. What is the first thing to write in a letter? In Spanish, as in English, the date is generally the first thing; it is written thus:

CADIZ, October 1st, 1866.

5. What comes next? The name and residence of the person we are writing to, thus:

Messrs. LAFUENTE, SONS & Co., Malaga:

6. So far there is little difference between the two languages. Very little; we next go on to say (*luego se pone*):

Gentlemen (or Sir, or My Dear Sir, or Dear Sirs, or, if we write to a lady, Madam):

7. Ah! there I observe a decided difference: is that the form always followed for commencing letters? For business letters, yes; but for familiar correspondence, we have many others; indeed,* they are mostly always suited to the taste of the writer.

8. Be good enough to show me one or two. With the greatest

---
* *El hecho es.*

pleasure: My Dear Friend: My Very Dear Alexander: Esteemed Friend: My Ever Dear Mother, &c., &c., &c.

9. How do you acknowledge (*acusar*) the receipt of a favor? In this manner: I have duly received your esteemed favor (or letter) of the 17th instant.

10. As for the body of the letter, the form depends entirely on the nature of the business; and, in general, all that is required is to say just what is necessary and nothing more, and to avoid obscurity (*oscuridad*), in order that our ideas may be completely understood by our correspondent (*corresponsal*).

11. The usual manners of closing a letter are:

     I am, dear sir,
      Your most obd't ser't; or,
     I am, sir,
      Yours very truly.

12. And for familiar letters:
I am, dear Charles,
   Your true friend and loving cousin; or,
With kindest expressions to your brother,
   Believe me to remain your ever faithful and loving friend.

LESSON LVII.

Abalanzarse.	To rush, to spring.
Concordar.	To agree.
Cumplir.	To fulfil, to keep, to do (duty).
Conversar.	To converse.
Entregar.	To give, to hand, to deliver.
Escapar.	To escape.
Honrar.	To honor.
Participar.	To participate, to partake.
Regir.	To govern.
Auxiliar.	To help.
Honrado.	Honest, honored.
Plural.	Plural.
Singular.	Singular.

LESSON LVII.

Barón.	Baron.	Alhaja.	Jewel.
Crédito.	Credit.	Agudeza.	Wit, witty saying.
Encargo.	Commission, charge, order.	Cocina.	Kitchen.
Género.	Kind, cloth.	Confianza.	Confidence.
Empleo.	Employment, office.	Espada.	Sword.
		Fuga.	Flight.
Plato.	Plate, dish.	Gracia.	Favor, good graces.
Número.	Number.	Manía.	Mania.
Régimen.	Regimen.	Promesa.	Promise.
Tema.	Theme, exercise.	Pretension.	Pretension, claim.
Diptongo.	Diphthong.	Concordancia.	Concord, agreement.
Triptongo.	Triphthong.		
Varon.	Man.	Version.	Version.
Error.	Error, mistake.	Tema.	Whim.

COMPOSITION.

Acordarse con alguno.	To agree with any one.
Acordarse de alguno.	To remember any one.
Caer á la plaza.	To front on the square (said of a house).
Caer en la plaza.	To fall in the square.
Caer de la gracia de alguno.	To fall from any one's favor (or good graces).
Caer en gracia á alguno.	To get into any one's favor (or good graces).
Contar una cosa.	To relate, to tell a thing.
Contar con una cosa.	To count upon a thing.
Convenir á uno.	To suit (to be convenient for) any one.
Convenir con uno.	To agree with any one.
Cumplir con uno.	To do one's duty toward any one.
Cumplir por uno.	To act in the place of any one.
Dar algo.	To give any thing.
Dar con algo.	To find any thing.
Dar en una cosa.	To be obstinate.
Dar por algo.	To give for any thing.
Dar crédito.	To give credit, to believe.
Dar á crédito.	To give on credit.
Dar la mano.	To give the hand (or to shake hands).
Dar de mano.	To lay aside, to abandon.
Dar en manos de.	To fall into the hands of.
Dar con el pié.	To despise, to scorn, to make light of.
Dar por el pié.	To overthrow.

LESSON LVII.

Dar fin (or cabo) á una cosa.	To bring to an end, to finish.
Dar fin de una cosa.	To destroy.
Declararse á alguno.	To confide one's secrets to any one.
Declararse por alguno.	To side with any one, to declare one's self in favor of any one.
Dejar hacer algo.	To let any thing be done.
Dejar de hacer algo.	To leave any thing undone.
Deshacerse alguna cosa.	(Speaking of things) to be destroyed.
Deshacerse de alguna cosa.	To dispose of (or part with) any thing.
Disponer sus alhajas.	To arrange one's jewelry.
Disponer de sus alhajas.	To dispose of one's jewelry.
Echar tierra á una cosa.	To forget any thing, to cast it into oblivion.
Echar un género en tierra.	To throw any thing on the ground (or down).
Entender una cosa.	To understand a thing.
Entender en una cosa.	To be a judge of a thing.
Entregarse al dinero.	To make a god of one's money.
Entregarse del dinero.	To receive, to take charge of money.
Escapar á buenas.	To make the best of one's escape.
Escapar de buenas.	To make a happy escape.
Estar en alguna cosa.	To be aware of any thing.
Estar sobre alguna cosa.	To push an affair.
Estar á todo.	To be ready for whatever may come.
Estar en todo.	To pay attention to every matter.
Estar con cuidado.	To be anxious, solicitous.
Estar de cuidado.	To be dangerously ill.
Estar en sí.	To have complete consciousness.
Estar sobre sí.	To be proud.
Estar con alguno.	To be with any one, to be of any one's opinion.
Estar por alguno.	To favor any one.
Estar en hacer alguna cosa.	To be resolved (or disposed) to do any thing.
Estar para hacer alguna cosa.	To be about to do any thing.
Estar por hacer alguna cosa.	To be inclined to do something.
Estar alguna cosa por hacer.	To remain to be done.
Gustar un plato.	To taste a dish (of any kind of food).
Gustar de un plato.	To be fond of a dish.
Hacer confianza á una persona.	To tell a secret to any one.
Hacer confianza de una persona.	To make a confident of any one, to trust to any one.
Hacer una cosa con tiempo.	To do a thing at one's leisure (so as not to be pressed for time).

Hacer una cosa en tiempo.	To do a thing in time, at a suitable time.
Hacerse á una cosa.	To get used to a thing.
Hacerse con una cosa.	To get (or procure) a thing.
Hacerse de una cosa.	To provide one's self with a thing.
Hallarse algo.	To find any thing.
Hallarse con algo.	To be in possession of (or have) any thing.
Ir con alguno.	To go with anybody, to be of any one's opinion, to be on any one's side, to listen to any one.
Ir sobre alguno.	To fall upon (or attack) any one.
Mayor de edad.	To be of age.
Mayor en edad.	To be older.
Participar una cosa.	To communicate any thing (to another).
Participar de una cosa.	To participate in any thing.
Poner una cosa en tierra.	To lay any thing on the ground.
Poner una cosa por tierra.	To make little of a thing.
Poner con cuidado.	To put (or place, or lay) with care.
Poner en cuidado.	To alarm, to give anxiety.
Preguntar á uno.	To ask any one (interrogate).
Preguntar por uno.	To ask (or inquire) for any thing.
Quedar en hacer una cosa.	To agree to do any thing.
Quedar una cosa por hacer.	To remain to be done (speaking of things).
Responder una cosa.	To answer something (giving an answer).
Responder de una cosa.	To answer for any thing.
Saber á cocina.	To smell (or taste) of the kitchen.
Saber de cocina.	To be skilful in (or to understand) cooking.
Salir con una empresa.	To carry out an enterprise.
Salir de una empresa.	To give up an enterprise.
Salir á su padre.	To resemble one's father.
Salir con su padre.	To go out with one's father.
Salir de su padre.	To be released from the wardship of one's father.
Salir por su padre.	To go bail for one's father.
Ser con alguno.	To be of any one's opinion.
Ser de alguno.	To belong to any one's party.
Ser para alguno.	To be for any one (of things).
Tener consigo.	To have with (or about) one.
Tener para sí.	To be persuaded.
Tener de hacer algo.	To be going to do any thing.
Tener que hacer algo.	To have to do any thing.
Tirar la espada.	To throw down (or away) one's sword.

Tirar de la espada.	To draw one's sword.
Tratar de vinos.	To talk about wines.
Tratar en vinos.	To deal in wines.
Vender al contado.	To sell for cash.
Vender de contado.	To sell on the instant.
Volver á la razon.	To recover one's reason.
Volver por la razon.	To stand up for reason (or what is right).
Volver en razon de tal cosa.	To return for such a reason (or motive).

EXPLANATION.

271. It is a general custom, amongst authors of Spanish grammars and Spanish methods, to copy entire the forty pages devoted by the Spanish Academy in its Grammar to a list of verbs requiring certain prepositions after them. But we, notwithstanding our most profound respect for the body just mentioned, refrain from following in the footsteps of our predecessors, and that not merely on account of the uselessness of the list, but for the more potent reason that we believe it to be calculated to misguide the student at every step. An example:—Any one not thoroughly acquainted with Spanish syntax would, on reading the very first article in the list above referred to, *Abalanzarse á los peligros,* naturally conclude therefrom that the verb *abalanzar* governs at all times and under all circumstances the preposition *á.* Now that would be absurd, for nothing is more usual than to see, and hear the expressions:—*Abalanzarse* contra (*or* sobre) *su enemigo, abalanzarse* con (*or* sin) *juicio, abalanzarse* para *sacudir*, de repente, &c. And so of all the other verbs, each of which may, according to the idea to be conveyed, govern almost any preposition in the language.

It would be vain to attempt to give, in a work of the nature of the present one, a complete set of rules for determining the various significations of every verb as decided or modified by the attendant preposition; but, as much can be done, even here, toward helping the student through the most difficult parts, we could not resist giving in this day's Composition a list composed of those verbs which are at the same time of most frequent occurrence in general every-day conversation, and susceptible of the greatest diversity of meaning, according to the preposition by which they are followed.

Before dismissing this subject we deem it convenient to remark that a large number of English verbs, to determine the meaning of which a preposition is indispensable, are rendered in Spanish by a verb alone. For example:

Bajar.	To go down.
Entrar.	To come in.
Salir.	To go out.
Subir.	To go up.
Sacar.	To draw out.
Partir.	To set out.
Caer.	To fall down.

This may be the reason why many Spanish grammarians have thought that in Spanish the same thing does not exist. We regret that the dimensions of our book do not allow of our giving a more complete list in corroboration of the fact that Spanish verbs too enjoy that transition of signification which is so frequent in English verbs.

CONVERSATION AND VERSION.

1. ¿A qué lado caen las ventanas de su cuarto de V.? Tres caen á la plaza de Madison y las otras tres caen á la calle Veinte y cinco.

2. ¿Le cae á V. en gracia ese muchachito? Sí, señor, porque responde con mucha agudeza.

3. ¿Puedo contar con su promesa de V.? V. puede contar con ella, porque yo cumplo siempre lo que prometo.

4. ¿Da V. crédito á todo lo que oye? No, señor, á ménos que conozca las personas.

5. ¿Da V. la mano á aquel pobre? Sí, señor, porque aunque pobre es honrado.

6. ¿Ha dado V. fin á su tarea? Todavía no; pero pronto daré de mano.

7. Si V. deja esos libros en manos de ese muchacho, pronto dará fin de ellos.—Así lo creo; pero es necesario que los niños tengan algo para entretenerse.

8. ¿Cómo ha dispuesto V. de sus alhajas? Las he guardado, porque pude encontrar dinero sin venderlas.

9. ¿Qué se hizo de aquel mal negocio en que se metió su primo de V.? Se le ha echado tierra, y nadie se acuerda mas de él.

10. ¿En qué se ocupa su amigo de V.? Entiende en vinos; pero es cosa que no entiende.

LESSON LVII.

11. ¿Cómo está su esposa de V.? Ella está de cuidado, y yo con cuidado.
12. ¿Está V. en hacer aquel negocio? Estoy para hacerlo.
13. ¿Queda V. en hacer ese encargo por mí? Quedo en hacerlo y pierda V. cuidado, que no se quedará por hacer.
14. ¿Es V. mayor de edad? No, señor, todavía no; pero soy mayor en edad con respecto á mis hermanos.
15. No ponga V. eso por tierra.—No lo pongo por tierra, sino en tierra.
16. ¿Piensa V. salir con su empresa? No, señor, pero pienso salir pronto de ella.
17. ¿Tiró ese hombre de la espada? Tiró de la espada, porque la sacó; pero el miedo le hizo emprender la fuga y la tiró.
18. Don Juan, ¿le gusta á V. vender al fiado? No, señor, me gusta vender al contado y de contado.
19. ¿Volvió D. Francisco por la razon? No, señor, D. Francisco no ha vuelto á la razon, y por consiguiente no volvió por la razon.
20. ¿Se acuerda ese hombre con su esposa? No, señor, no se acuerdan.
21. ¿Se acuerda V. de lo que le dije á V. ayer? No, señor, lo he olvidado.
22. ¿Conviene V. ahora conmigo en que el español es mas fácil que el inglés? Convengo con V. en ello.
23. ¿Le conviene á V. hacer eso? No, señor, no me conviene.
24. ¿Dió V. por fin con lo que buscaba? No, señor, todavía no lo he encontrado.
25. Este hombre ha dado en la tema de querer aprender sin estudiar; ¿no le parece á V. que es una pretension muy ridícula? Ridiculísima.

EXERCISE.

1. Has the Baron given up his project? He told me he would like to give it up, if he could do so honorably.
2. I understand he is an honorable man? Yes, and he is therefore respected by all who know him.
3. Has your brother come to an agreement with that dealer for the purchase of the horse he was speaking of? It appears not, and that, on the contrary, he desires to get rid of the one he has.
4. Did you inform the merchant of the order you received from the West? Not yet; but I intend to let him know of it this very day.
5. Does that woman understand cooking? She says she does; and she handed me a letter from a lady with whom she lived two years.
6. Did the captain draw his sword as soon as he heard his antagonist's reply? He had already drawn it; but when he heard the reply he threw down his sword, and ran and gave his hand to the man whom, a few moments before, he was resolved to kill.

7. Has your brother sent you the books he promised you? No, and that need not surprise you, for I can never rely (count) on him for any thing.

8. That is to say, he never keeps his promise? That is precisely what I mean to say.

9.. Do past participles always agree in gender and number with the subject of the verb? Yes, always, except when governed by the auxiliary *to have*.

10. Are there not some participles, past and present, that do not retain the regimen of the verbs to which they belong?—There are very many; and, if you like, I will mention some of them.—Be good enough to do so.

11. I hope you have provided yourself with every thing necessary for your journey? Every thing, except one or two articles which I have been unable to find.

12. How do you advise me to arrange (dispose) all these books? I have only one advice to give you in the matter, and that is, to dispose of them as quickly as you can.

13. Would you like to taste this dish? No, thank you, I am not fond of it.

14. Is he not of your opinion? Not at all; he always goes (sides) with his father.

LESSON LVIII.

Notar.	To note, to observe, to perceive.
Cazar.	To hunt, to chase.
Chancear.	To jest.
Combinar.	To combine.
Concertar.	To concert, to agree.
Concluir.	To conclude, to finish.
Enfriarse.	To cool, to get (or grow) cold.
Encargar.	To charge, to commission, to order.
Flotar.	To float.
Improvisar.	To improvise.
Inspirar.	To inspire.
Repartir.	To divide.
Saltar.	To leap, to jump.
Trinchar.	To carve, to cut.
Cobrar. Brindar.	To collect. To toast.

LESSON LVIII.

A lo léjos.	At a distance, in the distance.
A cuestas.	On one's back, on one's shoulder.
A la española.	In the Spanish fashion.
Atras.	Backward, ago, behind.

Blanco.	White.
Bonito.	Pretty.
Durable, duradero.	Durable.
Elocuente.	Eloquent.
Galante.	Gallant.
Bello sexo.	Fair sex.
Magnífico.	Magnificent.
Negro.	Black.
Rodeado.	Surrounded.
Vacío.	Empty.

Abanico.	Fan.	Ala.	Wing.
Apetito.	Appetite.	Botella.	Bottle.
Aficionado.	Amateur, one fond of.	Caza.	Hunt.
		Chanza.	Jest.
Baul.	Trunk.	Cima.	Top, summit.
Buey.	Ox.	Colina.	Hill.
Brindis.	Toast.	Dama.	Lady.
Carro.	Car, cart.	Imaginacion.	Imagination.
Canasto.	Basket.	Llave, clave.	Key.
Conductor.	Conductor.	Milla.	Mile.
Pretexto.	Pretext.	Pechuga.	Breast (of fowl).
Peñasco.	Rock.	Fuerza.	Force, strength.
Embarcadero.	Ferry.	Suerte.	Luck, sort.
Piropos (pl.).	Sweet things.	Tarea.	Task.
Pasaje.	Fare.	Vocal.	Vowel.
Sitio.	Place, spot.	Voz.	Voice, word.
Salon.	Saloon.	Sombra.	Shade, shadow.
Vocabulario.	Vocabulary.	Elocuencia.	Eloquence.

COMPOSITION.

Quedámos en que saldriamos á las cinco.	We agreed (or appointed) to set out (or start) at five o'clock.
Este canasto es superior á mis fuerzas.	This basket is more than I am able to manage.
A la salud de las señoras.	To the health of the ladies.

Decir piropos á las señoritas.	To say sweet things to the young ladies.
Sírvase V. pagar al conductor.	Please pay the conductor.
¡ Mire V. qué gracia!	Only think!
¿ Qué tal le gusta á V.?	How do you like?
Pongamos los canastos á la sombra.	Let us set the baskets in the shade.
La subida de la colina con un gran canasto á cuestas, me ha abierto el apetito.	Coming up the hill with a large basket on my back has sharpened my appetite.
Me alegro de ver á V.	I am glad to see you.
Se alegró de la noticia.	He was rejoiced at the news.
Lo siento mucho.	I am very sorry for it (i. e., I feel it much).
Me pesa mucho saberlo.	I am very sorry to know it (i. e., it grieves me much to know it).
¿ Cuántas personas caben en esta iglesia?	How many persons does this church hold?
No cabíamos todos en el salon.	The saloon could not hold us all.
¿ Puede caber en tu imaginacion tal cosa?	Can such a thing enter your imagination?
Cabe mucho en este baul.	This trunk holds a great deal.
No caber de piés.	To have no room to stand.
A mí me cupo en suerte venir á la América.	It was my lot to come to America.
No caber de gozo.	To be overjoyed.

EXPLANATION.

IDIOMATIC USE OF CERTAIN VERBS.

272. ALEGRARSE.—The verbs *to be glad* and *to be rejoiced at* are translated by the reflective verb *alegrarse*; as.

Me *alegro* de ver á V.	I am glad to see you.
Se *alegró* de la noticia.	He was rejoiced at the news.

273. SENTIR and PESAR.—*To be sorry* and *to grieve*, are translated by these verbs; as,

Lo siento mucho.	I am very sorry for it (i. e., I feel it much).
Me pesa mucho saberlo.	I am very sorry to know it (i. e., it grieves me much to know it).

274. CABER, to be capable of containing, &c.—This verb is employed in different manners in Spanish; as,

¿ Cuántas personas *caben* en esta iglesia?	How many persons does this church hold (or is it capable of containing)?

LESSON LVIII.

No *cabiamos* todos en el salon.	The saloon could not hold us all.
¿Puede *caber* en tu imaginacion tal cosa?	Can such a thing enter your imagination?
Cabe mucho en este baul.	This trunk holds a great deal.
No *caber* de piés.	To have no room to stand.
A mí me *cupo* en suerte venir á la América.	It was my lot to come to America.
No *caber* en sí.	To be well satisfied with one's self.
No *caber* de gozo.	To be overjoyed.

CONVERSATION AND VERSION.

1. Buenos dias, señores, ¿conque ya todos estan listos? Pues no habiamos de estar, si son ya las seis y quedámos en que saldriamos á las cinco.

2. Habriamos estado aquí de los primeros, si no hubiera sido que, despues de haber andado dos ó tres manzanas, echó de ver mi esposa que habia olvidado la llave del cuarto, el paraguas, el abanico, y yo no sé cuántas otras cosas mas; pero en fin ya estamos aquí, ¿cuándo partimos? Estamos esperando el carro que va al embarcadero de la calle Treinta y tres.

3. Señoras, esten Vds. prontas, porque veo venir el carro.—Don Martin, ayúdeme V. á llevar este canasto, porque es superior á mis fuerzas.—Llame V. á Don Pepito, que no hace mas que decir piropos á las señoritas, porque yo tengo ya dos paráguas y tres niños de que cuidar.

4. Don Pepe, V. que no tiene niños, ni canastos, etc., sírvase V. pagar al conductor.—(¡El diantre del hombre! ahora me pesa no haber tomado un canasto.)

5. ¡El pasaje caballeros! ¿Cuántos somos? uno, dos, tres, cuatro, caballeros; una, dos, tres, cuatro, siete señoras, esto es: once personas mayores y catorce niños.

6. Papá, ¿está muy léjos el sitio á donde vamos á pasar el dia? No, Luisita, solamente unas diez millas.

7. ¿De este lado ó del otro del rio? Del otro, desde aquí lo puedes ver.

8. ¿No ves allá á lo léjos, en la cima de aquella colina, una casa blanca en donde flota la bandera americana? Sí, señor, es muy bonito sitio y debe tener muy buenas vistas.

9. Cuidado con los niños al saltar en tierra, no se caiga alguno al agua.—¿Estan todos fuera? ¿No se ha olvidado nada?—No, señor.—Pues en marcha.

10. Don Pepito, tome V. ese canasto, y cuidado no lo deje caer y rompa las botellas que contiene.—¡Hombre, por Dios! con el pretexto de que venia con las manos vacías, me ha hecho V. pagar los carros y el va-

porcito por veinte y tres personas, y ahora me quiere V. hacer cargar con el canasto del vino.

11. Vamos, Don Pepito, llévelo V. ahora hasta la cima de aquella colina, que á la vuelta á casa yo me encargo de llevarlo.—¡Mire V. qué gracia! á la vuelta! qué es lo que quedará de una docena de botellas, despues de beber veinte y tres personas.

12. Nada; el que no ayude á llevar los canastos no participará de su contenido.—Sres., repartamos la tarea; que los hombres lleven los canastos, las mamás á los niños, los niños los paraguas, y las señoritas á Don Pepito.

13. Da. Delfina ¿qué tal le gusta á V. este sitio? ¡Oh! es delicioso; ¡qué vistas tan bonitas!

14. Pongamos los canastos á la sombra de ese hermoso árbol.—Sí, y pongámonos nosotros tambien á la sombra, que al sol hace calorcito.

15. ¿No le parece á V., Don Enrique, que es tiempo de poner la mesa? Así me parece, porque la subida de la colina con un gran canasto á cuestas me ha abierto el apetito.

16. Sres., la comida está en la mesa.—Señoras, ¿qué es lo que Vds. dicen? ¡en la mesa! ¡Ah! sí, ya vemos, sobre un gran peñasco á la sombra de aquel árbol ¡magnífica idea!

17. Don Pepito, traiga V. un par de sillas mas, que faltan para dos señoras. Allá voy, ¡cáspita con las sillitas! cada una pesa cien libras; pero, eso sí, son durables, no haya miedo de que se rompan.—Tomen Vds. asiento, señoras.

18. Pase V., Don Martin, primero. No, señor, despues de V.—Señores sin cumplimientos que se enfría la comida.

19. ¿Quién quiere sopa? ¡Hombre, sopa! yo, yo, sírvame V. un plato, Don Enrique.

20. Poco á poco, Don Pepito, en el campo, no tenemos sopa.—Pues yo creí que V. me la ofrecia.—Yo pregunté por saber quién era aficionado á la sopa.

21. Señor Don Pedro ¿quiere V. hacerme el favor de trinchar ese pollo? Con mucho gusto.

22. Da. Margarita ¿voy á mandarle á V. un pedazo de pechuga? No, señor, gracias, mándeme V. el ala ó la pierna, que me gusta mas.

23. Don Pepito, un brindis, vamos un brindis.—Excúsenme Vds., señores, yo no sé hacer, y ménos improvisar brindis.

24. Pero hombre, ¡eso dice V. que es tan galante y elocuente con las damas! ¿No le inspira á V. algo el bello sexo de que se halla V. rodeado? Pues bien, á la salud de las señoras.—Y ¿porqué no?

LESSON LVIII.

EXERCISE.

1. Has the baker not come yet? You are in a jesting mood (*humor*) this morning; he came long before you were up.

2. Never mind; I have got change enough to pay for all.—You are too late, I have already paid; the conductor has no time to wait half an hour collecting the fare of each passenger.

3. Your appetite seems to be a little better to-day than usual; how do you account for that? Really you flatter my appetite beyond what it deserves; I am happy to say that it is at all times in excellent order.

4. Do you not find it good exercise to climb to the top of the hill with that heavy basket on your arm? The fact is I shall have to give it to some one else for a while, for my strength is not equal to the task.

5. I wonder whom you can give it to; you see that we have each of us something to carry. Well, in that case, I must change with some one that has a lighter burden (*carga*) than my own.

6. Does not John intend to become a soldier? He does, though entirely contrary to the will of his father, who set his face against it in the most determined manner.

7. How many trunks is each passenger (*pasajero*) allowed to keep with him in his berth (*camarote*)? Only one, supposed to contain the articles he will require to have at hand during the passage.

8. Did you ever go to a lion-hunt while you were in South Africa? Several times, and I can assure you it is a most interesting and exciting scene.

9. Did you go there entirely for pleasure? No, I managed to combine business and pleasure, otherwise I should probably never have seen that country, for you know that such a voyage as that costs a great deal of money.

10. Did they drink many toasts during the dinner? A good many, and the first one I proposed was to the fair sex.

11. Nothing surprising in that; I know it would scarcely be possible to surpass you in gallantry. You are flattering me now, for the ladies agree on all hands in calling you the most gallant young gentleman in the country.

12. Just try if your eloquence will not succeed in persuading your young friend to come with us to-morrow. With all my heart; but unfortunately he does not speak French, and you know how much my eloquence loses in English.

13. Does the art of pleasing depend on what we do and what we say? It does not, in my opinion, depend so much on what we do and say as on how we do things and how we say them.

14. Is it not surprising that your sister has not yet come? I believe she has gone *round* to see her young Spanish friend (*fem.*), although she left me but half an hour ago, under pretext of having to write a letter.

15. Do you generally dine in the Spanish fashion at home? We generally eat in the French fashion, notwithstanding we are all very fond of the Spanish manner of cooking.

LESSON LIX.

Amenazar.	To menace.
Cojear.	To be lame, to limp.
Colgar.	To hang.
Corregir.	To correct.
Cubrir.	To cover.
Cubrirse.	To put on one's hat.
Descubrir.	To discover, to uncover.
Descubrirse.	To take off one's hat.
Despedir.	To send away, to put away, to give up.
Definir.	To define.
Durar.	To last.
Rodar.	To roll, to run on wheels.
Prestar.	To lend.
Vencer.	To conquer.
Cosa de.	About.
Capaz.	Capable, able.
Condicional.	Conditional.
Cariredondo.	Roundfaced.
Casero.	Household, family, domestic.
Compañero.	Companion.
Claro.	Clear.
Copulativo.	Copulative.
Generoso.	Generous.
Defectivo.	Defective.
Libre.	Free, unembarrassed.
Vulgar.	Vulgar, common, usual.
Vistoso.	Showy.

LESSON LIX.

Asesino.	Assassin.	Barba.	Beard, chin.
Aumento.	Increase, augmentation.	Carcajada.	Burst of laughter.
		Decena.	About ten.
Cerrojo.	Bolt.	Definicion.	Definition.
Campo.	Field, country.	Evidencia.	Evidence.
Corredor.	Broker.	Espalda.	Back.
Dedo.	Finger.	Gana.	Desire, mind.
Diálogo.	Dialogue.	Hoja.	Leaf.
Dolor de costado.	Pain in the side.	Lotería.	Lottery.
Deseo.	Desire, wish.	Llave.	Key.
Descuido.	Carelessness.	Pena.	Difficulty, pain.
Grito.	Shout.	Pera.	Pear.
Gemido.	Groan, moan.	Pobreza.	Poverty.
Pagaré.	Promissory note.	Pascua.	Easter.
Presidio.	State-prison.	Rodilla.	Knee.
Peral.	Pear-tree.	Vuelta.	Turn, change.
Pésame.	Condolence.	Posicion.	Position.
Premio.	Prize, premium, reward.	Excusa.	Excuse, apology.
Salto.	Jump, spring.		
Semblante.	Look.		
Trago.	Draught, drink.		

COMPOSITION.

Su pagaré de V. cae el mes que viene.	Your note falls due next month.
Le ha caido la lotería.	He has won a prize in the lottery.
Este edificio cae al (*or* hácia el) Norte.	This building looks toward the North.
Mis ventanas caen á la mano derecha.	My windows are on the right hand.
Este vestido te cae bien.	This dress fits her well.
No cayó en la cuenta.	He did not see the drift (of what was said).
Ya caigo en ello.	Ah, now I see!
Estar al caer.	To be about to take place.
Caer de piés, de rodillas.	To fall on one's feet, on one's knees.
Lo doy por hecho.	I take for granted it is done.
Lo dieron por libre.	They let him free.
Me doy por vencido.	I give it up.
Le dió un dolor de costado.	He took a pain in his side.
La lectura de ese libro te dará ganas de dormir.	Reading this book will put you asleep (or make you sleep).
Al fin dió en la dificultad.	Finally he fell upon the difficulty.
Dar los buenos dias.	To wish one good day.
Dar las pascuas.	To wish a happy Easter.

LESSON LIX.

Dar el pésame.	To express condolence.
Dar la enhorabuena.	To congratulate.
Dar gritos.	To give shouts.
Dar gemidos.	To utter groans.
Dió una carcajada.	He burst out laughing.
Dar á comprender.	To give to understand.
Darse á conocer.	To make one's self known.
Dar una vuelta.	To take a turn, to go round.
Dar pena.	To cause displeasure.
Dar gusto.	To give pleasure.
Dar gana.	To have a mind; to take the notion.
Dar saltos.	To jump about.
Dió que decir.	He left room for talk.
Esto no dice bien con aquello.	This is not in strict accordance with that.
El blanco dice bien con el azul.	White goes very well with blue.
Su vestido dice su pobreza.	Her dress tells of her poverty.
El semblante de Juan dice bien su mal genio.	John's bad temper is pictured on his countenance.
Este peral echa muchas peras.	This pear-tree bears a great many pears.
Esta planta no ha echado hojas.	This plant has not had any leaves.
He echado un trago.	I have taken a drink.
Eche V. la llave á la puerta.	Lock the door.
Echar pié á tierra.	To dismount.
Echar el cerrojo.	To draw the bolt.
Echarlo á juego (or chanza).	To take it in play (or in jest).
Hoy echan la comedia nueva.	The new play comes out to-night.
Ha echado coche.	He has bought a carriage.
Echar á presidio.	To send to State-prison.
Echar por los campos.	To set out across the fields.
Echaron á correr.	They set out running.
Lo echó todo á perder.	He spoiled all.
Echar á rodar.	To send rolling.
No echo de ver este defecto.	I do not perceive the defect.
¿Echa V. de ménos algo?	Do you miss any thing?
No, señor; echo de ménos á álguien.	No, sir; I miss some one.
Me eché á dormir.	I went asleep.
Se echó á reir.	He began to laugh.
Se echó á corredor.	He became a broker.
Lo puso de patitas en la calle.	He threw him into the street.

EXPLANATION.

275. The verbs *caer*, to fall; *dar*, to give; *decir*, to tell, or to say; *echar*, to throw; differ from the English in meaning as conveyed by the sentences which are given in the Composition, and to which we refer without putting them here, in order to avoid repetition.

There they are to be found, with their English translations, which is the only explanation they admit of.

CONVERSATION AND VERSION.

1. Don Gonzalo, ¿le ha caido á V. la lotería? No, señor; pero mi pagaré ha caido.

2. Luisita, ¿quién ha hecho ese vestido que te cae tan bien? Mi mamá lo cortó y yo lo cosí.

3. ¿No sabe V. porqué me hace ahora tantos cumplimientos Don Enrique? No, señor, no sé qué motivo tenga para ser ahora mas político con V. que lo ha sido hasta aquí.

4. ¿No sabe V. que me ha caido el premio de los cien mil pesos en la lotería de la Habana? Sí, señor; ya me lo ha dicho V. ántes.

5. Pues bien, ¿no cae V. ahora en la cuenta? ¡Ha! ya caigo en ello. Don Enrique quiere pedirle á V. dinero prestado.

6. ¿Han dado las doce? Estan al caer.

7. ¿Dieron garrote á los asesinos? No, señor, al fin los dieron por libres, porque no habia evidencia suficiente para sentenciarlos.

8. ¿Qué ha tenido su hermano de V. que no lo he visto por tanto tiempo? Le dió un dolor de costado y ha tenido que guardar cama por una semana.

9. ¿A que no adivina V. lo que acabo de hacer? Seguramente que no lo adivinaré, porque V. es capaz de hacer muchas cosas buenas y malas.

10. ¿Se da V. por vencido? Me doy.—Pues vengo de echar un trago.

11. ¿Qué comedia echan hoy? Hoy dan la tragedia de "Medea," en donde representa la Señora Ristori; ¿irá V.?

12. Siendo en italiano no iré, porque no comprendo el italiano y me daria ganas de dormir.

13. Sr. D. Alejandro, vengo á darle á V. los buenos dias.—Téngalos V. muy buenos.

14. ¿No me quiere V. dar alguna otra cosa? Sí, señor, le doy á V. la enhorabuena por el aumento que ha tenido V. en su familia.—Viva V. mil años.

15. Todo eso es muy bueno, D. Pepito; pero sea V. generoso y deme V. alguna cosita mas.—Hombre, si V. no se da á comprender yo no sé qué mas darle á V. ¡Ha! sí, ya caigo! que estamos en tiempo de. . . . Doy á V. felices pascuas.

16. Dale, Dale, si no es eso, yo hablo del dinero que presté á V. hace

mas de un año.—¡Ha! Señor D. Alejandro, no crea V. que yo lo haya echado en saco roto.

17. Pues bien; ¿porqué no me lo da V.? ¡Porqué! hombre, ahora ha dado V. en la dificultad, y esta es que yo no tengo dinero, y por consiguiente no puedo darlo.

18. Entónces, ¿qué es lo que V. puede dar? ¡O! en cuanto á eso yo puedo dar muchas cosas.

19. ¡Ha! me alegro mucho, veamos lo que V. puede dar.—En primer lugar puedo dar gemidos.

20. ¡Puf! (*pshaw*).—Tambien puedo dar gritos.

21. ¡Dale!—Puedo dar, ... que decir.

22. No lo dudo.—Puedo dar un pésame.

23. ¡Dios me libre!—Puedo dar saltos.

24. Vaya acabe V., hombre, acabé V.—Puedo dar á comprender.

25. Sí, eso sí, demasiado comprendo.—Puedo darme á conocer.

26. Ya, ya, conozco de qué pié cojea V.—Puedo dar una vuelta.

27. Pues vuélvase V., por donde ha venido y nunca dé V. mas vueltas por esta casa.—Y todavía mas, puedo dar una carcajada.

28. ¡Juan! ¡Juan! echa á ese hombre de casa, y despues echa la llave y el cerrojo á la puerta. ¡Haya pícaro! lo he de echar á un presidio!

29. ¿Has echado á ese hombre á la calle? Sí, señor, ya lo puse de patitas en la calle.

30. Y ¿qué dijo? Primero se echo á reir, yo le amenacé que lo echaria á rodar y entónces echo á correr.

31. El diantre del hombre siempre está pidiendo dinero prestado y sobre no pagarlo se viene á reir de uno en sus barbas.—Señor, ¿manda V. alguna otra cosa? No, te puedes ir, yo voy á echarme á dormir, ese bribon me ha dado un gran dolor de cabeza.

EXERCISE.

1. Is there any thing in the papers this morning relative to the trial of the murderer of Smith? I understand his trial is not to take place before a month from this time.

2. Why did you not bring your friend with you? He is not able to walk very far to-day, owing to a pain in his side, which has troubled him for the last three days.

3. Did you tell the servant to draw the bolt of the door? No, but I told him to lock the door.

4. Who is that I hear groaning? You hear no one groaning; it is some one shouting in the distance.

5. How did your cousin lose his situation? He owes that misfortune entirely to his own carelessness.

6. Charles, are you not going to say good morning to that gentleman? I need not say good morning to him now, for I have already wished him a happy Easter.

7. Did that merchant pay his correspondent at Malaga after all? He did not pay him; but he gave him a note at three months.

8. What do you understand by parlor plays (household comedies) in Spain? They are plays represented by private individuals* sometimes in private houses, from which circumstance they take their name.

9. Do you know that round-faced little man who is sitting next to your uncle? That is one of the principal actors (*actor*) in the parlor plays given at Mr. Gutiérrez'.

10. What became of the offender? The evidence not being sufficient to prove the crime of which he was accused† he was let off; otherwise he would have been sent to State-prison.

11. Did they refuse to give him the things he wanted on credit? Of course they did, because no one can rely on him nor give credit to any thing he says.

12. Will that young man probably obtain the employment he has applied for? Most probably he will, because he has had the good fortune to get into the president's favor.

13. How! do you not attend your classes this week? No, I am not very well; and so a friend of mine was good enough to offer to act in my place.

14. Was the error corrected before the letter was dispatched? No, it was not discovered in time to be corrected.

LESSON LX.

Decidir.	To decide.
Ejecutar.	To execute.
Ejercer.	To exercise.
Ensuciar.	To dirty, to soil.
Enemistar.	To put at enmity.
Escuchar.	To listen to, to hearken to.
Exagerar.	To exaggerate.
Exhibir.	To exhibit.
Extrañar.	To wonder at, to find strange.
Enfriarse.	To grow cold, to get (become) cold.

* *Aficionados.* † *Acusar.*

LESSON LX.

Encargar.	To commission, to order, to give charge.
Exclamar.	To exclaim.
Exceptuar.	To except.
Esforzar.	To endeavor, to make effort.
Estrechar.	To press.
Sospechar.	To suspect.
Tardar.	To delay.

Extra.	Extra.
Empero.	But.

Elíptico.	Elliptical.
Agrio.	Sour.
Estrecho.	Close, narrow.
Preciso.	Essential, indispensable, precise.
Elocuente.	Eloquent.
Tonto.	Foolish, stupid.
Travieso.	Mischievous.

Entrámbos.	Both.
Entretanto.	In the mean time.
Excepto.	Except.

Atolladero.	Difficulty.	Casaca.	Coat, dress-coat.
Camino.	Road, way.	Colocacion.	Situation.
Astrónomo.	Astronomer.	Civilizacion.	Civilization.
Cólera.	Cholera.	Cólera.	Anger.
Cometa.	Comet.	Corte.	Court.
Cofre.	Chest.	Cometa.	Kite.
Cajon.	Drawer, box.	Cita.	Appointment.
Capricho.	Caprice.	Charla.	Chat.
Cuello.	Neck.	Claridad.	Clearness.
Cargo.	Cargo, charge.	Compañía.	Company.
Exterior.	Exterior, outside.	Caja.	Box, case, cash (*commercial*).
Extranjero.	Foreigner.		
Embarcadero.	Landing.	Cartilla.	Primer.
Espejo.	Mirror, looking-glass.	Calentura.	Fever.
		Casualidad.	Chance.
Estrecho.	Strait.	Cantidad.	Quantity.
Elemento.	Element.	Capa.	Cloak.
Gobernador.	Governor.	Cara.	Face.
Grado.	Grade, degree.		

LESSON LX.

Horno.	Oven.
Luto.	Mourning.
Litro.	Litre.*
Matemático.	Mathematician.
Tonel.	Cask.
Termómetro.	Thermometer.
Ferro-carril.	Railroad.
Fruto.	Fruit (result).
Fondo.	Bottom.
Flúido.	Fluid.
Carga.	Charge (of a gun, &c.).
Cuchara.	Spoon.
Culpa.	Fault, blame.
Criatura.	Creature, infant.
Costa.	Cost, coast.
Disculpa.	Apology.
Estacion.	Season.
Existencia.	Existence.
Fragata.	Frigate.
Máscara.	Mask.
Tontera.	Foolish action.
Pretension.	Pretension, claim.
Yerba.	Grass.

COMPOSITION.

Hoy entra la primavera.	Spring commences to-day.
Mañana entra el mes de Octubre.	The month of October commences to-morrow.
Entra en el número de los sabios.	He is of the number of the learned.
Entró á reinar á los quince años.	He began to reign at fifteen years of age.
Este tonel hace cien litros.	This cask holds 100 litres.
No le hago tan tonto.	I do not take him for such a fool.
Yo le hacia mas rico.	I took him to be richer.
Haz por venir.	Try to come.
Hace de gobernador.	He is acting as governor.
Esa pobre muchacha está haciendo de madre á sus hermanos.	That poor girl is acting the part of a mother to her brothers and sisters.
A eso voy.	That is the point I am coming to.
Voy de paseo.	I am going for pleasure.
Van de máscara.	They are going in masks.
Va de luto.	He is in mourning.
Le va en ello la vida.	His life is at stake.
Vengo en ello.	I agree to that.
¿Cuánto me lleva V. por esto?	How much will you charge me for this?
Estos dos amigos se llevan muy bien.	These two friends agree very well together.
No nos llevamos bien.	We do not agree well together.
Este camino lleva á Madrid.	This road leads to Madrid.
Le llevo dos años y medio.	I am two years and a half older than he.
Me llevé chasco.	I was disappointed.

* Equal to 2.113 American pints.

LESSON LX.

Lleva una casaca á la francesa.	He wears a coat made in the French fashion.
Se hizo á la vela.	He set sail.
Manda que nos traigan el almuerzo.	Order the breakfast to be served up.
Haré que nos lo traigan.	I shall have it brought to us.
¿Hace V. teñir su vestido de azul?	Are you getting your dress dyed blue?
No, señor, lo he mandado teñir de verde.	No, sir, I have ordered it to be dyed green.
Saldrá buen matemático.	He shall turn out (to be) a good mathematician.
Salió muy travieso.	He (or she—the child) turned out very naughty.
Ya he salido de todos mis granos.	I have got rid of all my grain.
Me salió una buena colocacion.	A good situation turned up for me.
Este negocio me ha salido bien.	This business has turned out well for me.
Le salió mal su empresa.	His undertaking turned out badly.
Este niño ha salido á su padre.	This child resembles his father.
Salió de la regla.	He departed from the rule.
Pronto saldré de hijo de familia.	I shall soon be of age.
Esta capa me sale en cincuenta pesos.	This cloak cost me fifty dollars.
Se salió con su pretension.	He obtained what he desired.
Sírve al rey.	He serves the king.
No sirve para nada.	It is good for nothing.
Sírvase V. admitir mis disculpas.	Be good enough to accept my apology.
Él tarda mucho en decidir.	He is slow in deciding.
¡Cuánto tarda en responder!	How long he is in answering!
¡Adios! Volveré á ver á V., y le volveré á hablar de eso.	Good-by! I shall see you again, and talk more to you on the subject.
Este vino se vuelve agrio.	This wine is turning sour.
Se volverá bueno con el tiempo.	It will become good again in time.
Este melon sabe á melocoton.	This melon has the taste of a peach.
Este vino huele á vinagre.	This wine smells of vinegar.
D. Juan hace un gran papel en la corte.	John makes a great noise at court.
Napoleon III hace un gran papel en la política del mundo.	Napoleon III. plays a great part in the politics of the world.

EXPLANATION.

276. In the Composition of this lesson we give the principal idioms with the verbs *entrar*, to go (or come) in; *hacer*, to do, to make; *ir*, to go; *llevar*, to take, to charge; *mandar*, *hacer*, in the sense of to order, to cause to be done; *oler á*, to to smell of; and *saber á*, to taste of; *salir, servir, tardar* and *volver*.

LESSON LX.

CONVERSATION AND VERSION.

1. ¿Cuándo entra la primavera? Debo confesar francamente que no sé el dia preciso en que entra y sale cada estacion.

2. Entónces V. no entra en el número de los sabios, puesto que no sabe cuándo estamos en invierno y cuando en verano.—Poco á poco, señor Don Pedro, eso seria hacerme entrar en el número de los idiotas.

3. ¿Pues no acaba V. de decirlo? Yo acabo de decir que no sé el dia preciso en que entra cada estacion; pero cuando veo crecer la yerba y las hojas de los árboles, y abrirse las flores, sospecho que estamos en la primavera.

4. ¡Ha! V. sospecha! Vamos, ya es algo.—Sí, señor, y del mismo modo, cuando veo el termómetro en la sombra, que marca 98°, creo adivinar que estoy, una de dos, ó en un horno ó en Nueva York en la estacion del verano.

5. Vamos, yo le hacia á V. mas ignorante de lo que en efecto es; ¿y cómo adivina V., ó sospecha, que se encuentra V. en el otoño? Cuando los melocotones se acaban y las hojas caen.

6. ¡Bien! bien! ¿y el invierno? Cuando por la mañana no puedo lavarme por hallar que se ha helado el agua en la palangana.

7. Ya veo que es V. un sabio perfecto. Veamos en historia ¿á qué edad entró á reinar el Rey Pepino?—¡Cáspita! Señor Don Pedro! es mas fácil criticar que ejecutar, y mas fácil hacer preguntas que responderlas, y sino respóndame V. que la echa de sabio.

8. ¿Cuántos litros hace ese tonel? ¡Hombre! yo ¿qué he de entender de medir toneles?

9. Pues cambiaré de materia, ¿quién hace de gobernador en Manila? ¡Y á mí qué me importa!

10. ¡Vaya! ese es un buen modo de salir del atolladero.—No, señor, sírvase V. recibir mis disculpas, tengo que irme ahora, pero volveré á ver á V., y volverémos á tratar de esa materia. Adios, señores.

11. ¿Qué le parece á V., Don Enrique, de ese caballero? Me parece que este jóven saldrá buen matemático, porque ha salido en todo á su padre.

12. ¿Sabe V. si salió bien ó mal de su empresa? Es un negocio que le ha salido muy bien.

13. ¿Se lleva bien Luisa con sus hermanos? Sí, señor, y aunque no les lleva mas de tres ó cuatro años, les sirve de madre.

14. ¿Cuánto le cuesta á V. esa capa? Me sale en unos cincuenta pesos.

15. ¿Cuánto tardará la fragata en hacerse á la vela? No sé, creo que el capitan es hombre que tarda en decidirse.

16. ¿De qué color hace V. teñir su vestido? Lo mandé teñir de amarillo.

17. Don Manuel, mande V. que nos suban el almuerzo.—Haré que nos lo traigan.

EXERCISE.

1. When does Spring commence? It commences in March and ends in May.

2. Has your young friend passed his examination yet? The examinations have not taken place; but when they do, he will prove to be the best Spanish scholar in the country.

3. In what month does the cold weather generally commence in the North of Spain? Winter usually sets in about the middle of November.

4. How much does this cask hold? It holds from 100 to 120 litres.

5. How soon do you set out for Europe? As soon as the fine weather sets in.

6. Are you going on business, or for pleasure? For pleasure only.

7. How are they going to the ball? They are going in masks.

8. How much did your tailor charge you for that coat? It cost me forty-five dollars.

9. What age do you take my cousin to be? I would take him to be about the same age as his friend.

10. You had better guess again. I give it up.

11. How old is he, then? He is two years and four months older than his friend.

12. Do you know whether the pianist's brother succeeded in obtaining the position he applied for? He did not; but an excellent situation turned up for him a short time after.

13. How long will you take to dye this dress for me? About a week.

14. What color do you wish it to be dyed? I wish to have it dyed blue.

15. Do you think this boy will turn out to be as good a musician as his father? I have not the least doubt about it, for he resembles him in every respect (*en todo*).

16. Be good enough to accept my apology for not having come yesterday as I had promised. Certainly, sir; I know very well that you have a great deal of business to attend to.

17. Who is Mr. Terrero in mourning for? For his uncle, who died about a year ago in Manila.

LESSON LXI.

Felicitar.	To felicitate, to congratulate.
Fiar.	To trust.
Ignorar.	To be ignorant of, unaware of.
Lastimar.	To hurt, to wound.
Improvisar.	To improvise, to do (any thing) off-hand.
Inquietar.	To make uneasy, to cause anxiety.
Intentar.	To attempt, to intend.
Interrogar.	To interrogate, to question.
Invertir.	To invert, to invest.
Interesar.	To interest, to be of interest.
Invitar.	To invite.
Imprimir.	To print.
Obligar.	To force, to oblige.
Rehusar.	To refuse.
Lisonjear.	To flatter.
Llevar.	To carry, to take, to charge.
Descuidado.	Careless.
Final.	Final.
Ignorante.	Ignorant.
Impersonal.	Impersonal.
Increible.	Incredible.
Indefinido.	Indefinite.
Inexplicable.	Inexplicable.
Ingenioso.	Ingenious.
Inmediato.	Immediate, close by, next.
Inquieto.	Uneasy, restless.
Justo.	Just, right.
Ultimo.	Last.
Lisonjero.	Flattering.
Especiero.	Grocer.
Loco.	Mad.
Lento.	Slow.
Solemne.	Solemn, cruel.
De Zeca en Meca.	To and fro.
A ciegas.	With one's eyes shut.
A gatas.	On all fours.
En el interin.	In the mean time.

LESSON LXI.

Ampo de la nieve.	Whiteness of snow.
Asno.	Ass.
Descuido.	Carelessness.
Hueso.	Bone.
Golpe.	Blow, stroke.
Dares y tomares.	Dispute.
Indice.	Index.
Ingenio.	Genius.
Insecto.	Insect.
Instinto.	Instinct.
Instrumento.	Instrument.
Interrogante.	Question, note of interrogation.
Italiano.	Italian.
Arco íris.	Rainbow.
Galicismo.	Gallicism.
Hierro.	Iron.
Juego.	Play.
Loco.	Madman.
Lugar.	Place.
Latin.	Latin.
Sonido, Son.	Sound.
Pico.	Beak.
Levita.	Levite.
Uso.	Use, custom.
Objeto.	Object.
Oido.	Ear, hearing.
Olfato.	Smell.
Anchuras (*f. pl.*).	Ease.
Cuba.	Cask, toper, drunkard.
Cara.	Face.
Cartilla.	Primer.
Calabaza.	Pumpkin, refusal.
Imaginacion.	Imagination.
Intencion.	Intention.
Interrogacion.	Interrogation.
Inversion.	Inversion.
Justicia.	Justice.
Llave.	Key.
Lluvia.	Rain.
Lista.	List.
Lisonja.	Flattery.
Luna.	Moon.
Luz.	Light.
Latitud.	Latitude.
Longitud.	Longitude.
Legua.	League.
Letra.	Letter.
Limosna.	Alms.
Limpieza.	Cleanness.
Línea.	Line.
Levita.	Frock-coat.
Rama.	Branch.
Teja.	Tile.
Ocasion.	Occasion.
Vergüenza.	Shame.

COMPOSITION.

A mas tardar.	At latest.
A media palabra.	At the slightest hint.
A medida de sus deseos.	According to one's wishes.
A sus anchuras.	At one's ease.
Al descuido y con cuidado.	Studiously careless.
Abrir el ojo.	To be upon the alert.
Allá se las haya.	Let him look to that.
Andar á ciegas.	To grope in the dark.
Andar á gatas.	To creep on all fours.
A todo correr.	With all speed.

LESSON LXI.

Vaya V. con Dios.	Go in peace.
El va de capa caida.	He is crest-fallen.
El va de Zeca en Meca.	He goes roving about, to and fro.
Ir de puntillas.	To go on tiptoe.
Andar en dares y tomares.	To quarrel.
Andarse por las ramas.	Not to come to the point.
De tejas abajo.	Humanly speaking.
Asir la ocasion por los cabellos.	To take time by the forelock.
Bailar al son que se toca.	To go with the stream.
Beber los aires *or* los vientos.	To desire anxiously.
Beber como una cuba.	To drink like a fish.
Blanco como el ampo de la nieve.	White as the driven snow.
Bocado sin hueso.	An employment without labor; a sinecure.
Burla burlando.	Between joke and earnest.
Buscar cinco piés al gato.	To pick a quarrel.
No caber de gozo.	To be overjoyed.
No caber en sí.	To be bursting with pride.
No cabe en él.	He is not capable of such a thing.
Caer de su asno.	To acknowledge one's fault.
Caérsele á uno la cara de vergüenza.	To blush with shame.
Callar el pico.	To hold one's tongue.
Chanzas aparte.	Jesting aside.
Con mil amores.	Most willingly.
Con su pan se lo coma.	That is his own business.
Conque, hasta la vista.	I hope we may soon meet again.
Cosa que no está en la cartilla.	Something out of the common way.
Dar á alguno con las puertas en la cara.	To shut the door in one's face.
Dar á luz.	To publish; to give birth to.
Dar por supuesto, *or* por sentado.	To take for granted.
Dar chasco.	To disappoint.
Dar el sí.	To consent.
Dar golpe una cosa.	To strike one with admiration, or astonishment (said of things).
Dar calabazas.	To give the mitten.
No se le da nada.	He cares nothing about it.

CONVERSATION AND VERSION.

1. ¿Le salen á V. las cosas á medida de sus deseos? Chanzas aparte, Don Juan, V. sabe bien que de tejas abajo eso nunca sucede.

2. Sí, pero como V. baila al son que se toca y sabe asir la ocasion por los cabellos, siempre está á sus anchuras y tiene siempre algun bocado sin hueso.—Amigo, caiga V. de su asno y confieso de buena fé que si

anda de capa caida, es porque va siempre de Zeca en Meca, y porque bebe mas que una cuba.

3. Adios, Don Pedro, me voy, porque no quiero buscar cinco piés al gato.—Vaya V. con Dios, Don Juan.

4. Don Pedro, me parece que V. ha dado con la puerta en la cara á Don Juan.—No, señor, Don Enrique, á otro se le caeria la cara de vergüenza, pero á él no se le da nada, y pronto lo volverá V. á ver por acá.

5. Entónces él no entiende á media palabra.—A mas tardar lo verá V. aquí otra vez dentro de media hora.

6. El pobre hombre anda á ciegas, y si no abre el ojo, irá á parar á un hospital.—Con su pan se lo coma, y allá se las haya; yo lo siento solamente por su niña, que es una señorita perfecta.

7. Me han dicho que V. queria casarse con ella, ¿es verdad, Don Enrique?—Sí, señor, y lo hubiera hecho con mil amores, porque además de ser muy amable é instruida, es muy bonita, tiene ojos negros muy hermosos y es tan blanca como el ampo de la nieve.

8. Pues ¿porqué no se casó V. con ella? Por una pequeña dificultad.

9. Quizá V. se andaria por las ramas y no sabria asir la ocasion por los cabellos.—No, señor, nada de eso, ántes al contrario yo lo daba todo por supuesto, porque V. sabe que soy rico, y creí que la niña me daria el sí sin hacerse de rogar.

10. ¿Pues qué, no se lo dió? No, señor, no me dió el sí, pero me dió calabazas.

11. ¡Miren la rapazuela! ¿y V. qué hizo? Yo que bebia los vientos por ella, y creia que sus calabazas eran cosa que no estaban en la cartilla, recurrí á su padre, creyendo que él no me negaria la mano de su hija.

12. ¿Y bien y qué? Que me llevó un solemne chasco, el padre me rehusó la mano de su hija ni mas ni ménos que ella lo habia hecho.

13. ¿Pero qué razon le dió á V. para ello? Me dijo que su hija, aunque pobre, era hija de un caballero y que ni ella querria ni él la obligaria jamás á casarse con un especiero comun é ignorante; que el dinero era una gran cosa, pero que no lo compraba todo.

14. ¿Y V. qué dijo? Yo, por no andar en dares y tomares y dimes y dirétes, me callé el pico y salí de su casa á todo correr.

EXERCISE.

1. Would you not be more likely to obtain what you wish, if you came to the point at once? Perhaps I would; but the matter is an important one, and I considered it necessary to enter into some explanation relative to it.

2. Do you think he would understand me? Of course he would, at the slightest hint.

3. How did your cousin Charles succeed in that affair? Every thing turned out according to his wishes.

4. How soon do you suppose this book will be published? I hope it will be published in a very short time; I know they are working at it with all possible speed.

5. Have you ever seen a more active man than that merchant? Never; and I have never seen a less active man than his brother, he always goes with the stream, and troubles himself about nothing.

6. Ought you not to have shown that letter to your brother? I would have done so, of course, but I took for granted that he had already heard the news.

7. You had better tell your friend to be upon the alert, and not get into a quarrel with that man. That is his own business, let him look to it himself.

8. Is it possible that he could be capable of such an action? Yes, but the worst of all is, that he is not ashamed to acknowledge it to every one he meets.

9. When is Peter to be married? I cannot say certainly; but I suppose in about a month at latest.

10. I don't know any one who has a better position than your uncle: plenty of money and scarcely any thing to do. That is a fact, his situation is a real sinecure.

11. What has occurred to that gentleman? he looks quite crest-fallen. Do not be astonished at that; he has been unfortunate in business, and has lost almost all he possessed in the world.

12. Are you trying to pick a quarrel with me? No, I assure you, jesting aside, that the matter stands exactly as I say.

13. How was he received by the lady's father? He was not received at all, they shut the door in his face.

14. If you desire so anxiously to see him, why do you not go to his house? I cannot make up my mind (*decidirme*) to do that; you know he is bursting with pride, and he would very probably refuse to receive me.

15. Well, I hope we may soon meet again; present my respects to your family. With the greatest pleasure.—Please not to forget the letter.

16. That I care nothing about; all I desire to know is whether he will be here in time or not. I think you may rely on his being punctual.

17. I have been told that your brother was about to be married to Miss Ramirez; is it true? I really cannot say how the matter will turn out; so far every thing seems to go on according to the desire of both parties.

LESSON LXII.

Aplicar.	To apply.
Cebarse.	To feed, to gloat.
Echar á perder.	To spoil.
Errar.	To err, to miss.
Ocurrir.	To occur.
Murmurar.	To murmur, to grumble.
Madrugar.	To rise early.
Medir.	To measure.
Montar.	To mount, to amount.
Mudar.	To change, to move.
Nacer.	To be born, to spring up, to proceed.
Sazonar.	To season, to ripen.
Reunirse.	To unite, to collect together, to assemble.
Modificar.	To modify.
Desprevenido.	Unawares, unprepared.
Intachable.	Unimpeachable, unquestionable.
Maldito.	Perverse, confounded.
Mayúscula.	Capital (letter).
Minúscula.	Small (letter).
Numeral.	Numeral.
Noble.	Noble.
Nominativo.	Nominative.
Neutro.	Neuter.
Masculino.	Masculine.
Objetivo.	Objective.
Quieto.	Quiet, at rest.

Cumpleaños.	Birthday.	Apariencia.	Appearance.
Menoscabo.	Detriment, lessening.	Bravata.	Bravado.
		Botica.	Drug store.
Pique.	Point, verge.	Fiesta.	Feast, holiday.
Rayo.	Thunderbolt.	Centella.	Spark, flash.
Socio.	Associate, partner.	Siesta.	Siesta (afternoon nap).
Sabor.	Taste, savor.		
Menudo.	Change, small change.	Suerte.	Luck, fortune, chance.

LESSON LXII.

Meridiano.	Meridian.	Murmuracion.	Murmurings.
Metal.	Metal.	Malicia.	Malice.
Miembro.	Member.	Mente.	Mind.
Mineral.	Mineral.	Muestra.	Sample, sign.
Momento.	Moment.	Manera.	Manner.
Mozo.	Youth, waiter.	Manteca, *or* man-	Butter.
Macho.	Male.	tequilla.	
Maestro.	Master, teacher.	Medida.	Measure.
Manuscrito.	Manuscript.	Olla podrida.	Sort of mixed dish.
Mar.	Sea.		
Olor.	Smell, odor.	Ostra.	Oyster.
Olivar.	Olive ground.	Negacion.	Negation.
Ostion. (See *Ostra*.)	Oyster.	Mar.	Sea.
		Negativa.	Negative.
Palo.	Wood, stick.	Nota.	Note.
Polvo.	Dust, powder.	Zaga.	Rear-guard.
Paño.	Cloth.		
Parabien.	Felicitation, congratulation.		

COMPOSITION.

De buenas á primeras.	Without ceremony.
De buena fé.	With sincerity.
De mala fé.	Deceitfully.
De intento.	On purpose.
De oidas.	By hearsay.
Decir por decir.	To talk for the sake of talking.
Dejar á uno colgado.	To frustrate one's hopes.
Dejar á uno en la calle.	To strip one of his all.
Dejar atras los vientos.	To go quicker than the wind.
Dejar correr.	To go with the world.
Dejar el campo libre.	To yield to one's competitors.
Dejar en blanco.	To leave blank.
Dejarse alguna cosa en el tintero.	To forget to say something.
Dia de cumpleaños.	Birthday.
Saber algo de buena tinta.	To know any thing on good authority.
De dia en dia.	From day to day.
De un dia para otro.	From one day to another.
De hoy en ocho dias.	This day week.
Un dia sí y otro no.	Every other day.
Hoy dia.	Now-a-days.
Dicho y hecho.	No sooner said than done.

LESSON LXII.

Dormir á pierna suelta.	To sleep at one's ease.
Dormir la siesta.	To take an afternoon nap.
Echar á perder algo.	To spoil any thing.
Echar bravatas.	To brag, to boast.
Echar rayos y centellas.	To be furious, enraged.
Echar la culpa á alguno.	To throw the blame on any one.
Echar suertes.	To cast lots.
Empeñarse en hacer algo.	To insist upon doing any thing.
Empeñarse por alguno.	To interest one's self for any one.
En un abrir y cerrar de ojos.	In the twinkling of an eye, in a trice.
Encenderse en cólera.	To fly into a passion.
Errar el tiro.	To miss one's aim.
Erre que erre.	Obstinately.
Escarmentar en cabeza agena.	To take warning by others' misfortunes.
Estar á pique de perderse.	To be within an ace of being lost.
Estar de casa.	To be in dishabille.
Estar de fiesta.	To be merry.
Estar en ascuas.	To be upon thorns.
Estar en lo que se dice.	To comprehend what is said.
Estar á sus anchuras.	To be at one's ease.
Estar sobre sí.	To be on one's guard.
Estar desprevenido.	To be off one's guard.
Estar mano sobre mano.	To be idle.
¿Estás en tus cinco sentidos?	Are you in your senses?

CONVERSATION AND VERSION.

1. Señores, dejen Vds. el campo libre, que aquí viene Don Pepito echando bravatas y rayos y centellas.—Bien venido, Don Pepito, ¿qué trae V. de nuevo, que parece estar fuera de sí?

2. No, señor, yo estoy en mis cinco sentidos, pero hay gentes de mala fé que hablan por hablar y se ocupan de criticar al prójimo.—¿Y eso á qué viene?

3. Yo no lo digo por V., Don Enrique, pero V. sabe que hay muchos desocupados que se vienen á su botica de V. y critican á todo el mundo.— ¡Vamos, vamos! Don Pepito, que á V. tambien le gusta un poquito la murmuracion.

4. Ciertamente, porque sino ¿qué seria de la conversacion sin un poquito de crítica que la sazone y le dé interés? Muy bien, pero entónces no eche V. la culpa á nadie de hacer lo mismo que V. hace.

5. Sí, pero yo hablo sin malicia, de buena fé y digo lo que me ocurre por decirlo, nada mas.—Así pueden decir los demás.

6. Sí, pero yo no soy como Don Cárlos, que viene aquí de dia en dia,

y de la mañana á la tarde hablando mas que un sacamuelas y sin dejar á nadie hueso sano.—Sí, pues aplíquese V. el cuento.

7. No, señor, yo no soy ni tan hablador ni tan murmurador como ninguno de los que se reunen aquí, y si no, observe V. un poquito á cada uno de ellos, D. Gonzalo, por ejemplo, ¿ha venido hoy? No, señor, no ha venido, ni vendrá, porque es el dia de su cumpleaños y lo celebra con su familia en el campo, por consiguiente puede V. cebarse en él á su sabor.

8. D. Gonzalo es hombre de buenos sentimientos y hombre honrado, no haya miedo que yo diga nada en menoscabo suyo, pero tiene un maldito genio que le hace echar á perder toda conversacion.

9. Pues yo no habia observado eso.—¡Cómo hombre! pues si viene aquí un dia sí y otro no, á criticar á los que se reunen en la botica de la esquina, y los dias que no viene aquí va á la botica de la esquina á criticarnos á nosotros.

10. ¿Y qué es lo que le hace echar á perder las conversaciones como decia V. pocos minutos há? Que en un abrir y cerrar de ojos se enciende en cólera.

11. Bien, por D. Gonzalo, ¿y nuestro vecino, D. Alberto, ese sí que es intachable, no le parece á V.? ¡Ho! en efecto es un excelente hombre, lástima que errase el tiro.

12. ¿Qué quiere V. decir con eso de errar el tiro? Hablo con respecto á sus negocios.

13. Y bien, ¿qué le sucedió? Que escogió malos socios, y le han dejado en la calle.

14. Pero eso no puede ser, Don Alberto goza de muy buena reputacion, V. habla de oidas.—No, señor, que lo sé de buena tinta, y hoy dia está á pique de perderse.

15. Pues él parece dormir á pierna suelta.—Está obligado á hacerlo así por guardar las apariencias.

16. ¿No se ha dejado V. algo en el tintero? Sin duda que me he dejado, pero es tarde y voy á dormir la siesta.

EXERCISE.

1. Is the custom of taking an afternoon nap as common in Spain now-a-days as in former times? It is quite as common now-a-days as it ever was, not only in Spain, but in almost every country of Europe.

2. Are you perfectly certain that he acted with sincerity in that matter? I am quite sure, as I know it on good authority.

3. Who told you that young man had acted deceitfully toward your cousin? I do not care to say much in the matter, especially as all I know respecting it I only know by hearsay.

4. Can you tell me how that merchant's enterprise turned out? Very badly; for shortly after he had engaged in it, he heard of his brother's misfortune, which frustrated all his hopes.

5. Did Alexander manage to pay his debts after all? No, he did not; and although his intentions were strictly honorable, his creditors (*acreedores*) would wait no longer, and they stripped him of all he possessed in the world.

6. What date do you wish me to put here? Just leave a blank, and Charles will put in the date before he sends the letter off.

7. When do you think they will be able to give me some of the papers? Probably by this day week.

8. What did he say when he saw how the tailor had spoiled his coat? Fortunately for the latter he was in a merry mood, and did not fly into a passion as he usually does when any thing occurs to displease him.

9. Are you in your senses, my dear friend? are you not aware that such a thing is impossible?

10. Did he shut the door on purpose? Yes, but he sent his servant to take us into another room, for he was in dishabille, and did not wish to be seen until he had dressed.

11. How often do you go to dine at your uncle's? I generally go every other day.

12. Have your friends returned yet from the country? No, they have been putting it off* from day to day for some time, and I shall not be in the least astonished if they do not return before November.

13. Why did you not bring your sister with you? I did all I possibly could to persuade her to come, but she insisted upon staying at home.

14. How did they decide on who should go first? They cast lots for it

---

LESSON LXIII.

Retirar.	To retire, to withdraw.
Pegar.	To stick, to adhere, to beat.
Pescar.	To fish.
Posponer.	To place after.
Preceder.	To precede.
Prometer.	To promise.
Razonar.	To reason.
Resfriarse,	To take cold.
Regalar,	To regale, to present.

* *Posponer.*

LESSON LXIII.

En frente. / Frente por frente.	In front, opposite.
De hito en hito.	Fixedly, with open eyes.
De grado.	By fair means.
Por fas ó por nefas.	Justly or unjustly.

¡Cascaras!	Dear me! Oh!

Afortunado.	Fortunate.
Ageno.	Foreign, belonging to others.
Formal.	Formal, steady, respectable.
Pasivo.	Passive.
Perezoso.	Lazy.
Personal.	Personal.
Posesivo.	Possessive.
Potencial.	Potential.
Preciso.	Precise, necessary, obligatory.
Preliminar.	Preliminary.
Pretérito.	Preterit.
Puntual.	Punctual.
Partitivo.	Partitive.
Radical.	Radical.
Raro.	Rare, curious.
Recíproco.	Reciprocal.
Reflexivo.	Reflective.
Rubio.	Fair (of the hair and complexion).
Ruin.	Mean.

Alarde.	Boast.	Bulla.	Noise, uproar.
Bulto.	Bulk, bundle.	Baza.	Trick (card-playing).
Ganso.	Goose.		
Bledo.	Straw.	Huéspeda.	Hostess.
Diente.	Tooth.	Puntuacion.	Punctuation.
Desafío.	Challenge, duel.	Puntualidad.	Punctuality.
Espadachin.	Bully.	Paciencia.	Patience.
Estribo.	Stirrup.	Paja.	Straw.
Mequetrefe.	Trifling fellow, meddler.	Pólvora.	Gunpowder.
		Perseverancia.	Perseverance.
Pasaje.	Passage.	Porcion.	Portion, number.
Pedazo.	Piece.	Prenda.	Good quality, jewel.
Perro.	Dog.		
Plazo.	Term.	Pronunciacion.	Pronunciation.
Plomo.	Lead.		

LESSON LXIII.

Porqué.	Reason why.	Propiedad.	Propriety, property.
Público.	Public.		
Principio.	Principle, beginning.	Pulgada.	Inch.
		Raíz.	Root.
Rasgo.	Trait.	Rebanada.	Slice.
Recado.	Message, errand.	Reforma.	Reform, reformation.
Recibo.	Receipt.		
Rector.	Rector, director.	Regla.	Rule.
Refran.	Proverb.	Reina.	Queen.
Relámpago.	Flash of lightning.	Repeticion.	Repetition, rehearsal.
Relojero.	Watchmaker.	Resolucion.	Resolution.
Regalo.	Present.	Rosa.	Rose.
Reposo.	Rest, repose.	Rutina.	Routine.
Resfriado.	Cold.	Suma.	Sum.
Reumatismo.	Rheumatism.	Sutileza.	Subtilty, fineness.
Revés.	Wrong side, back.	Salida.	Departure.
Rincon.	Corner.	Sílaba.	Syllable.
Ruiseñor.	Nightingale.	Soledad.	Solitude.
		Sustancia.	Substance.
		Subida.	Rising ground, going up.
		Suegra.	Mother-in-law.

COMPOSITION.

Faltar á su palabra.	To break one's word.
Guardarse de alguna cosa.	To take care not to do a thing (not to attempt to do a thing).
Hablar á bulto.	To speak at random.
Hablar á tontas y á locas.	To speak without rhyme or reason.
Hablar al aire.	To talk vaguely.
Hablar al oido.	To whisper into one's ear.
Hablar al alma.	To speak one's mind.
Hablar entre dientes.	To mutter.
Hablar por boca de ganso.	To echo what another has said.
Hacer á uno perder los estribos.	To make one lose his temper.
Hacer de las suyas.	To show off one's tricks.
Hacer alarde de.	To boast of.
Hacer la cuenta sin la huéspeda.	To reckon without the host.
Hacer caso de.	To pay attention (or respect) to.
Haberla (or habérselas) con alguno.	To dispute (or contend) with any one.
Irse de la memoria.	To escape one's memory.
Irsele á uno la cabeza.	To lose one's reason.

LESSON LXIII.

Van cien duros á que es cierto.	I wager a hundred dollars that it is true.
Llevar á mal.	To take any thing amiss.
Mal de su grado.	Unwillingly.
Mal que le pese.	In spite of him.
Manos á la obra.	To set about a work.
Meter bulla.	To make a noise, a bustle.
Meterse á caballero.	To assume the gentleman.
Meterse á sabio.	To affect learning and knowledge.
Meterse con alguno.	To pick a quarrel with any one.
Meterse en camisa de once varas.	To interfere in other people's business.
Meterse en todo.	To meddle in every thing.
Meterse en vidas agenas.	To dive into other people's affairs.
Mirar de hito en hito.	To look steadfastly at.
Mostrar las suelas de los zapatos.	To take to one's heels.
Nacer de piés.	To be born to good luck.
Nada se me da de ello.	I care nothing about it.
No dejar meter baza.	Not to allow one to slip in a word.
No cabe mas.	Nothing more can be desired.
No estar para fiestas.	To be out of temper.
No le pesa de haber nacido.	He has no mean opinion of himself.
No se me da un bledo.	I do not care a straw.
No tener arte ni parte en alguna cosa.	To have no hand in any thing.
Perder cuidado.	Not to fear, to make one's self easy.
Por ce ó por be.	Some way or other.
Por fas ó nefas.	Right or wrong.
No llegará la sangre al rio.	There is nothing to be feared.

CONVERSATION AND VERSION.

1. D. Pepito ha faltado á su palabra, ó ¿cree V. qué vendrá todavía? ¡Qué ha de venir! Si él habla siempre á tontas y á locas.

2. Pues yo creí que prometió formalmente venir hoy.—Don Pepito no habla nunca formalmente.

3. ¿De qué manera habla entónces? De muchas, él habla al aire, á bulto, al oido, entre dientes, por boca de ganso; pero nunca habla al alma.

4. Esto hará perder á cualquiera los estribos.—A esto le llama él, haciendo alarde, hacer de las suyas.

5. Sí; pero él se las habrá conmigo, porque ha hecho la cuenta sin la huéspeda.—D. Luis, no haga V. caso, es un mequetrefe, si Vds. quieren yo iré á su casa y le haré venir mal de su grado, ó mejor dicho, mal que le pese.

6. No, señor, no vaya V., es un hombre que se mete en todo.—Y en eso tiene V. razon, porque él se mete con todo el mundo.

LESSON LXIII.

7. Y hasta se mete á sabio y á caballero.— Lo peor es que mete mucha bulla.

8. ¿Vamos, señores, en qué mas se mete el pobre D. Pepito? Se mete en camisa de once varas, en vidas agenas, etc., etc.

9. Pero, señores, no olviden Vds. que si por ce ó por be, lo llegase á saber, D. Pepito, y por fas ó por nefas hubiese un desafío, no lo olviden Vds., vuelvo á repetir que Don Pepito es un gran espadachin. ¡Vaya! pierda V. cuidado, que no llegará la sangre al rio.

10. ¡Don Pepito espadachin! Cáscaras!—Van cien pesos á que si le miro de hito en hito, muestra las suelas de los zapatos.

11. V. no debe llevarlo á mal, aunque Don Pepito sea tan su amigo; pero es muy hablador y no deja á nadie meter baza.—Yo no tengo arte ni parte en ello y no se me da un bledo.

12. ¿Se acordó V. de decir aquello á su vecino el Sr. Foster? No, señor, se me fué de la memoria.

13. ¿Es un jóven muy afortunado? Sí, señor, ha nacido de piés; pero sé que no le pesa de haber nacido.

14. V. no debe criticarlo, porque ahora no está para fiestas.—A mí no se me da un bledo de que esté ó no de mal humor.

15. Hable V. bajo ó hábleme V. al oido, porque veo al Señor Foster allí en frente y V. debe guardarse de que le oiga hablar de ese modo, porque lo llevaria á mal.—Pierda V. cuidado que no llegará la sangre al rio.

EXERCISE.

1. Does that man always keep his word? I have never known him to break his word on a single occasion.

2. Peter is very sorry that Alexander went away without him, and I do not know what he would have done if John had left him.

3. John took good care not to start at the same time as his elder brother, for he well knew that he would have been obliged to show him every thing worth seeing in the city.

4. He very often talks for hours together without rhyme or reason, to the very great annoyance of those who have to listen to him.

5. Believe me, it is no proof of talent to talk away at random for an hour at a time, without saying any thing that could be called either new or agreeable.

6. I cannot support a man who is so ignorant as to come and whisper something in my ear while I am engaged in conversation with another.

7. Not one of those ideas is his own, he only echoes what he has heard said by others.

8. I would advise you to pay no attention to any thing he tells you.

9. Judging by his manner of speaking, one would say he had lost his reason.

10. I will wager fifty dollars that not one word of all you have read and heard on that score (*sobre esa materia*) is true.

11. I suppose you have already heard of my good fortune? I have; and I need not tell you how glad I was to know you had succeeded.

12. Did you hear all the president said? Every thing; he spoke very loud, so that all those that were present might not lose a word.

13. Although he affects great learning and knowledge, I have had occasion to find out (discover) that he is a very ignorant man.

14. I know very well that he has no mean opinion of himself; but, after all, his greatest fault is to dive a little too much into other people's affairs.

LESSON LXIV.

Alumbrar.	To light.
Soltar.	To loose, to let go.
Suponer.	To suppose.
Situar.	To situate.
Significar.	To signify.
Saludar.	To salute, to bow to.
Sobrar.	To remain over, to be too much, too many.
Sonreirse.	To smile.
Soplar.	To blow, to prompt.
Sonrojarse.	To blush.
Sufrir.	To suffer, to bear.
Suplicar.	To supplicate, to beseech.
Suspirar.	To sigh, to long after.
Rasgar.	To tear.
Rebajar.	To lower.
Rebanar.	To cut in slices.
Recitar.	To recite.
Recomendar.	To recommend.
Referir.	To refer, to tell, to relate.
Regular.	To regulate.
Remendar.	To mend.
Remediar.	To remedy, to help.

Repasar.	To look over (a lesson, &c.).
Representar.	To represent, to lay before.
Resolver.	To resolve.
Zafar.	To disembarrass.

De gorra.	Sponging, at the expense of others.
De perilla.	To the purpose, at the proper time.
Cascos á la gineta.	On one's high horse.
A raya.	Within bounds, at bay.
A solas.	All alone.
Siquiera.	Even, only.
En suma.	In a word, in fine.

Santo.	Holy, saintly.
Sutil.	Subtil, fine.
Silencioso.	Silent.
Sordo.	Deaf.
Sustantivo.	Substantive.
Sucio.	Dirty, filthy.

Atrevimiento.	Assurance, daring.	Blanca.	Mite.
		Bula.	Bull (of the Pope).
Cuerpo.	Body.	Flaqueza.	Weakness.
Inconveniente.	Objection.	Gorra.	Cap, lady's bonnet.
Esfuerzo.	Effort, endeavor.		
Descaro.	Barefacedness.	Calzas (*fem. pl.*).	Breeches.
Fondos (*pl.*).	Funds.	Pieza.	Piece.
Matrimonio.	Matrimony.	Trastienda.	Back shop.
Modismo.	Idiom.	Tienda.	Store, shop.
Provecho.	Profit, benefit.	Tigeras.	Scissors.
Yugo.	Yoke.	Tarjeta.	Card (visiting or business).
Trapo.	Rag.		
Saber.	Learning, knowledge.	Traza.	Mien, appearance.
		Trampa.	Trap, cheat.
Sacacorchos.	Corkscrew.	Traduccion.	Translation.
Saldo.	Balance.		
Salto.	Leap, jump.		

COMPOSITION.

Quedarse en blanco.	To be left in the lurch.
Quedarse hecho una pieza (*or* helado).	To be thunderstruck, to remain astonished.

LESSON LXIV.

Querer decir.	To mean.
Sacar fuerzas de flaqueza.*	To make a virtue of a necessity.
Sacar provecho.	To turn to account.
Sacudir el yugo.	To shake off the yoke.
Salir á luz.	To be produced, to be published.
Salir con algo.	To gain one's end.
Salir los colores á la cara.	To blush.
Salga lo que saliere.	Come what may.
Salirse con la suya.	To have one's own way, to accomplish an object.
Santo y bueno.	Well and good.
Sin mas acá ni mas allá.	Without ifs and ands.
Sin qué ni para qué.	Without rhyme or reason.
En nombrando al ruin de Roma luego asoma.	Speak of the devil, and his imps appear.
Sobre la marcha.	Off-hand (instantly).
Tan claro como el sol (or como el agua).	As clear as daylight.
Tener á ménos hablar á uno.	Not to deign to speak to one.
Tener á uno á raya.	To keep one at bay.
Tener algo en la punta de la lengua.	To have any thing on the tip of one's tongue.
Tener buen diente.	To have a good appetite.
Tener bula para todo.	To have permission to do what one likes.
Tener el pié en dos zapatos.	To have two strings to one's bow.
Tener los cascos á la gineta.	To be hare-brained, to have little judgment.
Tener su alma en su cuerpo.	To do what one thinks proper.
Tomar el cielo con las manos.	To be transported with rapture, to be enraged.
Tomar la ocasion por los cabellos.	To profit by the occasion.
Tomar las (calzas) de Villadiego.	To take to one's heels.
Vamos claros.	Let us understand one another.
Venir á ménos.	To decline in any way.
Venir al caso.	To come to the point.
Venir con las manos lavadas.	To wish to enjoy the fruit of another's labor.
Venir de perilla.	To come at the nick of time, or to fit exactly.
Venir una cosa pintada.	A thing to suit (or fit) exactly.
Verse negro.	To be afflicted, embarrassed.
Vestirse con veinte y cinco alfileres.	To be dressed in style, to be decked out.
Dicho y hecho.	No sooner said than done.

* *Hacer de la necesidad virtud.*

LESSON LXIV.

Vivir de gorra.	To live at another's expense.
Vivir á sus anchas (anchuras).	To live at one's ease.
Zafarse de alguna cosa.	To get clear (or rid of) any thing.

CONVERSATION AND VERSION.

1. ¿Qué quiere decir quedarse en blanco? Quiere decir lo mismo que quedarse á la luna de Valencia, esto es, quedarse sin nada.

2. ¿Y quedarse hecho una pieza ó helado, qué quiere decir? Son modismos que indican admiracion ó sorpresa.

3. ¿Quiere V. explicarme algunos modismos españoles? No tengo inconveniente, pregúnteme V. el significado de los que no comprenda V. —Muy bien.

4. Sacar fuerzas de flaqueza, ¿qué quiere decir? Yo creo que es hacer esfuerzos; pero tambien significa, hacer de la necesidad virtud.

5. Sacar provecho, creo que no necesita explicacion y si la ocasion se presenta, creo que sabré sacarlo.—¿Y qué me dice V. acerca de sacudir el yugo? Que aquellos que tengan algun mal yugo que sacudir deben hacerlo sobre la marcha.

6. Santo y bueno, pero V., ¿no tiene ningun yugo que sacudir? No, señor, es verdad que estoy bajo el yugo del matrimonio; pero no deseo zafarme de él, porque para mí aunque es yugo, es un yugo santo que me ha hecho muy feliz y bajo el cual deseo vivir todavía muchos años.

7. ¿No le parece á V. que aquel hombre vive de gorra? Sí, señor, aquí se venia todos los dias con sus manos lavadas y se nos comia un codo.

8. ¿Y porqué no lo echó V. de su casa? ¡Así lo hice ayer, y si V. lo hubiera visto! parecia querer tomar el cielo con las manos!

9. ¡Vaya un atrevimiento! Al fin me ví obligado á amenazarle con una silla, y entónces tomó las de Villadiego.

10. Creo que ántes era rico, pero ahora ha venido á ménos.—No, lo que es tener, todavía tiene.

11. No hombre, si no tiene sobre qué caerse muerto.—Perdone V., si V. quiere que, para practicar en los modismos del verbo tener, le diga á V. lo que ese buen señor tiene, se lo diré á V.

12. Santo y bueno.—Pues entónces allá va sin qué ni para qué.

13. Pero hombre, ¿para qué sacar á la colada los trapos de ese buen hombre? Si eso es tan claro como el sol que nos alumbra.

14. Vamos claros, ¿quiere V. ó no que le diga lo que ese señor, que se viste con veinte y cinco alfileres, tiene? Pero si no viene al caso.

15. Entónces se acabará el ejercicio sin poder introducir en la práctica la mitad de los modismos que tenemos en la leccion.—¡Ah! sí, sí, tiene V. mil razones, escucho, ¿qué es lo que ese buen señor tiene?

LESSON LXIV.

16. En primer lugar tiene buen apetito y buen diente.—¡Caspita! qué si lo tiene! ¿y á quien se lo cuenta V.?

17. Tiene siempre algo en la punta de la lengua y nunca tiene nada en el bolsillo.

18. Y segun el descaro con que obra, parece tener bula para todo; tambien tiene los cascos á la gineta y con tanto tener creo que es mas lo que le falta que lo que tiene.

19. Yo no sé cómo tenerlo á raya, ¿no me hará V. el favor de aconsejarle que no venga mas por aquí? Amigo mio, dígaselo V. mismo, porque yo tengo á ménos hablar á una persona de su especie.

20. Y sin embargo, vea V., él tiene el pié en dos zapatos, ¿y qué mas tiene?

21. Déjeme V. pensar, ¡ah! sí, el pobre señor tiene todavía otra cosa mas.—Bien, pues, dígala V., que se acaba el ejercicio.

22. Tiene su alma en su cuerpo. Hombre, calle V., que aquí viene él en persona.—Sí, en nombrando al ruin de Roma, luego asoma.

23. Buenos dias, D. Juan.—Téngalos V. muy buenos, D. Periquito, ¿qué se ofrece? Vengo á pedirle á V. diez pesos prestados, que me vendrian de perilla, ¡porque me veo negro!

24. Hombre pídaselos V. al Sr. De V. que está en fondos, en cuanto á mí me encuentro sin blanca.

EXERCISE.

1. I understand your brother was left entirely in the lurch? Not at all; on the contrary, he came off (turned out) much better than I did.

2. How did he feel when he learned that I had heard of the whole matter? He was thunderstruck, and could not give me any reply.

3. How are you going to manage in such a case as that? I have only to make a virtue of necessity.

4. I think there is little danger of his not succeeding; what do you think (what appears to you)? Not the least; he is very prudent, and knows how to turn every thing to account.

5. Do you remember when that article was published? I do not remember exactly; but it appears to me it must have been some time in last November.

6. You see that is what I told you the other day would take place. Yes, that is true; but you seem to have forgotten the condition I mentioned to your friend as he was going out.

7. Is Mr. Martinez not going to be here, as he promised? I am expecting him.—We shall wait until seven o'clock; if he comes before that time, well and good; if not, we shall go on with the business of the evening without him.

8. Well, let us understand each other before going any farther. It seems to me we understand each other perfectly; the thing is as clear as daylight.

9. Oh, Charles! I am so glad to see you! you have just come at the nick of time; we shall have the pleasure of your company at dinner. You are very kind; but really you must excuse me; I have a friend waiting for me.

10. You lost your coat? how did you come home in the cold without it? Alexander lent me one of his that fitted me exactly.

11. No sooner said than done; he took his hat and went out in search of him, notwithstanding it rained in torrents.

12. You may be at ease in your mind on that score; I shall manage to get rid of him very soon.

13. I wish you would come to the point, for up to the present I have been unable to find out what you mean.

14. One would have said, from the manner in which he was (*viéndolo*) decked out, that he was going to the theatre or to a ball instead of to the office.

LESSON LXV.

Aventurarse.	To venture.
Apretar.	To tighten, to urge.
Cobrar.	To collect.
Desafiar.	To challenge.
Escaldar.	To scald.
Enhebrar.	To thread (a needle), to link.
Enzarzar.	To sow discord.
Enfadarse.	To get angry.
Hilar.	To spin.
Juntar.	To join.
Madrugar.	To rise early.
Prevenir.	To warn, to inform.
Relucir.	To shine.
Sustentar.	To sustain.
Trasquilar.	To shear.
Tapar.	To cover up, to close up.
Trampear.	To impose upon, to deceive.
Tragar.	To swallow.

LESSON LXV.

Trasnochar.	To sit up all night.
Terminar.	To terminate.
Tolerar.	To tolerate.
Tornar.	To return, to do over again.
Tranquilizar.	To tranquillize, to make any one's mind easy.
Tutear.	To address any one in the second person singular, to speak familiarly to.

Expresivo.	Expressive.
Justo.	Just.
Duro.	Hard.
Necio.	Silly, foolish.
Práctico.	Practised, experienced.
Ciego.	Blind.
Tuerto.	Blind of one eye.
Trigueño.	Dark (of the complexion).
Tinto.	Colored, red.
Tonto.	Foolish.
Tramposo.	Deceitful, swindling.
Terminante.	Decided.
Tranquilo.	Tranquil, quiet.

A borbotones.	Bubbling, hurriedly, confusedly.
Palabras mayores.	Offensive words or expressions.
No ser rana.	To be able and expert.

¡Caramba!	Dear me ¡ Hah!

Asador.	Spit (for roasting).	Cola.	Tail.
Copo.	Flake (of snow).	Danza.	Dance.
Entendedor.	One who understands.	Divisa.	Motto.
		Familiaridad.	Familiarity.
Herrero.	Blacksmith.	Miel.	Honey.
Menosprecio.	Scorn, contempt.	Mona.	Monkey.
Hortelano.	Gardener.	Fama.	Fame, notoriety.
Dado.	Dye.	Moderacion.	Moderation.
Proverbio.	Proverb.	Oveja.	Sheep.
Sayo.	Sort of loose coat or jacket.	Necesidad.	Necessity.
		Pareja.	Pair.
Pecho.	Breast.	Rana.	Frog.

LESSON LXV.

Raton.	Mouse.	Viga.	Beam.
Tio.	Uncle.	Tenacidad.	Tenacity.
Bebedor.	Toper, tippler.	Tos.	Cough.

(All these are masculine.)

Soliloquio.	Soliloquy.	Tirabuzon.	Corkscrew.
Suegro.	Father-in-law.	Trineo.	Sleigh.
Sugeto.	Person, individual.	Tacto.	Touch.
		Talento.	Talent.
Sobrino.	Nephew.	Telégrafo.	Telegraph.
Sinónimo.	Synonyme.	Tenedor.	Fork.
Silencio.	Silence.	Término.	Term.
Sentido.	Sense.	Trigo.	Wheat.
Semblante.	Countenance, looks.	Termómetro.	Thermometer.
		Torno.	Lathe.
Secreto.	Secret.	Toque.	Touch, ringing (of bells).
Trato.	Intercourse, treatment.	Título.	Title.
Través.	Breadth (of a thing).	Trago.	Draught, drink.

COMPOSITION.

A buena gana no hay pan duro.	Hunger is the best sauce.
A lo hecho pecho.	What is done cannot be helped.
A quien se hace de miel las moscas se lo comen.	Smear yourself with honey, and you will be devoured by flies.
A quien madruga Dios le ayuda.	The early bird catches the worm.
Al buen entendedor con media palabra basta.	A word to the wise is sufficient.
Al fin se canta la gloria.	Boast not till the victory is won.
Antes que te cases mira lo que haces.	Look before you leap.
Antes cabeza de raton que cola de leon.	Better be the head of a mouse than the tail of a lion.
Aunque la mona se vista de seda mona se queda.	A hog in armor is still but a hog.
Bien vengas mal si vienes solo.	Misfortune never comes alone.
Cada oveja con su pareja (*or* Dios los cria y ellos se juntan).	Birds of a feather flock together.
Cada uno juzga por su corazon el ageno.	Every man measures other people's corn in his own bushel.
Cada uno hace de su capa un sayo.	Every one may do as he likes with his own.

LESSON LXV.

Cada uno sabe donde le aprieta el zapato.	Every one knows where the shoe pinches him.
Cobra buena fama y échate á dormir.	Get the name of early rising, and you may lie a-bed all day.
Como el perro del hortelano, que ni come ni deja comer.	Like the dog in the manger.
Cuenta y razon sustentan amistad.	Short reckoning and long friends.
Del mal el ménos.	Of two evils, the lesser.
Debajo de una mala capa se encuentra un buen bebedor.	We should not judge the book by the cover.
Dime con quién andas, y te diré quién eres.	Tell me your company and I will tell you what you are.
Donde fueres haz como vieres.	When at Rome, do as Rome does.
Lo mejor de los dados es no jugarlos.	The best throw at dice is to throw them away.
En boca cerrada no entran moscas.	A close mouth catches no flies.
En casa del herrero asador de palo.	No one goes worse shod than the shoemaker's wife.
En tierra de ciegos el tuerto es rey.	In the land of the blind, the one-eyed man is king.
Gato escaldado del agua fria huye.	A burnt child dreads the fire.
Ir por lana y volver trasquilado.	The biter bit.
Hombre prevenido nunca fue vencido.	Forewarned, forearmed.
La caridad bien ordenada empieza por uno mismo.	Charity begins at home.
La mucha familiaridad es causa de menosprecio.	Too much familiarity breeds contempt.
La necesidad carece de ley.	Necessity has no law.
La tenacidad es divisa del necio.	A wise man will change his mind; a fool never.
Lo que no se puede remediar se ha de aguantar.	What can't be cured must be endured.
Mas vale tarde que nunca.	Better late than never.
Mar vale pájaro en mano que ciento volando.	A bird in the hand is worth two in the bush.
Miéntras en mi casa estoy rey soy.	A man's house is his castle.
Nadie puede decir de esta agua no beberé.	No one can tell what is to happen to him.
No es oro todo lo que reluce.	All is not gold that glitters.
No hay mal que por bien no venga.	It's an ill wind that blows nobody good.
No la hagas no la temas.	Do no evil, and fear no harm.
Poquito á poco hilaba la vieja el copo.	Rome was not built in a day.
Quien bien te quiere te hará llorar.	Spare the rod, and you will spoil the child.
Quien mucho habla mucho yerra.	Who speaks much often blunders.

Quien no se aventura no pasa la mar.	Never venture, never win.
Ya que la casa se quema calentémonos.	Let us make the best of a bad job.
Vemos la paja en el ojo ageno y no la viga en el nuestro.	We see the mote in our neighbor's eye, and not the beam in our own.
Tu enemigo es de tu oficio.	Two of a trade never agree.

CONVERSATION AND VERSION.

1. ¿Hay muchos proverbios en español? Hay muchísimos; en todas las lenguas los hay, pero en la española creo que hay tantos que si se reuniesen todos formarian varios volúmenes.

2. ¿Le gustan á V. los proverbios? Sí, señor, son muy expresivos, pero debemos usarlos, como decia D. Quijote, con moderacion y no á borbotones como Sancho Panza.

3. En eso tiene V. razon, porque quien mucho habla mucho yerra.—V. acaba de aplicar ese muy bien; pero es imposible que practiquemos con todos los que trae esta leccion, en este ejercicio.

4. Sin embargo, al que madruga Dios le ayuda.—V. dice bien, y quien no se aventura no pasa la mar.

5. Espero que quien nos oiga conversar introduciendo tanto refran, no diga de ellos lo que se dice de los males.—¿Qué dicen de los males? Bien vengas mal si vienes solo.

6. ¡Oh! no, señor, en primer lugar los proverbios no son males, y en segundo lugar á nosotros nos gustan, y queremos practicar con ellos, para aprenderlos.—V. está en lo justo, y además, cada uno hace de su capa un sayo.

7. ¡Ola, amiguito! V. me parece práctico en la materia, pero no piense V. que yo soy rana, porque debajo de una mala capa se encuentra un buen bebedor.—Caramba ¡que no me deja V. meter baza! no se dirá de V. aquello de, en boca cerrada no entran moscas.

8. Vamos amigo, ese refran vino por los cabellos.—Pues si vino por los cabellos, á pelo vino, además, que V. me parece ser de aquellos que ven la paja en el ojo ageno y no la viga en el suyo.

9. No se enfade V., amigo, que quien bien lo quiero le hará llorar.—No, señor, no me enfado, pero ya veo que no es oro todo lo que reluce.

10. ¡Bravo! bravo! ya va V. aprendiendo á enzarzar refranes, lo hace V. cual otro Sancho Panza, y yo, con toda mi práctica, he ido por lana y he vuelto trasquilado.—Su ejemplo de V. me irá enseñando; poquito á poco hilaba la vieja el copo, y dime con quién andas y te diré quién eres.

11. ¡Qué hombre! si V. va á ganar á su maestro! pero no hay mal que por bien no venga; V. me hace reir con sus refranes.—Bien, del mal el ménos, pero D. Manuel, ¿es posible que le haya de ganar su discípulo?

LESSON LXV.

12. No sé, no puedo decir de esta agua no beberé, y lo que no se puede remediar se ha de aguantar, y al fin se canta la gloria.—¡Zape, como los enhebra! pero yo no me doy por vencido, señor maestro, porque yo ya sé aquello de cobra buena fama y échate á dormir.

13. La tenacidad es divisa del necio, y al buen entendedor con media palabra basta.—Sí, pero esas ya son palabras mayores, y á quien se hace de miel las moscas se lo comen, y miéntras en mi casa estoy, rey soy.

14. Espero, D. Cárlos, que no me quiera V. poner fuera de su casa.—No hombre, pero estos refranes son tan expresivos que le hacen decir á uno mas de lo que quiere; pero á lo hecho pecho y ya que V. me desafió, siga la danza.

15. Bueno, si V. lo quiere, ya que la casa se quema calentémonos; pero bien haria V. ántes que se case en mirar lo que hace, porque cada uno sabe donde le aprieta el zapato.—Amigo mio, V. no sabe de la misa la media; yo nunca doy mi brazo á torcer, y ántes quiero ser cabeza de raton que cola de leon.

16. Sí, señor, pero aunque la mona se vista de seda, mona se queda, no sea V. como el perro del hortelano, que ni come ni deja comer, y acuérdese V. que cuenta y razon sustentan amistad y lo mejor de los dados es no jugarlos.—Basta, basta, hombre me doy por vencido.

17. No la hagas no la temas; tu enemigo es de tu oficio.—Pero, D. Cárlos, le repito. . . .

18. La caridad bien ordenada entra por sí misma.—Pero si repito que. . . .

19. Donde quiera que fueres haz como vieres.—Señor, me rindo.—Mas vale tarde que nunca.

EXERCISE.

1. Well, Charles, so you have come at last. Yes, better late than never, you know; but if it had continued raining I would not have come at all.

2. Are you going out? I thought we were going together to the theatre this evening.—I must go out now; but should I get back as soon as I expect, we shall still have time to go to the theatre.

3. If you undertake that journey, I should like to be your companion. It is rather doubtful at present whether I shall; but if I do, I would be delighted to have your company.

4. If the directors establish that as a general rule, very many persons will suffer great loss.

5. The conditions were, that if he did not discover the error, or if, after having discovered it, he could not rectify it, he should lose his place.

6. He said he would have no rest until he should hear some news of that poor young man.

7. He promised that I should have the place, if it were in his power to procure it for me.

8. In case his efforts should not be attended with success, you may rely upon me to do all in my power to advance (*promover*) your interests.

9. Their embarrassments will not cease so long as they do not introduce some system of reasonable economy.

10. Peter tells his stories so well, and with such an appearance of truth, that one is actually tempted to believe them.

11. They made so many conditions, that it was clear they had no wish to help us.

12. Why did you not take that book? I would not take it because some leaves were wanting.

13. If there is any thing within (in) my reach with which I can serve you, *just** let me know.

14. Whatever he may have been in his youth, he is now a respectable man, and beloved (loved) by everybody that knows him.

* English words in *italics*, not to be translated.

GENERAL OBSERVATIONS

ON SOME

GRAMMATICAL AND IDIOMATICAL PECULIARITIES OF THE SPANISH LANGUAGE, NOT HITHERTO TREATED OF IN THE GRAMMAR.

In order to acquire a thorough knowledge of a language, it is necessary to compare carefully the different uses of the several parts of speech in the native language and in the one proposed to be learned.

The sense of a whole passage is very often changed by the undue suppression or omission of an article, a preposition, or a conjunction; by using one tense of a verb for another; placing an adjective before its noun when, in order to convey the idea intended, it should go after it; and not unfrequently by translating a certain part of speech by a word which, although its appearance would lead us to take it for the equivalent of the word to be interpreted, bears in reality no relation to the sense designed to be expressed.

We have deemed it convenient, therefore, to devote a few pages of our COMBINED METHOD to such general remarks as are necessary to guide the learner, and which, if attentively observed, will, after the study of the Spanish exercises contained in the preceding lessons, enable him to compose purely and idiomatically in the Castilian language.

The Definite Article.

1. It has already been observed in previous lessons, which are the most usual cases where the definite article is expressed in the Spanish language; but there are many others in which it would be altogether incorrect to express or omit it in Spanish, as in English, as may be seen from the following examples, which may serve as a general rule for all those of the same kind:

¿Está el rey en palacio?	Is the king in *the* palace?
Es costumbre en España.	It is *the* custom in Spain.
Su tio firmó por él, en ausencia de su padre.	His uncle signed for him, in *the* absence of his father.
Decia verdad.	He told *the* truth.
A tres de junio.	On *the* 3d of June.
Tuvo valor para responder.	He had *the* courage to answer.
A mediados de agosto.	In *the* middle of August.

2. In Spanish the article is at times accompanied by a preposition not required in English; as,

Hace *del* caballero.	He plays *the* gentleman.

Indefinite Article.

3. The so-called indefinite article (more properly adjective) is, as has been observed in one of the early lessons, frequently employed in English; and when translating from the latter language into Spanish, we either suppress it entirely or render it by some other part of speech; as,

Tiene derecho sobre este caudal.	He has *a* right to (or *a* claim upon) this capital.
A distancia de . . .	At *a* distance of . . .
Cádiz es puerto de mar.	Cadiz is *a* seaport (town).
Es otro Alejandro.	He is *a*nother Alexander.
En medio siglo (*or* dentro de medio siglo).	In half *a* century.
Volvérémos dentro de media hora.	We shall return in half *an* hour.
Las obras de otro (*or* obras agenas).	The works of *a*nother (or *a*nother's works).
Hubo tiempo en que . . .	There was *a* time in which . . .

Personal and Possessive Pronouns.

4. The use and repetition of the personal and possessive pronouns are more frequent in English than in Spanish; and that seeming redundance is essential to the clearness and precision of the English language; but Spanish syntax does not

submit to such encumbrances, and they are, therefore, generally suppressed, as will be seen from the following examples:

Es verdad.	*It* is true.
Llueve.	*It* is raining (or *it* rains).
Hace frio.	*It* is cold.
¿Porqué es menester?	Why is *it* necessary?
El mismo príncipe.	The prince *himself*.
Su misma madre.	His mother *herself*.
Él mismo lo vió.	He saw it *himself*.

5. Before leaving the pronouns, it is proper to remark that *one* and *ones*, so often used in English composition, to avoid the unpleasant repetition of nouns, have no equivalent whatever in Spanish, and are hence to be left out in translating from the former language to the latter; as,

¿Tiene V. caballos?	Have you horses (or any horses)?
Tengo dos buenos.	I have two good *ones*.

6. Personal pronouns, when used redundantly in English, as in the following example, are never expressed in Spanish:

Ambos perecieron.	Both *of them* perished (or were lost).

7. Even whole members of sentences are, not unfrequently, suppressed in translating from English into Spanish; as,

Todo no podia entrar en un elogio, mas sí en una sátira.	All could not find place in a eulogy, but *all could find place* in a satire.

Observe that the repetition of the words *italicized* in the English sentence is avoided by means of the adverb *sí* in Spanish, which serves to correct the negation expressed in the first member of the phrase, thus rendering the latter at once shorter and more elegant.

Ellipsis.

8. There are certain short modes of expression, certain grammatical laconicisms, peculiar to the English language, which are not admissible in Spanish; the ellipses must in such cases often be filled up; as,

Jamás *hubo* orador *que* hablase mejor.	Never did orator speak better.
De ahí *dimanan* estos errores.	Hence these errors.

No puede pensar en *hacer* mal.	He cannot think of evil.
La ciudad *reducida* á cenizas.	The city in ashes.
No *va* mal para *ser* niño.	Not bad for a child.
Su madre *bañada* en lágrimas.	Her mother in tears.
Aunque todos estuviesen juntos.	They were all together.
Esto *es* por *lo que toca á* su persona.	So much for his person (or personal appearance).
En pro y *en* contra.	For and against.
Con la espada en *la* mano.	Sword in hand.

N. B.—It is also correct to say, *Espada en mano.*

Inversion.

Although we have spoken at some length, in Lesson LI., on the subject of inversion, we imagine the learner will not be displeased to meet here a few well-chosen examples which will give him a still clearer idea of the order observed in Spanish for the expression of ideas, and the consequent difference of construction between that language and the English.

9. The substantive often precedes its adjective; as,

Es el hombre mas perfecto del mundo.	He is the most perfect man in the world.
Llave falsa.	False key.
Testigo falso.	False witness.
Su hijo mas jóven.	Her youngest son.

10. Instances occur, however, of the inversion taking place in English, while the natural construction is followed in Spanish; especially in the case of past participles acting as verbal adjectives; as,

Una vez destruido este fundamento, todo se viene abajo.	This foundation being once destroyed, the whole (edifice) comes to the ground.
Admitida esta libertad, el hombre puede . . .	This liberty (being) once admitted, man may . . .

11. In all cases similar to that of the following example, the possessives *mio, tuyo, suyo* are placed after the substantive, and then, of course, they retain their final syllable; as,

El otro hijo *suyo.*	His other son.

12. The same ideas are in not a few instances presented in

Spanish in an order very different from that followed in English; as,

No ha venido para destruir, sino para edificar.	It is not to destroy that he has come, but to build up.
Bien veo que . . .	I see (very) well that . . .
Si tuviese V. que hacer una contrata.	If you had an agreement to make.

(*If you had to make an agreement* would, of course, also be an allowable construction in English.)

No tenia razon aquel filósofo que decia que . . .	That philosopher who said that . . . was wrong.
Toca remunerar los servicios al que los recibió.	It is for him who received the services to reward them.
Entre los Griegos, los que . . .	Those amongst the Greeks, who . . .
Él que mas hablaba.	He who spoke the most.
Cien veces mas quisiera yo que . . .	I would prefer a thousand times that . .
Solo Dios es inmutable.	God alone is unchanging.

Nouns.

13. There is a striking difference to be observed in the use of nouns in the two languages; we sometimes meet nouns in the singular in English, while in Spanish they are used in the plural only, and *vice-versâ*:

Plural.	*Singular.*
Mirar con *malos ojos*.	To look with evil *eye*.
Puso *los ojos* en mí.	He set his *eye* on me.
Dar *oidos* á . . .	To give *ear* to . . .
Prestar *oidos*.	To lend an *ear*.
De *piés* á cabeza.	From head to *foot*.
Por *todas partes*.	In every *direction*.
Juego de *manos*.	Sleight of *hand*.
Se presentó con *los ojos* en el suelo.	He came forward with downcast *eye*.

Singular.	*Plural.*
A *pié* descalzo.	With bare *feet* (or in (his) bare *feet*)
Estar en *pié*.	To stand on (one's) *feet*.
A *remo y vela*.	With *oars* and *sails*.
En toda *suerte* de negocios.	In all *sorts* (or kinds) of business.
No son dueños de *sí*.	They are not masters of *themselves*.

One Part of Speech for Another.

14. It is not uncommon, in comparing English and Spanish composition, to see adjectives translated by substantives, adverbs by substantives, substantives by verbs, and *vice-versâ*. Sometimes, in translating, difficulties, appearing at first sight almost insurmountable, are overcome by the simple substitution of one part of speech for another.

Adjectives for Substantives.

Pica de *guapo* (*or* presumido de *guapo*).	He piques himself on his *bravery*.
Es acusado de *impío*.	He is accused of *impiety*.
Se pone *furioso*.	He gets into a *fury*.

Substantives for Adverbs, and vice-versâ.

Aunque idólatras de *orígen*.	Although *originally* idolaters.
Come *excesivamente*.	He eats to *excess*.
Tuvo la *dicha* de salvarse.	*Happily* for him he escaped.
Por *desgracia* nada oyeron.	*Unfortunately* they heard nothing.

Substantives for Verbs, and vice-versâ.

Habló lo mejor que *pudo*.	He spoke to the best of his *ability*.
Debe probar su *dicho*.	He must prove what he *says*.
Como *acostumbra*.	According to his *custom*.
Despues de *almorzar*.	After *breakfast*.
Antes de *comer*.	Before *dinner*.

Verbs for Pronouns.

Hay historiadores que aseguran que . . .	*Some* historians assure us that . . .

Of Verbs in General.

15. We very often find verbs active with the indefinite *se*, and sometimes the passive verb with the particle *se*, used in Spanish to express the same idea conveyed in English by passive, and sometimes also by active verbs; one tense translated by another different tense, one number substituted in the place of another, one person for other persons, and at times even the same person translated by any or all the others, according to the sense desired to be conveyed.

Passive in English.

El concilio *se celebraba* en Pisa.	The council *was held* at Pisa.
El libro que *se* le *atribuye*.	The book which *is attributed* to him.
Esto *se encierra* en la proposicion.	That *is contained* in the proposition.
Esto debe *contarse* por nada.	This is to *be counted* for nothing.
Cuando *se* les ruega que respondan.	When they *are requested* to answer.

GRAMMATICAL PECULIARITIES. 361

Active in English.

Viene á *juntarse* con su familia.	He comes to *join* his family.
Se *casó* con la duquesa.	He *married* the duchess.
Se *hicieron* á la vela.	They *set* sail.

The Indicative or Subjunctive for the Infinitive.

Le mandó que *callase*.	He ordered him *to hold* his tongue (or *to be* silent).
Es reputado por hombre que nada *posee*.	He is supposed *to possess* nothing.
Espero me *responda* V.	I expect you *to answer* me.

One Tense for Another.

¿Te *habré* yo *dado* un derecho que no tengo?	Have I then *given* thee a right which I do not possess myself?
¿Porqué solo los hombres *habrán de degenerar*?	Why must mankind alone degenerate?
Cuanto mas *hagan*, ménos ganarán.	The more they *do*, the less they will gain.
Que un muerto *resuscite*, no es cosa comun.	It is no common thing for a dead (man) *to resuscitate*.

One Number for Another in Verbs.

Son las seis.	It *is* six o'clock.
No le *quedan* mas que tres hijos.	He *has* only three children left.

One Person for Another.

Nosotros *somos* los bárbaros.	It *is* we that are barbarians.
Si *hubiesen* sido ellos los vituperados.	If it *had* been they that they had blamed.

Mode of Asking Questions and forming Negations with Verbs.

16. The auxiliary *do*, used in English in asking questions, whether negatively or positively, is to be lost sight of in translating into Spanish, inasmuch as the simple form of the verb contains all that is required for that purpose, as may be seen in the following examples:

¿*Van* Vds. algunas veces á la ópera?	*Do* you sometimes go to the opera?
¿*Sabia* V. que debiamos venir tan temprano?	*Did* you know that we were to come so early?
No *creia* que debiesen Vds. venir hasta las tres.	I *did* not think you were to come until three o'clock.

17. Nor is it to be translated into Spanish when it stands in the English sentence merely for the purpose of giving more emphasis to the expression; as,

Yo creia que no iban nunca al teatro. Sí, señor, van á menudo.	I thought they never went to the theatre. Yes, sir, they *do* go often.

18. It sometimes takes the place of a verb, to avoid the repetition of the latter; in all such cases it is to be rendered into Spanish by a simple particle (positive or negative, as required by the sense), or else the verb expressing the action must itself be repeated; as,

¿Escribe V. todos los meses á su tio? Sí, señor (*or* le escribo todos los meses).	Do you write to your uncle every month? Yes, sir, I *do*.

19. To what has already been remarked relative to conjugations, we have but a few words to add, respecting a limited number of verbs of the third conjugation. Those which have either of the letters *ch*, *ll*, or *ñ*, immediately preceding the termination, make their past participle in *endo*, instead of *iendo*; as, *ciñendo, mullendo, riñendo, hinchendo, bruñendo, gruñendo, tañendo,* instead of *ciñiendo, mulliendo, riñiendo, hinchiendo, bruñiendo, gruñiendo, tañiendo.*

For the same reason the *i* is also suppressed in the third persons singular and plural of the preterit definite of the indicative, and in all the persons of the second and third terminations of the imperfect subjunctive, and of the future of the same mood; as, *ciñó, mulló, riñeron, hinchera, bruñese, gruñere,* instead of *ciñió, mullió, riñieron, hinchiera, bruñiese, gruñiere.*

There is but one exception allowable to this rule, and that occurs in the verb *henchir*, which generally retains the *i* in the third person singular preterit definite of the indicative, making it *hinchió*, in order to avoid confounding it with *hinchó*, same person and tense of *hinchar*, a regular verb of the first conjugation.

The reason of the suppression of the *i* in the cases pointed out above is obvious, inasmuch as the letters *ch*, *ll*, or *ñ*, when forming a syllable with *e*, cannot be sounded without the concurrence of the *i* element to a certain extent. If, therefore, the *i* were retained in those combinations, a forced and disagreeable sound would be the result.

GRAMMATICAL PECULIARITIES. 363

20. There are in English certain verbs of very frequent occurrence, and whose signification, if not determined by some other part of speech, it would often be difficult to explain. Amongst this class, the verb *to get* plays a very important, if not the most important part, and English persons are sometimes at as great a loss to know how exactly to translate it into a foreign language, as foreigners are to know how and when to use it idiomatically in English. This verb (*to get*) has no exact equivalent in Spanish, but there are in that language many verbs of something of a like nature, and by which it may at times be correctly rendered, according to the signification in which it is used. We venture to say that, in the most knotty cases, a little thought, a moment's reflection would go far in removing all difficulty.

Before making some uncouth makeshift of a translation, pause a moment, and look what is the real meaning of *to get* in the case before you; then see what other verb would serve in its place, or what other form of expression you can substitute for the one proposed to be translated. This you will soon discover, for perhaps in no language can an instance be found of the impossibility to express the same idea in more than one way. For instance, let it be required to translate into Spanish, To GET IN by the window; here is a difficulty just as great as any other case where the verb *to get* can be used.

Let us now see how else we can express that idea: To GO IN, or to *come* in by the window; that is to say, we have to convey the idea of motion *into*. This same idea is to be expressed thus: To ENTER by the window=ENTRAR *por la ventana*; ENTRAR then is the standard and usual verb expressive of motion into. Let us now change the preposition and reverse the sense, for the preposition *in* determines the signification of *get* in the case under consideration.

Required to translate: To GET OUT by the window; the same process as above gives us motion *out*; hence, SALIR *por la ventana*, SALIR being the standard and usual Spanish verb expressive of motion *out*.

This mode of reasoning will in all cases lead to the desired end. Let your object be to find some verb in English which *alone* will mean the same thing as *get* and its determining preposition together.

GET, used in connection with adjectives, is no more difficult to be disposed of than when accompanied by prepositions, and it may in general be turned into Spanish by one of the three verbs *ponerse, hacerse,* or *volverse* (according to the nature of the case), and an adjective corresponding to the English one determining *get*; as,

Hacerse rico.	To *get* rich.
Volverse or *ponerse* rojo.	To *get* red.
Ponerse furioso.	To *get* furious.

These ideas in Spanish may be expressed by single verbs derived from each of the adjectives respectively; as,

Enriquecerse.	To *get* rich.
Enrojecerse.	To *get* red (*i. e.*, to redden).
Enfurecerse.	To *get* furious.

21. To GET, as an active verb, is usually translated into Spanish by any of these : *conseguir, obtener, procurar, hacerse de, hacerse con,* according to the sense; as,

Consiguió lo que deseaba.	He *got* what he wanted.
Obtendrán el privilegio.	They will *get* the patent.
¿Puede V. *conseguirme* or *procurarme* un ejemplar de ese libro?	Can you *get* me a copy of that book?
Se hizo de un caballo para el viaje.	He *got* (*i. e.*, bought) a horse for his journey.

22. As for *to get*, used redundantly (and incorrectly) with the verb *to have*, it disappears in the Spanish translation; as,

Tenemos uno.	We have *got* one.

23. The above remarks are equally applicable to all verbs of the class alluded to, as for instance *to become*; which latter, as well as *to get*, is often elegantly translated by *llegar á ser*; as,

Se hizo ciudadano de los Estados Unidos.	He *became* a citizen of the United States.
Llegó á ser hombre muy distinguido.	He *became* a very distinguished man

RECAPITULACION
DE LAS REGLAS DE LA GRAMÁTICA.

LECCION I.

1. ¿En qué letras acaban los infinitivos de todos los verbos en español?
— ¿Cuántas conjugaciones hay?

2. ¿Cómo se llaman las letras que anteceden (*precede*) á las terminaciones *ar*, *er*, *ir*?

3. ¿Cómo se forman las conjugaciones de todos los verbos regulares de la lengua?
— ¿Se puede suprimir el pronombre nominativo?
— ¿Porqué?
— ¿Puede suprimirse el pronombre *Usted*?

4. ¿En qué persona se pone el verbo cuando se emplea el pronombre *Usted*?
— ¿En qué casos se emplea la segunda persona del verbo? esto es, ¿cuándo se *tutea* en español?

LECCION II.

5. ¿Qué significa la palabra *señor* cuando se usa en vocativo?
— ¿Qué palabra se debe emplear en lugar de *señor* en el caso vocativo?
— ¿Cuándo se emplea la palabra *señor*?
— ¿Cuándo se emplean las palabras *señora*, *señorita* y *señorito*?

6. ¿De qué modo se usan los vocablos (*words*) *Don* y *Doña*?

7. ¿En dónde se coloca la negacion *no*, con respecto al verbo?

LECCION III.

8. ¿Cuándo se cambia la conjuncion *y* por la vocal *é*?

9. ¿Cuándo se escribe el acento sobre el *que*?

10. ¿En qué casos se traduce *but* por *sino?*

11. ¿En qué caso se traduce *but* por *pero?*

12. ¿Pueden las palabras *español, frances, bien,* y otras muchas, pertenecer á diferentes partes de la oracion (*speech*)?

LECCION IV.

13. ¿Cuándo rigen los verbos activos á su objeto con ayuda de la preposicion *á?*

14. ¿Qué preposicion sirve para denotar la posesion ó la materia de que una cosa está hecha?

15. ¿Qué nombres determina el artículo *el?*

— ¿Qué variacion sufre el artículo *el* cuando viene despues de la preposicion *á* ó *de?*

16. ¿Delante de qué parte de la oracion se coloca el artículo indefinido *un?*

— ¿Cuál es el uso de la palabra *uno?*

LECCION V.

17. ¿Cuántos géneros hay en español?

— ¿Cuándo se emplea el artículo femenino *una?*

18. ¿Cómo se traduce *your?*

LECCION VI.

19. ¿En qué letra acaban todos los verbos en la primera persona de indicativo?

— ¿En qué se diferencia la segunda conjugacion de la primera, en el presente de indicativo?

20 ¿Cómo se traduce *muy?*

21. ¿Cómo se forma la terminacion femenina de los nombres acabados en *o?*

LECCION VII.

22. ¿Cómo forman su terminacion femenina los adjetivos que acaban en *o, an* ú *on?*

— ¿Y los gentilicios?

— ¿En dónde se colocan generalmente los adjetivos con respecto á los sustantivos?

— ¿En dónde se colocan los adjetivos usados metafóricamente (*metaphorically*)?

— ¿Pierden algunos adjetivos su última letra ó sílaba cuando se colocan delante de los sustantivos?

LECCION VIII.

23. ¿En qué se diferencian las terminaciones de la segunda y tercera conjugacion en el presente de indicativo?

24. ¿Cuándo se cambia la conjuncion *ó* por la letra *ú?*

25. ¿Cómo se traduce *neither* y *nor?*

26. ¿Cómo se forma el plural de los nombres?

27. ¿Concuerda el adjetivo con el sustantivo?

28. ¿Concuerda el artículo con el nombre á que se refiere?

— ¿Qué nombres femeninos toman el artículo masculino?

29. ¿Cuándo se usa el artículo neutro *lo?*

LECCION IX.

30. ¿Cómo forman el plural los nombres *papá, mamá* y *pié?*

31. ¿Cómo forman el plural los nombres de mas de una sílaba que acaban en *s*, tales como *lúnes, mártes?*

— ¿Cuál es el plural de *juez, lápiz,* y demás nombres que acaban en *z?*

32. ¿Cómo se forma el plural de los nombres compuestos?

33. ¿Cuándo toman artículo los dias de la semana?

34. ¿Qué lugar ocupan en la oracion los adverbios *dónde, adónde* y *cuándo?*

35. ¿Cuándo requieren el acento los adverbios *donde, adonde* y *cuando?*

LECCION X.

36. ¿Qué son verbos irregulares?

— ¿Qué se advierte acerca de *tener* y los demás verbos auxiliares?

— ¿Cómo se traduce los pronombres, régimen directo de un verbo inglés?

37. ¿Cómo se usará del *le* y el *lo* en el caso acusativo, esto es, como régimen directo?

— ¿Cómo se traducen en algunos casos *it* y *so?*

38. ¿Requieren el artículo los pronombres interrogativos *quién, cuál, qué, de quién?*

39. Cuando en una pregunta está regido un pronombre interrogativo por una preposicion ¿qué debe hacerse en la respuesta?

LECCION XI.

40. ¿Cuándo se emplea *álguien*, y cuándo *alguno?*
— ¿En qué caso se traducirá *any one*, ó *anybody* por *cualquiera?*

41. ¿Cómo se usa de *nadie* y *ninguno?*

42. ¿Cuándo pierden *alguno* y *ninguno* la *o* final?

43. ¿En qué caso se usará de *algo* y *alguna cosa?*

44. ¿Cuándo se usará de *nada* y *ninguna cosa?*

45. ¿Qué negaciones se colocan delante del verbo?
— ¿Qué efecto producen en español, dos negativas en la misma sentencia?

46. ¿En qué casos no se traduce el artículo indefinido *a* ó *an?*

LECCION XII.

47. ¿Cuándo se usa del verbo *haber* y cuándo del verbo *tener?*
— ¿Cómo se traducen los auxiliares *to have* y *to be* seguidos de un infinitivo?

48. ¿En qué casos se emplea el *pretérito indefinido?*

LECCION XIII.

49. ¿De qué modo forman su terminacion femenina los pronombres *mio, tuyo, suyo, nuestro, vuestro?*

50. ¿Qué concordancia tienen los pronombres posesivos?

51. ¿En dónde se colocan y qué letras pierden cuando se usan como adjetivos pronominales?

52. ¿En dónde se coloca el pronombre *mio*, cuando se usa en el caso vocativo?

53. ¿Qué concordancia tienen los adjetivos posesivos cuando se usan como pronombres?

— ¿Requieren el artículo en esta caso?

54. ¿Qué artículo requieren cuando se usan de un modo indefinido?

55. ¿Cuándo se omite el artículo con los pronombres posesivos?

56. ¿Cuándo se emplean los pronombres *vuestro* y *vuestra*?

LECCION XIV.

57. ¿Qué órden se sigue en la formacion de los números compuestos?

58. ¿Cuáles son los números declinables?

59. ¿Cuándo pierde *uno* la letra *o*?

60. ¿Qué concordancia tiene *ciento* y cuándo pierde la última sílaba?

LECCION XV.

61. ¿Qué concordancia tienen los números ordinales y dónde se colocan?

— ¿Qué números ordinales pierden su última letra?

62. ¿Qué números ordinales se usan y cuándo?

LECCION XVI.

63. ¿Cuándo se usa el *pretérito definido*, y en qué se diferencia del *pretérito indefinido*?

64. ¿Qué significa la preposicion *ante*?

65. ¿Cómo se usan los adverbios *mas* y *ménos*, y en dónde se colocan en la oracion?

LECCION XVII.

66. ¿De qué modo se emplea el pronombre relativo *quien*?

67. ¿Cuándo se traduce *who* por *que* y cuándo por *quien*?

68. ¿*Cual* y *que* pueden referirse á personas y cosas?

69. ¿Con qué palabra concuerda *cuyo*?

— ¿Qué especie de pronombre es?

70. ¿Se usa del pronombre relativo en español del mismo modo que en inglés; esto es, precedido ó no de una preposicion?

71. ¿Puede suprimirse el pronombre relativo?

LECCION XVIII.

72. ¿Cómo se declinan los pronombres demostrativos *este, ese, aquel*?

73. ¿En qué caso se emplea *este*?

74. ¿Qué sucedia en lo antiguo cuando *este* y *ese* precedian al adjetivo *otro*?

75. ¿Cómo se emplean los pronombres demostrativos en su calidad de adjetivos?

76. ¿Cómo se traducen las palabras *the former* y *the latter*?

77. ¿Cómo se traduce el pronombre demostrativo inglés *that*, seguido de la preposicion *of*, ó de cualquiera de los relativos *who* ó *which*?

78. ¿Cómo se traducen generalmente los pronombres personales ingleses, cuando van seguidos de un relativo?

79. ¿Qué diferencia hay entre el significado de los adverbios *aquí* y *allí*, y *acá* y *allá*?

LECCION XIX.

80. ¿Cuándo debe usarse de la preposicion *para*, y cuándo de *por*?

81. ¿Cuál es el significado de la preposicion *entre*?

82. ¿Cuál es el significado de la preposicion *hasta*?

LECCION XX.

83. ¿Cuándo pierden los adverbios *tanto* y *cuanto* su última sílaba?

84. ¿Cómo se forma el comparativo de *igualdad*?

85. ¿En qué caso puede emplearse *cuan*?

86. ¿Cómo se forma el comparativo de *superioridad*?

87. ¿Cómo se forma el comparativo de *inferioridad?*

88. ¿Porqué los adjetivos *mayor, menor, mejor y peor*, no necesitan de las palabras *mas* ó *ménos*, para formar sus grados de comparacion?

89. ¿En qué caso se traduce *than* por *de* y en cuál otro por *qué?*

90. ¿Pueden tambien formar grados de comparacion los nombres, verbos y adverbios?

LECCION XXI.

91. ¿Cómo se traducen los superlativos ingleses que acaban por *est*, ó se forman con la palabra *most?*

92. ¿En qué caso se traduce *most*, ó *most of*, por *la mayor parte?*

93. ¿Qué preposicion corresponde en español al *in* inglés despues de un superlativo?

94. Los superlativos que se forman en inglés por medio de *most, very*, &c., ¿cómo se forman en español?

95. ¿Cuándo pierden los adjetivos la última vocal?

96. ¿Dígame V. lo que se advierte acerca de los superlativos en *érrimo?*

97. ¿Qué adjetivos cambian sus letras finales ántes de recibir la terminacion *ísimo?*

98. ¿Cuáles son los superlativos en *ísimo* formados irregularmente?

99. ¿Cuáles son los comparativos y superlativos irregulares?

100. ¿Cuándo admiten grados de comparacion los sustantivos?

LECCION XXII.

101. ¿Qué se advierte acerca de los verbos *ser* y *estar?*

102. ¿Cuándo se traduce el verbo *to be*, por *ser*, y cuándo por *estar?*

— ¿Cuáles son los verbos cuyos gerundios no admiten el verbo *estar* como auxiliar?

LECCION XXIII.

103. ¿Cuándo se emplea el *futuro simple?*

104. ¿Cómo se usan los numerales que indican las horas del dia?

105. ¿Porqué palabra se traduce *evening* ó *night?*

106. ¿En qué caso no rige al subjuntivo la conjuncion *si?*

LECCION XXIV.

107. ¿Cuándo se emplea el *futuro compuesto?*

108. ¿Cómo se traduce en inglés *acabar de?*

109. ¿En qué letra acaban en español la mayor parte de las palabras que en inglés terminan en *tion?*

110. ¿Con qué números se cuentan los dias del mes?

LECCION XXV.

111. ¿Qué diferencia se encuentra en el significado de los verbos *saber* y *conocer?*

112. ¿Qué diferencia existe entre los adverbios *aun, ya* y *todavia?*

— ¿Cómo se traduce *once, twice,* etc.?

— ¿Qué se observa en el uso de la palabras *miedo, valor, vergüenza, lástima,* y *tiempo?*

113. Cuando el verbo *to be* precede á los adjetivos *hungry, thirsty, afraid, ashamed, right, wrong, cold, sleepy,* ¿qué verbo se emplea en español?

114. ¿Cómo se emplean *jamás* y *nunca?*

LECCION XXVI.

115. ¿En dónde se colocan los pronombres nominativos con respecto al verbo?

116. ¿Qué peculiaridad se nota en los pronombres personales?

117. ¿En dónde se coloca el *complemento directo* (*objective case*) cuando no le precede una preposicion, y el verbo está en infinitivo ó imperativo?

118. ¿En qué tiempos pierde el verbo la letra final cuando se le añade uno de los pronombres *nos* ú *os?*

— ¿Con que objeto se hace esto?

119. ¿Cuándo podrá colocarse el pronombre complemento directo despues del verbo en el modo indicativo ó subjuntivo?

RECAPITULACION.

120. Cuando un verbo rija á otro en infinitivo, ¿en dónde se colocará el pronombre objeto?

121. ¿Qué caso rigen las preposiciones expresas?

122. ¿Qué se nota cuando la preposicion *con* antecede á los pronombres *mí, ti, sí?*

123. ¿Cuándo se usa de la preposicion *entre* con el caso nominativo?

124. ¿Qué pronombre complemento (*i. e.*, 1st objective or 2d objective case) se usa despues de los comparativos?

125. Cuando en inglés el caso objetivo de la primera ó segunda persona es el régimen del verbo ó de la preposicion *to*, tácita (*understood*) ó expresa, ¿cómo se traduce?

126. ¿Cómo se traduce el complemento indirecto inglés de la tercera persona?

LECCION XXVII.

127. Cuando la tercera persona va regida de la preposicion *to* en inglés, tácita ó expresa, siendo el régimen del verbo un pronombre de la tercera persona, ¿por qué palabra se traduce?

— ¿Cuál es la razon de esto?

128. En caso de encontrarse en una sentencia dos pronombres, uno complemento directo y el otro indirecto, ¿cuál se coloca primero?

129. ¿Y cuándo el régimen del verbo es un pronombre reflexivo?

130. ¿Qué se observa cuando, para dar mas energía á la frase, se ponen dos pronombres de la misma persona?

131. ¿Qué debe observarse con respecto á las frases, *á él quiero, á ti amo?*

132. ¿Qué se debe tener presente para no confundir los pronombres personales *él, la, lo, los* y *las*, con los artículos *el, la, lo, los* y *las?*

133. ¿Para qué sirve el adjetivo *mismo?*

LECCION XXVIII.

134. ¿Cuándo se usa el *imperfecto?*

135. ¿Cuándo se usa el *pluscuamperfecto?*

136. ¿Cómo se traducen las expresiones *to have just* y *to be just* delante de un participio pasado?

LECCION XXIX.

137. ¿Cuándo se usa el pretérito anterior?

138. ¿De dónde se derivan los adverbios de modo y calidad?

139. ¿Cómo se forman los adverbios que se derivan de adjetivos?

140. ¿Qué adverbios admiten grados de comparacion?

141. ¿Qué adverbios pueden sustituirse sin cambiar de significado?

LECCION XXX.

142. ¿Qué son verbos impersonales?

143. ¿En qué caso se usan los verbos *amanecer* y *anochecer* en las tres personas?

144. ¿Cómo se traducen en inglés los verbos *haber* y *hacer* cuando se usan como impersonales?

— ¿Qué se observa con respecto á la primera persona del presente de indicativo del verbo *haber*, usado impersonalmente?

— ¿Hay otros verbos que pueden usarse como impersonales?

145. ¿En qué caso no se traduce el pronombre inglés *it?*

— ¿Requieren artículo los nombres tomados en sentido indefinido?

— ¿Toman el artículo los nombres usados en toda la extension de su significado?

146. ¿Llevan artículo los nombres de naciones, países, provincias, montes, rios y estaciones?

147. ¿Cuándo no admiten artículo los nombres de naciones, países y provincias, etc.

— ¿Cuáles requieren siempre el artículo?

LECCION XXXI.

148. ¿Cómo se conjuga el verbo *gustar* cuando significa *to please?*

149. ¿Qué significa el verbo *gustar* seguido de la preposicion *de?*

150. ¿Qué significa y cómo se conjuga el verbo *gustar* como verbo activo?

151. ¿Qué otros verbos requieren la misma construccion idiomática del verbo *gustar*?

152. ¿Qué se observa en la conjugacion del verbo *pesar* cuando significa *to regret*?

LECCION XXXII.

153. ¿Cómo se forma la voz pasiva?

— ¿Cuándo se forma con el verbo *estar*?

154. ¿En qué caso no podrá usarse la voz pasiva con el verbo *ser* en el presente y el imperfecto de indicativo?

155. ¿Cuándo se usará de la preposicion *de* y cuándo de *por* en la voz pasiva?

156-157. ¿En qué casos se forma la voz pasiva con el pronombre *se*?

LECCION XXXIII.

158. ¿Cómo se conjugan los verbos reflexivos?

159. ¿Cuándo se usa la forma reflexiva?

160. ¿Cómo se conjugan los verbos recíprocos?

LECCION XXXIV.

161. ¿Qué constituye la irregularidad de los verbos?

162. ¿Qué debe tenerse presente para no confundir con los verbos irregulares algunos que aunque sufren un cambio ortográfico no dejan por eso de ser regulares?

163. ¿Qué cambio sufren los verbos que acaban en *eer*?

164. ¿Qué cambio se nota en los que acaban en *uir*?

165. ¿En cuántas clases ó grupos se dividen los verbos irregulares?

166. ¿Qué se observa en la construccion del verbo *pagar*?

LECCION XXXV.

167. ¿Cuál es la irregularidad del verbo *acostar*?

168. ¿Cuándo se usa el modo imperativo?

RECAPITULACION.

169. ¿Qué letras pierde, y en qué personas, el modo imperativo cuando se le añade el pronombres *nos* y *os*?

170. ¿En dónde se colocan los pronombres en español cuando el imperativo se usa en la forma negativa?

171. ¿Puede usarse el futuro de indicativo por el imperativo?

172. ¿Cómo se traducen en español los adjetivos ingleses acabados en *ous*?

173. ¿Y los nombres y adjetivos ingleses que acaban en *ic* ó *ical*?

LECCION XXXVI.

174. ¿Cuál es la irregularidad del verbo *mover*?

175. Cuando se usa del *se* como pronombre indefinido, ¿á qué palabras corresponde en inglés?

176. ¿Cuáles son las cuatro funciones que desempeña el pronombre *se*?

177. ¿Cómo se traducen en español los nombres ingleses que acaban en *ty*?

— ¿A qué género pertenecen estos nombres?

178. ¿Qué peculiaridad se nota en el verbo *doler*?

LECCION XXXVII.

179. ¿Cuál es la irregularidad del verbo *atender*?

180-181-182-183. ¿Cuándo se emplea el modo subjuntivo?

184. ¿Cuándo se usa el presente de subjuntivo?

185. ¿Cuándo se usa el perfecto de subjuntivo?

LECCION XXXVIII.

186. ¿Tienen los verbos españoles otro participio además del pasado?

— ¿Qué terminacion tienen los participios presentes, y cómo se usan?

187. ¿Cuándo se usan los gerundios?

188. ¿Cuál es el auxiliar de los gerundios?

189. ¿Cómo se traduce en español el participio presente inglés, precedido de una preposicion?

190. ¿Puede usarse el infinitivo como nombre verbal?

191. ¿Cómo se traduce en inglés el infinitivo español, regido por otro verbo?

LECCION XXXIX.

192. ¿Cuál es la irregularidad del verbo *pedir?*

193. ¿Cuáles son las formas mas usuales para saludar?

LECCION XL.

194. ¿Cuál es la irregularidad del verbo *conducir?*

195. ¿Qué se nota sobre la palabra *segun?*

196. ¿Cómo concuerdan los nombres colectivos?

LECCION XLI.

197. ¿Qué son verbos defectivos?

198. ¿En qué personas y cuándo se usa el verbo *yacer?*

199. ¿En qué tiempos se usa el verbo *soler* y qué peculiaridad se nota en él?

200. ¿Qué significacion tiene la preposicion *desde?*

201. ¿Cómo se usa la preposicion *contra?*

202. ¿Cuál es la significacion de la preposicion *sobre?*

203. ¿Cuál es la significacion de la preposicion *tras?*

204. ¿Cuándo se usa de la conjuncion *pues?*

LECCION XLII

205. ¿En qué se dividen las conjunciones?

206. ¿Qué debe observarse acerca del régimen de las conjunciones?

207. ¿Qué conjunciones rigen el verbo al modo subjuntivo?

208. ¿Cuáles le rigen al modo infinitivo?

209. ¿Cuáles le rigen al modo indicativo?

LECCION XLIII.

210. ¿Cuándo se emplea el imperfecto de subjuntivo, y cuándo el pluscuamperfecto?

211. ¿Cómo se traducen en español los auxiliares *may, might, can, could, will, would* y *should*?

212. ¿De qué manera expresa la accion del verbo el imperfecto de subjuntivo?

213. ¿De qué manera la representa el pluscuamperfecto?

LECCION XLIV.

214. ¿Qué son nombres aumentativos y diminutivos, y cómo se forman?

215. ¿Hay algunos nombres que forman sus diminutivos con otras terminaciones distintas de las designadas por este objeto?

216. ¿Pueden formarse diminutivos con otras partes de la oracion?

217. ¿Qué nombres primitivos no admiten algunas de las terminaciones designadas?

218. ¿A qué nombres se designa con el de *despreciativos*?

LECCION XLV.

219. ¿Cómo representa la accion del verbo el futuro simple de subjuntivo?

220. ¿Cuándo puede sustituirse el presente de subjuntivo al futuro simple?

221. ¿Cómo representa la accion del verbo el futuro compuesto de subjuntivo?

222. ¿Cuándo puede sustituírsele el perfecto de subjuntivo?

223. ¿Qué debe tenerse presente para no confundir el imperfecto y pluscuamperfecto del modo subjuntivo, con el futuro simple y compuesto del mismo modo?

224. Cuando el verbo que está en futuro simple ó compuesto funciona como verbo determinante ¿á qué modo y tiempos puede regir al verbo determinado?

LECCION XLVI.

225-226. ¿Qué son conjunciones, y cuál es el significado de las principales?

LECCION XLVII.

227. ¿Qué partes de la oracion pueden llevar artículo?

228. ¿Llevan artículo los nombres comunes que se usan en toda la extension de su significacion?

229. ¿Se pone artículo delante de los nombres de imperios, reinos, provincias y países?

— ¿Cuándo se omite?

230. ¿Cuándo requieren artículo los nombres de medidas, pesos, &c.

231. ¿Cuándo se repite el artículo?

232. ¿En qué caso se pone el artículo delante de los nombres que expresan rango, oficio, profesion ó título de personas?

233. ¿En qué caso se usa el artículo en lugar del adjetivo posesivo?

234. ¿En qué caso se usa el artículo, como en inglés?

LECCION XLVIII.

235. ¿Cómo se corresponden los verbos cuando estan unidos por un relativo?

236. ¿Cuándo se pone en infinitivo el verbo determinado?

237. Si el verbo determinante fuere *ser*, ó cualquiera de los impersonales, ¿en qué modo se pondrá el verbo determinado, en el caso de carecer este de sugeto?

— ¿Porqué sucede esto así?

238. Y cuando dicho verbo tuviere sugeto, ¿en qué modo se pondrá?

— Los verbos que expresan mandato, ¿á qué modo rigen el verbo determinado?

239. Cuando el verbo determinante está en infinitivo, en presente ó futuro de indicativo, ó en imperativo unido al verbo determinado por una conjuncion ¿en que modo se pone este último?

240. ¿A qué modo y en qué tiempos rige al verbo determinado el

determinante, cuando este último se encuentra en el pretérito indefinido ó en el futuro compuesto de indicativo?

241. Cuando el nominativo es el mismo para ámbos verbos y el determinante se encuentra en indicativo, ¿á que modo rige este al determinado?

LECCION XLIX.

242. ¿Qué son nombres derivados?

243, 244, 245, 246, 247, 248, 249, 250, 251, 252. ¿Qué denotan, y cuáles son las principales terminaciones?

LECCION L.

253. ¿Cómo se forman los nombres compuestos?

LECCION LI.

254. ¿Cuál es la construccion natural?

255. ¿Cuál es la figurada?

256. ¿De cuántos modos puede construirse una frase?

257. ¿Qué construccion es la preferible?

LECCION LII.

258. ¿Conservan algunos participios el régimen de sus verbos?

259. ¿Cuál es la concordancia del participio pasado?

260. Cuando un verbo tiene dos participios pasados, uno regular y otro irregular, ¿cómo se emplean?

261. ¿Cuáles son los participios pasados irregulares que se pueden usar con el verbo haber?

262. ¿Qué irregularidad peculiar tiene el verbo *morir?*

263. ¿Hay algunos participios pasados ó pasivos que toman una significacion activa?

264. ¿Pueden algunos participios pasados hacer las veces de sustantivo?

265. ¿Qué se debe observar acerca de otros tiempos que algunos gramáticos agregan al modo infinitivo?

LECCION LIII.

266. ¿Qué son modismos ó idiotismos?

— ¿Cómo se traducen en español las frases en que la preposicion inglesa toma un significado diferente de aquel que generalmente se le atribuye?

LECCION LIV.

267. ¿Cómo se traducen en español las conjunciones inglesas que se usan frecuentemente en lugar de otras palabras?

268. ¿Hay tambien en español conjunciones que se usan en lugar de otras palabras?

— ¿Cuáles son los principales usos de la conjuncion *si*?

LECCION LV.

269. ¿Cuáles son los principales usos de la conjuncion *que*?

LECCION LVI.

270. ¿Cuáles son las formas mas usuales para principiar y acabar cartas?

LECCION LVII.

271. ¿Qué se advierte acerca de las preposiciones que cambian su significado de los verbos á que se juntan?

LECCION LVIII.

272. ¿Cómo se traducen los verbos *to be glad* y *to be rejoiced at*?

273. ¿Cómo se traducen los verbos *to be sorry* y *to grieve*?

274. ¿Cómo se emplea el verbo *caber*?

LECCION LIX.

275. ¿A qué modismos se prestan los verbos *caer, dar, decir* y *echar*?

LECCION LX.

276. ¿Cuáles son los principales idiotismos á que se prestan los verbos *entrar, hacer, ir, llevar, mandar, oler á, saber á, salir, servir, tardar* y *volver*?

COMPLETE LIST

OF THE

CONJUGATIONS OF ALL THE SPANISH VERBS, AUXILIARY, REGULAR, IRREGULAR, REFLECTIVE, IMPERSONAL AND DEFECTIVE, WITH AN EXAMPLE OF THE PASSIVE VOICE.

AUXILIARY VERBS.

INFINITIVE.

PRESENT.

To have.			*To be.*	
Haber.	Tener.		Ser.	Estar.

GERUND.

Having.			*Being.*	
Habiendo.	Teniendo.		Siendo.	Estando.

PAST PARTICIPLE.

Had.			*Been.*	
Habido.	Tenido.		Sido.	Estado.

INDICATIVE.

PRESENT.

	I have.		*I am.*	
1. He.	Tengo.		Soy.	Estoy.
2. Has.	Tienes.		Eres.	Estas.
3. Ha.	Tiene.		Es.	Está
1. Hemos.	Tenemos.		Somos.	Estamos.
2. Habeis.	Teneis.		Sois.	Estais.
3. Han.	Tienen.		Son.	Estan.

IMPERFECT.

	I had.		*I was.*	
1. Habia.	Tenia.		Era.	Estaba.
2. Habias.	Tenias.		Eras.	Estabas.
3. Habia.	Tenia.		Era.	Estaba.

1. Habiamos.	Teniamos.	Eramos.	Estabamos.
2. Habiais.	Teniais.	Erais.	Estabais.
3. Habian.	Tenian.	Eran.	Estaban.

PRETERIT DEFINITE.

I had.   *I was.*

1. Hube.	Tuve.	Fuí.	Estuve.
2. Hubiste.	Tuviste.	Fuiste.	Estuviste.
3. Hubo.	Tuvo.	Fué.	Estuvo.
1. Hubimos.	Tuvimos.	Fuimos.	Estuvimos.
2. Hubisteis.	Tuvisteis.	Fuisteis.	Estuvisteis.
3. Hubieron.	Tuvieron.	Fueron.	Estuvieron.

FUTURE SIMPLE.

I shall have.   *I shall be.*

1. Habré.	Tendré.	Seré.	Estaré.
2. Habrás.	Tendrás.	Serás.	Estarás.
3. Habrá.	Tendrá.	Será.	Estará.
1. Habrémos.	Tendrémos.	Serémos.	Estarémos.
2. Habréis.	Tendréis.	Seréis.	Estaréis.
3. Habrán.	Tendrán.	Serán.	Estarán.

IMPERATIVE.

Let me have.   *Let me be.*

2. Have thou.	Ten tú.	Sé.	Está.
3. Let him have.	Tenga él.	Sea.	Esté.
1. Let us have.	Tengamos.	Seamos.	Estemos.
2. Have ye.	Tened.	Sed.	Estad.
3. Let them have.	Tengan.	Sean.	Esten.

SUBJUNCTIVE.
PRESENT.

I may have.   *I may be.*

1. Haya.	Tenga.	Sea.	Esté.
2. Hayas.	Tengas.	Seas.	Estes.
3. Haya.	Tenga.	Sea.	Esté.
1. Hayamos.	Tengamos.	Seamos.	Estemos.
2. Hayais.	Tengais.	Seais.	Esteis.
3. Hayan.	Tengan.	Sean.	Esten.

CONJUGATIONS.

IMPERFECT.—*First Termination.**

	I would have.		*I would be.*
1. Habria.	Tendria.	Seria.—	Estaria.
2. Habrias.	Tendrias.	Serias.	Estarias.
3. Habria.	Tendria.	Seria.	Estaria.
1. Habriamos.	Tendriamos.	Seriamos.	Estariamos.
2. Habriais.	Tendriais.	Seriais.	Estariais.
3. Habrian.	Tendrian.	Serian.	Estarian.

Second Termination.

	I would have.		*I would be.*
1. Hubiera.	Tuviera.	Fuera.	Estuviera.
2. Hubierais.	Tuvieras.	Fueras.	Estuvieras.
3. Hubiera.	Tuviera.	Fuera.	Estuviera.
1. Hubieramos.	Tuvieramos.	Fueramos.	Estuvieramos.
2. Hubierais.	Tuvierais.	Fuerais.	Estuvierais.
3. Hubieran.	Tuvieran.	Fueran.	Estuvieran.

Third Termination.

	I should have.		*I should be.*
1. Hubiese.	Tuviese.	Fuese.	Estuviese.
2. Hubieses.	Tuvieses.	Fueses.	Estuvieses.
3. Hubiese.	Tuviese.	Fuese.	Estuviese.
1. Hubiesemos.	Tuviesemos.	Fuesemos.	Estuviesemos.
2. Hubieseis.	Tuvieseis.	Fueseis.	Estuvieseis.
3. Hubiesen.	Tuviesen.	Fuesen.	Estuviesen.

FUTURE.

	I might or should have.		*I might or should be.*
1. Hubiere.	Tuviere.	Fuere.	Estuviere.
2. Hubieres.	Tuvieres.	Fueres.	Estuvieres.
3. Hubiere.	Tuviere.	Fuere.	Estuviere.
1. Hubieremos.	Tuvieremos.	Fueremos.	Estuvieremos.
2. Hubiereis.	Tuviereis.	Fuereis.	Estuviereis.
3. Hubieren.	Tuvieren.	Fueren.	Estuvieren.

* It will be observed that, differing from almost all other grammars, we give *ria* as the first termination, this order appearing to us more logical and, above all, more grammatical, and more in accordance with the signification and uses of the three terminations.

MODELS OF THE THREE REGULAR CONJUGATIONS.

FIRST CONJUGATION.

INFINITIVE.

Hablar. | To speak.

GERUND.

Hablando. | Speaking.

PAST PARTICIPLE.

Hablado. | Spoken.

INDICATIVE.

PRESENT.

Singular.
1. Hablo.   I speak.
2. Hablas.
3. Habla.

Plural.
1. Hablamos.
2. Hablais.
3. Hablan.

IMPERFECT.

1. Hablaba.   I spoke, was speaking, &c.
2. Hablabas.
3. Hablaba.

1. Hablabamos.
2. Hablabais.
3. Hablaban.

PRETERIT DEFINITE.

1. Hablé.   I spoke.
2. Hablaste.
3. Habló.

1. Hablámos.
2. Hablasteis.
3. Hablaron.

FUTURE SIMPLE.

1. Hablaré.   I shall or will speak.
2. Hablarás.
3. Hablará.

1. Hablarémos.
2. Hablaréis.
3. Hablarán.

IMPERATIVE.

2. Habla.   Speak (thou).
3. Hable.

1. Hablemos.
2. Hablad.
3. Hablen.

SUBJUNCTIVE.

PRESENT.

1. Hable.	I may speak.	1. Hablemos.
2. Hables.		2. Hableis.
3. Hable.		3. Hablen.

IMPERFECT.—*First Termination.*

1. Hablaria.	I should or would speak.	1. Hablariamos.
2. Hablarias.		2. Hablariais.
3. Hablaria.		3. Hablarian.

Second Termination.

1. Hablara.	I might, could, would, or should speak.	1. Hablaramos.
2. Hablaras.		2. Hablarais.
3. Hablara.		3. Hablaran.

Third Termination.

1. Hablase.	I might, &c., speak.	1. Hablasemos.
2. Hablases.		2. Hablaseis.
3. Hablase.		3. Hablasen.

FUTURE.

1. Hablare.	I might, &c., speak.	1. Hablaremos.
2. Hablares.		2. Hablareis.
3. Hablare.		3. Hablaren.

SECOND CONJUGATION.

INFINITIVE.

Aprender. | To learn.

GERUND.

Aprendiendo. | Learning.

PAST PARTICIPLE.

Aprendido. | Learned.

INDICATIVE.

PRESENT.

1. Aprendo.	I learn.	1. Aprendemos.
2. Aprendes.		2. Aprendeis.
3. Aprende.		3. Aprenden.

IMPERFECT.

1. Aprendia.	I learned, was learning, &c.	1. Aprendiamos.
2. Aprendias.		2. Aprendiais.
3. Aprendia.		3. Aprendian.

PRETERIT DEFINITE.

1. Aprendí.	I learned.	1. Aprendimos.
2. Aprendiste.		2. Aprendisteis.
3. Aprendió.		3. Aprendieron.

FUTURE SIMPLE.

1. Aprenderé.	I shall or will learn.	1. Aprenderémos.
2. Aprenderás.		2. Aprenderéis.
3. Aprenderá.		3. Aprenderán.

IMPERATIVE.

		1. Aprendamos.
2. Aprende.	Learn (thou).	2. Aprended.
3. Aprenda.		3. Aprendan.

SUBJUNCTIVE.

PRESENT.

1. Aprenda.	I may learn.	1. Aprendamos.
2. Aprendas.		2. Aprendais.
3. Aprenda.		3. Aprendan.

IMPERFECT.—*First Termination.*

1. Aprenderia.	I would or should learn.	1. Aprenderiamos.
2. Aprenderias.		2. Aprenderiais.
3. Aprenderia.		3. Aprenderian.

CONJUGATIONS.

Second Termination.

1. Aprendiera.	I might, could, would, or should learn.	1. Aprendieramos.
2. Aprendieras.		2. Aprendierais.
3. Aprendiera.		3. Aprendieran.

Third Termination.

1. Aprendiese.	I might, &c., learn.	1. Aprendiesemos.
2. Aprendieses.		2. Aprendieseis.
3. Aprendiese.		3. Aprendiesen.

FUTURE.

1. Aprendiere.	I might, &c., learn.	1. Aprendieremos.
2. Aprendieres.		2. Aprendiereis.
3. Aprendiere.		3. Aprendieren.

THIRD CONJUGATION.

INFINITIVE.

Escribir.	To write.

GERUND.

Escribiendo.	Writing.

PAST PARTICIPLE.

Escrito.*	Written.

INDICATIVE.

PRESENT.

1. Escribo.	I write.	1. Escribimos.
2. Escribes.		2. Escribis.
3. Escribe.		3. Escriben.

IMPERFECT.

1. Escribia.	I wrote, was writing.	1. Escribiamos.
2. Escribias.		2. Escribiais.
3. Escribia.		3. Escribian.

* This is the only instance of irregularity in the verb *Escribir*.

PRETERIT DEFINITE.

1. Escribí. I wrote.   1. Escribímos.
2. Escribiste.   2. Escribisteis.
3. Escribió.   3. Escribieron.

FUTURE SIMPLE.

1. Escribiré. I shall (or will) write.   1. Escribirémos.
2. Escribirás.   2. Escribiréis.
3. Escribirá.   3. Escribirán.

IMPERATIVE.

                             1. Escribamos.
2. Escribe. Write (thou).   2. Escribid.
3. Escriba. Let him, &c., write.   3. Escriban.

SUBJUNCTIVE.

PRESENT.

1. Escriba. I may write.   1. Escribamos.
2. Escribas.   2. Escribais.
3. Escriba.   3. Escriban.

IMPERFECT.—*First Termination.*

1. Escribiria. I would (or should) write.   1. Escribiriamos.
2. Escribirias.   2. Escribiriais.
3. Escribiria.   3. Escribirian.

Second Termination.

1. Escribiera. I might, could, would, or should write.   1. Escribieramos.
2. Escribieras.   2. Escribierais.
3. Escribiera.   3. Escribieran.

Third Termination.

1. Escribiese. I might, could, would, or should write.   1. Escribiesemos.
2. Escribieses.   2. Escribieseis.
3. Escribiese.   3. Escribiesen.

CONJUGATIONS.

FUTURE.

1. Escribiere.   I might, &c., write.
2. Escribieres.
3. Escribiere.

1. Escribieremos.
2. Escribiereis.
3. Escribieren.

COMPOUND TENSES.

These are formed by joining the several tenses of the auxiliary *haber* to the past participle of the verb expressing the action.

INDICATIVE MOOD.

PRETERIT INDEFINITE.

I have spoken.
I have learned.
I have written.

Yo he hablado.
Yo he aprendido.
Yo he escrito.

1. He } hablado.
2. Has } aprendido.
3. Ha } escrito.

Hemos } hablado.
Habeis } aprendido.
Han   } escrito.

PLUPERFECT.

I had spoken.
I had learned.
I had written.

Yo habia hablado.
Yo habia aprendido.
Yo habia escrito.

1. Habia } hablado.
2. Habias } aprendido.
3. Habia } escrito.

Habiamos } hablado.
Habiais } aprendido.
Habian   } escrito.

PRETERIT ANTERIOR.

I had spoken.
I had learned.
I had written.

Yo hube hablado.
Yo hube aprendido.
Yo hube escrito.

1. Hube   } hablado.
2. Hubiste } aprendido.
3. Hubo   } escrito.

Hubimos } hablado.
Hubisteis } aprendido.
Hubieron } escrito.

COMPOUND FUTURE.

I shall have spoken.
I shall have learned.
I shall have written.

Yo habré hablado.
Yo habré aprendido.
Yo habré escrito.

1. Habré } hablado.
2. Habrás } aprendido.
3. Habrá } escrito. *

* The other compound tenses are conjugated in like manner.

THE SEVEN PRINCIPAL CLASSES OF IRREGULAR VERBS.

FIRST CLASS.

ACERTAR. | *To hit the mark.*

INDICATIVE.
PRESENT.

1. Acierto.   I hit the mark.   1. Acertamos.
2. Aciertas.   2. Acertais.
3. Acierta.   3. Aciertan.

IMPERATIVE.

                             1. Acertemos.
2. Acierta.   2. Acertad.
3. Acierte.   3. Acierten.

SUBJUNCTIVE.
PRESENT.

1. Acierte.   1. Acertemos.
2. Aciertes.   2. Acerteis.
3. Acierte.   3. Acierten.

The following verbs, and their compounds, are conjugated like ACERTAR:

Acrecentar.	To increase.	Derrengar.	To break the back.
Adestrar.	To render skilful.	Despernar.	To cut off the legs.
Alentar.	To breathe.	Despertar.	To awake.
Apacentar.	To feed.	Desterrar.	To banish.
Apretar.	To squeeze.	Empedrar.	To pave.
Arrendar.	To hire.	Empezar.	To begin.
Asentar.	To place.	Encerrar.	To lock up.
Aserrar.	To saw.	Encomendar.	To recommend.
Aterrar.	To throw down.	Enterrar.	To bury.
Atestar.	To stuff.	Escarmentar.	To take warning.
Atravesar.	To cross.	Fregar.	To rub.
Aventar.	To winnow.	Gobernar.	To govern.
Calentar.	To warm.	Helar.	To freeze.
Cegar.	To blind.	Herrar.	To shoe.
Cerrar.	To shut.	Invernar.	To winter.
Comenzar.	To commence.	Mentar.	To mention.
Concertar.	To agree.	Merendar.	To take a collation.
Confesar.	To confess.	Negar.	To deny.
Decentar.	To taste for the first time.	Nevar.	To snow.
		Pensar.	To think.

CONJUGATIONS.

Quebrar.	To break.	Sosegar.	To quiet.
Recomendar.	To recommend.	Soterrar.	To bury.
Regar.	To water.	Temblar.	To tremble.
Reventar.	To burst.	Tentar.	To tempt.
Segar.	To cut down.	Trasegar.	To rake.
Sembrar.	To sow.	Tropezar.	To stumble.
Sentar.	To set.		

SECOND CLASS.

ACOSTAR. | To put in bed.

INDICATIVE.

PRESENT.

1. Acuesto.	I put in bed.	1. Acostamos.	
2. Acuestas.		2. Acostais.	
3. Acuesta.		3. Acuestan.	

IMPERATIVE.

	1. Acostemos.
2. Acuesta.	2. Acostad.
3. Acueste.	3. Acuesten.

SUBJUNCTIVE.

PRESENT.

1. Acueste.	1. Acostemos.
2. Acuestes.	2. Acosteis.
3. Acueste.	3. Acuesten.

The following verbs, and their compounds, are conjugated like ACOSTAR:

Acordar.	To agree.	Consolar.	To console.
Agorar.	To divine.	Contar.	To count.
Almorzar.	To breakfast.	Costar.	To cost.
Amolar.	To grind.	Degollar.	To behead.
Aporcar.	To hoe.	Demostrar.	To demonstrate.
Apostar.	To bet.	Descollar.	To surpass.
Aprobar.	To approve.	Desconsolar.	To discourage.
Asolar.	To waste.	Desolar.	To desolate.
Atronar.	To thunder.	Desollar.	To skin.
Avergonzar.	To shame.	Desvergonzarse.	To be impudent.
Colar.	To strain.	Emporcar.	To dirty.
Colgar.	To hang.	Encordar.	To string.
Comprobar.	To verify.	Encontrar.	To meet.

17*

Engrosar.	To engross.	Resollar.	To breathe.
Forzar.	To force.	Rodar.	To roll.
Holgar.	To rest.	Rogar.	To entreat.
Hollar.	To tread.	Soldar.	To solder.
Mostrar.	To show.	Soltar.	To lessen.
Poblar.	To people.	Sonar.	To sound.
Probar.	To prove.	Soñar.	To dream.
Recordar.	To remind.	Tostar.	To toast.
Recostar.	To lie down.	Trocar.	To barter.
Regoldar.	To belch.	Tronar.	To thunder.
Renovar.	To renew.	Volar.	To fly.
Reprobar.	To reprove.	Volcar.	To overturn.
Rescontar.	To compensate.		

THIRD CLASS.

Mover. | To move.

INDICATIVE.
PRESENT.

1. Muevo. | 1. Movemos.
2. Mueves. | 2. Moveis.
3. Mueve. | 3. Mueven.

IMPERATIVE.

  | 1. Movamos.
2. Mueve. | 2. Moved.
3. Mueva. | 3. Muevan.

SUBJUNCTIVE.
PRESENT.

1. Mueva. | 1. Movamos.
2. Muevas. | 2. Movais.
3. Mueva. | 3. Muevan.

The following verbs, and their compounds, are conjugated like Mover.

Absolver.	To absolve.	Morder.	To bite.
Disolver.	To dissolve.	Retorcer.	To twist again.
Doler.	To grieve.	Solver.	To solve.
Llover.	To rain.	Torcer.	To twist.
Moler.	To grind.	Volver.	To turn.

FOURTH CLASS.

Atender. | *To attend.*

INDICATIVE.
PRESENT.

1. Atiendo.	1. Atendemos.
2. Atiendes.	2. Atendeis.
3. Atiende.	3. Atienden.

IMPERATIVE.

	1. Atendamos.
2. Atiende.	2. Atended.
3. Atienda.	3. Atiendan.

SUBJUNCTIVE.
PRESENT.

1. Atienda.	1. Atendamos.
2. Atiendas.	2. Atendais.
3. Atienda.	3. Atiendan.

The following verbs, and their compounds, have the same irregularities as ATENDER:

Ascender.	To ascend.	Entender.	To understand.
Cerner.	To sift.	Extender.	To extend.
Condescender.	To condescend.	Heder.	To stink.
Contender.	To contend.	Hender.	To split.
Defender.	To defend.	Perder.	To lose.
Desatender.	To neglect.	Tender.	To stretch out.
Descender.	To descend.	Trascender.	To transcend.
Encender.	To kindle.	Verter.	To pour out.

FIFTH CLASS.

SENTIR. | *To feel.*

INDICATIVE.
PRESENT.

1. Siento.	1. Sentimos.
2. Sientes.	2. Sentis.
3. Siente.	3. Sienten.

IMPERATIVE.

	1. Sintamos.
2. Siente.	2. Sentid.
3. Sienta.	3. Sientan.

SUBJUNCTIVE.
PRESENT.

1. Sienta.	1. Sintamos.
2. Sientas.	2. Sintais.
3. Sienta.	3. Sientan.

IMPERFECT.
First Termination.
1. Sentiria, &c.

Second Termination.

1. Sintiera.	1. Sintieramos.
2. Sintieras.	2. Sintierais.
3. Sintiera.	3. Sintieran.

Third Termination.

1. Sintiese.	1. Sintiesemos.
2. Sintieses.	2. Sintieseis.
3. Sintiese.	3. Sintiesen.

FUTURE.

1. Sintiere.	1. Sintieremos.
2. Sintieres.	2. Sintiereis.
3. Sintiere.	3. Sintieren.

The following verbs, and their compounds, have the same irregularities as SENTIR:

Adherir.	To adhere.	Digerir.	To digest.
Advertir.	To advert.	Herir.	To wound.
Arrepentirse.	To repent.	Hervir.	To boil.
Asentir.	To assent.	Ingerir.	To ingraft.
Conferir.	To confer.	Invertir.	To invert.
Consentir.	To consent.	Pervertir.	To pervert.
Controvertir.	To controvert.	Preferir.	To prefer.
Convertir.	To convert.	Referir.	To refer.
Diferir.	To defer.	Requerir.	To require.
Diferir.	To differ.		

SIXTH CLASS.

PEDIR.   *To ask.*

INDICATIVE.
PRESENT.

1. Pido.	1. Pedimos.
2. Pides.	2. Pedis.
3. Pide.	3. Piden.

PRETERIT.

1. Pedí.	1. Pedimos.
2. Pediste.	2. Pedisteis.
3. Pidió.	3. Pidieron.

IMPERATIVE.

2. Pide.	1. Pidamos.
3. Pida.	2. Pedid.
	3. Pidan.

SUBJUNCTIVE.

PRESENT.

1. Pida.	1. Pidamos.
2. Pidas.	2. Pidais.
3. Pida.	3. Pidan.

IMPERFECT.—*First Termination.*

1. Pediria, &c.

Second Termination.

1. Pidiera.	1. Pidieramos.
2. Pidieras.	2. Pidierais.
3. Pidiera.	3. Pidieran.

Third Termination.

1. Pidiese.	1. Pidiesemos.
2. Pidieses.	2. Pidieseis.
3. Pidiese.	3. Pidiesen.

FUTURE.

1. Pidiere.	1. Pidieremos.
2. Pidieres.	2. Pidiereis.
3. Pidiere.	3. Pidieren.

The following verbs, and their compounds, have the same irregularities as PEDIR:

Arrecir.	To benumb.	Gemir.	To groan.
Ceñir.	To belt.	Medir.	To measure.
Colejir.	To collect.	Regir.	To rule.
Competir.	To contend.	Rendir.	To render.
Concebir.	To conceive.	Reñir.	To quarrel.
Constreñir.	To constrain.	Repetir.	To repeat.
Derretir.	To melt.	Seguir.	To follow.
Desleir.	To dissolve.	Servir.	To serve.
Elejir.	To elect.	Teñir.	To dye.
Embestir.	To attack.	Vestir.	To dress.

SEVENTH CLASS.

CONDUCIR. | *To conduct.*

INDICATIVE.
PRESENT.

1. Conduzco.
2. Conduces, &c.

1. Conducimos.
2. Conducis, &c.

PRETERIT.

1. Conduje.
2. Condujiste.
3. Condujo.

1. Condujimos.
2. Condujisteis.
3. Condujeron.

IMPERATIVE.

2. Conduce.
3. Conduzca.

1. Conduzcamos.
2. Conducid.
3. Conduzcan.

SUBJUNCTIVE.
PRESENT.

1. Conduzca, &c. | 1. Conduzcamos, &c.

IMPERFECT.—*First Termination.*

1. Conduciria, &c. | 1. Conduciriamos, &c.

Second Termination.

1. Condujera, &c. | 1. Condujeramos, &c.

Third Termination.

1. Condujese, &c. | 1. Condujesemos, &c.

FUTURE.

1. Condujere, &c. | 1. Condujeremos, &c.

The following verbs are conjugated like CONDUCIR.

Aducir.	To adduce.	Producir.	To produce.
Deducir.	To deduce.	Reducir.	To reduce.
Introducir.	To introduce.	Traducir.	To translate.

N. B.—*Conocer*, and all verbs ending in *cer*, of more than two syllables, follow the irregularity of *Conducir* in the present indicative and subjunctive, and in the imperative. Elsewhere regular.

LIST OF IRREGULAR VERBS

CONJUGATED DIFFERENTLY FROM THOSE OF THE SEVEN CLASSES ALREADY GIVEN.

Infinitive. Adquirir, *to acquire.*
Gerund. Adquiriendo, *acquiring.*
Past Part. Adquirido, *acquired.*

			Singular.			Plural.		
			1.	2.	3.	1.	2.	3.
Indicative.	*Present.*		Adquiero,	adquieres,	adquiere.	Adquirimos,	adquiris,	adquieren.
	Imperfect.		Adquiria,	adquirias,	adquiria.	Adquiriamos,	adquiriais,	adquirian.
	Pret. Def.		Adquiri,	adquiriste,	adquirió.	Adquirimos,	adquiristeis,	adquirieron.
	Future.		Adquiriré,	adquirirás,	adquirirá.	Adquirirémos,	adquiriréis,	adquirirán.
Imperative.				adquiere,	adquiera.	Adquiramos,	adquirid,	adquieran.
Subjunctive.	*Present.*		Adquiera,	adquieras,	adquiera.	Adquiramos,	adquirais,	adquieran.
	Imperfect	1st Ter.	Adquiriria,	adquiririas,	adquiriria.	Adquiririamos,	adquiririais,	adquiririan.
		2d Ter.	Adquiriera,	adquirieras,	adquiriera.	Adquirieramos,	adquirierais,	adquirieran.
		3d Ter.	Adquiriese,	adquirieses,	adquiriese.	Adquiriesemos,	adquirieseis,	adquiriesen.
	Future.		Adquiriere,	adquirieres,	adquiriere.	Adquirieremos,	adquiriereis,	adquirieren.

LIST OF IRREGULAR VERBS.—(Continued.)

INFINITIVE. Andar, *to go, to walk.*
GERUND. Andando, *walking.*
PAST PART. Andado, *walked.*

		Singular.			Plural.		
		1.	2.	3.	1.	2.	3.
INDICATIVE.	*Present.*	Ando,	andas,	anda.	Andamos,	andais,	andan.
	Imperfect.	Andaba,	andabas,	andaba.	Andabamos,	andabais,	andaban.
	Pret. Def.	Anduve,	anduviste,	anduvo.	Anduvimos,	anduvisteis,	anduvieron.
	Future.	Andaré,	andarás,	andará.	Andarémos,	andaréis,	andarán.
IMPERATIVE.			anda,			andad,	
SUBJUNCTIVE.	*Present.*	Ande,	andes,	ande.	Andemos,	andeis,	anden.
	Imperfect. {1st Ter.	Andaria,	andarias,	andaria.	Andariamos,	andariais,	andarian.
	2d Ter.	Anduviera,	anduvieras,	anduviera.	Anduvieramos,	anduvierais,	anduvieran.
	3d Ter.	Anduviese,	anduvieses,	anduviese.	Anduviesemos,	anduvieseis,	anduviesen.
	Future.	Anduviere,	anduvieres,	anduviere.	Anduvieremos,	anduviereis,	anduvieren.

CONJUGATIONS.

			Singular.			Plural.		
			1.	2.	3.	1.	2.	3.
INDICATIVE.	Present.		Asgo,	ases,	ase.	Asimos,	asis,	asen.
	Imperfect.		Asia,	asias,	asia.	Asiamos,	asiais,	asian.
	Pret. Def.		Asi,	asiste,	asió.	Asimos,	asisteis,	asieron.
	Future.		Asiré,	asirás,	asirá.	Asirémos,	asiréis,	asirán.
IMPERATIVE.				ase,	asga.	Asgamos,	asid,	asgan.
SUBJUNCTIVE.	Present.		Asga,	asgas,	asga.	Asgamos,	asgais,	asgan.
	Imperfect.	1st Ter.	Asiria,	asirias,	asiria.	Asiriamos,	asiriais,	asirian.
		2d Ter.	Asiera,	asieras,	asiera.	Asieramos,	asierais,	asieran.
		3d Ter.	Asiese,	asieses,	asiese.	Asiesemos,	asieseis,	asiesen.
	Future.		Asiere,	asieres,	asiere.	Asieremos,	asiereis,	asieren.

LIST OF IRREGULAR VERBS.—(Continued.)

Infinitive. Bendecir, *to bless.*
Gerund. Bendiciendo, *blessing.*
Past Part. { Bendecido, } *blessed.*
{ Bendito. }

		Singular.			Plural.		
		1.	2.	3.	1.	2.	3.
Indicative.	*Present.*	Bendigo,	bendices,	bendice.	Bendecimos,	bendecis,	bendicen.
	Imperfect.	Bendecia,	bendecias,	bendecia.	Bendeciamos,	bendeciais,	bendecian.
	Pret. Def.	Bendije,	bendijiste,	bendijo.	Bendijimos,	bendijisteis,	bendijeron.
	Future.	Bendeciré,	bendecirás,	bendecirá.	Bendecirémos,	bendeciréis,	bendecirán.
Imperative.			bendice.			bendecid,	
Subjunctive.	*Present.*	Bendiga,	bendigas,	bendiga.	Bendigamos,	bendigais,	bendigan.
	Imperfect. 1st Ter.	Bendeciria,	bendecirias,	bendeciria.	Bendeciriamos,	bendeciriais.	bendecirian.
	2d Ter.	Bendijera,	bendijeras,	bendijera.	Bendijeramos,	bendijerais,	bendijeran.
	3d Ter.	Bendijese,	bendijeses,	bendijese.	Bendijesemos,	bendijeseis,	bendijesen.
	Future.	Bendijere,	bendijeres,	bendijere.	Bendijeremos,	bendijereis,	bendijerem.

CONJUGATIONS. 403

		Singular.			Plural.		
		1.	2.	3.	1.	2.	3.
INDICATIVE.	*Present.*	Quepo,	cabes,	cabe.	Cabemos,	cabeis,	caben.
	Imperfect.	Cabia,	cabias,	cabia.	Cabiamos,	cabiais,	cabian.
	Pret. Def.	Cupe,	cupiste,	cupo.	Cupimos,	cupisteis,	cupieron.
	Future.	Cabré,	cabrás,	cabrá.	Cabrémos,	cabreis,	cabrán.
IMPERATIVE.			cabe,			cabed,	
SUBJUNCTIVE.	*Present.*	Quepa,	quepas,	quepa.	Quepamos,	quepais,	quepan.
	Imperfect 1st Ter.	Cabria,	cabrias,	cabria.	Cabriamos,	cabriais,	cabrian.
	2d Ter.	Cupiera,	cupieras,	cupiera.	Cupieramos,	cupierais,	cupieran.
	3d Ter.	Cupiese,	cupieses,	cupiese.	Cupiesemos,	cupieseis,	cupiesen.
	Future.	Cupiere,	cupieres,	cupiere.	Cupieremos,	cupiereis,	cupieren.

LIST OF IRREGULAR VERBS.—(*Continued.*)

INFINITIVE. *Cocer, to cook.*
GERUND. *Cociendo, cooking.*
PAST PART. *Cocido, cooked.*

		Singular.			Plural.		
		1.	2.	3.	1.	2.	3.
INDICATIVE.	*Present.*	Cuezo,	cueces,	cuece.	Cocemos,	coceis,	cuecen.
	Imperfect.	Cocia,	cocias,	cocia.	Cociamos,	cociais,	cocian.
	Pret. Def.	Cocí,	cociste,	coció.	Cocimos,	cocisteis,	cocieron.
	Future.	Coceré,	cocerás,	cocerá.	Cocerémos,	coceréis,	cocerán.
IMPERATIVE.			cuece,	cueza.	Cozamos,	coced,	cuezan.
SUBJUNCTIVE.	*Present.*	Cueza,	cuezas,	cueza.	Cozamos,	cozais,	cuezan.
	Imperfect. 1st Ter.	Coceria,	cocerias,	coceria.	Coceriamos,	coceriais,	cocerian.
	2d Ter.	Cociera,	cocieras,	cociera.	Cocieramos,	cocierais,	cocieran.
	3d Ter.	Cociese,	cocieses,	cociese.	Cociesemos,	cocieseis,	cociesen.
	Future.	Cociere,	cocieres,	cociere.	Cocieremos,	cociereis,	cocieren.

CONJUGATIONS.

		Singular.			Plural.		
		1.	2.	3.	1.	2.	3.
INDICATIVE.	*Present.*	Doy,	das,	da.	Damos,	dais,	dan.
	Imperfect.	Daba,	dabas,	daba.	Dabamos,	dabais,	daban.
	Pret. Def.	Dí,	diste,	dió.	Dimos,	disteis,	dieron.
	Future.	Daré,	darás,	dará.	Darémos,	daréis,	darán.
IMPERATIVE.			da,	de.	Demos,	dad,	den.
SUBJUNCTIVE.	*Present.*	Dé,	des,	de.	Demos,	deis,	den.
	Imperfect. 1st Ter.	Daria,	darias,	daria.	Dariamos,	dariais,	darian.
	2d Ter.	Diera,	dieras,	diera.	Dieramos,	dierais,	dieran.
	3d Ter.	Diese,	dieses,	diese.	Diesemos,	dieseis,	diesen.
	Future.	Diere,	dieres,	diere.	Dieremos,	diereis,	dieren.

LIST OF IRREGULAR VERBS.—(Continued.)

INFINITIVE. Decir, *to say, to tell.*
GERUND. Diciendo, *saying, telling.*
PAST PART. Dicho, *said, told.*

		Singular.			Plural.		
		1.	2.	3.	1.	2.	3.
INDICATIVE	*Present.*	Digo,	dices,	dice.	Decimos,	decis,	dicen.
	Imperfect.	Decia,	decias,	decia.	Deciamos,	deciais,	decian.
	Pret. Def.	Dije,	dijiste,	dijo.	Dijimos,	dijisteis,	dijeron.
	Future.	Diré,	dirás,	dirá.	Diremos,	diréis,	dirán.
IMPERATIVE			di,			decid,	
SUBJUNCTIVE	*Present.*	Diga,	digas,	diga.	Digamos,	digais,	digan.
	Imperfect. 1st Ter.	Diria,	dirias,	diria.	Diriamos,	diriais,	dirian.
	2d Ter.	Dijera,	dijeras,	dijera.	Dijeramos,	dijerais,	dijeran.
	3d Ter.	Dijese,	dijeses,	dijese.	Dijesemos,	dijeseis,	dijesen.
	Future.	Dijere,	dijeres,	dijere.	Dijeremos,	dijereis,	dijeren.

CONJUGATIONS.

INFINITIVE. Dormir, *to sleep.*
GERUND. Durmiendo, *sleeping.*
PAST PART. Dormido, *slept.*

		Singular.			Plural.		
		1.	2.	3.	1.	2.	3.
INDICATIVE.	*Present.*	Duermo,	duermes,	duerme.	Dormimos,	dormis,	duermen.
	Imperfect.	Dormia,	dormias,	dormia.	Dormiamos,	dormiais,	dormian.
	Pret. Def.	Dormí,	dormiste,	durmió.	Dormímos,	dormisteis,	durmieron.
	Future.	Dormiré,	dormirás,	dormirá.	Dormirémos,	dormiréis,	dormirán.
IMPERATIVE.			duerme,	duerma.	Durmamos,	dormid,	duerman.
SUBJUNCTIVE.	*Present.*	Duerma,	duermas,	duerma.	Durmamos,	durmais,	duerman.
	Imperfect. { 1st Ter.	Dormiria,	dormirias,	dormiria.	Dormiriamos,	dormiriais,	dormirian.
	2d Ter.	Durmiera,	durmieras,	durmiera.	Durmieramos,	durmierais,	durmieran.
	3d Ter.	Durmiese,	durmieses,	durmiese.	Durmiesemos,	durmieseis,	durmiesen.
	Future.	Durmiere,	durmieres,	durmiere.	Durmierémos,	durmiereis,	durmieren.

N. B.—The verb *Morir* is conjugated like *Dormir*.

LIST OF IRREGULAR VERBS.—(Continued.)

INFINITIVE. Erguir, *to hold upright (as the head, &c.).*
GERUND. Irguiendo, *holding upright.*
PAST PART. Erguido, *held upright.*

			Singular.			Plural.		
			1.	2.	3.	1.	2.	3.
INDICATIVE.	*Present.*		**Yergo,**	**yergues,**	**yergue.**	Erguimos,	erguís,	**yerguen.**
	Imperfect.		Erguía,	erguías,	erguía.	Erguíamos,	erguíais,	erguían.
	Pret. Def.		Erguí,	erguiste,	**Irguió.**	Erguimos,	erguisteis,	**irguieron.**
	Future.		Erguiré,	erguirás,	erguirá.	Erguirémos,	erguiréis,	erguirán.
IMPERATIVE.				**yergue,**	**yerga.**	**Irgamos,**	**irgais,**	**yergan.**
SUBJUNCTIVE.	*Present.*		**Yerga,**	**yergas,**	**yerga.**	**Irgamos,**	**irgais,**	**yergan.**
	Imperfect.	1st Ter.	Erguiría,	erguirías,	erguiría.	Erguiríamos,	erguiríais,	erguirían.
		2d Ter.	Irguiera,	irguieras,	irguiera.	Irguiéramos,	irguierais,	irguieran.
		3d Ter.	Irguiese,	irguieses,	irguiese.	Irguiésemos,	irguieseis,	irguiesen.
	Future.		Irguiere,	irguieres,	irguiere.	Irguiéremos,	irguiereis,	irguieren.

CONJUGATIONS.

		Singular.			Plural.		
		1.	2.	3.	1.	2.	3.
INDICATIVE.	Present.	Yerro,	yerras,	yerra.	Erramos,	erraís,	yerran.
	Imperfect.	Erraba,	errabas,	erraba.	Errabamos,	errabais,	erraban.
	Pret. Def.	Erré,	erraste,	erró.	Errámos,	errasteis,	erraron.
	Future.	Erraré,	errarás,	errará.	Errarémos,	erraréis,	errarán.
IMPERATIVE.		Yerre,	yerra,	yerre.	Erremos,	errad,	yerren.
SUBJUNCTIVE.	Present.	Yerre,	yerres,	yerre.	Erremos,	erreis,	yerren.
	Imperfect. 1st Ter.	Erraria,	errarias,	erraria.	Errariamos,	errariais,	errarian.
	2d Ter.	Errara,	erraras,	errara.	Erraramos,	errarais,	erraran.
	3d Ter.	Errase,	errases,	errase.	Errasemos,	erraseis,	errasen.
	Future.	Errare,	errares,	errare.	Erraremos,	errareis,	erraren.

18

LIST OF IRREGULAR VERBS.—(*Continued.*)

INFINITIVE. Hacer, *to make, to do.*
GERUND. Haciendo, *making, doing.*
PAST PART. Hecho, *made, done.*

		Singular.			Plural.		
		1.	2.	3.	1.	2.	3.
INDICATIVE	Present.	Hago,	haces,	hace.	Hacemos,	haceis,	hacen.
	Imperfect.	Hacia,	hacias,	hacia.	Haciamos,	haciais,	hacian.
	Pret. Def.	Hice,	hiciste,	hizo.	Hicimos,	hicisteis,	hicieron.
	Future.	Haré,	harás,	hará.	Haremos,	haréis,	harian.
IMPERATIVE			haz,	haga.	Hagamos,	haced,	hagan.
SUBJUNCTIVE	Present.	Haga,	hagas,	haga.	Hagamos,	hagais,	hagan.
	Imperfect. 1st Ter.	Haria,	harias,	haria.	Hariamos,	hariais,	harian.
	2d Ter.	Hiciera,	hicieras,	hiciera.	Hicieramos,	hicierais,	hicieran.
	3d Ter.	Hiciese,	hicieses,	hiciese.	Hiciesemos,	hicieseis,	hiciesen.
	Future.	Hiciere,	hicieres,	hiciere.	Hicieremos,	hiciereis,	hicieren.

CONJUGATIONS.

			Singular.			Plural.		
			1.	2.	3.	1.	2.	3.
INDICATIVE.	Present.		Voy,	vas,	va.	Vamos,	vais,	van.
	Imperfect.		Iba,	ibas,	iba.	Ibamos,	ibais,	iban.
	Pret. Def.		Fuí,	fuiste,	fué.	Fuimos,	fuisteis,	fueron.
	Future.		Iré,	irás,	irá.	Irémos,	iréis,	irán.
IMPERATIVE.				ve,	vaya.	Vayamos, or vamos,	id,	vayan.
SUBJUNCTIVE.	Present.		Vaya,	vayas,	vaya.	Vayamos,	vayais,	vayan.
	Imperfect	1st Ter.	Iria,	irias,	iria.	Iriamos,	iriais,	irian.
		2d Ter.	Fuera,	fueras,	fuera.	Fueramos,	fuerais,	fueran.
		3d Ter.	Fuese,	fueses,	fuese.	Fuesemos,	fueseis,	fuesen.
	Future.		Fuere,	fueres,	fuere.	Fueremos,	fuereis,	fueren.

LIST OF IRREGULAR VERBS.—(*Continued*)

INFINITIVE. *Jugar, to play.*
GERUND. *Jugando, playing.*
PAST PART. *Jugado, played.*

			Singular.			Plural.		
			1.	2.	3.	1.	2.	3.
INDICATIVE.	*Present.*		Juego,	juegas,	juega.	Jugamos,	jugais,	juegan.
	Imperfect.		Jugaba,	jugabas,	jugaba.	Jugabamos,	jugabais,	jugaban.
	Pret. Def.		Jugué,	jugaste,	jugó.	Jugámos,	jugasteis,	jugaron.
	Future.		Jugaré,	jugarás,	jugará.	Jugarémos,	jugareis,	jugarán.
IMPERATIVE.				juega,	juegue.	Juguemos,	jugad,	jueguen.
SUBJUNCTIVE.	*Present.*		Juegue,	juegues,	juegue.	Juguemos,	jugueis,	jueguen.
	Imperfect.	1st Ter.	Jugaria,	jugarias,	jugaria.	Jugariamos,	jugariais,	jugarian.
		2d Ter.	Jugara,	jugaras,	jugara.	Jugaramos,	jugarais,	jugaran.
		3d Ter.	Jugase,	jugases,	jugase.	Jugasemos,	jugaseis,	jugasen.
	Future.		Jugare,	jugares,	jugare.	Jugaremos,	jugareis,	jugaren.

CONJUGATIONS. 413

		Singular.			Plural.		
		1.	2.	3.	1.	2.	3.
INDICATIVE.	Present.	Oigo,	oyes,	oye.	Oimos,	ois,	oyen.
	Imperfect.	Oia,	oias,	oia.	Oiamos,	oiais,	oian.
	Pret. Def.	Oí,	oiste,	oyó.	Oimos,	oisteis,	oyeron.
	Future.	Oiré,	oirás,	oirá.	Oirémos,	oiréis,	oirán.
IMPERATIVE.			oye,	oiga.	Oigamos,	oid,	oigan.
SUBJUNCTIVE.	Present.	Oiga,	oigas,	oiga.	Oigamos,	oigais,	oigan.
	Imperfect. 1st Ter.	Oiria,	oirias,	oiria.	Oiriamos,	oiriais,	oirian.
	2d Ter.	Oyera,	oyeras,	oyera.	Oyeramos,	oyerais,	oyeran.
	3d Ter.	Oyese,	oyeses,	oyese.	Oyesemos,	oyeseis,	oyesen.
	Future.	Oyere,	oyeres,	oyere.	Oyeremos,	oyereis,	oyeren.

LIST OF IRREGULAR VERBS.—(Continued.)

INFINITIVE. Oler, *to smell.*
GERUND. Oliendo, *smelling.*
PAST PART. Olido, *smell.*

			Singular.			Plural.		
			1.	2.	3.	1.	2.	3.
INDICATIVE.	*Present.*		**Huelo,**	**hueles,**	**huele.**	Olemos,	oleis,	**huelen.**
	Imperfect.		Olia,	olias,	olia.	Oliamos,	oliais,	olian.
	Pret. Def.		Olí,	oliste,	olió.	Olimos,	olisteis	olieron.
	Future.		Oleré,	olerás,	olerá.	Olerémos,	oleréis,	olerán.
IMPERATIVE.				**huele,**	**huela.**	Olamos,	oled,	**huelan.**
SUBJUNCTIVE.	*Present.*		**Huela,**	**huelas,**	**huela.**	Olamos,	oluis,	**huelan.**
	Imperfect.	1st Ter.	Oleria,	olerias,	oleria.	Oleriamos,	oleriais,	olerian.
		2d Ter.	Oliera,	olieras,	oliera.	Olieramos,	olierais,	olieran.
		3d Ter.	Oliese,	olieses,	oliese.	Oliesemos,	olieseis,	oliesen.
	Future.		Oliere,	olieres,	oliere.	Olieremos,	oliereis,	olieren.

CONJUGATIONS.

			Singular.			Plural.	
		1.	2.	3.	1.	2.	3.
INDICATIVE.	*Present.*	Puedo,	puedes,	puede.	Podemos,	podeis,	pueden.
	Imperfect.	Podia,	podias,	podia.	Podiamos,	podiais,	podian.
	Pret. Def.	Pude,	pudiste,	pudo.	Pudimos,	pudisteis,	pudieron.
	Future.	Podré,	podrás,	podrá.	Podrémos,	podréis,	podrán.
IMPERATIVE.			*Wanting.*				
SUBJUNCTIVE.	*Present.*	Pueda,	puedas,	pueda.	Podamos,	podais,	puedan.
	Imperfect. 1st Ter.	Podria,	podrias,	podria.	Podriamos,	podriais,	podrian.
	2d Ter.	Pudiera,	pudieras,	pudiera.	Pudieramos,	pudierais,	pudieran.
	3d Ter.	Pudiese,	pudieses,	pudiese.	Pudiesemos,	pudieseis,	pudiesen.
	Future.	Pudiere,	pudieres,	pudiere.	Pudieremos,	pudiereis,	pudieren.

LIST OF IRREGULAR VERBS.—(Continued.)

Infinitive Podrir,* *to rot.*
Gerund. Pudriendo, *rotting.*
Past Part. Podrido, *rotten.*

		Singular.			Plural.		
		1.	2.	3.	1.	2.	3.
Indicative	*Present.*	Pudro,	pudres,	pudre.	Podrimos,	podris,	pudren.
	Imperfect.	Podria,	podrias,	podria.	Podriamos,	podriais,	podrian.
	Pret. Def.	Podrió,	podriste,	pudrió.	Podrimos,	podristeis,	pudrieron.
	Future.	Podriré,	podrirás,	podrirá.	Podrirémos,	podriréis,	podrirán.
Imperative			pudre,			podrid,	
Subjunctive	*Present.*	Pudra,	pudras,	pudra.	Pudramos,	pudrais,	pudran.
	Imperfect. 1st Ter.	Podriria,	podririas,	podriria.	Podririamos,	podririais,	podririan.
	2d Ter.	Pudriera,	pudrieras,	pudriera.	Pudrieramos,	pudrierais,	pudrieran.
	3d Ter.	Pudriese,	pudrieses,	pudriese.	Pudriesemos,	pudrieseis,	pudriesen.
	Future.	Pudriere,	pudrieres,	pudriere.	Pudrieremos,	pudriereis,	pudrieren.

* The Spanish Academy, and many of the best Spanish writers, now substitute u for o throughout the whole of this verb, except the past participle.

CONJUGATIONS.

		Singular.			Plural.		
		1.	2.	3.	1.	2.	3.
INDICATIVE.	*Present.*	Pongo,	pones,	pone.	Ponemos,	poneis,	ponen.
	Imperfect.	Ponia,	ponias,	ponia.	Poniamos,	poniais,	ponian.
	Pret. Def.	Puse,	pusiste,	puso.	Pusimos,	pusisteis,	pusieron.
	Future.	Pondré,	pondrás,	pondrá.	Pondrémos,	pondreis,	pondrán.
IMPERATIVE.			pon,	ponga.	Pongamos,	poned,	pongan.
SUBJUNCTIVE.	*Present.*	Ponga,	pongas,	ponga.	Pongamos,	pongais,	pongan.
	Imperfect 1st Ter.	Pondría,	pondrías,	pondria.	Pondríamos,	pondríais,	pondrían.
	2d Ter.	Pusiera,	pusieras,	pusiera.	Pusiéramos,	pusierais,	pusieran.
	3d Ter.	Pusiese,	pusieses,	pusiese.	Pusiésemos,	pusieseis,	pusiesen.
	Future.	Pusiere,	pusieres,	pusiere.	Pusiéremos,	pusiereis,	pusieren.

LIST OF IRREGULAR VERBS.—(*Continued.*)

INFINITIVE. Querer, *to wish, &c.*
GERUND. Queriendo, *wishing.*
PAST PART. Querido, *wished.*

		Singular.			Plural.		
		1.	2.	3.	1.	2.	3.
INDICATIVE.	*Present.*	Quiero,	quieres,	quiere.	Queremos,	queréis,	quieren.
	Imperfect.	Quería,	querías,	quería.	Queríamos,	queríais,	querían.
	Pret. Def.	Quise,	quisiste,	quiso.	Quisimos,	quisisteis,	quisieron.
	Future.	Querré,	querrás,	querrá.	Querrémos,	querréis,	querrán.
IMPERATIVE.			*Wanting.*				
SUBJUNCTIVE.	*Present.*	Quiera,	quieras,	quiera.	Queramos,	queráis,	quieran.
	Imperfect. 1st Ter.	Querria,	querrias,	querria.	Querriamos,	querriais,	querrian.
	2d Ter.	Quisiera,	quisieras,	quisiera.	Quisiéramos,	quisierais,	quisieran.
	3d Ter.	Quisiese,	quisieses,	quisiese.	Quisiésemos,	quisieseis,	quisiesen.
	Future.	Quisiere,	quisieres,	quisiere.	quisiéremos,	quisiereis,	quisieren.

CONJUGATIONS. 419

Infinitive. Reir, *to laugh.*
Gerund. Riendo, *laughing.*
Past Part. Reido, *laughed.*

		Singular.			Plural.		
		1.	2.	3.	1.	2.	3.
Indicative.	*Present.*	Rio,	ries,	rie.	Reimos,	reis,	rien.
	Imperfect.	Reia,	reias,	reia.	Reiamos,	reiais,	reian.
	Pret. Def.	Rei,	reiste,	rió.	Reimos,	reisteis,	rieron.
	Future.	Reiré,	reirás,	reirá.	Reirémos,	reiréis,	reirán.
Imperative.			rie,		Riamos,	reid,	rian.
Subjunctive.	*Present,*	Ria,	rias,	ria.	Riamos,	riais,	rian.
	Imperfect. 1st Ter.	Reiria,	reirias,	reiria.	Reiriamos,	reiriais,	reirian.
	2d Ter.	Riera,	rieras,	riera.	Rieramos,	rierais,	rieran.
	3d Ter.	Riese,	rieses,	riese.	Riesemos,	rieseis,	riesen.
	Future.	Riere,	rieres,	riere.	Rieremos,	riereis,	rieren.

LIST OF IRREGULAR VERBS.—(*Continued.*)

INFINITIVE. Saber, *to know.*
GERUND. Sabiendo, *knowing.*
PAST PART. Sabido, *known.*

		Singular.			Plural.		
		1.	2.	3.	1.	2.	3.
INDICATIVE	*Present.*	Sé,	sabes,	sabe.	Sabemos,	sabeis,	saben.
	Imperfect.	Sabia,	sabias,	sabia.	Sabiamos,	sabiais,	sabian.
	Pret. Def.	Supe,	supiste,	supo.	Supimos,	supisteis,	supieron.
	Future.	Sabré,	sabrás,	sabrá.	Sabrémos,	sabréis,	sabrán.
IMPERATIVE.			sabe,	sepa.	Sepamos,	sabed,	sepan.
SUBJUNCTIVE.	*Present.*	Sepa,	sepas,	sepa.	Sepamos,	sepais,	sepan.
	Imperfect. 1st Ter.	Sabria,	sabrias,	sabria.	Sabriamos,	sabriais,	sabrian.
	2d Ter.	Supiera,	supieras,	supiera.	Supieramos,	supierais,	supieran.
	3d Ter.	Supiese,	supieses,	supiese.	Supiesemos,	supieseis,	supiesen.
	Future.	Supiere,	supieres,	supiere.	Supieremos,	supiereis,	supieren.

CONJUGATIONS. 421

		Singular.			Plural.		
		1.	2.	3.	1.	2.	3.
INDICATIVE.	Present.	Salgo,	sales,	sale.	Salimos,	salis,	salen.
	Imperfect.	Salia,	salias,	salia.	Saliamos,	saliais,	salian.
	Pret. Def.	Salí,	saliste,	salió.	Salimos,	salisteis,	salieron.
	Future.	Saldré,	saldrás,	saldrá.	Saldrémos,	saldréis,	saldrán.
IMPERATIVE.			sal,			salid,	
SUBJUNCTIVE.	Present.	Salga,	salgas,	salga.	Salgamos,	salgais,	salgan.
	Imperfect. 1st Ter.	Saldria,	saldrias,	saldria.	Saldriamos,	saldriais,	saldrian.
	2d Ter.	Saliera,	salieras,	saliera.	Salieramos,	salierais,	salieran.
	3d Ter.	Saliese,	salieses,	saliese.	Saliesemos,	salieseis,	saliesen.
	Future.	Saliere.	salieres,	saliere.	Salieremos,	saliereis,	salieren.

LIST OF IRREGULAR VERBS.—(Continued.)

INFINITIVE. Traer, *to bring*.
GERUND. Trayendo, *bringing*.
PAST PART. Traido, *brought*.

			Singular.			Plural.		
			1.	2.	3.	1.	2.	3.
INDICATIVE.	Present.		Traigo,	traes,	trae.	Traemos,	traeis,	traen.
	Imperfect.		Traia,	traias,	raia.	Traiamos,	traiais,	traian.
	Pret. Def.		Traje,	trajiste,	trajo.	Trajimos,	trajisteis,	trajeron.
	Future.		Traeré,	traerás,	traerá.	Traerémos,	traeréis,	traerán.
IMPERATIVE.				trae,	traiga,	Traigamos,	traed,	traigan.
SUBJUNCTIVE.	Present.		Traiga,	traigas,	traiga.	Traigamos,	traigais,	traigan.
	Imperfect.	1st Ter.	Traeria,	traerias,	traeria.	Traeriamos,	traeriais,	traerian.
		2d Ter.	Trajera,	trajeras,	trajera.	Trajeramos,	trajerais,	trajeran.
		3d Ter.	Trajese,	trajeses,	trajese.	Trajesemos,	trajeseis,	trajesen.
	Future.		Trajere,	trajeres,	trajere.	Trajeremos,	trajereis,	trajeren.

Caer and its compounds are conjugated like *Traer*, in the present indicative and subjunctive, and in the imperative. Regular elsewhere.

CONJUGATIONS.

		Singular.			Plural.		
		1.	2.	3.	1.	2.	3.
INDICATIVE.	Present.	Valgo,	vales,	vale.	Valemos,	valeis,	valen.
	Imperfect.	Valia,	valias,	valia.	Valiamos,	valiais,	valian.
	Pret. Def.	Valí,	valiste,	valió.	Valimos,	valisteis,	valieron.
	Future.	Valdré,	valdrás,	valdrá.	Valdrémos,	valdréis,	valdrán.
IMPERATIVE.			vale,		Valgamos,	valed,	valgan.
SUBJUNCTIVE.	Present.	Valga,	valgas,	valga.	Valgamos,	valgais,	valgan.
	Imperfect 1st Ter.	Valdria,	valdrias,	valdria.	Valdriamos,	valdriais,	valdrian.
	Imperfect 2d Ter.	Valiera,	valieras,	valiera.	Valieramos,	valierais,	valieran.
	Imperfect 3d Ter.	Valiese,	valieses,	valiese.	Valiesemos,	valieseis,	valiesen.
	Future.	Valiere,	valieres,	valiere.	Valieremos,	valiereis,	valieren.

LIST OF IRREGULAR VERBS.—(Continued.)

INFINITIVE. Venir, *to come.*
GERUND. Viniendo, *coming.*
PAST PART. Venido, *come.*

		Singular.			Plural.		
		1.	2.	3.	1.	2.	3.
INDICATIVE.	Present.	Vengo,	vienes,	viene.	Venimos,	venis,	vienen.
	Imperfect.	Venia,	venias,	venia.	Veniamos,	veniais,	venian.
	Pret. Def.	Vine,	viniste,	vino.	Vinimos,	vinisteis,	vinieron.
	Future.	Vendré,	vendrás,	vendrá.	Vendrémos,	vendréis,	vendrán.
IMPERATIVE.			ven,			venid,	
SUBJUNCTIVE.	Present.	Venga,	vengas,	venga.	Vengamos,	vengais,	vengan.
	Imperfect. 1st Ter.	Vendria,	vendrias,	vendria.	Vendriamos,	vendriais,	vendrian.
	2d Ter.	Viniera,	vinieras,	viniera.	Vinieramos,	vinierais,	vinieran.
	3d Ter.	Viniese,	vinieses,	viniese.	Viniesemos,	vinieseis,	viniesen.
	Future.	Viniere,	vinieres,	viniere.	Vinieremos,	viniereis,	vinieren.

CONJUGATIONS.

INFINITIVE. **Ver,** *to see.*
GERUND. **Viendo,** *seeing.*
PAST PART. **Visto,** *seen.*

		Singular.			*Plural.*		
		1.	2.	3.	1.	2.	3.
INDICATIVE	*Present.*	Veo,	ves,	ve.	Vemos,	veis,	ven.
	Imperfect.	Veia,	veias,	veia.	Veiamos,	veiais,	veian.
	Pret. Def.	Ví,	viste,	vió.	Vimos,	visteis,	vieron.
	Future.	Veré,	verás,	verá.	Verémos,	veréis,	verán.
IMPERATIVE.			ve,	vea.	Veamos,	ved,	vean.
SUBJUNCTIVE.	*Present.*	Vea,	veas,	vea.	Veamos,	veais,	vean.
Imperfect.	1st Ter.	Veria,	verias,	veria.	Veriamos,	veriais,	verian.
	2d Ter.	Viera,	vieras,	viera.	Vieramos,	vierais,	vieran.
	3d Ter.	Viese,	vieses,	viese.	Viesemos,	vieseis,	viesen.
	Future.	Viere,	vieres,	viere.	Vieremos,	viereis,	vieren.

CONJUGATION OF A VERB IN THE REFLECTIVE FORM.

INFINITIVE.

Lavarse.	To wash one's self.

GERUND.

Lavándose.	Washing one's self.

PAST PARTICIPLE.

Lavádose.	Washed one's self.

INDICATIVE.

PRESENT.

1. Me lavo.	I wash myself.	1. Nos lavamos.
2. Te lavas.		2. Os lavais.
3. Se lava.		3. Se lavan.

IMPERFECT.

1. Me lavaba.	I was washing, washed, or used to wash myself.	1. Nos lavabamos.
2. Te lavabas.		2. Os lavabais.
3. Se lavaba.		3. Se lavaban.

PRETERIT DEFINITE.

1. Me lavé.	I washed myself.	1. Nos lavámos.
2. Te lavaste.		2. Os lavasteis.
3. Se lavó.		3. Se lavaron.

FUTURE SIMPLE.

1. Me lavaré.	I shall wash myself.	1. Nos lavarémos.
2. Te lavarás.		2. Os lavaréis.
3. Se lavará.		3. Se lavarán.

IMPERATIVE.

		1. Lavémonos.
2. Lávate.	Wash thyself.	2. Lavaos.
3. Lávese.		3. Lávense.

SUBJUNCTIVE.

PRESENT.

1. Me lave.	I may wash myself.	1. Nos lavemos.
2. Te laves.		2. Os laveis.
3. Se lave.		3. Se laven.

IMPERFECT.—*First Termination.*

1. Me lavaria.	I would wash myself.	1. Nos lavariamos.
2. Te lavarias.		2. Os lavariais.
3. Se lavaria.		3. Se lavarian.

Second Termination.

1. Me lavara.	I might, could, would, or should wash myself.	1. Nos lavaramos.
2. Te lavaras.		2. Os lavarais.
3. Se lavara.		3. Se lavaran.

Third Termination.

1. Me lavase.	I might, could, would, or should wash myself.	1. Nos lavasemos.
2. Te lavases.		2. Os lavaseis.
3. Se lavase.		3. Se lavasen.

FUTURE.

1. Me lavare.	I might or should wash myself.	1. Nos lavaremos.
2. Te lavares.		2. Os lavareis.
3. Se lavare.		3. Se lavaren.

INFINITIVE.

Ayudarse. | To help each other.

GERUND.

Ayudándose. | Helping each other.

PAST PARTICIPLE.

Ayudádose. | Helped each other.

INDICATIVE.

PRESENT.
1. Nos ayudamos.   We help each other.
2. Os ayudais.
3. Se ayudan.

IMPERFECT.
1. Nos ayudabamos.   We used to help each other.
2. Os ayudabais.
3. Se ayudaban.

PRETERIT DEFINITE.
1. Nos ayudámos.   We helped each other.
2. Os ayudasteis.
3. Se ayudaron.

FUTURE SIMPLE.
1. Nos ayudarémos.   We shall help each other.
2. Os ayudaréis.
3. Se ayudarán.

IMPERATIVE.

1. Ayudémonos.   Let us help each other.
2. Ayudaos.   Help each other.
3. Ayúdense.   Let them help each other.

SUBJUNCTIVE.

PRESENT.
1. Nos ayudemos.   We may help each other.
2. Os ayudeis.
3. Se ayuden.

IMPERFECT.—*First Termination.*
1. Nos ayudariamos.   We would help each other.
2. Os ayudariais.
3. Se ayudarian.

Second Termination.
1. Nos ayudaramos.   We might, could, would, or should help each other.
2. Os ayudarais.
3. Se ayudaran.

Third Termination.
1. Nos ayudasemos.   We might, could, would, or should help each other.
2. Os ayudaseis.
3. Se ayudasen.

FUTURE.
1. Nos ayudaremos.   We might or should help each other.
2. Os ayudareis.
3. Se ayudaren.

IMPERSONAL VERBS.

Amanecer. | To grow light.

INDICATIVE.

Simple Tenses.

Present.	Amanece.	It grows light.
Imperfect.	Amanecia.	It was growing light.
Pret. Def.	Amaneció.	It grew light.
Fut. Simple.	Amanecerá.	It will grow light.

Compound Tenses.

Pret. Indef.	Ha amanecido.	It has grown light.
Pluperfect.	Habia amanecido.	It had grown light.
Anterior.	Hubo amanecido.	It had grown light.
Comp. Future.	Habrá amanecido.	It will have grown light.

IMPERATIVE.

Amanezca. | Let it grow light.

SUBJUNCTIVE.

Simple Tenses.

Present. Amanezca. It may grow light.

Imperfect. { Amaneceria. / Amaneciera. / Amaneciese. } It { might, / should, or / would } grow light.

Future. Amaneciere. It should grow light.

Compound Tenses.

Perfect. Haya amanecido. It may have grown light.

Pluperf. { Habria / Hubiera / Hubiese } amanecido. It { might have, / should have, or / would have } grown light.

Comp. Future. Hubiere amanecido. It should have grown light.

N. B.—*Anochecer*, to grow dark, is conjugated in the same manner, and has the same irregularity.

CONJUGATIONS.

NEVAR. | To snow.

INDICATIVE.

SIMPLE TENSES.

Present.	Nieva.		It snows.
Imperfect.	Nevaba.		It was snowing.
Pret. Def.	Nevó.		It snowed.
Future.	Nevará.		It will snow.

COMPOUND TENSES.

Pret. Indef.	Ha nevado.		It has snowed.
Pluperfect.	Habia nevado.		It had snowed.
Anterior.	Hubo nevado.		It had snowed.
Comp. Future.	Habrá nevado.		It will have snowed.

IMPERATIVE.

Nieve. | Let it snow.

SUBJUNCTIVE.

SIMPLE TENSES.

Present. Nieve. — It may snow.

Imperfect. { Nevaria. / Nevara. / Nevase, } — It { might, / should, or / would } snow.

Future. Nevare. — It should snow.

COMPOUND TENSES.

Perfect. Haya nevado. — It may have snowed.

Pluperfect. { Habria / Hubiera / Hubiese } nevado. — It { might have, / should have, or / would have } snowed.

Comp. Future. Hubiere nevado. — It should have snowed.

N. B.—*Helar*, to freeze, is conjugated in the same manner, and has the same tenses irregular.

CONJUGATIONS.

TRONAR. | *To thunder.*

INDICATIVE.
SIMPLE TENSES.

Present.	Truena.	It thunders.
Imperfect.	Tronaba.	It was thundering.
Pret. Def.	Tronó.	It thundered.
Future.	Tronará.	It will thunder.

COMPOUND TENSES.

Pret. Indef.	Ha tronado.	It has thundered.
Pluperfect.	Habia tronado.	It had thundered.
Anterior.	Hubo tronado.	It had thundered.
Comp. Future.	Habrá tronado.	It will have thundered.

IMPERATIVE.

Truene. | Let it thunder.

SUBJUNCTIVE.
SIMPLE TENSES.

Present.	Truene.	It may thunder.
Imperfect.	{ Tronaria. / Tronara. / Tronase. }	It { might, / should, or / would } thunder.
Future.	Tronare.	It should thunder.

COMPOUND TENSES.

Perfect.	Haya tronado.	It may have thundered.
Pluperfect.	{ Habria / Hubiera / Hubiese } tronado.	It { might have, / should have, or / would have } thundered.
Comp. Future.	Hubiere tronado.	It should have thundered.

N. B.—*Llover*, to rain, is conjugated like this verb, and changes also the *o* into *ue* in the same tenses. *Escarchar*, to freeze; *granizar*, to hail; *lloviznar*, to drizzle; and *relampaguear*, to lighten, are all regular.

HACER, *to be* (when employed in reference to time and weather).

INDICATIVE.
SIMPLE TENSES.

Present.	Hace.	It is.
Imperfect.	Hacia.	It was.
Pret. Def.	Hizo.	It was.
Future.	Hará.	It will be.

COMPOUND TENSES.

Pret. Indef.	Ha hecho.	It has been.
Pluperfect.	Habia hecho.	It had been.
Anterior.	Hubo hecho.	It had been.
Comp. Future.	Habrá hecho.	It will have been.

IMPERATIVE.

Haga.	Let it be.

SUBJUNCTIVE.
SIMPLE TENSES.

Present.	Haga.	It may be.
Imperfect.	{ Haria. / Hiciera. / Hiciese. }	It { might, should, or would } be.
Future.	Hiciere.	It should be.

COMPOUND TENSES.

Perfect.	Haya hecho.	It may have been.
Pluperfect.	{ Habria / Hubiera / Hubiese } hecho.	It { might have, should have, or would have } been.
Comp. Future.	Hubiere hecho.	It should have been.

HABER, when signifying *there to be.*

Hay.	{ There is, / There are. }	Ha habido.	{ There has been. / There have been. }
Habia.	{ There was. / There were. }	Habia habido.	There had been.
Hubo.		Hubo habido.	There had been.
Habrá.	There will be.	Habrá habido.	There shall have been.

Haya.	Let there be.	Haya habido.	There may have been.
Haya.	There may be.		
Habria.	There might, could, would, or should be.	Habria habido. Hubiera habido. Hubiese habido.	There might, could, would, or should have been.
Hubiera.			
Hubiese.			
Hubiere.	There might or should be.	Hubiere habido.	There might or should have been.

DEFECTIVES.

The following verbs are found used only in the tenses and persons given in the annexed examples:

PLACER. | To please.

INDICATIVE.

Present, 3d pers. sing.,	Place.	It pleases.
Imperf. " "	Placia.	It was pleasing.
Pret. Def. " "	Plugo.	It pleased.

SUBJUNCTIVE.

Present. 3d pers., sing.,	Plegue.	It may please.
Imperf. " "	Pluguiera.	It would please.
	Pluguiese.	It might please.
Comp. Future. "	Pluguiere.	It should please.

SOLER. | To be wont.

INDICATIVE.

PRESENT.

Suelo.	I am wont.
Sueles.	Thou art wont.
Suele.	He is wont.
Solemos.	We are wont.
Soleis.	You are wont.
Suelen.	They are wont.

IMPERFECT.

Solia.	I was wont.
Solias.	Thou wast wont.
Solia.	He was wont.
Soliamos.	We were wont.
Soliais,	You were wont.
Solian.	They were wont.

YACER.	*To lie dead.*

No part of this verb is made use of except the third persons of the present indicative, *yace* and *yacen*, which are generally inscribed on tombstones.

CONJUGATION OF A VERB IN THE PASSIVE VOICE.

INFINITIVE.

Ser perdonado.	To be pardoned.

GERUND.

Siendo perdonado.	Being pardoned.

PAST PARTICIPLE.

Habiendo sido perdonado.	Having been pardoned.

INDICATIVE.

PRESENT.

1. Soy perdonado.	I am pardoned.	1. Somos perdonados.
2. Eres perdonado.		2. Sois perdonados.
3. Es perdonado,		3. Son perdonados.

IMPERFECT.

1. Era perdonado.	I was or used to be pardoned.	1. Eramos perdonados.
2. Eras perdonado.		2. Erais perdonados.
3. Era perdonado,		3. Eran perdonados.

PRETERIT DEFINITE.

1. Fuí perdonado. I was pardoned.
2. Fuiste perdonado.
3. Fué perdonado.

1. Fuimos perdonados.
2. Fuisteis perdonados.
3. Fueron perdonados.

FUTURE SIMPLE.

1. Seré perdonado. I shall be pardoned.
2. Serás perdonado.
3. Será perdonado.

1. Serémos perdonados.
2. Seréis perdonados.
3. Serán perdonados.

IMPERATIVE.

2. Sé perdonado. Be pardoned.
3. Sea perdonado.

1. Seamos perdonados.
2. Sed perdonados.
3. Sean perdonados.

SUBJUNCTIVE.

PRESENT.

1. Sea perdonado. I may be pardoned.
2. Seas perdonado.
3. Sea perdonado.

1. Seamos perdonados.
2. Seais perdonados.
3. Sean perdonados.

IMPERFECT.—*First Termination.*

1. Seria perdonado. I would be pardoned.
2. Serias perdonado.
3. Seria perdonado.

1. Seriamos perdonados.
2. Seriais perdonados.
3. Serian perdonados.

Second Termination.

1. Fuera perdonado. I might, could, would, or should be pardoned.
2. Fueras perdonado.
3. Fuera perdonado.

1. Fueramos perdonados.
2. Fuerais perdonados.
3. Fueran perdonados.

Third Termination.

1. Fuese perdonado.	I might, could, would, or should be pardoned.	1. Fuesemos perdonados.
2. Fueses perdonado.		2. Fueseis perdonados.
3. Fuese perdonado.		3. Fuesen perdonados.

FUTURE.

1. Fuere perdonado.	I might or should be pardoned.	1. Fueremos perdonados.
2. Fueres perdonado.		2. Fuereis perdonados.
3. Fuere perdonado.		3. Fueren perdonados.

Compound Tenses.
INDICATIVE.
PRETERIT INDEFINITE.

1. He sido perdonado.	I have been pardoned.	1. Hemos sido perdonados.
2. Has sido perdonado.		2. Habeis sido perdonados.
3. Ha sido perdonado.		3. Han sido perdonados.

PLUPERFECT.

1. Habia sido perdonado.	I had been pardoned.	1. Habiamos sido perdonados.
2. Habias sido perdonado.		2. Habiais sido perdoandos.
3. Habia sido perdonado.		3. Habian sido perdonados.

ANTERIOR.

1. Hube sido perdonado.	I had been pardoned.	1. Hubimos sido perdonados.
2. Hubiste sido perdonado.		2. Hubisteis sido perdonados.
3. Hubo sido perdonado.		3. Hubieron sido perdonados.

COMPOUND FUTURE.

1. Habré sido perdonado. — I shall have been pardoned.
2. Habrás sido perdonado.
3. Habrá sido perdonado.

1. Habrémos sido perdonados.
2. Habréis sido perdonados.
3. Habrán sido perdonados.

SUBJUNCTIVE.
PERFECT.

1. Haya sido perdonado. — I may have been pardoned.
2. Hayas sido perdonado.
3. Haya sido perdonado.

1. Hayamos sido perdonados.
2. Hayais sido perdonados.
3. Hayan sido perdonados.

PLUPERFECT.—*First Termination.*

1. Habria sido perdonado. — I would have been pardoned.
2. Habrias sido perdonado.
3. Habria sido perdonado.

1. Habriamos sido perdonados.
2. Habriais sido perdonados.
3. Habrian sido perdonados.

Second Termination.

1. Hubiera sido perdonado. — I might, could, would, or should have been pardoned.
2. Hubieras sido perdonado.
3. Hubiera sido perdonado.

1. Hubieramos sido perdonados.
2. Hubierais sido perdonados.
3. Hubieran sido perdonados.

Third Termination.

1. Hubiese sido perdonado. — I might, could, would, or should have been pardoned.
2. Hubieses sido perdonado.
3. Hubiese sido perdonado.

1. Hubiesemos sido perdonados.
2. Hubieseis sido perdonados.
3. Hubiesen sido perdonados.

FUTURE COMPOUND.

1. Hubiere sido perdonado.	I might or should have been pardoned.	1. Hubieremos sido perdonados.
2. Hubieres sido perdonado.		2. Hubiereis sido perdonados.
3. Hubiere sido perdonado.		3. Hubieren sido perdonados.

LIST

OF THE PRINCIPAL IRREGULAR VERBS IN THE SPANISH LANGUAGE.

N B.—*The figures placed after each verb refer to the page at which the model conjugation for that verb is to be found. For instance, the number 398 shows that* ADUCIR *is conjugated like* CONDUCIR, *found at page 398.*

Absolver, 394.
Abstraer, 422.
Acertar, 392.
Acordar, 393.
Acostar, 393.
Acrecentar, 392.
Adestrar, 392.
Adherir, 395.
Adquirir, 399.
Advertir, 395.
Aducir, 398.
Agorar, 393.
Alentar, 392.
Almorzar, 393.
Amolar, 393.
Andar, 400.
Apacentar, 392.
Apostar, 393.
Aprobar, 393.
Apretar, 392.
Arrecirse, 390.
Arrendar, 392.
Arrepentirse, 395.
Ascender, 394.
Asentar, 392.
Asentir, 395.
Aserrar, 392.
Asestar, 392.
Asir, 401.
Asolar, 393.
Asoldar, 393.
Atender, 394.
Atentar, 392.
Aterrar (echar por tierra), 392.
Atestar (rellenar), 392.
Atraer, 422.
Atravesar, 392.
Aventar, 392.
Aventarse, 392.
Avergonzar, 393.

Bendecir, 402.

Caber, 403.
Caer, 422.
Calentar, 392.
Cegar, 392.
Ceñir, 396.
Cerner, 394.
Cerrar, 392.
Cimentar, 392.
Cocer, 404.
Colar, 393.
Colegir, 396.
Colgar, 393.
Comedirse, 396.
Comenzar, 392.
Competir, 396.
Concebir, 396.
Concernir, 395.
Concertar, 392.
Concordar, 393.
Condescender, 394.
Condolerse, 394.
Conducir, 398.
Conferir, 395.
Confesar, 392.
Conocer, 398.
Conseguir, 396.
Consentir, 395.
Consolar, 393.
Constreñir, 396.
Contar, 393.
Contener, like TENER.
(See auxiliary verbs.)
Contender, 394.
Contradecir, 406.
Controvertir, 395.
Contraer, 422.
Convertir, 395.
Corregir, 396.

Dar, 405.
Decaer, 422.
Decentar, 392.
Decir, 406.

Deducir, 398.
Defender, 394.
Deferir, 395.
Degollar, 393.
Demoler, 394.
Demostrar, 393.
Denegar, 392.
Denostar, 393.
Derrengar, 392.
Derretir, 396.
Desavenir, 424.
Descender, 394.
Descollar, 393.
Descordar, 393.
Descomedirse, 396.
Desflocar, 393.
Deshacer, 410.
Deshelar, 392.
Destelr, 396.
Desembrar, 392.
Desolar, 393.
Desollar, 393.
Desovar, 393.
Despedir, 396.
Despernar, 392.
Despertar, 392.
Desterrar, 392.
Desplegar, 392.
Desvergonzarse, 393.
Dezmar, 392.
Discernir, 395.
Diferir, 395.
Digerir, 395.
Discordar, 393.
Disolver, 394.
Divertir, 395.
Doler, 394.
Dormir, 407.

Elegir, 396.
Embestir, 396.
Empedrar, 392.

440 LIST OF IRREGULAR VERBS.

Empezar, 392.
Emporcar, 393.
Encender, 394.
Encensar, 392.
Encerrar, 392.
Encomendar, 392.
Encontrar, 393.
Encordar, 393.
Engreirse, 396.
Engrosar, 393.
Enmendar, 392.
Enrodar, 393.
Ensangrentar, 392.
Entender, 394.
Enterrar, 392.
Envestir, 396.
Erguir, 408.
Errar, 409.
Escarmentar, 392.
Escocer, 404.
Esforzar, 393.
ESTAR. (See auxiliary verbs.)
Estreñir, 396.
Expedir, 396.
Extender, 394.

Forzar, 393.
Fregar, 392.

Gemir, 396.
Gobernar, 392.

HABER. (See auxiliaries and impersonals.)
Hacer, 410.
Heder, 394.
Helar, 392.
Henchir, 396.
Hender, 394.
Heñir, 396.
Herir, 395.
Herrar, 392.
Hervir, 395.
Holgar, 393.
Hollar, 393.

Impedir, 396.
Incensar, 392.
Inducir, 398.
Inferir, 395.
Ingerir, 396.
Inquirir, 390.
Introducir, 398.
Invernar, 392.
Invertir, 395.
Investir, 396.
Ir, 411.

Jugar, 412.

Llover, 394.

Maldecir, 402.
Manifestar, 392.
Mantener, like TENER. (See auxiliary verbs.)
Medir, 396.
Mentar, 392.
Mentir, 395.
Merendar, 392.
Moler, 394.
Morder, 394.
Morir, 407.
Mostrar, 392.
Mover, 394.

Negar, 392.
Nevar, 392.

Oir, 413.
Oler, 414.

Pedir, 396.
Pensar, 392.
Perder, 394.
Pervertir, 395.
Placer, 433.
Plegar, 392.
Poblar, 393.
Poder, 415.
Podrir, 416.
Poner, 417.
Preferir, 395.
Probar, 393.
Producir, 398.
Proferir, 395.

Quebrar, 392.
Querer, 418.

Raer, 422.
Recomendar, 392.
Recordar, 393.
Recostar, 393.
Reducir, 398.
Referir, 395.
Regar, 392.
Regir, 396.
Regoldar, 392.
Reir, 419.
Remendar, 392.
Rendir, 396.
Renovar, 393.
Reñir, 396.
Repetir, 396.
Requebrar, 392.
Requerir, 395.
Rescontrar, 393.

Resollar, 393.
Retentar, 392.
Reventar, 392.
Revolcar, 393.
Rodar, 393.
Roer.
Rogar, 393.

Saber, 420.
Salir, 421.
Satisfacer, 410.
Segar, 392.
Seguir, 396.
Sembrar, 392.
Sentar, 392.
Setir, 395.
SER. (See auxiliary verbs.)
Servir, 396.
Serrar, 392.
Soldar, 393.
Soler, 433.
Soltar, 393.
Solver, 394.
Sonar, 393.
Soñar, 393.
Sosegar, 392.
Soterrar, 392.
Sugerir, 395.

Temblar, 392.
Tender, 394.
TENER. (See auxiliary verbs.)
Teñir, 396.
Tentar, 392.
Torcer, 404.
Tostar, 393.
Traducir, 398.
Traer, 422.
Trascender, 394.
Trascordarse, 393.
Trasegar, 392.
Trocar, 393.
Tronar, 393.
Tropezar, 392.

Valer, 423.
Venir, 424.
Ver, 425.
Verter, 394.
Vestir, 396.
Volar, 393.
Volcar, 393.
Volver, 394.

Yacer, 434.

Zaherir, 395.

VOCABULARY,

CONTAINING ALL THE SPANISH WORDS USED IN THE GRAMMAR.

N. B.—*The figures after each definition refer to the lessons in which the words have been explained in the Grammar.*

A.

A, *ah*, prep., to, at, in.—Voy á Francia, I am going to France; á lo menos, at least; á la verdad, indeed; á la española, in the Spanish fashion. L. 4.
Abajo, *ah-bah'-ho*, adv., below, down, down-stairs. L. 33.
Abalanzar, *ah-bah-lan-thar'*, to spring, to rush. L. 57.
Abandonar, *ah-ban-do-nar'*, to abandon, to give up, to leave. L. 58.
Abanico, *ah-bah-ne'-co*, s. m., fan. L. 52.
Abierto, *ah-bĕ-air'-to*, p. p. irr. of ABRIR, (which see). L. 52.
Abogado, *ah-bo-gah'-do*, s. m., lawyer, advocate. L. 49.
Aborrecible, *ah-bor-rai-thĕ'-blai*, adj., hateful. L. 24.
Abril, *ah-breel'*, s. m., April. L. 28.
Abrir, *ah-breer'*, to open. *Abrirse*, to be opened, to blow (of flowers). L. 23.
Acá, *a'h-ca'*, adv., here.—*Acá y allá*, here and there. L. 18.
Acabar, *ah-cah-bar'*, to finish, to end.—*Acabar de*, to be just, to have just.—*Acabar con*, to kill, to put an end to, to destroy. L. 23.
Academia, *ah-cah-dai'-mĕ-a*, s. f., academy. L. 51.
Acaso, *ah-cah'-so*, adv., perchance, by chance.—*Si acaso*, if at all.—*Por si acaso*, in case that. L. 32.
Accidente, *ac-thĕ-dain'-tai*, s. m., accident. L. 40.
Accion, *ac-thĕ-ōne'*, s. f., action, share. L. 24.
Acento, *ah-thain'-to*, s. m., accent. L. 47.
Aceptar, *ah-thaip-tar'*, to accept. L. 45.
Acerca, *ah-thair'-ca*, prep. *Acerca de*, about. L. 49.
Acertar, *ah-thair-tar'*, to make out, to hit the mark, to succeed, to be right (*i. e.*, to conjecture right). L. 34.
Acierto, *ah-thĕ-air'-to*, s. m., success. L. 52.
Acomodar, *ah-cō-mō-dar'*, to accommodate, to suit. L. 31.
Acompañar, *ah-cōm-pan-yar'*, to accompany. L. 47.
Aconsejar, *ah-cōn-sai-har'*, to counsel, to advise. L. 45.
Acordar, *ah-cōr-dar'*, to accord, to agree, to tune.—*Acordarse*, to remember. L. 46.

Acostar, *ah-cōs-tar'*, to lay down.—*Acostarse*, to lie down, to go to bed. L. 35.
Actual, *ac-twal'*, adj., present. L. 52.
Acudir, *ah-coo-deer'*, to haste, to run, to turn (to), to refer (to). L. 49.
Acuerdo, *ah-cwair'-do*, s. m., agreement, accord, decision (of a court). L. 42.
Acullá, *ah-cool-ya'*, adv., there.—*Aquí y acullá*, to and fro; here and there. L. 18.
Adelantar, *ah-dai-lan-tar'*, to advance, to make progress. L. 36.
Adelante, *ah-dai-lan'-tai*, adv., forward.—*En adelante*, henceforward.—¡ *Adelante!* go on! go ahead! L. 43.
Ademan, *ah-dai-man'*, s. m., posture, air. L. 44.
Además, *ah-dai-mas'*, prep., besides; adv., moreover, besides. L. 37.
Adentro, *ah-dain'-tro*, adv., in, within, inside. L. 47.
Adivinar, *ah-dee-vee-nar'*, to guess, to divine. L. 46.
Adjetivo, *ad-hai-tee'-vo*, s. m., adjective. L. 43.
Admirable, *ad-mee-rah'-blai*, adj., admirable, wonderful. L. 51.
Admiracion, *ad-mee-rah-thĕ-ōne'*, s. f., admiration, wonder. L. 51.
Admirar, *ad-mee-rar'*, to admire, to wonder at. L. 46.
Adonde. (See DONDE.) L. 9.
Adquirir, *ad-kĕ-reer'*, to acquire. L. 42.
Adverbial, *ad-vair-bĕ-al'*, adj., adverbial. L. 50.
Adverbio, s. m., adverb. L. 43.
Advertir, *ad-rair-teer'*, to advise, to mention, to point out, to warn, to observe. L. 43.
Aéreo, *ah-ai'-rai-o*, adj., aërial. L. 48.
Afectacion, *ah-faik-tah-thĕ-ōne'*, s. f., affectation. L. 24.
Afectar, *ah-faik-tar'*, to affect. L. 45.
Afeitar, *ah-fai-ĕ-tar'*, to shave, to paint (the face). L. 33.
Afirmacion, *ah-feer-mah-thĕ-ōne'*, s. f., affirmation. L. 24.
Afirmar, *ah-feer-mar'*, to affirm, to make firm, to strengthen. L. 48.
Afligir, *ah-flee-heer'*, to afflict. L. 48.
Afortunado, *ah-fōre-too-nah'-do*, adj., fortunate. L. 63.
Ageno, *ah-hai'-no*, adj., foreign, belonging to others. L. 63.

442   VOCABULARY.

Agitacion, *ah-hes-tah-thĕ-ōne'*, s. f., agitation. L. 24.
Agradar, *ah-grah-dar'*, to please. L. 53.
Agradecer, *ah-grah-dai-thair'*, to thank, to be obliged to. L. 39.
Agregar, *ah-grai-gar'*, to add, to unite. L. 49.
Agrio, *ah'-grĕ-o*, adj., sour. L. 22.
Agua, *ah'-gwa*, s. f., water. L. 7.
Aguantar, *ah-gwan-tar'*, to support, to put up with, to bear, to bear with. L. 53.
Aguardiente, *ah-gwar-dĕ-ain'-tai*, s. m., brandy. L. 50.
Agudeza, *ah-goo-dai'-tha*, s. f., wit, witty saying. L. 57.
Agüero, *ah-gwai'-ro*, s. m., augury, omen. L. 45.
Ahora, *ah-ō-ra*, adv., now. L. 27.
Aire, *i'-rai*, s. m., air. L. 46.
Ajedrez, *ah-hai-draith'*, s. m., chess. L. 42.
Ala, *ah'-la*, s. f., wing. L. 58.
Alabanza, *ah-lah-ban'-tha*, s. f., praise. L. 53.
Alarde, s. m.—Hacer *alarde*, to boast. L. 63.
Alberto, *al-bair'-to*, s. m., Albert. L. 38.
Alcance, *al-kan'-thai*, s. m., reach. L. 53.
Alcanzar, *al-can-thar'*, to reach, to overtake, to take up with, to catch. L. 53.
Alegrar, *ah-lai-grar'*, to give joy, to make glad. L. 37.
Alegre, *ah-lai'-grai*, adj., joyful, glad, merry. L. 21.
Alejandro, *ah-lai-han'-dro*, s. m., Alexander. L. 3.
Alelí, *ah-lai-lee'*, s. m., gilliflower. L. 9.
Aleman, *ah-lai-man'*, s. m., German (language). L. 2.
Aleman, s. m., German; adj., German. L. 3.
Alemania, *ah-lai-mah-nĕ-a*, s. f., Germany. L. 9.
Alfiler, *al-fee-lair'*, s. m. and f., pin. L. 46.
Algazara, *al-gah-thah'-ra*, s. f., shouts of joy. L. 54.
Algodon, *al-gō-dōne'*, s. m., cotton. L. 5.
Alguien, *al'-gain*, pron., somebody, anybody, some one, any one. L. 17.
Alguno, a, *al-goo'-no*, adj., some. L. 17.
Alguno, a, pron. ind., and adj., somebody, some one, anybody, any one, some. L. 17.
Alhaja, *al-ah'-ha*, s. f., jewel. L. 57.
Alimentar, *ah-lee-main-tar'*, to feed.—*Alimentarse* de esperanzas, to live on hope. L. 53.
Alimento, s. m., food. L. 49.
Allá, *al-ya'*, adv., there, yonder. L. 18.
Alma, *al'-ma*, s. f., soul. L. 47.
Almacen, *al-mah-thain'*, s. m., store. L. 62.
Almorzar, *al-mōr-thar'*, to breakfast, to take breakfast. L. 35.
Almuerzo, *al-mu-air'-tho*, s. m., breakfast. L. 55.
Alrededor, *al-rai-dai-dōr'*, adv., around. L. 56.
Alteracion, *al-tah-rah-thĕ-ōne'*, s. f., alteration, change. L. 56.
Alto, *al'-tō*, adj., high, tall. L. 21.
Altura, *al-too'-ra*, s. f., height. L. 37.
Alumbrar, *ah-loom-brar'*, to light. L. 64.
..mable, *ah-mah'-blai*, adj., amiable. L. 47.
Amador, *ah-mah-dōr'*, s. m., lover. L. 49.

Amanecer, *ah-mah-nai-thair'*, to get morning, to be in a place at daybreak, or morning. L. 30.
Amante, *ah-man'-tai*, p. p. and s., loving, lover, sweetheart. L. 33.
Amar, *ah-mar'*, to love. L. 21.
Amarillo, *ah-mah-reel'-yō*, adj., yellow. L. 54.
Ambicion, *am-bĕ-thĕ-ōne'*, s. f., ambition. L. 60.
Ambos, *am'-bōs*, pron., both. L. 28.
Amenazar, *ah-nai-nah-thar'*, to menace, to threaten. L. 59.
Amenidad, *ah-mai-nĕ-dath'*, s. f., amenity. L. 32.
Amigo, *ah-mĕ'-go*, s. m., friend. L. 13.
Amistad, *ah-mees-tath'*, s. f., friendship. L. 61.
Amor, *ah-more'*, s. m., love. L. 43.
Amplio, *am'-plĕ-o*, adj., ample. L. 52.
Ampo, s. m., whiteness (of snow). L. 61.
Analítico, *ah-nah-lĕ'-tĕ-co*, adj., analytical. L. 35.
Anaranjado, *ah-nah-ran-hah'-do*, adj., orange (color). L. 54.
Ancho, *an'-chō*, adj., wide, broad. L. 47.
Anchura, *an-choo'-ra*, s. f., width, breadth. L. 61.
Anciano, *an-thĕ-ah'-no*, adj. and s., old, old man. L. 48.
Andar, *an-dar'*, to walk, to go. L. 44.
Anécdota, *ah-naik'-dō-ta*, s. f., anecdote. L. 44.
Angel, *an'-hail*, s. m., angel. L. 60.
Angulo, *an'goo-lo*, s. m., angle.—En *ángulos rectos*, at right angles. L. 60.
Animal, *ah-nĕ-mal'*, s. m., animal. L. 62.
Animar, *ah-nĕ-mar'*, to animate, to encourage. L. 38.
Anoche, *ah-nō'-chai*, adv., last night. L. 28.
Anochecer, *ah-nō-chai-thair'*, to get night, to be (in such a place) at nightfall. L. 30.
Antagonista, *an-tah-gō-nees'-ta*, s. m., antagonist. L. 36.
Ante, *an'-tai*, prep., before, in presence of. L. 16.
Anteayer, *an-tai-ah-yair'*, adv., the day before yesterday. L. 16.
Antecedente, *an-tai-thai-dain'-tai*, s. m., antecedent. L. 61.
Antenoche, *an-tai-nō'-chai*, the night before last. L. 23.
Anteojo, *an-tai-ō'-ho*, s. m., eye-glass.—*Anteojos*, spectacles. L. 53.
Antepenúltimo, *an-tai-pai-nool'-tĕ-mo*, adj. and s. m., antepenultimate. L. 50.
Anterior, *an-tai-rĕ-or'*, adj., preceding, foregoing, previous, former. L. 49.
Antes, *an'-tais*, prep.—*Antes* de, before. L. 42.
Antes, adv., rather, first, sooner than. L. 16.
Antepuesto, *an-tai-pwais'-to*, p.p., prefixed; s., prefix. L. 52.
Antiguo, *an-tĕ'-gwo*, adj., ancient, old. L. 52.
Antisocial, *an-tĕ-sō-thĕ-al'*, adj., antisocial. L. 50.
Antojo, *an-tō'-ho*, s. m., whim, longing. L. 63.
Añadir, *an-yah-deer'*, to add. L. 49.
Añil, *an-yeel'*, s. m., indigo (color). L. 54.
Año, *an-yo*, s. m., year. L. 10.
Apariencia, *ah-pah-rĕ-ain'-thĕ-a*, s. f., appearance. L. 53.

VOCABULARY. 443

[L. 46.

Apegar, *ah-pai-gar*, to adhere, to attach. L. 54.
Apénas, *ah-pai'-nas*, adv., scarcely, hardly. L. 29.
Aplicar, *ah-plē-car'*, to apply. L. 62.
Apostar, *ah-pōs-tar'*, to bet, to wager. L. 63.
Apoyar, *ah-pō-yar'*, to lean, to support, to protect. L. 50.
Apreciable, *ah-prah-thē-ah'-blai*, appreciable, respectable. L. 56.
Apremiar, *ah-prai-mē-ar'*, to press, to urge. L. 45.
Aprender, *ah-prain-dair'*. L. 6.
Apretar, *ah-prai-tar'*, to tighten, to press, to urge. L. 65.
Aprisa, *ah-prē'-sa*, adv., quickly. L. 6.
Aprobacion, *ah-prō-bah-thē-ōne'*, s. f., approbation. L. 24.
Aprobar, *ah-prō-bar'*, to approve. L. 35.
Aprovechar, *ah-prō-vai-char'*, to progress, to make the most of. L. 52.
Aproximar, *ah-prō-ksē-mar'*, to approximate, to approach. L. 44.
Apto, *ap'-to*, adj., apt, fit. L. 51.
Apurado, *ah-poo-rah'-do*, adj., embarrassed. L. 44.
Aquel, *ah-kail'*, pron., that one, he; the former. L. 18.
Aquí, *ah-kē'*, adv., here. L. 18.
Arbol, *ar'-bōl*, s. m., tree. L. 49.
Arboleda, *ar-bō-lai'-da*, s. f., grove. L. 49.
Arenal, *ah-rai-nal'*, s. m., sandy ground. L. 49.
Argüir, *ar-goo-eer'*, to argue. L. 34.
Aristocracia, *ah-rees-tō-krah'-thē-a*, s. f., aristocracy. L. 60.
Aristocrático, adj., aristocrat. L. 35.
Aritmética, *ah-reet-mai'-tē-ka*, s. f., arithmetic. L. 21.
Armar, *ar-mar'*, to arm. L. 59.
Arpa, *ar'-pa*, s. f., harp. L. 15.
Arquitecto, *ar-kē-taik'-to*, s. m., architect. L. 48.
Arquitectura, *ar-kē-taik-too'-ra*, s. f., architecture. L. 51.
Arreglar, *ar-rai-glar'*, to regulate, to arrange, to settle. L. 60.
Arrepentirse, *ar-rai-pain-teer'-sai*, to repent. L. 38.
Arrestar, *ar-rais-tar'*, to arrest. L. 37.
Arriba, *ar-rē'-ba*, adv., above, up-stairs. L. 33.
Arte, s. *ar'-tai*, m. and f., art. L. 31.
Artículo, *ar-tē'-coo-lo*, s. m., article. L. 43.
Artificial, *ar-tē-fē-thē-al'*, adj., artificial. L. 49.
Artista, *ar-tees'-ta*, s. m., artist. L. 36.
Asador, s. m., spit (for roasting). L. 65.
Ascender, *as-thain-dair'*, to ascend, to amount. L. 37.
Ascension, *as-thain-sē-ōne'*, s. f., ascension. L. 49.
Asegurar, *ah-sai-goo-rar'*, to secure, to assure. L. 38.
Asesino, *ah-sai-sē'-no*, s. m., assassin. L. 59.
Así, *ah-sē'*, adv., so, thus. L. 20.—*Así* que, so that, as soon as. L. 29.—*Así así*, so so. L. 39.
Asiento, *ah-sē-ain'-to*, s. m., seat. L. 39.
Asir, *ah-seer'*, to seize, to make the most of. L. 42.
Asno, *as'-no*, s. m., ass. L. 61.

Asombro, *ah-sōm'-bro*, s. m., amazement.
Astronomía, *ass-trō-nō-mē'-a*, s. f., astronomy. L. 49.
Atencion, *ah-tain-thē-ōne'*, s. f., attention. L. 56.
Atender, *ah-tain-dair'*, to attend. L. 37.
Atlántico, *at-lan' tē-ko*, s. m. and adj., Atlantic. L. 46.
Atolladero, *ah-tōl-lya-dai'-ro*, s.m., difficulty. L. 60.
Atraccion, *ah-trak-thē-ōne'*, s. f., attraction. L. 24.
Atrás, *ah-tras'*, adv., behind, ago. L. 58.
Atreverse, *ah-trai-vair'-sai*, to dare. L. 48.
Atrevimiento, *ah-trai-ve-mē-ain'-to*, s. m., assurance, daring. L. 64.
Atrocidad, *ah-trō-thē-dath'*, s. f., atrocity. L. 36.
Atropellar, *a-trō-pail-yar'*, to trample upon, to run over. L. 51.
Aullar, *ah-ool-yar'*, to howl. L. 44.
Aumento, *ah-oo-main'-to*, s. m., augmentation, increase. L. 59.
Aun, *ah-oon'*, adv., still, yet. L. 25.
Aunque, *ah-oon-ke'*, adv., although, though. L. 36.
Ausencia, *ah-oo-sain'-thē-a*, s. f., absence. L. 35.
Ausente, *ah-oo-sain'-tai*, adj., absent. L. 59.
Autor, *ah-oo-tōr'*, s. m., author. L. 47.
Autoridad, *ah-oo-tō-rē-dath'*, s. f., authority. L. 59.
Auxiliar, *ah-oo-ksē-lē-ar'*, s.m. and adj., auxiliary. L. 57.
Auxiliar, to help, to aid. L. 62.
Auxilio, *ah-oo-ksē'-lē-o*, s. m., help, assistance. L. 55.
Avenida, *ah-vai-nē'-da*, s. f., avenue. L. 15.
Aventurarse, *ah-vain-too-rar'-sai*, to venture. L. 65.
Avisar, *ah-vē-sar'*, to inform, to let know. L. 45.
Ay! *ah-e'*, int., alas! L. 46.
Ayer, *ah-yair'*, adv., yesterday. L. 16.
Ayudar, *ah-yoo-dar'*, to aid, to help. L. 38.
Azul, *ah-thool'*, adj., blue. L. 54.

B.

Bailar, *bah-ē-lar'*, to dance. L. 28.
Baile, *bah-ē-lai*, s. m., dance, ball. L. 30.
Bajar, *bah-har'*, to go or come down, to lower. L. 53.
Bajo, *bah'-ho*, adj., low, base, mean. L. 21.
Banco, *ban'-ko*, s. m., bench, bank. L. 31.
Bandera, *ban-dai'-ra*, s. f., flag, standard. L. 58.
Bañar, *ban-yar'*, to bathe. L. 49.
Barato, *bah-rah'-to*, adj., cheap. L. 13.
Barba, *bar'-ba*, s. f., chin, beard. L. 59.
Barbería, *bar-bai-rē'-a*, s. f., barber's shop. L. 50.
Barbero, *bar-bai'-ro*, s. m., barber. L. 33.
Barbilampiño, *bar-bē-lam-peen'-yo*, adj., having a thin beard. L. 50.
Barco, s. m., vessel, boat. L. 60.
Baron, *bah-rōne'*, s. m., baron. L. 51.
Barrer, *bar-rair'*, to sweep. L. 24.
Basta! *bas'-ta*, int., enough! L. 30.
Bastante, *bas-tan'-tai*, adv., enough. L. 25.

444 VOCABULARY.

Bastar, *bas-tar'*, to be enough, sufficient. L. 30.
Baston, *bas-tōne*, s. m., cane, stick. L. 10.
Baza, *bah'-tha*, s. f., trick (at cards).—No dejar meter *baza*, not to let any one put in a single word. L. 63.
Bebedor, *bai-bai-dōre'*, s. m., tippler, toper, drinker. L. 65.
Beber, *bai-bair'*, to drink.—*Beber* los vientos por algo, to solicit with much eagerness, to desire ardently.—*Beber* como una cuba, to drink like a fish. L. 7.
Belleza, *bail-yai'-tha*, s. f., beauty. L. 51.
Bello, *bail'-yo*, adj., beautiful, handsome. L. 31.
Bendecir, *bain-dai-theer'*, to bless. L. 41.
Bendito, *bain-dě'-to*, adj., blessed. L. 52.
Besar, *bai-sar'*, to kiss. L. 39.
Beso, *bai'-so*, s. m., kiss. L. 39.
Biblioteca, *bě-blě-ō-tai'-ka*, s. f., library. L. 52.
Bien, *bě-ain'* (pronounce in one syllable), adv., well. L. 3.—Está *bien*, very well, all right.—No *bien*, scarcely, no sooner. L. 29.
Bienhechor, *bě-ain-ai-chōr'*, s. m., benefactor. L. 50.
Bien venido! *bě-ain' vai-ně'-do*, int., welcome! L. 45.
Billete, *beel-yai'-tai*, s. m., note, ticket. L. 7.
Blanca, *blan'-ka*, s. f.—Encontrarse sin *blanca*, not to have a cent. L. 64.
Blanco, *blan'-ko*, adj., white. L. 58.
Blanco, s. m., mark (to aim at).—Quedarse en *blanco*, to be left in the lurch. L. 57.
Bledo, *blai'-do*, s. m., straw.—No se me da un *bledo*, I do not care a straw for it. L. 63.
Boca, *bō'-ka*, s. f., mouth. L. 44.—Hablar por *boca* de ganso, to repeat what another has said. L. 63.
Bocado, *bō-kah'-do*, s. m., mouthful, bite.—*Bocado* sin hueso, sinecure. L. 61.
Bolsa, *bōl'-sa*, s. f., purse. L. 45.
Bolsillo, *bōl-seel'-yo*, s. m., pocket, purse. L. 47.
Bondad, *bōne-dath'*, s. f., goodness, kindness. L. 39.
Bondadoso, *bōne-dah-dō'-so*, adj., good, kind. L. 54.
Bonito, *bō-ně'-to*, adj., pretty. L. 58.
Borboton, *bōre-bō-tōne'*.—A *borbotones*, bubbling, hurriedly, confusedly. L. 63.
Bosque, *bōs'-kai*, s. m., wood, woody place. L. 40.
Bota, *bō'-ta*, s. f., boot. L. 10.
Botica, *bō-lě'-ka*, s. f., drug-store. L. 62.
Boticario, *bō-lě-kah'-rě-o*, s. m., druggist. L. 49.
Bravata, *brah-vah'-ta*, s.f., bravado.—Echar *bravatas*, to brag, to boast. L. 62.
Bravo, *brah'-vo*, adj., brave. L. 44.
Bravo! int., bravo! L. 48.
Brazo, *brah'-tho*, s. m., arm. L. 44.
Bribon, *brě-bonè'*, s. m., scoundrel, rascal. L. 32.
Bruto, *broo'-to*, s. m., brute, ignorant person. L. 48.
Bruto, adj., brutish, ignorant. L. 48.
Bueno, *bwai'-no*, adj., good. L. 7.—*Buenos* dias, good morning, good day.—De *buenas* á primeras, all at once. L. 62.

Buey, *bwai'-ě*, s. m., ox. L. 58.
Bula, *boo'-la*, s. f.—Tener *bula* para todo, to act according to one's fancy. L. 64.
Bulla, *bool'-ya*, s. f., noise.—Meter *bulla*, to make a noise. L. 63.
Bullicio, *bool-yě'-thě-o*, s. m., bustle, noise, uproar. L. 54.
Bulto, *bool'-to*, s. m., bundle.—Hablar á *bulto*, to talk at random. L. 63.
Burla, *boor'-la*, s. f., jest, joke.—Hablar de *burlas*, to speak in jest. L. 33.
Burlar, *boor-lar'*, to jest.—*Burlarse* de alguno, to make fun of, to laugh at any one.—*Burla burlando*, half jest, half earnest. L. 33.
Burlon, *boor-lōne'*, s. m., wag, jester. L. 44.
Busca, *boos'-ka*, s. f., search.—En *busca* de, in search of. L. 55.
Buscar, *boos-kar'*, to search, to look for. L. 4.—*Buscar* cinco piés al gato, to pick a quarrel. L. 4.

C.

Caballejo, *kah-bal-yai'-ho*, s.m. (*dim.* of CABALLO), nag, contemptible old horse. L. 49.
Caballero, *kah-bal-yai'-ro*, s. m., gentleman, knight.—Buenos tardes, *caballero*, good afternoon, sir. L. 2.
Caballo, *kah-bal'-yo*, s. m., horse. L. 4.
Cabello, *kah-bail'-yo*, s. m., hair. L. 33.—Tomar la ocasion por los *cabellos*, to profit by the occasion. L. 61.
Caber, *kah-bair'*, to hold, to contain.—No *caber* de gozo, to be overjoyed.—¿Puede *caber* en tu imaginacion? can such a thing enter into your imagination?—No *cabe* mas, nothing more can be desired. L. 42.
Cabeza, *kah-bai'-tha*, s. f., head. L. 28.
Cable, *kah'-blai*, s. m., cable. L. 46.
Cabo, *kah'-bo*, s. m., end.—Al *cabo*, at last. L. 51.
Cada, *kah'-da*, pron., each, every.—*Cada* vez, every time.—*Cada* uno, each, every one. L. 43.
Caer, *kah-air'*, to fall, to see, to understand, to be, fall due. L. 41.—*Caer* de piés, to fall on one's feet.—Ya *caigo* en ello, now I see, understand.—Las ventanas *caen* á la plaza, the windows look on the square.—*Caérsele* á uno la cara de vergüenza, to blush with shame. L. 59.
Café, *kah-fai'*, s. m., coffee, coffee-house. L. 14.
Caja, *kah'-ha*, s. f., case, box, cash (commercial). L. 60.
Cal, s. f., lime.—De *cal* y canto, of stone. L. 48.
Calabaza, *kah-lah-bah'-tha*, s. f., pumpkin.—Dar *calabazas*, to give the mitten. L. 61.
Calcular, *kal-koo-lar'*, to calculate. L. 51.
Caldo, *kal'-do*, s. m., broth. L. 44.
Calducho, *kal-doo'-cho*, s. m., poor broth. L. 44.
Calentar, *kah-lain-tar'*, to heat, to warm. L. 34.
Calentura, *kah-lain-too'-ra*, s. f., fever. L. 60.
Caliente, *kah-lě-ain'-tai*, adj., hot, warm. L. 41.

Callado, *kal-yah'-do*, adj., silent, taciturn. L. 20.
Callar, *kal-yar'*, to be silent, to keep silence.—*Callar su pico*, to hold one's tongue, to say nothing. L. 42.
Calle, *kal'-yai*, s. f., street.—*Dejar á uno en la calle*, to strip one of his all. L. 15.
Calor, *kah-lor'*, s. m., heat, warmth. L. 25.
Calva, *kal'-va*, s. f., bald place, bald part of the head. L. 45.
Calvo, *kal'-vo*, adj., bald. L. 45.
Calza, *kal'-tha*, s. f., stockings.—*Tomar las calzas de Villadiego*, to make off, to make a hurried escape. L. 50.
Cama, *kah'-ma*, s. f., bed.—*Guardar cama*, to be confined to one's bed. L. 14.
Cambiar, *kam-bē-ar'*, to change. L. 59.
Cambio, *kam'-bē-o*, s. m., change. L. 46.
Camino, *kah-mē'-no*, s. m., way, road. L. 60.
Camisa, *kah-mē'-sa*, s. f., shirt.—*Meterse en camisa de once varas*, to interfere in other people's affairs. L. 46.
Campo, *kam'-po*, s. m., field, camp.—*Dejar el campo libre*, to leave the field to one's competitors. L. 59.
Canasto, *kah-nas'-to*, s. m., basket. L. 58.
Cándidamente, *kan'-dē-dah-main-tai*, adv., candidly. L. 48.
Cansado, *kan-sah'-do*, adj., tired, tiresome.—*Estar cansado*, to be tired.—*Ser cansado*, to be tiresome. L. 20.
Cansar, *kan-sar'*, to tire, to fatigue. L. 33.
Cantar, *kan-tar'*, to sing. L. 15.
Cantatriz, *kan-tah-treeth'*, s. f., singer. L. 15.
Cantidad, *kan-tē-dath'*, quantity, sum. L. 60.
Canto, *kan'-to*, s. m., singing, stone.—*De cal y canto*, of stone. L. 48.
Cantor, *kan-tor'*, s. m., singer. L. 15.
Cañon, *kan-yōne'*, s. m., cannon. L. 44.
Cañonazo, *kan-yō-nah'-tho*, s. m., cannon-shot, gun-shot. L. 44.
Capa, *kah'-pa*, s. f., cloak.—*Andar de capa caida*, to be crestfallen. L. 60.
Capacidad, *kah-pah-thē-dath'*, s. f., capacity, capability. L. 36.
Capaz, *kah-path'*, adj., capable. L. 59.
Capitan, *kah-pē-tan'*, s. m., captain. L. 52.
Capricho, *kah-prē'-cho*, s. m., caprice, fancy, whim. L. 60.
Cara, *kah'-ra*, s. f., face.—*Dar á alguno con la puerta en la cara*, to shut the door in any one's face. L. 60.
Carácter, *kah-rak'-tair* (pl. caractéres), s. m., character, disposition. L. 40.
Caramba! *kah-ram'-ba*, inter., strange! zounds! L. 65.
Carcajada, *kar-kah-hah'-da*, s. f., loud laugh, burst of laughter. L. 54.
Cárcel, *kar'-thail*, s. f., prison. L. 34.
Carga, *kar'-ga*, s. f., load, burden, charge. L. 60.
Cargar, *kar-gar'*, to charge, to load, to heap. L. 47.
Cargo, *kar'-go*, s. m., load, employment, charge, office. L. 60.
Caridad, *kah-rē-dath'*, s. f., charity. L. 41.
Cariredondo, *kah-rē-rai-dōne'-do*, adj., roundfaced. L. 59.
Carne, *kar'-nai*, s. f., flesh, meat. L. 7.
Carnero, *kar-nai'-ro*, s. m., mutton, sheep. L. 40.

Carnicería, *kar-nē-thai-rē'-a*, s. f., butcher's shop, meat market. L. 11.
Carnicero, *kar-nē-thai'-ro*, s. m., butcher. L. 11.
Carnuza, *kar-noo'-tha*, s. f., bad, disgusting, spoiled meat. L. 49.
Caro, *kah'-ro*, adj., dear, at a high price. L. 13.
Carpintero, *kar-peen-tai'-ro*, s. m., carpenter. L. 33.
Carrera, *kar-rai'-ra*, s. f., career, course, race, profession. L. 48.
Carro, *kar'-ro*, s. m., car, wagon. L. 58.
Carruage, *kar-roo-ah'-hai*, s. m., carriage. L. 51.
Carta, *kar'-ta*, s. f., letter. L. 7.
Cartilla, *kar-teel'-ya*, s. f., primer.—*Cosa que no está en la cartilla*, something strange or uncommon. L. 61.
Casa, *kah'-sa*, s. f., house. L. 9.
Cáscaras! *kas'-kah-ras*, int., oh! dear me! L. 63.
Casero, *kah-sai'-ro*, adj., domestic, household.—*Comedia casera*, parlor play. L. 59.
Casi, *kah'-sē*, adv., almost. L. 32.
Caso, *kah'-so*, s. m., case, event.—*No haga V. caso de eso*, take no notice of that. L. 60.
Castaña, *kas-tan'-ya*, s. f., chestnut. L. 40.
Castellano, *kas-tail-yah'-no*, s. m., Castilian language. L. 55.
Castellano, adj., Castilian. L. 55.
Castillo, *kas-teel'-yo*, s. m., castle.—*Hacer castillos en el aire*, to build castles in the air. L. 48.
Casualidad, *kah-soo-ah-lē-dath'*, s. f., casualty, chance, hazard. L. 60.
Casucha, *kah-soo'-cha*, s. f., contemptible old house. L. 41.
Catolicismo, *ka-tō-lē-thcess'-mo*, s. m., Catholicism. L. 49.
Catorce, *kah-tor'-thai*, num. adj., fourteen.—*Luis Catorce*, Louis the Fourteenth. L. 14.
Causa, *kah'-oo-sa*, s. f., cause.—*A causa de*, on account of. L. 40.
Causar, *kah-oo-sar'*, to cause. L. 51.
Caza, *kah'-tha*, s. f., chase, hunt, hunting.—*Ir á la caza*, to go hunting. L. 58.
Cazar, *kah-thar'*, to chase, to hunt. L. 58.
Celebracion, *thai-lai-brah-thē-ōne'*, s. f., celebration. L. 39.
Celebrar, *thai-lai-brar'*, to celebrate.—*Celebro que V. haya venido*, I am glad you have come. L. 39.
Celeste, *thai-lais'-tai*, adj., heavenly, celestial.—*Los cuerpos celestes*, the heavenly bodies. L. 49.
Celestial, *thai-lais-tē-al'*, adj., celestial, heavenly. (See CELESTE.) L. 49.
Célico, *thai'-lē-ko*, adj., heavenly (used in poetry only). L. 49.
Celo, *thai'-lo*, s. m., zeal. L. 55.
Cena, *thai'-na*, s. f., supper, Last Supper. L. 52.
Cenar, *thai-nar'*, to sup, to take supper. L. 39.
Centavo, *thain-tah'-vo*, s. m., cent. L. 14.
Centella, *thain-tail'-ya*, s. f., flash, spark.—*Echar rayos y centellas*, to foam with rage. L. 62.
Centena, *thain-tai'-na*, s. f., about a hundred. L. 40.

VOCABULARY.

Contenar, *thain-tai-nar'*, s. m., a hundred, L. 40.
Cerca, *thair'-ka*, adv., near, close by. Cerca de su casa, near his house. L. 31.
Ceremonial, *thai-rai-mō-nē-al'*, adj., ceremonial, ceremonious. L. 54.
Cerrar, *thair-rar'*, to shut, to close. L. 34.
Cerrojo, *thair-rō'-ho*, s. m., bolt. L. 59.
Cerveza, *thair-vai'-tha*, s. f., ale, beer. L. 7.
Chaleco, *chah-lai'-ko*, s. m., vest. L. 10.
Chancear, *chan-thai-ar'*, to jest, to joke. L. 58.
Chanza, *chan'-tha*, s. f., jest, joke. L. 58.
Charla, *char'-la*, s. f., chit-chat, prattle. L. 60.
Charlar, *char-lar'*, to chat, to prattle. L. 37.
Chasco, *chas'-ko*, s. m., disappointment.—Llevarse un chasco solemne, to be greatly disappointed. L. 46.
Chelin, *chai-leen'*, s. m., shilling. L. 61.
Chico, *chē'-ko*, adj., little, small. L. 44.
Chiquirrítico, *chē-keer-rē-tē'-ko*, adj., very small, very little. L. 41.
Chito! *chē'-to*, int., hush! silence! L. 46.
Chocolate, *chō-kō-lah'-tai*, s. m., chocolate. L. 14.
Ciego, *thē-ai'-go*, s. m. and adj., blind.—A ciegas, blindly, in the dark. L. 48.
Cielo, *thē-ai'-lo*, s. m., heaven, sky.—Tomar el cielo con las manos, to be transported with joy, grief, or passion. L. 45.
Cien, *thē-ain'*, num. adj., a hundred.—(See CIENTO.) L. 14.
Ciencia, *thē-ain'-thē-a*, s. f., science. L. 49.
Ciento, *thē-ain'-to*, num. adj., a hundred.—(See CIEN.) L. 14.
Cierto, *thē-air'-to*, adj., certain. L. 48.
Cimiento, *the-mē-ain'-to*, s. m., foundation. L. 59.
Cinco, *theen'-ko*, num. adj., five, fifth. L. 14.
Cincuenta, *theen-kwain'-ta*, num. adj., fifty, fiftieth. L. 14.
Circumspección, *theer-koonss-paik-thē-ōne'*, s. f., circumspection. L. 24.
Circunstancia, *theer-koonss-tan'-thē-a*, s. f., circumstance. L. 40.
Cita, *thē'-ta*, s. f., appointment, quotation. L. 60.
Citar, *thē-tar'*, to make an appointment (with any one), to quote. L. 52.
Ciudadano, *thē-oo-dah-dah'-no*, citizen. L. 47.
Civilización, *thē-rē-lē-thah-thē-one'*, s. f., civilization. L. 60.
Claridad, *klah-rē-dath'*, s. f., clearness, perspicuity. L. 36.
Claro, *klah'-ro*, adj., clear, bright. L. 59.
Clase, *klah'-sai*, s. f., class. L. 54.
Clásico, *klah'-sē-ko*, adj., classic, classical. L. 35.
Clasificación, *klah-sē-fē-ka-thē-one'*, s. f., classification. L. 24.
Clima, *klē'-ma*, s. m., climate. L. 40.
Cocer, *kō-thair'*, to boil, to cook. L. 42.
Coche, *kō'-chai*, s. m., coach, carriage in general.—Ir en coche, to go in a carriage. L. 42.
Cocinero, *kō-thē-nai'-ro*, s. m., cook. L. 11.
Cofre, *kō'-frai*, s. m., chest, trunk. L. 60.
Coger, *kō-hair'*, to catch, to take, to pick up. L. 46.
Cojear, *kō-hai-ar'*, to limp, to walk lame. L. 39.

Cojo, *kō'-ho*, adj. and s. m., lame. L. 44.
Colada, *kō-lah'-da*, s. f., stiffening of clothes. —Todo saldrá en la colada, all will be brought to light. L. 65.
Colectivo, *kō-laik-tē'-vo*, adj., collective. L. 40.
Colgar, *kōle-gar'*, to hang. L. 59.
Colina, *kō-lē'-na*, s. f., hill. L. 58.
Colocación, *kō-lō-kah-thē-ōne'*, s. f., employment, place, situation. L. 60.
Colocar, *kō-lō-kar'*, to put, to arrange, to place, to employ. L. 46.
Colorado, *kō-lō-rah'-do*, adj., red. L. 54.
Colorido, *kō-lō-rē'-do*, s. m., coloring (painting). L. 52.
Color, *kō-lōr'*, s. m., color. L. 52.
Combatir, *kōme-bah-teer'*, to combat, to fight. L. 54.
Combinación, *kōme-bē-nah-thē-ōne'*, s. f., combination. L. 24.
Combinado, *kōme-bē-nah'-do*, p. p. and adj., combined. L. 58.
Combinar, *kōme-bē-nar'*, to combine. L. 58.
Comedia, *kō-mai'-dē-a*, s. f., comedy. L. 52.
Comer, *kō-mair'*, to eat, to dine. L. 7.
Comerciante, *kō-mair-thē-an'-tai*, s. m., merchant. L. 5.
Cometa, *kō-mai'-ta*, s. m., comet; s. f., kite (toy). L. 60.
Cometer, *kō-mai-tair'*, to commit. L. 43.
Cómico, *kō'-mē-ko*, s. m., actor, comedian. L. 63.
Cómico, adj., comic, comical. L. 35.
Como, *kō'-mo*, adv., how, as.—¿Cómo está V.? how are you?—Yo seré tan rico como él, I shall be as rich as he. L. 15.
Comodidad, *kō-mō-dē-dath'*, s. f., commodity, convenience, comfort. L. 29.
Cómodo, *kō'-mō-do*, adj., commodious, comfortable. L. 29.
Compañero, *kōme-pan-yai'-ro*, s. m., companion, comrade. L. 60.
Compañía, *kōme-pan-yē'-a*, s. f., company. L. 60.
Comparativo, *kōme-pah-rah-tē'-vo*, adj., comparative. L. 61.
Compasión, *kōme-pah-sē-ōne'*, s. f., compassion. L. 45.
Complacencia, *kōme-plah-thain'-thē-a*, s. f., complacency, pleasure. L. 39.
Complemento, *kōme-plai-main'-to*, s. m., complement. L. 51.
Componente, *kōme-pō-nain'-tai*, part., component. L. 49.
Componer, *kōme-pō-nair'*, to compose, to mend, to arrange, to compound. L. 49.
Composición, *kōme-pō-sē-thē-ōne'*, s. f., composition, mending, arranging, compounding. L. 24.
Comprar, *kōme-prar'*, to buy, to purchase. L. 4.
Comprender, *kōme-prain-dair'*, to comprehend, to understand, to comprise. L. 50.
Con, *kōne*, prep., with, by. L. 10.
Concebir, *kōne-thai-beer'*, to conceive of. L. 54.
Conceder, *kōne-thai-dair'*, to grant, to concede. L. 53.
Concertar, *kōne-thair-tar'*, to concert, to agree. L. 58.
Conciencia, *kōne-thē-ain'-thē-a*, s. f., conscience. L. 40.

VOCABULARY. 447

Concierto, *kōne-thě-air'-to*, s. m., concert, agreement. L. 17.
Concluir, *kōne-cloo-eer'*, to conclude, to finish, to be over. L. 58.
Concordancia, *kōne-kōre-dan'-thě-a*, s. f., concordance, agreement. L. 50.
Condescender, *kōne-dais-thain-dair'*, to condescend, to agree. L. 43.
Condicion, *kōne-dě-thě-ōne'*, s. f., condition. L. 43.
Condicional, *kōns-dě-thě-ōne-al'*, adj., conditional. L. 50.
Conducir, *kōne-doo-theer'*, to conduct, to convey, to lead. L. 40.
Confesar, *kōns-fai-sar'*, to confess, to acknowledge, to avow. L. 34.
Confuso, *kōns-foo'-so*, adj., confused, confounded. L. 54.
Conjugacion, *kōne-hoo-gah-thě-ōne'*, s. f., conjugation. L. 43.
Conjugar, *kōne-hoo-gar'*, to conjugate. L. 43.
Conjuncion, *kōns-hoon-thě-ōne'*, s. f., conjunction. L. 43.
Conmigo, *kōne-mě'-go*, pron., with me, with myself. L. 26.
Conocer, *kō-nō-thair'*, to know, to be acquainted with. L. 25.
Conocimiento, *kō-nō-thě-mě-ain'-to*, s. m., knowledge, bill of lading (commerce). L. 43.
Consecuencia, *kōne-sai-kwain'-thě-a*, s. f., consequence. L. 34.
Conseguir, *kōne-sai-gheer'*, to obtain, to get, to succeed. L. 42.
Consejo, *kōns-sai'-ho*, s. m., counsel, advice. L. 53.
Consentir, *kōns-sain-teer'*, to consent, to agree (to). L. 33.
Consistir, *kōne-sees-teer'*, to consist. L. 52.
Consolar, *kōns-sō-lar'*, to console. L. 35.
Constancia, *kōns-tan'-thě-a*, s. f., constancy, steadiness. L. 46.
Construccion, *kōns-trook-thě-ōne'*, construction. L. 51.
Contante, *kōns-tan'-tai*, s. m. and adj., ready money. L. 33.
Contar, *kō.is-tar'*, to count, to relate, to tell. L. 33.
Contener, *kōns-tai-nair'*, to contain, to restrain, to stop, to check. L. 49.
Contenido, *kōns-tai-nee'-do*, s. m., contents. L. 49.
Contentar, *kōns-tain-tar'*, to content, to make glad. L. 33.
Contento, *kōns-tain'-to*, adj., content, contented, glad, satisfied. L. 33.
Contigo, *kōns-tě'-go*, pron., with thee. L. 26.
Continuar, *kōns-tě-noo-ar'*, to continue. L. 54.
Contra, *kōns'-tra*, prep., against. L. 41.
Contradecir, *kōns-trah-dai-theer'*, to contradict. L. 41.
Contrario, *kōne-trah'-rě-o*, adj., contrary.— Al *contrario*, on the contrary. L. 53.
Convencer, *kōne-vain-thair'*, to convince. L. 43.
Convenir, *kōne-vai-neer'*, to suit, to be convenient, to agree. L. 30.
Conversacion, *kōne-vair-sah-thě-ōne'*, s. f., conversation. L. 24.
Conversar, *kōne-vair-sar'*, to converse. L. 53.

Convertir, *kōne-vair-teer'*, to convert. L. 45.
Convicto, *kōne-veek'-to*, irr. past part. (of CONVENCER), convicted. L. 52.
Convite, *kōne-vee'-tai*, s. m., invitation, feast or banquet to which any one is invited. L. 56.
Copulativo, *kō-poo-lah-tě'-vo*, adj., copulative. L. 59.
Coqueta, *kō-kai'-ta*, s. f., coquette. L. 32.
Corazon, *kō-rah-thōne'*, s. m., heart. L. 56.
Corbata, *kōre-bah'-ta*, cravat. L. 10.
Corona, *kō-rō'-na*, s. f., crown. L. 56.
Correcto, *kōr-raik'-to*, adj., correct. L. 29.
Corredor, *kōr-rai-dōre'*, s. m., corridor, broker. L. 49.
Corregir, *kōr-rai-heer'*, to correct.— *Corregirse*, to mend. L. 59.
Correo, *kōr-rai'-o*, s. m., courier, post.— Casa de *correos*, post-office. L. 29.
Correr, *kōr-rair'*, to run.— *Correrse*, to be ashamed or confused, to blush. L. 51.
Corretear, *kōr-rai-tai-ar'*, to run about. L. 53.
Correveidile, *kōr-rai-vai-ě-dě'-lai*, s. m., talebearer, tattler. L. 50.
Corriente, *kōr-rě-ain'-tai*, adj., current; s. m., al *corriente* de, aware of; s. f., current, stream. L. 56.
Corrientemente, *kōr-rě-ain-tai-main'-tai*, adv., currently, fluently. L. 49.
Corro, *kōr'-ro*, s. m., circle of people collected together for talking. L. 44.
Cortante, *kōre-tan'-tai*, adj., cutting, sharp, edged. L. 38.
Cortaplumas, *kōre-tah-ploo'-mass*, penknife. L. 9.
Cortar, *kōre-tar'*, to cut. L. 33.
Corto, *kōre'-to*, adj., short. L. 21.
Cosa, *kō'-sa*, s. f., thing.— A *cosa* de las seis, about six o'clock. L. 11.
Coser, *kō-sair'*, to sew. L. 24.
Cosmopolita, *kōs-mō-pō-lee'-ta*, s. m., cosmopolite. L. 51.
Costa, *kōce'-ta*, s. f., cost, coast.— A *costa mia*, at my expense.— A *costa* de, at the expense of. L. 60.
Costado, *kōs-tah'-do*, s. m., side. L. 61.
Costar, *kōs-tar'*, to cost. L. 61.
Costumbre, *kōs-toom'-brai*, s. f., custom, habit. L. 54.
Creacion, *krai-ah-thě-ōne'*, s. f., creation. L. 41.
Crear, *krai-ar'*, to create. L. 41.
Crédito, *krai'-dě-to*, s. m., credit, credence. L. 57.
Creencia, *krai-ain'-thě-a*, s. f., credence, belief. L. 49.
Creer, *krai-air'*, to believe, to think. L. 27.
Creyente, *krai-yain'-tai*, present part. (of CREER), s. m. and f., believing, believer. L. 38.
Criado, *krě-ah'-do*, s. m., servant. L. 17.
Criado, past part. of CRIAR. L. 54.
Criar, *krě-ar'*, to breed, to bring up. L. 54.
Criatura, *krě-ah-too'-ra*, s. f., creature, infant. L. 60.
Crimen, *krě'-main*, s. m., crime. L. 59.
Criticar, *krě-tě-kar'*, to criticise. L. 48.
Crítico, *krě'-tě-ko*, s. m., critic. L. 45.
Cronologista, *krō-nō-lō-heess'-ta*, chronologist. L. 36.
Crueldad, *kroo-all-dath'*, s. f., cruelty. L. 30.

VOCABULARY.

Cuaderno, *cwah-dair'-no*, s. m., copy-book. L. 4.
Cual, *cwal*, pron., which. L. 10.
Cualidad, *cwah-lē-dath'*, s. f., quality. L. 36.
Cualquiera, *cwal-kē-ai'-ra*, pron. and adj., any one, whosoever, some one. L. 34.
Cuan, *cwan*, adv., how, as (used only before adjectives or other adverbs). L. 14.
Cuando, *cwan'-do*, adv., when. L. 9.
Cuánto? *cwan'-to*, adj., how much? how many?—*Cuanto ántes*, at once, immediately.—Por *cuanto*, inasmuch as. L. 14.
Cuarto, *cwar'-to*, ord. adj. and s. m., fourth, room, chamber. L. 40.
Cuatro, *cwah'-tro*, num. adj., four. L. 15.
Cuba, *koo'-ba*, s. f., cask, tub.—Cuba (island of). L. 61.
Cubrir, *koo-breer'*, to cover. L. 59.
Cuchara, *koo-chah'-ra*, s. f., spoon. L. 60.
Cuchillo, *koo-cheel'-yo*, s. m., knife. L. 33.
Cuello, *cwail'-yo*, s. m., neck, collar. L. 60.
Cuenta, *cwain'-ta*, s. f., account, bill. L. 46.
Cuento, *cwain'-to*, s. m., story, tale. L. 44.
Cuerpo, *cwair-po*, s. m., body. L. 64.
Cuervo, *cwair'-vo*, s. m., crow. L. 45.
Cuesta, *cwaiss'-ta*, s. f., hill.—A *cuestas*, on one's back or shoulders. L. 63.
Cuestion, *cwais-tē-ōne'*, s. f., question. L. 40.
Cuidado, *cwē-dah'-do*, s. m., care.—Estar de *cuidado*, to be dangerously ill.—Estar con *cuidado*, to be very anxious. L. 28.
Cuidar, *cwe-dar'*, to care, to take care. L. 44.
Culpa, *kool'-pa*, s. f., fault, blame. L. 60.
Culpar, *kool-par'*, to blame. L. 60.
Cultivar, *kool-tē-var'*, to cultivate. L. 60.
Cumpleaños, *koom-plai-an'-yos*, s.m., birthday. L. 62.
Cumplimiento, *koom-plē-mē-ain'-to*, s. m., compliment. L. 40.
Cumplir, *koom-pleer'*, to accomplish, to fulfil.—*Cumplir* por otro, to act for or in the name of another. L. 57.
Cuñado, a, *koon-yah'-do, da*, s. m. and f., brother-in-law, sister-in-law. L. 64.
Curioso, *koo-rē-ō'-so*, adj., curious, worthy of note. L. 51.
Curso, *koor'-so*, s. m., course. L. 64.
Custodia, *koos-tō'-dē-a*, s. f., custody. L. 53.
Cútis, *koo'-teess*, s. m. and f., skin. L. 64.
Cuyo, *koo'-yo*, pron., of whom, of which, whose, which. L. 17.

D.

Dale! *dah'-lai*, int., have at it! L. 64.
Dama, *dah'-ma*, s. f., lady, dame.—*Damas*, draughts, or checkers. L. 58.
Danza, *dan'-tha*, s. f., dance. L. 64.
Dañar, *dan-yar'*, to damage, to hurt, to harm. L. 47.
Daño, *dan'-yo*, s. m., damage, hurt, harm. L. 42.
Dar, to give.—*Dares* y tomares, disputes, ifs and ands.—*Darse* á la vela, to set sail. L. 26.
De, *dai*, prep., of, from.—*De* dia, by day.—*De* intento, on purpose. L. 4.
Deber, *dai-bair'*, s. m., duty. L. 28.
Deber, to owe, must.—*Deben* ser las ocho, it must be eight o'clock. L. 28.

Decena, *dai-thai'-na*, s. f., about ten. L. 59.
Decidir, *dai-thē-deer'*, to decide. L. 60.
Décimo, *dai'-thē-mo*, ord. adj., and s. m., tenth. L. 15.
Decir, *dai-theer'*, to say, to tell. L. 27.
Declarar, *dai-clah-rar'*, to declare. L. 48.
Dedal, *dai-dal'*, s. m., thimble. L. 24.
Dedo, *dai'-do*, s. m., finger. L. 59.
Defectivo, *dai-faik-tē'-vo*, adj., defective. L. 63.
Defecto, *dai-faik'-to*, s. m., defect, failing. L. 55.
Defender, *dai-fain-dair'*, to defend. L. 37.
Definicion, *dai-fē-nē-thē-ōne'*, s. f., definition. L. 59.
Definir, *dai-fē-neer'*, to define. L. 59.
Dejar, *dai-har'*, to leave, to let, to allow. L. 44.
Delante, *dai-lan'-tai*, prep.—*Delante* de, before, in the presence of. L. 18.
Deleitar, *dai-lai-ē-tar'*, to delight. L. 47.
Delicado, *dai-lē-kah'-do*, adj., delicate. L. 39.
Delicioso, *dai-lē-thē-ō'-so*, adj., delicious. L. 35.
Delincuente, *dai-leen-cwain'-tai*, s. m., delinquent, transgressor. L. 34.
Delinquir, *dai-leen-keer'*, to transgress. L. 34.
Delito, *dai-lē'-to*, s. m., crime, transgression. L. 51.
Demás, *dai-mass'*, adv., over and above, too much; adj. (generally used with lo, los, las), the rest, the others, others. L. 43.
Demasiado, *dai-mah-sē-ah'-do*, adj. and adv., too much, too. L. 25.
Dentro, *dain'-tro*, prep., in, within, inside (always followed by *de*). L. 31.
Derecho, *dai-rai'-cho*, adj., right, even, straight. L. 50.
Desafiar, *dai-sah-fē-ar'*, to challenge. L. 63.
Desafío, *dai-sah-fē'-o*, s.m., challenge, duel. L. 63.
Desanimar, *dai-sah-nē-mar'*, to dishearten, to discourage. L. 38.
Descansadamente, *dais-kan-sah-dah-main'-tai*, adv., easily, at one's case. L. 33.
Descansado, *dais-kan-sah'-do*, adj., easy, quiet, refreshed. L. 33.
Descansar, *dais-kan-sar'*, to rest. L. 33.
Descanso, *dais-kan'-so*, s. m., rest, repose, ease. L. 33.
Descaro, *dais-kah'-ro*, s. m., barefacedness. L. 64.
Descender, *dais-thain-dair'*, to descend. L. 37.
Descomponer, *dais-kōme-pō-nair'*, to disarrange, to discompose, to put out of order. L. 53.
Descompuesto, *dais-kōme-pwaiss'-to*, adj., disarranged, discomposed, out of order, disorderly. L. 53.
Desconfiar, *dais-kōne-fē-ar'*, to distrust, to mistrust. L. 43.
Desgracia, *dais-grah'-thē-a*, s. f., misfortune, ill-luck. L. 48.
Deshacer, *dais-ah-thair'*, to undo, to destroy, to take or put asunder. L. 57.
Desierto, *dai-sē-air'-to*, s. m., desert, wilderness. L. 54.
Desigual, *dai-sē-gwal'*, adj., unequal, uneven. L. 53.

VOCABULARY. 449

Desocupar, *dai-sō-koo-par'*, to quit, to evacuate, to empty. L. 56.
Despacio, *dais-pah'-thē-o*, adv., slowly. L. 6.
Despedir, *dais-pai-deer'*, to dismiss, to send or put away, to discharge. L. 59.
Despertar, *dais-pair-tar'*, to awake, to awaken, to arouse, to rouse. L. 34.
Despierto, *dais-pē-air'-to*, adj., awake, brisk, sprightly, lively. L. 52.
Desproporcionadísimamente, *dais-prō-pōre-thē-ōne-ah-dē'-sē-mah-main-tai*, adv., out of all proportion. L. 50.
Despues, *dais-pwaiss'*, prep. and adv., after, afterward. L. 16.
Determinante, *dai-tair-mē-nan'-tai*, adj., determining.—Verbo *determinante*, determining verb. L. 53.
Determinar, *dai-tair-mē-nar'*, to determine. L. 53.
Detrás, *dai-trass'*, prep. and adv., behind. L. 33.
Deudor, *dai-oo-dōre'*, s. m., debtor. L. 45.
Devolver, *dai-vōle-vair'*, to return, to give back. L. 43.
Dia, *dē'-a*, s. m., day.—De *dia*, by day, in the daytime.—Dar los *dias*, to say good morning (to any one). L. 9.
Diablo, *dē-ah'-blo*, s. m., devil. L. 65.
Dialecto, *dē-ah-laik'-to*, s. m., dialect. L. 55.
Diálogo, *dē-ah'-lō-go*, s.m., dialogue. L. 59.
Diantre, *dē-an'-trai*, s. m., deuce. L. 46.
Dibujo, *dē-boo'-ho*, s. m., drawing, design. L. 51.
Diccionario, *deek-thē-ō-nah'-rē-o*, s. m., dictionary. L. 49.
Dicha, *dē'-cha*, s. f., happiness, good luck, good fortune. L. 64.
Dicho, *dē'-cho*, s. m., saying. L. 54.
Diciembre, *dē-thē-aim'-brai*, s. m., December. L. 24.
Diente, *dē-ain'-tai*, s.m., tooth.—Hablar entre *dientes*, to mumble, to mutter. L. 63.
Diez, *dē-aith'*, num. adj., ten. L. 14.
Diferencia, *dē-fai-rain'-thē-a*, s. f., difference. L. 48.
Diferenciar, *dē-fai-rain-thē-ar'*, to differ. L. 48.
Difícil, *dē-fē'-theel*, adj., difficult. L. 21.
Dificultad, *dē-fē-kool-tath'*, s. f., difficulty. L. 36.
Digno, *deeg'-no*, adj., worthy, deserving. L. 53.
Diluviar, *dē-loo-vē-ar'*, to rain like a deluge, to pour. L. 30.
Dimes, *dē'-maiss*.—Andar en *dimes* y diretes, to use ifs and ands, to quibble. L. 47.
Diminutivo, *dē-mē-noo-tē'-vo*, s. m., diminutive. L. 44.
Dinero, *dē-nai'-ro*, s. m., money. L. 13.
Dios, *dē-oce'*, s. m., God. L. 21.
Diptongo, *deep-tōne'-go*, s. m., diphthong. L. 57.
Direccion, *dē-raik-thē-ōne'*, s. f., direction, address. L. 24.
Directo, *dē-raik'-to*, adj., direct. L. 51.
Director, *dē-raik-tor'*, director. L. 50.
Dirigir, *dē-rē-heer'*, to direct.—*Dirigirse*, to apply. L. 63.
Discípulo, *dees-thē'-poo-lo*, s. m., pupil, disciple. L. 18.
Discreto, *dees-krai'-to*, adj., discreet, circumspect. L. 39.

Disculpa, *dees-kool'-pa*, s. f., apology, excuse. L. 60.
Discurso, *dees-koor'-so*, s. m., discourse, speech, course. L. 53.
Disgustar, *dees-goos-tar'*, to disgust, to displease. L. 50.
Disgusto, *dees-goos'-to*, s. m., disgust, displeasure, unpleasantness. L. 50.
Disponer, *dees-pō-nair'*, to dispose, to lay out, to arrange, to prepare. L. 48.
Disposicion, *dees-pō-sē-thē-ōne'*, s. f., disposition, arrangement, distribution. L. 33.
Distancia, *dees-tan'-thē-a*, s. f., distance. L. 51.
Distante, *dees-tan'-tai*, adj., distant. L. 38.
Distar, *dees-tar'*, to be distant, far from. L. 53.
Distinguir, *dees-teen-gheer'*, to distinguish. L. 43.
Divertir, *dē-vair-teer'*, to divert, to amuse. L. 39.
Dividir, *dē-vē-deer'*, to divide. L. 51.
Divisar, *dē-vē-sar'*, to descry, to perceive, to catch a glimpse of. L. 42.
Doble, *dō'-blai*, adj., double. L. 40.
Doble, s. m., double. L. 40.
Doce, *dō'-thai*, num. adj. and s. m., twelve, twelfth. L. 14.
Docena, *dō-thai'-na*, s. f., dozen. L. 40.
Doler, *dō-lair'*.—*Dolerlo* á uno la cabeza, los dientes, to have a headache, toothache. L. 36.
Dolor, *dō-lore'*, s. m., pain. L. 50.
Domingo, *dō-meen'-go*, s. m., Sunday. L. 9.
Donde, *dōne'-dai*, adv., where. L. 9.
Doña, *dōne'-ya*, s. f., lady, madam, Mrs. L. 2.
Dormir, *dōre-meer'*, to sleep. L. 41.
Dos, *dōce*, num. adj. and s. m., two, second. L. 14.
Drama, *drah'-ma*, s. m., drama. L. 52.
Dramático, *drah-mah'-tē-ko*, adj., dramatic. L. 52.
Duda, *doo'-da*, s. f., doubt. L. 43.
Dudar, *doo-dar'*, to doubt. L. 28.
Durable, *doo-rah'-blai*, adj., durable. L. 58.
Durante, *doo-ran'-tai*, pres. part., during. L. 59.
Durar, *doo-rar'*, to last, to continue. L. 59.
Duro, *doo'-ro*, adj. and s. m., hard; dollar. L. 60.

E.

Ea! *at'-a*, int., say! hollo! L. 46.
Echar, *ai-char'*, to throw, to put, to cast.—*Echar* de ver, to notice, to observe.—*Echar* á correr, to run away.—*Echar* á perder, to spoil. L. 35.
Económico, *ai-kō-nō'-mē-ko*, adj., economical. L. 35.
Edad, s. f., age. L. 53.
Edicion, *ai-dē-thē-ōne'*, s. f., edition. L. 60.
Edificar, *ai-dē-fē-kar'*, to edify. L. 48.
Efecto, *ai-faik'-to*, s. m., effect. L. 47.
Ejecutar, *ai-hai-koo-tar'*, to execute, to put into execution, to put into practice. L. 60.
Ejemplo, *ai-haim'-plo*, s. m., example. L. 32.
Ejercer, *ai-hair-thair'*, to exercise, to practise. L. 60.

Ejercicio, *ai-hair-thĕ'-thĕ-o*, s. m., exercise. L. 8.
El, la, lo, los, las, def. art., the. L. 1.
Él, ella, *ail, ail'-ya*, pers. pron., he, she, it. L. 1.
Eleccion, *ai-laik-thĕ-ōne'*, s. f., election, choice. L. 21.
Elegancia, *ai-lai-gan'-thĕ-a*, s. f., elegance. L. 52.
Elegante, *ai-lai-gan'-tai*, adj., elegant. L. 63.
Elegir, *ai-lai-heer'*, to elect, to choose. L. 39.
Elemento, *ai-lai-main'-to*, s. m., element, constituent part. L. 60.
Elena, *ai-lai'-na*, s. f., Helena, Ellen. L. 19.
Elíptico, *ai-leep'-tĕ-ko*, adj., elliptic, elliptical. L. 60.
Embarcadero, *aim-bar-kah-dai'-ro*, s. m., landing, ferry. L. 58.
Embargo, *aim-bar'-go*, s. m., embargo.—*Sin embargo*, notwithstanding, however. L. 48.
Empeñar, *aim-pain-yar'*, to engage, to pledge, to bind.—*Empeñarse*, to bind one's self, to persist, to desire eagerly. L. 45.
Empero, *aim-pai'-ro*, conj., yet, however, but. L. 60.
Emplear, *aim-plai-ar'*, to employ. L. 44.
Empleo, *aim-plai'-o*, s. m., employ, employment, office. L. 57.
En, *ain*, prep., in, at, on. L. 8.
Enamorar, *ai-nah-mō-rar'*, to court, to make love to.—*Enamorarse de*, to be enamoured of, to fall in love with. L. 39.
Encargo, *ain-kar'-go*, s. m., charge, commission, command. L. 57.
Encargar, *a'n-kar-gar'*, to charge, to commission, to order. L. 58.
Encender, *ain-thain-dair'*, to light, to kindle. L. 37.
Encerrar, *ain-thair-rar'*, to shut up, to contain, to comprehend. L. 63.
Encima, *ain-thĕ'-ma*, prep. and adv., above, over. L. 33.
Encontrar, *ain-kōne-trar'*, to meet, to find. L. 35.
Enemigo, *ai-nai-mĕ'-go*, s. m., enemy. L. 51.
Enemistar, *ai-nai-meess-tar'*, to set at enmity.—*Enemistar* á alguno con otro, to put any one at enmity with, or against another. L. 60.
Energía, *ai-nair-hĕ'-a*, s. f., energy. L. 61.
Enfermar, *ain-fair-mar'*, to become or get sick. L. 38.
Enfermo, *ain-fair'-mo*, adj., sick, ill. L. 48.
Enfrente, *ain-frain'-tai*, adv., opposite, in front. L. 51.
Engañar, *ain-gan-yar'*, to deceive, to take in. L. 32.
Enhebrar, *ain-ai-brar'*, to thread, to link. L. 65.
Enhorabuena, *ai-nō-rah-bwai'-na*, s. f., congratulation, felicitation. L. 39.
Enrique, *ain-rĕ'-kai*, s. m., Henry. L. 15.
Enseñar, *ain-sain-yar'*, to show, to teach. L. 27.
Ensuciar, *ain-soo-thĕ-ar'*, to dirty, to soil, to daub. L. 60.
Entendedor, *ain-tain-dai-dōre'*, s. m., he who understands.—A buen *entendedor* media palabra basta, a word to the wise is sufficient. L. 63.

Entender, *ain-tain-dair'*, to understand. L. 37.
Entónces, *ain-tōne'-thaiss*, adv., then. L. 23.
Entrámbos, *ain-tram'-bōce*, pron. pl., both. L. 60.
Entrar, *ain-trar'*, to enter, to begin, to commence, to come or go in, to get in. L. 28.
Entre, *ain'-trai*, prep., between, in the course of. L. 19.
Entretanto, *ain-trai-tan'-to*, adv., in the mean time. L. 60.
Entretener, *ain-trai-tai-nair'*, to entertain, to amuse, to divert.—*Entretenerse*, to spend one's time, to be engaged in. L. 48.
Entusiasmo, *ain-too-sĕ-ass'-mo*, s. m., enthusiasm. L. 54.
Enviar, *ain-vĕ-ar'*, to send. L. 14.
Envidiar, *ain-vĕ-dĕ-ar'*, to envy. L. 40.
Equivocacion, *ai-kĕ-vō-kah-thĕ-ōne'*, s. f., mistake, misconception. L. 60.
Equivocar, *ai-kĕ-vō-kar'*, to mistake.—*Equivocarse*, to be mistaken. L. 47.
Erguir, *air-gheer'*, to hold erect (as the head, &c.). L. 42.
Errar, *air-rar'*, to err, to miss. L. 41.
Erudicion, *ai-roo-dĕ-thĕ-ōne'*, s. f., erudition. L. 52.
Escaldar, *aiss-kal-dar'*, to scald. L. 65.
Escena, *aiss-thai'-na*, s. f., scene. L. 65.
Escéptico, *aiss-thaip'-tĕ-ko*, adj., skeptical. L. 45.
Escoba, *aiss-kō'-ba*, s. f., broom. L. 49.
Escobajo, *aiss-kō-bah'-ho*, s. m. (augmentative of ESCOBA), stump of a broom. L. 49.
Escoger, *aiss-kō-hair'*, to choose. L. 65.
Escribano, *aiss-krĕ-bah'-no*, s. m., notary. L. 19.
Escribiente, *aiss-krĕ-bĕ-ain'-tai*, s. m., amanuensis, clerk, writer (in an office). L. 33.
Escribir, *aiss-krĕ-beer'*, to write. L. 8.
Escritor, *aiss-krĕ-tōre'*, s. m., writer, author. L. 19.
Escritura, *aiss-krĕ-too'-ra*, s. f., writing, document, conveyance. L. 19.
Escuchar, *aiss-koo-char'*, to hearken, to listen. L. 60.
Escuela, *aiss-kwai'-la*, s. f., school. L. 21.
Escultor, *aiss-kool-tōre'*, s. m., sculptor. L. 31.
Escultura, *aiss-kool-too'-ra*, s. f., sculpture. L. 31.
Esforzar, *aiss-fōre-thar'*, to strengthen, to exert.—*Esforzarse*, to make effort, to endeavor. L. 60.
Esfuerzo, *aiss-fwair'-tho*, s. m., effort, endeavor (pl.), courage, bravery. L. 47.
Espacio, *aiss-pah'-thĕ-o*, s. m., space. L. 48.
Espada, *aiss-pah'-da*, s. f., sword. L. 57.
Espadachin, *aiss-pah-dah-cheen'*, s. m., bully. L. 63.
Espalda, *aiss-pal'-da*, s. f., shoulder, (pl.) back. L. 59.
España, *aiss-pan'-ya*, s. f., Spain. L. 9.
Español, *aiss-pan-yōle'*, s. and adj., Spanish language; Spanish.—A la *española*, in the Spanish fashion. L. 2.
Especie, *aiss-pai'-thĕ-ai*, s. f., species, kind, sort. L. 40.
Especiero, *aiss-pai-thĕ-ai'-ro*, s. m., grocer. L. 65.

VOCABULARY.   451

Espejo, *aiss-pai'-ho*, s. m., looking-glass. L. 60.
Esperanza, *aiss-pai-ran'-tha*, s. f., hope. L. 21.
Esperar, *aiss-pai-rar'*, to hope, to await, to wait for. L. 32.
Espíritu, *aiss-pē'-rē-too*, s. m., spirit. L. 45.
Esposa, *aiss-pō'-sa*, s. f., spouse, wife. L. 39.
Esposo, *aiss-pō'-so*, s. m., spouse, husband. L. 39.
Esquela, *aiss-kai'-la*, s. f., note. L. 56.
Esquina, *aiss-kē'-na*, s. f., corner. L. 51.
Establecer, *aiss-tah-blai-thair'*, to establish. L. 42.
Estacion, *aiss-tah-thē-ōne'*, s. f., station, season. L. 60.
Estado, *aiss-tah'-do*, s. m., state, State.—Los *Estados* Unidos, the United States. L. 19.
Estar, *aiss-tar'*, to be, to understand.— *Estar* para salir, to be about to set out.— *Estar* por alguno, to be for, or in favor of, any one.—¿*Está* V.? do you understand? L. 22.
Este, *aiss'-tai*, s. m., east. L. 22.
Este, esta, esto, dem. pron., this, this one. L. 18.
Estilo, *aiss-tē'-lo*, s. m., style. L. 52.
Estimable, *aiss-tē-mah'-blai*, adj., estimable. L. 39.
Estimar, *aiss-tē-mar'*, to esteem, to estimate. L. 39.
Esto, *aiss'-to*. (See Este.) L. 18.
Estocada, *aiss-tō-kah'-da*, s. f., stab, thrust. L. 53.
Estraño, *aiss-tran'-yo*, adj., strange, foreign. L. 48.
Estratagema, *aiss-trah-tah-hai'-ma*, s. f., stratagem, ruse. L. 44.
Estrechar, *aiss-trai-char'*, to tighten, to make narrow, to squeeze, to press. L. 60.
Estrecho, *aiss-trai'-cho*, adj., narrow, tight, close, intimate.—*Estrecho*, s. m., strait. L. 60.
Estribo, *aiss-trē'-bo*, s. m., stirrup. L. 38.
Estudiante, *aiss-too-dē-an'-tai*, s. m., student. L. 38.
Estudiar, *aiss-too-dē-ar'*, to study. L. 3.
Estudio, *aiss-too'-dē-ō*, s. m., study. L. 25.
Eternidad, *ai-tair-nē-dath'*, s. f., eternity. L. 36.
Eterno, *ai-tair'-no*, adj., eternal. L. 41.
Evidencia, *ai-vē-dain'-thē-a*, s. f., evidence. L. 59.
Evitar, *ai-vē-tar'*, to avoid, to help (do otherwise than has been done). L. 47.
Exageracion, *aik-sah-hai-rah-thē-ōne'*, s. f., exaggeration. L. 48.
Exagerar, *aik-sah-hai-rar'*, to exaggerate. L. 60.
Exámen, *aik-sah'-main*, s. m., examination. L. 38.
Examinar, *aik-sah-mē-nar'*, to examine. L. 41.
Exceder, *aiks-thai-dair'*, to exceed, to overstep, to surpass. L. 53.
Excelente, *aiks-thai-lain'-tai*, adj., excellent. L. 53.
Excepcion, *aiks-thaip-thē-ōne'*, s. f., exception. L. 45.
Exceptuar, *aiks-thaip-too-ar'*, to except. L. 60.

Exclamacion, *aiks-klah-mah-thē-ōne'*, s. f., exclamation. L. 24.
Exclamar, *aiks-klah-mar'*, to exclaim. L. 60.
Excusa, *aiks-koo'-sa*, s. f., excuse, apology. L. 60.
Excusar, *aiks-koo-sar'*, to excuse, to apologize. L. 27.
Exhibicion, *aik-sē-bē-thē-ōne'*, s. f., exhibition. L. 48.
Exhibir, *aik-sē-beer'*, to exhibit. L. 60.
Exigir, *aik-sē-heer'*, to exact, to require, to demand. L. 38.
Existencia, *aik-seess-tain'-thē-a*, s. f., existence, (pl.) stock. L. 52.
Existir, *aik-seess-teer'*, to exist. L. 40.
Exito, *aik'-sē-to*, s. m., result, issue.—Con buen *éxito*, successfully. L. 46.
Experiencia, *aiks-pai-rē-ain'-thē-a*, s. f., experience. L. 41.
Explicacion, *aiks-plē-kah-thē-ōne'*, s. f., explanation. L. 48.
Explicar, *aiks-plē-kar'*, to explain. L. 45.
Exponer, *aiks-pō-nair'*, to expose, to expound, to explain. L. 51.
Expresar, *aiks-prai-sar'*, to express. L. 52.
Expresion, *aiks-prai-sē-ōne'*, s. f., expression. L. 56.
Expresivo, *aiks-prai-sē'-vo*, adj., expressive. L. 65.
Exterior, *aiks-tai-rē-ōre'*, exterior. L. 48.
Extra, *aiks'-tra*, adv., extra. L. 60.
Extrangero, *aiks-tran-hai'-ro*, s. m., foreigner. L. 60.
Extrañar, *aiks-tran-yar'*, to wonder at, to find (a thing) strange. L. 60.
Extraño, *aiks-tran'-yo*, adj., strange. L. 48.
Extraordinario, *aiks-trah-ōre-dē-nah'-rē-ō*, adj., extraordinary. L. 46.
Extremado, *aiks-trai-mah'-do*, adj., extreme. L. 55.

F.

Fabricar, *fah-brē-kar'*, to make, to manufacture, to build. L. 48.
Faccion, *fak-thē-ōne'*, s. f., feature; faction. L. 35.
Fácil, *fah'-theel*, adj., easy. L. 21.
Facilidad, *fah-thē-lē-dath'*, s. f., facility, ease. L. 36.
Facilitar, *fah-thē-lē-tar'*, to facilitate, to make easy, to procure. L. 49.
Fácilmente, *fah'-theel-main-tai*, adv., easily. L. 49.
Factura, *fak-too'-ra*, s. f., invoice. L. 63.
Facultad, *fah-kool-tath'*, s. f., faculty, power of doing any thing, liberty to do any thing. L. 63.
Falso, *fal'-so*, adj., false. L. 45.
Falta, *fal'-ta*, s. f., fault, want. L. 27.
Faltar, *fal-tar'*, to want, to lack, to be lacking. L. 31.
Fama, *fah'-ma*, s. f., fame, reputation, repute. L. 65.
Familia, *fah-mē'-lē-a*, s. f., family. L. 23.
Familiar, *fah-mē-lē-ar'*, adj., familiar. L. 49.
Familiaridad, *fah-mē-lē-ah-rē-dath'*, s. f., familiarity. L. 65.
Famoso, *fah-mō'-so*, adj., famous. L. 45.
Fanático, *fah-nah'-tē-ko*, adj., fanatical. L. 65.

Fas, *fass.*—Por *fas* ó por *néfas*, right or wrong; justly or unjustly. L. 63.
Fastidio, *fass-tē'-dē-o*, s. m., trouble, annoyance. L. 47.
Favor, *fah-vōre'*, s. m., favor, mercy, help.—A *favor* de, in behalf of. L. 39.
Favorecer, *fah-vō-rai-thair'*, to favor. L. 56.
Favorito, *fah-vō-rē'-to*, adj., favorite. L. 54.
Fé, *fai*, s. f., faith. L. 45.
Febrero, *fai-brai'-ro*, s. m., February. L. 24.
Fecha, *fai'-cha*, s. f., date. L. 20.
Felicidad, *fai-lē-thē-dath'*, s. f., happiness, felicity. L. 48.
Felicitar, *fai-lē-thē-tar'*, to felicitate, to congratulate. L. 61.
Feliz, *fai-leeth'*, adj., happy, fortunate, lucky. L. 21.
Felizmente, *fai-leeth-main'-tai*, adv., happily, fortunately, luckily. L. 49.
Femenino, *fai-mai-nē'-no*, adj., feminine. L. 47.
Feo, *fai'-o*, adj., ugly, unbecoming. L. 7.
Feroz, *fai-rōth'*, adj., ferocious, fierce, ravenous. L. 54.
Ferrocarril, *fair-rō-car-reel'*, s. m., railroad. L. 60.
Fiado, *fē-ah'-do*, adj., confident, trusting.—Al *fiado*, on credit, on trust. L. 61.
Fiar, *fē-ar'*, to trust, to bail. L. 61.
Fiel, *fē-ail'*, adj., faithful. L. 21.
Fiesta, *fē-aiss'-ta*, s. f., feast, festival.—Día de *fiesta*, holiday. L. 62.
Figura, *fē-goo'-ra*, s. f., figure, form, shape.—Hacer *figura*, to make, to cut a figure. L. 63.
Figurado, *fē-goo-rah'-do*, adj., figurative. L. 51.
Filosofastro, *fē-lō-sō-fass'-tro*, s. m., philosophaster. L. 49.
Filósofo, *fē-lō'-sō-fo*, s. m., philosopher. L. 49.
Fin, *feen*, s. m., end, object, point.—A *fin* de, in order to. L. 45.
Final, *fē-nal'*, s. m. and adj., end, termination; final. L. 61.
Finalmente, *fē-nal-main'-tai*, adv., finally. L. 49.
Fino, *fē'-no*, adj., fine. L. 56.
Firma, *feer'-ma*, s. f., signature. L. 56.
Fisonomia, *fē-sō-nō-mē'-a*, s. f., physiognomy. L. 45.
Flaqueza, *flah-kai'-tha*, s. f., leanness, weakness, foible, frailty. L. 64.
Fondo, *fōne'-do*, s. m., bottom, ground (of colored articles); pl., funds, cash, money. L. 60.
Formal, *fōre-mal'*, adj., formal, reliable, respectable. L. 45.
Formalidad, *fōre-mah-lē-dath'*, s. f., formality, reliability, respectability. L. 45.
Formar, *fōre-mar'*, to form, to shape. L. 43.
Fortuna, *fōre-too'-na*, s. f., fortune, luck. L. 42.
Fragata, *frah-gah'-ta*, s. f., frigate. L. 60.
Fraile, *frah'-ē-lai*, s. f., friar. L. 41.
Francés, *fran-thaiss'*, s. m. and adj., French (language), French. l. 8.
Francia, *fran'-thē-a*, s. f., France. L. 9.
Francisco, *fran-theess'-ko*, s. m., Francis. L. 44.
Franco, *fran'-ko*, adj., frank, free, open-hearted, intimate. L. 34.

Franqueza, *fran-kai'-tha*, s. f., frankness, open-heartedness, intimacy. L. 48.
Frase, *frah'-sai*, s. f., phrase, sentence. L. 51.
Fray, *frah'-ē*, s. m., friar. L. 41.
Frecuente, *frai-kwain'-tai*, adj., frequent. L. 29.
Freir, *frai-eer'*, to fry. L. 52.
Frente, *frain'-tai*, s. f., forehead, front.—En*frente*, opposite. L. 45.
Fresco, *fraiss'-ko*, adj., fresh, cool.—Pintura al *fresco*, fresco painting. L. 46.
Fresco, s. m., cool breeze, cool, refreshing air, fresco (painting). L. 46.
Frio, *frē'-o*, adj. and s. m., cold. L. 25.
Friolera, *frē-ō-lai'-ra*, s. f., trifle. L. 37.
Fruta, *froo'-ta*, s. f., fruit. L. 31.
Fruto, *froo'-to*, s. m., fruit (produce). L. 40.
Fuego, *fwai'-go*, s. m., fire. L. 34.
Fuente, *fwain'-tai*, s. f., fountain, spring, source. L. 52.
Fuera, *fwai'-ra*, adv., out.—*Fuera* de que, besides. L. 81.
Fuera! inter., out! be gone! away! L. 31.
Fuerza, *fwair'-tha*, s. f., force, strength.—A *fuerza* de, by dint of. L. 58.
Fuga, *foo'-ga*, s. f., flight, escape. L. 57.
Fulano, *foo-lah'-no*, s. m., such a one. L. 5.
Fumar, *foo-mar'*, to smoke. L. 42.
Fusil, *foo-seel'*, s. m., gun. L. 49.
Fusilar, *foo-sē-lar'*, to shoot (military). l. 45.
Futuro, *foo-too'-ro*, s. m., future (tense). L. 43.
Futuro, adj., future. L. 43.

G.

Galán, *gah-lan'*, s. m. and adj., gallant, actor; gallant. L. 58.
Galante, *gah-lan'-tai*, adj., gallant, courtly. L. 58.
Galicismo, *gah-lē-theess'-mo*, s. m., gallicism. L. 61.
Gallego, *gal-yai'-go*, s. m., Galician. L. 55.
Gallina, *gal-yē'-na*, s. f., hen. L. 5.
Gana, *gah'-na*, s. f., desire, will, appetite. L. 59.
Ganapierde, *gah-nah-pē-air'-dai*, s. m., game of draughts, or checkers, at which the loser wins. L. 50.
Ganar, *gah-nar'*, to gain, to win. L. 27.
Ganso, *gan'-so*, s. m., goose.—Hablar por boca de *ganso*, to echo what has been said by others. L. 63.
Garrotazo, *gar-rō-tah'-thō*, s. m., blow with a cudgel. L. 44.
Garrote, *gar-rō'-tai*, s. m., cudgel. L. 44.
Gastar, *gass-tar'*, to waste, to use, to spend, to expend. L. 50.
Gatillo, *gah-teel'-yo*, s. m. (dim.), little cat, trigger of a gun. L. 53.
Gato, *gah'-to*, s. m., cat. L. 46.
Gemido, *hai-mē'-do*, s. m., groan, lamentation, moan, howling. L. 59.
General, *hai-nai-ral'*, s. m. and adj., general. L. 45.
Género, *hai'-nai-ro*, s. m., gender, genus, kind, sort, cloth. L. 57.
Gentilicio, *hain-tē-lē'-thē-ō*, adj., peculiar to a nation. L. 49.

VOCABULARY. 453

Gentío, *hain-tĕ'-ŏ*, s. m., great crowd, multitude. L. 40.
Gentualla, *hain-too-al'-ya*, s. f., rabble, dregs of the people. L. 49.
Gerundio, *hai-roon'-dĕ-ŏ*, s. m., gerund. L. 43.
Gigantesco, *hĕ-gan-taiss'-ko*, adj., gigantic. L. 49.
Gineta, *hĕ-nai'-ta*.—Tener los cascos á la *gineta*, to be hare-brained. L. 64.
Globo, *glŏ'-bo*, s. m., globe, balloon. L. 37.
Gobernador, *gŏ-bair-nah-dōre'*, s. m., governor. L. 60.
Gobernante, *gŏ-bair-nan'-tai*, pres. part., governing. L. 38.
Gobernar, *gŏ-bair-nar'*, to govern. L. 34.
Gobierno, *gŏ-bĕ-air'-no*, s. m., government. L. 40.
Goce, *gŏ'-thai*, s. m., enjoyment. L. 54.
Golpe, *gōle'-pai*, s. m., blow, stroke. L. 61.
González, *gŏne-thah'-laith*, s. m. (dim.), Spanish proper name signifying son of *Gonzalo*. L. 49.
Gorra, *gōre'-ra*, s. f., bonnet.—Vivir de *gorra*, to live at others' expense, to sponge. L. 64.
Gozar, *gŏ-thar'*, to enjoy. L. 25.
Gozo, *gŏ'-tho*, s. m., joy, satisfaction, pleasure. L. 51.
Grabado, *grah-bah'-do*, s. m., engraving, cut (picture). L. 52.
Grabar, *grah-bar'*, to engrave. L. 52.
Gracia, *grah'-thĕ-a*, s. f., grace, favor, gracefulness, pardon. L. 51.
Gracias, s. m. pl., thank you. L. 23.
Grado, *grah'-do*, s. m., grade, degree.—De *grado*, willingly. L. 60.
Gramática, *grah-mah'-tĕ-ka*, s. f., grammar. L. 5.
Gramatical, *grah-mah-tĕ-kal'*, adj., grammatical. L. 51.
Grande, *gran'-dai*, adj., great, large. L. 7.
Granizar, *grah-nĕ-thar'*, to hail. L. 30.
Grato, *grah'-to*, adj., grateful, pleasing, agreeable. L. 56.
Grito, *grĕ'-to*, s. m., cry, shout, scream. L. 59.
Guerra, *gair'-ra*, s. f., war. L. 56.
Guiñada, *gheen-yah'-da*, s. f., wink. L. 54.
Guipúzcoa, *ghĕ-pooth'-kwa*, s. f., Guipuzcoa (province in Spain). L. 53.
Gustar, *gooss-tar'*, to like, to please, to taste. L. 31.
Gusto, *gooss'-to*, s. m., taste, pleasure.—Con mucho *gusto*, with great pleasure. L. 23.

H.

Habana (La), *lah-ah-bah'-na*, s. f., Havana. L. 12.
Habanero, *ah-bah-nai'-ro*, adj. and s. m., Havanese. L. 49.
Haber, *ah-bair'*, to have (used only as an auxiliary verb in this signification; for exceptions see Lesson 66); impersonal verb, there to be.—Hay dos iglesias en esta calle, there are two churches in this street. L. 12.
Hábil, *ah'-beel*, adj., able, skilful, expert, clever. L. 21.
Habilidad, *ah-bĕ-lĕ-dath'*, s. f., ability, skilfulness, expertness, cleverness. L. 36.

Habitante, *ah-bĕ-tan'-tai*, s. m., inhabitant. L. 40.
Hablador, *ab-lah-dōre'*, adj. and s. m., talkative; talker. L. 20.
Hablar, *ab-lar'*, to talk, to speak.—Hablar á bulto, to talk at random. L. 1.
Hacer, *ah-thair'*, to do, to make.—Hacer muy bien, to do well or right, to be right.—Hacer de, to act as. L. 19.
Hácia, *ah'-thĕ-a*, adv., toward, towards. L. 19.
Hallar, *al-yar'*, to find. L. 37.
Hambre, *am'-brai*, s. f., hunger.—Tener *hambre*, to be hungry. L. 25.
Hasta, *ass'-ta*, adv., until, till, as far as, even. L. 19.
Hazmereir, *ath-mai-rai-eer'*, s. m., laughingstock. L. 50.
He! *ai*, inter., ho! what? what do you say? L. 44.
Hecho, *ai'-cho*, s. m., action, fact. L. 52.
Helar, *ai-lar'*, to freeze. L. 30.
Helena, *ai-lai'-na*, s. f., Helen, Ellen. L. 19.
Hermanastro, *air-mah-nass'-tro*, s. m., aug., step-brother, half-brother. L. 49.
Hermano, *air-mah'-no*, s. m., brother. L. 6.
Hermoso, *air-mŏ'-so*, adj., beautiful, handsome. L. 7.
Hermosura, *air-mŏ-soo'-ra*, s. f., beauty, handsomeness. L. 53.
Herrero, *air-rai'-ro*, s. m., blacksmith. L. 65.
Hielo, *yai'-lo*, s. m., ice, frost. L. 30.
Hierro, *yair'-ro*, s. m., iron. L. 61.
Higo, *ĕ'-go*, s. m., fig. L. 40.
Hijastro, *ĕ-hass'-tro*, s. m., step-son. L. 49.
Hijo, *ĕ'-ho*, s. m., son. L. 6.
Hilar, *ĕ-lar'*, to spin. L. 65.
Hilo, *ĕ'-lo*, s. m., thread. L. 21.
Hinchar, *een-char'*, to swell. L. 53.
Historia, *eess-tŏ'-rĕ-a*, s. f., history. L. 15.
Hoja, *ŏ'-ha*, s. f., leaf (of a tree or a book). L. 59.
Hola! *ŏ'-la*, inter., hallo! L. 46.
Holgazán, *ŏle-gah-than'*, adj. and s. m., idle, lazy, loitering; idler, loiterer. L. 6.
Hombre, *ŏme'-brai*, s. m., man.—Es mas *hombre* que su hermano, he is more of a man than his brother. L. 6.
Honor, *ŏ-nōre'*, s. m., honor. L. 39.
Honroso, *ŏne-rŏ'-so*, adj., honorable. L. 52.
Hora, *ŏ'-ra*, s. f., hour. L. 23.
Horno, *ōre'-no*, s. m., oven.—Cocer en *horno*, to bake. L. 60.
Horrendo, *ōre-rain'-do*, adj., horrific (poet.). L. 55.
Hortelano, *ōre-tai-lah'-no*, s. m., gardener. L. 65.
Hospital, *ōce-pĕ-tal'*, s. m., hospital. L. 47.
Hotel, *ŏ-tail'*, s. m., hotel. L. 17.
Hueso, *wai'-so*, s. m., bone.—Bocado sin *hueso*, sinecure. L. 61.
Huésped, *waiss'-paid*, s. m., guest, host.—Echar la cuenta sin la *huéspeda*, to reckon without the host. L. 63.
Huir, *weer*, to flee, to make off. L. 34.
Humano, *oo-mah'-no*, adj., human. L. 48.
Humor, *oo-mōre'*, s. m., humor, wit. L. 27.

I.

Idea, *ĕ-dai'-a*, s. f., ideal. L. 54.
Ideal, *ĕ-dai-al'*, adj., ideal. L. 43.

Idioma, *ĭ-dĕ-ŏ'-ma*, s. m., idiom, language. L. 55.
Idiota, *ĭ-dĕ-ŏ'-ta*, s. m., idiot. L. 48.
Idiotismo, *ĭ-dĕ-ŏ-teess'-mo*, s. m., idiom, form of expression peculiar to a language. L. 49.
Iglesia, *ĭ-glai'-sĕ-a*, s. f., church. L. 16.
Ignorancia, *eeg-nŏ-ran'-thĕ-a*, s. f., ignorance. L. 52.
Ignorante, *eeg-nŏ-ran'-tai*, adj., ignorant. L. 61.
Ignorar, *eeg-nŏ-rar'*, to be ignorant of, not to know. L. 61.
Igual, *ĭ-gwal'*, adj., equal, alike, like. L. 48.
Igualdad, *ĭ-gwal-dath'*, s. f., equality. L. 55.
Ilusion, *ĭ-loo-sĕ-ōne'*, s. f., illusion. L. 43.
Imaginacion, *ĭ-mah-hĕ-nah-thĕ-ōne'*, s. f., imagination. L. 58.
Impedir, *eem-pai-deer'*, to impede, to hinder. L. 43.
Imperativo, *eem-pai-rah-tĕ'-vo*, adj. and s. m., imperative, imperative mood. L. 43.
Imperfeccion, *eem-pair-faik-thĕ-ōne'*, s. f., imperfection. L. 55.
Imperfecto, *eem-pair-faik'-to*, adj., imperfect. L. 43.
Impersonal, *eem-pair-sŏ-nal'*, adj., impersonal. L. 61.
Imponer, *eem-pŏ-nair'*, to impose, to inform, to acquaint. L. 44.
Importante, *eem-pōre-tan'-tai*, adj., important. L. 38.
Importar, *eem-pōre-tar'*, to import, to be of importance, to amount to. L. 31.
Imposible, *eem-pŏ-sĕ'-blai*, adj., impossible. L. 31.
Impreso, *eem-prai'-so*, past part. of IMPRIMIR. L. 61.
Imprimir, *eem-prĕ-meer'*, to print. L. 61.
Improvisar, *eem-prŏ-vĕ-sar'*, to improvise, to extemporise. L. 53.
Improviso, *eem-prŏ-vĕ'-so*.—De *improviso*, unexpectedly, on a sudden. L. 32.
Imprudencia, *eem-proo-dain'-thĕ-a*, s. f., imprudence. L. 43.
Imprudente, *eem-proo-dain'-tai*, adj., imprudent. L. 20.
Impuesto, *eem-pwaiss'-to*, past part. of IMPONER. L. 52.
In, *een*, Latin prep. used in Spanish as a prefix only, and generally with a negative signification. L. 50.
Incendiar, *een-thain-dĕ-ar'*, to kindle. L. 51.
Incluir, *een-cloo-eer'*, to include. L. 49.
Incómodamente, *een-kŏ'-mŏ-dah-main-tai*, adv., incommodiously, inconveniently, uncomfortably. L. 29.
Incomodar, *een-kŏ-mŏ-dar'*, to incommode, to put out. L. 47.
Incómodo, *een-kŏ'-mŏ-do*, adj., incommodious, inconvenient, uncomfortable. L. 29.
Incompleto, *een-kome-plai'-to*, adj., incomplete. L. 48.
Inconveniente, *een-kŏne-vai-nĕ-ain'-tai*, s. m., difficulty, obstacle, objection. L. 61.
Increible, *een-krai-ĕ'-blai*, adj., incredible. L. 61.
Indefinido, *een-dai-fĕ-nĕ'-do*, adj., indefinite. L. 61.
Independencia, *een-dai-pain-dain'-thĕ-a*, s. f., independence. L. 35.
Indicativo, *een-dĕ-kah-tĕ'-vo*, adj., indicative. L. 43.

Indice, *een'-dĕ-thai*, s. m., index. L. 61.
Indigno, *een-deeg'-no*, adj., unworthy, undeserving. L. 53.
Indigo, *een'-dĕ-go*, s. m. L. 54. (See AÑIL.)
Indirecto, *een-dĕ-raik'-to*, adj., indirect. L. 51.
Individuo, *een-dĕ-vĕ'-doo-ŏ*, s. m., individual, member (of academies, universities, &c.). L. 51.
Industrioso, *een-doos-trĕ-ŏ'-so*, adj., industrious. L. 35.
Inepto, *een-aip'-to*, adj., inept, unfit. L. 51.
Inexplicable, *een-aiks-plĕ-kuh'-blai*, adj., inexplicable. L. 61.
Infancia, *een-fan'-thĕ-a*, s. f., infancy. L. 54.
Inferior, *een-fai-rĕ-ōre'*, adj., inferior. L. 21.
Infimo, *een'-fĕ-mo*, adj., lowest. L. 21.
Infinidad, *een-fĕ-nĕ-dath'*, s. f., infinity. L. 40.
Infinitivo, *een-fĕ-nĕ-tĕ'-vo*, adj., infinitive. L. 43.
Infinito, *een-fĕ-nĕ'-to*, adj., infinite. L. 39.
Influir, *een-floo-eer'*, to influence. L. 43.
Infortunio, *een-fōre-too'-nĕ-o*, s. m., misfortune. L. 41.
Ingenio, *een-hai'-nĕ-o*, s. m., genius. L. 61.
Ingenioso, *een-hai-nĕ-ŏ'-so*, adj., ingenious. L. 61.
Inglaterra, *een-glah-tair'-ra*, s. f., England. L. 9.
Inglés, *een-glaiss'*, s. m. and adj., English. L. 2.
Inicial, *ĭ-nĕ-thĕ-al'*, adj., initial. L. 56.
Injusticia, *een-hooss-tĕ'-thĕ-a*, s. f., injustice. L. 45.
Inmediato, *een-mai-dĕ-ah'-to*, adj., immediate, near, next. L. 61.
Inmemorial, *een-mai-mŏ-rĕ-al'*, adj., immemorial. L. 55.
Inocente, *ĭ-nŏ-thain'-tai*, adj., innocent. L. 34.
Inquietar, *een-kĕ-ai-tar'*, to make uneasy. L. 61.
Inquieto, *een-kĕ-ai'-to*, adj., uneasy, restless. L. 61.
Insecto, *een-saik'-to*, s. m., insect. L. 61.
Inspirar, *eens-pĕ-rar'*, to inspire. L. 58.
Instante, *eens-tan'-te*, s. m., instant.—Al *instante*, immediately. L. 42.
Instinto, *eens-teen'-to*, s. m., instinct. L. 61.
Instruccion, *een-trook-thĕ-ōne'*, s. f., instruction, learning. L. 52.
Instruido, *eens-troo-ĕ'-do*, adj., instructed, learned, educated. L. 49.
Instruir, *eens-troo-eer'*, to instruct, to teach. L. 47.
Instrumento, *eens-troo-main'-to*, s. m., instrument. L. 61.
Intachable, *een-tah-chah'-blai*, adj., unimpeachable, irreproachable. L. 62.
Intencion, *een-tain-thĕ-ōne'*, s. f., intention. L. 61.
Intentar, *een-tain-tar'*, to attempt. L. 61.
Interés, *een-tai-raiss'*, s. m., interest. L. 54.
Interesante, *een-tai-rai-san'-tai*, adj., interesting. L. 47.
Interesar, *een-tai-rai-sar'*, to interest. L. 61.
Interin, *een'-tai-reen*, adv., in the interim. L. 61.
Interior, *een-tai-rĕ-ōre'*, adj., interior. L. 48.
Interior, s. m., interior. L. 45.

VOCABULARY. 455

Interjeccion, *een-tair-haik-thĕ-ōne'*, s. f., interjection. L. 43.
Interrogacion, *een-tair-rŏ-gah-thĕ-ōne'*, s. f., interrogation. L. 61.
Interrogante, *een-tair-rŏ-gan'-tai*, s.m., note of interrogation. (Pres. part. of INTERROGAR.) L. 61.
Interrogar, *een-tair-rŏ-gar'*, to interrogate, to question. L. 61.
Interrumpir, *een-tair-room-peer'*, to interrupt. L. 64.
Intimidad, *een-tĕ-mĕ-dath'*, s. f., intimacy. L. 56.
Intimo, *een'-tĕ-mo*, adj., intimate. L. 56.
Introducir, *een-trŏ-doo-theer'*, to introduce. L. 40.
Inútil, *een-oo'-teel*, adj., useless. L. 50.
Invariable, *een-vah-rĕ-ah'-blai*, adj., invariable. L. 56.
Inversion, *een-vair-sĕ-ōne'*, s. f., inversion. L. 61.
Invertir, *een-vair-teer'*, to invert. L. 61.
Invierno, *een-vĕ-air'-no*, s. m., winter. L. 24.
Invitar, *een-vĕ-tar'*, to invite. L. 56.
Ir, *eer*, to go. L. 18.
Iris, *ē'-reess*, s. f., rainbow. L. 61.
Irlanda, *eer-lan'-da*, s. f., Ireland. L. 40.
Irregular, *eer-rai-goo-lar'*, adj., irregular. L. 49.
Irregularidad, *eer-rai-goo-lah-rĕ-dath'*, s. f., irregularity. L. 55.
Isabel, *ē-sah-bail'*, s. f., Isabella, Elizabeth. L. 55.
Isla, *eess'-la*, s. f., island. L. 61.
Italia, *ē-tah'-lĕ-a*, s. f., Italy. L. 40.
Italiano, *ē-tah-lĕ-ah'-no*, s. m. and adj., Italian. L. 61.
Izquierdo, *eeth-kĕ-air'-do*, adj., left-handed.—Mano *izquierda*, left hand. L. 50.

J.

Jabon, *hah-bōne'*, s. m., soap. L. 5.
Jamás, *hah-mass'*, adv., never. L. 25.
Jaque, *hah'-kai*, check (at chess).—*Jaque y mate*, checkmate. L. 42.
Jardin, *har-deen'*, s. m., garden. L. 18.
Jardinero, *har-dĕ-nai'-ro*, s. m., gardener. L. 34.
José, *hŏ-sai'*, s. m., Joseph. L. 43.
Jóven, *hŏ'-vain*, adj. and s. m. and f., young; young man, young woman. L. 13.
Juan, *whan*, s. m., John. L. 17.
Juana, *whah'-na*, s. f., Jane. L. 17.
Juego, *whai'-go*, s. m., game, play, set. L. 61.
Juéves, *whai'-vaiss*, s. m., Thursday. L. 9.
Juez, *whaith*, s. m., judge. L. 9.
Jugar, *hoo-gar'*, to play. L. 41.
Juicio, *whē'-thĕ-ō*, s. m., judgment, sense, trial. L. 53.
Julio, *hoo'-lē-ō*, s. m., July, (prop. name) Julius. L. 24.
Juntar, *hoon-tar'*, to join, to place together. L. 65.
Junto, *hoon'-to*, adv., near, close to. L. 39.
Juramento, *hoo-ra-main'-to*, s. m., oath, affidavit. L. 53.
Justicia, *hooss-tē'-thē-a*, s. f., justice. L. 61.
Justo, *hooss'-to*, adj., just, right. L. 61.
Juventud, *hoo-ven-tooth'*, s. f., youth. L. 48.

L.

La, def. art. f. sing., the. L. 5.
La, pron. f. sing., her, it. L. 8.
Lacónico, *lah-kŏ'-nĕ-ko*, adj., laconic. L. 38.
Laboriosidad, *lah-bo-rĕ-ō-sĕ-dath'*, s. f., industry. L. 51.
Lacre, *lah'-krai*, s. m., sealing-wax. L. 5.
Lado, *lah'-do*, s. m., side. L. 18.
Ladron, *lah-drōne'*, s. m., thief. L. 44.
Lago, *lah'-go*, s. m., lake. L. 40.
Lágrima, *lah'-grĕ-ma*, s. f., tear. L. 51.
Lápiz, *lah'-peeth*, s. m., pencil. L. 51.
Largo, *lar'-go*, adj., long.—*Largo tiempo*, a long time.—*A lo largo*, alongside. L. 21.
Lástima, *lass'-tĕ-ma*, s. f., pity. L. 25.
Lastimar, *lass-tĕ-mar'*, to hurt, to wound, to offend. L. 61.
Latin, *lah-teen'*, s. m., Latin. L. 61.
Latinajo, *lah-tē-nah'-ho*, s. m. aug., Dog-Latin. L. 49.
Latitud, *lah-tē-tooth'*, s. f., width, latitude. L. 61.
Lavandera, *lah-van-dai'-ra*, s. f., washerwoman. L. 5.
Lavar, *lah-var'*, to wash. L. 24.
Le, *lai*, pron., him, it; to him, to it. L. 10.
Leccion, *laik-thē-ōne'*, s. f., lesson. L. 8.
Leche, *lai'-chai*, s. f., milk. L. 7.
Lectura, *laik-too'-ra*, s. f., reading. L. 38.
Leer, *lai-air'*, to read. L. 7.
Legua, *lai'-gwa*, s. f., league. L. 61.
Leido, *lai-ē'-do*, adj.—*Hombre bien leído*, a well-read man. (Past pt. of LEER.) L. 52.
Léjos, *lai'-hōce*, adv., far off.—*A lo léjos*, in the distance. L. 31.
Lengua, *lain'-gwa*, s. f., tongue, language. L. 23.
Lenguaje, *lain-gwa'-hai*, s. m., language, manner of speaking or writing. L. 66.
Lento, *lain'-to*, adj., slow, tardy. L. 61.
Leon, *lai-ōne'*, s. m., lion. L. 54.
Letra, *lai'-tra*, s. f., letter (character), handwriting, letter (of credit); pl., letters, literature.—*Bellas letras*, Belles-lettres. L. 61.
Levantar, *lai-van-tar'*, to raise, to lift up.—*Levantarse*, to rise, to get up. L. 33.
Levita, *lai-vē'-ta*, s. m., Levite.—*Levita*, s. f., frock-coat. L. 61.
Ley, *lai'-ē*, s. f., law. L. 8.
Liberal, *lē-bē-ral'*, adj., liberal. L. 62.
Libertad, *lē-bair-tath'*, s. f., liberty. L. 40.
Libra, *lē'-bra*, s. f., pound.—*Libra esterlina*, pound sterling. L. 47.
Librar, *lē-brar'*, to free, to deliver: (commercial) to draw. L. 45.
Libre, *lē'-brai*, adj., free. L. 59.
Librería, *lē-brai-rē'-a*, s. f., bookstore, bookseller's shop, book-trade. L. 11.
Librero, *lē-brai'-ro*, s. m., bookseller. L. 11.
Libro, *lē'-bro*, s. m., book. L. 4.
Ligero, *lē-hai'-ro*, adj., light, swift.—*A la ligera*, lightly. L. 46.
Limosna, *lē-mōce'-na*, s. f., alms. L. 61.
Limpiar, *leem-pē-ar'*, to clean. L. 64.
Limpieza, *leem-pē-ai'-tha*, s. f., cleanliness. L. 61.
Limpio, *leem'-pē-ō*, adj., clean, cleanly. L. 20.
Línea, *lē' nai-a*, s. f., line. L. 61.
Lisboa, *leess-bō'-a*, s. f., Lisbon. L. 55.
Lisonja, *lē-sōne'-ha*, s. f., flattery. L. 61.

Lisonjear, *lē-sōne-hai-ar'*, to flatter. L. 61.
Lisonjero, *lē-sōne-hai'-ro*, adj. and s. m., flattering, flatterer. L. 61.
Lista, *leess'-ta*, s. f., list. L. 61.
Listo, *leess'-to*, adj., ready, sharp, quick. L. 46.
Literato, *lē-tai-rah'-to*, s. m., man of letters, literatus. L. 51.
Literatura, *lē-tai-rah-too'-ra*, s. f., literature. L. 52.
Litro, *lē'-tro*, s. m., litre. L. 60.
Lo, art. neut., the. (See explanations in Lesson 8.)
Lo, pron., it, (and sometimes) him. L. 26.
Local, *lō-kal'*, adj., local. L. 51.
Loco, *lō'-ko*, adj., mad —A toutas y á *locas*, inconsiderately, without reduction. L. 61.
Loco, s. m., madman. L. 61.
Lodo, *lō'-do*, s. m., mud, mire. L. 45.
Lograr, *lō-grar'*, to succeed, to obtain. L. 38.
Lóndres, *lōns'-dra!ss*, s. m., London. L. 12.
Longitud, *lōns-hē-tooth'*, s. f., length, longitude. L. 61.
Lotería, *lō-tai-rē'-a*, s. f., lottery. L. 63.
Lucir, *loo-theer'*, to shine, to glitter. L. 63.
Luego, *loo-ai'-go*, adv., by and by, immediately;—conj., then, therefore. L. 33.
Lugar, *loo-gar'*, s. m., place, village.—En *lugar* de, instead of. L. 29.
Luis, *loo-eess'*, s. m., Lewis, Louis. L. 15.
Luisa, *loo-ē'-sa*, s. f., Louisa. L. 2.
Luna, *loo'-na*, s. f. moon. L. 61.
Luto, *loo'-to*, s. m., mourning. L. 60.
Luz, *looth*, s. f., light.—Dar á *luz*, to publish, to give birth to. L. 61.

LL.

Llamar, *lyah-mar'*, to call, to know. L. 27.
Llave, *lyah'-vai*, s. f., key. L. 53.
Llegar, *lyai-gar'*, to arrive.—*Llegar* á ser, to become. L. 37.
Llenar, *lyai-nar'*, to fill, to fulfil. L. 54.
Lleno, *lyai'-no*, adj., full. L. 54.
Llevar, *lyai-var'*, to take, to carry, to bear, to bring forth. L. 14.
Llorar, *lyō-rar'*, to cry, to weep. L. 51.
Lloro, *lyō'-ro*, s. m., tear, act of crying. L. 51.
Llover, *lyō-vair'*, to rain.—*Llover* á cántaros, to pour. L. 3).
Lloviznar, *lyo-veeth-nar'*, to drizzle. L. 30.
Lluvia, *lyoo'-vē-a*, s. f., rain. L. 30.

M.

Macho, *mah'-cho*, s. m., male (of animals), mule. L. 62.
Madera, *mah-dai'-ra*, s. f., wood, timber, lumber. L. 4.
Madrastra, *mah-drass'-tra*, s. f., step-mother. L. 49.
Madre, *mah'-drai*, s. f., mother.—Lengua *madre*, an original language. L. 6.
Madrid, *mah-dreeth'*, s. m., Madrid. L. 12.
Madrileño, *mah-drē-lnin'-yo*, s. m., Madrilenian, native of Madrid. L. 49.
Madrugada, *mah-droo-gah'-da*, s. f., that part of the night from 12 P. M. until sun rise. L. 65.

Madrugar, *mah-droo-gar'*, to rise very early. L. 62.
Madurez, *mah-doo-raith'*, s. f., maturity, ripeness. L. 51.
Maestro, *mah-ass'-tro*, s. m., master, teacher. L. 62.
Magnífico, *mag-nē'-fē-ko*, adj., magnificent. L. 58.
Mal, s. m., evil, harm, disease. L. 48.
Mal, adv., badly.—*Mal* de su grado, in spite of him. L. 3.
Maldito, *mal-dē'-to*, adj., accursed, perverse. L. 62.
Malicia, *mah-lē'-thē-a*, s. f., malice, wickedness. L. 62.
Malo, *mah'-lo*, adj., bad, ill, wicked.—Estar *malo*, to be sick.—Ser *malo*, to be bad, to be wicked. L. 7.
Mamá, *mah-ma'*, s. f., mamma. L. 5.
Mandar, *man-dar'*, to send, to command, to order. L. 17.
Manera, *mah-nai'-ra*, s. f., manner.—De *manera* que, so as, so that. L. 42.
Manía, *mah-nē'-a*, s. f., mania, whim. L. 57.
Manifestar, *mah-nē-fuiss-tar'*, to manifest, to show. L. 51.
Manifiesto, *mah-nē-fē-aiss'-to*, adj., manifest. L. 52.
Mano, *mah'-no*, s. f., hand, quire (of paper).—Venir con sus *manos* lavadas, to wish to enjoy the fruit of another's labor. L. 28.
Manteca, *man-tai'-ka*, s. f., butter, lard (South America). L. 62.
Mantequilla, *man-tai-keel'-ya*, s. f., butter (South America), lard. L. 62.
Manuel, *mah-noo-ail'*, s. m., Emanuel. L. 2.
Manuscrito, *mah-nooss-krē-to*, s. m., manuscript. L. 62.
Manzana, *man-thah'-na*, s. f., apple, block (of houses). L. 31.
Manzanar, *man-thah-nar'*, s. m., apple-orchard. L. 49.
Mañana, *man-yah'-na*, s. f., morning, tomorrow.—Pasado *mañana*, the day after to-morrow. L. 30.
Mar, s. m. and f., sea.—Quien no se arriesga no pasa la *mar*, faint heart never won fair lady. L. 62.
Marca, *mar'-ka*, s. f., mark, brand. L. 42.
Marcha, *mar'-cha*, s. f., march.—Sobre la *marcha*, off-hand, on the spot. L. 51.
Marchar, *mar-char'*, to march. L. 19.
Margarita, *mar-gah-rē'-ta*, s. f., Margaret. L. 3.
María, *mah-rē'-a*, s. f., Mary. L. 44.
Mártes, *mar'-taiss*, s. m., Tuesday. L. 9.
Marzo, *mar'-thō*, s. m., March. L. 24.
Mas, *mass*, adv., more.—*Mas* que (or de), more than. L. 16.
Máscara, *mass'-kah-ra*, s. f., mask. L. 60.
Masculino, *mass-koo-lē'-no*, adj., masculine. L. 47.
Matar, *mah-tar'*, to kill. L. 44.
Matemático, *mah-tai-mah'-tē-ko*, s. m., mathematician; adj., mathematical. L. 60.
Materia, *mah-tai'-rē-a*, s. f., matter, subject, affair. L. 54.
Material, *mah-tai-rē-al'*, adj., material. L. 48.
Materialista, *mah-tai-rē-ah-leess'-ta*, s. m., materialist. L. 36.

VOCABULARY. 457

Matrimonio, *mah-trē-mō'-nē-o*, s. m., matrimony, wedlock, marriage. L. 64.
Maulhdo, *mah-ool-yē'-do*, s. m., mew (of a cat). L. 46.
Máximo, *mak'-sē-mo*, adj. (superlative of GRANDE), chief, principal, very great. L. 21.
Mayo, *mah'-yo*, s. m., May. L. 24.
Mayor, *mah-yōre'*, adj., greater, larger.—El *mayor*, the greatest, the largest. L. 20.
Mayúscula, *mah-yooss'-koo-la*, adj., capital (said of letters). L. 62.
Me, *mai*, pron., me, to me. L. 26.
Meca, *mai'-ka*, s. f.—De zeca en *meca*, from pillar to post, to and fro. L. 61.
Media, *mai'-dē-a*, s. f., stocking. L. 10.
Medianamente, *mai-dē-ah-nah-main'-tai*, adv., middling. L. 39.
Medianía, *mai-dē-ah-nē'-a*, s. f., mediocrity, moderation. L. 52.
Mediano, *mai-dē-ah'-no*, adj., medium, middling, moderate. L. 39.
Médico, *mai'-dē-ko*, s. m., physician. L. 19.
Medida, *mai-dē'-da*, s. f., measure. L. 53.
Medio, *mai'-dē-o*, adj., half.—*Media*día, midday, noon.—*Media*noche, midnight. L. 30.
Medio, s. m., middle, means.—Por *medio de*, by means of. L. 37.
Mediodía, *mai-dē-ō-dē'-a*, s. m., noon, midday, south. L. 30.
Medir, *mai-deer'*, to measure. L. 39.
Mejicano, *mai hē-kah'-no*, s. m. and adj., Mexican. L. 47.
Méjico, *mai'-hē-ko*, s. m., Mexico. L. 20.
Mejor, *mai-hōre'*, adj. and adv., better.—El *mejor*, the best. L. 20.
Melocoton, *mai lō-kō-tōne'*, s. m., peach. L. 31.
Melon, *mai-lōne'*, s. m., melon. L. 31.
Memoria, *mai-mō'-rē-a*, s. f., memory, recollection.—Aprender de *memoria*, to learn by heart. L. 38.
Memorias, *mai-mō-rē-as*, s. f. pl., my compliments. L. 39.
Mencion, *main-thē-ōne'*, s. f., mention. L. 52.
Mencionar, *main-thē-ō-nar'*, to mention. L. 45.
Menester, *mai-naiss-tair'*, s. m., need, want, necessity.—Ser *menester*, to be necessary; must.—Haber *menester*, to want, to require. L. 30.
Menor, *mai-nōre'*, adj., less, smaller, minor, younger; s. m., minor. L. 20.
Ménos, *mai'-nōce*, adv., less.—A lo *ménos*, at least.—Ni mas mi *ménos*, neither more nor less. L. 16.
Menoscabo, *mai-nōce-kah'-bo*, s. m., deterioration, detriment, prejudice, diminution. L. 62.
Menosprecio, *mai-nōce-prai'-thē-ō*, s. m., contempt, scorn.—Mucha familiaridad es causa de *menosprecio*, much familiarity breeds contempt. L. 65.
Mente, *main'-tai*, s. f., mind. L. 62.
Mentir, *main-teer'*, to lie. L. 45.
Menudo, *mai-noo'-do*, adj., small, slender, mean.—A *menudo*, often. L. 25.
Mequetrefe, *mai-kai-trai'-fai*, s. m., trifler, jackanapes. L. 63.
Mercader, *mair kah-dair'*, s. m., dealer, trader, shopkeeper. L. 52.
Mercado, *mair-kah'-do*, s. m., market. L. 17.

Mercantil, *mair-kan-teel'*, adj., mercantile. L. 56.
Merecer, *mai-rai-thair'*, to merit, to deserve. L. 52.
Merendar, *mai-rain-dar'*, to lunch. L. 34.
Meridiano, *mai-rē-dē-ah'-no*, s. m., meridian. L. 62.
Merino, *mai-rē'-no*, s. m., merino (sort of Spanish sheep). L. 40.
Mérito, *mai'-rē-to*, s. m., merit. L. 55.
Mes, *maiss*, s. m., month.—Al *mes*, by the month. L. 16.
Mesa, *mai'-sa*, s. f., table. L. 14.
Metal, *mai-tal'*, s. m., metal. L. 62.
Meter, *mai-tair'*, to put, to place.—*Meter* ruido, to make noise. L. 46.
Metódico, *mai-tō'-dē-ko*, adj., methodical. L. 35.
Método, *mai'-lō-do*, s. m., method. L. 47.
Metrópoli, *mai-trō' pō-lē*, s. f., metropolis. L. 51.
Mí, *mē*, pron., me. L. 25.
Mi, poss. pron., my. L. 5.
Miedo, *mē-ai'-do*, s. f., fear.—Tener *miedo*, to be afraid. L. 25.
Miel, *mē-ail'*, s. f., honey. L. 65.
Miembro, *mē-aim'-bro*, s. m., member, limb. L. 62.
Miércoles, *mē-air'-kō-laiss*, s. m., Thursday. L. 9.
Mil, *meel*, num. adj. and s. m., a thousand, one thousand. L. 14.
Milla, *meel'-ya*, s. f., mile. L. 62.
Millar, *meel-yar'*, s. m., the number of a thousand, thousand. L. 40.
Millon, *meel-yōne'*, num. adj. and s. m., million.—*Millones* de pesos, millions of dollars. L. 40.
Mineral, *mē-nai-ral'*, s. m., mineral. L. 62.
Minúscula, *mē-nooce'-koo-la*, adj., small (said of letters), as opposed to capital. L. 62.
Minuto, *mē-noo'-to*, s. m., minute. L. 23.
Mio, mia, *mē'-ō*, *mē'-a*, poss. pron. and poss. adj., mine. (As a poss. adj., *mio* is always placed after the substantive.) L. 13.
Mirar, *mē-rar'*, to look, to look at, to observe. L. 29.
Mismo, *meess'-mo*, adj., same, self, selfsame.—El *mismo*, he himself. L. 27.
Mitad, *mē-tath'*, s. f., half. L. 40.
Moda, *mō'-da*, s. f., fashion. L. 25.
Modelo, *mō-dai'-lo*, s. m., model. L. 55.
Moderacion, *mō-dai-rah-thē-ōne'*, s. f., moderation. L. 65.
Moderno, *mō-dair'-no*, adj., modern. L. 52.
Modificar, *mō-dē-fē-kar'*, to modify. L. 61.
Modismo, *mō-deess'-mo*, s. m., peculiar manner of expressing the same ideas in the same language. L. 64.
Modo, *mō'-do*, s. m., mode, manner.—De ningun *modo*, by no means.—De *modo que*, so that. L. 42.
Molestar, *mō-laiss-tar'*, to molest, to disturb, to trouble. L. 43.
Momento, *mō-main'-to*, s. m., moment. L. 62.
Mona, *mō'-na*, s. f., female monkey.—Aunque la *mona* se vista de seda, *mona* se queda, a hog in armor is still but a hog. L. 65.
Monárquico, *mō-nar'-kē-ko*, adj., monarchical. L. 35.

20

VOCABULARY.

Moneda, *mŏ-nai'-da*, s. f., money, coin.—*Papel moneda*, paper money. L. 55.
Montar, *mŏne-tar'*, to mount, to ascend, to ride (on horseback). L. 62.
Montaraz, *mŏne-tah-rath'*, adj., mountain, wild. L. 54.
Monte, *mŏne'-tai*, s. m., mountain.—*Monte de piedad*, pawn-office. L. 40.
Morder, *mŏre-dair'*, to bite, to nip.—*No se muerde los labios*, he speaks out his mind. L. 36.
Moribundo, *mŏ-rē-boon'-do*, adj., dying. L. 47.
Morir, *mŏ-reer'*, to die. L. 41.
Mosca, *mŏce'-ka*, s. f., fly. L. 44.
Mostrar, *mŏce-trar'*, to show. L. 35.
Motivo, *mŏ-tē'-vo*, s. m., motive. L. 34.
Mover, *mŏ-vair'*, to move. L. 36.
Mozo, *mŏ'-tho*, s. m., youth, young man, waiter. L. 62.
Muchacha, *moo-chah'-cha*, s. f., girl. L. 6.
Muchacho, *moo-chah'-cho*, s. m., boy. L. 6.
Mucho, *moo'-cho*, adj. and adv., much. a great deal, very. L. 8.
Mudable, *moo-dah'-blai*, adj., mutable, changeable, fickle. L. 49.
Mudar, *moo-dar'*, to change.—*Mudarse*, to move (from one place to another). L. 62.
Muela, *moo-ai'-la*, s. f., back tooth.—*Dolor de muelas*, toothache. L. 50.
Muerte, *moo-air'-tai*, s. f., death. L. 38.
Muerto, *moo-air'-to*, past part. (of Monir), dead, killed. L. 52.
Muestra, *moo-aiss'-tra*, s. f., sample, sign. L. 62.
Mujer, *moo-hair'*, s. f., woman, wife. L. 6.
Multitud, *mool-tē-tooth'*, s. f., multitude. L. 40.
Mundo, *moon'-do*, s. m., world.—*Todo el mundo*, everybody. L. 35.
Murmuracion, *moor-moo-rah-thē-ōne'*, s. f., murmuring, backbiting. L. 62.
Murmurar, *moor-moo-rar'*, to murmur, to backbite. L. 62.
Museo, *moo-sai'-o*, s. m., museum. L. 51.
Música, *moo'-sē-ka*, s. f., music. L. 15.
Músico, *moo'-sē-ko*, s. m., musician. L. 15.
Muy, *moo'-ē*, very. L. 6.

N.

Nacer, *nah-thair'*, to be born.—*Nacer de piés*, to be born to good luck. L. 62.
Nacion, *nah-thē-ōne'*, s. f., nation. L. 24.
Nada, *nah'-da*, adv., in no degree.—*Nada ménos*, nothing less. L. 11.
Nada, s. f., nothing, nonentity. L. 11.
Nadar, *nah-dar'*, to swim. L. 53.
Nadie, *nah'-dē-ai*, ind. pron., nobody, no one. L. 11.
Nápoles, *nah'-pō-laiss*, s. f., Naples. L. 47.
Naranja, *nah-ran'-ha*, s. f., orange. L. 31.
Natural, *nah-too-ral'*, s. m. and adj., natural; native. L. 44.
Naturaleza, *nah-too-rah-lai'-tha*, s. f., nature. L. 40.
Naturalista, *nah-too-rah-leess'-ta*, s. m., naturalist. L. 36.
Navarra, *nah-var'-ra*, s. f., Navarre. L. 55.
Navarro, *nah-rar'-ro*, s. m., Navarrese (native of Navarre). L. 55.

Navegacion, *nah-vai-gah-thē-ōne'*, s. f., navigation. L. 24.
Navidad, *nah-vē-dath'*, s. f., nativity, Christmas. L. 43.
Navío, *nah-vē'-o*, s. m., ship. L. 53.
Necesario, *nai-thai-sah'-rē-o*, adj., necessary. L. 27.
Necesidad, *nai-thai-sē-dath'*, s. f., necessity, need, want. L. 44.
Necesitar, *nai-thai-sē-tar'*, to be necessary, to necessitate, to require, to want. L. 5.
Necio, *nai'-thē-o*, adj. and s. m., foolish; fool. L. 65.
Nefas, *nai'-fass*.—*Por fas ó por nefas*, right or wrong. L. 63.
Negacion, *nai-gah-thē-ōne'*, s. f., negation. L. 62.
Negar, *nai-gar'*, to deny. to refuse. L. 34.
Negativa, *nai-gah-tē'-va*, s. f., negation. negative, refusal. L. 62.
Negligente, *nai-glē-hain'-tai*, adj., negligent. L. 50.
Negocio, *nai-gō'-thē-o*, s. m., business, affair, matter. L. 27.
Negro, *nai'-gro*, s. m. and adj., negro; black. L. 62.
Neutro, *nai'-oo-tro*, adj., neuter. L. 62.
Nevar, *nai-var'*, to snow. L. 30.
Ni, *nē*, conj., neither, nor.—*Ni mas ni ménos*, neither more nor less. L. 8.
Nieve, *nē-ai'-vai*, s. f., snow. L. 30.
Ninguno, *neen-goo'-no*, pron., no one, nobody.—*Ninguna cosa*, nothing. L. 11.
Niña, *neen'-ya*, s. f., little girl, young girl, maiden. L. 17.
Niño, *neen'-yo*, s. m., child, infant. L. 17.
No, adv., no, not. L. 1.
Noble, *nō'-blai*, adj., noble. L. 62.
Nobleza, *nō-blai'-tha*, s. f., nobleness, nobility. L. 55.
Noche, *nō'-chai*, s. f., evening, night.—*Buenas noches*, good evening, good night.—*Noche buena*, Christmas eve.—*Anoche*, last night. L. 28.
Nombrar, *nōme-brar'*, to name, to appoint. L. 48.
Nombre, *nōme'-brai*, s. m., name, noun.—*Nombre propio*, proper name, proper noun. L. 40.
Nominativo, *nō-mē-nah-tē'-ro*, s. m., nominative. L. 62.
Nono. (See Noveno.) L. 15.
No obstante, *nō-ōbe-stan'-tai*, adv., nevertheless, notwithstanding, however. L. 54.
Norte, *nōre'-tai*, s. m., north. L. 22.
Nos, *nōce*, pers. pron., us, to us. L. 26.
Nosotros, *nō-sō'-trōce*, pron., we, ourselves. L. 1.
Nota, *nō'-ta*, s. f., note. L. 62.
Notar, *nō-tar'*, to note, to observe. L. 58.
Noticia, *nō-tē'-thē-a*, s. f., notice, news; pl., news. L. 27.
Notorio, *nō-tō'-rē-o*, adj., notorious. L. 45.
Novecientos, *nō-vai-thē-ain'-tōce*, num. adj., nine hundred. L. 14.
Novedad, *nō-vai-dath'*, s. f., novelty, trouble. L. 39.
Novela, *nō-vai'-la*, s. f., novel, romance. L. 52.
Noveno, *nō-vai'-no*, ord. adj. and s. m., ninth. L. 15.
Noventa, *nō-vain'-ta*, num. adj., ninety. L. 14.

VOCABULARY.   459

Noviembre, *nŏ-vē-aim'-brai*, s. m., November. L. 24.
Nuestro, *noo-aiss'-tro*, poss. pron., our, ours. L. 13.
Nueva, *noo-ai'-va*, s. f., news (generally used in the pl.). L. 60.
Nueva York, *noo-ai'-va*, s. f., New York. L. 9.
Nueve, *noo-ai'-vai*, num. adj., nine. L. 14.
Nuevo, *noo-ai'-vo*, adj., new.—De *nuevo*, anew. L. 21.
Nuez, *noo-aith'*, s. f., walnut. L. 40.
Numeral, *noo-mai-ral'*, adj., numeral. L. 14.
Número, *noo'-mai-ro*, s. m., number.—¿Qué *número* tiene su casa de V.? what is the number of your house? L. 14.
Nunca, *noon'-ka*, adv., never. L. 25.

O.

O, conj., or, either. L. 8.
O! inter., oh! L. 39.
Obedecer, *ŏ-bai-dai-thair'*, to obey. L. 48.
Objetivo, *ŏbe-hai-tē'-vo*, adj. and s. m., objective. L. 62.
Objeto, *ōbe-hai'-to*, s. m., object. L. 48.
Obligacion, *ŏ-blē-gah-thē-ŏne'*, s. f., obligation, duty. L. 24.
Obligar, *ŏ-blē-gar'*, to oblige, to force, to compel. L. 61.
Obra, *ŏ'-bra*, s. f., work (any thing made, as a book, a house, &c.). L. 15.
Obrar, *ŏ-brar'*, to work, to act, to operate. L. 40.
Observar, *ŏbe-sair-var'*, to observe, to remark. L. 48.
Obstante, *ŏbe-stan'-tai*, present part.—No *obstante*. (See NO OBSTANTE.) L. 54.
Obvio, *ŏbe'-vē-ŏ*, adj., obvious. L. 43.
Ocasion, *ŏ-kah-sē-ŏne'*, s. f., occasion, opportunity.—Tomar la *ocasion* por los cabellos, to take time by the forelock. L. 39.
Occidente, *ŏke-thē-dain'-tai*, s. m., the west. L. 51.
Ochenta, *ŏ-chain'-ta*, num. adj., eighty. L. 14.
Ocho, *ŏ'-cho*, num. adj., eight. L. 14.
Ochocientos, *ŏ-cho-thē-ain'-toce*, num. adj., eight hundred. L. 14.
Octavo, *ŏke-tah'-vo*, ord. adj., eighth.—Eu *octavo*, 8vo. L. 15.
Octubre, *ŏke-too'-brai*, s. m., October. L 24.
Ocultar, *ŏ kool-tar'*, to hide. L. 48.
Oculto, *ŏ-kool'-to*, adj., hidden. L. 52.
Ocupacion, *ŏ koo-pah-thē-ŏne'*, s. f., occupation, business, concern. L. 54.
Ocupar, *ŏ-koo-par'*, to occupy, to engage, to fill (a post). L. 47.
Ocurrir, *ŏ-koor-reer'*, to occur, to strike.— Le *ocurre* una idea, an idea strikes him. L. 62.
Oeste, *ŏ-aiss'-tai*, s. m., west. L. 51.
Ofender, *ŏ-fain-dair'*, to offend. L. 27.
Oficio, *ŏ-fē'-thē-o*, s. m., office, employ, trade. L. 38.
Ofrecer, *ŏ-frai-thair'*, to offer L. 49.
Oido, *ŏ-ē'-do*, s. m., hearing, ear.—Hablar al *oido*, to whisper in one's ear. L. 61.
Oir, *ŏ-eer'*, to hear.—*Oiga!* Just listen! L. 41.

Ojalá! *ŏ-hah-la'*, inter., would to God! L. 37.
Ojo, *ŏ'-ho*, s. m., eye. L. 29.
Oler, *ŏ-lair'*, to smell. L. 41.
Olfato, *ŏle-fah'-to*, s. m., the sense of smell. L. 61.
Olla, *ŏle'-ya*, s. f., earthen pot.—*Olla* podrida, Spanish mixed dish of meats, vegetables, &c., cooked together. L. 62.
Olor, *ŏ-lōre'*, s. m., odor, scent, smell. L. 62.
Olivar, *ŏ-lē-var'*, s. m., olive ground. L. 62.
Olvidar, *ŏle-vē-dar'*, to forget. L. 40.
Omnibus, *ŏme'-nē-booce*, s. m., omnibus. L. 51.
Once, *ŏne'-thai*, num. adj., eleven.—Hacer las *once*, to lunch about noon. L. 14.
Opera, *ŏ'-pai-ra*, s. f., opera. L. 25.
Opinion, *ŏ-pē-nē-ŏne'*, s. f., opinion. L. 42.
Oponer, *ŏ-pŏ-nair'*, to oppose. L. 51.
Optimo, *ŏpe' tē-mo*, adj., best, extremely good. L. 21.
Opuesto, *ŏ-pwaiss'-to*, adj., opposite, opposed. (Irreg. past. part. of OPONER.) L. 52.
Oracion, *ŏ-rah-thē-ŏne'*, s. f., prayer, speech, discourse. L. 45.
Orden, *ŏre'-dain*, s. m. and f., order.—A la *órden* de V., at your service. L. 39.
Ordenar, *ŏre-dai-nar'*, to order, to command. L. 51.
Organista, *ŏre-gah-neess'-ta*, s. m., organist. L. 36.
Oriente, *ŏ-rē-ain'-tai*, east. L. 51.
Oro, *ŏ'-ro*, s. m., gold.—No es *oro* todo lo que reluce, all is not gold that glitters. L. 8.
Os, *ŏce*, pron., you (objective of verbs). L. 26.
Ostion, *ŏce-tē-ŏne'*, s. m. (See OSTRA.) L. 62.
Ostra, *ŏce'-tra*, s. f., oyster. L. 62.
Otoño, *ŏ-tŏne'-yo*, s. m., autumn, fall. L. 24.
Otro, *ŏ'-tro*, indef. pron., other, another. L. 18.
Oveja, *ŏ-vai'-ha*, s. f., sheep. L. 65.
Ox! *ŏks*, inter. used to frighten off fowls, &c. L. 46.

P.

Paca, *pah'-ka*, s. f., Fanny. L. 44.
Paciencia, *pah-thē-ain'-thē-a*, s. f., patience. L. 63.
Paco, *pah'-ko*, s. m., (contraction of FRANCISCO, Francis), Frank. L. 44.
Padecer, *pah-dai-thair'*, to suffer pain. L. 47.
Padrastro, *pah-drass'-tro*, s. m., step-father. L. 49.
Padre, *pah'-drai*, s. m., father.—*Padre* nuestro, the Lord's prayer. L. 6 and 45.
Pagar, *pah-gar'*, to pay. L. 14.
Pagaré, *pah-gah-rai'*, s. m., (comm.) promissory note. L. 59.
Página, *pah'-hē-na*, s. f., page (of a book, &c.). L. 50.
Pais, *pah-eess'*, s. m., country.—¿Cuánto tiempo hace qué está V. en este *país*? how long have you been in this country? L. 19.
Paisano, *pah-ē-sah'-no*, s. m., countryman (one from the same country). L. 50.
Paja, *pah'-ha*, s. f., straw. L. 63.

Pájaro, *pah'-hah-ro*, s. m., bird. L. 48.
Pajarraco, *pah-har-ruh'-ko*, s. m., (aug. of PÁJARO), an ugly, clumsy bird. L. 49.
Palabra, *pah-lah'-bra*, s. f., word, promise.—*Palabras* mayores, offensive words. L. 15 and 65.
Palacio, *pah-lah'-thē-o*, s. m., palace. L. 48.
Falangana, *pah-lan-gah'-na*, s. f., washbowl. L. 46.
Palo, *pah'-lo*, s. m., stick of wood. L. 62.
Pan, *pan*, s. m., bread, loaf. L. 7.
Panadería, *pah-nah-dai-rē'-a*, s. f., bakery. L. 11.
Panadero, *pah-nah-dai'-ro*, s. m., baker. bit. L. 11.
Pantalon, *pan-tah-lōne'*, s. m., pantaloons, trousers. L. 17.
Paño, *pan'-yo*, s. m., cloth. L. 62.
Pañuelo, *pan-yoo-ai'-lo*, s. m., pocket-handkerchief. L. 5.
Papá, *pah-pa'*, s. m., papa. L. 5.
Papel, *pah-pail'*, s. m., paper, part (in a play).—Hacer *papel*, to cut a figure. L. 4.
Paquito, *pah-kē'-to*, s. m., (contraction of FRANCISCO, Francis), Franky. L. 44.
Par, *par*, s. m., pair, couple. L. 40.
Para, *pah'-ra*, prep., for, to, in order to, toward.—Tiene una carta *para* V., he has a letter for you.—Está *para* partir, he is about to set out. L. 19.
Parabien, *pah-rah-bē-ain'*, s. m., congratulation, compliment.—Dar el *parabien*, to congratulate. L. 62.
Paráguas, *pah-rah'-gwass*, s. m., umbrella. L. 50.
Parar, *pah-rar'*, to stop, to end (in). L. 51.
Parasol, *pah-rah-sōle'*, s. m., parasol. L. 50.
Parecer, *pah-rai-thair'*, to appear, to seem. L. 30.
Pared, *pah-raith'*, s. f., wall. L. 50.
Paris, *pah-reess'*, s. m., Paris. L. 12.
Parque, *par'-kai*, s. m., park. L. 17.
Parte, *par'-tai*, s. f., part.—Alguna *parte*, somewhere.—Ninguna *parte*, nowhere.—De ocho dias á esta *parte*, for the last eight days;—s. m., message, dispatch, information. L. 27.
Participar, *par-tē-thē-par'*, to participate, to partake. L. 57.
Participio, *par-tē-thē'-pē-ō*, s. m., participle. L. 43.
Partícula, *par-tē'-koo-la*, s. f., particle. L. 50.
Particular, *par-tē-koo-lar'*, adj., particular, private. L. 49.
Partida, *par-tē'-da*, s. f., departure. L. 42.
Partir, *par-teer'*, to depart, to set out, to divide, to split. L. 19.
Partitivo, *par-tē-tē'-vo*, adj., partitive. L. 63.
Pasaje, *pah-sah'-hai*, s. m., passage, fare. L. 58 and 63.
Pasar, *pah-sar'*, to pass, to go (from place to place). L. 16.
Pascua, *pass' kwa*, s. f., Easter. L. 50.
Paseante, *pah sai-an'-tai*, s. m., passer-by, walker, promenader. (Pres. part. of PASEAR.) L. 38.
Pasear, *pah-sai-ar'*, to walk, to promenade. L. 24.
Paseo, *pah-sai'-o*, s. m., walk, promenade. L. 51.

Pasiva, *pah-sē'-va*, s. f., the passive voice. L. 50.
Pasivo, *pah-sē'-vo*, adj., passive. L. 63.
Paso, *pah'-so*, s. m., step, pace. L. 54.
Patio, *pah'-tē-o*, s. m., yard, pit (in theatres). L. 46.
Patronímico, *pah-trō-nē'-mē-ko*, adj., patronymic. L. 49.
Paz, *path*, s. f., peace. L. 43.
Pecho, *pai'-cho*, s. m., breast.—A lo hecho *pecho*, what is done cannot be helped. L. 63.
Pechuga, *pai-choo'-ga*, s. f., breast of fowl. L. 58.
Pedazo, *pai-dah'-tho*, s. m., piece, morsel. bit. L. 63.
Pedir, *pai-deer'*, to ask, to demand, to ask for.—A *pedir* de boca, as well as could be desired. L. 39.
Pedro, *pai'-dro*, s. m., Peter. L. 19.
Pegar, *pai-gar'*, to stick, to paste, to beat. L. 63.
Peinar, *pai-ē-nar'*, to comb. L. 46.
Peine, *pai-ē'-nai*, s. m., comb. L. 46.
Peligro, *pai-lē'-gro*, s. m., danger, peril. L. 51.
Pelo, *pai'-lo*, s. m., hair.—A *pelo*, to the purpose. L. 32 and 44.
Pelota, *pai-lō'-ta*, s. f., ball (for playing). L. 54.
Pena, *pai'-na*, s. f., pain, penalty.—A duras *penas*, with much difficulty. L. 59.
Pensamiento. *pain-sah-mē-ain'-to*, s. m., thought. L. 48.
Pensar, *pain-sar'*, to think, to intend. L. 31.
Penúltimo, *pai-nool'-tē-mo*, adj., penultimate, last but one. L. 50.
Peñasco, *pain-yass'-ko*, s. m., a large rock. L. 56.
Peor, *pai-ōre'*, adj. and adv., worse. L. 20.
Popa, *pai'-pa*, s. f., (contraction of FRANCISCA, Frances), Fanny. L. 44.
Pepe. (See PEPITO.) L. 44.
Pepito, *pai-pē'-to*, s. m. (contraction of JOSÉ, Joseph), Joe. L. 44.
Pequeño, *pai-kain'-yo*, adj., small, little, young. L. 7.
Per, *pair*, Latin prep. used in Spanish as a prefix only; as, *perturbar*. L. 50.
Pera, *pai'-ra*, s. f., pear. L. 59.
Peral, *pai-ral'*, s. m., pear-tree. L. 59.
Perder, *pair-dair'*, to lose. L. 37.
Perdonar, *pair-dō-nar'*, to pardon. L. 27.
Perezoso, *pai-rai-thō'-so*, adj., lazy, slothful. L. 38.
Perfeccionar, *pair-faik-thē-ō-nar'*, to perfect, to improve. L. 38.
Perfecto, *pair-faik'-to*, adj., perfect. L. 29.
Perilla, *pai-reel'-ya*, s. f., small pear.—Venir de *perilla*, to suit exactly. L. 64.
Periódico, *pai-rē-ō'-dē-ko*, s. m., newspaper. L. 8.
Permanecer, *pair-mah-nai-thair'*, to remain, to stop, to stay. L. 45.
Permanencia, *pair-mah-nain'-thē-a*, s. f., permanence, duration, stop, stay. L. 51.
Permitir, *pair-mē-teer'*, to permit, to allow. L. 44.
Pero, *pai'-ro*, conj., but. L. 3.
Perpendicular, *pair-pain-dē-koo-lar'*, adj., perpendicular. L. 51.
Perro, *pair'-ro*, s. m., dog. L. 63.

VOCABULARY.

Perseverancia, *pair-sai-vai-ran'-thĕ-a*, s. f., perseverance. L. 63.
Persistir, *pair-seess-teer'*, to persist. L. 50.
Persona, *pair-sō'-na*, s. f., person. L. 38.
Personal, *pair-sō-nal'*, adj., personal. L. 63.
Pesa, *pai'-sa*, s. f., weight (for weighing). L. 55.
Pésame, *pai'-sah-mai*, s. m., condolence. L. —.
Pesar, *pai-sar'*, to weigh, to regret.—No le pesa de haber nocido, he has an excellent opinion of himself. L. 31.
Pesar, s. m., regret, grief, sorrow.—A pesar de, in spite of, notwithstanding. L. 31.
Pescado, *paiss-kah'-do*, s. m., fish. L. 7.
Pescar, *paiss-kar'*, to fish. L. 63.
Pésimo, *pai'-sĕ-mo*, adj., worst, very bad. L. 21.
Peso, *pai'-so*, s. m., weight, heaviness, dollar. L. 14.
Pianista, *pĕ-ah-neess'-ta*, s. m., pianist. L. 15.
Piano, *pĕ-ah'-no*, s. m., piano. L. 15.
Picante, *pĕ-kan'-tai*, adj., piquant, high-seasoned, pungent. L. 54.
Picar, *pĕ-kar'*, to prick, to bite, to pique. L. 46.
Picaresco, *pĕ-kah-raiss'-ko*, adj., roguish. L. 49.
Pícaro, *pĕ'-kah-ro*, adj., rogue, rascal, scoundrel. L. 32.
Pico, *pĕ'-ko*, s. m., beak, bill.—Callarse el pico, to hold one's tongue. L. 61.
Pié, *pĕ-ai'*, s. m., foot.—A pié, on foot.—Nacer de piés, to be born to good luck. L. 39.
Pierna, *pĕ-air'-na*, s. f., leg. L. 33.
Pieza, *pĕ-ai'-tha*, s. f., piece. L. 64.
Pinar, *pĕ-nar'*, s. m., pine-grove. L. 49.
Pino, *pĕ'-no*, s. m., pine. L. 49.
Pintar, *peen-tar'*, to paint, to represent. L. 54.
Pintor, *peen-tōre'*, s. m., painter. L. 31.
Pintura, *peen-too'-ra*, s. f., painting. L. 31.
Pipa, *pĕ'-pa*, s. f., pipe. L. 42.
Pique, *pĕ'-kai*, s. m., pique, offence.—Estaba pique de perderse, he was on the brink of ruin. L. 62.
Piropos (Decir), *pĕ-rō'-pōce*, to say soft things (to the ladies). L. 58.
Pisaverde, *pĕ-sah-vair'-dai*, s. m., fop, coxcomb. L. 50.
Piso, *pĕ'-so*, s. m., floor, story (of a house).—Tercer piso, third floor. L. 53.
Pistola, *peess-tō'-la*, s. f., pistol. L. 44.
Pistoletazo, *peess-tō-lai-tah'-tho*, s. m., pistol-shot. L. 44.
Placer, *plah-thair'*, to please. L. 31.
Placer, s. m., pleasure. L. 31.
Plata, *plah'-ta*, s. f., silver. L. 8.
Plato, *plah'-to*, s. m., plate, dish (of viands). L. 57.
Plaza, *plah'-tha*, s. f., place, situation, square; market-place.—Plaza de toros, Arena (for bull-fights). L. 17 and 54.
Plazo, *plah'-tho*, s. m., term (of payment). L. 63.
Plomo, *plō'-mo*, s. m., lead. L. 63.
Pluma, *ploo'-ma*, s. f., pen, feather. L. 5.
Plural, *ploo-ral'*, adj., plural. L. 57.
Pluscuamperfecto, *ploose-kwam-pair-faik'-to*, s. m., pluperfect. L. 43.

Pobre, *pō'-brai*, adj., poor, needy, wretched. L. 13.
Pobreza, *pō-brai'-tha*, s. f., poverty. L. 59.
Poco, *pō'-ko*, adv., little; pl., few.—Poco á poco, gently, softly. L. 32.
Poco, s. m., little. L. 6.
Poder, *pō-dair'*, to be able.—No poder mas, to be exhausted. L. 32.
Poder, s. m., power, possession. L. 35.
Podrir, *pō-dreer'*, to rot. L. 41.
Poesía, *pō-ai-sĕ'-a*, s. f., poesy, poetry. L. 31.
Poeta, *pō-ai'-ta*, s. m., poet. L. 31.
Poetastro, *pō-ai-tass'-tro*, s. m., poetaster. L. 44.
Poético, *pō-ai'-tĕ-ko*, adj., poetic, poetical. L. 35.
Polca, *pōle'-ka*, s. f., polka. L. 23.
Política, *pō-lĕ'-tĕ-ka*, s. f., politics; politeness. L. 52.
Político, *pō-lĕ'-tĕ-ko*, adj., political; polite. L. 52.
Político, s. m., man of politics. L. 52.
Pollo, *pōle'-yo*, s. m., chicken. L. 5.
Polvo, *pōle'-vo*, s. m., powder, dust. L. 62.
Pólvora, *pōle'-vō-ra*, s. f., gunpowder. L. 63.
Ponderar, *pōne-dai-rar'*, to exaggerate, to cry up. L. 54.
Poner, *pō-nair'*, to put, to place, to lay, to set (as the sun).—Ponerse, to become, to get.—Se puso serio, he became serious. L. 41.
Por, *pōre*, prep., by, for, in behalf of, in favor of, about, through.—Por las calles, through the streets.—Ir por pan, to go for bread.—Por si acaso, in case, if by any chance. L. 19.
Porcion, *pōre-thĕ-ōne'*, s. f., portion, part, lot, number, quantity. L. 63.
Pormenor, *pōre-mai-nōre'*, s. m. (generally used in the plural).—Pormenores, details, particulars. L. 50.
Porque, *pōre'-kai*, conj., because. L. 18.
Porqué, *pōre-kai'*, conj., why? for what reason?—s. m., reason wherefore. L. 18.
Portarse, *pōre-tar'-sai*, to behave, to conduct one's self. L. 55.
Portugal, *pōre-too-gal'*, s. m., Portugal. L. 60.
Portugues, *pōre-too-ghaiss'*, s. m. and adj., Portuguese (language), Portuguese (native of Portugal). L. 34.
Poseer, *pō-sai-air'*, to possess. L. 34.
Posesivo, *pō-sai-sĕ'-vo*, adj., possessive. L. 63.
Posible, *pō-sĕ'-blai*, adj., possible. L. 31.
Positivo, *pō-sĕ-tĕ'-vo*, adj., positive. L. 48.
Posponer, *pōce-pō-nair'*, to postpone, to place after. L. 63.
Potencial, *pō-tain-thĕ-al'*, adj., potential. L. 63.
Práctica, *prak'-tĕ-ka*, s. f., practice. L. 23.
Practicante, *prak-tĕ-kan'-tai*, s. m., practitioner. (Present part. of PRACTICAR.) L. 38.
Practicar, *prak-tĕ-kar'*, to practise. L. 23.
Práctico, *prak'-tĕ-ko*, adj., practical. L. 65.
Pre, *prai*, Latin prep. used in Spanish as a prefix only. L. 50.
Preceder, *prai-thai-dair'*, to precede, to go before. L. 63.
Precepto, *prai-thaip'-to*, s. m., precept. L. 53.

Precio, *prai'-thē-ŏ*, s. m., price, prize. L. 50.
Preciso, *prai-thē'-so*, adj., necessary, obligatory, precise.—Es *preciso* que la lean, they must read it. L. 63.
Preferir, *prai-fai-reer'*, to prefer. L. 38.
Pregunta, *prai-goon'-ta*, s. f., question, inquiry. L. 33.
Preguntar, *prai-goon-tar'*, to ask questions, to question. L. 33.
Preliminar, *prai-lē-mē-nar'*, adj., preliminary. L. 63.
Premiar, *prai-mē-ar'*, to reward. L. 62.
Premio, *prai'-mē-ŏ*, s. m., premium, reward, prize. L. 53.
Prenda, *prain'-da*, s. f., pledge, jewel; pl., endowments, talents, parts. L. 41, 63.
Prender, *prain-dair'*, to take, to take up, to arrest. L. 39.
Preposicion, *prai-pŏ-sē-thē-ōne'*, preposition. L. 43.
Presencia, *prai-sain'-thē-a*, s. f., presence.— *Presencia* de ánimo, presence of mind. L. 63.
Presentar, *prai-sain-tar'*, to present, to introduce, to offer. L. 39.
Presente, *prai-sain'tai*, adj., present.—Tener *presente*, to bear in mind. L. 43.
Presidente, *prai-sē-dain'-tai*, s. m., president. L. 46.
Presidio, *prai-sē'-dē-ŏ*, s. m., state prison. L. 59.
Presidir, *prai-sē-deer'*, to preside. L. 51.
Preso, *prai'-so*, irreg. past part. (of PRENDER), taken. L. 52.
Prestar, *praiss-tar'*, to lend. L. 59.
Presto, *praiss'-to*, adj., quick, ready, prompt. L. 20.
Presto, adv., soon, quickly. L. 20.
Pretender, *prai-tain-dair'*, to pretend, to lay claim to, to claim, to solicit. L. 48.
Pretension, *prai-tain-sē-ōne'*, s. f., pretension, claim, thing solicited. L. 57.
Pretérito, *prai-tai'-rē-to*, adj., preterit. L. 63.
Pretesto, *prai-taiss'-to*, s. m., pretext. L. 58.
Prevenir, *prai-vai-neer'*, to prevent, to foresee, to warn, to prepare. L. 63.
Prever, *prai-vair'*, to foresee. L. 39.
Primavera, *prē-mah-vai'-ra*, s. f., Spring. L. 21.
Primero, *prē-mai'-ro*, adj., first.—De buenas á *primeras*, all at once, rashly.—adv., first, rather, sooner. L. 15.
Primo, *prē'-mo*, s. m., cousin. L. 13.
Principal, *preen-thē-pal'*, adj., principal, chief. L. 36.
Principiante, *preen-thē-pē-an'-tai*, s. m. and pres. part. (of PRINCIPIAR), beginner. L. 38.
Principiar, *preen-thē-pē-ar'*, to begin, to commence. L. 23.
Principio, *preen-thē'-pē-ŏ*, s. m., beginning, commencement, principle. L. 63.
Prisa, *prē'-sa*, s. f., haste, hurry.—Tener *prisa*, to be in a hurry. L. 30.
Prisionero, *prē-sē-ŏ-nai'-ro*, s. m., prisoner. L. 48.
Prisma, *preess'-ma*, s. m., prism. L. 54.
Probable, *prŏ-bah'-blai*, adj., probable. L. 29.
Probar, *prŏ-bar'*, to try, to prove, to taste.—El clima de este pais le *prueba* bien, the climate of this country agrees well with him. L. 35.
Procesion, *prŏ-thai-sē-ōne'*, s. f., procession. L. 46.
Procurar, *prŏ-koo-rar'*, to procure, to endeavor, to try. L. 51.
Produccion, *prŏ-took-thē-ōne'*, s. f., production. L. 40.
Producir, *prŏ-doo-theer'*, to produce. L. 40.
Proeza, *prŏ-ai'-tha*, s. f., prowess. L. 54.
Profecia, *prŏ-fai-thē'-a*, s. f., prophecy. L. 45.
Profesion, *prŏ-fai-sē-ōne'*, s. f., profession. L. 38.
Profesor, *prŏ-fai-sōre'*, s. m., professor. L. 18.
Prohibir, *prŏ-ē-beer'*, to prohibit. L. 53.
Prójimo, *prŏ'-hē-mo*, s. m., neighbor (fellow-creature). L. 28.
Promesa, *prŏ-mai'-sa*, s. f., promise. L. 57.
Prometer, *prŏ-mai-tair'*, to promise. L. 25.
Pronombre, *prŏ-nōme'-brai*, s. m., pronoun. L. 43.
Pronominal, *prŏ-nŏ-mē-nal'*, adj., pronominal. L. 61.
Prontitud, *prōne-tē-tooth'*, s. f., promptness, promptitude, quickness. L. 43.
Pronto, *prōne'-to*, adj., prompt, quick, ready; —adj., soon, promptly, quickly. L. 26.
Pronunciacion, *prŏ-noon-thē-ah-thē-ōne'*, s. f., pronunciation. L. 63.
Pronunciar, *prŏ-noon-thē-ar'*, to pronounce. L. 15.
Propiedad, *prŏ-pē-ai-dath'*, s. f., propriety, property. L. 63.
Propio, *prŏ'-pē-ŏ*, adj., proper, own, selfsame, same. L. 49.
Proponer, *prŏ-pŏ-nair'*, to propose. L. 51.
Prosa, *prŏ'-sa*, s. f., prose. L. 31.
Proporcionar, *prŏ-pōre-thē-ŏ-nar'*, to proportion, to procure, to offer. L. 48.
Protestante, *prŏ-taiss-tan'-tai*, s. m., Protestant. L. 49.
Protestantismo, *prŏ-taiss-tan-teess'-mo*, s. m., Protestantism. L. 40.
Provecho, *prŏ-vai'-cho*, s. m., profit, benefit. L. 64.
Proveer, *prŏ-vai-air'*, to provide. L. 34.
Proverbio, *prŏ-vair'-bē-ŏ*, s. m., proverb. L. 65.
Provincia, *prŏ-veen'-thē-a*, s. f., province. L. 19.
Provisto, *prŏ-veess'-to*, past part. (of PROVEER), provided. L. 52.
Próximo, *prŏke'-sē-mo*, adj., proximo, next, nearest.—El sábado *próximo*, next Saturday. L. 23.
Prudencia, *proo-dain'-thē-a*, s. f., prudence. L. 34.
Prudente, *proo-dain'-tai*, adj., prudent. L. 20.
Prueba, *proo-ai'-ba*, s. f., proof. L. 46.
Prusia, *proo'-sē-a*, s. f., Prussia. L. 46.
Publicar, *poo-blē-kar'*, to publish. L. 48.
Público, *poo'-blē-ko*, s. m. and adj., public. L. 51.
Pueblo, *pwai'-blo*, s. m., town, people. L. 50.
Puerta, *pwair'-ta*, s. f., door. L. 27.
Pues, *pwaiss*, conj., then, therefore, inasmuch as, since, because;—inter., well!— *Pues*, qué? well, what of it? L. 41.
Puesto que, *pwaiss'-to*, adv., since, inasmuch as, supposing that. L. 57.

Pulgada, *pool-gah'-da*, s. f. inch. L. 63.
Puntapié, *poon-tah-pĕ-aí'*, s. m., kick. L. 50.
Punta, *poon'-ta*, point, stitch. L. 50.
Puntilla, *poon-teel'-ya*, s. f., small point.—De *puntillas*, on tiptoe. L. 44.
Punto, *poon'-to*, s. m., point (of time or space), spot, place.—Al *punto*, at once. L. 51.
Puntuacion, *poon-too-ah-thĕ-ōne'*, s. f., punctuation. L. 63.
Puntual, *poon-too-al'*, adj., punctual, exact, accurate. L. 63.
Puntualidad, *poon-too-ah-lĕ-dath'*, s. f., punctuality. L. 63.
Purista, *poo-reess'-ta*, s. m., purist. L. 36.

Q.

Que, *kai*, rel. pron., that, which, who.— ¡*Qué* bueno! how good!—¡*Qué* desgracia! what a misfortune!—*Que* venga, let him come.—¿*Qué* se dice de bueno? what is the good news?—Tarde *que* temprano, sooner or later. L. 3, 16, 17.
Quebrar, *kai-brar'*, to break, to smash. L. 34.
Quedar, *kai-dar'*, to stay, to stop, to remain, to become.—El campo *quedó* por los Americanos, the Americans were victorious. L. 38.
Quejarse, *kai-har'-sai*, to moan, to complain. L. 48.
Quemar, *kai-mar'*, to burn. L. 32.
Querer, *kai-rair'*, to wish, to desire, to will, to love, to like, to be willing. L. 13.
Querido, *kai-rĕ'-do*, adj., dear. (Past part. of QUERER.) L. 13.
Queso, *kai'-so*, s. m., cheese. L. 7.
Quien, *kĕ-ain'*, rel. pron., who, whom. L. 17.
Quienquiera, *kĕ-ain-ke-ai'-ra*, indef. pron., whosoever. L. 50.
Quieto, *kĕ-ai'-to*, adj., quiet, still, at rest. L. 62.
Quijada, *kĕ-hah'-da*, s. f., jaw. L. 50.
Quince, *keen'-thai*, num. adj., fifteen. L. 14.
Quinientos, *kĕ-nĕ-ain'-tōce*, adj., five hundred. L. 14.
Quinto, *keen'-to*, ord. adj. and s. m., fifth. L. 50.
Quitar, *kĕ-tar'*, to remove, to take away, off, out; to prevent. L. 53.
Quitasol, *kĕ-tah-sōle'*, s. m., parasol. L. 50.
Quizá, quizás, *kĕ-thah', -thass'*, adv., perhaps. L. 34.

R.

Radical, *rah-de-kal'*, adj., radical. L. 63.
Raíz, *rah-eeth'*, s. f., root. L. 63.
Rama, *rah'-ma*, s. f., branch (of trees, families, &c.) L. 61.
Ramillete, *rah-meel-yai'-tai*, s. m., bouquet. L. 27.
Ramo, *rah'-mo*, s. m., branch, department. L. 56.
Rana, *rah'-na*, s. f., frog.—No ser *rana*, to be wide awake, expert. L. 65.
Rapaza, *rah-pah'-tha*, s. f., little girl.—¡Miren la *rapazuela!* the little vixen! L. 61.
Raro, *rah'-ro*, adj., rare, odd, curious, scarce. L. 63.

Rasgar, *rass-gar'*, to tear, to scratch. L. 64.
Rasgo, *rass'-go*, s. m., trait, stroke, instance. L. 63.
Rato, *rah'-to*, s. m., while, moment.—A *ratos*, from time to time. L. 44.
Raton, *rah-tōne'*, s. m., mouse. L. 65.
Raya, *rah'-ya*, s. f., stroke, dash.—Tener á *raya*, to keep within bounds. L. 64.
Rayo, *rah'-yo*, s. m., ray, thunderbolt.— Echar *rayos* y centellas, to foam with rage. L. 62 and 63.
Razon, *rah-thōne'*, s. f., reason, right.— Tener *razon*, to be right. L. 25.
Razonar, *rah-thō-nar'*, to reason. L. 63.
Re, *rai*, always used as a prefix. L. 50.
Real, *rai-al'*, adj., real, royal; —s. m., real (Spanish coin). L. 47 and 48.
Realidad, *rai-ah-lĕ-dath'*, s. f., reality. L. 48.
Rebajar, *rai-bah-har'*, to reduce, to abate, to lower (prices, &c.). L. 64.
Rebanada, *rai-bah-nah'-da*, s. f., slice (of bread, &c.). L. 63.
Rebanar, *rai-bah-nar'*, to slice. L. 64.
Rebaño, *rai-ban'-yo*, s. m., flock of sheep. L. 40.
Recado, *rai-kah'-do*, s. m., message, errand. L. 63.
Recepcion, *rai-thaip-thĕ-ōne'*, s. f., reception. L. 54.
Recibimiento, *rai-thĕ-bĕ-mĕ-ain'-to*, s. m., act of receiving, reception. L. 55.
Recibir, *rai-thĕ-beer'*, to receive. L. 8.
Recibo, *rai-thĕ'-bo*, s. m., receipt. L. 63.
Recíproco, *rai-thĕ'-prō-ko*, adj., reciprocal. L. 63.
Recitar, *rai-thĕ-tar'*, to recite. L. 64.
Recomendacion, *rai-kō-main-dah-thĕ-ōne'*, s. f., recommendation. L. 60.
Recomendar, *rai-kō-main-dar'*, to recommend. L. 64.
Reconocer, *rai-kō-nō-thair'*, to recognize, to acknowledge. L. 39.
Recordar, *rai-kōre-dar'*, to remember, to remind. L. 35.
Recto, *raik'-to*, adj., right.—En ángulos *rectos*, at right angles. L. 55.
Rector, *raik-tōre'*, s. m., rector, director. L. 63.
Recurrir, *rai-koor-reer'*, to recur, to have recourse. L. 50.
Recurso, *rai-koor'-so*, s. m., recourse, resource. L. 40.
Reducir, *rai-doo-theer'*, to reduce. L. 54.
Referir, *rai-fai-reer'*, to refer, to relate. L. 64.
Reflexivo, *rai-flaik-sĕ'-vo*, adj., reflective. L. 63.
Reflexionar, *rai-flaik-sĕ-ō-nar'*, to reflect. L. 48.
Reforma, *rai-fōre'-ma*, s. f., reform, reformation. L. 63.
Reformar, *rai-fōre-mar'*, to reform, to form anew, to discharge (from an employment or office). L. 48.
Refran, *rai-fran'*, s. m., refrain, proverb. L. 63 and 65.
Regalar, *rai-gah-lar'*, to regale, to present with, to make a present of. L. 63.
Regalo, *rai-gah'-lo*, s. m., gift, present. L. 63.
Régimen, *rai'-hĕ-main*, s. m., regimen, government, object (of verbs). L. 57.

Regimiento, *rai-hē-mē-ain'-to*, s. m., regimiento. L. 19.
Regir, *rai-heer'*, to govern. L. 57.
Regla, *raig'-la*, s. f., rule, ruler. L. 63.
Regular, *rai-goo-lar'*, adj., regular, tolerable, moderate, ordinary;—adv., tolerably, middling;—v., to regulate. L. 27, 57, and 64.
Regularidad, *rai-goo-lah-rē-dath'*, s. f., regularity. L. 55.
Regularizar, *rai-goo-lah-rē-thar'*, to regulate. L. 48.
Rehusar, *rai-oo-sar'*, to refuse. L. 61.
Reina, *rai-ē'-na*, s. f., queen. L. 63.
Reinante, *rai-ē-nan'-tai*, pres. part., reigning. L. 38.
Reinar, *rai-ē-nar'*, to reign. L. 15.
Reino, *rai-ē'-no*, s. m., kingdom. L. 45.
Reir, *rai-eer'*, to laugh. L. 41.
Relacion, *rai-lah-thē-ōne'*, s. f., relation, account, recital. L. 43.
Relámpago, *rai-lam'-pah-go*, s. m., flash of lightning. L. 63.
Relampaguear, *rai-lam-pah-gai-ar'*, to lighten. L. 30.
Relatar, *rai-lah-tar'*, to relate. L. 45.
Religion, *rai-lē-hē-ōne'*, s. f., religion. L. 35.
Religioso, *rai-lē-hē-ō'-so*, adj., religious. L. 35.
Reloj, *rai-lo'*, s. m., watch, clock. L. 28.
Relojero, *rai-lō-hai'-ro*, s. m., watchmaker. L. 63.
Relucir, *rai-loo-theer'*, to sparkle, to glitter.—No es oro todo lo que *reluce*, all is not gold that glitters. L. 65.
Remediar, *rai-mai-dē-ar'*, to remedy. L. 64.
Remedio, *rai-mai'-dē-ō*, s. m., remedy. L. 53.
Remendar, *rai-main-dar'*, to repair, to mend. L. 64.
Remunerar, *rai-moo-nai-rar'*, to remunerate. L. 52.
Rendir, *rain-deer'*, to render, to subdue.—*Rendirse*, to surrender. L. 39.
Reñir, *rain-yeer'*, to quarrel, to dispute, to scold. L. 39.
Reo, *rai'-o*, s. m., culprit, offender. L. 53.
Repartir, *rai-par-teer'*, to divide. L. 58.
Repasar, *rai-pah-sar'*, to repass, to reëxamine, to glance over again. L. 64.
Repaso, *rai-pah'-so*, s. m., revision, act of going over anew. L. 61.
Repente, *rai-pain'-tai*,—De *repente*, suddenly, on a sudden. L. 51.
Repeticion, *rai-pai-tē-thē-ōne'*, s. f., repetition. L. 63.
Repetir, *rai-pai-teer'*, to repeat. L. 39.
Reposar, *rai-pō-sar'*, to repose, to rest. L. 39.
Reposo, *rai-pō'-so*, s. m., repose, rest. L. 63.
Reprender, *rai-prain-dair'*, to reprehend, reprimand. L. 42.
Representar, *rai-prai-sain-tar'*, to represent, to make appear; to perform (a part), to enact. L. 64.
Reprobar, *rai-prō-bar'*, to reprove, to upbraid. L. 60.
República, *rai-poo'-blē-ka*, s. f., republic. L. 35.
Reputacion, *rai-poo-tah-thē-ōne'*, s. f., reputation. L. 24.

Resarcir, *rai-sar-theer'*, to indemnify, to compensate, to make up for. L. 59.
Resentirse, *rai-sain-teer'-sai*, to feel the effects (of), to resent. L. 59.
Resfriado, *raiss-frē-ah'-do*, s. m., cold (disease caused by cold). L. 63.
Resfriarse, *raiss-frē-ar'-sai*, to catch cold. L. 63.
Residente, *rai-sē-dain'-tai*, adj. and part. (of RESIDIR), resident, residing. L. 38.
Residir, *rai-sē-deer'*, to reside. L. 9.
Resistir, *rai-seess-teer'*, to resist. L. 51.
Resolucion, *rai-sō-loo-thē-ōne'*, s. f., resolution. L. 63.
Resolver, *rai-sōle-vair'*, to solve, to resolve. L. 64.
Respecta, *raiss-paik'-ta*.—En lo que *respecta*, with respect to. L. 51.
Respetable, *raiss-pai-tah'-blai*, adj., respectable. L. 39.
Respetar, *raiss-pai-tar'*, to respect. L. 36.
Respeto, *raiss-pai'-to*, s. m., respect, regard. L. 56.
Responder, *raiss-pōne-dair'*, to respond, to answer. L. 33.
Respondon, *raiss-pōne-dōne'*, adj., always ready to reply. L. 33.
Respuesta, *raiss-pwaiss'-ta*, s. f., response, reply, answer. L. 30.
Restante, *raiss-tan'-tai*, s. m., and pres. part. (of RESTAR), remainder, rest; remaining. L. 46.
Resultar, *rai-sool-tar'*, to result, to turn out, to occur. L. 43.
Retirar, *rai-tē-rar'*, to retire, to withdraw, to retreat. L. 63.
Retrato, *rai-trah'-to*, s. m., portrait, likeness. L. 17.
Reumatismo, *rai-oo-mah-teess'-mo*, s. m., rheumatism. L. 63.
Reunir, *rai-oo-neer'*, to reunite, to assemble. L. 52.
Revés, *rai-vaiss'*, s. m., back part, wrong side.—Al *revés*, on the contrary; upside down. L. 63.
Revoltoso, *rai-vōle-tō'-so*, adj., turbulent, rebellious. L. 44.
Rey, *rai'-ē*, s. m., king. L. 15.
Reyezuelo, *rai-yai-thwai'-lo*, s. m. (dim. of REY), petty king. L. 44.
Ricacho, *rē-kah'-cho*, adj., very rich. L. 49.
Rico, *rē'-ko*, adj., rich. L. 13.
Ridiculez, *rē-dē-koo-laith'*, s. f., ridicule. L. 45.
Ridiculizar, *rē-dē-koo-lē-thar'*, to ridicule. L. 48.
Ridículo, *rē-dē'-koo-lo*, adj. and s. m., ridiculous, reticule (sort of lady's basket). L. 5.
Rigodon, *rē-gō-dōne'*, s. m., rigadoon, country dance. L. 23.
Rincon, *reen-kōne'*, s. m., corner. L. 51.
Rio, *rē'-ō*, s. m., river. L. 40.
Riqueza, *rē-kai'-tha*, s. f., riches. L. 48.
Risa, *rē'-sa*, s. f., laugh, laughter. L. 48.
Rivalizar, *rē-rah-lē-thar'*, to rival, to vie with. L. 51.
Robar, *rō-bar'*, to rob, to steal. L. 44.
Rodar, *rō-dar'*, to roll. L. 54.
Rodear, *rō-dai-ar'*, to surround, to go round, to revolve. L. 54.
Rodeado, *rō-dai-ah'-do*, adj. and past part. (of RODEAR), surrounded. L. 53.

Rodilla, *rŏ-deel'-ya*, s. f., knee.—De *rodillas*, on one's knees. L. 59.
Rodriguez, *rŏ-drē-gaith'*, s. m., Rodriguez. L. 49.
Rogar, *rŏ-gar'*, to pray, to beg of. L. 35.
Rojo, *rŏ'-ho*, adj., red. L. 54.
Romano, *rō-mah'-no*, adj., Roman. L. 54.
Romper, *rōme-pair'*, to break, to tear.—*Romper el silencio*, to break the silence. L. 46.
Ropa, *rŏ'-pa*, s. f., clothes, wearing apparel. L. 28.
Rosa, *rŏ'-sa*, s. f., rose. L. 63.
Roto, *rŏ'-to*, irr. past part. (of ROMPER), broken. L. 52.
Rubio, *roo'-bē-ŏ*, adj., fair (of the complexion), ruddy. L. 63.
Ruido, *roo-ē'-do*, s. m., noise. L. 46.
Ruin, *roo-een'*, adj., mean, churlish. L. 63.
Ruindad, *roo-een-dath'*, s. f., meanness, churlishness. L. 48.
Ruiseñor, *roo-ē-sain-yōre'*, s. m., nightingale. L. 63.
Rumor, *roo-mōre'*, s. m., rumor. L. 54.
Rutina, *roo-tē'-na*, s. f., routine. L. 63.

S.

Sábado, *sah'-bah-do*, s. m., Saturday. L. 9.
Saber, *sah-bair'*, to know, to have knowledge of, to hear from; to savor, to taste; —s. m., learning, knowledge. L. 42 and 21.
Sabio, *sah'-bē-o*, adj., wise, sage, learned. L. 21.
Sabor, *sah-bōre'*, s. m., savor, taste.—A su *sabor*, at his pleasure, taste. L. 62 and 66.
Sacacorchos, *sah-kah-kōre'-chŏce*, s. m., corkscrew. L. 64.
Sacamuelas, *sah-kah-mwai'-lass*, s. m., tooth-drawer, dentist. L. 50.
Sacar, *sah-kar'*, to take or draw out, to pull out. L. 50 and 66.
Saco, *sah'-ko*, s. m., sack, bag. L. 61.
Sacudir, *sah-koo-deer'*, to shake off, to shake. L. 54.
Sal, s. f., salt, wit. L. 55.
Saldo, *sal'-do*, s. m., balance (of accounts, &c.). L. 64.
Salida, *sah-lē'-da*, s. f., going out, departure, start. L. 63.
Saliente, *sah-lē-ain'-tai*, adj. and pres. part. (of SALIR), projecting, sallent. L. 38.
Salir, *sah-leer'*, to go or come out, to set out, to leave, to start, to go out, to end or finish, to rise (said of the sun, &c.): to turn out, to turn up.—*Salió á su padre*, he resembled his father. L. 20.
Salon, *sah-lōne'*, s. m., saloon, large hall. L. 53.
Saltar, *sal-tar'*, to jump, to leap, to bound, to spring. L. 58.
Salto, *sal'-to*, s. m., leap, jump, bound, spring. L. 59.
Salud, *sah-looth'* s. f., health.—A la *salud de las señoras*, to the good health of the ladies. L. 25.
Saludar, *sah-loo-dar'*, to salute. L. 64.
Sánchez, *san'-chaith*, s. m., Spanish family name, signifying son of *Suncho*. L. 49.
Sangre, *san'-grai*, s. f., blood. L. 64.
Santificar, *san-tē-fē-kar'*, to sanctify. L. 45.

Santo, *san'-to*, adj., holy, saintly.—*Santo y bueno*, well and good. L. 64.
Sastre, *sass'-trai*, s. m., tailor. L. 11.
Sastreria, *sass-trai-rē'-a*, s. f., tailor's shop. L. 11.
Satirico, *sah-tē'-rē-ko*, adj., satirical. L. 35.
Satisfacer, *sah-teess-jah-thair'*, to satisfy. L. 42.
Satisfecho, *sah-teess-fai'-cho*, adj. and past part. (of SATISFACER), satisfied. L. 44 and 52.
Sayo, *sah'-yo*, s. m., sort of loose coat or jacket. L. 65.
Sazonar, *sah-thŏ-nar'*, to season. L. 62.
Se, *sai*, pers. pron. (instead of LE, LES, to him, to her, to them). L. 26.—Pron. (used to form the passive voice). L. 32.—Reflective pron. L. 33.—Impers. pron., we, they, people, &c.—*Se dice*, they say.—*Se cree*, it is believed. L. 36.
Se, prep., used as a prefix in composition. L. 50.
Secreto, *sai-krai'-to*, s. m., secret, secrecy. L. 65.
Sed, *saith*, s. f., thirst.—*Tener sed*, to be thirsty. L. 25.
Seda, *sai'-da*, s. f., silk. L. 5.
Seguir, *sai-gheer'*, to follow; to continue. L. 39.
Segun, *sai-goon'*, prep., according to.—*Segun y como*, just as. L. 40 and 66.
Segundo, *sai-goon'-do*, ord. adj. and s. m., second. L. 15 and 23.
Seguro, *sai-goo'-ro*, adj., sure, secure. L. 43.
Seis, *sai'-eess*, num. adj., six. L. 14.
Seiscientos, *sai-cess-thē-ain'-tŏce*, num. adj., six hundred. L. 14.
Semana, *sai-mah'-na*, s. f., week. L. 8.
Semblante, *saim-blan'-tai*, s. m., countenance, face, aspect, appearance, look. L. 59.
Sentar, *sain-tar'*, to set down, to enter (in a book); to fit, to become. L. 34.
Sentencia, *sain-fain'-thē-a*, s. f., sentence, phrase. L. 43.
Sentido, *sain-tē'-do*, s. m., sense. L. 65.
Sentir, *sain-teer'*, to feel; to be sorry for. L. 38.
Señor, *sain-yōre'*, s. m., Lord, sir, Mr.—Muy *señor mio*, my dear sir. L. 1.
Señora, *sain-yŏ'-ra*, s. f., lady, madam, Mrs. L. 2.
Señorita, *sain-yŏ-rē'-ta*, s. f., young lady, miss. L. 2.
Señorito, *sain-yŏ-rē'-to*, s. m., young gentleman, sir (used generally by servants), Mr. L. 2.
Séptimo, *saip'-tē-mo*, ord. adj., seventh. L. 15.
Ser, *sair*, to be, to exist. (Not to be confounded with ESTAR, which see.) L. 11 and 22.
Ser, s. m., being, existence. L. 54.
Servidor, *sair-vē-dōre'*, s. m., servant.—*Servidor de V.*, your servant. L. 39.
Servir, *sair-veer'*, to serve, to oblige, to do a service.—*Servirse*, to be good enough, kind enough, to please.—*Sírvase V.* tomar asiento, please to take a seat.—*Servirse de*, to use. L. 39.
Sesenta, *sai-sain'-ta*, num. adj., sixty. L. 14.
Setenta, *sai-tain'-ta*, num. adj., seventy. L. 14.

VOCABULARY.

Setecientos, *sai-tai-thě-ain'-tŏce*, num. adj., seven hundred. L. 14.
Setiembre, *sai-tě-aim'-vrai*, s. m., September. L. 24.
Sexo, *saik'-so*, s. m., sex.—El bello *sexo*, the fair sex. L. 58.
Sexto, *saiks'-to*, ord. adj. and s. m., sixth. L. 15.
Sí, *see*, adv., yes. L. 1.
Sí, Indef. pron., self, one's self.—Habló para *sí*, he spoke to himself. L. 26.
Si, conj., if; but.—*Si* no viene, hombre, but he is not coming, my dear fellow. L. 23.
Siempre, *sě-aim'-prai*, adv., always.—Por *siempre jamás*, for ever and ever. L. 25.
Siesta, *sě-aiss'-ta*, s. f., siesta, afternoon nap. L. 62.
Siete, *sě-ai'-tai*, num. adj., seven. L. 14.
Siglo, *seeg'-lo*, s. m., century. L. 52.
Significado, *seeg-ně-fě-kah'-do*, s. m., signification, meaning. L. 40.
Significar, *seeg-ně-fě-kar'*, to signify. L. 64.
Sílaba, *sě'-lah-ba*, s. f., syllable. L. 63.
Silencio, *sě-lain'-thě-o*, s. m., silence. L. 65.
Silencioso, *sě-lain-thě-ŏ'-so*, adj., silent. L. 64.
Silla, *seel'-ya*, s. f., chair. L. 14.
Simpatizar, *seem-pah-tě-thar'*, to sympathize. L. 51.
Simple, *seem'-plai*, adj., simple, single; simple, silly. L. 43.
Sin, *seen*, prep., without.—*Sin* embargo, notwithstanding, however.—*Sin* qué ni para qué, without any cause or reason. L. 19.
Sinceridad, *seen-thai-rě-dath'*, s. f., sincerity. L. 45.
Sincero, *seen-thai'-ro*, adj., sincere. L. 40.
Singular, *seen-goo-lar'*, adj., singular. L. 57.
Sino, *sě'-no*, conj., but; if not.—No es él, *sino* su hermano, it is not he, but his brother. L. 3.
Sinónimo, *sě-nŏ'-ně-mo*, s. m., synonyme. L. 65.
Sinrazon, *seen-rah-thŏne'*, s. f., wrong, injustice. L. 50.
Siquiera, *sě-kě-ai'-ra*, conj., even, at least. L. 40.
Sitio, *sě'-tě-ŏ*, s. m., place, position, siege. L. 58.
Situado, *sě-too-ah'-do*, past. part. of SITUAR. L. 20.
Situar, *sě-too-ar'*, to situate. L. 64.
So, *sŏ*, prep., under.—*So* pretesto de, under pretext of. L. 41.
Sobrar, *sŏ-brar'*, to be over and above, to have more of any thing than one needs. L. 64.
Sobre, *sŏ'-brai*, prep., upon, above, over, about.—Vino *sobre* las ocho, he came about eight o'clock. L. 41.
Sobrescrito, *sŏ-brai-aiss-krě'-to*, s. m., superscription, address (of a letter). L. 56.
Sobrina, *sŏ-brě'-na*, s. f., niece. L. 65.
Sobrino, *sŏ-brě'-no*, s. m., nephew. L. 65.
Socialismo, *sŏ-thě-ah-leess'-mo*, s. m., socialism. L. 50.
Sociedad, *sŏ-thě-ai-dath'*, s. f., society, firm, partnership (commercial). L. 32.
Socio, *sŏ'-thě-o*, s. m., partner, companion. L. 62.
Sofá, *sŏ-fa'*, s. m., sofa. L. 34.

Sol, *sŏle*, s. m., sun. L. 45.
Solas (A), *sŏ'-lass*, all alone. L. 64.
Soldado, *sŏle-dah'-do*, s. m., soldier. L. 52.
Soledad, *sŏ-lai-dath'*, s. f., solitude, loneliness. L. 63.
Solemne, *sŏ-laim'-nai*, adj., solemn; thorough, downright. L. 61.
Soler, *sŏ-lair'*, to be accustomed to, to be wont. L. 41.
Solicitar, *sŏ-lě-thě-tar'*, to solicit. L. 47.
Soliloquio, *sŏ-lě-lŏ'-kě-ŏ*, s. m., soliloquy. L. 65.
Solo, *sŏ'-lo*, adj., alone;—adv., only. L. 25.
Soltar, *sŏle-tar'*, to untie, to loose, to liberate, to let go, to let free. L. 64.
Soltero, *sŏle-tai'-ro*, s. m., bachelor, unmarried man. L. 51.
Sombra, *sŏme'-bra*, s. f., shade, shadow. L. 58.
Sombrero, *sŏme-brai'-ro*, s. m., hat. L. 10.
Son, *sŏne*, s. m., sound.—Sin ton y sin *son*, without rhyme or reason. L. 47.
Sonar, *sŏ-nar'*, to sound. L. 45.
Sonido, *sŏ-ně'-do*, s. m., sound. L. 47.
Sonreirse, *sŏne-rai-eer'-sai*, to smile. L. 64.
Sonrisa, *sŏne-rě'-sa*, s. f., smile. L. 54.
Sonrojar, *sŏne-rŏ-har'*, to make one blush. L. 64.
Soñar, *sŏne-yar'*, to dream. L. 35.
Sopa, *sŏ'-pa*, s. f., soup. L. 44.
Sopeton, *sŏ-pai-tŏne'*.—De *sopeton*, unexpectedly. L. 44.
Soplar, *sŏ-plar'*, to blow; to prompt. L. 64.
Sordo, *sŏre'-do*, adj., deaf. L. 64.
Sorprender, *sŏre-prain-dair'*, to surprise. L. 42.
Sorpresa, *sŏre-prai'-sa*, s. f., surprise. L. 51.
Sospechar, *sŏce-pai-char'*, to suspect. L. 60.
Su, *soo*, pron. adj., his, her, its, their. L. 5.
Sub, *soob*, Latin prep. used in Spanish as a prefix only. L. 56.
Subida, *soo-bě'-da*, s. f., rising, rise; ascent. L. 63.
Subir, *soo-beer'*, to go or come up, to ascend, to mount, to rise. L. 50.
Subjuntivo, *soob-hoon-tě'-vo*, adj., subjunctive. L. 43.
Suceder, *soo-thai-dair'*, to happen, to take place, to succeed (come after). L. 45.
Sucesivo, *soo-thai-sě'-vo*.—En lo *sucesivo*, in future. L. 32.
Sucio, *soo'-thě-ŏ*, adj., dirty. L. 64.
Sud, *sood*, s. m., south. L. 26.
Suegra, *swai'-gra*, s. f., mother-in-law. L. 63.
Suegro, *swai'-gro*, s. m., father-in-law. L. 63.
Suela, *swai'-la*, s. f., sole. L. 61.
Suelo, *swai'-lo*, s. m., ground, floor, soil. L. 54.
Suelto, *swail'-to*, adj. and past part. (of SOLTAR), loose, free.—A rienda *suelta*, with loose rein. L. 64.
Sueño, *swain'-yo*, s. m., sleep, dream.—Tener *sueño*, to be sleepy. L. 25.
Suerte, *swair'-tai*, s. f., luck, chance, sort. Echar *suertes*, to cast lots. L. 58.
Suficiente, *soo-fě-thě-ain'-tai*, adj., sufficient. L. 49.
Sufrir, *soo-freer'*, to suffer, to bear with, to undergo. L. 64.
Sugeto, *soo-hai'-to*, s. m., individual, person; topic, matter, subject. L. 27.

VOCABULARY. 467

Sujeto, *soo-hai'-to*, adj. and past part. (of SUJETAR) subject; subjected, tied, fastened. L. 65.
Suma, *soo'-ma*, s. m., sum.—En *suma*, in short. L. 63 and 64.
Superior, *soo-pai-rē-ōre'*, adj., superior. L. 21.
Superlativo, *soo-pair-lah-tē'-vo*, adj., superlative. L. 50.
Supersticioso, *soo-pairss-tē-thē-ō'-so*, adj., superstitious. L. 45.
Suplicar, *soo-plē-kar'*, to supplicate, to beg, to crave. L. 64.
Suponer, *soo-pō-nair'*, to suppose. L. 64.
Supremo, *soo-prai'-mo*, adj., supreme, highest, most excellent. L. 21.
Supuesto, *soo-pwaiss'-to*, past part. of SUPONER.—Por *supuesto*, of course. L. 64.
Sur. (See SUD.) L. 66.
Sus! *sooce*, inter., holla! L. 46.
Suspirar, *sooce-pē-rar'*, to sigh. L. 64.
Sustancia, *sooce-tan'-thē-a*, s. f., substance. L. 63.
Sustantivo, *sooce-tan-tē'-ro*, s. m. and adj., substantive. L. 64.
Sustentar, *sooce-tain-tar'*, to sustain. L. 65.
Sutil, *soo-teel'*, adj., subtle, thin, slender. L. 64.
Sutileza, *soo-tē-lai'-tha*, s. f., subtlety, cunning, thinness, slenderness. L. 63.
Suyo, *soo'-yo*, his, hers, its, theirs, one's. L. 13.

T.

Tabaco, *tah-bah'-ko*, s. m., tobacco, cigar. L. 42.
Tablero, *tah-blai'-ro*, s. m., a smooth board.—*Tablero* de ajedrez, chess-board. L. 51.
Tacto, *tak'-to*, s. m., the sense of touch. L. 65.
Tal, adj., such, so.—*Tal* cual, middling, so so.—*Tal* vez, perhaps. L. 32.
Talento, *tah-lain'-to*, s. m., talent, abilities. L. 65.
Tambien, *tam-bē-ain'*, conj. and adv., also, as well, morever. L. 29.
Tampoco, *tam-pō'-ko*, adv., neither, not either, nor. L. 20.
Tan, adv., so, so much, as, as much. L. 20.
Tanto, *tan'-to*, adj., so, in such a manner.—*Tanto* mejor, so much the better.—Por lo *tanto*, therefore. L. 20.
Tapar, *tah-par'*, to cover up, to stop up (with a cover). L. 65.
Tapete, *tah-pai'-tai*, s. m., table-cover. L. 61.
Tardar, *tar-dar'*, to delay, to put off. L. 60.
Tarde, *tar'-dai*, s. f., afternoon;—adv., late.—Algo *tarde*, rather late. L. 20.
Tarea, *tah'-rai-a*, s. f., task. L. 58.
Tarjeta, *tar-hai'-ta*, s. f., card, visiting card. L. 64.
Tate! *tah'-tai*, inter., easy! take care! L. 49.
Taza, *tah'-tha*, s. f., cup. L. 55.
Té, *tai*, s. m., tea. L. 55.
Te, pron., thee, to thee. L. 26.
Teatro, *tai-ah'-tro*, s. m., theatre. L. 17.
Teja, *tai'-ha*, s. f., tile.—De *tejas* abajo, humanly speaking. L. 61.
Telegráfico, *tai-lai-grah'-fē-ko*, adj., telegraph. L. 65.

Telégrafo, *tai-lai'-grah-fo*, s. m., telegraph. L. 46.
Tema, *tai'-ma*, s. m., theme, exercise;—s. f., dispute, contention. L. 57.
Temer, *tai-mair'*, to fear. L. 28.
Temerario, *tai-mai-rah'-rē-ō*, adj., rash, inconsiderate. L. 54.
Temor, *tai-mōre'*.—Por *temor* de, for fear of. L. 42.
Temprano, *taim-prah'-no*, adv., early, soon. L. 20.
Tenacidad, *tai-nah-thē-dath'*, s. f., tenacity. L. 65.
Tenedor, *tai-nai-dōre'*, s. m., fork. L. 65.
Tener, *tai-nair'*, to have, to hold: to be, to take (place).—*Tener* hambre, frio, sed, to be hungry, cold, thirsty.—*Tener* lugar, to take place.—*Tener* que hacer, to have something to do.—Yo *tengo* para mí, it is my opinion.—*Tenga* V. la bondad de decirme, be good enough to tell me. L. 10.
Tentacion, *tain-tah-thē-ōne'*, s. m., temptation. L. 61.
Teñir, *tain-yeer'*, to dye. L. 39.
Teoría, *tai-ō-rē'-a*, s. f., theory. L. 23.
Tercero, *tair-thai'-ro*, ord. adj., third. L. 15.
Tercio, *tair'-thē-ō*, s. m., third, third part. L. 40.
Terminacion, *tair-mē-nah-thē-ōne'*, s. f., termination. L. 49.
Terminante, *tair'-mē-nan'-tai*, adj., conclusive. L. 65.
Terminar, *tair-mē-nar'*, to terminate. L. 65.
Término, *tair'-mē-no*, s. m., termination, end; term. L. 65.
Termómetro, *tair-mō'-mai-tro*, s. m., thermometer. L. 60.
Terrenal, *tair-rai-nal'*, adj., terrestrial. L. 49.
Terreno, *tair-rai'-no*, s. m., ground. L. 55.
Terrible, *tair-rē'-blai*, adj., terrible. L. 53.
Terron, *tair-rōne'*, s. m., turned up earth. L. 49.
Terroso, *tair-rō'-so*, adj., terreous, earthy. L. 49.
Terrestre, *tair-raiss'-trai*, adj., terrestrial, earthly. L. 49.
Tertulia, *tair-too'-lē-a*, s. f., party. L. 39.
Tí, *tē*, pron., thee (governed by a prep.). L. 26.
Tiempo, *tē-aim'-po*, s. m., time, weather.—Con el *tiempo*, in the course of time. L. 23.
Tienda, *tē-ain'-da*, s. f., store, shop. L. 64.
Tierra, *tē-air'-ra*, s. f., earth, land, native soil. L. 45.
Tijeras, *tē-hai'-ras*, s. f. pl., scissors. L. 64.
Tinta, *teen'-ta*, s. f., ink. L. 5.
Tintero, *teen-tai'-ro*, s. m., inkstand.—Dejarse algo en el *tintero*, to forget to say something. L. 4.
Tinto, *teen'-to*, adj., red (said of wines). L. 65.
Tío, *tē'-ō*, s. m., uncle. L. 65.
Tirabuzon, *tē-rah-boo-thōne'*, s. m., corkscrew. L. 63.
Tiránico, *tē-rah'-nē-ko*, adj., tyrannical. L. 35.
Tirar, *tē-rar'*, to throw, to cast, to take (speaking of a road).—*Tire* V. por aquí, take this way. L. 54.

Tiro, *tē'-ro*, s. m., throw, cast.—A *tiro* de pistola, within a pistol-shot. L. 53.
Título, *tē'-too-lo*, s. m., title. L. 55.
Tocante á, *tō-kan'-tai a*, prep., concerning, relating to, touching. L. 38.
Tocar, *tō-kar'*, to touch, to play (on an instrument). L. 15.
Todavía, *tō-dah-vē'-a*, adv., yet, still. L. 25.
Todo, *tō'-do*, adj., all.—*Todos* los días, every day.—Del *todo*, entirely.—Con *todo*, however, notwithstanding. L. 11.
Todo, s. m., the whole. L. 61.
Tolerar, *tō-lai-rar'*, to tolerate. L. 65.
Toma! *tō'-ma*, inter., indeed! L. 45.
Tomar, *tō-mar'*, to take. L. 14.
Tomo, *tō'-mo*, s. m., volume.—Un libro de tres *tomos*, a book in three volumes. L. 15.
Tonel, *tō-nail'*, s. m., cask, barrel. L. 60.
Tonto, *tōne'-to*, adj., foolish.—A *tontas* y á locas, at random. L. 60.
Tontera, *tōne-tai'-ra*, s. f., foolish action. L. 60.
Toque, *tō'-kai*, s. m., roll (of a drum), ringing (of bells).—Ahí está el *toque*, that is where the difficulty lies. L. 65.
Torero, *tō-rai'-ro*, s. m., bull-fighter. L. 53.
Tornar, *tōre-nar'*, to return, to begin anew. L. 65.
Torno, *tōre'-no*, s. m., lathe.—En *torno*, round about. L. 65.
Toro, *tō'-ro*, s. m., bull. L. 53.
Tos, *tōce*, s. f., cough. L. 65.
Trabajador, *trah-bah-hah-dōre'*, adj. and s. m., hardworking, worker. L. 17.
Trabajar, *trah-bah-har'*, to work, to labor. L. 17.
Trabajo, *trah-bah'-ho*, s. m., work, labor, occupation. L. 47.
Traducción, *trah-dook-thē-ōne'*, s. f., translation. L. 61.
Traducir, *trah-doo-theer'*, to translate. L. 40.
Traer, *trah-air'*, to bring, to carry, to wear. L. 42.
Tragar, *trah-gar'*, to swallow. L. 65.
Tragedia, *trah-hai'-dē-a*, s. f., tragedy. L. 52.
Trágico, *trah'-hē-ko*, adj., tragic. L. 35.
Trago, *trah'-go*, s. m., draught, drink.—Echar un *trago*, to take a dram. L. 59.
Traje, *trah'-hai*, s. m., dress, costume. L. 54.
Trampa, *tram'-pa*, s. f., trap, swindle.—Caer en la *trampa*, to fall into the snare. L. 64.
Trampear, *tram-pai-ar'*, to swindle, to impose upon. L. 65.
Tramposo, *tram-pō'-so*, adj., deceitful, swindling:—s. m., cheat, swindler. L. 65.
Tranquilidad, *tran-kē-lē-dath'*, s. f., tranquillity, peace, quietness. L. 46.
Tranquilizar, *tran-kē-lē-thar'*, to tranquillize. L. 65.
Tranquilo, *tran-kē'-lo*, adj., tranquil, quiet, peaceful. L. 60.
Trapo, *trah'-po*, s. m., rag. L. 64.
Tras, prep., behind, after. L. 41.
Trascurso, *trass-koor'-so*, s. m., course, process (of time). L. 51.
Trasnochar, *trass-nō-char'*, to sit up all night. L. 65.

Trasquilar, *trass-kē-lar'*, to shear (sheep).—Ir por lana y volver *trasquilado*, the biter bit. L. 65.
Trastienda, *trass-tē-ain'-da*, s. f., back shop. L. 61.
Tratado, *trah-tah'-do*, s. m., treatise, treaty. L. 46.
Tratante, *trah-tan'-tai*, s. m., dealer. L. 38.
Tratar, *trah-tar'*, to treat, to have intercourse or relations with, to trade, to deal, to traffic, to try. L. 32.
Trato, *trah'-to*, s. m., treatment, dealings, intercourse. L. 65.
Través, *trah-vaiss'*, prep.—Al *través* de, through. L. 65.
Travesura, *trah-vai-soo'-ra*, s. f., trick, mischief, naughtiness. L. 53.
Travieso, *trah-vē-ai'-so*, adj., tricky, naughty, mischievous. L. 52.
Traza, *trah'-tha*, s. f., trace.—Tener buena *traza*, to look well. L. 64.
Trece, *trai'-thai*, num. adj., thirteen. L. 14.
Treinta, *trai-een'-ta*, num. adj., thirty. L. 14.
Tres, *traiss*, num. adj., three. L. 14.
Tribunal, *trē-boo-nal'*, s. m., tribunal, court of justice. L. 53.
Trigo, *trē'-go*, s. m., wheat. L. 65.
Trigueño, *trē-gain'-yo*, adj., brown, dark (complexion). L. 65.
Trinchar, *treen-char'*, to cut up, to carve. L. 58.
Trineo, *trē-nai'-ō*, s. m., sleigh. L. 65.
Trinidad, *trē-nē-dath'*, s. f., Trinity. L. 21.
Triptongo, *treep-tōne'-go*, s. m., triphthong. L. 57.
Triste, *treess'-tai*, adj., sad, mournful, dull. L. 21.
Tristeza, *treess-tai'-tha*, s. f., sadness, dulness. L. 41.
Tronar, *trō-nar'*, to thunder. L. 30.
Tropa, *trō'-pa*, s. f., troop. L. 40.
Trueco, *trwai'-ko*, s. m., barter, exchange.—A *trueco*, provided that. L. 61.
Trueno, *trwai'-no*, s. m., thunder, clap of thunder. L. 30.
Trueque. (See Trueco.) L. 48.
Tú, *too*, pers. pron., thou;—poss. adj., thy. L. 1.
Tuerto, *twair'-to*, adj., blind of one eye. L. 65.
Tutear, *too-tai-ar'*, to speak familiarly (in the second person singular). L. 65.
Tuteo, *too-tai'-ō*, s. m., theuing. L. 65.
Tuyo, *too'-yo*, poss. pron., thine. L. 13.

U.

U, *oo*, conj., used instead of *ó*, before words beginning with *o* or *ho*. L. 8.
Uf! *oof*, inter., ugh! L. 46.
Ultimo, *ool'-tē-mo*, adj., last.—Por *último* at last, finally. L. 61.
Un, *oon*, adj. and indef. art., one, a (always used before, never after, words). L. 4.
Una, *oo'-na*, fem. of Uno, which see. L. 5.
Universidad, *oo-nē-vair-sē-dath'*, s. f., university. L. 55.
Uno, *oo'-no*, indef. art. and adj., a, one.—*Uno á uno*, one by one. L. 14.
Uña, *oon'-ya*, s. f., finger-nail. L. 33.
Usar, *co-sar'*, to use. L. 62.

VOCABULARY.

Uso, *oo'-so*, s. m., use. L. 61.
Usted, *coss-taith'*, s. m. and f., you. (Contraction of VUESTRA MERCED, your worship.) L. 1.
Util, *co'-teel*, adj., useful. L. 13.
Uva, *oo'-va*, s. f., grape. L. 40.

V.

Vaca, *vah'-ka*, s. f., cow, beef. L. 55.
Vacío, *vah-thē'-ō*, adj., empty. L. 58.
Valencia, *vah-lain'-thē-a*, s. f., Valencia. L. 53.
Valentía, *vah-lain-tē'-a*, s. f., valor, bravery. L. 54.
Valer, *vah-lair'*, to be worth, to be good for.—Mas *vale* tarde que nunca, better late than never.—*Válgame* Dios! bless me! L. 41.
Valiente, *vah-lē-ain'-tai*, adj., valiant, brave. L. 47.
Valor, *vah-lōre'*, s. m., valor, bravery; worth, value. L. 25.
Vals, *valce*, s. m., waltz. L. 23.
Vamos! *vah'-moce*, inter., come! come along! L. 46.
Vapor, *vah-pōre'*, s. m., steam, steamboat, steamer. L. 37.
Vara, *vah'-ra*, s. f., rod; yard measure. L. 47.
Vario, *vah'-rē-o*, adj., various, variable;—pl., several. L. 43.
Varon, *vah-rōne'*, s. m., man, male human being. L. 62.
Vascongadas, (LAS PROVINCIAS), *vass-kōne-gah'-dass*, s. f. pl., the three Spanish provinces of Alava, Guipuzcoa, and Biscay. L. 55.
Vascuence, *vass-kwain'-thai*, s. m., the Biscayan dialect. L. 55.
Vasija, *vah-sē'-ha*, s. f., cask for liquors. L. 52.
Vaso, *vah'-so*, s. m., vase, glass (for drinking), tumbler. L. 61.
Vaya! *vah'-ya*, inter., come now! indeed! L. 42.
Vecino, *vai-thē'-no*, s. m., neighbor. L. 28.
Veinte, *vai'-een-tai*, num. adj., twenty. L. 14.
Vela, *vai'-la*, s. f., sail (of a ship), candle. L. 53.
Vencer, *vain-thair'*, to vanquish, to overcome, to conquer. L. 59.
Vender, *vain-dair'*, to sell. L. 6.
Venir, *vai-neer'*, to come; to fit, to suit.—*Venir* á pelo, to be just the thing.—No hay mal que por bien no *venga*, it's an ill wind that blows good to nobody. L. 18.
Ventaja, *vain-tah'-ha*, s. f., advantage. L. 43.
Ventana, *vain-tah'-na*, s. f., window. L. 28.
Ver, *vair*, to see, to look.—A *ver*, let us see.—*Verse* negro, to be in great distress. L. 29.
Verano, *vai-rah'-no*, s. m., summer. L. 24.
Verbal, *vair-bal'*, adj., verbal. L. 49.
Verbo, *vair'-bo*, s. m., verb. L. 41.
Verdad, *vair-dath'*, s. f., truth.—A la *verdad*, truly; indeed. L. 43.
Verdaderamente, *vair-dah-dai-rah-main'-tai*, adv., truly, veritably. L. 39.
Verde, *vair'-dai*, adj. green. L. 54.

Verdura, *vair-doo'-ra*, s. f., verdure; vegetables. L. 34.
Vergüenza, *vair-gwain'-tha*, s. f., shame.—Tener *vergüenza*, to be ashamed. L. 25.
Version, *vair-sē-ōne'*, s. f., version. L. 64.
Verso, *vair'-so*, s. m., verse; line of poetry. L. 52.
Vestido, *vaiss-tē'-do*, s. m., dress, wearing apparel. L. 39.
Vestir, *vaiss-teer'*, to dress, to clothe. L. 25.
Vez, *vaith*, s. f., time.—Una *vez*, once.—Dos *veces*, twice.—En *vez* de, instead of.—Hacer las *veces* de, to act as, serve as.—Tal *vez*, perhaps.—A mi *vez*, in my turn.—A *veces*, at times. L. 25.
Viajar, *vē-ah-har'*, to travel. L. 21.
Vicerector, *vē-thai-raik-tōre'*, s. m., vicerector. L. 50.
Vice versa, *vē'-thai vair'-sa*, vice versá. L. 47.
Vicio, *vē'-thē-ō*, s. m., vice. L. 41.
Victoria, *veek-tō'-rē-a*, s. f., victory. L. 46.
Vida, *vē'-da*, s. f., life. L. 50.
Viejo, *vē-ai'-ho*, adj., old. L. 13.
Viena, *vē-ai'-na*, s. f., Vienna. L. 12.
Viento, *vē-ain'-to*, s. m., wind. L. 30.
Viérnes, *vē-air'-naiss*, s. m., Friday.—*Viérnes* santo, Good Friday. L. 9.
Viga, *vē'-ga*, s. f., beam. L. 65.
Villadiego, *veel-yah-vē-ai'-go*, s. m.—Tomar las de *Villadiego*, to run away; to take to one's heels. L. 50.
Vinacho, *vē-nah'-cho*, s. m., bad wine. L. 49.
Vino, *vē'-no*, s. m., wine. L. 7.
Violado, *vē-ō-lah'-do*, s. m. and adj., violet (color). L. 54.
Violeta, *vē-ō-lai'-ta*, s. f., violet. L. 54.
Violin, *vē-ō-leen'*, s. m., violin. L. 15.
Violinista, *vē-ō-lē-neess'-ta*, s. m., violinist. L. 36.
Virtud, *veer-tooth'*, s. f., virtue.—En *virtud* de, by virtue of. L. 41.
Visita, *vē-sē'-ta*, s. f., visit. L. 28.
Visitar, *vē-sē-tar'*, to visit; to examine. L. 52.
Vista, *veess'-ta*, s. f., view, sight.—A *vista*, at sight.—Perder de *vista*, to lose sight of. L. 29 and 51.
Visto, *veess'-to*, past part. (of VER), seen. L. 52.
Vistoso, *veess-tō'-so*, adj., conspicuous, showy. L. 54.
Viva! *vē'-va*, inter., long live! hurrah! huzza! L. 46.
Viviente, *vē-vē-ain'-tai*, s. m. and pres. part., living being; living, animated. L. 38.
Vivir, *vē-veer'*, to live. L. 9.
Vivo, *vē'-vo*, adj., alive, lively, sprightly. L. 20.
Vizcaino, *reeth-kah-ē'-no*, s. m. and adj., Biscayan. L. 55.
Vizcaya, *veeth-kah'-ya*, s. f., Biscay. L. 55.
Vocabulario, *vō-kah-boo-lah'-rē-ō*, s. m., vocabulary. L. 58.
Vocal, *vō-kal'*, adj. and s. m., vocal; vowel. L. 58.
Volar, *vō-lar'*, to fly. L. 45.
Volúmen, *vō-loo'-main*, s. m., volume. L. 15.
Voluntad, *vō-loon-tath'*, s. f., will. L. 45.
Volver, *vōle-vair'*, to come or go back, to return, to do again, to turn.—*Volver* en sí, to recover one's senses.—*Volver* á las

andadas, to return to one's old habits. L. 36.
Vos, *vōce*, pers. pron., you. L. 66.
Vosotros, *vō-sō'-trōce*, pers. pron., you, ye. L. 1.
Voz, *vōth*, s. f., voice; word; rumor; report.—Corre la *voz* que . . . , it is rumored that . . . L. 58.
Vuelta, *vwait'-ta*, s. f., return, turn, trip.—A *vuelta* de correo, by return mail.—Dar una *vuelta*, to take a walk.—Dar la *vuelta* al parque, to go round the park. L. 46.
Vuelto, *vwait'-to*, past part. (of VOLVER), returned. L. 52.
Vuestro, *vwaisse'-tro*, poss. adj., your. L. 13.
Vulgar, *vool-gar'*, adj., vulgar. L. 59.

Y.

Y, *ē*, conj., and. L. 3.
Ya, adv., already, yet; sometimes.—*Ya* lo uno, *ya* lo otro, sometimes one, sometimes the other. L. 25 and 37.
Yacer, *yah-thair'*, to lie. L. 41.
Yerba, *yair'-ba*, s. f., herb, grass. L. 60.
Yerno, *yair'-no*, s. m., son-in-law. L. 60.

Yo, pers. pron., I.—*Yo mismo*, I myself. L. 1.
Yugo, *yoo'-go*, s. m., yoke. L. 64.

Z.

Zafarse, *thah-far'-sai*, to escape, to get rid of. L. 64.
Zaga, *thah'-ga*, s. f., rear.—No irle ń uno en *zaga*, not to be far behind any one. L. 44.
Zapatería, *thah-pah tai-iē'-a*, s. f., shoe trade; shoemaker's shop. L. 17.
Zapatero, *thah pah-tai'-ro*, s. m., shoemaker. L. 8.
Zapato, *thah-pah'-to*, s. m., shoe. L. 10.
Zape! *thah'-pai*, inter., used to frighten away the cats; God forbid! L. 46.
Zas! zas! *thass*, inter., used to imitate the sound of repeated knocks or blows. L. 62.
Zeca en Meca (ANDAR DE), *thai'-ka ain mai'-ka*, to wander about from pillar to post. L. 61.
Zutano, *thoo-tah'-no*, s. m., such a one. L. 55.

www.ingramcontent.com/pod-product-compliance
Lightning Source LLC
Chambersburg PA
CBHW021422300426
44114CB00010B/611